AGRICULTURE IN DEVELOPMENT THEORY

A Publication of the Economic Growth Center, Yale University

# AGRICULTURE
# IN
# DEVELOPMENT THEORY

## EDITED BY LLOYD G. REYNOLDS

New Haven and London, Yale University Press, 1975

773090

Designed by Sally Sullivan
and set in Times Roman type.
Printed in the United States of America by
The Murray Printing Co., Forge Village, Massachusetts.

Published in Great Britain, Europe, and Africa by
Yale University Press, Ltd., London.
Distributed in Latin America by Kaiman & Polon,
Inc., New York City;
in India by UBS Publishers' Distributors Pvt.,
Ltd., Delhi; in Japan by John Weatherhill, Inc., Tokyo.

# Contents

Foreword    vii
Preface    ix

1. Agriculture in Development Theory: An Overview    1
   Lloyd G. Reynolds

PART I    THE ECONOMICS OF PEASANT PRODUCTION

2. Smallholder Decision Making: Tropical African
   Evidence    27
   GERALD K. HELLEINER

3. The Response of Nonmonetary Production Units to
   Contact with the Exchange Economy
   E. K. FISK    53

4. A Pure Theory of Underdeveloped Economies
   JAMES A. MIRRLEES    84

PART II    TENURE SYSTEMS AND ECONOMIC RESPONSES

5. The Choice of Rental Contract in Peasant
   Agriculture
   DAVID M. G. NEWBERY    109

6. An Economic Theory of Tenant and Landlord
   Based on a Philippine Case
   MAHAR MANGAHAS    138

PART III    GENERATING AND DIFFUSING NEW
AGRICULTURAL TECHNOLOGY

7. Technology Transfer, Institutional Transfer, and
   Induced Technical and Institutional Change in
   Agricultural Development
   VERNON W. RUTTAN    165

8. Technology Generation in Agriculture
   ROBERT EVENSON    192

9. Agricultural Research Organization in Economic
   Development: A Review of the Japanese Experience
   YUJIRO HAYAMI AND SABURO YAMADA    224

PART IV   AGRICULTURAL SECTOR PERFORMANCE

10.  Special Problems of Policy Making in a
Technologically Heterogeneous Agriculture: Colombia
R. A. BERRY                                          253

11.  Measurement of the Direct and Indirect Employment
Effects of Agricultural Growth with Technical
Change
RAJ KRISHNA                                          297

PART V   AGRICULTURE, GROWTH, AND TRADE

12.  Agriculture and Economic Development in the Open
Economy
HLA MYINT                                            327

13.  Agriculture in Two Types of Open Economies
JOHN C. H. FEI AND GUSTAV RANIS                      355

14.  The Political Economy of Rice Production and
Trade in Asia
C. PETER TIMMER AND WALTER P. FALCON                 373

PART VI   COMPARATIVE STUDIES

15.  Agriculture in the Economic Growth of the East
European Socialist Countries
Z. KOZLOWSKI                                         411

16.  Peasant Families and the Agrarian Community in
the Process of Economic Development
SHIGERU ISHIKAWA                                     451

Contributors                                         497
Index                                                499

# Foreword

This volume is one in a series of studies supported by the Economic Growth Center, an activity of the Yale Department of Economics since 1961. The Center is a research organization with worldwide activities and interests. Its research interests are defined in terms of both method of approach and subject matter. In terms of method, the Center sponsors studies which are designed to test significant general hypotheses concerning the problem of economic growth and which draw on quantitative information from national economic accounts and other sources. In terms of subject matter, the Center's research interests include theoretical analysis of economic structure and growth, quantitative analysis of a national economy as an integral whole, comparative cross-sectional studies using data from a number of countries, and efforts to improve the techniques of national economic measurement. The research program includes field investigation of recent economic growth in twenty-five developing countries of Asia, Africa, and Latin America.

The Center administers, jointly with the Department of Economics, the Yale training program in International and Foreign Economic Administration. It presents a regular series of seminar and workshop meetings and includes among its publications both book-length studies and journal reprints by staff members, the latter circulated as Center Papers.

Gustav Ranis, Director

# Preface

The papers in this volume were presented at a conference held in Bellagio, Italy, in May 1973, under the auspices of the Economic Growth Center, Yale University. The conference had two distinctive features. First, the discussions were pitched at an analytical and research level, though policy concerns were certainly not absent from the minds of the participants. Second, the participants were drawn about equally from among general development economists and specialists in agricultural development. It was felt that closer interaction between these groups would be mutually beneficial.

The strategy of the conference was to work from narrower to broader topics, from problems internal to the agricultural sector to problems of the interaction of agriculture and nonagriculture in the growth process. This strategy has guided the sequence of the published papers. We begin in Part I with problems of a very "micro" character, involving decision making at the level of the individual farm unit. This micro emphasis continues in Part II, which is concerned with the determination of tenancy arrangements through the interaction of landlords' and tenants' preferences.

The question of how agricultural research resources can be organized most effectively, and how research results can be translated into farm production practices, is an important frontier of current research. Two of the papers in Part III discuss these questions in general terms, while an additional paper reviews one of the most successful experiences in agricultural innovation—the case of Japan.

In Part IV we attempt to answer two questions about agricultural sector performance: First, where there is marked dualism between large and small farms *within* the agricultural sector, what are the growth consequences of pushing technological advance on large farms as against a policy of diffusing progress more evenly throughout the sector? Second, to what extent does the new "green revolution" technology generate increases in farm and nonfarm employment?

Most models of early economic growth are closed-economy models. What happens to the role of agriculture when the model is opened to foreign trade? Two of the papers in Part V attack this issue in general terms, while one presents a case study of international trade in a major foodstuff. Finally, two papers of very broad scope, which cut across all the previous discussion, comprise the concluding Part VI.

We are grateful to several institutions without whose aid the conference would not have been possible. The Rockefeller Foundation made available its excellent conference facilities at the Villa Serbelloni. Travel funds were provided by the Ford Foundation and by the Agricultural Development Council. The administrative staff of the Yale Economic Growth Center handled a variety of practical arrangements. Special thanks are due to Gail Ross, who bore the brunt of the work of reproducing and circulating the conference papers, and of preparing this volume for publication.

L. G. R.

# 1

# Agriculture in Development Theory: An Overview

LLOYD G. REYNOLDS

The development literature now contains a dozen or so models of early economic growth. These invariably contain an agricultural sector; but the internal structure of agriculture often remains shadowy. Some models depend on specific institutional assumptions about agriculture, and a different set of assumptions would lead to quite different results. The industrial sector, on the other hand, is specified more clearly and more consistently from one model to the next. This doubtless stems from the fact that industry tends to be regarded as the focal point of economic development, with agriculture playing the role of a resource reservoir. Existing models are also typically closed-economy models, and their aim is to depict a capitalist (or "mixed economy") growth path.

The conventional treatment of agriculture raises several questions, on which I propose to comment briefly in this paper:

1. In setting out to construct a multisector model, what assumptions about agricultural structure are more plausible than others? This involves such matters as tenure form, whether tenure form should be treated as exogenous or endogenous, the significance of "dualistic" agricultural structures, the choice of factors of production, and the characteristics of agricultural production functions.

2. Is it reasonable to postulate "economic" behavior by low-income farmers? What, concretely, do we mean by economic behavior?

3. In what sense does agriculture in some economies contain a "labor surplus"? Is labor surplus more characteristic of agriculture than of other economic sectors?

4. How is technical progress in agriculture generated and diffused? What are the requirements for effective diffusion?

5. To what extent should agriculture be regarded as a resource reservoir for development? Are resource transfers out of agriculture during

1

early economic growth inevitable, or desirable, or historically documented?

6. What are the implications for agriculture of moving from a closed to an open economy? How does the comparative advantage-specialization-trade view of growth differ from the internal self-sufficiency approach?

7. How does the role of agriculture in socialist less developed countries (hereafter, LDCs) differ from its role in nonsocialist systems? Are there differences in the economic functions of agriculture, or only in the control instruments available to policy makers?

This agenda is ambitious to the point of appearing foolhardy; so I hasten to add several disclaimers. First, I share with most of my development colleagues the disadvantage of not being an agricultural economist. My comments should be regarded as those of a concerned amateur, who begs forgiveness of the specialists for any naive remarks. Second, I am clearly not going to *answer* the questions listed above. My objective is the more modest one of specifying why these questions are important, and of commenting briefly on the current state of knowledge concerning them. Third, I shall be forced inevitably to oversimplify and overgeneralize. Agriculture is a complex bundle of activities, highly variable within and among countries. It is probably impossible to make any statement that would be true of all agricultural activities everywhere. Here, as elsewhere in economics, we must aim at *judicious* simplification without going to the point of caricature.

### AGRICULTURAL ORGANIZATION

Suppose one were setting out afresh to build a multisector development model. What assumptions about agricultural organization would one choose as having the widest range of applicability?

As regards the tenure system, it is most plausible to assume owner-operated "family farming." This is much the commonest system on a world scale. Other "pure" systems are: share tenancy, fixed-rent tenancy, hired wage labor, and collective farming. In practice, of course, several tenure systems may coexist in a country; but it is a reasonable simplification to assume a predominant form.

A model based on large landowners hiring wage labor is not very plausible because, while such landowners exist in many countries, they rarely predominate. Tenancy systems are more frequent but are quite heterogeneous. They vary widely on such matters as permanence of tenure, sharing of input costs, provision of and charges for current finance, responsibility for choice of crops and production methods, and supervision of production activities. Tenancy should thus be regarded, not as a *single* tenure form, but as a large family of potential tenure arrangements. A model assuming a tenancy system in agriculture must specify the detailed characteristics of the system.

To assume a certain tenure system as an exogenous feature of the model is a general and, I believe, warranted practice. But it bypasses several important problems. For example, the existing tenure system can be regarded, not as a fact of nature, but as reflecting the interests and preferences of landowners and cultivators, plus production characteristics of agriculture. This effort to treat tenure systems as endogenous, and to explain their origin in economic terms, has spread rapidly in recent years. Chapters 5 and 6 in this volume deal with this frontier area.

There is also a large literature on the question whether one tenure system is preferable to another on productivity grounds. The traditional view that family farming leads necessarily to better factor combinations than does a tenancy system has been attacked along two lines. First, several writers have demonstrated that it is possible to specify tenancy arrangements that will produce the same factor combination and the same output result as owner operation. Second, it can be argued that in any event the important issue is not static resource allocation, toward which the traditional reasoning was directed, but rather what tenure system is most conducive to rapid adoption of new production technology. This question will come up again in my later discussion of technical progress.

These interesting issues, however, I set aside as tangential to the present inquiry. I take it as valid to assume an exogenous tenure system, without asking where it came from or whether it is preferable in production terms; and I assert that it makes most sense to assume an agricultural sector consisting of owner-operated family farms. A simple model could assume that the sector consists of farm units of equal size, with each farm family providing all labor inputs for its farm and selling no labor off the farm. But it is possible also to complicate the picture by admitting, first, the possibility of variation in farm sizes and, second, the sale and purchase of labor by farmers in an agricultural labor market.

Many countries, indeed, exhibit a "dualistic" agricultural structure consisting of (1) small "peasant farms," on which labor inputs are supplied mainly by family members; and (2) larger farms employing substantial amounts of wage labor. Research from countries as diverse as Colombia and India indicates that the small farms apply more labor and other variable inputs per acre of land and achieve higher yields per acre. Large farms are less labor intensive and achieve lower yields per acre but higher yields per man-hour. This poses interesting analytical and policy problems. Chapter 10 in this volume explores these issues with respect to Colombian agriculture.

In addition to assumptions about tenure form, we need assumptions about production functions. For industry, one automatically writes out a production function incorporating labor, capital, and technology. There is a strong temptation to do the same for agriculture, and some model-builders have yielded to it. All nonhuman inputs, including land, are lumped together in the capital term.

For agriculture, and especially for premodern agriculture, this is not very plausible. Land is different from other material inputs. Capital takes mainly the form of circulating capital—seeds plus a "wages fund" to enable the family to subsist between harvests. Fixed capital is limited to simple tools and perhaps a little animal power. Without undue simplification, then, one can posit a production function including only land and labor inputs, with labor's average and marginal productivity curves having the conventional shape.

In some agricultural regimes, to be sure, capital formation enters in the form of land improvements. Thus in irrigated rice cultivation the farm family's labor is allocated between current production and land improvements (small irrigation channels, terracing, drainage) designed to achieve a higher level of water control. Government also invests in dams and large irrigation channels, and the farmers' investment of time is complementary to these large projects. When a higher stage of water control is achieved, it becomes possible to apply an improved "package" of fertilizer, seed, and other current inputs, which raises the labor productivity schedules. Capital in this sense is complementary to labor rather than a substitute factor, as in manufacturing production functions.

The production function at any moment assumes a given technology. In premodern agriculture there are historical grounds for this assumption, since the technology in use has undergone only minor modifications for decades or centuries. Agricultural modernization, however, implies an effort to shift production functions by developing and diffusing improved technology. But one cannot safely assume that agricultural technology advances in the same fashion as industrial technology. It does not, and the differences are important enough to deserve a separate section below.

### THE POSTULATE OF ECONOMIC BEHAVIOR

I visualize, then, a farm family with a given amount of land and family labor power. The family has a set of production possibilities and market options. It produces $z$ goods, one or more food crops, perhaps a non-food crop. It can sell these crops in product markets and can buy food, other consumer goods, and agricultural inputs. In the labor market it can sell family labor time or buy outside labor at a cash wage.

Given the production functions, the market price parameters, and the family's preferences concerning goods and leisure, it is a simple exercise to write out the marginal equalities necessary to maximize the family's satisfaction. This is done, for example, in Chihiro Nakajima's contribution to the recent Wharton symposium.[1] But there remains a question whether the element of maximizing behavior in peasants' decisions is strong enough to make this a meaningful exercise. Some writers have presented models of the "inert peasant," bound by custom and tradition, unresponsive to new production and consumption possibilities; or the "satisficing peasant," who will put forth only the effort needed to achieve a fixed income target.

Against these constructs, T. W. Schultz and others have defended the "optimizing peasant," a shrewd fellow who has learned through experience to allocate efficiently and who is responsive to economic incentives within his perceived opportunity set.[2] The weight of available research evidence supports this view. There is much evidence of allocative efficiency in input combinations and output choices, and also in longer-range investment decisions such as cocoa and coffee planting. True, one usually finds marked efficiency differences among farms in the same region. But Yujiro Hayami and Vernon Ruttan conclude that these differences are no greater than those among farmers in the United States.[3]

Apparent deviations from optimizing behavior, then, are not to be

1. C. R. Wharton, ed., *Subsistence Agriculture and Economic Development* (Chicago: Aldine, 1969).
2. T. W. Schultz, *Transforming Traditional Agriculture* (New Haven: Yale University Press, 1964).
3. Y. Hayami and V. W. Ruttan, *Agricultural Development: An International Perspective* (Baltimore: Johns Hopkins Press, 1971).

explained by peculiarities of motivation. Rather, they stem from a variety of constraints on economic behavior. These can retard or even prevent movement toward a hypothetical equilibrium, or they may cause adjustment to stop at peculiar values of one or more variables. The more important constraints are: the uncertainties inherent in agricultural production, and the aversion to risk natural to families with low incomes and negligible cash reserves; heterogeneity of "family labor" and "hired labor," which are not regarded as fully interchangeable; peculiarities of land as an asset; and serious imperfections in rural capital markets. The consequences of these things for farmers' behavior have been explored at length in the agricultural literature.

More interesting than static allocation is the question whether peasant producers respond to change in the direction predicted by economic reasoning. Especially important are changes in price parameters, in the man/land ratio, and in technology (which I leave for discussion under the next heading).

Most of the research literature deals with the effects of a change in *relative* prices. Typical examples of such change are: (1) a change in the price of a food crop, part of which is marketed; (2) a change in the price of a cash crop relative to a food crop, or of one cash crop relative to others; (3) a change in the market wage rate; (4) a change in the price of an agricultural input—for example, a reduction in fertilizer prices relative to farm output prices. There is by now an overwhelming body of evidence that peasant producers' responses to such changes are in the "correct" direction, though the magnitude of the response varies with circumstances. The postulate of economic behavior works well.

More complicated and ambiguous are the effects of a *general* shift in the terms of trade between agriculture and nonagriculture. Here the income effect, which can be treated as minor for a single crop, becomes important and runs counter to the substitution effect, making the outcome unpredictable. It seems plausible that an improvement in agriculture's terms of trade will (1) increase total labor input by the farm family; (2) produce a reallocation of labor time away from $z$ goods toward crop production; and (3) in consequence raise crop output. But will an increase in output also increase the "marketed surplus" sold to the cities? This issue has been much debated in the literature, because of the obvious need for increased food marketings in countries with a growing urban population. Theoretical efforts to prove that a certain result *must* follow have not been very successful.

A basic problem is that it is hard to estimate the income elasticity of farmers' demand for food because of the difficulty of measuring their real income, much of which is in noncash form.

It is possible, however, to measure the elasticity of marketed surplus with respect to *output,* and this usually turns out to be positive. If, then, the elasticity of output with respect to price is also positive, one can multiply the two coefficients to derive an elasticity of marketings. There is thus some basis for concluding that improvement in agriculture's terms of trade is likely to result in larger marketings of foodstuffs.

A similar problem, attended by similar difficulties, is that of predicting farmers' response to tax changes. There is a large and inconclusive literature on this subject. There are' of course many kinds of taxes—on acreage, output, potential output, marketings, income—and their effects need not run in the same direction. The art of public finance consists partly of developing an agricultural tax structure with minimum disincentive effect. In model-building terms, if the model includes (as it should) a government sector, then one must assume an agricultural tax structure and a relation between tax rates and output decisions. It is unfortunate that the empirical basis for choice of assumptions in this area is still weak.

A kind of change that has been less investigated is population growth, leading to a rise in the man/land ratio. Yet this kind of change is in practice very important. In most LDCs rural population is continuing to rise at 1.5 to 2.0 percent per year. Using plausible parameters, Folke Dovring projects that agricultural population in these countries will still be rising fifty years from now.[4]

This aspect of rural change has perhaps been neglected because its impact is almost self-evident and is profoundly discouraging. In a system of family farming, with static technology, the result will be larger inputs of man-hours per acre and a sliding down the labor productivity schedules toward the point of bare subsistence. What constitutes subsistence may also be redefined downward. Efforts to escape this discouraging conclusion by finding natural brakes on the process of deterioration—for example, Ester Boserup's thesis of endogenous technical change induced by population pressure—have not

4. Carl Eicher and Lawrence Witt, eds., *Agriculture in Economic Development,* "The Share of Agriculture in a Growing Population," pp. 78–98. (New York: McGraw-Hill, 1964).

been very successful. The Boserup argument has a very long time perspective and is geared to a very gradual rate of population growth.[5] With present LDC population growth rates, peasant producers might well starve before they could innovate. In areas such as Bangla Desh, the reality of Malthus's positive checks on population growth is already evident.

TECHNICAL PROGRESS IN AGRICULTURE

If population growth is the villain in the agricultural drama, technical change is generally regarded as the hero. How does technical change occur in agriculture, and how can it be incorporated in a development model? Technical change in agriculture has several basic characteristics which differentiate it from the corresponding process in manufacturing.

1. Generating technical change in agriculture is inherently a *public responsibility*. The reasons for this are, first, the small scale and limited financial resources of production units in agriculture. Second, the impossibility of restricting the use of new agricultural knowledge—its strong external effects—means that the optimal level of research is much larger than any one producer would be willing to support. Third, the possibilities of borrowing technology from advanced countries are more limited in agriculture than in industry. This is because crops are sensitive to rainfall, soil, length of day during the growing season, and other local conditions. Successful innovation is very location specific. International and interregional diffusion of technology thus requires local research investment to adapt new seed strains to local conditions.

For these reasons agricultural progress in an LDC is contingent on public investment in research laboratories, experiment stations, and training of agricultural scientists. The payoff to research activity has been tested both within large countries, such as the United States and India, and also on a cross-country basis. Robert Evenson has assembled indicators of research activity for a large number of countries, both developed and less developed, and finds a marked relation between research expenditures and crop yields. Some of his findings are reviewed in his contribution to this volume, Chapter 8.

Because of the gradual spread of new technology, productivity improvement should probably be treated as a lagged function of prior agricultural research. The degree of lag depends partly on the effective-

5. Ester Boserup, *The Conditions of Agricultural Growth* (Chicago: Aldine, 1965).

ness of grassroots extension activities. But the diffusion problem can readily be exaggerated. There is much evidence that, if an innovation is profitable, and if the necessary inputs (including finance) are readily available, diffusion occurs with surprising speed.

2. Technical progress in agriculture usually has a strong *factor bias*. Innovations in agriculture are of two main kinds: (a) mechanical innovations, which are labor saving; and (b) biological-chemical innovations, such as those involved in the recent "revolution" in rice and wheat production in some LDCs, which are land saving and labor using.

Hayami and Ruttan argue that the direction of technical change can be regarded as endogenous, as a response to relative resource availabilities and resource prices.[6] A country gets the innovations it needs. Research is directed toward saving resources whose relative price is rising. They believe that this explains the dominance of mechanical innovations in U.S. agriculture, and the dominance of biological-chemical innovations in Japanese agriculture. Some of their reasoning is incorporated in the Ruttan paper in this volume, Chapter 7. In what follows, I shall be concerned entirely with the biological-chemical line of development, which is most relevant to LDC factor endowments.

3. Technical change is typically embodied in *new inputs:* tubewells, irrigation channels, seeds and livestock varieties, fertilizers, pesticides, improved hand tools. The pace of diffusion depends partly on physical availability of the necessary inputs, and also on their cost. Witness the demonstration in Chapter 14 in this volume that fertilizer use per acre in rice cultivation is strongly influenced by the rice/fertilizer price ratio. Purchase of the new inputs also requires more circulating capital, so credit availability is a limiting factor in adoption of innovations. One reason why large cultivators are often quicker than small ones to profit from new technology is their greater ability to finance input purchases.

4. Use of improved current inputs requires *complementary fixed investment*. This investment, most of which must be organized by government, is of several kinds. There is construction of factories to produce fertilizer and other improved inputs. There is transport investment to facilitate marketing of increased farm output, and expansion of warehousing and processing facilities. In regions of sparse or irregular rainfall investment in water supply can be critically important. This may take the form of tubewells, as in parts of India and Pakistan; or it may take the form of irrigation canals and ditches to distribute river

6. See their *Agricultural Development: An International Perspective*.

water. Better control of water supply permits use of better seed-fertilizer combinations, which shift productivity schedules upward. It may also permit double- and even triple-cropping on the same land.

5. Biological-chemical innovations lead to a substantial increase in farm and nonfarm *employment*. The most obvious effect is an increase of labor inputs per acre in current crop production. More labor is required for soil preparation and sowing. For example, the "Japanese" technique of rice cultivation requires much labor for transplanting of seedlings. There is more careful weeding and application of pesticides during the growing season. To the extent that yields are increased, more labor is needed for harvesting, threshing, and marketing the crop.

There has already been some research on the magnitude of the employment gains associated with the green revolution in Asian agriculture. These studies indicate that man-hour inputs per acre rise considerably less than yields per acre, i.e., there is a substantial increase in man-hour productivity. Labor's average and marginal productivity curves are raised sufficiently so that, even with larger labor inputs, one ends up at a higher point on the productivity schedule.

A study of the adoption of high-yielding varieties (HYV) of rice in the Philippines[7] found that labor input per hectare was increased by 10 percent on rather traditional farms and by up to 25 percent on more progressive farms. For the Philippine agricultural sector as a whole, these authors estimate the employment elasticity of output at 0.7 (compared with 0.5 in manufacturing and 1.2–1.3 in trade and services). A different kind of study has compared labor inputs per hectare in rice cultivation in a number of Asian countries.[8] These show striking intercountry differences, with Japanese labor inputs four to five times as great as those in West Bengal. One must remember, of course, that Japan has reached this level of labor intensity through an evolution extending over several centuries. The LDCs can scarcely duplicate this experience in a matter of ten or twenty years. But the comparison does dramatize the potential for labor absorption *within* the agricultural sector.

Moreover, analysis of the direct increase in labor inputs considerably

7. Randolph Barker, Mahar Mangahas, and William H. Meyers, "The Probable Impact of the Seed-Fertilizer Revolution on Grain Production and on Farm Labor Requirements" (Paper presented at the Conference on Strategies for Agricultural Development in the 1970s, Stanford University, December 1971).

8. Shigeru Ishikawa, *Economic Development in Asian Perspective* (Tokyo: Kinokuniya Bookstore, 1967).

understates the employment impact of agricultural development. One must consider also (1) increased farm labor inputs of an investment character, in water control, ditching, terracing, and the like; (2) increased labor inputs in government-organized investment, which, as we noted earlier, is a necessary complement to the new technology; (3) increased employment in the production of new farm inputs; and (4) increased farm purchases of consumer goods and services, made possible by larger farm incomes, with a consequent rise in urban employment. In Chapter 11 of this volume, using Indian input-output data, Raj Krishna suggests the size of these indirect employment effects.

THE AGRICULTURAL LABOR SURPLUS

The question how far, or in what sense, traditional agriculture contains a labor surplus has perhaps occupied more space in the literature than it really deserves. It is a remarkably confused discussion. There is often a basic confusion as to whether the discussion involves laborers or man-hours of labor. Yet the question of what happens when more man-hours are applied to a given land area is quite distinct from the question of what happens when people are added to or withdrawn from the agricultural labor force. I shall try to be clear on which concept is being used, in my later discussion.

Further, the supposed "surplus" has been defined in a variety of ways, some of which are not readily testable, and which in any case require different kinds of tests. At least six variants of the concept can be distinguished:

1. People are working fewer hours than they would be willing to work, at the existing earnings level, if demand for labor were higher. This concept, developed by Shigeru Ishikawa and Amartya Sen, assumes that, when hours are short, the schedule of the disutility of labor may be flat over a considerable range. How far people work into this range depends on the level of demand. The implication is that, if some people are withdrawn from agriculture, those remaining can be persuaded to work more (for the same *hourly* return, which means an increased *total* return), so that total man-hour input need not fall.

This contention is difficult to test empirically. Efforts to compare "available" man-hours in agriculture with man-hours actually worked are not very persuasive, because of the arbitrariness of the definition of availability. Hours that appear short to the observer may partly reflect deficiencies of nutrition and physical strength, plus the fact that heavy physical labor does have disutility. A further complicating factor is the seasonality of agricultural operations. Research studies suggest that, even in such densely populated countries as Egypt, the rural labor force is quite fully employed at the seasonal peak.

2. The curve of labor supply to the industrial sector is perfectly elastic at a constant real wage. This is what Arthur Lewis calls "unlimited supplies of labor." It seems to be supported by the fact that manufacturers and other "modern" employers in the LDCs rarely have any difficulty in recruiting a labor force. But this does not demonstrate that the labor supply curve is horizontal. It is quite possible that employers, for one reason or another, are paying more than the supply price of labor. If industrial wages are being forced upward by minimum wage legislation, trade union pressure, or other institutional forces, then their movement over time does not necessarily say anything about labor supply conditions, or about labor's productivity in agriculture.

3. The private marginal productivity of labor in agriculture is zero. This is the "redundant labor" of the Fei-Ranis model.[9] This concept can scarcely apply to people, if there is efficient work-sharing within the family, but must apply rather to the last man-hour of labor input. Marginal productivity in this sense could be zero only if, over a certain range, increased hours of work had zero disutility, i.e., leisure had zero value. This is a conceivable case; but research studies in which production functions are fitted to cross-section farm data usually show a positive marginal product of additional man-hours.

4. The private marginal product of a man-hour of labor, while positive, is below the hourly return to labor. This could readily happen in family farming, where each family member's share of output reflects the average rather than the marginal product of labor. A corollary is that the supply price of labor for nonfarm work, and hence the rural wage level, will reflect average productivity on the farm. For employers of hired labor, however, it would seem that marginal productivity could not fall below the wage rate unless the employer ignores profitability or unless he is obliged to hire a fixed number of workers. In the latter case, the worker's daily earnings become an overhead cost. If the employer can set the hours of work without worker consent or resistance, it will pay him to increase hours until marginal productivity approaches zero.

The case of a divergence between earnings and marginal product is

9. J. C. H. Fei and Gustav Ranis, *Development of the Labor Surplus Economy: Theory and Policy* (Homewood, Ill.: Richard D. Irwin, 1964).

often termed "disguised unemployment," a concept developed originally in the 1930s with respect to depression unemployment in developed countries. In such periods, many workers are forced downward on the skill ladder. While they may still be employed, their productivity in their current employment is below their potential productivity on their regular job. There is thus a hidden labor potential which can be activated as demand rises during recovery. It does not seem helpful to apply this terminology—quite clear-cut in its original meaning—to the very different circumstances of agricultural workers in the LDCs.

5. Another conceivable situation is one in which, given the social objective of maximizing the value of current income, the combination of techniques and resources is such that the shadow wage and hence the *social marginal productivity* of labor is zero. The existence of surplus labor in this sense does not necessarily imply its existence in the other senses listed. To test the existence of this situation would require use of programming techniques, and the assumptions used in constructing a programming model are so restrictive that little significance could be attached to the results.

6. Finally, it is said that surplus labor exists if workers can be withdrawn from the agricultural sector without reducing agricultural output. This must mean that, as workers are withdrawn, the remaining workers put in enough additional hours to keep total man-hour input as high as before. This would imply the kinds of assumption about disutility of labor used in cases 1 or 3 above.

The realism of this case has been strongly denied by T. W. Schultz and others. It is difficult to put the argument to an empirical test, because one hardly ever observes an actual decline of the farm labor force except at an advanced stage of economic development. However, it is intuitively plausible to think that, if the rural labor force shrank absolutely, and if there were no other change in the situation, agricultural output would also decline.

In sum: there has been a tendency to confuse several different concepts of labor surplus. One of these does not necessarily imply the others. One or more of them can be true without all being true. For example, it is not inconsistent to maintain that:

i. Labor surplus does not exist in sense 3. The marginal productivity of *man-hours* worked in agriculture is significantly positive.

ii. Nor does labor surplus exist in sense 6. Withdrawal of *people* from agriculture would, ceteris paribus, reduce output.

iii. Yet labor surplus does exist in sense 2.—elastic supply of labor to the industrial sector. A possible reason for this is overpricing of industrial labor.

However one rationalizes it, there seems to be substantial labor force slack in most LDCs—low labor force participation rates of female and even male prime-age workers, short hours per week and per year, low intensity of work, low output per man-hour, plus a good deal of open unemployment. This slack is not confined to agriculture. It pervades the traditional trade, service, and handicraft activities and even penetrates the modern sector through such devices as compulsory overstaffing.

Mobilization of this unused labor potential requires mainly an intensification of demand, but two caveats are in order. First, within the agricultural sector, intensification of demand means mainly technical changes that shift labor productivity curves upward. Second, technical change would be needed in any event to compensate workers who are being asked to work harder and who will demand a reward in terms of higher consumption, including higher food consumption. The notion of a "costless" labor transfer from agriculture in the original Nurkse model, and the accompanying notion that technical progress in agriculture is required only at some later stage of development, seems fundamentally wrong. A development process that does not incorporate technical change in agriculture from the beginning must quickly grind to a halt—at least under closed-economy assumptions. Even when the possibility of trade is admitted, few LDCs have sufficiently dependable nonfood exports to sustain a growing food deficit.

### AGRICULTURE AS A RESOURCE RESERVOIR

The labor surplus discussion is one aspect of a larger issue. In most development models, modern industry is the cutting edge of economic growth, while agriculture plays the role of a resource reservoir which can be drawn on for supplies of food, labor, and finance to fuel the growth of urban activities. It is argued that this is both a logical necessity and a matter of historical experience, illustrated especially by the case of Japan.

In commenting on this view, I must emphasize a distinction that is often not clearly drawn: (1) It is one thing to assert that, in an economy where agricultural output is not rising, the agricultural sector contains potential surpluses of labor time, food output, and saving capacity requiring only appropriate public policies for their release. This we may term the static view of resource transfer. (2) It is quite a different thing to assert that, in an economy where agricultural output is being raised by a combination of investment and technical progress, part of the increment in farm output and income is available for transfer to non-agriculture. This we may term the dynamic view of resource transfer. The model-building implications of this approach are different, and its policy implications are decidely different.

## Transfers of Labor

Consider first a static economy with no growth in population or farm output. In such an economy there might well be an urban-rural income gap large enough to provide an incentive to migration; but it would seem that such migration must soon cease. If the people moving to the city are employed there at higher wages, demand for food will rise, while for reasons suggested in the previous section their departure from agriculture will probably cause food output to fall. The economy thus runs immediately into the Ricardian food bottleneck.

The situation is not basically changed if we allow population to rise with no change in cultivated area or agricultural technology. Food output will then rise but, because of diminishing returns, it will rise less rapidly than population. There are more people available for transfer to the city, but there is not enough food to feed them there. The food bottleneck remains.

A plausible model of labor transfer, then, seems to require technical progress. An internally consistent model, for example, might involve population growth of 3 percent (in country and city), agricultural output rising at 5 percent, and direct farm labor requirements rising at 2 percent. This would *permit* rural-urban migration because food supplies would be adequate; and it would *require* such migration to avert growing rural underemployment.

In short, the notion of a costless labor transfer from agriculture to industry under static conditions is a mirage. The reality is that part of the increment of a growing labor force can be transferred, if the necessary food supply conditions are met. Such transfers are then not only feasible but necessary as a condition of continuing balanced growth.

## Transfers of Food

Most of what might be said under this heading has already been implied. If the static argument for a costless labor transfer is implausible, the notion of a costless food transfer is equally suspect. Given the low levels of farm consumption prevailing in most LDCs, the possibility of putting a further "squeeze" on farmers by diverting food to the cities is clearly limited. But this view is quite compatible with a dynamic argument for a potential food surplus. Given technical progress, availability of modern inputs and improved rural infrastructure, agricultural output can be substantially increased; and part of the increment to output is available for off-farm sale.

## Transfers of Finance

Development models tend to incorporate an increase in industrial and infrastructure investment, financed partly by an increase in agricultural savings transferred for urban use. Institutionally, this transfer is viewed as occurring through some combination of private capital markets and the fiscal system. The implication is that agricultural investment is not required, or that investment possibilities in agriculture have been pushed to the margin of profitability.

From a dynamic view, however, there is need for rising agricultural output per man and per acre, associated with changes in technique. These changes require substantial investment: public investment in transportation, irrigation facilities, fertilizer factories, and agricultural research and development; and private investment by farmers in land improvement, tools, and improved inputs. Thus private saving, tax levies, private investment, and public investment should be viewed as going on simultaneously in both agriculture and nonagriculture. Financial flows are going in both directions, with the gross flows substantially larger than the net flow.

One should not assume a priori that the net flow will be from agriculture to industry. Clearly, one could construct assumptions that would produce the opposite result. Historically, this is a matter for empirical investigation. As for policy, allocation of investment funds should presumably be guided by relative returns rather than by doctrinaire notions of the absolute superiority of industry (or agriculture). R. A. Berry's forthcoming volume on Colombian agriculture concludes that, as of 1970, prospective returns to agricultural investment considerably exceeded returns to manufacturing. But this is something to be investigated country by country, and any general conclusion would be premature.

To the extent that net transfers are expected from agriculture, these will clearly be facilitated by rising agricultural incomes. Marginal savings rates are typically higher than average rates. As regards fiscal transfers, it is obviously easier to tax away part of the increment to a rising income than it is to cut into a stationary income without adverse incentive effects.

THE OPEN ECONOMY

The burden of the argument thus far has been that closed-economy development models need to be restructured in important respects. But there is a further question whether even the most sophisticated closed-economy model can have much relevance for LDCs that are heavily involved in international trade. Preoccupation with the closed economy has tended to draw attention away from difficult issues relating to agriculture's role in the open economy.

The nature of these difficulties is outlined in Hla Myint's contribution to this volume, Chapter 12. As he points out, agriculture is usually expected to contribute to overall growth in several ways:

i. by increasing domestic food supplies
ii. by providing a growing market for domestic manufactures
iii. by contributing to domestic saving and capital formation
iv. by providing foreign exchange through agricultural exports

When we add this fourth item, however, we slip over into an open-economy setting; and when we do this, the necessity for the first three contributions is no longer self-evident. Trade flows will in some measure reflect comparative advantage; and a developing economy may have comparative advantage in either agricultural or industrial goods, or in some items from each category. Thus it is conceivable that growing food requirements may be met from imports. The growing market for industrial products need not necessarily be a domestic market. Domestic savings may be supplemented by foreign capital, and so on.

Further, as Myint correctly argues, the four contributions may become inconsistent with each other. Policies of import substitution, designed to direct farmers' demand toward domestic manufactures (item ii) and heavier farm taxation to augment the national savings fund (item iii) will reduce real farm income and reduce production incentives (items i and iv). Moreover, increased production of food for home consumption (item i) may be competitive with increased production of agricultural exports (item iv). The shift to an open-economy setting thus requires a fundamental rethinking of agriculture's role.

Reasoning on this front is closely linked with arguments over the applicability of conventional trade theory to LDC conditions and is often linked also with policy analysis. Without venturing far into this vast terrain, I will comment briefly on the familiar models of export-led growth, and of import substitution.

## Export-Led Growth

By "exports" here we mean primary exports, and more specifically exports of agricultural products. Export-led growth is an old idea, going back at least to Adam Smith. More recently, it has been restated as the "staple hypothesis." Exports of primary staples are alleged to have been important in the early growth of economies as diverse as Argentina, the United States, the British Dominions, Denmark, and Russia. More recently, the economic expansion of some West African and Southeast Asian countries has involved a rapid increase in exports of cocoa, rice, and other peasant-produced crops.

Two questions immediately arise: first, can supplies of agricultural exports be increased without encroaching on simultaneous growth of food for domestic consumption? An affirmative answer requires that we assume either: (1) a dualistic agriculture in which exports come from plantations not readily convertible to food production; (2) unused land and labor resources that can be mobilized for export crops without encroaching on food output, as in the West African cocoa story; or (3) technical progress of a land-saving sort, in cases where land shortage is the binding constraint on output. While these conditions do not always exist, they exist frequently enough to make export-led growth a realistic possibility for many countries.

The second problem is that of markets. "Export pessimists" such as Raul Prebisch and Gunnar Myrdal have argued that world demand for primary exports is now rising too slowly to provide an adequate rate of increase in foreign exchange availability to the LDCs, and that efforts to push exports will also lead to secular deterioration of the terms of trade. But one should not overgeneralize. The outcome varies with the product: livestock, poultry, feed grains, and temperate-zone cereals may have better prospects than tea, coffee, and cocoa. But even for tropical products, W. A. Lewis points out that from 1955 to 1965 the physical volume of exports from tropical countries grew at 4.5 percent per year, about the same as the average GNP growth rate of the OECD

(Organization for Economic Cooperation and Development) countries excluding Japan.[10] Over the whole period from 1883 to 1965, Lewis finds that a linear relation between the log of (tropical) agricultural exports and the log of (developed country) industrial production has a slope of 0.84. Agricultural exports do not grow as fast, but almost as fast.

Moreover, export performance is not given exogenously from the developed world. It depends on what the exporting country does. Irving Kravis recently analyzed the export performance of 58 LDCs from 1959 to 1965, dividing them into "superior," "middle," and "inferior" groups. For each group he calculated: (1) a "world market factor," showing what each country's exports would have been, had its exports changed only in response to changes in world demand for its traditional exports; (2) a "competitiveness" factor, based on the change in each country's *share* of world demand for its traditional exports; and (3) a "diversification" factor, equivalent to the ratio of the share of traditional exports in the country's total exports in the initial period to the share of traditional exports in the terminal period. The "superior" group of countries increased their export earnings by 78 percent over the period; and two-thirds of this good performance was accounted for by the competitiveness and diversification factors rather than by growth of world markets.[11]

It is not difficult, then, to construct a believable growth model in which peasant-produced agricultural exports are rising at, say, 5 percent a year, and in which the foreign exchange thus earned is used initially for consumer goods imports but, with the passage of time, increasingly for imports of capital goods and industrial materials. Domestic manufacturing industries appear, in Hirschman fashion, as the size of the domestic market approaches the capacity of an optimum-sized producing unit. The nascent industrial sector grows mainly by reinvestment of profits, gradually replacing both consumer good imports and domestic handicraft outputs. Food output rises at an appropriate rate; and government, by implication, participates actively by building infrastructure and by modernizing economic institutions.

10. W. A. Lewis, *Aspects of Tropical Trade, 1883–1965* (Stockholm: Almquist and Wiksell, 1969).
11. Irving Kravis, "Trade as a Handmaiden of Growth: Similarities between the Nineteenth and Twentieth Centuries," *Economic Journal*, December 1970, pp. 850–72.

This may be viewed as a gradual, unexciting growth path; but one can scarcely deny that it is a viable path.

## Import Substitution

A more popular model in the less developed world has been that of import-substitution growth, designed to accelerate creation of a modern industrial base. The reasoning used in support of this approach is "infant economy" reasoning, strongly reminiscent of traditional infant industry arguments, but often reinforced by labor-surplus and factor-price distortion arguments as well. There is no doubt that this, too, is a viable growth path, particularly for countries of substantial size. For a time, at least, it can raise the rate of increase in industrial output. Whether the rate of increase in total output is higher than it would have been under more outward-looking policies is less certain.

The essence of import-substitution policy is to make domestic manufacturing profitable. The available instruments are exchange rate policy, inflation, and tariff protection. In large measure these are substitutable for each other; the same degree of profit transfer to industry can be achieved by different policy packages. The economic effects are not identical, however, and there are sometimes political reasons for preferring one package to another.

A full analysis of these policies would go beyond my present purpose. The main point here is that they produce a double squeeze on the agricultural sector. The overvalued exchange rate penalizes exporters of farm products, while the artificial enhancement of the prices of domestic manufactures turns the domestic terms of trade against farmers. This must reduce incentives for agricultural production. Experienced observers such as T. W. Schultz have concluded that this discouraging effect is substantial. Thus, apart from any limitations of foreign demand, export expansion may be slowed down from the supply side. Export pessimism, often urged as a reason for import substitution, can readily become self-fulfilling.

A further characteristic of import substitution is that it must necessarily come to an end. The extent of import substitution achieved at any time can be measured in either of two ways: by the percentage of foreign exchange allocated to purchase of capital and intermediate goods as against consumer goods, or by imports of manufactured consumer goods as a percentage of domestic consumption of manufactures. The former percentage cannot rise above one hundred, nor can the latter fall below zero. So, while domestic output of manufactures can for a while rise faster than domestic consumption, its growth rate must eventually fall to correspond with that of the domestic market —unless, that is, the country can shift to an export position in manufactures. Unfortunately, the hothouse atmosphere of high protectionism is not conducive to productive efficiency and attainment of international competitiveness. Development of export potential in manufactures requires a drastic shift in domestic policies, which few countries have yet managed to accomplish.

## AGRICULTURE IN SOCIALIST DEVELOPMENT

By a socialist LDC I mean one in which government is dominated by a communist party, in which agriculture is (usually) organized in collective farms, and in which industrial enterprises are state owned and operated. Examples are China, Cuba, North Korea, North Vietnam, and several of the less developed East European countries. Chapter 15 in this volume analyzes agricultural development in Eastern Europe since 1945.

The requirements for agricultural progress, and the significant interactions between the agricultural and nonagricultural sectors, seem similar in socialist and nonsocialist economies. But the institutional organization is different; and agricultural performance is also a function of government policies. In the Soviet Union and Eastern Europe, these policies have had a strong proindustry bias, which must partially account for lagging agricultural performance. It is not yet demonstrated that collective agriculture need perform as poorly as it has done in the past.

By far the largest of the socialist LDCs is China; and, though information on Chinese agriculture is fragmentary, a few observations can be made. The Chinese government, after an initial concentration on heavy industry, reverted in the 1960s to balanced development of industry and agriculture. The policy stance is clearly more proagriculture than in Eastern Europe or the Soviet Union.

The city price of food grains has remained unchanged for many years. Farm prices, on the other hand, have been raised several times. Farm and city prices are now approximately equal, which implies a government subsidy of transport and handling costs. Prices of manufactures have declined somewhat, as unit costs have been reduced through rising productivity with relatively stable money wages. Agriculture's terms of trade have thus been improving. Direct taxation of agriculture is moderate, being estimated at present at about 7 percent of gross farm income. Communes located near city markets also have considerable opportunity to increase income by selling nonstaple products (such as vegetables, fruit, poultry, eggs, milk, and fish) at prices negotiated with the municipal authorities.

The output results have thus far been modest. Dwight Perkins estimates that between 1957 and 1972 agricultural output rose at an average annual rate of 3 percent.[12] Population is thought to be growing at not more than 2 percent. The implication is that the population is able to eat a little better each year. The control system has also proven capable of transferring sufficient food from the farms to feed the 20 percent of the population in urban areas.

In interpreting the output results, one must recall that land limitations are severe. Increases in cropped acreage have been small and have been accomplished more by double-cropping than by actual extension of cultivation. In addition, supplies of chemical fertilizer and other modern inputs, while growing rapidly in percentage terms, remain very small on an absolute basis.

An interesting feature of Chinese economic policy is the effort to restrain rural-urban migration, in order to reduce pressure on urban housing and community facilities and to avoid urban unemployment. Official policy is that existing urban centers, particularly the large cities on the eastern seaboard, should not increase in size, and that the present 80:20 rural-urban balance should be maintained for the foreseeable future. Movement of labor toward the cities is restrained in several ways. (1) Industrial location policy: the emphasis is on location of new industries in suburban areas rather than central cities, and on industrial development within the commune structure to absorb surplus farm labor. (2) Employment controls: one cannot get a city job except through the municipal employment bureau, which will accept migrants from the country only if there is a genuine need for additional workers, and only if existing urban labor supplies are fully mobilized. (3) Housing allocations: if a country worker applies for housing in the city, the first question is "Do you have a job?" If the answer is no, the applicant is back to square one. (4) Purchasing controls: permission is required to change one's ration book location, and this is not easy to get. This interlocking network of controls makes it virtually impossible

12. Dwight H. Perkins, "Looking Inside China: An Economic Reappraisal," *Problems of Communism* 13 (1973): 1–13.

to move to and remain unemployed in the city. At some times, indeed, the flow of labor has been in the other direction. If in a particular year the number of new jobs becoming available in, say, Shanghai is less than the available supply of school leavers, the surplus is dispatched to the countryside for farm labor.

One's first thought might be that this is simply shifting the burden of surplus labor from city to country, with an intensification of rural underemployment. Chinese spokesmen maintain, however, that everyone in the countryside is fully employed, and that there would be work for additional hands if they were available. How can such statements be interpreted?

The main sources of increased rural employment seem to have been as follows. First, there has been a marked expansion of small-scale industrial production, in workshops employing typically from 20 to 200 people, within the commune structure. These rural industries produce partly for farm use—bricks, cement, fertilizer, and farm tools—and repair implements, but they also turn out consumer goods for off-farm sale and even for export. At seasonal peaks of harvest activity, most of these workers go into the fields; but their main activity is factory work, which helps to fill in the valleys of the agricultural cycle. They are paid, in cash or in work points, at about what they would receive for the same amount of time spent in farm labor. Second, there has also been a marked increase of labor time invested in infrastructure activities: construction of roads, water control and irrigation systems, land terracing, reforestation, building of schools, hospitals, and public buildings as well as housing. This work is also done mainly in the agricultural off-season. Third, these infrastructure activities, and especially improved water control, have made possible a considerable shift of acreage from single- to double-cropping. They also make possible greater use of fertilizer and more sophisticated input "packages." All this requires more labor. Fourth, in areas near city markets there has been some diversification of farm activity into fruit and vegetable production and into animal husbandry. These activities are more labor intensive than grain growing.

All in all, there seems no reason to question the claim of substantially full employment. Some of this employment—for example, creating new land by carrying baskets of earth from another area—probably has a low marginal yield. There is doubtless a tendency to treat the available labor time as an overhead cost, and to regard even a slight addition to output as worthwhile.

While the institutional context is very different, there are interesting similarities between recent Chinese development and Japanese development from, say, 1880 to 1905. In both cases one observes: (1) marked emphasis on agricultural development, leading to output increases of about 1 percent per capita per year; (2) marked development of rural-based industries, in relatively small, labor-intensive workshops employing mainly farm family members; (3) rapid development of roads, railroads, and communication facilities; and (4) the beginnings of heavy industrial development, stimulated partly by military requirements. There are obvious differences as well, in such matters as rate of labor transfer from agriculture, degree of involvement in foreign trade, and trends in income distribution. But China-Japan comparisons should eventually tell us more about whether economies starting with similar factor endowments and income levels tend to follow a similar development path despite institutional differences.

In view of the already summary character of this survey, further summarizing would be pointless. The burden of our story, in this book, is the central importance of agriculture in development economics, at both empirical and analytical levels. As data accumulate over the years, it should soon become possible to distinguish the LDCs that have managed to embark on sustained growth from those that have not. We hypothesize that, when this is done, the countries that can be classified as "success cases" will show a strong performance in the agricultural sector, and conversely.

Model builders, too, should concentrate more heavily than they sometimes have done on the design of the agricultural sector, which is more difficult than the industrial sector but at the same time critically important. Particularly important are assumptions about the conditions and characteristics of technical progress. The central problem is to generate a rate of progress high enough to meet both food-transfer and labor-absorption objectives in a context of rapid population growth.

PART I: THE ECONOMICS OF PEASANT PRODUCTION

# 2

# Smallholder Decision Making:
# Tropical African Evidence

GERALD K. HELLEINER

In agricultural economics as in other fields, the study of Africa has been much influenced by thought and research from other parts of the Third World. In recent years there has also been emerging an "indigenous" literature of African agricultural development which, while still related to theory and evidence from elsewhere, is increasingly based upon knowledge of African farming systems. This chapter will not seek to develop a new theoretical model of smallholder decision making. Rather it seeks to summarize the present state of knowledge and thought about smallholder decision making in Africa.

The African focus of this paper derives not from a view that there is something uniquely African which makes it possible to generalize across that continent, although some knowledgeable observers do assert that African "peasants" are different from those theorized about elsewhere in the development literature.[1] It grows, rather, from a consciousness that research results from the African continent are not adequately represented in many of the existing general analyses of agricultural development.[2]

I am grateful for comments on an earlier draft from Carl Eicher, Jan Hogendorn, Bruce Johnston, Peter McLoughlin, Jerome Wells, and Lloyd Reynolds, none of whom is at all responsible for the content of the present version.

1. Peter F. M. McLoughlin, ed., *African Food Production Systems: Cases and Theory* (Baltimore: Johns Hopkins Press, 1970), p. 11.
2. Such as John W. Mellor, *The Economics of Agricultural Development* (Ithaca, N. Y.: Cornell University Press, 1966); Herman M. Southworth and Bruce F. Johnston, eds., *Agricultural Development and Economic Growth* (Ithaca, N. Y.: Cornell University Press, 1967); C. R. Wharton, ed., *Subsistence Agriculture and Economic Development* (Chicago: Aldine, 1969); indeed, the evidence to be summarized here is not totally representative of all of Africa anyway, in that the literature cited is primarily that available in English.

Dominating all other research results in recent years is the awareness that African agricultural systems are diverse, changing, and complex. As in the rest of the development literature, there is growing hesitancy about generalization. At the same time, at a very general level, evidence accumulates which runs directly counter to some of the earlier wisdom regarding African agriculture but which accords with recent evidence from other continents; particularly noteworthy in this respect is that bearing upon "orthodox" supply response.

The discussion in this chapter will be organized as follows. Section 1 will be concerned with the traditional questions of African agriculture —disguised unemployment and/or "laziness," migrant labor, shifting cultivation, the backward-bending supply curve, and the like. Section 2 focuses on the historical and more recent evidence bearing on the nature and extent of smallholder supply response. Section 3 addresses the issue of smallholder resource allocation and response to technological innovations.

## 1. TRADITIONAL ISSUES IN AFRICAN AGRICULTURE

### Disguised Unemployment and the Labor Constraint

On one traditional question in the literature of agriculture and economic development there is now virtual unanimity in Africa. The marginal productivity of labor in agriculture is positive. Disguised unemployment is a concept no longer much employed in the African context since the evidence that it is peak season labor which is typically the operative constraint in African farming systems is by now overwhelming.[3] Discussions in this sphere are much more likely to be cast

3. See, for example, D. W. Norman, "Labour Inputs of Farmers: A Case Study of the Zaria Province of the North-Central State of Nigeria," *Nigerian Journal of Economic and Social Studies* 11, no. 1 (1969); H. A. Luning, *Economic Aspects of Low Labour-Income Farming* (Wageningen: Centre for Agricultural Publications and Documentation, 1967); M. P. Collinson, "Experience with a Trial Management Farm in Tanzania," *East African Journal of Rural Development* 2, no. 2 (1969); Derek Byerlee and Carl K. Eicher, "Rural Employment, Migration, and Economic Development: Theoretical Issues and Empirical Evidence from Africa," African Rural Employment Study, Rural Employment Paper no. 1 (Department of Agricultural Economics, Michigan State University, East Lansing, September 1972); Judith Heyer, "A Linear Programming Analysis of Constraints on Peasant Farming," *Food Research Institute Studies* 10, no. 1 (1971): 55–68; John C. de Wilde et al., *Experiences with Agricultural Development in Tropical Africa* (Baltimore: Johns Hopkins Press, 1967); John H. Cleave, "Labour in the Development of African Agriculture: The Evidence from Farm Surveys" (Ph.D. diss., Stanford University, 1970); Marvin

in terms of whether or not there still exists a land surplus, in the sense that the marginal product of further inputs of labor, with unchanged technology, is constant.[4]

Yet the typically pronounced seasonality in the demand for farm labor does have implications for development theory and policy which are not unrelated to the earlier discussions of disguised unemployment. The seasonally "surplus" labor, which the casual observer assumed was a permanent phenomenon, can be and is mobilized in a variety of ways. Where seasonal peaks in nearby agricultural systems do not coincide, as in the case of the West African savannah zone and the adjoining tree-crop zones to the south, there is an obvious potential for highly productive short-term labor (and farmer) migration and labor market participation.[5] Thus the earlier condemnation of the widespread African practice of short-term labor migration was inappropriate, based as it was on an inadequate understanding of the patterns of African farming. Increased nonfarm economic activities of various sorts, including rural capital formation, are also obvious possibilities for off-season employment.

At the same time, recognition that labor is the major constraint upon agricultural expansion in existing systems carries implications for the development of nonfarm economic activity on a full-time basis. There may be considerable opportunity costs involved in the latter activities, particularly when they are located in the rural areas, unless of course the full-time labor is drawn from the ranks of the urban unemployed.[6] Nonfarm activity is now recognized as a major user not only of slack season but even of peak season rural labor; it may take as

P. Miracle, *Agriculture in the Congo Basin: Tradition and Change in African Rural Economies* (Madison: University of Wisconsin Press, 1967); and McLoughlin, *African Food Production Systems,* p. 310.

4. Gerald K. Helleiner, "Typology in Development Theory: The Land Surplus Economy (Nigeria)," *Food Research Institute Studies* 6 (1966): 181–94; E. M. Godfrey, "Labor-Surplus Models and Labor-Deficit Economies: The West African Case," *Economic Development and Cultural Change* 17, no. 3 (1969): 382–91.

5. Elliot J. Berg, "The Economics of the Migrant Labor System," in *Urbanization and Migration in West Africa,* ed. Hilda Kuper (Berkeley and Los Angeles: University of California Press, 1965); Ralph E. Beals and Carmen F. Menezes, "Migrant Labour and Agricultural Output in Ghana," *Oxford Economic Papers* 22, no. 1 (1970): 109–27; Marvin P. Miracle and Sara S. Berry, "Migrant Labour and Economic Development," *Oxford Economic Papers* 22, no. 1 (1970): 86–108.

6. For an attempt to develop a model that incorporates some of these elements see O. Aboyade, "The Development Process," in *Reconstruction and Development in Nigeria,* ed. A. A. Ayida and H. M. Onitiri (Ibadan: Oxford University Press, 1971).

much as half the total working time of African farmers.[7] The labor constraint also implies that agricultural innovations—new crops, improved practices, and so on—will be assessed by potential adopters with careful consideration of the seasonal pattern of their labor requirements.

### Target Incomes and the Backward-Sloping Supply Schedule[8]

The target income hypothesis is one of the hoariest of all of the bits of conventional wisdoms of old Africa hands. Although it originated with reference to labor supply schedules faced by foreign employers, it was presumed to apply to aggregate labor supply and thus to agricultural supply as well. Substitution effects were believed to be dominated by income effects in the relevant African decision makers' trade-offs as between work and leisure (or the production of $z$-goods,[9] although their existence was not generally considered at that time). The desire on the part of Africans to earn a specified money income (the target), whether for bride-price, tax obligations, particular consumer-good purchases, or whatever, led, according to this interpretation, to a backward bend in the labor supply schedule within the relevant ranges. What was true of individual decision makers was, of course, unlikely to be true of the aggregate of these decision makers, since their numbers could also be expected to respond to price alterations.[10] The accumulation of evidence of "normal" responses to economic incentives, particularly with respect to price relatives and rural earning opportunities (see below), called into question this hypothesis with respect to individual behavior but did not directly disprove it. In the continuing absence of empirical evidence on the question it began to be asserted increasingly that the "normality" of African responses had increased over time as the cash economy spread and as tastes were developed for goods and services purchasable only with cash. Recently that widespread interpretation has been directly challenged by evidence that there were sufficient changes in the economic incentives themselves, including the deterioration of earning opportunities on the land, to account for the

7. See also section 1.

8. Byerlee and Eicher, "Rural Employment, Migration, and Economic Development," p. 10.

9. Stephen Hymer and Stephen Resnick, "A Model of an Agrarian Economy with Non-Agricultural Activities," *American Economic Review* 59, no. 4 (1969): 493–506.

10. Elliot J. Berg, "Backward-Sloping Labor Supply Functions in Dual Economies: The Africa Case," *Quarterly Journal of Economics* 75 (1961): 468–92.

purported alteration in the degree of African responsiveness thereto.[11] It is difficult to take any but an agnostic position as to whether the target income approach ever applied to significant numbers of individual African farmers; but its applicability today is likely to be limited.[12]

## Traditional Practices

More careful analysis and the collection of more data have also led to revisions of conventional views as to the productivity of traditional methods of cultivation and farming systems. Shifting cultivation, of which the largest continuous belt in the world is in tropical Africa,[13] is now seen, for instance, as a rational land-intensive technique in a context in which land is effectively free.[14] Many of the innovations pushed upon unwilling African smallholders by colonial agriculturalists are now recognized as having been uneconomical.[15] African smallholders' early understanding of the need for shade cover and the carrying capacity of and suitable crop mixes and rotations for various kinds of soils is now seen as considerable.

## 2. SUPPLY RESPONSE

In African smallholder agriculture, since purchased inputs are typically few, supply responses are largely matters of labor and land reallocation. (The absence of specialized capital and other inputs in smallholder agriculture may, in the short run, make its acreage more price responsive but its yields less price responsive compared with estate agriculture.

11. Marvin P. Miracle and Bruce Fetter, "Backward-Sloping Labor-Supply Functions and African Economic Behavior," *Economic Development and Cultural Change* 18, no. 2 (1970): 240–51.

12. James McCabe has called my attention to the fact that there seems to have been an instance of negative supply response on the part of palm oil producers in Zaire following the 1967 devaluation; moreover, the fact that palm oil prices in Zaire rise as the distance between the urban retailing area and the producing site increases also suggests that there exist "abnormal" supply responses in this sector. On the first point see Jacques S. Kazadi and W. A. Dile, *Politiques salariales et développement* (Paris, 1970). On the second I am indebted to Mr. McCabe.

13. Miracle, *Agriculture in the Congo Basin*, p. iii.

14. Ibid.; Ralph Gerald Saylor, *The Economic System of Sierra Leone* (Durham, N.C.: Duke University Press, 1967); Polly Hill, *Studies in Rural Capitalism in West Africa* (Cambridge: at the University Press, 1970), p. 15.

15. For instance, Reginald H. Green and Stephen Hymer, "Cocoa in the Gold Coast: A Study in the Relations between African Farmers and Agricultural Experts," *Journal of Economic History* 16, no. 3 (1966): 299–319.

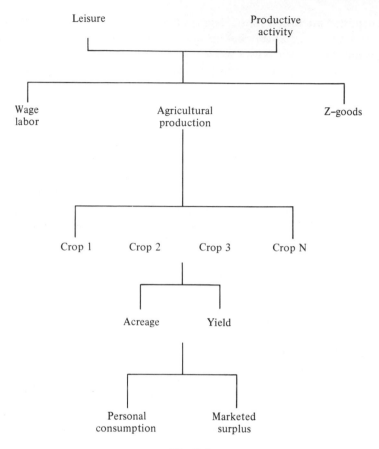

Fig. 2.1

This hypothesis is supported by the evidence on Kenyan coffee.)[16] Acreage, yield, and agricultural production responses to relative price changes in the agricultural sector do not constitute the entire story of economic response on the part of the smallholder. His total allocation of time as between agricultural production activities, other economic activities, and leisure can also be considered to be responsive to alterations in relative prices. Figure 2.1 illustrates the variety of supply de-

16. J. K. Maitha, "A Supply Function for Kenyan Coffee," *Eastern Africa Economic Review* 1, no. 1 (1969); idem, "Productivity Response to Price: A Case Study of Kenyan Coffee," *Eastern Africa Economic Review* 2, no. 2 (1970); Derek J. Ford, "Long-run Price Elasticities in the Supply of Kenyan Coffee: A Methodological Note," *Eastern Africa Economic Review*, n.s. no. 1 (1971).

cisions and trade-offs that are made by smallholders under study, each of which can be considered in the short or long run. (Clifton Wharton's otherwise admirable classification of supply responses did not distinguish, as it should have, among leisure, wage labor, and $z$-goods production as alternatives to agricultural production.)[17]

At each decision point, measures of risk and uncertainty must be introduced as explanatory variables, together with the relevant prices or rates of return. The failure of some earlier attempts at construction of models of smallholder decision making to introduce risk factors is striking.[18] (The risk factor is still lacking from the otherwise quite sophisticated models of urban-rural migration; the attraction of an urban job relative to rural income-earning opportunities may be a matter of its stability as much as its level.)

The discovery of a positive correlation between the price of a crop and sales to a marketing board thus tells the analyst very little about the nature of decision making among agricultural producers. It can reflect trade-offs between leisure and production, $z$-goods and agricultural production, wage labor and agricultural production, one crop and another, or personal consumption and marketed surplus; and, to the extent that production of the crop in question alters, this may have been achieved through changes in either labor, acreage, or other inputs, some of which may constitute adoptions of totally new technological innovations. To understand the observed correlation—and thus to derive generalizable results therefrom—one clearly requires far more detailed information than one customarily has: data concerning welfare functions that incorporate attitudes to risk, the constraints on existing farming systems, and the interrelationships between various inputs and outputs of such systems in the appropriate environmental context. The simple regression results in table 2.1 nevertheless represent more evidence than there used to be.

There is no reliable evidence on major elements of aggregate supply responses in Africa. The substitution of "productive activity" for "leisure" has gradually taken a smaller proportion of total smallholder time as the cash economy has made an impact upon African rural society; but, for obvious reasons, it has not been possible to verify this assumption empirically. Indeed it has not been possible even to test responsiveness of leisure to its price in the more recent periods,

17. Wharton, *Subsistence Agriculture and Economic Development*, p. 230.
18. For example, Chihiro Nakajima's essay in ibid.

for which data have become a little more numerous. Nor has it been possible to test the aggregate agricultural supply response (either production or marketed surplus) either of individual smallholders or of the smallholder sector as a whole to "total" agricultural prices or the agricultural/industrial or rural/urban terms of trade, since the estimates of total domestically consumed agricultural production are subject to such wide margins of error. The only test—that of Edwin Dean in Malawi—using responsiveness of labor supply to the consumer price index was inconclusive.[19]

On the one margin for which there are some data—that between smallholder farming and wage (particularly urban) labor—the evidence is fairly one-sided. Historically, relative attractiveness, including legal requirements or prohibitions of some sorts of economic activity, does seem to have influenced the Africans' choice between wage labor and smallholder production. The percentage of the male population in Zambia and Rhodesia who migrated from their region for employment in the 1940s and 1950s was correlated inversely with the cash crop potential of their region.[20] Malawi tobacco growers' sales from 1926 to 1960 were inversely and significantly related to wage rates in the Rhodesian and South African labor markets to which farmers could travel for work.[21] Several historians have by now made similar observations, frequently introducing other explanatory variables into their interpretations as well. Historical analysis of Rhodesian agriculture, for instance, demonstrated the relationship between wage earning and not only cash-cropping opportunities but also existing or preexistent rural social systems. Thus, Ndebele men participated far more than Shona men in the wage labor force at least partly because upper-caste Ndebele were thrown into a state of "structural underemployment" by the Pax Britannica, which forbade them their martial pursuits.[22]

19. Edwin Dean, *The Supply Responses of African Farmers: Theory and Measurement in Malawi* (Amsterdam: North Holland, 1966). Minford found a significant relationship between a measure of marketed agricultural surpluses (all crops) in Malawi and an index of farmer prices (with an elasticity of 0.6) between 1949 and 1969; but the sources of data and, in particular, the measure of marketed surplus were not stated in the paper in which this result was reported, so that it is difficult to evaluate it; see A. P. L. Minford, "A Model of Tax Incidence for Malawi," in "African Public Sector Economics," mimeographed (Centre of African Studies, University of Edinburgh, 1970).

20. William J. Barber, "Economic Rationality and Behaviour Patterns in an Underdeveloped Area: A Case Study of African Economic Behaviour in the Rhodesias," *Economic Development and Cultural Change* 8, no. 3 (1960): 237–51.

21. Dean, *Supply Responses of African Farmers*.

22. Giovanni Arrighi, "Labour Supplies in Historical Perspective: A Study of the

What was once perceived as growing rationality over time is now coming to be seen as continuing sophisticated calculation of the costs and benefits of wage earning as against rural production, with a gradual improvement in urban conditions, a lowering of transport costs, the deterioration of rural earning opportunities (the product of growing land shortage, deteriorating produce prices, and official discouragement), and increases in African demands for necessities[23] explaining the increasing "normality" of the labor supply schedule.

Rural-urban migration, which has been the object of so much attention in Africa in recent years, is also, of course, the product of decisions taken in the rural areas by smallholders. Fairly sophisticated models explaining the phenomenon have been erected on the basis of assumptions as to the basic economic rationality of these rural decision makers.[24] Migration, which is the product of a decision to seek urban wage employment, is related in these models to the mathematically expected value of rural as against urban real earnings. The calculation of expected value requires estimates of the probabilities of finding various types of employment; a useful simplifying hypothesis has related the probability of finding *some* employment to the current rate of unemployment in the relevant urban area. The variety of economic activities possible both in urban and in rural areas, the availability of sources of support other than direct employment, conceptual difficulties as to the appropriate decision-making unit,[25] the presence of "noneconomic" variables in the decision makers' welfare functions, and the usual problems of data collection are among the factors that have so far prevented any satisfactory statistical verification or estimation of

Proletarianization of the African Peasantry in Rhodesia," *Journal of Development Studies* 6, no. 3 (1970): 201–03.

23. Miracle and Fetter, "Backward-Sloping Labor-Supply Functions"; Arrighi, "Labour Supplies in Historical Perspective." It may be worth mentioning here, although it is not part of the main thrust of this chapter, that whether Africans entered the monetary sector as wage earners or as cash-crop farmers, and where precisely they first did so, may have exerted profound influences over the subsequent course of social, political, and economic development in particular countries.

24. Michael P. Todaro, "A Model of Labor Migration and Urban Unemployment in Less Developed Countries," *American Economic Review* 59, no. 1 (1969): 138–48; idem, "Income Expectations, Rural-Urban Migration, and Employment in Africa," *International Labour Review* 104, no. 5 (1971): 387–414; J. E. Stiglitz, "Rural-Urban Migration, Surplus Labour, and the Relationship between Urban and Rural Wages," *Eastern Africa Economic Review* 1, no. 2 (1969): 1–27. See also Byerlee and Eicher, "Rural Employment, Migration, and Economic Development."

25. For a particularly good analysis of these difficulties, see J. B. Knight, "Measuring Urban-Rural Income Differentials," in *Urban Unemployment in Africa*, ed. Richard Jolly and Rita Cruise O'Brien (forthcoming).

these models. The most that can be said is that there has not been
evidence inconsistent with their use. A study of interregional migration
rates using 1960 Ghanaian population data did indicate responsiveness
to income differentials and to "distance" (which probably incorporates
certain sociocultural variables as well as transport costs) as well as
other variables.[26]

While there is still very little reliable evidence on total agricultural
supply response, there now exists a good deal that bears on the response
to changes in the prices of particular commodities. As has been seen, it
is unfortunately not usually possible to uncover the precise underlying
form of the response—aggregate response or response to relative price
changes, acreage or yield response, production or marketed surplus
response, and so on. Since statistical testing is possible only for the cases
in which produce is marketed through official channels (because those
are where the data can be found), very little is known about food production supply responses. Nevertheless, as table 2.1 shows, positive
supply responses have been observed for a wide variety of smallholder
cash crops in Africa—cotton, cocoa, palm kernels, palm oil, tobacco,
coffee, and rubber.

This is not the place for a detailed discussion of the alternative
models of supply behavior and/or specifications of the supply function
that have been tested in the context of African agriculture. Suffice
it to say that there is obviously no single "correct" model or specification that can be universally applied. Some of the reported tests have
not defended very conclusively the underlying model on which econometric testing was based. All have been based on relatively few and not
very reliable data. The price actually received by the producer, for
example, may differ from that which is being measured in these studies
not only in its level (which is fairly obvious) but also in its degree or
even in its direction of change. In several instances only one of the
various possible forms of the supply relationship tested produced
significant results; and the "successful" forms varied from test to test.
Thus, cotton producers in Nigeria responded to producer prices lagged
one year, whereas those in Tanzania did not; but the latter proved
responsive to a "long-run" price as determined by a distributed lag

26. L. N. Moses, R. E. Beals, and M. B. Levy, "Rationality and Migration in
Ghana," *Review of Economics and Statistics* 49, no. 4 (1967): 480–86. See also John
C. Caldwell, *African Rural-Urban Migration: The Movement to Ghana's Towns* (New
York: Columbia University Press, 1969).

formulation.[27] Notably lacking from the tests made to date are any specifically relating supply (or planting) to farmer income or liquidity, rather than to price.[28]

Smallholder responses to price changes have been measured both for perennial tree crops, for which the existence of a gestation period complicates the relationship, and for annual crops. Supply responses have been calculated for Kenyan coffee and Tanzanian sisal estates as well, but this chapter concerns itself only with smallholder decision making.[29] The greatest variety of tests have been conducted upon West African smallholder cocoa. Planting data are not available but production (which, fortunately for statisticians, is synonymous with sales to marketing boards for export) is clearly related over the long run to real producer prices; tests relating cocoa sales to such prices, allowing for the length of time required for a tree to reach maturity, for various time periods from 1926 to the present, and with varying functional forms, show positive and significant results. The supply elasticities calculated at the relevant means vary between 0.20 and 1.81.[30] Short-

27. Nighoma A. Malima, "The Economics of Cotton Production in Tanzania: An Examination of Some of the Factors That Influence Agricultural Development" (Ph.D. diss., Princeton University, 1971); Victor P. Diejomaoh, "Rural Development in Nigeria: The Role of Fiscal Policy" (Paper presented to the Annual Conference of the Nigerian Economic Society, March 1972).

28. Merrill J. Bateman, "Supply Relations for Perennial Crops in the Less-Developed Areas," in Wharton, ed., *Subsistence Agriculture and Economic Development*, pp. 243–53; Reginald H. Green and Stephen Hymer, "Investment in the Ghana Cocoa Industry: Some Problems of Structure and Policy," *Economic Bulletin of Ghana* 9, no. 1 (1965).

29. J. K. Maitha, "Productivity Response to Price: A Case Study of Kenyan Cofee," *Eastern Africa Economic Review* 2, no. 2 (1970); idem, "Supply Function for Kenyan Coffee"; Ford, "Long-Run Price Elasticities"; G. D. Gwyer, "Long and Short-Run Elasticities of Sisal Supply," *Eastern Africa Economic Review* 3, no. 2 (1971).

30. Peter Ady, "Trends in Cocoa Production," *Oxford University Institute of Statistics Bulletin* 2 (1949): 389–404; idem, "Supply Functions in Tropical Agriculture," *Bulletin of the Oxford University Institute of Economics and Statistics* 30, no. 2 (1968): 157–88; Robert M. Stern, "The Determinants of Cocoa Supply in West Africa," in *African Primary Products and International Trade,* ed. I. G. Stewart and H. W. Ord (Edinburgh: Edinburgh University Press, 1965); Merrill J. Bateman, "Aggregate and Regional Supply Functions for Ghanaian Cocoa, 1946–1962," *Journal of Farm Economics* 47, no. 2 (1965): 384–401; idem, "Supply Relations for Perennial Crops"; Jere R. Behrman, *Supply Response in Underdeveloped Agriculture* (Amsterdam: North Holland, 1968); Saylor, *Economic System of Sierra Leone;* Godwin Okurume, "The Food Crop Economy in Nigerian Agricultural Policy," Consortium Study of Nigerian Rural Development no. 31 (East Lansing, Mich., Michigan State University, February 1969); S. Olajuwon Olayide, "Some Estimates

run supply response from alteration of current inputs to the available stock of trees has been statistically demonstrated only in a minority of studies.[31]

Coffee produced by smallholders has also proven to be responsive to producer prices, both lagged and current, in Kenya, Uganda, and Ethiopia.[32] Kenyan data permit the separation of acreage from yield effects and the comparison of smallholder response with that of the estate sector. In the 1946–64 period, smallholders' acreage and long-term yield responses exceeded those of the estate sector, while their short-term yield responses fell slightly short of them. Long-term responses were significantly greater than short-term (current price) responses, and surprisingly yield responses, even in the long term, exceeded acreage responses.[33] All but this last result are in keeping with a priori expectations.

Positive producer price supply responses have been tested for smallholder palm oil and palm kernels, which are also tree crops, but since the trees in the relevant areas grow "wild"[34] and the response is essentially the product of a harvesting rather than a planting decision, palm produce amounts to an annual crop. Significant palm oil supply responses were found in the 1950s and early 1960s among Nigerian smallholders, with a (short-term) elasticity between 0.22 and 0.81.[35]

of Supply Elasticities for Nigeria's Cash Crops," *Journal of Agricultural Economics* 23, no. 3 (1972).

31. Stern, "Determinants of Cocoa Supply"; Behrman, *Supply Response in Underdeveloped Agriculture;* Okurume, "Food Crop Economy in Nigerian Agricultural Policy." Stern found a short-run response only for Ghana in the prewar period. Behrman found it only for the data from the Cameroun Republic. Okurume's data relate to Western Nigeria; he found the current price of cocoa to be negatively correlated with (admittedly imperfect) measures of yam, cassava, and maize production. (This study also indicated that food prices were either irrelevant to the food/cocoa decision or poorly measured; cocoa prices were stated by farmers and measured to be more important than the cocoa/food price relative.)

32. Ady, "Supply Functions in Tropical Agriculture"; Maitha, "Supply Function for Kenyan Coffee," and "Productivity Response to Price"; Ford, "Long-Run Price Elasticities"; T. James Goering, Akilu Afework, and Abate Temesgen, "The Response of Ethiopian Farmers to Changes in Product Prices," forthcoming; Brian van Arkadie, "Trends in the Output of Cotton and Coffee in Uganda," Rural Development Research Paper no. 70 (Makerere University, 1965).

33. Maitha, ibid.; Ford, ibid.

34. Jan S. Hogendorn tells me that there are many references in the pre-1914 period to the establishment of new palm trees on cleared land in these areas. The usual references to oil palms as "wild" may therefore not be strictly accurate.

35. Diejomaoh, "Rural Development in Nigeria"; S. A. Oni, "Production Response

Palm oil, unlike many other export crops for which supply response has been tested, can also be consumed domestically; the share of Eastern Nigerian palm oil production sold for export has been found to be significantly related to the real producer price paid by the marketing boards, with an implicit supply elasticity of 0.41.[36] (This response is a matter of "disposal economics" rather than "production economics.") The supply of palm kernels, which are joint products with palm oil of the same (wild) tree, is also positively, although not as significantly, related to own-producer price; the Nigerian supply elasticity varies between 0.22 and 0.28.[37] Significant palm kernel supply response has also been found in Sierra Leone with respect to both own-producer price and, with still better results, the palm kernel/cocoa price relative.[38] Nigerian rubber has been shown to respond positively to world prices as well, although the statistical significance of the relationship was not great.[39]

Those annual export crops for which supply responses have been tested can be shown to have similar "normality" of response. Cotton production in Tanzania during the 1953–69 period was significantly and positively related to the normal, or expected, producer price.[40] Cotton supplies in Nigeria and Uganda were significantly related to shorter-term cotton prices or price relatives.[41] Malawi tobacco sales over the 1926–60 period were significantly related to producer prices lagged one year, with an implicit elasticity of 0.48.[42] (They were also significantly negatively related to wage rates in Rhodesia and South

in Nigerian Agriculture: A Case Study of Palm Produce, 1949–1966," *Nigerian Journal of Economic and Social Studies* 11, no. 1 (1969); Olayide, "Supply Elasticities for Nigeria's Cash Crops."

36. Helleiner, *Peasant Agriculture, Government, and Economic Growth in Nigeria*, pp. 60–62.

37. Diejomaoh, "Rural Development in Nigeria"; Oni, "Production Response in Nigerian Agriculture."

38. Saylor, *Economic System of Sierra Leone*, pp. 58–74.

39. Olayide, "Supply Elasticities for Nigeria's Cash Crops."

40. A distributed lag formulation of the price variable was employed to describe the expected normal price. See Nighoma A. Malima, "The Determinants of Cotton Supply in Tanzania," *Economic Research Bureau Paper 71.4* (Dar es Salaam: University of Dar es Salaam, 1971).

41. Van Arkadie, "Output of Cotton and Coffee in Uganda"; Diejomaoh, "Rural Development in Nigeria"; S. A. Oni, "Econometric Analysis of Supply Response among Nigerian Cotton Growers," *Bulletin of Rural Economics and Sociology* 4, no. 2 (1969); Olayide, "Supply Elasticities for Nigeria's Cash Crops."

42. Dean, *Supply Responses of African Farmers*.

Table 2.1: Evidence on African Smallholder Supply Elasticities[a]

| Product and country | Period | Short-run elasticity | Long-run elasticity | Positive response but no elasticity data[b] | Source[c] |
|---|---|---|---|---|---|
| Cocoa: | | | | | |
| Ghana | 1930–40 | | 0.43 | | Ady, 1949 |
| | 1920–39 | 0.17 | | | Stern, 1965 |
| | 1920–46 | .15 | | | Ibid. |
| | 1946–62 | | .32–.87 | | Bateman, 1965 |
| | 1946–62 | | .77–1.28 | | Ibid. |
| | 1947–64 | | .71 | | Behrman, 1968 |
| Nigeria | 1920–45 | | 1.29 | | Stern, 1965 |
| | 1947–64 | | .45 | | Behrman, 1968 |
| | 1948–67 | | .20 | | Olayide, 1972 |
| Ivory Coast | 1947–64 | | .80 | | Behrman, 1968 |
| Cameroun | 1947–64 | | 1.81 | | Ibid. |
| Ghana | 1947–64 | | | * | Ady, 1968 |
| Nigeria | 1947–65 | | | * | Ibid. |
| Sierra Leone | | | | * | Saylor, 1967 |
| Coffee: | | | | | |
| Kenya, estates acreage | 1946–64 | .16 | .47 | | Maitha, 1969; Ford, 1971 |
| Kenya, smallholder acreage | 1946–64 | .20 | .56 | | Ibid. |
| Kenya, estates yield | 1946–64 | .66 | .71 | | Maitha, 1970; Ford, 1971 |
| Kenya, smallholder yield | 1946–64 | .64 | 1.01 | | Ibid. |
| Ethiopia | 1964–70 | | | | Goering et al. |
| Uganda | 1950–64 | | | * | Ady, 1968 |
| Palm oil: | | | | | |
| Nigeria | 1950–64 | .81 | | | Diejomaoh, 1972 |
| | 1949–63 | .41 | | | Helleiner, 1966 |
| | 1948–67 | | .22–.26 | | Olayide, 1972 |
| Eastern Nigeria | 1949–66 | .41–.70 | | | Oni, 1969a |
| Palm kernels: | | | | | |
| Nigeria | 1950–64 | .25 | | | Diejomaoh, 1972 |
| | 1949–66 | .22–.28 | | | Oni, 1969a |
| Sierra Leone | | | | * | Saylor, 1967 |
| Cotton: | | | | | |
| Nigeria | 1950–64 | .67 | | | Diejomaoh, 1972 |
| | 1948–67 | .21–.38 | | | Oni, 1969b |
| | 1948–67 | 0.3 | | | Olayide, 1972 |
| Tanzania | 1953–69 | | 2.44 | | Malima, 1971 |
| Tobacco, Malawi | 1926–60 | .48 | | | Dean, 1966 |
| Rubber, Nigeria | 1948–67 | .21 | .17–.24 | | Olayide, 1972 |
| Haricot beans, Ethiopia | 1953–70 | 1.60 | | | Goering et al. |
| Civet, Ethiopia | 1957–70 | 3.16 | | | Ibid. |

·        ·        ·        ·

| Pulses, Ethiopia | 1952–70 | .72 | Ibid. |
| Lentils, Ethiopia | 1953–70 | 1.30 | Ibid. |
| Sesame, Ethiopia | 1957–70 | .61 | Ibid. |

a. It is difficult to summarize results in a number or two. A complete assessment of the meaning and value of these various estimates requires reference to the original source.

b. Asterisk indicates statistically significant response.

c. Full references are given below in source notes.

*Sources:* Peter Ady, "Trends in Cocoa Production," *Oxford University Institute of Statistics Bulletin* 2 (1949): 389–404; idem, "Supply Functions in Tropical Agriculture," *Bulletin of the Oxford University Institute of Economics and Statistics* 30, no. 2 (1968): 157–88; Robert M. Stern, "The Determinants of Cocoa Supply in West Africa," in *African Primary Products and International Trade*, ed. I. G. Stewart and H. W. Ord (Edinburgh: Edinburgh University Press, 1965); Merrill J. Bateman, "Aggregate and Regional Supply Functions for Ghanaian Cocoa, 1946–1962," *Journal of Farm Economics* 47, no. 2 (1965): 384–401; S. Olajuwon Olayide, "Some Estimates of Supply Elasticities for Nigeria's Cash Crops," *Journal of Agricultural Economics* 23, no. 3 (1972); J. K. Maitha, "A Supply Function for Kenyan Coffee," *Eastern Africa Economic Review* 1, no. 1 (1969); idem, "Productivity Response to Price: A Case Study of Kenyan Coffee," *Eastern Africa Economic Review* 2, no. 2 (1970); Derek J. Ford, "Long-run Price Elasticities in the Supply of Kenyan Coffee: A Methodological Note," *Eastern Africa Economic Review*, n.s. 3, no. 1 (1971); T. James Goering, Akilu Afework, and Abate Temesgen, "The Response of Ethiopian Farmers to Changes in Product Prices," forthcoming; Victor P. Diejomaoh, "Rural Development in Nigeria: The Role of Fiscal Policy" (Paper presented to the Annual Conference of the Nigerian Economic Society, March 1972); Gerald K. Helleiner, *Peasant Agriculture, Government, and Economic Growth in Nigeria* (Homewood, Ill.: Irwin, 1966); S. A. Oni, "Production Response in Nigerian Agriculture: A Case Study of Palm Produce, 1949–1966," *Nigerian Journal of Economic and Social Studies* 11, no. 1 (1969a); idem, "Econometric Analysis of Supply Response among Nigerian Cotton Growers," *Bulletin of Rural Economics and Sociology* 4, no. 2 (1969b); Edwin Dean, *The Supply Responses of African Farmers: Theory and Measurement in Malawi* (Amsterdam: North Holland, 1966); Jere R. Behrman, "Monopolistic Cocoa Pricing," *American Journal of Agricultural Economics* 58 (1968); Nighoma A. Malima, "The Determinants of Cotton Supply in Tanzania," *Economic Research Bureau Paper 71.4* (Dar es Salaam: University of Dar es Salaam, 1971); Ralph Gerald Saylor, *The Economic System of Sierra Leone* (Durham, N.C.: Duke University Press, 1967).

Africa, where wage employment constituted the main alternative activity to tobacco farming; see above.) In addition, a number of minor crops in Ethiopia seem to be significantly price responsive.[43]

The responsiveness of African smallholders to economic incentives has also been demonstrated in activities other than agricultural production. In processing and trade they have been found to behave with monotonous rationality. The introduction of quality differentials in Nigerian cocoa, palm oil, groundnuts, and cotton generated a rapid

43. Goering, Afework, and Temesgen, "Response of Ethiopian Farmers."

response in the quality composition of sales.[44] Whether this response was the product of better processing methods, more sophisticated mixing, or the influencing of inspectors, there is clearly an economic response of some sort taking place.

Evidence on food supply response is rather scarce and more impressionistic. There are some time-series data on maize in Zambia, Rhodesia, and Uganda,[45] groundnuts in Rhodesia,[46] and yam, cassava, and maize in Western Nigeria[47] which suggest a degree of elasticity with respect to producer prices. Supply responses have clearly taken place in other cases, such as Kenyan maize and Tanzanian rice, despite the inability of econometricians to analyze them statistically. There are several reasons for believing that price responses are likely to be greater for cash crops (e.g., the export crops) than for food crops. First, because of better marketing systems there are greater grounds for believing that farm prices will move with observed, or announced, prices. Second, the fact that they frequently occupy relatively small proportions of total labor time and total land permits reallocation to be made more easily in response to price changes than in those instances where, as with food production, a high proportion of available inputs is already so occupied. Third, farmers can be expected to take greater risks with nonfood crops than with food.[48]

Lest one gain the impression that the record is completely unambiguous, it should be pointed out again that not all of the tests reported showed significantly positive responses, and also that when the results do not prove "favorable" they are not always reported; the sales of groundnuts in Nigeria, for instance, are difficult to fit into this overall pattern,[49] although historically their expansion certainly was related to the improvement of incentives. Nor is the appropriate rational response always as clear as is implied by some of these comparatively simple

44. P.T. Bauer and B. S. Yamey, "A Case Study of Response to Price in an Underdeveloped Country," *Economic Journal* 69, no. 276 (1959): 800–05; Helleiner, *Peasant Agriculture, Government, and Economic Growth in Nigeria*, pp. 64–67; J. S. Hogendorn, "Response to Price Change: A Nigerian Example," *Economica* 34, no. 135 (1967): 325.

45. Marvin P. Miracle, *Maize in Tropical Africa* (Madison: University of Wisconsin Press, 1966), pp. 253–59; Montague Yudelman, *Africans on the Land* (Cambridge: Harvard University Press, 1964).

46. Yudelman, ibid.

47. Okurume, "Food Crop Economy in Nigerian Agricultural Policy."

48. United Nations, Food and Agriculture Organisation, *The State of Food and Agriculture, 1967* (Rome, 1968), chapter 3.

49. Diejomaoh, "Rural Development in Nigeria"; Olayide, "Supply Elasticities for Nigeria's Cash Crops."

regressions of sales volume on price.[50] At the same time, whether correlations between price and investments (planting) in agriculture are the product of orthodox supply responses or, rather, the product of an actual relationship between earnings and investment is not always clear. There is some evidence for the latter interpretation. Western Nigerian cocoa farmers appear to expand their food production through increased hiring of labor when the price of cocoa rises; the cocoa price is a better predictor of food/cocoa production decisions than is the food/cocoa price relative.[51] Ghanaian cocoa farmers' plantings also seem to be related to earnings rather than to prices.[52] Note too that Ghanaian cocoa production around 1970 had not fallen, as one would have expected had price rather than income determined plantings in the early 1960s.[53] Still, these results are not wildly out of line with those of similar econometric tests in other less developed areas,[54] and they are supportive of the "new orthodoxy" of agricultural supply response.

Producer price elasticity is only one type of elasticity in which the theoretician or policy maker should be interested. In addition to other price elasticities—other output prices, input prices—one ought, in principle, to be able to consider the elasticity of smallholder response to changes in inputs such as extension advice, credit facilities, improved roads, and so on, or perhaps to changes in total expenditures upon them. Cotton supply in Tanzania appears, for example, to be related to the number of buying stations.[55]

The systems approach to the understanding of agriculture suggests that the ceteris paribus assumptions of orthodox microanalysis may nevertheless not carry one very far.[56] Measuring the response to a change in only one of the myriad of influences upon smallholder deci-

50. Michael Lipton, "Should Reasonable Farmers Respond to Price Changes?" *Journal of Modern Asian Studies* 1, no. 1 (1966); and idem, "The Theory of the Optimising Peasant," *Journal of Development Studies* 4, no. 3 (1968): 327–51.

51. Okurume, "Food Crop Economy in Nigerian Agricultural Policy."

52. Polly Hill, *The Migrant Cocoa Farmers of Southern Ghana: A Study in Rural Capitalism* (Cambridge: at the University Press, 1963); Green and Hymer, "Cocoa in the Gold Coast."

53. Tony Killick, "The Economics of Cocoa," in *A Study of Contemporary Ghana,* vol. 1, *The Economy of Ghana,* ed. Walter Birmingham, I. Neustadt, and E. N. Omaboe (Chicago: Northwestern University Press, 1966), p. 376.

54. See, for example, Behrman, *Supply Response in Underdeveloped Agriculture,* pp. 15–18; Bateman, "Supply Relations for Perennial Crops," p. 251.

55. Malima, "Determinants of Cotton Supply in Tanzania."

56. Max F. Millikan and David Hapgood, *No Easy Harvest: The Dilemma of Agriculture in Underdeveloped Countries* (Boston: Little, Brown, 1967), pp. 13–18, 78–80.

sion making, even if it is as important a one as output price, is likely
ultimately to be unrewarding or even misleading. What one seeks to
understand is the effect of alterations in various packages of influences.
Price changes coupled with the increased provision of cheap credit
may induce responses totally different from price changes unaccom-
panied by credit innovations but concurrent with marketing or land
reforms. Simple supply responses are likely to be greater in the longer
term than in the short term; but in the longer term their importance is
likely to be dwarfed by the effects of new technologies, inputs, and
institutions. Therefore the efforts devoted to the establishment of the
price responsiveness of smallholders in African agriculture have, despite their relative youth, probably already reached a point of rapidly
diminishing returns.

### 3. SMALLHOLDER RESPONSES TO INNOVATION

Africa has been the scene of very rapid expansion in cash cropping in
the twentieth century. This has been achieved through the use of
leisure, that is, seasonally slack labor and labor previously engaged in
nonfarm activities ($z$-goods production), in unknown proportions.[57]
While most of this expansion appears to have taken place through expansion on the land frontier, some has been the product of improved
per acre and per man-hour yields. To the extent that this expansion
involved the introduction of new crops and new agricultural systems to
the smallholder economies, it implied a major response to innovation
on the part of thousands of African farmers whose numbers have increased with each passing year. These innovations were probably essentially labor saving and therefore can be interpreted as confirmation
of the Hayami-Ruttan thesis concerning the factor-saving bias in
agricultural innovation;[58] on the other hand, they were essentially
biological rather than mechanical innovations and therefore do not fit
into this model too comfortably. Evidence is accumulating of shifts in
traditional crop mixes and techniques of production in periods prior to
the opening up of cash cropping for export markets as well.[59]

57. Byerlee and Eicher, "Rural Employment, Migration, and Economic Development," p. 13.
58. Yujiro Hayami and Vernon W. Ruttan, *Agricultural Development: An International Perspective* (Baltimore: Johns Hopkins Press, 1971).
59. See, for example, Miracle, *Maize in Tropical Africa* and *Agriculture in the
Congo Basin.*

While there is now a great deal of rhetoric devoted to agricultural innovation in Africa, there is still a dearth of data that is even more serious than that in the field of general supply responses; what data there are, and they too have been multiplying recently, do not fit easily into a theoretical structure that can explain innovation.

To my knowledge there is only one empirical study that has sought to correlate measured yields (per hectare and, what is more important in Africa, per unit of available adult labor) with farm and farmer characteristics; it is a study of Tanzanian cotton farmers. This study found, among other things, no correlation between yields and age, education, or experience; there was a significant positive correlation between an index of farmer modernity and yields in a majority of the regression equations that were estimated.[60] The rest of the evidence relates to the adoption of innovations.

Understanding the decision making of the rural smallholder is particularly important now that the "transformation" and "settlement" approaches to agricultural development have been discredited in Africa, and there is a return to the more gradual and broader-based approaches to rural progress. African evidence on smallholder decisions relating to the adoption of innovations is essentially of two kinds. First, there is some (very limited) information concerning the rates of return and risks from alternative farming systems in selected areas that have been intensively studied; this can be and has been used to explain the responses of smallholders to proffered innovations, assuming alternative welfare functions, and constraints. Second, there are now quite a number of empirical studies addressing themselves to the question of who innovates or who adopts. These typically attempt to correlate the adoption of specific innovations, such as fertilizer applications or the use of pesticides, or overall modernity with a variety of particular characteristics of the population, such as educational attainment, land ownership, and the like. The latter data shade into the question of agricultural extension theory and practice and are also related to diffusion theory.

Farm management studies that shed light upon smallholder decision making are few and far between in Africa.[61] Production functions have

---

60. Saylor, *Economic System of Sierra Leone.*
61. For useful surveys of farm management studies in the African context, see Cleave, "Labour in the Development of African Agriculture"; and Malcolm Hall, "A Review of Farm Management Research in East Africa," *FCA/FAO Agricultural Economics Bulletin for Africa* 12 (1970): 11–24.

been estimated for samples of Rhodesian, Northern Nigerian, and Eastern Nigerian smallholders, all of which indicated that on average they allocated their labor and land quite efficiently.[62] This conclusion is not inconsistent with the existence of considerable dispersion of management skills within the samples. This evidence of "rationality" lends credence to other studies, employing programming or simpler methods, which have sought to analyze the economic implications of adopting various crop mixes or production innovations on the basis of assumptions as to the operative constraints, including knowledge.[63]

No doubt economic profitability (defined so as to include the risk factor) is a necessary element in smallholder adoption of innovations. It is possible to construct an economic theory of innovation, either individual or collective, which bases itself upon the familiar concepts of production functions, welfare functions, and so on, and takes risk aversion into account.[64] Yet there are some severe conceptual problems.

The specification of the appropriate decision-making unit for purposes of economic analysis, for instance, is a source of considerable difficulty in Africa. On the one hand, the sexual division of labor within the nuclear family at times suggests the need for more than one decision unit per household.[65] Females may be engaged exclusively in food production or marketing activities which are to a large extent independent of their husbands' economic activities. Analysis based on notions of using total household labor or maximizing household earnings may therefore be quite misleading. On the other hand, the extended family system and/or communal tenure systems may require

62. B. F. Massell and R. W. M. Johnson, "Economics of Smallholder Farming in Rhodesia: A Cross-Section Analysis of Two Areas," *Food Research Institute Studies in Agricultural Economics, Trade, and Development* 8, suppl. (1968); Luning, *Economic Aspects of Low Labour-Income Farming;* D. E. Welsch, "Response to Economic Incentive by Abakaliki Rice Farmers in Eastern Nigeria," *Journal of Farm Economics* 47, no. 4 (1965): 900–14.

63. Heyer, "Linear Programming Analysis of Constraints on Peasant Farming"; David Feldman, "An Assessment of Alternative Agricultural Strategies for Tobacco Development in Iringa District, Tanzania," *Economic Research Bureau Paper 68.21* (Dar es Salaam: University of Dar es Salaam, 1968); Collinson, "Evaluation of Innovations for Peasant Farming" and "Trial Management Farm in Tanzania."

64. John R. Harris, "Some Theory of Agricultural Innovation" (Paper prepared for the East African Agricultural Economic Society Conference, June 1969); Helleiner, *Peasant Agriculture, Government, and Economic Growth in Nigeria,* pp. 67–75.

65. It may be recalled that this led the first serious students of national income accounting in Africa to recommend the valuation of wives' services to husbands for the purposes of arriving at a figure for Nigerian national income. See A. R. Prest and I. G. Stewart, *The National Income of Nigeria, 1950–51,* Colonial Office, Colonial Research Studies no. 11 (London: H.M.S.O., 1953).

units larger than the household, for analytical purposes. Relationships among family, household, or even community members are believed by many to be qualitatively different from those with outsiders, with the latter more narrowly economic in the sense that they are market based. While the peasant may indeed sell his produce to outsiders "just as cunningly and egotistically as the stock exchange member his portfolio of shares,"[66] economic relationships within an extended family may be quite a different matter.

At the same time, evidence of economic ties within rural families some of whose members have migrated permanently or temporarily to the cities—remittances or loans by urban employed to their rural relatives, rural land purchase by urban dwellers, and the like—add a further dimension to this theoretical problem.[67] Indeed, one can add still more complexity by recognizing the possibility that education of selected members of the next generation for the purpose of obtaining high-paying urban jobs may also be part of an extended family's decision making. Some portray this assumed "duality" of the farm family's activity as a matter of subsistence versus market activity.[68] While there remains a dearth of hard statistical verification, there is now wide agreement, based upon numerous village-level and micro-level studies, that in much of the African rural scene food production is perceived as paramount—the first claim upon labor, land, and other inputs.[69] If "economic" relationships are truly subject to "dual" behavioral norms such as these, the analysis of smallholder decision making with respect to allocation, production, and distribution becomes still more difficult.[70]

66. Joseph A. Schumpeter, *The Theory of Economic Development* (Cambridge: Harvard University Press, 1934), p. 80. I owe this quotation to Nicholas Georgescu-Roegen, "The Institutional Aspects of Peasant Communities: An Analytical View," in Wharton, ed., *Subsistence Agricultural and Economic Development*, p. 84.

67. Colin Leys, "Politics in Kenya: The Development of Peasant Society," *British Journal of Political Science* 1, no. 3 (1971): 307–37, and references cited therein; Caldwell, *African Rural-Urban Migration;* R. H. Sabot, "Urban Migration in Tanzania," mimeographed (Economic Research Bureau, Dar es Salaam, September 1972).

68. Chihiro Nakajima, "Subsistence and Commercial Family Farms: Some Theoretical Models of Subjective Equilibrium," in Wharton, ed., *Subsistence Agriculture and Economic Development*.

69. McLoughlin, *African Food Production Systems;* Okurume, "Food Crop Economy in Nigerian Agricultural Policy."

70. See Raj Krishna, "Models of the Family Farm," in Wharton, ed., *Subsistence Agriculture and Economic Development,* pp. 185–90, for a succinct discussion of these issues.

The long-standing difficulty of applying orthodox analytical techniques to the behavior of decision makers who are not occupationally specialized also applies to the rural household sector. As has been seen, nonfarm activities may take as much as half the working time of rural African farmers.[71]

That adoption of an innovation sometimes involves a pattern of usage different from that recommended or expected by its purveyor can be very revealing. In Northern Nigeria, for example, fertilizer intended for application to the groundnut crop was applied to the food crop with the indirect result that acreage devoted to groundnuts may have expanded.[72] This sort of adaptability demonstrates both the sophistication of the smallholder's decision making and the necessity of analyzing the entire farming (indeed the total socioeconomic) system in which he operates rather than an isolated part of it, and of understanding his preference system.

The wide variety of individual and group experience and responses suggests that the simplified apparatus of microeconomics, in which factor inputs are varied so as to achieve that combination of material return and risk reduction which maximizes welfare, is, in any case, not sufficient for an explanation of African smallholder behavior. Marvin Miracle's studies of agricultural change in the Congo Basin demonstrate particularly dramatically the unevenness over time and over space of smallholder agricultural practices, which cannot, by any stretch of the imagination, be described as stagnant.[73]

One possible approach to the analysis of divergent behavior with respect to agricultural change is to seek to identify the characteristics of innovating smallholders or communities. This approach is analogous to the long-standing search for a theory of entrepreneurship. To the extent that divergent behavior is attributable to differing factor endowments, access to information, or input availabilities, behavior can readily be interpreted in terms of conventional micro-theory; but differences in welfare functions, including attitudes toward risk, require further investigation. A number of studies of innovation have been undertaken in Africa in recent years. Among the characteristics

71. Byerlee and Eicher, "Rural Employment, Migration, and Economic Development," p. 10.

72. C. K. Laurent, "Problems Facing the Fertiliser Distribution Program in the Six Northern States," Consortium Study of Nigerian Rural Development no. 27 (East Lansing, Mich., Michigan State University, January 1969).

73. Miracle, *Agriculture in the Congo Basin.*

found to be positively related to "adoption" were farm size, wealth, tenure status, extension contact, participation in local organizations, use of communications media, degree of full-time commitment to farming, commercial experience, and modernity.[74] Among the factors tested but found to be unrelated to adoption were age, educational attainment, religion, sex, and work or farming experience.[75] With the new emphasis in Africa upon nonformal education and other aspects of learning, one would like to be able to correlate response not merely with educational attainment but also with protein nutrition in infancy, incidence of disease and parasites,[76] and exposure to various institutions of traditional or nonformal schooling.

There have been no tests in Africa attempting similarly to uncover the characteristics of "rejectors" of innovations, although this, particularly if one could isolate the characteristics of *wise* rejectors, would undoubtedly prove equally interesting.

Without knowing more about the innovations themselves it is difficult to know whether one is learning, in these studies, about smallholders' innovativeness or their gullibility. (In some circumstances, one may even be uncovering their susceptibility to various forms of duress.) Adopters certainly need not be the best farmers. Hypotheses can also be constructed relating the characteristics of particular innovations and "change agents" to the likelihood of adoption. Apart from the obvious importance of profitability and riskiness, the innova-

74. A. C. Basu, "The Relationship of Farmer Characteristics to the Adoption of Recommended Farm Practices in Four Villages of Western State of Nigeria," *Bulletin of Rural Economics and Sociology* 4, no. 1 (1969); David W. Kidd, "Factors Affecting Farmers' Response to Extension in Western Nigeria," Consortium Study of Nigerian Rural Development no. 30 (East Lansing, Mich., Michigan State University, 1969); Robert C. Clark and I. A. Akinbode, "Factors Associated with Adoption of Three Farm Practices in Western Nigeria," University of Ife, Department of Extension Education and Rural Sociology, Department Research Monograph no. 1 (Ibadan, 1967); Ralph Gerald Saylor, "Variations in Sukumaland Cotton Yields and the Extension Service," *Economic Research Bureau Paper 70.5* (Dar es Salaam: University of Dar es Salaam, 1970); Akinsola Akiwowo and Arun C. Basu, "The Social Organisations of Tobacco Growers in Northern Oyo Division and Adoption of New Farming Ideas and Practices," mimeographed (Nigerian Institute of Social and Economic Research, November 30, 1968); H. U. E. Thoden van Velsen, "Staff, Kulak, and Peasant" (Paper presented to a conference of the East African Academy, September 1968); Edgar Bowden and Jon Moris, "Social Characteristics of Progressive Baganda Farmers," *East African Journal of Rural Development* 2, no. 1 (1969).

75. Basu, ibid.; Akiwowo and Basu, ibid., Bowden and Moris, ibid., Saylor, ibid.

76. John W. Mellor, "The Subsistence Farmer in Traditional Economies," in Wharton, ed., *Subsistence Agriculture and Economic Development*, p. 222.

tion's complexity and compatibility with traditional practices and tastes can be expected to matter. Many would attribute the rejections in Africa primarily to shortcomings in the original orientation and quality of agricultural research which failed sufficiently to consider the factors affecting farm-level acceptability. The potential adopter's relationship with the source of information concerning the innovation can also be a significant influence.

This research focus upon the characteristics of individual innovators of course has its roots in the study of American agriculture. In other contexts, it may be more fruitful to explore the characteristics of groups (e.g., cooperatives, settlement schemes, etc.) or whole societies in which innovations do or do not occur.[77] Among the factors to be investigated are attitudes toward deviance, social attitudes toward material progress, collective provision for the indigent and unlucky, decision-making structures, land tenure systems, or even, Hagen-like, child-rearing practices.[78]

All of this discussion has related to general smallholder decision making at a given point in time. Existing theory and analysis in Africa, as elsewhere, focuses explicitly or implicitly upon the representative smallholder, and plays down the variations in smallholder behavior. Yet not only can this variation be great but it is even possible for the vast majority (or even all) of the farmers in a sample to behave in a way totally different from that which is measured as average behavior.[79] For the purposes of understanding the role of agricultural producers in the development process one must, of course, be concerned with the evolution of successful farmers over time. Special attention must be devoted to the successful farmers (capitalists) since they are the ones at the heart of the process of change; what is taking place can be obscured by economic (or other) analyses based upon "the myth of the amorphous peasantry."[80] For them above all, but for the rest as well, analysis and evidence of decision making with respect to a whole series of decisions on savings, investment and spending allocation, borrowing

77. Beverley Brock, "The Sociology of the Innovator" (Paper presented at the East African Agricultural Economics Society Conference on Technical Innovation in East African Agriculture, 1969); Kidd, "Response to Extension in Western Nigeria."
78. Everett E. Hagen, *On the Theory of Social Change* (Homewood, Ill.: Dorsey, 1962).
79. Mellor, "Subsistence Farmer in Traditional Economies," p. 217.
80. Polly Hill, "The Myth of the Amorphous Peasantry: A Northern Nigerian Case Study," *Nigerian Journal of Economic and Social Studies* 10, no. 2 (1968): 239–61.

and lending, and even political participation, taken at various points in time, are then required in addition to the more static analyses of crop choice and innovations. Polly Hill has done pioneering empirical work in this sphere in Africa, but there does not exist much else, either theoretical or concrete, to illuminate these aspects of decision making.[81]

That there exists "normal" response to price incentives and profit opportunities seems now to be fairly firmly established, whether it is a matter of migration, production response, or the adoption of innovations. But there is as yet insufficient evidence as to the extent and sources of differentiation among individual or group responders. There now exist some studies identifying the characteristics of rural-urban migrants[82] and "early adopters,"[83] but none seeking to determine the characteristics of "conventional" supply responders, or the various factors that influence price responsiveness, whether economic or noneconomic. Tenure systems, social structure, educational attainment, proximity to urban areas, degree of land scarcity, levels of income, and wealth can all be expected to influence individual and collective response to price alterations, just as many of them influence responses to innovations.[84]

Our knowledge of what is necessary in order for smallholder decision making to contribute to agricultural development has increased greatly; but we still do not know what is sufficient. In particular, we do not know much about response to a mixed and rapidly changing barrage of new information stimuli, incentives, and programs. As John Mellor has written, "just because we often find farmers in traditional agricultures in good adjustment with their stable environment, we should not assume that they are quick and able decision-makers when their environment begins to change dramatically."[85] It is the variability in

81. Hill, *Migrant Cocoa Farmers of Southern Ghana* and *Studies in Rural Capitalism in West Africa*.

82. They tend, for instance, to be better educated and younger than the average populations. See Richard Jolly and Rita Cruise O'Brien, eds., *Unemployment in Africa* (forthcoming); and Derek Byerlee, "Research on Migration in Africa: Past, Present, and Future," African Rural Employment Study, Rural Employment Paper no. 2 (Department of Agricultural Economics, Michigan State University, East Lansing, September 1972).

83. See above.

84. The only evidence of this sort of which I am aware is Bateman's to the effect that cocoa supply elasticity appears to be related to the "age" of the cocoa-growing region in Ghana, and that may have more to do with technology than with socio-economics. See Bateman, "Aggregate and Regional Supply Functions" and "Supply Relations for Perennial Crops."

85. Mellor, "Subsistence Farmer in Traditional Economies," p. 217.

decision making in circumstances of change that is likely to shed the greatest light upon the sources of agricultural development, at least insofar as smallholder decision making has anything to do with it. What influences are associated with adaptability, responsiveness, and success—physical, social, economic? It is my impression that in Africa, as elsewhere, little more is known about these matters today than was known a decade or two ago.

# 3

## The Response of Nonmonetary Production Units
## to Contact with the Exchange Economy

E. K. FISK

In much of the Pacific region a monetary exchange economy is a relatively recent innovation—in some places very recent indeed. In the period since World War II it has been possible to observe substantial groups in the process of initial contact with an exchange economy, and even today large numbers of people, especially in parts of Melanesia, are still independent of the monetary economy for the main essentials of their livelihood. Economic planners in the region have been much concerned with the problem of how to accelerate the transition of these people from nonmonetary self-subsistent economic activity to full participation in the monetized exchange system of the market, and it must be admitted that their efforts in this direction have often met with a puzzlingly slow response. It is with the understanding of this phenomenon, and of the manner in which such response takes place, that this chapter is concerned.

In this transitional process there are many possible stages that could be defined, presenting an almost continuous range of degrees of market participation. However, in the interests of simplicity I have picked out four key stages that may be identified roughly in the real world. These are as follows:

1. *Pure subsistence in isolation.* At this stage there is no effective contact with the monetized sector, all consumption depends on self-subsistent production, and there is no specialization, no trade, and no division of labor outside the group.

2. *Subsistence with supplementary cash production.* At this stage the essentials of life are still mainly produced by the group that consumes them, but supplementary production is undertaken in order to secure

access to market goods and services not obtainable directly from the group's own resouces. Examples are the subsistence gardener who produces some extra staple foods for sale, or who adds a small grove of coffee trees to his garden, or who leaves his family on the subsistence garden and works for a time for wages.

3. *Cash orientation with supplementary subsistence.* In this state, the producer is oriented mainly toward the monetized economy, and his main productive efforts are directed at earning a money income; however, some, even a substantial part, of his basic foods and other necessities may be home produced because, in terms of factor cost, it is more economical to do so. An example is the sugar farmer in Fiji who may, as a sideline, produce the main food requirements of his family from land not in use for sugar production.

4. *Complete specialization for the market.* This is the stage where specialization and division of labor are exploited to the maximum, and the producer is dependent on the market for all the goods and services he requires. This is, of course, rarely reached in practice, even in the most sophisticated economies, for some of these goods and services will normally be produced internally within the family group. However, it is a stage approached closely by substantial components of the population of advanced countries, and, for these people at least, it is probably reasonable to ignore, for practical planning purposes, the nonmonetary component in their economic activity.

In what follows I shall be concerned mainly with stage 2, subsistence with supplementary cash production, and with how the extent of such supplementary production is determined. Subsequently I shall look briefly at some of the factors involved in the further transition into stage 3.

I propose to start by referring to a set of simple models that I first developed some twelve years ago in an attempt to understand the principles of self-subsistent nonmonetary production as we found them in Papua New Guinea, and the manner of their response to the opportunities presented by contact with a modern exchange economy. Since then more sophisticated and complete systems of analysis of subjective equilibrium on peasant-type farms have become available, of which I particularly admire those of A. K. Sen and Chihiro Nakajima.[1] These

1. A.K. Sen, "Peasants and Dualism with or without Surplus Labour," *Journal of Political Economy* 74 (1966): 425–50; Chihiro Nakajima, "Subsistence and Commercial Family Farms: Some Theoretical Models of Subjective Equilibrium," in

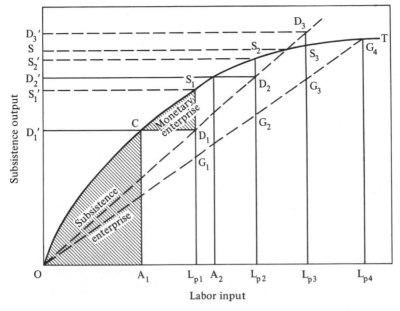

Fig. 3.1

models cover a great deal more than mine attempted to do and are generally much sharper analytical tools, to the extent that for most purposes I regard my earlier attempt as superseded, even for my own purposes. For this reason I shall convert to the Nakajima models, which are readily related to mine, for the finer analysis of some aspects of the problem I wish to discuss. However, in one or two respects, and especially in identifying a part of the problem that I find difficult to resolve with either of the two more sophisticated sets of models as originally propounded, I find my earlier model useful. Therefore, with apologies, I present a brief account of some of its main characteristics.

The situation with which the model deals initially is that of the self-subsistent, nonmonetary production unit (perhaps a family farm) in isolation, and it sets out to study the factors that determine the level of production within such a unit. This can be illustrated simply in diagrammatic form, as in figure 3.1.[2] The land available to the unit is assumed to be constant but quite substantial, so that at modest levels of popula-

---

*Subsistence Agriculture and Economic Development*, ed. C. R. Wharton (Chicago: Aldine, 1969), pp. 165–85. The models introduced by Nakajima will be discussed throughout the present chapter.

2. For full details of this model see E. K. Fisk, "Planning in a Primitive Economy: Special Problems of Papua New Guinea," *Economic Record* 38 (1962): 462–78; and

tion the unit does not need to use all its land to meet its subsistence requirements. There is one output, comprising a simple but adequate range of subsistence staple foods, the volume of which is measured along the vertical axis. Technology and capital are assumed to be constant and given, so that there is only one variable input, labor, and the quantity used is measured along the horizontal axis. The curve $OT$ shows the different quantities of subsistence goods and services that can be produced from the unit's land under these conditions, with varying levels of labor input.

Under these circumstances, the quantity of production will be wholly determined by the size of the labor input. If, therefore, we can determine the amount of labor that will be applied to production in our model, we can determine the amount of staples that will be produced, and vice versa.

One determinant of the labor input will necessarily be the size of the population. For each level of total population, $N$, there will be a maximum potential supply of labor, $L_p$, available within the production unit itself. This $L_p$ will be a function of $N$, but the nature of this function will be determined by the age and sex structure of the population, and by certain social values and institutions accepted by the population concerned. If, therefore, we assume that population increases over time at a steady rate (so that the age and sex structure remains constant), that its physical condition and its social values and institutions (i.e., its land, capital, and technology) remain constant, we can then say that the potential supply of labor available from within the unit at any level of population would be a constant function of the population size. This can be expressed in simple symbols as follows:

$$L_p = f(N),$$

where $f$ is simply a constant.

Under these defined conditions, the input of labor cannot exceed $L_p$ for any given level of population, though it can be (and often is) less than $L_p$. We can therefore mark on figure 3.1 a series of points along the horizontal axis representing the potential supply of labor that would be available from the specified production unit at different levels of total production. Three such points are shown on the figure as $L_{p1}$, $L_{p2}$, and $L_{p3}$. The lines drawn vertically from these points cut the

Fisk, "Labour Absorption Capacity of Subsistence Agriculture," *Economic Record* 47 (1971): 366–78.

production possibility curve, $OT$, at $S_1$, $S_2$, and $S_3$ respectively, thus showing on the vertical axis the level of production potentially accessible to the unit, under these conditions, at the different levels of population. The unit can choose a level of production at or below the point $S$ corresponding to its level of total population, subject to the limitation that there will be a point $G$ for each population below which production is insufficient to sustain the production power of the labor force, and $L_p$ will thus decline.

Given a constant physical structure of the population, this point $G$ will also be a constant, though different, function of total population, $N$. Accordingly, we can mark one of these points on figure 3.1 for the population level giving, for example, potential supply of labor $L_{p1}$, marking the corresponding point on the vertical from $L_{p1}$ as $G_1$. Then, as $G = g(N)$ always under our assumptions, all the possible positions of $G$ will fall on a radial from the origin $O$ passing through $G_1$, and we can mark in the corresponding points for $L_{p2}$ and $L_{p3}$ as $G_2$ and $G_3$ respectively.

There will also be another point, marked $D_1$ on figure 3.1, where the self-subsistent production unit at $L_{p1}$ will find its production of subsistence output adequate for its own consumption, until further production is not wanted for this purpose.[3] At this point, when the basic needs of staple foods, plus shelter and clothing, have been met to traditionally acceptable standards, the satisfactions and enjoyments that can be secured by the input of more labor fall off sharply per hour of work done, while the dissatisfactions involved in doing the work increase.

Once this level of production has been reached, after allowing a reasonable margin of safety to compensate for bad seasons, further production of these goods has little point, and the dissatisfaction involved in doing further such productive work on the land would not be justified. Under these circumstances one can meaningfully imagine a demand ceiling beyond which there is no adequate incentive to produce for own consumption. Given constant physical and social characteristics in the population, and constant age and sex structure, the level of production necessary to reach this demand ceiling will

---

3. Under some conditions, such as trading contact with the outside world, further production may be required for some *other* purpose, but this is a different matter to be dealt with later. Here let it be assumed that the unit is isolated and has no use for its output other than its own immediate consumption.

also be a constant function of population size. This can be expressed $D = d(N)$, and a radial $OD_1D_2D_3$ can be drawn as shown in figure 3.1, describing all possible values of $D$ as the population of the unit varies.[4]

The value of this model, as shown in figure 3.1, is that it illustrates some very important effects of differing levels of population pressure on land resources in such communities. For example, at the level of population corresponding to the potential supply of labor $L_{p1}$, the production unit could use $OL_{p1}$ units of labor to produce $OS_1'$ units of product, but in isolation, under the circumstances we have assumed, it would in fact have no incentive to produce above the level $OD_1'$, so that the actual level of labor input would not be $OL_{p1}$ but only $OA_1$. This means that there would be a substantial amount of available labor concealed within the operations of this subsistence production unit, amounting to $L_{p1}$ minus $A_1$, which could be used to produce an agricultural surplus $D_1S_1$, or for other new forms of production. Moreover, this could be done without in any way reducing the supply of goods and services with which the community was self-subsistent. *All that is necessary to draw this labor into productive use is a level of incentive sufficient to make it worthwhile.*

At the level of population corresponding to $L_{p1}$, as figure 3.1 shows, the unused labor available for leisure or for producing an agricultural surplus, or which can be released to wage labor without reducing family subsistence consumption, is substantial both in absolute terms and relative to the other parameters. However, if the population increases to the level corresponding to $L_{p2}$, this available labor is greatly reduced, while at $L_{p3}$ the maximum level of consumption attainable with their existing land, capital, and technology is well below the desired level and they are continually hungry though not yet starving. At a population level above that corresponding to $L_{p4}$, starvation would set in, and the population would be returned to $L_{p4}$ by the grim Malthusian controls of famine and disease. The affluence or otherwise of the self-subsistent farmer is thus determined largely by the relationship between the numbers he has to support and the availability of land.[5]

4. Here again the model does some violence to reality. In real life the demand ceiling is the product of a more complex process, even in an isolated self-subsistent agricultural community. The product of their agriculture is not confined simply to one or two staples but includes a range of foods and condiments. Moreover the produce is required not only for immediate consumption, but also for ceremonial uses, for gifts and exchange, perhaps for libations and sacrifices, and even for display. How, ever, it is only in the pretence that there is a sudden and complete transition, at one definite point, from strong and urgent demand to complete indifference, that the model exaggerates.

5. For the effects of changes in technology or the addition of capital in this situa-

In India most peasants with a substantial self-subsistent component in their production are poorly supplied with land, and their position on figure 3.1 would approximate that of a unit with a population/land situation indicated by $L_{p3}$ or $L_{p4}$, with some more fortunate peasants at perhaps $L_{p2}$. For India, and for peasants in many other heavily populated, less developed countries, the majority of the peasant population of interest for development planning is liable to be land poor, and the problem is not so much to induce these peasants to take part in the monetary economy but rather to raise the production possibility curve by the introduction of new techniques and capital, in order to enable them to do so on a scale sufficient to provide for an income above the starvation level. However, the situation I found in Papua New Guinea, and in many other of the larger Pacific territories was quite different. Here the situation of the self-subsistent production unit frequently was similar to that depicted by $L_{p1}$ in figure 3.1, or even better. Except in the atolls and one or two smaller territories whose populations have outgrown their land areas, such as Tonga, land is still available to most of the self-subsistent indigenous peasants of the Pacific[6] in relative abundance, and many of them live in a state of what I have called primitive affluence. This means that they are able to produce, from their own resources, as much as they can consume of the normal staple foods that they are used to, together with a reasonable surplus for entertainment, display and emergency, and a standard of housing, clothing, and entertainment requisites (e.g., kava) that is traditionally acceptable, with the employment of a relatively small part of the total potential resources of labor and land available to them. This means that within their self-subsistent, nonmonetary production system the productivity of their labor is very high, and it is still quite common in these regions to find substantial groups of peasants able to sustain this level of consumption from their own resources at the cost of an average labor input of about three hours per man-day or less.[7]

On the other hand, when they first respond to the opportunity of participating in the market economy, their productivity in the monetary sec-

tion, see the detailed exposition in my earlier technical articles, cited in note 2 in this chapter.

6. This usually does not apply to nonindigenous immigrants, such as the Indians in Fiji, who have been excluded from traditional land rights.

7. I have had no direct experience of Africa, but I was greatly encouraged to find that G. K. Helleiner, working in Nigeria, came to very similar conclusions about nonmonetary subsistence production there and independently arrived at an almost identical model in explanation of his findings. See Gerald K. Helleiner, "Typology in Development Theory: The Land Surplus Economy (Nigeria)," *Food Research Institute Studies* 6 (1966): 181–94.

tor tends to be very low. Transport costs, except for the few who happen to live in favored sites near the towns or other major links to the modern economy, are very high. As wage labor they are usually unskilled, and they are unaccustomed even to the idea of regular hours. As for commercial agriculture, the staple foods they are used to producing are much to their own taste and keep well in the ground until harvested, at least for moderate periods. (The crops are in this respect better suited to the needs of many peasants than even grain and flour, for which rats, mildew, and insects may present problems.) However, markets for these staples are slow to develop, for the staples are mainly sweet potato, yams, and taro, which are bulky, and thus difficult and expensive to transport, and which present problems of storage over any lengthy period. Consequently commerce and consumers in the advanced sector of the economy tend to prefer other foods that do not have these problems (such as rice, flour, tinned fish) or that are more to the accustomed taste of the large cash customers, who are mostly non-indigenous. In the rural peasant areas there is no market for the local staple goods, as everybody grows their own, and in addition there are often social objections to the idea of exchanging such foods among themselves on any basis other than the traditional prestation basis. The result is that, other than the lucky few on the outskirts of the main towns, peasants tend almost invariably to commence operations in the market either by engaging themselves or one of their family members in wage labor for a limited period, or by utilizing some of their spare labor on the farm to produce a purely cash crop (such as coffee, cocoa, or rubber) in small quantities over and above their own subsistence requirements. Moreover, with the cash thus earned there is also a strongly marked pattern of expenditure, in that the market goods and services that the peasant buys tend to be luxuries and supplements to his normal self-subsistent consumption rather than substitutes. There are of course exceptions; when a peasant buys a steel ax-head this does render his stone ax redundant, but generally the pattern holds. In other words, the peasant coming in contact with the market from the position $L_{p1}$ in figure 3.1 tends to continue his self-subsistent nonmonetary production very much as it was before contact, using labor input $A_1$ to produce the essentials of life at level $D_1$. However, he uses some of the remaining available labor ($L_{p1} - A_1$) to earn a cash supplement by wage labor or by the production of another cash crop. But the cash and self-subsistence activities are almost entirely separate; in effect the production and consumption in the subsistence region $OCA_1$ is quite separate from that in the monetary triangle $CS_1\,D_1$, and the production function will in most cases also be different.

In this situation my diagram is of use in indicating the level of nonmonetary production likely to be sustained, and in indicating whether a large or small amount of labor might be used for cash-earning activities without making it physically necessary to curtail the nonmonetary production. It can also show how the scope for such purely supplementary cash production will vary between production units with differing levels of population pressure on their land resources. But there, it seems to me, its usefulness ends. It provides no indication whatsoever as to how much of the available labor $(L_{p1} - A_1)$ will in fact be applied to cash-earning activities, nor how much such activities will earn. There will presumably be conceptually a point of subjective equilibrium at some labor input between $A_1$ and $L_{p1}$, but my diagram provides no means of determining it.[8]

It seems particularly important to understand the process whereby this equilibrium is reached, for the involvement of the rural peasant population in economic development is mainly to be achieved through their enhanced participation in the advanced monetized sector of the economy through wage labor or cash cropping. Knowledge of how to expedite and encourage this process is inevitably an important factor in development policy formation.

Both Sen and Nakajima have devised techniques for analyzing the factors determining the point at which subjective equilibrium will be achieved under these circumstances. Their answer in each case is that equilibrium will be reached when family welfare is maximized, and this will be when the marginal utility of the family income equals the marginal disutility of the family labor required to produce it. However, for their models to work for the transitional unit it is necessary to relate the utilities of the product retained for home consumption and the utilities of the goods purchased on the market, with the proceeds of the sale of some of the farm product, and/or the sale of some farm labor. This presents difficulties that will be further discussed a little later.

8. There is, however, considerable empirical evidence to suggest that this equilibrium is seldom *sustained* at a level anywhere approaching $L_{pl}$, even when the capital investment (e.g., in coffee gardens, rubber trees ready for tapping, etc.) has already been made—often as a result of noneconomic incentives, status considerations, or simply the wish to please the district commissioner. Agricultural officers throughout most of the Pacific region complain that indigenous-owned cash crop lands produce at levels far below the potential, often because they lack relatively minor maintenance, and often simply because the full crop has not been harvested.

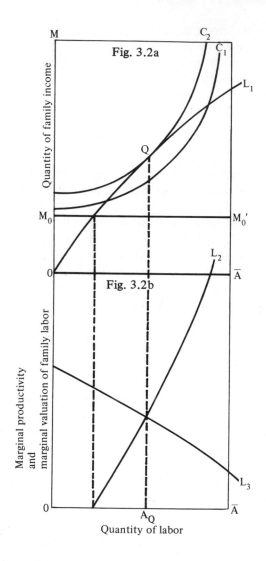

Marginal productivity and marginal valuation of family labor

Quantity of labor

Nakajima's model works roughly as follows. I shall use one of his simpler diagrams in illustration initially, in order to show its relation-ship to the diagram in figure 3.1. In figure 3.2a Nakajima shows on the vertical axis the quantity of family income, from whatever source, measured in terms of money, $M$. This corresponds to the vertical axis in my figure 3.1, except of course that the income in figure 3.1 is confined to nonmonetary product and is not measured in money terms. His horizontal axis, like mine, measures the quantity of labor. The vertical line passing through figure 3.2*a* and *b* on the right, marked *A*, stands for "the physiologically possible maximum of labor hours for the whole family" and corresponds roughly to my vertical line $L_p$ for the production unit or family concerned. The curve $OL_1$ is the production possibility curve for the family farm, corresponding to the curve $OT$ in my diagram. The horizontal line $M_0 M_0'$ is the "minimum subsistence standard of income for the whole family" and corresponds to the point of intersection of the line $OG_1 G_2 G_3 G_4$ with the appropriate vertical line $L_p$ for the unit concerned on my diagram. Curves $C_1$ and $C_2$ are indifference curves, and subjective equilibrium is reached at $Q$, where an indifference curve touches the production possibility curve. The indifference curves will approach the minimum subsistence line and the maximum labor line asymptotically. In figure 3.2*b* the curve $L_3$ is the marginal productivity of labor curve for the farm, and the curve $L_2$ is what Nakajima describes as the "marginal valuation of family labor curve," representing the marginal increment of money income the family requires to make the marginal unit of family labor input just worthwhile.

The basis of this situation is its assumption that the farm produces one product all of which is sold at a price $P_x$ to give a family income. $M$ is money over one year. $M_0$ is the minimum subsistence income. The land available is fixed and is represented by $B$. The only variable is the input of labor, and here there is no labor market, so only family labor is available. The amount of labor potentially available is $\bar{A}$, which is the physiological maximum the family can supply. The amount of labor used, in hours per year, is $A_0$. Therefore:

$$\bar{A} \geqq A_0 > O, \quad M \geqq M_0 > O. \tag{3.1}$$

The utility function is

$$U = U(A,M), \tag{3.2}$$

and it is assumed that

$$U_A > 0, \quad U_M > 0, \tag{3.3}$$

$$\frac{\delta}{\delta A}\left(\frac{U_A}{U_M}\right) > 0, \tag{3.4}$$

$$\frac{-U_A}{U_M} = \infty \text{ when } A = \bar{A}, \tag{3.5}$$

$$\frac{\delta}{\delta M}\left(\frac{-U_A}{U_M}\right) > 0, \tag{3.6}$$

and

$$\frac{-U_A}{U_M} = 0, \text{ when } M = M_0. \tag{3.7}$$

Thus, in figure 3.2, the equation of the production possibility curve of the farm, which is the family income curve in this case, is

$$M = P_x F(A, B) \tag{3.8}$$

and the slope of the indifference curve is $-U_A/U_M$, which is the marginal valuation of family labor. Then, assuming $F_A \geqq 0$, $F_{AA} < 0$, and maximizing $U$ of equation (3.2), we have

$$P_x F_A = \frac{-U_A}{U_M}, \tag{3.9}$$

and the equilibrium values of $A$ and $M$ are determined by the simultaneous equations (3.8) and (3.9).

This is Nakajima's basic model, for the pure commercial family farm without a labor market. Later he introduces the concept of an "achievement standard of income," which he defines as "that standard of income at and above which the slope of indifference curves becomes nearly vertical regardless of the distance from the vertical axis." This standard, represented in figures 3.3a and b by the line $\overline{MM}'$, can be high or low, depending on the stage of development. However, if this line were placed not very far above the minimum subsistence line, and if the farm were defined as a pure subsistence or nonmonetary production unit, the achievement standard of income would be very similar in effect to my greatly simplified (and therefore less accurate) concept of the demand ceiling, $DD'$ in figure 3.1.

For simplicity, let us consider next Nakajima's model of the pure commercial family farm with a competitive labor market. One case of this is shown in figures 3.4a and b. Here he has introduced the competitively determined wage rate $W$, represented in 3.4a by the straight line $CQR$ and in 3.4b by the horizontal line $WW'$. In the absence of the labor market, equilibrium would have been at $Q'$, but, as the labor market offers a higher return at this level of input of family labor, equilibrium will be reached by applying family labor to the family farm only to point $Q$ in figure 3.4a and then hiring family labor out to point $R$.

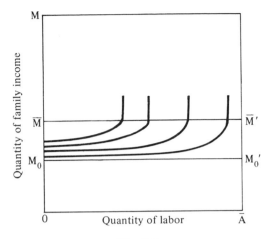

Fig. 3.3a

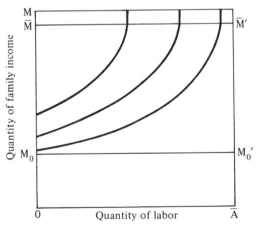

Fig. 3.3b

In this case the equation for family income becomes:

$$M = P_x F(A', B) + W(A - A'), \qquad (3.10)$$

where $A'$ represents the total labor input to the farm (whether family labor or hired labor) and $A$ represents the amount of family labor used (whether on the farm or hired out).

In figure 3.4, we have $A > A'$ and family labor is hired out, so that

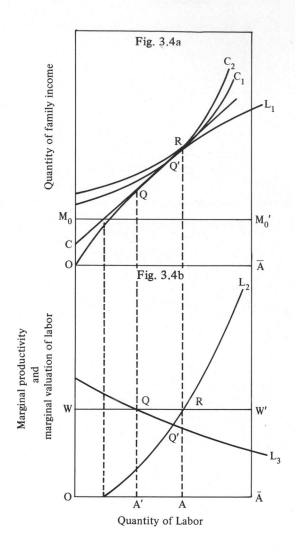

Fig. 3.4a

Fig. 3.4b

Quantity of Labor

the term $W(A - A')$ is positive, but the possibilities are that $A \gtreqless A'$, so that $W(A - A')$ can be zero or negative. In the latter case outside labor would be brought in to work on the farm.

Maximizing $U$ of equation (3.2) we have:

$$P_x F_{A'} = W \qquad (3.11)$$

and

$$\frac{-U_A}{U_M} = W. \tag{3.12}$$

Equation (3.11) determines the amount of labor that will be used on the farm; equations (3.10) and (3.12) determine $A$ and $M$.

It would be very useful if this analysis could be extended to the case I have described in figure 3.1, for Nakajima goes on to describe the effects of price changes, and to elaborate his model to cope with other more complex situations, where the farm is semisubsistence (i.e., consumes some of its product and sells some) and where there is more than one product. If we could impute a price for the subsistence staples one might be tempted to try, but this is, in my view, a dubious procedure. Basically the problem is that price is a market phenomenon, the function of which is to bring into equilibrium the value to the producers and the value to the consumers, who have access to the market, through the process of exchange. Where there is no such process there is nothing to bring about such equilibrium and there is no reason why the two sets of values should be equal. Imputing a price does not do this; the value to one producer may be quite different from the value to another, and neither need have any direct correspondence with the value to an imputed, but not existent, outside consumer. If the subsistence producer in the remote Star Mountains of New Guinea uses ten pounds of sweet potatoes a day to feed his family, and if we value this at the price current in the nearest market (two days' march away) at two cents a pound, and deduct three cents a pound for imputed costs of transport to market, the implication is that the poor man would be better off dead, for the more he produces, the poorer he will be. If we tell him that the rational thing for him to do as economic man is to stop all production and starve we may expect him to protest that he is not that sort of economic man.

The real difficulty is that the economic activity appertaining to the triangle $OCA_1$ in figure 3.1 is nonmonetary and is not effectively related to any monetary market. This means that there are in fact no money prices, and it does not really help to pretend that there are. As Nicholas Georgescu-Roegen argues, an economic system is characterized by its institutions,[9] and for an economic theory that characterization is fundamental. Money and markets are clearly important institutions in this respect. I therefore suggest that it is unprofitable to attempt to

9. Nicholas Georgescu-Roegen, "Economic Theory and Agrarian Economics," *Oxford Economic Papers* 12 (1960): 1–40.

apply the same theoretical tool of analysis to both parts of the semi-subsistence farm, and that we should do better to analyze the non-monetary and the monetary components separately, taking into account in each box the main cross-effects and influences from the other. This means that we have two related enterprises, one entirely nonmonetary and one entirely monetized. The first will comprise the economic activity of the triangle $OCA_1$ in figure 3.1, and the second that of the triangle $CS_1D_1$.

Let us therefore attempt this, using Nakajima's model from figure 3.3a and b adapted for pure subsistence production by measuring the utilities on the vertical axis in quantities of product instead of in money, and putting it side by side with an adaptation of his model from figure 3.4a and b for the monetary enterprise. This is done in figures 3.5 and 3.6, sections 3.5a and b being the subsistence enterprise, and sections 3.6a and b being the monetary enterprise.

In figure 3.5a the vertical axis measures the output of the subsistence enterprise in quantity only and not by price. $Q$ is therefore not related to $M$ by any price, $P$, at this stage. The income curve for the subsistence enterprise is therefore:

$$Q = F(A, B), \tag{3.13}$$

and the other equation determining equilibrium for the subsistence enterprise is

$$F_A = \frac{-U_A}{U_Q}. \tag{3.14}$$

Equilibrium is achieved at a level of family labor input to the subsistence enterprise equal to $A_Q$. Similarly the degree of land utilization for the subsistence enterprise might be denoted by $B_Q$, where $B_Q \leq B$.

Initially, in the "supplementary cash production" stage, the relationships between the subsistence enterprise and the monetary enterprise will be as follows. First the labor supply available in the monetary enterprise will be determined by the configurations of figures 3.6a and b and will be the residual of the physically possible labor, $\bar{A}$, after deducting $A_Q$, which is the amount of labor used in the nonmonetary enterprise. That is, the possible supply of labor to the monetary enterprise will be $\bar{A} - A_Q$. The supply of labor in the monetary enterprise is thus determined indirectly by the demographic characteristics of the family production unit, by the type and quantity of land available, by the techniques and improvements in use, all of which determine the

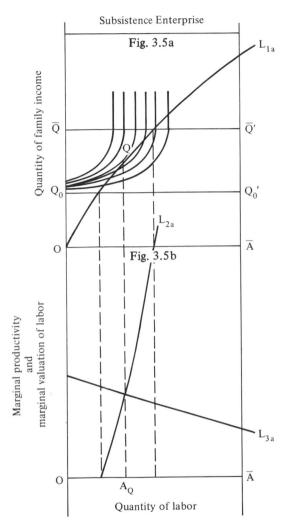

Subsistence Enterprise

**Fig. 3.5a**

$L_{1a}$

Quantity of family income

$\overline{Q}$

$\overline{Q}'$

$Q$

$Q_0$

$Q_0'$

$\overline{A}$

O

$L_{2a}$

**Fig. 3.5b**

Marginal productivity and marginal valuation of labor

$L_{3a}$

O

$\overline{A}$

$A_Q$

Quantity of labor

shape of the subsistence production possibility curve $OL_{1a}$ in figure 3.5*a*, and by the demographic and social characteristics of the population of the unit, which determine indifference curves, largely through the position of the subsistence line $Q_0Q_0'$ and the income aspiration line $\overline{Q}\overline{Q}'$ in figure 3.5*a*.

Second, the other initial correlation between figures 3.5 and 3.6 will be that the production possibility curve for the family farm in 3.6*a* will be determined partially by the land use in figure 3.5. The quantity and

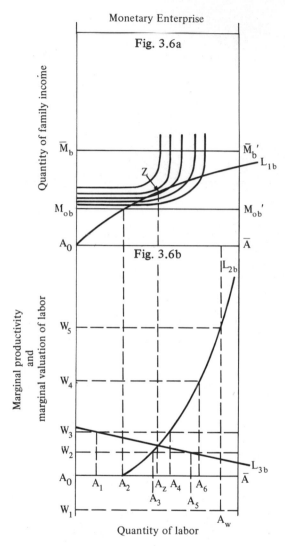

Monetary Enterprise
Fig. 3.6a
Quantity of family income
$\bar{M}_b$
$\bar{M}_b'$
$L_{1b}$
Z
$M_{ob}$
$M_{ob}'$
$A_0$
$\bar{A}$
Fig. 3.6b
$L_{2b}$
Marginal productivity and marginal valuation of labor
$W_5$
$W_4$
$W_3$
$W_2$
$L_{3b}$
$A_0$
$\bar{A}$
$A_1$ $A_2$ $A_z$ $A_4$ $A_6$
$A_3$ $A_5$
$W_1$
$A_w$
Quantity of labor

quality of land available after the needs of the subsistence enterprise have been satisfied will be influenced by the varying proportions of the line $D_1S_1$ to $CS_1$ in the upper shaded thriangle of figure 3.1, that is, by the shape of the curve from $C$ to $S_1$. However, it is not possible to construct the production possibility curve in the monetary enterprise directly from figure 3.1, because other factors, including type of crop,

prices, techniques, and other inputs, will be variable. Nevertheless it is possible to state as a general rule that, for any production unit with given land, the higher the level of subsistence production required for equilibrium in the subsistence enterprise, the lower and flatter will be the production possibility curve in the monetary enterprise, ceteris paribus. Conversely, a reduction in the aspiration level of the subsistence component would lead to a heightening and steepening of the production possibility curve in the monetary enterprise. This is most clearly seen in the special case where the subsistence crop and the monetary enterprise crop are the same (e.g., rice). Then, in quantitative terms there would be one production function for both enterprises, the subsistence enterprise taking first cut of the production and the surplus being sold. The monetary enterprise production possibility curve would then be the remaining segment of the subsistence production possibility curve to the right of $Q$, as modified by the price, $P_x$.

The equation for income in the monetary enterprise will thus be

$$M = P_x F(A^{*1}, B^*) \, W(A^* - A^{*1}), \qquad (3.15)$$

where $A^*$ and $B^*$ are the amounts of family labor and family land utilized in the monetary enterprise, $A^{*1}$ is the total labor (from all sources) used on the farm component of the monetary enterprise, and where

$$A^* \leqq (\bar{A} - A_Q), \text{ and } B^* < (B - B_Q). \qquad (3.16)$$

Maximizing $U$ in the monetary enterprise, we shall have

$$P_X F_A{}^{*1} = W \qquad (3.17)$$

and

$$\frac{-U_A{}^*}{U_M} = W, \qquad (3.18)$$

with equation (3.17) determining the level of total labor input to the farm component of the monetary enterprise, and the simultaneous equations (3.15) and (3.18) determining $M$ and $A^*$.

Third, the shape of the indifference curves in figures 3.5 and 3.6 will be independently determined, for all practical purposes, until stage 3 is reached, that is, until substitution between subsistence and market consumption goods begins to take place on a significant scale. In the subsistence enterprise the slope of the indifference curve will be:

$$\frac{-U_A}{U_Q},\tag{3.19}$$

whereas in the monetary enterprise it will be:

$$\frac{-U_A{}^*}{U_M}.\tag{3.20}$$

In these two functions the numerators are related to the extent that the maximum possible value of $A^*$ is $\bar{A} - A$. However, in the absence of an effective local market for subsistence goods, in which the farm family can always operate at will, there is no necessary relationship between $U_Q$ and $U_M$.

This will cease to be the case when stage 3 is reached. In most cases an effective local market sufficient to make this possible will also tend to make specialization in the monetary enterprise worthwhile, and the subsistence component as a separate enterprise will tend to fade away. It is characteristic of this third stage that the family tends to consume its own produce only when it is advantageous in money terms, so that the denominator in both (3.19) and (3.20) is effectively $U_M$. The conditions upon which this important next stage of transition eventuates will be discussed briefly at the end of this chapter; but they are not applicable at the stage now being considered.

At this earlier stage markets are distant, wages as well as the prices of produce produced for sale are low, and family labor is unskilled and relatively unproductive in the monetary sector. In other words, the cost of earning money (as distinct from subsistence) in terms of effort is very high. At the same time, the utility of money on the family farm or near it is also limited, for local cash incomes are small, the range of goods and services readily available for money is restricted, and prices tend to be high.[10] Though the demand for some money income may be very strong, with the effect that initially the indifference curves in the monetary enterprise will tend to be very nearly horizontal for some distance to the right of $A_Q$ in figure 3.6$a$, or to the right of $M_{0b}$, the intensity of that demand tends to fall off quickly. The "minimum money income line" (which is what $M_{0b}M_{0b}'$ would in effect be here), if there is one, would represent some minimum money income essential to enable the production unit to produce, as for example to meet a monetary land tax or rent.

10. For a detailed discussion of these aspects see my essay "Planning in a Primitive Economy: From Pure Subsistence to the Production of a Market Surplus," *Economic Record* 40 (1964): 156–74.

On the other hand, once a few urgently felt needs have been met, the high effort cost of earning money at such low levels of productivity, together with the restricted purchasing power of the incomes accessible at the levels of income to which they can aspire, will tend to turn the indifference curves steeply upward at quite a low level. In Nakajima's terms, this could be represented by introducing an "aspiration level line," $\bar{M}_b\bar{M}'_b$, as shown in figure 3.6a.

The effect of these factors on the shape of the marginal productivity curve $L_{3b}$ and the marginal valuation of labor curve $L_{2b}$ is shown in figure 3.6b.

I have omitted drawing any wage line in figure 3.6a, since what I wish to show would unduly complicate the diagram. However, in 3.6b I have shown five wage lines, $W_1$, $W_2$, $W_3$, $W_4$, and $W_5$. The first of these, $W_1$, is a low wage which is shown as negative in total income. This has been a very common level of wage in the Pacific region, particularly for estate and other rural labor. It is shown as negative in figure 3.6b because the situation of family labor on the family farm is that the essentials of life are met on an adequate scale from the subsistence enterprise, and this applies not only to the adult worker but also to his dependents. For the employment of estate labor, on the other hand, it has in many of these areas been common practice to employ adult males only, for the most part, and to provide them with a wage made up often of a component in kind, comprising adequate food, housing, and clothing for the worker, plus a small cash supplement. For the ordinary unskilled novice worker, the cash supplement is quite insufficient to support a family of dependents, and therefore for the average worker the wage $W_1$ is insufficient to put him on an equal footing with the families remaining in the production unit here considered, even before they have started to earn a cash income. The fact that such low wage rates do produce some labor is dependent on the ability to recruit unmarried workers or workers who are prepared to leave their dependents behind in the subsistence sector for the period of their engagement. When this is done, the effect on the original production unit within which the wage worker's family remains can be to eliminate the worker's productive labor from the unit but not to eliminate his dependents' claim on its product. The effect on total (extended) family income can thus be negative. In other words, for these models a basic assumption is that goods and thus utilities are equally shared among the total population of the production unit, and that labor, and thus disutilities, are equally shared among the working component of that population. If this assumption were dropped, the situation for an individual, acting on his own account, could be different, as will be shown below.

From the individual worker's point of view, there are also two ways of looking at a wage in this context. One is the wage as it appears to the wage earner considered as a continuing member of the transitional subsistence production unit depicted in figures 3.5 and 3.6. The other is the wage as it appears to a member as an individual, breaking away from the transitional subsistence group with a view to becoming a permanent member of the monetized labor force. The low wage $W_1$ would appear to be below $O\bar{A}$ to the latter, assuming either that he is already or proposes within a year or two to become a family man with dependents. This is the man who is ultimately of the most interest from the point of view of development of an advanced economy, because this is the man who will become a committed member of the wage labor force, and whose cumulative improvement in experience and skill in the advanced monetary sector may be expected to be the basis for increasing productivity and thus increasing earning capacity. As the model shows, the existence of these low wages as the norm will tend to make such committed wage earning unattractive and to confine wage employment largely to inexperienced novices on their first contract, uninterested in the long-term improvement of their earning capacity as wage employees. As a corollary such low wages, tied to the low productivity of inexperienced novices, tend to be self-perpetuating from the employer's point of view also, and there is a strong tendency for wage labor under such circumstances to be caught in a kind of low income–low productivity trap.[11]

However, from the point of view of the man interested in remaining in the long run a member of the transitional subsistence production group, wage level $W_1$ may appear quite different. If he is a young man not yet married, for example, he may be prepared to postpone marriage and to go away to work as a single man for a year or two. In this case $W_1$ would put him in a position, income-wise, above the line $O\bar{A}$, for the wage will provide full subsistence needs for himself plus a cash supplement over and above these needs. Depending upon the size of the supplement, this could put him in a position equivalent to that shown as $W_2$, $W_3$, or even perhaps $W_4$ or $W_5$ in figure 3.6b. However, it must

11. Very similar conclusions were reached by Barber concerning an African population in Rhodesia. See William J. Barber, *The Economy of British Central Africa* (Stanford: Stanford University Press, 1961).

be remembered that in an "affluent" subsistence unit the input of labor, $A_Q$, in the nonmonetary enterprise is liable to be no more than twenty hours per week per man, while at the low level of productivity and aspiration indicated in figure 3.6a the additional labor input, $A_QA_3$, to the monetary enterprise is liable to be no more than about another five or six hours per week per man. On the other hand the full-time wage worker may be required to work a minimum of, say, fifty hours a week if he is to keep his job at all. This would mean that, to earn his wage, his labor input would be somewhere near that indicated in figure 3.6b as $A_W$. Therefore, on the particular configurations shown in figure 3.5, contract wage labor would not be attractive even to the noncommitted worker unless the effective wage were at least $W_5$.[12]

This brings up another important distinction that needs to be drawn in considering wage labor. For members of a transitional subsistence production unit, casual labor, which can be provided in small amounts of a few days or a week at a time while the worker still draws his main subsistence needs from the subsistence enterprise, can be of particular interest and importance at wage rates substantially below $W_5$. The reason for this is clear from figure 3.6b, which shows that if casual labor could be obtained at wage $W_4$ there would be no supplementary cash farm production undertaken, but instead $A_QA_6$ of the labor would be directed into this casual wage labor. On the other hand, if the wage for casual labor were $W_3$, it would pay them to put $A_Q-A_1$ of their available labor into cash farm production, and a further amount, $A_1A_4$, into casual wage labor. Finally, if there were a market in which casual wage labor were freely available to be hired at $W_2$, the transitional production unit would provide an input of only $A_QA_3$ into the farm monetary enterprise from its own labor resources and then hire a further amount, $A_3A_5$, on the market to supplement this.

From a policy point of view, the path to economic development in a society of transitional subsistence production units lies to a very large extent in increasing the level of participation in the monetary economy, for only with the catalysis of money do the full advantages of

12. This refers to an ex ante assessment by the prospective wage earner, and his experience ex post may be disappointing to him. This also ignores the "bright lights" effects, such as the attractions of adventure, of seeing strange and interesting places, and of possible access at times to urban entertainments and amenities. These factors may modify for a time the shape and position of the curve $L_{2b}$ in 3.6b for the individual worker by moving it to the right of where it would be for further work on the family farm. On the other hand, absence from friends, relatives, and the familiar and secure environment of home may eventually tend to move it back the other way.

specialization, division of labor, and large-scale capital formation, upon which most economic development depends, become accessible. For this reason, the response of the subsistence production units to the opportunities and incentives offered by contact with the monetary sector, and the means available for intervention to accelerate and enhance that response, are of particular theoretical and practical interest. Let us therefore examine the models to see, first, what they suggest about means of increasing the level of activity of the monetary enterprise in the transitional subsistence production unit, and, subsequently, what light they shed on the next stage of development in which specialization in monetary activity develops and the monetary enterprise begins to replace, rather than merely to supplement, the nonmonetary enterprise.

Taking the monetary and nonmonetary enterprises as separate and coexistent in the first instance, the first policy question concerns the monetary enterprise in this combination, and how to raise the effective participation of the combined unit in the monetary economy by stimulating the monetary enterprise. This, as the model shows, can be achieved in three ways.

1. The first way is to increase the supply of family labor and family land to the monetary enterprise. This can be achieved basically by two types of intervention. One would be to lower and flatten the indifference map in the subsistence enterprise by *lowering* the aspiration level $\bar{Q}\bar{Q}'$ in figure 3.5a, thus moving Q to the left in the figure. This is basically a belt-tightening process which, though possible in some cases through exhortation and leadership, is unlikely to have much appeal as a measure of development policy unless the peasants concerned are very land poor, or unless a very rapid and dramatic transition to market dependence and specialization at a noticeably higher level of living could be expected as a result.

The other type of intervention, much neglected in Pacific territories at least, is to raise the production possibility curve, $L_{1a}$, in the subsistence enterprise by improving the level of technology, using improved planting materials, and improving other inputs, such as fertilizer and water. Many departments of agriculture in Pacific territories have regarded subsistence agriculture as a major obstacle to economic development, and as something to be discouraged rather than improved. It is my contention that this view is mistaken, and that intensive research and extension work to enhance the productivity of subsistence crops would enhance the capacity of the transitional production unit to participate in the market economy.

Either of these two types of intervention, if effective, would raise productivity in the monetary enterprise by simultaneously releasing more labor and land to the monetary enterprise, thus flattening the indifference curves somewhat (by increasing the length of $A_Q\bar{A}$ in figure 3.6) and raising and steepening the production possibility curve of the farm monetary activity.

2. Next, one can operate directly on the production possibility curve of the monetary enterprise, steepening and raising it by enhancing physical productivity (by improved technology, improved inputs, and/ or capital additions) or by enhancing the effective farm-gate price of the product (usually through improvement of transport and marketing efficiency). The model shows some very interesting features of this effect, however, particularly where there is a minimum essential level of monetary income ($M_{0b}M_{0b}'$ in figure 3.6a) and where the maximum aspiration level, $\bar{M}_b\bar{M}_b'$, is not far above this.

Nakajima has shown that, where a minimum subsistence level is operative, the effect of an increase in price will always be to move the point of equilibrium to a higher level of family income (i.e., $Q$ will be raised vertically), but that the equilibrium level of input of family labor is indefinite, depending on the relative magnitude of the substitution effect and the income effect, as determined by the shape and location of the indifference curves. However, he points out, if the price (and the same would apply to other determinants of productivity in money terms, such as techniques) were so low that the production possibility curve just passed through $M_{0b}'$ (using figure 3.6a to illustrate), the equilibrium point would have to be precisely at $M_{0b}'$. Consequently, at productivity or price levels not much above $M_{0b}M_{0b}'$ the path of points of equilibrium will move upward and to the left as productivity or price increases. In other words, increases in price or productivity at these low levels will reduce the equilibrium level of family labor input.

Similarly it can be readily seen that, if the production possibility curve rises and steepens until it cuts the maximum aspiration level, $M_bM_b'$, the point of equilibrium cannot be to the right of that point of intersection, as all indifference curves by definition become vertical at that level. Therefore, any increase in productivity or price beyond that which makes the maximum aspiration level just physically possible must again move the point of equilibrium to the left and thus reduce the level of input of family labor. The result is that, where these maximum and minimum levels exist, even though there may be an intermediate range where increases in productivity produce increases in the equilibrium level of family labor input, there will be sizable ranges close to the upper or lower limits of aspired income where the reverse is the case. This to me makes some of the apparently conflicting empirical reports about price reactions of peasants less difficult to comprehend.

3. The third way to stimulate the monetary enterprise is to operate on these upper or lower limits, thus modifying the pattern of the indifference map and changing the marginal valuation (or marginal disutility) of family labor in that enterprise.

The minimum $M_{0b}M'_{0b}$ level can be raised or lowered by raising or lowering rents, taxes, and other costs without which production cannot be sustained. This device was once fairly popular in some colonial situations, using a poll tax or a land tax as a means of forcing self-subsistent peasants into wage labor or production for the market. The model shows that its effect will be to raise the point of origin from which the lowest indifference curves commence at right angles to the vertical axis, and thus to reduce the steepness of the curves in the lower ranges. The result is that such a measure can be effective in raising the level of input of family labor into the monetary enterprise where productivity is low and the production possibility curve does not rise steeply above the minimum income level of $M_0M'_b$. This is because the point of origin of the marginal valuation (or disutility) of family labor curve, $L_{3b}$, is moved to the right. However, so long as the maximum level, $\bar{M}_b\bar{M}'_b$, is unaffected, the point at which the marginal valuation of family labor approaches infinity remains the same, so that the effect decreases at higher levels of productivity.

On the other hand, the maximum level $\bar{M}_b\bar{M}'_b$ may be raised by increasing the utility of money income at the farm. This process has been discussed in detail elsewhere,[13] but an increase in the range and a decrease in the price of market goods and services available near the farm gate will have such a result. The effect on the motivation of the unit is to move the upper end of the marginal valuation of family labor curve to the right, reducing its slope throughout, thus increasing the equilibrium level of input of family labor at all levels of productivity, but particularly at the higher levels.

Finally, when supplementary production or labor supply for the

13. Fisk, "Planning in a Primitive Economy" (1964).

market sector reaches a high level in the transitional production unit, there comes a point where further advance will depend upon gradual abandonment of subsistence production and the development of specialization for the market in the form of pure commercial farming on the one hand and a committed wage labor force on the other. These developments make accessible further economies and efficiencies in the productive processes of the farm, and the development of higher skills and experience in the wage labor force.

This further step has sometimes proved more difficult in practice and fraught with more side effects than we have expected. Disappointment at the slow speed and unevenness of development at this stage has been common. This has been particularly so in much of the Pacific region and, I suspect, in areas elsewhere where "primitive affluence" is found.

The reason is that, for specialization to develop, the monetary enterprise, whether in farming or in wage labor, has to become more productive, in terms of the effort cost of obtaining the essentials of life, than the subsistence enterprise. Moreover, this generally applies to the product of the whole family as a unit and not just to that of an individual. In a situation of primitive affluence this is a very much larger step than is sometimes realized, simply because labor in the subsistence enterprise is so highly productive.

As we have seen, the fundamental characteristic of the earlier transitional stage is a clear dichotomy in the flow of goods and services consumed. The essentials of life are produced within the transitional unit itself and are either not available at all, or available only at much greater effort cost, from the market sector. On the other hand there are other goods and services, available only on the market, that are keenly desired even at great effort cost.[14] Under these circumstances specialization for the market, including dependence on the market for most of the essentials of life, cannot be expected to develop. Specialization will develop only when wage labor or cash cropping provides a more rewarding means of acquiring the essentials of life than self-subsistent production. This requires first that an acceptable range of such goods and services, or acceptable substitutes for them, be reliably available from the market sector, and second that the effort involved in acquiring them by market specialization cease to be notably greater

14. The keenness of this desire, and the readiness to work for quite low returns in the monetary enterprise to satisfy it, has at times led planners to false hopes that the peasant sector is ready to specialize. Such expectations derive from the premature treatment of nonmonetary production as though it were a part of the monetary enterprise.

than that in self-subsistent production. In other words, returns in the monetary enterprise must substantially increase, or those in the subsistence enterprise must fall.

Once this has taken place, the productive activities of the production unit, and its consumption, can be analyzed in money terms and the need for two diagrams disappears. Nakajima's model in figure 3.4, and its more sophisticated derivatives, then provide suitable tools of analysis for the whole enterprise. However, this is not yet the case, and we are still faced with the difficulty of comparing the utilities of market goods and services with those of goods and services not related to the market. This in general is almost impossible to do with any validity, for reasons already discussed. However, there is one level of consumption, which I will call the "full belly" situation, which I think can be used as one point of comparison between monetary and nonmonetary living, and in particular between living in a transitional subsistence production unit on the one hand and as a full-time wage laborer on the other. This is the point in the transitional or the pure subsistence unit where subsistence production provides as much as the unit needs of the basic foods, plus clothing, housing, and entertainment of a type and quantity acceptable by customary standards. This I take to be an identifiable and recognizable level of consumption that can be matched in the monetary sector by a level of expenditure that would similarly provide adequate basic foods, housing, clothing, and entertainment to a roughly equivalent level of satisfactions. Where this level of living is just attained and no more, whether in the monetary sector or the subsistence sector, the *gross* satisfactions enjoyed therefrom are assumed to be comparable.

In figure 3.7 this is represented by the line *FBFB'* which shows the level of utility attained by persons in this consumption position, the gross utility of their satisfactions being measured on the left vertical axis. The horizontal axis measures labor input in hours per man per week, and the right-hand vertical axis measures the gross disutility of work. Units of utility and disutility are equal, but of opposite sign. The curve *XD* represents the cost of work in terms of the units of disutility incurred for each level of labor input.

Let us now postulate two groups of subsistence production units. One, designated *A*, has abundant land, its labor is highly productive in the subsistence sector, and it is generally in a situation of primitive affluence. The full belly level of living is achieved at the cost of a labor input of somewhat less than 20 hours per man per week (as is by no

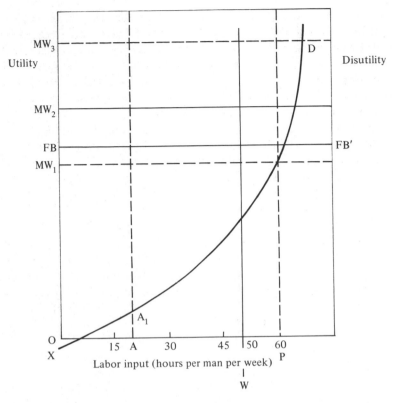

Fig. 3.7

means uncommon in the Pacific region). The other, designated *P*, is land hungry, its labor is relatively unproductive, and to achieve the full belly level of consumption it requires a labor input of 60 man-hours per week.

On these assumptions the two sets of production units achieve the same level of living (*FB*) in the subsistence enterprise, but the level of their net satisfactions will be quite different. Net satisfactions may be measured by the surplus of utility remaining after deducting the disutilities incurred in the process of laboring, or, in the particular case here described, by the difference between the level of gross utility achieved (*FB*) and a point on *XD* corresponding to the relevant labor input. For *A*, this surplus, *A′ − FB*, is very large, while for *P* it is very small.

Now let us introduce a money wage, *W*, in the advanced sector, at

which novice workers from the subsistence sector may obtain employment but in which they are required to work 50 hours per week. If the
money wage is the amount of cash income necessary just to sustain the
*FB* level of living in the monetary sector, this will afford workers from
*P* an opportunity of increasing their net satisfactions, even though
their level of consumption would not be raised, because there would
be a substantial saving in disutility because of the lower work input
involved. Even the lower level of wage and living implied by $MW_1$
would probably attract workers from *P*. However, workers from *A*
would not be attracted at either of these wage levels, nor even at the
higher level $MW_2$, as the disutility of the additional labor required
would outweigh the increase in income until a very much higher level
of wage, say $MW_3$, were offered. And why should any employer raise
the wage that high so long as labor is available at a lower wage from *P*?

The difficulties previously mentioned make it impossible to measure
the comparative utilities of money levels above and below *FB* on this
diagram, which makes it a singularly blunt instrument for analysis. It
provides a rough illustration of one feature and nothing more. For
example, it shows nothing of the opportunities and effects of the supplementary cash-earning activities illustrated in figures 3.5*b* and 3.6*b*.
However, a review of earlier parts of the chapter will show that the
opportunities for a substantial supplementary monetary enterprise are
far greater for units in the situation *A* than for those in situation *P*,
because for *P* most of the land and labor resources available will already
be taken up in the nonmonetary enterprise, leaving the scope for the
supplementary monetary enterprise much more restricted. If the effects
of such supplementary cash earning could be introduced into figure
3.7, therefore, the result would be to accentuate rather than to reduce
the relatively higher attraction of various wage rates for full-time
labor to *P* as against *A*.

As a result, certain identifiable development patterns become discernible in countries where primitive affluence is found. First, where
land is relatively abundant and all the indigenous population tend to
be in a position somewhere near *A* in figure 3.7, wage labor from the
subsistence sector is hard to attract, uncommitted, desultory, and persistently unskilled. Its productivity in the monetary sector is low, and
its lack of commitment makes its instruction costly and unfruitful. In
industries (such as most export agriculture) where world markets are
competitive and often oversupplied, and in which labor is a large element in total costs, low productivity necessitates low wage rates, and

the pattern becomes fixed. In the past, some employers in some such countries have imported labor from other countries, where poor peasants at level *P* abound. This has quite naturally led to serious social and political problems, as in Fiji and Malaysia, for example, because, as our analysis shows only too clearly, it is among the poorer, *P*-type groups that the incentive to join and succeed as committed wage labor is strongest, with the result that in Malaysia the Chinese and in Fiji the Indians soon dominated the job market in the advanced monetary sector of the economy, while the indigenous peasants of the *A*-type groups are left experimenting with minor supplementary cash-cropping enterprises grafted onto their main subsistence activities. When substantial economic growth takes place, the main income benefits thus tend to accrue to the highly motivated nonindigenous workers already in the advanced sector of the economy, leaving the once affluent indigenous peasantry stagnant and largely outside the ambit of such growth.

There has been insufficient understanding of the underlying rationale of these responses to what has appeared to be economic opportunity, and they have too often been passed off as the result of insufficient moral fiber, or laziness, or other reprehensible forms of irrationality. It is my view that, on the contrary, these responses are in fact quite rational, at least in the short run, and that it is incumbent on the economic planner to make a closer study of the motivational pattern of peasant agriculture as it is, rather than as it might have been imagined to be by allusion from our Western, capitalist, monetized economy.

# 4

# A Pure Theory of Underdeveloped Economies

JAMES A. MIRRLEES

There are a number of reasons for thinking that man's productivity depends upon his consumption, at least where incomes are low. Not only does more food make possible more and better work; good health, higher standards of comfort, and the well-being of dependents might all be expected to help a man do more. In some richer countries, these influences may be reversed. But many who know developing countries believe there is some such relationship, though there may be disagreement about its importance. Several writers have looked at the theoretical implications of the hypothesis that consumption affects productivity and have recognized that it may change the implications of more orthodox economic analysis.[1] In particular, it is one reason for expecting to find relatively high urban wages coexisting with substantial unemployment. The implications have not, as yet, been pushed much further than that. It is particularly interesting to consider what equilibrium in rural

Various imperfect versions of this paper have been given over the years. I remember particularly helpful comments and discussions when it was given in Oxford, at Cornell, and in Cambridge.

1. The relationship between productivity and consumption was first used in theory by Harvey Leibenstein, who, however, assumed full employment (Leibenstein, *Economic Backwardness and Economic Growth* [New York: Wiley, 1957]). The peculiarity of that assumption was pointed out by D. Mazumdar, in "The Marginal Productivity Theory of Wages and Disguised Unemployment," *Review of Economic Studies* 26, no. 3 (1959). J. C. H. Fei and Alpha D. Chiang developed a growth model using the relationship in "Maximum-Speed Development through Austerity," *The Theory and Design of Economic Development,* ed. I. Adelman and E. Thorbecke (Baltimore: Johns Hopkins Press, 1966). There are some interesting further developments in Pradhan H. Prasad, *Growth with Full Employment* (Bombay: Allied Publishers, 1970). Gunnar Myrdal has emphasized the relationship but does not do much with it; see *Asian Drama* (New York: Pantheon, 1968).

Some relevant evidence on a relationship that has not received much attention from econometricians is contained in the booklet *Nutrition and Working Efficiency,* produced for the Freedom from Hunger Campaign, as Basic Studies no. 5, and published by the FAO.

areas might be like in these circumstances. That will be the main task of this chapter. It does not provide anything like a complete analysis, but the techniques to be presented perhaps make one possible and at least help to make the theoretical relationships clear. I shall also explore implications for the shadow pricing of labor, both in rural and urban production.

The analysis to be presented is called a "pure" theory because it ignores many important features of underdeveloped economies, so as to concentrate on one relationship. One must of course simplify in order to get an analysis going, and in any case it is interesting to see how much of what we observe in the less developed economies might be explained by the productivity relationship. Pure theory has the attraction that it concentrates on rational action in the face of intrinsic constraints and may therefore point to underlying long-run tendencies.

## 1. FACTORIES AND WAGE LABOR

I begin by reviewing what is already known. Laborers work in factories, which are run by profit-maximizing employers. If they do not obtain employment, they may return whence they came, starve, or share in some fixed pool of charitable gifts; if a man obtains a job, he consumes the wage he is paid. We assume—bearing in mind that this means leaving aside some interesting problems—that the quantity and quality of labor a man provides can together be measured by a single number, $h$, which is a function of the wage, $w$, he receives, and that the labor ($h$) provided by different employees can simply be added up to give the total labor input. Thus a factory with production function $f$ produces output (measured in the same units as the wage)

$$y = f[nh(w)], \tag{4.1}$$

where $n$ is the number of men working in the factory and all workers receive wage $w$. We can consider the possibility of employing people at different wages, but the assumptions to be made in fact imply that producers do not want to.

Assume that $f$ is a concave, increasing function, zero at zero. The function $h$ is supposed to have the shape indicated in figure 4.1. The shape is plausible—as the production function for a typical piece of capital equipment designed for relatively specific purposes—consistent with such scant evidence as I have seen, and broadly necessary if the theory is to have any interest.

The producer's profits are

*James A. Mirrlees*

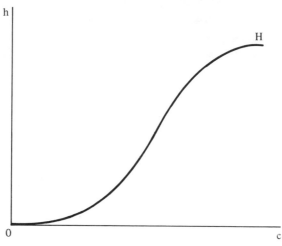

Fig. 4.1

$$\Pi = f[nh(w)] - nw. \tag{4.2}$$

Not only does he choose $n$; he has a certain degree of control over $w$ as well. The point is that employers can always pay more than the supply price of laborers to them; though, in the absence of the productivity relationship, they would have no reason to do so. Since we can write (4.2) in the form

$$\Pi = f[nh(w)] - nh(w) \cdot \frac{w}{h(w)},$$

the producer does best for himself if he chooses $w$ so as to make $w/h(w)$ as small as possible and then, having chosen $w$ in this way, chooses $nh$ to maximize $\Pi$.[2] Referring to figure 4.2, we see that $w/h$ is least when $w = c^*$, the consumption level at which the tangent to the $h$-curve passes through the origin. If the supply price of laborers is in any case above $c^*$, then the employer cannot do better than pay the supply price; but if it is less than $c^*$, he will not pay less than $c^*$. Thus, the profit-maximizing wage rate is

$$w = \text{Max}\,(c^*, w_S), \tag{4.3}$$

where $c^*$ maximizes $h/w$, and $w_S$ is the supply price of labor.

2. Since $\Pi$ is not a concave function of $w$, it is not sufficient to look at necessary conditions for maximization, but the argument given is rigorous, for if $c^*$ minimizes $w/h$ and $x^*$ maximizes $f(x) - xc^*/h(c^*), f(x^*) - x^*c^*/h(c^*) \geq f(nh) - nhc^*/h(c^*) \geq f(nh) - nhc/h = f(nh) - nc.$

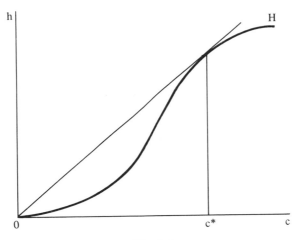

Fig. 4.2

Where there is a fixed supply of laborers available, and a number of factories, the supply price of labor will be greater than $c^*$ only if there would be an excess demand for labor by producers were the wage equal to $c^*$. If on the contrary there is an excess supply of labor when $w = c^*$, the supply price of labor is lower, but it ceases to operate: we have an equilibrium with unemployed laborers who do not choose to be unemployed.

If employers were unaware of the productivity relationship embodied in the function $h$, the natural outcome would be the usual competitive equilibrium, in which the wage might be lower than $c^*$. From that point of view, the "efficiency wage" notion introduces a new concept of equilibrium. From another point of view, we can think of the supply and demand for labor, rather than the supply and demand for laborers. If the wage is $w$, the price of labor to the employer is $v = w/h$. We have seen that this has a minimum value, or, to put it differently, the supply of labor is zero if $v$ is less than $v^* = c^*/h(c^*)$. Thus there is a discontinuity in the labor supply at $v^*$. If we look for a competitive equilibrium in the markets for goods and labor, we shall find that none exists when the supply of labor at $v^*$ exceeds the demand. But that is precisely the case in which $c^*$ is the equilibrium wage in the sense just defined.[3]

Notice that the producer we have just been considering would not

3. If all persons have different $h$ functions, and there is a continuum of consumers, a competitive equilibrium may exist, with some people at the zero consumption point. The equilibrium discussed in the text is the limit of such a competitive equilibrium as we move all consumer types into identity with one another.

want to pay different wages to different groups of laborers, even if the supply of laborers were large enough to make that possible. But the nature of work to be done varies from one industry to another, and from one department of a firm to another. One ought, therefore, to allow for various functions, $h$, applying to different factories. Corresponding to each, there will be a $c^*$. Consider different supplies of laborers. The higher the supply price of laborers, the more factories will be paying $w_S$ to their laborers, rather than the $c^*$ corresponding to them. When the supply of laborers is sufficiently large, all wage rates will be determined by the productivity relationship. When it is sufficiently small, a single wage rate will apply to all employment. In between, the range of wage rates being paid will be greater the lower the supply price of laborers.[4] There will be open unemployment only when $c^*$-level wages apply everywhere. Thus the productivity hypothesis has interesting implications even when there is no unemployment. We can expect that in general it applies to some jobs and not to others. Notice that this argument has been conducted on the assumption that all workers are alike. The wage differences we are talking about should arise even between people of similar abilities.

A third striking implication of the productivity hypothesis is that wage rates need not change over time in the way that earlier economic theory may have led us to expect. While technology changes, capital accumulates, and population grows, $c^*$ changes only insofar as the function $h$ changes. There is no reason why that function should change in such a way that $c^*$ increases over time. Thus, in a growing economy with initial unemployment we can expect real wages to remain constant; or at any rate we can claim that the appearance of fairly constant real wages in a growing economy is consistent with the productivity hypothesis, though not (special cases apart) with competitive equilibrium models. In a growing economy, one does expect unemployment to diminish eventually, especially if the real wage is not rising. The argument of the previous paragraph then leads one to expect that wage differences will diminish over time, with the highest wages for untrained labor remaining relatively constant. This particular suggestion would, in a world with skilled labor, be rather hard to test.

A further implication, which I have not seen mentioned elsewhere, relates to investment in labor quality. It is often argued—though, on

4. It is theoretically possible that the aggregate demand curve for laborers may not be a monotonic function of the wage in these circumstances, for an increased wage can lead to substitution of higher-paid laborers for lower-paid laborers.

the face of it, fallaciously—that when employment confers skills it generates an external economy. This argument is fallacious if the unskilled worker willingly accepts a lower wage because of the higher wage his acquired skill will later make available to him. But when the employer is in any case paying above the supply price for labor, this argument may not apply. True, the government may wish to subsidize employment in such an economy as I am discussing. I suspect it would want to subsidize it by more if employment conferred skills. The productivity hypothesis appears to provide support for the old training-externality argument. We should also recognize an externality arising from lags between consumption and productivity, which are surely quite substantial. A well-paid worker will be a better worker for months, perhaps years, to come. His current employer receives no immediate benefit from these lagged effects.

For both these reasons, the theory leads one to expect that employers will be willing to pay more to workers who contract (reliably) for longer periods of employment. This might manifest itself in arrangements for attaching labor to the firm on a semipermanent basis (as, to a considerable extent, in Japan); or at least in the development of "company towns," tied pension rights, and payment by the month (in arrears).

## 2. WELFARE ECONOMICS OF THE SIMPLE CASE

Consider next an economy in which all production is done in a factory with production possibilities described by equation (4.1), and the population, which may as well be identified with the supply of laborers, is so large that the equilibrium we have been discussing implies unemployment of laborers. It seems clear that this outcome, with zero consumption for the unemployed, is not optimal by any acceptable criterion. But we shall see that the optimum for such an economy of identical people may well prescribe different consumption levels for different groups.

We ought to have a welfare function that treats all individuals alike and favors equality. Such a welfare function is the familiar additive criterion

$$W = \sum_i u(c_i), \quad u \text{ increasing and concave,} \tag{4.4}$$

which expresses a rather individualistic point of view. With that reminder of its restrictive nature, I shall use equation (4.4), since it greatly simplifies the analysis.

$W$ is to be maximized, subject to the production constraint

$$\Sigma c_i \leq f[\Sigma h(c_i)]. \tag{4.5}$$

Necessary conditions for the optimum are easily written down, if we introduce a Lagrange multiplier $s$ for the constraint given in equation (4.5). Differentiating with respect to $c_i$ yields

$$u'(c_i) + s[f'(\Sigma h)h'(c_i) - 1] = 0. \tag{4.6}$$

One may be tempted to think that only one value of $c_i$ will satisfy this equation. But if, as that would imply, everyone has the same consumption level, it may be impossible to satisfy the production constraint: there may be no number $c$ such that $nc \leq f[nh(c)]$. Such a case is shown in figure 4.3, where the curve $OF$ shows for each level of $c$ the level of $h$ (per person) that would be required to produce it in a population of size $n$. The equation of the curve $OF$ is

$$c = \frac{1}{n}f(nh). \tag{4.7}$$

Since $OF$ does not intersect the curve $OH$ (with equation $h = h(c)$),

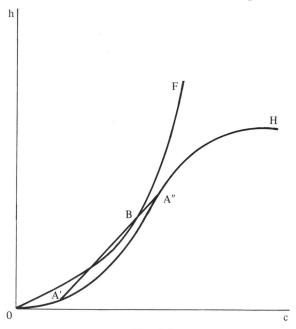

Fig. 4.3

no uniform level of $c$ can be produced with the labor that would be forthcoming.

It is possible, however, for the economy to have two different consumption levels coexisting. Such an allocation is shown by the line $A'BA''$ in the diagram. The two consumption levels are $c'$ and $c''$. If $\bar{c}$ is the average level of consumption in the economy, achieved by dividing the population between $c'$ and $c''$ in the proportions $A''B : A'B$, this can be achieved by an average labor input of $\bar{h}$, which is precisely what the population can, in these circumstances, provide. Thus no more than two consumption levels are required for feasibility. The question is whether more levels may be optimal. To answer this, and to bring out some other features of the optimum, I will introduce the more complicated diagram shown in figure 4.4.

In figure 4.4, the top right-hand quadrant corresponds to the diagram in figure 4.3: the curve $OH$ again shows the relationship between a man's consumption and the labor he can provide, while $OF$ shows production possibilities (in terms of average labor and average output). We will suppose that optimum production is represented by the point $B$, with average consumption equal to $\bar{c}$, and average labor equal to $\bar{h}$. At this stage of the argument, we do not predict the number of different consumption levels, so $c'$ and $c''$ should be ignored for the moment. The line $OQ$ has the same slope as the tangent to the production set at $B$, which is (seen from the vertical axis) the marginal product of labor (*not* laborers) at the optimum, $q$. This is used to construct the diagram in the top left-hand quadrant of the figure, where for each value of $h$ we take the horizontal distance between the line $OQ$ and the curve $OF$ to obtain $OF'$, and between $OQ$ and $OH$ to obtain $OH'$. We are subtracting $qh$ from the horizontal coordinate in each case.

Lowering our vision to the utility curves in the lower half of the figure, we see the utility function itself graphed in the lower right-hand quadrant. For convenience, $u$ is taken to be negative in the range that concerns us, so that the utility curve is convex in relation to the origin. The curve $U'V'$ in the lower left-hand quadrant is derived from the rest of the figure: it shows the relationship between $u$ and $c - qh$ that is implied by the curves $UV$ and $OH$. Having constructed that curve, we draw the *double tangent* to it. (It can be shown that if the curve $U'V'$ were concave, so that there was no double tangent, we would not be at the optimum. One can show that a neighboring production point is better.) It is clear that, in general, this will be a double, not a treble, tangent, and that it will be uniquely defined by the property of being

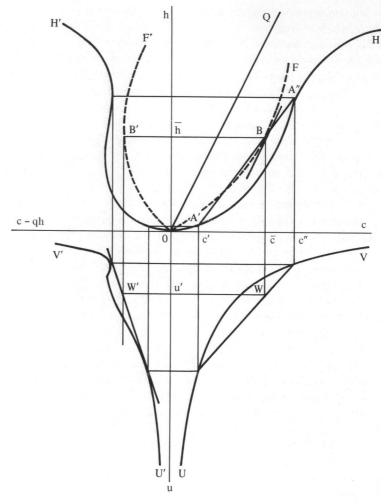

Fig. 4.4

double. The two points of tangency correspond to consumption levels $c'$ and $c''$, as shown in the figure; their respective coordinates are $c' - qh(c')$, $u(c')$ and $c'' - qh(c'')$, $u(c'')$. At the same time, there is a point $W'$ on the double tangent corresponding to the utility level $\bar{u}$ which is, by our initial specification, the maximum attainable utility level.

This point $W'$ must correspond to the point $B$ in the upper right-hand quadrant: that is, its horizontal coordinate must be $\bar{c} - q\bar{h}$. For since $W'$ lies on the line joining the two points corresponding to $A'$ and

$A''$, the point corresponding to $W'$ must lie on the line joining $A'$ and $A''$. Since its horizontal coordinate is $\bar{c}$, that point must indeed be $B$.

Because of our construction, $\bar{u}$ is certainly the maximum utility level consistent with the production point $B$, i.e., with given average levels $\bar{h}$ and $\bar{c}$. For, corresponding to every individual in the economy, there is a point on the curve $U'V'$ showing his utility and the value of $c - qh$ for him. The average of these points will show the average utility level, and $\bar{c} - q\bar{h}$. Any such average point (being in the convex hull of the curve $U'V'$) that has given $\bar{c} - \bar{q}\bar{h}$ must lie on the vertical line $W'B'$, at or below $W'$. The greatest average utility is obtained by dividing the population between consumption levels $c'$ and $c''$, as shown in the figure.

Since we specified $B$ originally as the optimum production point, it follows from this argument that there are (in general) two consumption levels in the optimum state of the economy. If the slope of the double tangent is $s$, we see that $c'$ and $c''$ maximize

$$u(c) + s\,[qh\,(c) - c], \tag{4.8}$$

where $q = f'(\bar{h})$. Thus we can now say more than equation (4.6), which merely asserted that the derivative of equation (4.8) vanished at those consumption levels that actually occur. In particular, notice that (4.8) takes the same value for $c'$ and $c''$.

By examing figure 4.4 more closely, we can deduce some other properties of the optimum for this economy:

  i. I have already remarked that the curve $U'V'$ must not be concave. This puts a lower bound to $q$, which we can call $q_1$. (It is not, I think, very important, so I will explain the deduction of its value in a footnote.[5]) We can also assign an upper bound to $q$. If the line $OQ$ were to

---

5. For each $q$, $t$ is chosen so that $tu(c) + qh(c) - c$ has two equal maxima. As $q \to q_1$, $tu + qh - c$ becomes concave for all $c_1$ with the first and second derivatives zero at one point, $c_1$. (The first derivative is zero because the maxima when $q > q_1$ are equal.) Since that is the maximum value of the second derivative, the third derivative is also zero. Therefore $q_1$ and $c_1$ satisfy (along with some number $t_1$) the following:

$$t_1 u'(c_1) + q_1 h'(c_1) = 1$$
$$t_1 u''(c_1) + q_1 h''(c_1) = 0$$
$$t_1 u'''(c_1) + q_1 h'''(c_1) = 0.$$

Therefore $c_1$ is defined by

$$h'''(c_1)u''(c_1) - h''(c_1)u'''(c_1) = 0,$$

and

cut the curve $OH$, $B$ could not be optimal, for a small increase in production would be possible by letting those consuming most consume more. Therefore $q$ must be less than $q* = c*/h(c*)$, the slope of the ray that is tangent to the $OH$ curve. Since $q_1 < q < q*$, the slope of the double tangent (negative as the diagram is drawn), $s$, is positive, and $c'' - qh(c'')$ is bigger than $c' - qh(c')$, i.e.,

$$c'' - c' > q(h'' - h'), \tag{4.9}$$

where I use the obvious notation $h' = h(c')$, $h'' = h(c'')$. This tells us that $B$ is the upper intersection of the line $A'A''$ with the curve $OF$.

ii. On the other hand $A''$ is the lower bound of the two possible intersections of $A'A''$ with the curve $OH$. For if the upper consumption level were shifted to the outer intersection, while $B$ remained fixed, the average utility level would fall, being the intersection of the appropriate chord of the utility curve with the vertical line $BW$. Also, $A'A''$ has a steeper slope than the curve $OH$ at $c'$. These two facts imply that

$$\frac{1}{h'(c')}(h'' - h') \geq c'' - c' \geq \frac{1}{h'(c'')}(h'' - h'). \tag{4.10}$$

The latter inequality also implies what is directly more interesting, i.e., that

$$c'' < c*. \tag{4.11}$$

iii. Because of the way that $c'$ and $c''$ were derived, they are functions of $q$ alone. Of course, given the functions $f$, $u$, and $h$ as data, we do not know in advance what $q$ is going to be, but it is nevertheless very useful that knowledge of $q$, the marginal product of labor, is the only information about production possibilities that we need in order to calculate the consumption levels. Given $q$, variations in the average product are accommodated, so long as uniform consumption for everyone is impossible, by varying the proportions of the population at the two consumption levels. One particular implication of this dependence of $c'$ and $c''$ on $q$ alone is that only certain pairs of values of $c'$ and $c''$ are

$$q_1 = \frac{u''(c_1)}{h'(c_1)u''(c_1) - h''(c')u'(c_1).}$$

Notice that

$$\frac{1}{q_1} = h'(c_1) + \frac{u'(c_1)}{-u''(c_1)}h''(c_1) > h'(c_1),$$

since $h''(c_1) = -(t_1/q_1)u''(c_1) > 0$. This fact is incorporated in figure 4.5.

possible. Indeed, we shall see in a moment that the consumption levels are monotonic functions of one another.

I do not yet see how to deduce, from the diagram alone, the manner in which the consumption levels depend on $q$. Instead, I resort to analytical methods. First $c'$ and $c''$ are determined, given $q$, by the equations

$$tu'(c') + qh'(c') = 1 \qquad (4.6')$$

$$tu'(c'') + qh'(c'') = 1 \qquad (4.6'')$$

$$tu(c') + qh(c') - c' = tu(c'') + qh(c'') - c'', \qquad (4.12)$$

where, for convenience, I have divided the earlier equations by $s$ and written $t$ for $1/s$. Since $t$ is to be eliminated from these equations to determine $c'$ and $c''$, we determine $dt/dq$ from equation (4.12). Differentiating the equation with respect to $q$, we notice that, because of equations (4.6') and (4.6''), the terms in derivatives of the consumption levels drop out, and we have

$$\frac{dt}{dq} = -\frac{h(c'') - h(c')}{u(c'') - u(c')}. \qquad (4.13)$$

Turning to equation (4.6') and differentiating, we get

$$[tu''(c') + qh''(c')] \frac{dc'}{dq} = -u'(c') \frac{dt}{dq} - h'(c)$$

$$= [h(c'') - h(c')] \frac{u'(c')}{u(c'') - u(c')} - h'(c'), \qquad (4.14)$$

using (4.13). The factor $tu'' + qh''$ is the second derivative of $tu + qh$ $-c$ and is therefore nonpositive, since $c'$ maximizes. Therefore, the sign of $dc'/dq$ is the opposite of the sign of the expression on the right of equation (4.14). The concavity of $u$ implies that $u(c'') - u(c') \le u'(c')$ $(c'' - c')$. It follows, using the left-hand inequality in equation (4.10), that the right-hand side of (4.14) is nonnegative. Therefore,

$$\frac{d}{dq} c' \le 0. \qquad (4.15)$$

In a similar way, using the right-hand inequality in equation (4.10), and the concavity inequality $u(c'') - u(c') \ge u'(c'')(c'' - c')$, it can be shown that

$$\frac{d}{dq} c'' \ge 0. \qquad (4.16)$$

Summarizing these results, for the optimum when uniform consumption is impossible, we find that the marginal product of labor, $q$, lies between two limits, $q_1$ and $q^*$, and as it increases from $q_1$ to $q^*$ the upper limit of consumption increases (in fact from $c_1$ to $c^*$, where $c_1$ is defined in footnote 5, and $c^*$ was defined earlier as the equilibrium wage), and the lower level of consumption decreases (from $c_1$ to 0).

It is interesting to consider how $q$ might be expected to vary over time, as production possibilities improve, i.e., as the curve $OF$ moves to the right. In figure 4.5, I show various possible $A'A''$ lines. These lie further to the right, with decreasing values of $q$ (indicated by arrows, with slope $1/q$), suggesting that as production possibilities expand, $q$ should become smaller and the consumption levels come closer together. There might be exceptions to that general tendency, but it is unambiguously the case that as population ($n$) falls (or, equivalently, when there is labor-augmenting technical progress) $q$ falls. To prove this, observe that, as $n$ varies, the marginal product of labor is always constant along rays going out from the origin: for on any such ray, $\bar{c}/\bar{h} = f(n\bar{h})/(n\bar{h})$ being constant, so are $n\bar{h}$, and $q = f'(n\bar{h})$. If, then, $n$ were to become smaller, the curve $OF$, described by equation (4.7), would move out, and if $q$ were to rise $\bar{c}/\bar{h}$ would have to fall, which is manifestly inconsistent with production being on an $A'A''$ line to the left of the previous one.

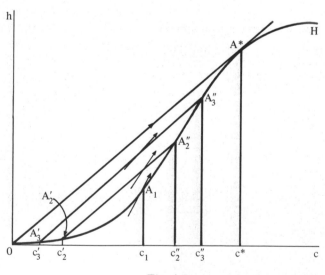

Fig. 4.5

Thus optimal development over time would appear to require a narrowing of consumption differentials, with the higher consumption level falling, until uniform consumption becomes possible (geometrically the $OF$ curve hits the $OH$ curve). At this point, there would in general be a discontinuous change of $q$ and the consumption levels, since it is very unlikely that the $OF$ curve would hit the $OH$ curve first at $c = c_1$. Notice that, according to equation (4.6″), $h'(c'') < 1/q$. It is therefore true, unless the functions are very peculiar, that the uniform consumption level to which the economy switches is less than $c''$, since at the new level $h' = 1/f'$. Actually, since (apart from anything else) capital has been ignored in this discussion, the analysis as yet provides no more than indications about optimal development. But we shall see later that the results are of considerable interest in a rather different context.

### COMPETITIVE REALIZATION OF THE OPTIMUM

It is quite clear that equilibrium in the absence of state intervention cannot possibly be optimal in this economy, because employers, who are concerned merely to maximize labor input per unit wage, $h(c)/c$, have no incentive to employ anyone at a wage other than $c^*$. Since this involves unemployment, one would suppose that the government ought to introduce wage subsidies to correct the equilibrium, with a particularly large subsidy for the employment of low-wage workers. Actually, however, it turns out that the subsidy should be greater for high-wage workers.

Suppose an employer is paid the following subsidy for each worker he employs at wage $w$:

$$\sigma(w) = a + tu(w). \qquad (4.17)$$

(It is not clear, a priori, whether equation (4.17) defines a tax or a subsidy, but we shall see that it is in fact positive for those values of $w$ that actually occur.) Let the parameters $a$ and $t > 0$ be determined so that there is full employment of laborers, and total output is just sufficient to cover consumption requirements. Then employers choose the number they employ, $m$, and the wages at which they are employed, $w_1, w_2, \ldots, w_m$ so as to maximize

$$f[\Sigma h(w_i)] - \Sigma w_i + \Sigma \sigma(w_i)$$
$$= f(\Sigma h(w_i)) - \Sigma w_i + ma + t\Sigma u(w_i). \qquad (4.18)$$

The government has chosen $a$ and $t$ so that employers choose $m$ to be $n$, the actual population, and $f[\Sigma h(w_i)] = \Sigma w_i$. Therefore this maximization of equation (4.18) tells us that $t\Sigma u(w_i)$ is greater than it would be for any alternative $w_1, w_2, \ldots, w_n$. In other words, the optimum has been realized.

How do we know $a$ and $t > 0$ can be found to achieve this desirable end? We know because we have already found such numbers in analyzing the optimum: $t$ is $1/s$, and $a$ is $c' - tu(c') - qh(c') = c'' - tu(c'')-qh(c'')$. With these values of $t$ and $a$, it is easy to verify that the optimum actually does maximize in equation (4.18). Since $\sigma(c') = c' - qh(c')$ and $\sigma(c'') = c'' - qh(c'')$, we know from figure 4.4 that the transfer is a subsidy (not a tax) at both $c'$ and $c''$.

It is interesting that the economy can be "put right" by using knowledge of only the utility function, in conjunction with market clearing: no knowledge of the $h$ function is required. Notice that employers end up with positive profit, equal to the total subsidy, which must be taxed away as a profit tax if the full optimum is to be achieved. Thus $f$ must be defined net of any profits required as incentives to producers.

## 4. THE PEASANT ECONOMY WITHOUT FACTOR MARKETS

The chief object of analysis in this chapter is a peasant economy, for which the productivity relationship holds, wherein each peasant family consists of a number of identical people, who possess a certain amount of land, with production possibilities described (in terms of average consumption and effort) by

$$c \leq \frac{1}{n} f(nh). \tag{4.7}$$

Obviously the assumption of identical people is made for analytical convenience and should cause no difficulty. What does cause difficulty is deciding what criteria would motivate such a family. We are discussing cases where it is impossible for everyone in the family to have the same consumption. The family is forced, therefore, to discriminate between its members. No doubt seniority, convention, brute force, and impulse may have influence, but I shall follow the extreme assumption that allocations within the family maximize a welfare function.

With this hypothesis, the theory of a peasant economy, in the absence of markets for labor and land, is formally identical to the welfare economics of a factory economy, a theory that we have already to some extent worked out. It is true that the assumption of an additively separable welfare function is less plausible in the case of a family than it is for groups in an economy, but one may reasonably hope that the theory for the separable case is a good predictor of the more general theory.

Applying the previous theory, then, we have the following propositions: (1) There are two consumption levels in a family; (2) the difference between the two consumption levels is greater the larger the family (per unit of land): as size increases, the higher consumption level becomes yet higher, though a smaller proportion of the family enjoys that level; and (3) total output is a decreasing function of family size.

The last proposition follows from the fact that $q = f'(n\bar{h})$ is an increasing function of $n$, for that means $n\bar{h}$ is a decreasing function of $n$, which in turn implies that output, $f(n\bar{h})$, is a decreasing function of $n$. We have deduced that the marginal product of laborers, in the sense one would observe it if one did cross-section studies, is negative. On the other hand the marginal product of labor, $q$, is positive.

## 5. MARKETS IN LABOR AND LAND

In an economy where different peasant families have different labor/land ratios, it is to be expected that land and labor markets will have developed. Of the two, the land market is easier to analyze, so let us take it up first. The model I use is one in which the same production function applies to all land, and the same utility function rules all intrafamilial allocations, so that families differ only in the value of $n$ appropriate to them, $n$ being interpreted as the number of family members per unit of land owned.

Let there be a perfect market in land, the price of a unit of land being $r$. Consider a family owning a unit of land. It could receive $r$ for that land, distributing the proceeds among its members (who would get an average of $r/n$ each), or it could keep its land, using its production function, or it could rent out some of its land or rent in additional land from other families. The production possibilities available to it have thus been expanded, the effective frontier now being the tangent from the all-land-rented-out point $(r/n, 0)$ to the ordinary production frontier, as shown in figure 4.6. It follows that $r$ determines $q$ uniquely, through the following equations:

$$q = f'(nh),$$
$$f(nh) - qnh = r. \tag{4.19}$$

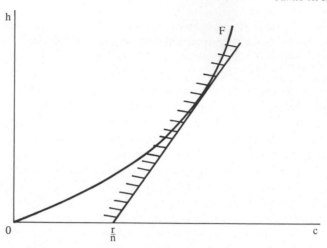

Fig. 4.6

Different families will therefore, according to our theory, all have the same two consumption levels, $c'$ and $c''$, except for those families who either have so much land that they can give all members a consumption level $c$ greater than $c''$, or have so little land that they are unable to provide all members with $c'$ and have to be content with a uniform consumption level below $c'$. The situation is portrayed in figure 4.7. Families with $n \geq n'$ have uniform consumption; families with $n' > n > n_2$ have two consumption levels, $c'$ and $c''$, and rent out some of their land; families with $n_2 > n > n_3$ have consumption levels $c'$ and $c''$ and rent in some land; families with $n_3 > n > n_4$ have uniform consumption (greater than $c_3$) and rent in land; families with $n_4 > n$ have uniform consumption and rent out land.

It will be seen that the poorest families (with the largest $n$) rent out almost all their land, as do the richest families (with small $n$); it is families of intermediate wealth who rent in land, being able to use the opportunity to increase both the consumption and the productivity of their members. The equilibrium level of $r$ is determined by the level of $q$ that ensures equality between the supply of and demand for land.

The perfect land market has the effect, in this model, of making the marginal product of labor the same on all units of land, so that output per unit of land is the same for all families. However, the number of people working the land varies from family to family: since the total labor input per unit area is constant, the number per unit area worked by the family (after allowing for renting) is inversely proportional to the average effort per person that family can provide. The poorer the family, the less its average effort in equilibrium, and therefore the higher the labor/land ratio on the land it works. An outside observer would deduce from such an economy, if he were ignorant of the productivity relationship, that the marginal product of laborers was zero, since he would see a variety of plots of land being worked, with varying numbers of workers per acre, yet all producing the same output per acre.

In fact one can make no unambiguous statement about the sign of the marginal product of laborers for the economy taken as a whole. If one could pretend that the average family must be one that neither rents in nor rents out land (or is at least indifferent between the options), one could apply the results of the previous section, treating the whole economy as a single family. But that is not legitimate; the distribution of land ownership influences the outcome, and even if equalization of land ownership would bring about an equilibrium with a negative marginal product of laborers, that marginal product may still be positive given the actual distribution of land ownership. Consider what happens if some people leave the economy, with proportionate reductions in the size of all families. The richer families will, for any $r$, increase their supply of land, since they have moved further out along the $OB$ line. But, for the same reason, the poorer families will reduce their supply of land. If in aggregate there is an increased supply of land, equilibrium $r$ must be lower (for a reduction in $r$ will increase excess demand for every family); but if the effect in aggregate is to reduce the supply of land, $r$ will rise. Lower $r$ means lower aggregate output, and higher $r$ means greater aggregate output. Thus, whether the departure of average laborers increases or reduces output depends upon the distribution of property. What one can say is that the marginal product will probably be negative in an economy where there are few large landholders (i.e., few people in families represented by points in the upper right-hand part of figure 4.7), or where most of those drawn away from the local economy (or added to it by population growth) are members of the poorer families.

The labor market in our economy is a little harder to deal with because, at first sight, it seems to be rather odd. If there were a ruling wage rate, resulting from optimal employment policies by families with the most land, one might think that the considerations discussed in section 1 of this chapter would apply. But a ruling wage at $c^*$ could hardly be maintained, since it would be possible for families to offer

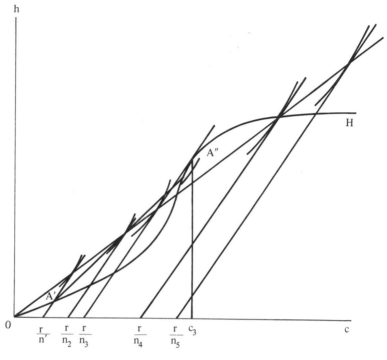

Fig. 4.7

family members for employment along with a guaranteed consumption subsidy. This is not a farfetched idea: the consumption subsidy would be apparent in the general good health and nutrition of the worker seeking employment, and the better favored men could expect to be employed before the less favored. It would be to the benefit of poorer families to subsidize their members to seek employment, since, as we have seen, their departure makes possible some increase in output.

The effect of any such arrangements would, implicitly, be to establish a market in labor rather than laborers. For employers always prefer workers who cost them less per unit of effort, and it would not pay the worker's family to subsidize him beyond the point where a unit of his labor costs the same as anyone else's. Now a market in labor is the same in effect, for our timeless economic model without indivisibilities, transaction costs, or uncertainty, as a market in land. It extends the possibilities open to a family in the same kind of way. In the real world, one could expect the two kinds of markets, taken together, to allow an approximately linear expansion of production possibilities, in the way described by figure 4.6. Thus we already have a theory for the effects of a market in labor. The price is $q$; a man with consumption $c$ gets a wage $qh(c)$.

The way one might expect equilibrium to work out in the model is that the poorest families would sell all their land and earn what they could in the labor market. In this model, unlike the simpler one of section 1, their income from land allows them to seek employment at a wage low enough to offset their low productivity. One would expect them to gain employment with the richer families. The land market could adjust matters between the richer and the middle peasants.

It will be recognized that there is no readily observable relationship between the wage rates that would operate in such a labor market and the marginal productivity of laborers. What wage rates are equal to are the marginal products of the laborers at constant consumption levels; but a change in family numbers normally means a change in the consumption of some of its members. Observed marginal products would include the effect of these changes. One odd implication of the theory is a certain diversity of wage rates. There may be some labor-supplying families so poor that their consumption is less than $c'$. Other families who wish to supply labor will fall into two categories: those with consumption $c'$, and those with consumption $c''$. So long as poor families keep their land rather than join the labor market, we would not expect to observe $c'$-laborers. But if, as often happens in developing countries, the poorest do sell their land, the theory predicts a two-level labor market. This may bode ill for the theory, but it should be remembered that age and sex can provide a basis for such discrimination.

6. SHADOW WAGE RATES

One reason for developing models of the rural economy is to seek a basis for estimating the cost and benefits of providing employment, both in urban and rural areas. I shall discuss two extreme cases: that of local employment, in which the government employs a number of people locally, at some wage, these people continuing to be part of their families, sharing their consumption with them or receiving consumption subsidies from them according to the family interest; and that of urban employment, where employment takes a man away from his family completely, so that there is no further transfer of goods between him and his family.

I will use two propositions for a family of the kind discussed above in section 4:

$$\frac{\partial}{\partial n}(n\bar{u}) = \bar{u} - s(\bar{c} - q\bar{h}) \tag{4.20}$$

$$\frac{\partial}{\partial C}(n\bar{u}) = s, \tag{4.21}$$

where $C$ is a gift of consumption goods to the family. The proof of these propositions follows lines familiar to devotees of Lagrange multipliers. The multiplier $s$ was introduced so that the family's constrained maximization could be expressed as maximization of

$$L = n\bar{u} + s(f(n\bar{h}) + C - n\bar{c}). \tag{4.22}$$

Of course $C$ was zero before, and we are now considering only small changes in $C$ away from zero. Consumption levels $c'$ and $c''$, the allocation of family members between them, and $s$ are chosen so that the derivatives of $L$ with respect to all of them are zero. Therefore the derivative of $L$ with respect to $C$ is $s$ and is also equal to the derivative of $n\bar{u}$ with respect to $C$. Similarly, if one differentiates with respect to $n$, one has $\partial L/\partial n = \bar{u} - s\bar{c} + sf'(n\bar{h})\bar{h} = \partial/\partial n\,(n\bar{u})$. In this way, both equations (4.20) and (4.21) are proved.

Suppose now the government comes in and offers employment to one man at the going wage. That wage, for a man with consumption $c''$ (which one may take to be the normal case), is $w = qh(c'')$. The man who gets the job has utility $u(c'')$. The family (not counting the new employee, once he has the job) has an increase in utility of $s(\bar{c} - q\bar{h}) - \bar{u}$ because of the change in numbers, and a reduction of $s[c'' - qh(c'')]$ because of the consumption subsidy paid to the employee. Thus the net gain in utility is $u(c'') + s(\bar{c} - q\bar{h}) - \bar{u} - s(c'' - qh'')$, which vanishes, since $u(c'') - s(c'' - qh'') = u(c') - s(c' - qh') = u - s(\bar{c} - q\bar{h})$, taking the average.

I thus conclude that the shadow wage rate for local employment when the market wage is paid is equal to the market wage $qh''$. If a higher wage is paid, the difference between $w$ and $qh''$ is a consumption subsidy to the family, to be evaluated as such. If the utility function is so measured that a unit of public funds has marginal (social) utility of unity, $s$ is the shadow price of a gift to the family. Its value could be assessed by using the formula

$$s = \frac{h'(c'')u'(c') - h'(c')u'(c'')}{h'(c'') - h'(c')} \tag{4.23}$$

which is readily deduced from equations (4.6') and (4.6''). Notice that $s$ is larger, and could be much larger, than $u'(c')$, the marginal utility of the poorest member of the family. The reason for this is the "multiplier" effects of the extra consumption through increased productivity within the family.

In the case of a man who leaves the rural community entirely, to enjoy (by consuming) a wage $w$, the gain in utility is, according to equation (4.20),

$$u(w) - \bar{u} + s(\bar{c} - q\bar{h}), \tag{4.24}$$

in which the direct utility increase for the man in question is combined with a multiple of the difference between the average product and the marginal product of the laborer, assuming that effort is constant. This is the same formula one would obtain if the productivity effects of consumption were ignored. The difference comes in the assessment of $s$, which, as we have seen, is influenced by multiplier effects, and may be substantially larger than one would think if average consumption were taken as a guide. It will be appreciated that the consumption value of employment, given by equation (4.24), should be set off against the wage-cost of employment, $w$.

We can round off our picture of a developing economy by considering the optimum employment and wage policy for the urban sector. Let $f$ and $h$ now apply to industry, and let us suppose that the marginal utility of public income is unity; $n$ is urban employment. Then public sector production should maximize

$$f[nh(w)] - nw + n[u(w) - \bar{u} + s(\bar{c} - q\bar{h})].$$

Therefore,

$$f'(nh)h'(w) = 1 - u'(w) \tag{4.25}$$

$$f'(nh)h(w) - w + u(w) - \bar{u} + s(\bar{c} - q\bar{h}) = 0. \tag{4.26}$$

Equation (4.26) equates the marginal product of laborers to something much less than $w$ (assuming that $u(w) > \bar{u}$ and $s$ is large.) Dividing equation (4.26) in terms of equation (4.25), we have

$$\frac{h(w)}{wh'(w)} = 1 - \frac{u(w) - wu'(w) - \bar{u} + s(\bar{c} - q\bar{h})}{1 - u'(w)}, \tag{4.27}$$

which would generally, but not necessarily, be less than one. We can therefore expect $w$ to be somewhat less than $c^*$.

The model discussed here has excluded much of what is believed to be important in developing countries. At the same time, it emphasizes something that might be important and yet has suffered neglect from economists. I think that a number of the implications of the productivity hypothesis might be taken to refute it—particularly the quite wide consumption differences within families, and the wide range of consumption levels that are not supposed to occur. Yet in fact there are large consumption differences within families; and of course $u$ and $h$ vary greatly between families and individuals, so that the striking results should not be interpreted very strictly. Also, the results are in other ways rather encouraging—in suggesting diversity of wage rates, for example, and predicting land sale by the poorest families. Among the simplifications made, I neglected the effect of the consumption level on population growth (that is, in terms of the models, the reaction of $c$ on $n$). Even today, this may be important, particularly for the poorest families. The consumption-productivity relationship explored in this chapter seems sufficiently promising to deserve critical empirical research into its form and importance.

# PART II: TENURE SYSTEMS AND ECONOMIC RESPONSES

# 5

## The Choice of Rental Contract in Peasant Agriculture

DAVID M. G. NEWBERY

The two main types of rental contract found in agriculture are fixed-rent tenancies and share tenancies.[1] In both the landlord supplies the land, the tenant supplies labor, and either party may supply other inputs, though under fixed rent it is unusual for the landlord to supply recurrent nonlabor inputs. Under fixed rent the tenant pays a fixed annual rent and bears all the risk, whereas a share tenant pays an agreed proportion of the crop and correspondingly shares the risk with the landlord. The first type of contract presents no difficulty to economic analysis and indeed has provided a paradigm for classical and neoclassical economists to extend to other fields of economic analysis. Share tenancies, in contrast, have proved difficult to analyze and have been a fruitful source of error and confusion for writers from Adam Smith down to the present.[2] There are several reasons for this difficulty, at successively deeper levels of analysis, which is part of the explanation for the considerable lapse of time between recognition of the problem and adequate resolution of it.

1. The increasing complexity of some forms of modern agriculture, with its close dependence on the availability of costly equipment, processing factories, and certified quality control, has resulted in a great diversity of farming and marketing contracts, which are discussed in *Contract Farming: Report of the Committee of Inquiry on Contract Farming,* HMSO cmnd. 5099 (London: HMSO, 1972). Quite complicated contracts also exist in peasant agriculture, but the focus here is on simple paradigms.

2. Two good surveys of the history of economic analysis of sharecropping are available: an earlier one in D. Gale Johnson, "Resource Allocation under Share Contracts," *Journal of Political Economy* 58 (1950): 111–23; and a more recent one in S. N. S. Cheung, *The Theory of Share Tenancy* (Chicago: University of Chicago Press, 1969).

The main aim of this chapter is to broaden the question "How do tenancy contracts affect productive behavior?" to the more fundamental question "What determines the type of contract that will be devised and agreed upon in given circumstances?" First of all, though, it is instructive to explore the reasons for the difficulty in analyzing share tenancy, and at the same time to examine and criticize recent contributions to the subject. This examination suggests additional factors that will affect the choice of contract. Finally, I will present a new model of the agricultural economy within which to analyze the choice of tenancy contract. It is sufficiently rich to account for a wider range of phenomena than earlier models, while at the same time avoiding assumptions that are earlier shown to be inconsistent with share tenancy.

### 1. THEORIES OF SHARE TENANCY

It is convenient to summarize the assumptions that, explicitly or implicitly, seem to be common to almost all attempts to analyze share tenancy. They are conventional neoclassical assumptions, and as such they form a natural starting point, since with them we can appeal to very powerful methods which typically lead to simple, general propositions and predictions. Indeed, without these assumptions, particularly those implying perfect competition, it is difficult to imagine producing a general theory (there is, for example, no satisfactory general theory of imperfect competition). Unfortunately for our theoretical ambitions, it will be shown that these simplifying assumptions are incapable of explaining the existence of share contracts, which, given their widespread occurrence, is rather damaging. But first let me set out the assumptions.

*Assumptions*

1. Land, $H$, and labor, $L$, are perfectly homogeneous and are the only factors of production. Output, $Y$, depends on both factor inputs and the "state of nature," or the particular sequence of environmental events such as weather, disease, pests, and so on, which can be represented by $z$. Then

$$Y = \Theta(z) F(H, L). \tag{5.1}$$

The mean of $\Theta$, $E\Theta$, is taken as unity, and if there is no uncertainty $\Theta = 1$ and will be ignored. For most purposes we have in addition the following:

1a. There are constant returns to scale, and equation (5.1) can be rewritten

$$Y = \Theta H f(l) = \Theta L g(h); \quad h = l^{-1} = H/L. \tag{5.2}$$

2. The labor market is perfect and certain in that the wage rate, $w$, is parametrically given to all agents.

3. Landlords are numerous and noncollusive.

4. There are no transaction or information costs: buyers and sellers face the same known prices.

5. Agents can enter into different contracts with different parties.

6. Agents maximize the expected utility of income, $EU(Y)$, which is a concave function. Agents know the distribution of $\Theta(z)$.

*Remarks*

Assumption 1 can be relaxed to include other inputs (fertilizer, etc.) but their treatment is conveniently deferred to section 3 below. Uncertainty (or more precisely risk, since agents know the probabilities of different states of nature occurring) is hardly ever explicitly introduced, though it is clearly important in any theory of sharecropping. Assumption 6 can be relaxed so that utility includes leisure as well as income, but in the presence of assumption 2 this adds little, since the latter implies that the opportunity cost of labor is always well defined. It is simpler to endow workers with $\bar{L}$ units of labor. Assumption 1a is not usually mentioned explicitly but is convenient. It could be replaced by a convexity assumption, which is clearly needed for perfect competition, as are assumptions 2 and 3. Assumption 4 is usually made implicitly (its strength will become apparent); similarly with assumption 5. With these assumptions we can illustrate some of the analyses and predictions made by earlier writers on share tenancy.

The traditional view was that, as the share tenant received only a fraction of the output, and in particular of the marginal product of any tenant-supplied input, he would be encouraged to undersupply these inputs and thus produce inefficiently compared with fixed-rent and owner-operated contracts. This is easy to show, but we can prove a rather stronger result, since we can show that with only fixed rent and wage contracts production will be efficient, so that we have an absolute standard of reference against which to compare share tenancy.

*Theorem 1*

Under assumptions 1–6, a competitive equilibrium with fixed-rent and wage contracts only, if it exists, will be production efficient.

*Proof*

The $i^{th}$ agent maximizes $EU^i(Y_i)$, where $i$ reminds us that utility functions as well as income will vary from person to person. Dropping subscripts we have

$$Y = \Theta F(H, L) - RH - wL + R\bar{H} + w\bar{L}. \qquad (5.3)$$

Here $\bar{H}$ and $\bar{L}$ are endowments (possibly zero) of land and labor; $H$ and $L$ are land and labor (owned or hired, it makes no difference) applied to production controlled by the agent. Maximizing $EU(Y)$ with respect to $L$ and $H$ gives

$$\frac{\partial EU(Y)}{\partial L} = F_L EU'\Theta - wEU' = 0. \qquad (5.4)$$

$$\frac{\partial EU(Y)}{\partial H} = F_H EU'\Theta - REU' = 0. \qquad (5.5)$$

$$\therefore \frac{F_L}{F_H} = \frac{w}{R}; 0 < \frac{EU'\Theta}{EU'} = \frac{w}{F_L} = \frac{R}{F_H} < 1. \qquad (5.6)$$

Under assumption la (constant returns), equation (5.6) implies that all producers will adopt the same man/land ratio, and marginal products will be the same everywhere, so that production will be efficient.

Q.E.D.

In contrast, under sharecropping we have

$$Y = (1 - r)\Theta F(H_1, L_1) - wL_1 + \Theta F(H, L) - RH - wL + w\bar{L} + R\bar{H}, \qquad (5.7)$$

where $r$ is the rental share, and the tenant also hires (or owns, in which case $H = \bar{H}$) land under fixed rent. Maximizing expected utility with respect to $L$, $L_1$, leads to

$$F_L = \frac{wEU'}{EU'\Theta} \qquad (5.8)$$

$$F_{L_1} = \frac{w}{1 - r}\frac{EU'}{EU'\Theta} = \frac{F_L}{1 - r}, \qquad (5.9)$$

$$\left.\begin{array}{c} (1 - r) F_{H_1} EU'\Theta \geq 0 \\ \\ H_1 \leq H^* \end{array}\right\} \text{complementarily}, \qquad (5.10)$$

where $H^*$ is the maximum amount of land the tenant is allowed to lease under share tenancy. Under normal assumptions $EU'\Theta > 0$, so equation (5.10) shows that, if he is allowed, the tenant will lease in land until its marginal product has fallen to zero, since such land is costless to hold.

Equation (5.9) shows that the marginal product of labor is higher under share rent than on fixed-rent (or owned) land, so that the labor/land ratio will be lower and production will be inefficient (absolutely, by theorem 1). Thus the theory predicts that output per acre will be lower under share tenancy.

D. Gale Johnson notes these predictions (though he is dealing with a model without uncertainty, the predictions are essentially the same) and finds them implausible, particularly the prediction that the marginal product of land will be driven down to zero. Moreover, the sketchy empirical data suggests that share rents are typically higher than fixed rents (though this does not in itself establish efficiency).[3] He therefore looks to solutions that would be evolved to rule out these anomalies and concludes that it will be in the landlord's interest to enforce a minimum intensity of cultivation:

> Three techniques are available to the landlord for enforcing the desired intensity of cultivation. The first is to enter into a lease contract that specifies in detail what the tenant is required to do. A second is to share in the payment of expenses to the same extent as in the sharing of the output. The third is to grant only a short term lease, which makes possible a periodic review of the performance of the tenant.[4]

Johnson concentrates on the last technique, since he argues that the first, while common in parts of Europe, is unusual in the United States. Steven Cheung has dealt with the first technique at some length,[5] and I will return later to his solution. Johnson argues that the tenant knows that he must on average ensure that the share rent is at least equal to $S$ per acre, where $\Theta S$ is an attractive rent to the landlord; otherwise the tenancy will not be renewed and he will incur heavy relocation costs. Thus the tenant maximizes equation (5.7), except that $(1 - r)\Theta F(H_1, L_1)$ is replaced by $\Theta[F(H_1, L_1) - SH_1]$, which has the required property of being a *share* contract yielding the required *average* rent $S$. Then

$$F_{L_1} = w \frac{EU'}{EU'\Theta} = F_L, \tag{5.11}$$

$$F_{H_1} = S. \tag{5.12}$$

3. Johnson, ibid., p. 118, n. 20.
4. Ibid., p. 118.
5. Cheung, *Theory of Share Tenancy.*

The landlord maximizes expected utility with

$$Y = \Theta S H_1 + \Theta F(H, L) - wL + R(\bar{H} - H_1 - H), \quad (5.13)$$

$$F_H EU'\Theta = R = SEU'\Theta. \quad (5.14)$$

Equations (5.14) and (5.12) imply that the marginal product of land is equated on share rented and owned land, equation (5.11) that the marginal product of labor is also equated, so that production is efficient on all classes of land. Note that $S > R$ from (5.14), the excess corresponding to the risk premium found empirically. Thus Johnson has identified a satisfactory method for eliminating the inefficiencies conventionally associated with share tenancy.

Recent empirical work has further tended to undermine the proposition that share tenancy is less efficient than fixed-rent tenancy. Vernon Ruttan exemplifies the theoretical inefficiency of labor input [equation (5.9)] by constructing hypothetical partial budgets for the use of fertilizer and herbicide on the assumption that the landlord shares in costs. He notes:

> The analysis is consistent with the proposition that share tenancy does reduce the incentive for intensive use of labor inputs and for the use of output increasing technical inputs such as fertiliser and insecticides. However, it appears that share tenancy may actually encourage a more rapid rate of adoption of labor saving technology than would occur under fixed rent leasehold or owner operator systems.[6]

Empirical evidence collected in the Philippines tended to show that on small farms a *higher* output per hectare under share tenancy than under leasehold for the same size of farm growing the same crops; the converse was found for larger farms. Moreover, output per man was *lower* on share tenancy, again on small farms. It is difficult to assess the statistical significance of these findings[7] but also difficult to claim support from them for the traditional view. Ruttan emphasizes the difficulty in predicting unambiguous results in transitional economies where other factors are important, and he suggests that access to credit may be easier for share tenants than for leasehold tenants and

6. Vernon W. Ruttan, "Tenure and Productivity of Philippine Rice Producing Farms," *Philippine Economic Journal* 79 (1971): 587–95.

7. The data show a rather odd and very variable relationship between land productivity and farm size, particularly tables 2 and 3, which suggests a high variation between farms.

may explain the Philippine observations. Moreover, he seems to suggest that lack of monetization in the product market may also be a factor. Neither proposition is very convincing, unless it is argued that fixed-rent tenancies are preferred by absentee landlords who do not wish to be involved in any farm management activities, though even here it is not clear that a straight loan repayable with the rent would be much trouble. The evidence is, however, consistent with the model developed in section 2 below.

Cheung, as mentioned above, took a different approach to the problem of ruling out the anomalous zero marginal product of land predicted by traditional theory.[8] His analysis ignored uncertainty on the grounds that, if share tenancy could be justified (i.e., shown to be as efficient as alternative contracts) without uncertainty, it would certainly be attractive with uncertainty, since the share tenant bears less risk.

Rather than repeat Cheung's analysis it seems preferable to extend it to deal with uncertainty. With constant returns we can replace $F(H_1, L_1)$ in equation (5.7) with $H_1 f(l)$, and $L_1$ with $lH_1$, and let the tenant maximize expected utility subject to a minimum contractual intensity $l^*$, which, to make sense, will be a binding constraint, so that $l = l^*$. The tenant will now demand such tenancies only if $\partial EU(Y)/\partial H \geqq 0$, i.e., if

$$(1 - r)f(l^*) \geqq wl^* \frac{EU'}{EU'\Theta} = l^*F_L.^9 \tag{5.15}$$

The landlord in turn maximizes his share rent subject to this constraint:

$$\text{Max } rf(l) + \lambda [(1 - r)f(l) - lF_L]. \tag{5.16}$$

Differentiating (5.16) with respect to $r$ shows that $\lambda = 1$, so that the constraint binds, $(1 - r)f(l^*) = l^*F_L$, and differentiating with respect to $l$ shows that $f'(l) = F_{L_1} = F_L$, and marginal products of labor are equated everywhere. It is also clear that marginal products of land are equated, and indeed, that $rf(l^*) = S$ of equation (5.12).

Cheung provides evidence to show that share contracts do specify

8. S. N. S. Cheung, "Private Property Rights and Sharecropping," *Journal of Political Economy* 76 (1968): 1107–22; and Cheung, *Theory of Share Tenancy*.

9. An interior solution with positive amounts of land under fixed rent or ownership is implied; this can be justified if it is assumed that a tenant may rent in land at fixed rent and rent it out at share rent which he will do if fixed rent tenancies seem unattractive to him.

minimum input levels.[10] What he does not show is that even with uncertainty share cropping offers no advantages over combinations of wage and fixed-rent contracts, so that one has to find additional reasons to account for the widespread existence of sharecropping. (The same criticism applies to Johnson's argument.)

*Theorem 2*

Under assumptions 1–6 above, share tenancy is at best equivalent to a combination of fixed-rent and fixed-wage contracts.

*Proof*

The best share tenancy has been shown to be efficient. Using the notation of equation (5.2) and the results of the previous section together with equation (5.6) we have:

$$\frac{R}{w} = \frac{F_H}{F_L} = \frac{F_{H_1}}{F_{L_1}} = \frac{rl}{1-r} = \frac{r}{h(1-r)}. \tag{5.17}$$

Now compare the difference between allocating 1 unit of labor to share rent and the alternative of allocating $1-r$ units to fixed rent, $r$ units to wage labor:

$$= (1-r)\,g\Theta - [(1-r)\,(g\Theta - Rh) + rw] \tag{5.18}$$

$$= 0, \text{ using (5.17).}$$

Thus there is no advantage in share tenancies. Q.E.D.

We have now established the contention advanced at the beginning that conventional neoclassical assumptions are unable to attribute any advantage to share tenancy, so that an adequate theory of share tenancy will have to abandon these attractive and simplifying assumptions. It is no wonder there has been such a discrepancy between theory and experience. Before abandoning these assumptions, however, there are two critiques of Cheung's work that raise important ideas and thus merit attention here.

## Enforcement Costs and the Type of Contract

Cheung makes the important point that different types of contract (fixed rent as opposed to sharecropping, and various combinations for the different inputs) not only yield different benefits (specifically, risk sharing, substitutes for credit, etc.) but have different enforcement

10. Cheung, *Theory of Share Tenancy*, pp. 76–77.

costs. Any theory that tries to account for the prevalence of specific types of tenancy must pay attention to these costs and benefits, whether the contract is formally stipulated or informal.[11]

C. H. H. Rao takes up the question of enforcing the contract and makes a perceptive distinction between crops with limited scope for the exercise of entrepreneurial skills, and crops for which the converse is true. This distinction is on the face of it quantifiable,[12] since entrepreneurial income is measured as the residual of gross return less costs (actual or opportunity) of the inputs. He argues that

> the existence of a significant scope for entrepreneurship may occasion fixed-cash rents, because the latter at the same time permit the tenants to capture the returns expected in consequence of their decision making and protect the suppliers of land services against the possible risks arising from the production decisions of the tenants.[13]

There is some danger of confusion here. We can distinguish four reasons why a fixed-rent contract will be preferred for a crop requiring these entrepreneurial skills:

i. Entrepreneurial tenants will not wish to share their special talents with landlords.

ii. Landlords are more wary of risks than are entrepreneurial tenants.

iii. Landlords face the problem of "moral hazard," i.e., they may find it difficult to establish whether the contract has been fulfilled, so that enforcement costs for this type of contract are high. (Obviously they are minimal for fixed-rent contracts.)

iv. Landlords may not be able to measure the entrepreneurial skill of a prospective tenant at the time of drawing up the contract.

Only the first two of these reasons seem to be implied in the quotation and elsewhere in the statement of Rao's hypothesis.[14] I shall argue that these first two do not provide a convincing argument for the hypothesis, though the last two do. In most cases Rao's conclusions

11. A formal contract is more likely if (1) the relationship between tenant and landlord is impersonal, (2) there exists a variety of possible specifications of rights and obligations, or (3) the tenant has security or the leases are long term. Conversely, informal contracts are likely if (1) the contract is face to face, (2) custom has evolved a well-defined and satisfactory specification, or (3) leases are frequently renegotiated.

12. But see below for the distinction between the reward to true entrepreneurial skill and merely bearing uncertainty.

13. C. H. H. Rao, "Uncertainty, Entrepreneurship, and Sharecropping in India," *Journal of Political Economy* 79 (1971): 580.

14. Ibid., pp. 579–83.

are upheld (as these arguments are likely to hold simultaneously), though the rather fine distinctions drawn here may have some use in predicting the existence of a different form of contract under certain circumstances.

Before continuing I must emphasize another distinction made by Rao. A decision maker faces two types of uncertainty. Any decision may lead to a variety of outcomes (we could call this "outcome uncertainty"), and there may exist several alternatives that might lead to the best result, given as yet unknown information on subsequent events (I will call this "choice uncertainty"). It is the ability to choose in the face of choice uncertainty that Rao described as entrepreneurial skill: "the existence of entrepreneurial function is indicated not by the existence of uncertainty as such but by the scope of decision-making in the face of uncertainty."[15] With this distinction (or definition) in mind we can turn to the various arguments given above.

Argument ii can be dispatched most readily. It is almost definitional that an entrepreneur (one who is willing to undertake risks) will be less averse to risk than a nonentrepreneur, *ceteris paribus*. But it is also plausible that the willingness to bear risks will increase with wealth (which in a peasant society will be highly correlated with land ownership); certainly this will be true at low levels of wealth, where risk reduces the probability of survival. Entrepreneurs will be more willing than nonentrepreneurs of similar wealth to accept a fixed-rent contract for a given piece of land as opposed to a given share-rental contract, but they will conceivably be less willing than large landholders, or than nonentrepreneurs offered a larger holding. In short, the degree of risk aversion (measured by the curvature of the utility functions) and the opportunities for gaining at least a minimum return (provided by farming sufficient land) should be distinguished. This is important for the empirical test, as Rao finds in comparing rice and tobacco production. The latter is characterized by higher (entrepreneurial) profits, a prevalence of fixed rents, and larger landholdings. Moreover, it appears that small landowners lease out land for tobacco farming to tenants with larger holdings, in contrast to rice farmers. Thus one possible explanation for the phenomenon of fixed rent would be that economies of scale in tobacco farming (fixed indivisible factors) lead to large optimal holdings. These are built up by transfers from smaller, more risk-averse farmers to larger and therefore less risk-averse tenants, with the favored contract shifting risk to the less risk-averse; in this

15. Ibid., p. 580.

case a fixed-rent contract will have the desired property. A significant residual income accrues to the farmer for bearing all the risk, though it will be the case that no skill in selecting one strategy rather than another is implied. In short, the contract has been chosen because of the size requirements of the crop and the source of the leased land, rather than because of the apparent entrepreneurial requirement of the crop. The empirical test does not refute the latter possibility but neither does it guarantee that it is the best explanation.

The first argument is interesting. Consider the following model. There are two types of tenants: "entrepreneurs" and "workers." Both receive the same wage when hired as laborers, but they are able to produce different amounts when farming:

$$Y = \Theta F(H, L) \text{ for workers.}$$

$$Y = \Theta G(H, L) \text{ for entrepreneurs.} \tag{5.19}$$

The previous discussion is perfectly general, as it states that there exists an efficient share contract $(r, l^*)$, which is as good as (but no better than) alternative fixed-rent and wage contracts. For the entrepreneur $(r, l^*)$ must be such that $G_L = F_L$, $rG/H = F_H$, and in general these values will differ from those taken by contracts for workers: intuitively we expect $r < r_W$ (workers' share rent).

Thus the possession of special skills by a prospective tenant does not preclude share contracts which are as attractive to both parties as fixed-rent contracts, provided the skills can be identified and the rental contract adjusted accordingly. If the skills cannot be identified, and if the rental share is not adjusted, the tenant will prefer a fixed-rent contract.[16] Argument iv has therefore been shown to provide a convincing case for the existence of fixed rents.

The third argument is also convincing and applies to formal and informal contracts. If the optimal input mix is well defined and does not depend upon the expected future state of the environment, then there is little scope for entrepreneurial skills. Provided the *random* variations

---

16. An interesting consequence of this is that it is unlikely that the correct share-rental contract will emerge, since the potential tenant will find it difficult to demonstrate his skill without the existence of a fixed-rent contract. If he attempts to demonstrate his skill under an existing worker-oriented contract he will be bargaining with the landlord to reduce the landlord's present income. Unless there exists an alternative fixed-rent contract the tenant's threat to leave and go to a landlord who presumably knows even less about his skill will carry little weight. So it might be argued that the existence of skilled tenants will encourage the emergence of fixed-rent contracts even if they do not all avail themselves of them.

in output for a given level of inputs are small, or sufficiently highly correlated with output in the observable neighborhood so that the residual variation is known to be small, it should be possible to tell with reasonable certainty at the time of the harvest whether the tenant devoted adequate inputs. In contrast, if there is a significant element of choice uncertainty (and hence scope for entrepreneurial skill) it will be difficult to establish *expost* whether the *exante* decisions were defensible in the light of expectations prevailing at that time. If for given decisions the outcomes on neighboring farms are sufficiently correlated it would, however, be possible to devise an alternative contract in which the rent was a proportion of the average yield in the relevant neighborhood. This would have the incentive effects of a fixed-rent contract and the insurance aspects of a share-rental contract, and it would be fairly cheap to enforce provided yield data were available (and could be trusted).

Rao subjects his empirical data to rather more careful analysis than previous writers, since he is aware of the complex interdependence between type of crop, scale of operation, and the relative enforcement costs and risk-sharing benefits of different contracts. He calculates the "marginal product of land" (MP land) at each size of holding,[17] presumably from his regression of log (land in standard acres) against log (output), and shows that above a certain minimum size (somewhere between 0 and 20 acres) the MP land is *higher* on share-rented land. If large owners lease to small share tenants they will receive a rent above their own MP land. However, the evidence must be treated with caution since (1) at small scales the traditional finding is apparently confirmed; and (2) if the estimation procedure is as described the "marginal product of land" is misnamed. For, under constant returns,

$$Y = H\Theta f(l), \tag{5.20}$$

with $l$ equated across farms and determined exogenously. Then $dY/dH = \Theta f(l)$, which is not the conventional marginal product of land.

To return to the main theme of Rao's article, we can perhaps conclude that if we can find some additional advantages for sharecropping (to justify it at all in the presence of enforcement costs) then the considerations discussed above will become relevant in influencing the choice of contract.

The final contribution that must be assessed is that of P. K. Bardhan

17. Rao, "Uncertainty, Entrepreneurship, and Sharecropping in India," p. 590, table 7.

and T. N. Srinivasan, since this brings out sharply some of the difficulties in describing a sharecropping equilibrium. In their model, landless laborers maximize a utility function of income (= consumption $C$) and leisure; there is no uncertainty and the choice is restricted to share renting or laboring: the argument is that either share renting or fixed renting will be preferable and that the two cannot coexist.[18] This argument rests on there being different production functions for the different tenancy types. On Rao's theory this could be defended by supposing that different crops lent themselves to different contracts, but so far this merely states that the *cost* of enforcing share-rental contracts varies with different crops. If fixed-rent and wage contracts are costless, share renting will never be observed. The only escape (not explicitly mentioned by Bardhan and Srinivasan) is to suppose that wage contracts are costly to enforce, so that share-rental contracts, even allowing for evasion and/or enforcement costs, are a cheaper means of sharing risk than wage contracts plus fixed-rent contracts. This is consistent with their assumption (again undefended) that the landowner's production function, $G(H,L)$, is less efficient than the tenants', $F(H,L)$. Presumably the difference is attributable to supervision costs: $T(H,L)$ [$\geq F(H,L) - G(H,L)$]. Even so, this is unsatisfactory since the choice of contract cannot be made until the comparative costs of the two types are known, and the efficiency loss (a measure of the cost of share contracts) will depend on the share rent, $r$, which in turn is not known independently of the equilibrium. In short, the reasons for confining attention to wage- and sharecropping ought to be given explicitly for a satisfactory analysis.

With some misgivings I now return to consider the tenants maximizing $U(C, 1 - L_1 - L_2)$ (using my notation):

$$C = (1 - r) F(H, L_1) + wL_2. \qquad (5.21)$$

They claim to be seeking a competitive equilibrium with no constraints on land and labor hiring, and they require that $F$ be strictly concave. In this equilibrium they conclude that $F_H$ must be zero and $F_L = w/(1 - r)$, as in equations (5.9) and (5.10). Landowners likewise maximize $U(C, 1 - L)$ so that

$$C = G(\bar{H} - H, L + L_1) - wL_1 + rF(H, L_2), \qquad (5.22)$$

18. P. K. Bardhan and T. N. Srinivasan, "Cropsharing Tenancy in Agriculture: A Theoretical and Empirical Analysis," *American Economic Review* 61 (1971): 51, n. 8.

where $\bar{H}$ is total land, and $L_1$ is hired labor; $G$ is the production function for owner-operators and, as has been pointed out, it must be inferior to $F$. In equilibrium,

$$G_H = rF_H; G_L = w. \qquad (5.23)$$

Bardhan and Srinivasan proceed to find the value of $r$ and the amount of land leased out, $H$, at which all these marginal conditions (together with marginal utility conditions which add little but complexity) are satisfied.

They argue that in this competitive equilibrium no landlord will be able to influence the share rental specified in the contract, which will be determined by the intersection of the aggregate supply and demand for tenancies. They criticize Cheung for ignoring his own assumption that "the percentage shares and area rented under share tenancy . . . are competitively determined in the market,"[19] when analyzing share-tenancy contracts, and they argue that the difference in their conclusions "lies in the kind of maximisation process Cheung carried out in Section III pp. 1113–14 of his paper. There he maximises only from the landlord's point of view, whereas in this paper we determine the demand side from maximisation by the tenant, just as the supply side is determined from landlord's maximising decision."[20] Thus Bardhan and Srinivasan themselves raise the question of the properties of a share-tenancy equilibrium, which is the root problem in analyzing this contract.

The first point to notice is that my presentation of Cheung's result arrives at the same solution by a route that clearly avoids Bardhan and Srinivasan's strictures: both parties maximize subject to constraints, and in equilibrium all contracts must be equally favorable. Their objection is presumably to Cheung's equilibrium condition on the supply of tenants. In my notation, and ignoring uncertainty,

$$(1 - r) F (H, L) = wL, \qquad (5.24)$$

which is the only way Cheung takes account of tenants. While Cheung's method of exposition may be rather misleading, it does seem fair to characterize his solution as a competitive equilibrium, given the alternative method of reaching the same result. Ironically, the same can certainly not be said of Bardhan and Srinivasan's "equilibrium."

19. Cheung, "Private Property Rights and Sharecropping," p. 1120.
20. Bardhan and Srinivasan, "Cropsharing Tenancy in Agriculture," p. 52.

Equation (5.24) is a condition for there to be zero excess demand for tenancies by the elastic supply of potential tenants implied in assuming a strictly exogenous wage rate. It cannot be simultaneously satisfied with the condition

$$(1 - r) F_L = w \qquad\qquad (5.25)$$

with a concave production function; tenants will earn intramarginal surpluses no matter what the rental share, and each landlord will be faced with an excess demand, so that each landlord is a potential monopolist. (Even if the wage rate were endogenous the same problem would arise.) There is a further difficulty, which is that there may be no feasible solution to $F_H = 0$, given the amount of land available (for example, many common production functions such as the Cobb-Douglas would yield an infinite demand for land at zero [marginal] price). It certainly cannot be said that an equilibrium is competitive if it is characterized by an excess supply of tenants and an excess demand for land by each tenant. Notice that in both of the previous models (i.e., Johnson's and Cheung's) neither problem arose, because of the underlying efficiency theorem. If sharecropping is equivalent to fixed-rent and wage contracts which are themselves consistent with a competitive equilibrium, then sharecropping itself will be. Conversely, if for some reason the combination of fixed-rent and wage contracts is unattractive, then our suspicion should be aroused as to whether competitive equilibrium is possible. Indeed, the model constructed in the next section is a specific example of probably the only general proposition one can make about share tenancy, namely, that a share-tenancy equilibrium will not be competitive in the usual sense. Typically tenants would prefer to increase their share-rent holdings on the contracted terms, while the landlord will find it profitable to restrict supply at these terms. This situation, which must be a general feature of sharecropping, is a consequence of the inadequacy of the price system used in the contracts. There are more inputs (land, labor, effort, skill, etc.) and outputs (harvests in each of a large number of states of nature) than there are prices, so that quantitative restrictions increase the range of controls available. Thus we see the sharp contrast with competitive neoclassical theories.[21]

There are further minor criticisms that can be leveled at the analysis

21. These arguments are examined in greater detail in D. M. G. Newbery, "Crop-sharing Tenancy in an Equilibrium Model" (Paper presented to the Econometric Society, Oslo, August 1973).

of Bardhan and Srinivasan, which are subsidiary to their failure to establish a satisfactory equilibrium concept, and a consequent empirical criticism. For example, they claim to be dealing with strictly concave production functions, but in their equation (20)[22] they allow landlords to divide up their land into parcels of size $h$, and tenants to hire from $n$ landlords, and claim that tenant consumption will then be

$$c = n(1 - r) F(h, L_1) + wL_2,  \tag{5.26}$$

instead of

$$c = (1 - r) F(nh, nL_1) + wL_2.  \tag{5.27}$$

Equation (5.26) implies that there are *constant* returns, in that each parcel increases output *pari passu*, and it suggests that, even if the tenant did not hire from different landlords, since the land is homogeneous he is at liberty to divide his total holding up into parcels (or plots) of optimal size and thus escape the diminishing returns. This almost suggests to Bardhan and Srinivasan that they have an existence problem, which would have become unavoidable if they *had* explicitly assumed constant returns, for they find in their next equation that tenants will have an excess demand for parcels. They further argue that there is for some unspecified reason a minimum plot size below which the landlord will not choose to subdivide his total holding,[23] so that their attempted resolution of the problem to limit both the number of parcels that each tenant can rent and the size of each parcel implies a limit on the *amount* of land each tenant can rent.

It is interesting to pursue the implications of allowing landlords to have monopoly power, though it should be emphasized that a satisfactory treatment requires a specification of the rest of the contractual framework within which this power is exercised, a point I have argued at some length elsewhere.[24] Suppose there are constant returns: $F = Hf(l) = Lg(h)$. If $g$ has no maximum (the conventional assumption for production function theory, but less plausible for extensive agriculture) then there will be an excess demand for land at all share-rental rates. If on the other hand $g$ has a maximum at $h_0$ there will be

22. Bardhan and Srinivasan, "Cropsharing Tenancy in Agriculture," p. 53.
23. Of course, the obvious reason is that the production function is not strictly concave everywhere but has a $U$-shaped cost function; i.e., there are initially at least some increasing returns. The necessity of some such assumption should be familiar from discussions of imperfect competition, e.g., N. Kaldor, "Market Imperfection and Excess Capacity," *Economica,* n.s. 2 (1935): 33–50.
24. Newbery, "Cropsharing Tenancy in an Equilibrium Model."

excess demand unless the solution to equation (5.25) is $h = h_0$. This will occur when

$$r = 1 - \frac{w}{g(h_0)} = \underset{h}{\text{Max}} \left[ 1 - \frac{w}{g(h)} \right]. \tag{5.28}$$

Either this will maximize the landlord's income per acre, $rf(l)$, or the landlord is free to choose a lower value of $r$ and ration the amount of land as in the first case. In both cases the landlord is free to maximize his return regardless of the decision of other landlords. The conditions for this maximum are readily derived by maximizing $rf(l)$ subject to equation (5.25)

$$\frac{d}{dr} [rf(l)] = f + rf' \frac{dl}{dr} = 0. \tag{5.29}$$

But $f' = w/(1 - r)$. Therefore:

$$f'' \frac{dl}{dr} = \frac{w}{(1 - r)^2} = \frac{f'}{(1 - r)}. \tag{5.30}$$

Therefore, since $\sigma = -f'(f - lf')/lff''$, the elasticity of substitution between land and labor

$$\frac{1 - r}{r} = \frac{f'^2}{f''} = \frac{lf'\sigma}{f - lf'} = \frac{1 - \rho}{\rho} \sigma, \tag{5.31}$$

or

$$r = \rho/[\sigma + \rho(1 - \sigma)], \tag{5.32}$$

where $\rho$ is the imputed share of land in total product $(= hg'/g)$. The rental share will be greater or less than the efficient fixed-rent *share* as $\sigma$ is less than or greater than unity.

Equation (5.31) characterizes the share-rental maximizing value which in general will depend on $w$ (unless $f$ is isoelastic). The amount of land leased will be completely determined by the landlords and is independent of the amount of labor available to tenants except insofar as this influences the wage rate, $w$, an influence precluded by assumption.

A direct consequence of this new formulation is that we can no longer unambiguously predict the direction of the change in the area of land leased in response to a parametric change in the wage rate. Let $R(w)$ be the return per acre to land leased out $(= \text{Max } rf)$ so that in equation (5.23) $G_H = R(w)$. The effect of a change in $w$ is given by

$$\frac{dH}{dw} = - \begin{vmatrix} R_W & G_{12} \\ 1 & G_{22} \end{vmatrix} \Big/ \begin{vmatrix} G_{11} & G_{12} \\ G_{21} & G_{22} \end{vmatrix}. \tag{5.33}$$

The denominator is positive for a strictly concave function, while

$$\frac{dR}{dw} = \frac{\partial R}{\partial w} + \frac{\partial R}{\partial r}\frac{dr}{dw}.$$

But $\partial R/\partial r = 0$, as $R$ is maximized with respect to $r$, so from (5.30)

$$\frac{\partial R}{\partial w} = \frac{rw}{(1-r)^2 f''} < 0. \tag{5.34}$$

The sign of $H_W$ is the sign of $(G_{12} - R_W G_{22})$, which is ambiguous though quite likely to be negative, in direct contrast to the Bardhan and Srinivasan argument.

A graphical illustration will serve to emphasize the difference in the arguments. Figure 5.1 reproduces their figure 1 and shows the effect of a shift in $w$, given their argument.

It is argued that a rise in $w$ will raise the amount leased out at any given $r$ from $q$ to $\bar{q}$, say, and will lower the tenants' demand from $H$ to $\bar{H}$. The net result is to lower the "equilibrium" rental share from $r_0$ to $r_1$, and raise the amount leased from $H_0$ to $H_1$. The argument here shows that an increase in $w$ lowers the attractiveness to the landlord of farming his own land and leasing it out, though it does not eliminate the tenants' excess demand for land. The final outcome will depend on the relative strengths of the two effects and cannot be predicted a priori.

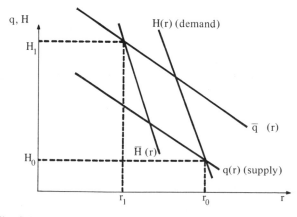

Fig. 5.1:  Demand and Supply in the Market for Land Leases

## The Stability of Share Tenancy Equilibrium

The situation just described was characterized by excess demand and inefficiency. Any tenant who can persuade a landlord that he will reduce this inefficiency to the benefit of the landlord will clearly be preferred by the landlord. Thus tenants will be prepared to bind themselves to supply minimum inputs if this constitutes a credible contract (i.e., if it can be observed or confirmed) since to do so will move nearer efficient production and so increase both parties' receipts. Thus it could be argued that the equilibrium described by Bardhan and Srinivasan (modified to meet the existence problem) is not only noncompetitive but also unstable, in that it would tend to be replaced by efficient contractual input tenancies.

### 2. THE EFFECT OF LABOR MARKET IMPERFECTIONS ON TENANCY CONTRACTS

The previous discussion assumed the existence of a perfect labor market, and it is clearly important to examine the strength of this assumption. The alternative to leasing land is to hire out one's labor, so there is a presupposition that the form of labor-hiring contracts available will affect the relative attractiveness of land-leasing contracts. By and large this apparently obvious point has been completely overlooked.[25]

For example, share-rental agreements are argued to be preferable to fixed-rent contracts for the tenant as they reduce the uncertainty in his income. He will therefore pay on average a higher rent than under a fixed-rent contract, sufficient to compensate the landlord for sharing the uncertainty and any extra costs involved in enforcing the contract. But, as we have seen, if there were a perfectly safe, freely available labor-hire contract available a tenant could also insure himself against uncertainty by allocating part of his labor to a fixed-rent contract and part to a wage contract. Thus the existence of a perfect labor market permits the tenant to enter into a combination of contracts (fixed-rent tenancy plus wage labor )with the same advantages as share tenancy but lower enforcement costs.

A moment's reflection suggests that unless the peasant economy is

25. Except by Johnson, who notes briefly that "if the unit is small and the share cropper is restricted in outside earnings, he must apply his labour and that of his family until he has achieved at least some minimum level of income" (see his "Resource Allocation under Share Contracts," p. 119).

extensively integrated into the outside world the competitive, risk-free labor markets of conventional theory are unlikely to exist or, more precisely, would not fill the role usually ascribed to them. The uncertainty that faces the farmers and tenants is pervasive and will have repercussions in the labor market. The simple algebraic/geometric models of productive activity ignore the essential time structure of decision making in agriculture and the comparative absence of future markets and forward contracting. A prospective tenant deciding whether to lease land or sell labor has to make a decision before the outcome is known. A decision to rely on wage income during the next crop year is a gamble on the continued availability of employment during the course of the year, so that neither farming nor wage employment avoids uncertainty, nor can he gain much insurance even by diversification. If the weather is unfavorable the crop will be poor and the demand for labor low. The following simplified model provides a framework for examining some of the interactions between labor and land-hire contracts in the presence of general uncertainty.

## A Simple Model of Labor Allocation under Uncertainty

For simplicity we will suppose that the tenant is risk neutral, at least in his allocation of labor between farming his plot and working for others.[26] Next suppose that, given the land available for cultivation, the number of days to be worked on it is determined in advance. In many ways this is more plausible than the alternative model considered in the appendix to this chapter, because it captures the interdependence of decisions taken at different points in the crop year. The amount of labor that can usefully be expended at harvest time is almost completely determined by earlier labor inputs. In an illustrative case (which could be made substantially more plausible and less extreme without altering the nature of the conclusions) there are $N$ "seasons," each of length $n$ days. A season is defined as a period during which certain essential agricultural activities must take place for there to be a successful harvest (thus planting, weeding, transplanting, etc., define seasons). Suppose that $m_i$ days in the $i$th season are devoted to these activities, and suppose that all $m_i$ days are equally valuable.[27] Finally, suppose

26. This is not unreasonable if the nature and degree of uncertainty facing both activities are the same, as is likely in peasant societies. Otherwise we have a portfolio selection problem.

27. "Days" may be redefined if work must be consecutive when started.

there is complete complementarity in the simplified sense that output, $Y$, is a lexicographic function of these inputs:

$$Y = F[H, \text{Min} (m_i : i = 1, \ldots N)]. \qquad (5.35)$$

Then, under a wide range of circumstances output will be determined by the initial labor input, $m_1 = m$, with all subsequent inputs the same, $m_i = m$. For as time passes knowledge about the likely harvest increases and the previous decision may be seen to be inappropriate, but, given the decreasing amount of work left to do to gain the fruits of all previous inputs, it may still be optimal to continue allocating $m$ inputs.

How is $m$ determined? Suppose the tenant believes that on any given day during a future season there is probability $p$ that a man seeking work will be successful in finding employment for that day at a wage $w$. It is theoretically and empirically plausible that both $w$ and $p$ will be beyond the influence of the individual tenant, though they may of course depend on each other, and on the season. Suppose that if the tenant is unsuccessful in finding work he can still complete a full day's work on his own land. Within the season of $n$ days it is assumed preferable to do at least $m$ days of farm work and no more, and so no more than $s$ days are available for wage employment ($s = n - m$). We want to find the expected revenue to be derived from increasing $s$ to $s + 1$, so that this can be compared with the expected revenue foregone in reducing farm labor from $m$ to $m - 1$. The following argument gives a simple formula in the case in which the probability of success in finding work, $p$, is independent of previous success or failure but is not confined to this case.[28]

Increasing the number of days potentially available for work from $s$ to $s + 1$ will result in another day's wage employment if and only if there are jobs available on more than $s$ days, i.e., if $n$ visits to the labor market would lead to more than $s$ successful (day) wage contracts. Thus the expected income from wage labor (equal to the given wage times the expected number of days employed) is *increased* by $P_S$, where $P_S$ is the probability that jobs are available on more than $s$ days. In this example $P_s$ is given by the Binomial Formula:

$$P_S = \sum_{t=s+1}^{n} \binom{t}{n} p^t q^{n-t}, \quad q \equiv 1 - p. \qquad (5.36)$$

The graph of the expected marginal return to wage employment of

28. I am indebted to D. G. Champernowne for this much shorter derivation of the formula.

allocating one less day for farming, which is to be compared to the expected return from the extra day's farming, is shown graphically in figure 5.2. Under sharecropping the expected marginal product of labor on the tenant's farm will be

$$MPL = (1 - r) F_2 (H, m), \tag{5.37}$$

while under a fixed-rent contract it will be

$$MPL_F = F_2 (H, m). \tag{5.38}$$

There is no advantage to a landlord in limiting the amount of land leased out to any one tenant under a fixed-rent contract, as the return per acre is specified in advance and is independent of the tenant. Thus a fixed-rent tenant will both wish to and be allowed to continue renting land until the marginal product is equal to $w$/day. This can be immediately seen from figure 5.2, where increases in $H$ raise the $MPL$ curve from $MPL_1$ to $MPL_2$ and, given $p$, raise the expected return from point $D$ to point $E$. This will continue until $W$ is reached (beyond which the cost of hiring labor will absorb all nonrental income).

In contrast, there is an advantage to the landlord in restricting the acreage leased out to a tenant farmer, since the smaller the area the lower will be the marginal product of tenant labor on this land (point $D$ rather than $E$) and hence the higher the return to the landlord (given the share rental). Viewed from a slightly different perspective, the

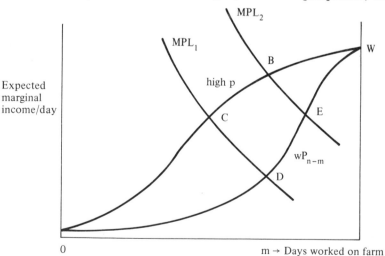

Fig. 5.2:   Marginal Product of Tenant Labor

smaller the amount of land leased, the lower will be the cost to the landlord of enforcing a given tenant labor input. If, however, the landlord is
too greedy in restricting acreage, the tenant will be able to find other
landlords willing to lease him land to bring his total area up to the
equilibrium amount, say $A$. If it were impossible to enforce contractual
labor inputs this equilibrium would be characterized by

$$(1 - r) F_2 (A, m) = w P_{n-m} = w (1 - r), \tag{5.39}$$

$$rF (A, m) = \bar{R}A, \tag{5.40}$$

where $\bar{R}$ is the fixed rent per acre considered equivalent in risk to the
average rent under share tenancy. This uniquely defines $r$ and $A$:

$$P_{n-m} = 1 - r \tag{5.41}$$

whence:

$$m = m (r, p, n). \tag{5.42}$$

Let $Af(m/A) = F(A, m)$ under constant returns, so that:

$$f' (m/A) = w \quad m/A = l (w). \tag{5.43}$$

Then

$$rf (m/A) = \bar{R}, \tag{5.44}$$

$$r = \bar{R}/f [l (w)], \tag{5.45}$$

$$A = m (r)/l (w). \tag{5.46}$$

Of course, $\bar{R}$ will be largely determined by $w$, so that $r = r(w)$, $A = A(p, n, w)$. An increase in the probability of finding work, $p$, will reduce
$A$ but leave $r$ unchanged (equivalent to a move from $E$ to $C$ in figure
5.2). This will tend to force more tenants to seek wage employment
and will tend to lower the probability of success in the labor market.
Thus the model has interesting consequences for the elasticity of labor
supply under sharecropping. Of course, a full equilibrium model would
have to inquire into the allocation of land previously under share
tenancy to fixed-rent contracts, and managed farms with hired labor,
with possible further repercussions for $p$, $w$, and $r$. An increase in $w$
leaving $p$ constant will raise $r$ if the elasticity of substitution of labor
for land, $\sigma$, is greater than unity, and will lower it if otherwise. The
amount of land leased under sharecropping will increase unless $d/dw$
$[(1 - r) w]$ is negative, i.e., unless $\sigma > 1/r$, which for normal values
of $r$ (between 1/5 and 2/3) seems unlikely.

Note that this last result is consistent with the (incorrectly derived) result of Bardhan and Srinivasan. The findings of this model can be summarized as follows. Uncertainty in the labor market of the type discussed here can be measured by the discrepancy between the casual wage rate and the average wage of the permanent laborer.[29] Its existance makes sharecropping more attractive to landlords (since enforcement costs are reduced), while it is likely that the same mechanisms that give rise to uncertainty in the labor market provide an incentive to the tenant to seek share contracts and spread risk. Variety in the types of labor contract available (casual, permanent, etc.) is to be expected when there is variety in the types of tenancy contract.

Finally, there are likely to be important interactions between the nature and degree of the labor market imperfections, the type of tenancy agreement prevalent, and the supply price of labor to the rest of the economy. The details of this, however, I leave for another time.

### Size of Holding and Choice of Contract

The labor market models described in the previous section are able to account for another widely observed phenomenon in peasant agriculture, namely, the tendency of output per acre to fall with the size of holding.[30] The smaller the holding the more time is available for work outside the holding and the lower the expected marginal return to an extra day's outside work.[31]

29. For an excellent discussion of the theoretical determinants of wage rates for casual and permanent or attached workers see P. Sanghvi, *Surplus Manpower in Agriculture and Economic Development* (New York: Asia Publishing House, 1969), chap. 4. He gives empirical evidence of the gap between the two (see pp. 99–103) and shows that the all-India average wage rate of casual workers was 17.5 annas, while that of attached workers was 12.3 annas. The range of the ratio of the casual to the attached wage rate across the country was from 1.04 (Madhya Pradesh) to 1.64 (Bombay), and in no zone or state was it less than unity.

30. The most carefully documented statistical evidence is presented in the Indian Farm Management Studies and is accessibly summarized in M. Paglin, "'Surplus' Agricultural Labour and Development: Facts and Theories," *American Economic Review* 55 (1965): 815–34. A more extensive and recent bibliography is given in J. N. Bhagwati and S. Chakravarty, "Contributions to Indian Economic Analysis: A Survey," *American Economic Review* 59, suppl. (1969): 1–73.

31. Two remarks are in order. The higher output per acre of small holdings is sometimes observed to result from the choice of more valuable (higher yield per acre) crops. Again, output per acre of these crops is frequently higher on large holdings (see especially World Bank, *Economic Growth of Colombia: Problems and Prospects,* Country Economic Report [Baltimore: Johns Hopkins Press, 1972], chap. 14). This is not inconsistent with the argument that smallholders have a comparative advantage in these crops, and that given the technology available to them output per acre will

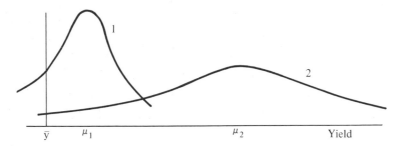

Fig. 5.3: Choice between Risky Alternatives

On the other hand, when a farmer is near the survival level it is plausible to describe his behavior as minimizing the chance that he will fall below the survival level. This is not quite the same as describing his behavior as highly risk averse, as the following example shows. Suppose there are two choices open to the farmer, each of which has a normally distributed range of outcomes, mean $\mu_i$, variance $\sigma_i^2$. Let $\bar{y}$ be the survival level, and $\beta_i = (\mu_i - \bar{y})/\sigma_i$. Then the probability of survival is an increasing function of $\beta$, and not necessarily of $\mu_i/\sigma_i$. Shown graphically in figure 5.3, this becomes obvious; the riskier choice 2 may be preferred to the less risky choice 1. Bearing in mind that the $\mu_i$ are total net yields, and that sharecropping tenancies must be below a certain size, it is then clearly possible for tenants to prefer larger, riskier fixed-rent tenancies. Bearing in mind the basic labor market model we would also expect workers with a regular source of income but some free time to be excluded from share contracts but to be prepared to accept fixed-rent contracts, and similarly with farmers owning a significant amount of land.

If we were to examine a region in which sharecropping and fixed-rent tenancies were both to be found, on land of given characteristics we would expect to find a tendency for small holdings to be under share rent and larger ones under fixed rent, except where the tenant had an alternative and secure form of income. Both the landlords and tenants would favor such a relation between tenancy type and size of holding. This is indeed what Rao found in West Godavari, where tobacco and

tend to fall. Other factors, particularly differential fertility by size of holding, access to different technology, and/or economies of scale in the use of the advanced technology will tend to confuse the empirical record (ibid.). The other point is that, relative to freehold or fixed-rent holdings of the same size, a share tenancy is still inefficient; therefore empirical work relating intensity to size of holding should distinguish the type of land tenure operative.

rice can both be grown.[32] Tobacco is grown on larger holdings (average size, 11.2 acres) under fixed rent (68 percent of tenancies) while rice is grown on smaller holdings (average size, 6.7 acres) under share tenancies (42 percent, though 58 percent are still fixed rent).[33]

Although we might expect to find small share tenancies yielding higher outputs per acre than small fixed-rent tenancies (since the latter might indicate the existence of an alternative risk-free source of steady income) we would nevertheless predict that small owner-occupiers (facing the same labor market as share tenants) would be even more productive. Thus we can reconcile Rao's findings discussed earlier with Ruttan's observations.

### 3. OTHER INPUTS AND COST SHARING

The basic model of share tenancy in the presence of a risky labor market is one in which the landlord can compel the tenant to devote his labor to the leased land by restricting the acreage leased, subject to competition by other landlords, who will be prepared to lease additional land to the tenant (and thus reduce tenant labor inputs on the originally leased land) if the landlord is too restrictive or too greedy in setting the share rent. (Of course, in some countries and regions competition from other landlords will be weak, and monopolistic rents will be extracted. This seems to be the case in parts of Latin America.[34] Of course, monopoly rents *could* similarly be extracted from fixed-rent contracts, but only by restricting the acreage and hence their total yield to the tenant. The previous arguments about uncertainty will then cause these tenants to prefer a share-rental agreement. The prevalence of sharecropping might be a reflection of the exercise of this monopoly power.)

However, while the landlord can rely on the imperfect labor market to give him control over tenant labor inputs, the same is not true of most other inputs, such as fertilizers, irrigation (where this is metered

32. Rao, "Uncertainty, Entrepreneurship, and Sharecropping in India," pp. 584–88.

33. Rao's main point is that the entrepreneurial requirements of the two crops differ, though he is clearly aware of the relationship between size and tenancy; see, for example, ibid., p. 587, n. 17.

34. For a rather different explanation (resting on imperfect product markets) of the mechanism of monopoly rent setting and some empirical evidence see A. Bottomley, *Factor Pricing and Economic Growth in Underdeveloped Rural Areas* (London: Crosby, Lockwood, 1971), chap. 6.

and charged), insecticides, and so on. (The exceptions might include implements and animal power, if the market in their services was similarly imperfect). Two possibilities present themselves.

## Cost Sharing of Inputs

Suppose output can be increased by additional inputs of $M$ (called fertilizer for convenience), whose price is $p$; and suppose the landlord pays a fraction $\beta$ of the cost. Then equilibrium in the share-tenancy market requires:

$$(1 - r) F_L = wP_{n-m} = (1 - r) w, \tag{5.47}$$

$$rF - pM = \bar{R}A = F^* - pM^* - wL^*, \tag{5.48}$$

$$(1 - r) F_M = (1 - \beta) p. \tag{5.49}$$

(Asterisks denote efficient levels of input chosen under fixed-rental contracts.)

Clearly, if $\beta = r$ efficient levels of labor and fertilizer inputs can be ensured by a suitable choice of $A$. Given that competition in the lease market will limit the rent per acre to the landlord, as shown in equation (5.48), any change in the contract that improves the tenant's position without worsening the landlord's will be preferred by the tenant, who will thereby be led to choose contracts with $\beta$ as close to $r$ as possible (with the obvious proviso that $r$ and $\beta$ are assumed to satisfy equation (5.49). Note the immediate conclusion (derived after some effort under different assumptions by Bardhan and Srinivasan) that holding $\bar{R}A$ constant implies that $r$ is an increasing function of $\beta$.)[35]

Exactly the same effect as setting $\beta = r$ can be achieved by deducting all nonlabor inputs from the harvest yield before dividing the crop between the tenant and landlord:

$$\operatorname*{Max}_{M} (1 - r) [F(A, M, L) - pM] : F_M = p. \tag{5.50}$$

(See equation [5.49], above). Examples of such contracts have been noted by Polly Hill for West Africa, where shallot growing and seine fishing typically involve sharecropping contracts, and expenses incurred are deducted before the proceeds are shared.[36]

35. Perhaps not immediately obvious. Differentiate equation (5.48), bearing in mind that $M$ is a function of $r$ and $\beta$ from equation (5.49).

36. Polly Hill, *Studies in Rural Capitalism in West Africa* (Cambridge: at the University Press, 1970), p. 40.

## Alternative Contracts

A somewhat less efficient solution occurs when the landlord supplies an amount he determines in return for a higher share rental. There is no difficulty in persuading the tenant to apply the fertilizer (assuming it cannot be resold without detection, a proviso that is also important under cost sharing) but the larger equilibrium rental share can be sustained only at lower plot sizes. The attraction of this kind of contract lies in the joint provision of inputs and credit for the farmer, and the certainty that the correct inputs are being used for the landlord. Where credit is costly and holdings small in my case, the system may be preferred despite its inefficiency.[37]

Similarly, if cost sharing is traditionally not practiced, the landlord can ensure the same return from share renting as fixed renting by sufficiently restricting acreage. The system will then be in equilibrium, provided no cost-sharing contracts are available, but inefficient. Such a system might survive if it were very costly to prevent fertilizers from being resold, and if the population pressure led to small plots and uncertain labor markets in any case. Unfortunately, this combination of circumstances makes it difficult to improve matters by selective government policies, despite the obvious urgency of reform and improvement.

## APPENDIX: A SECOND MODEL OF LABOR ALLOCATION UNDER UNCERTAINTY

Here I consider the (more complex) problem of the determination of area leased under share rental when the number of days worked on the land is not decided in advance. Suppose again there are $n$ days available in the relevant period, but that output on the farm is a function of the number of days worked on the farm, $t$. All days not spent in wage employment will be spent on the farm. Let $s$ be the number of days for which

$$(1 - r) F_2 (A, s) = w. \qquad (5.51)$$

Then at least $s$ days will be spent on the farm. Let $Q(t)$ be the distribu-

---

37. This type of contract would correspond to the *Krishabi* system described in the "Farm Management Survey in West Bengal" cited by Bardhan and Srinivasan ("Cropsharing Tenancy in Agriculture").

tion function: the probability of up to and including $t$ successful wage contracts in $n$ attempts. Let $ø(t)$ be the probability of having to farm exactly $t$ days. Then

$$ø(t) = Q(n - t) - Q(n - t - 1), \quad s < t \leqq n \qquad (5.52)$$

when $Q(n - t)$ is the probability of gaining wage employment for $n - t$ days or less, so that the right-hand side is the probability of exactly $n - t$ days wage employment. The value of $ø$ at the end-point $s$, $ø(s)$, is the probability of finding work for $n - s$ days *or more*:

$$ø(s) = 1 - Q(n - s - 1). \qquad (5.53)$$

Expected farm output is then

$$EY = \sum_{t=s}^{n} F(A, t)\, ø(t).$$

$$EY = F(A, s) + \sum_{i=1}^{n-s-1}(F(A, s + i) - F(A, s + i - 1))\, Q(n - s - i)$$

$$= F(A, s) + \sum_{i=0}^{n-s-2} F_2(A, s + i)\, Q(n - s - i + 1) > F(A, s)$$

where

$$Q(t) = \sum_{j=0}^{t} \binom{n}{j} p^j q^{n-j}.$$

Again, expected output per acre is greater than that which would prevail if there were no labor market uncertainty. The rented area, $A$, and the share, $r$, will be determined by the same considerations as before. One would suspect that a share tenancy would be more efficient for a given size leased (higher output per acre) if the labor allocated to the farm were determined in advance as in the previous model, since in the present model the ex post income from all days' work remains positive, in contrast to the former. The costs of not working on the farm are thus higher in the former model. This adds another dimension to Rao's concept of the scope for entrepreneurship. The more patterned or complementary are labor inputs at different seasons, the easier it is to ensure the correct labor input. This remains true even if there is considerable scope for varying the *average* intensity of labor input. The important component is the degree of complementarity between labor inputs, not the elasticity of output to aggregate labor.

# 6

## An Economic Theory of Tenant and Landlord
## Based on a Philippine Case

MAHAR MANGAHAS

About twenty years ago, share tenancy was being decried as inefficient in the use of resources, in comparison to conditions of the leaseholder or the owner-operator. A typical statement of the theory is Gale Johnson's, in which the share tenant is pictured as making all the farm decisions and bearing all the costs;[1] the experience leading to this theory was American. Later the theory was modified to allow for the landlord bearing part of the costs but still leaving all decisions on inputs to the share tenant. In this case efficient resource use might or might not be attained, depending on whether or not the product share and the cost share were equal.

However, the implications of this theory have been supported not at all by the Philippine experience. Productivity on share-tenant farms in the Philippines is very often no different from that on owner-operated or leasehold farms, and, where different, it is almost always greater. Nor have share tenants lagged behind with respect to adoption of high-yielding varieties of rice. The data supporting this case have come from the agricultural censuses, and from several surveys.[2]

This chapter reports on part of a research project on land reform and agricultural development in Nueva Ecija, undertaken by the Institute of Philippine Culture, Ateneo de Manila University, to which the author is project consultant.

Some time after this paper was written, more accurate information became available on the nature of contractual relationships in Nueva Ecija, and my model of the landlord-tenant contract (p. 150 below) was consequently revised. The revision is contained in Mahar Mangahas, Virginia A. Miralas, and Romana P. de los Reyes, *Tenants, Lessees, Owners: Welfare Implications of Tenure Change* (Quezon City: Institute of Philippine Culture, Ateneo de Manila University, 1975).

1. D. Gale Johnson, "Resource Allocation under Share Contracts," *Journal of Political Economy* 58, no. 4 (1950): 111–23.

2. J. P. Estanislao, "A Note on Differential Farm Productivity by Tenure,"

138

In 1968 Steven Cheung introduced a theory in which the landlord makes all the decisions, including how much of the tenant's own labor he is to apply to the land, and imposes an income-maximizing rental share, subject to the restriction that the tenant earns the equivalent of his opportunity wage income. Citing data from China, Cheung came to the conclusion that share tenancy, owner-operatorship, and leasehold are equally efficient.[3] Economists then began to turn their attention to the determination of the distribution of contracts according to tenure, some analysts concentrating on the implications of different types of contracts for the landlord,[4] and others on the implications for the tenant.[5]

Although Philippine experience is consistent with the results of Cheung's model, the assumptions of his model are not easy to accept completely. There does appear to be a substantial amount of landlord participation in decision making, at least as far as choice of plant variety and choice of fertilizer are concerned (table 6.1), but it is not necessary to turn to a model that assigns all decision-making power to the landlord. More recently, P. K. Bardhan and T. N. Srinivasan have proposed that the optimizing behavior of tenant and landlord be studied separately, leading to separate preference schedules for farm size, labor, and other inputs, as functions of the rental share and other contractual parameters.[6] The meeting of tenant and landlord in a competitive market then determines equilibrium contractual terms.

This chapter follows the Bardhan-Srinivasan approach in that the tenant and landlord are analyzed separately. It is assumed that each

---

*Philippine Economic Journal* 4, no. 1 (1965): 120–24; Vernon W. Ruttan, "Tenure and Productivity of Philippine Rice Producing Farms," *Philippine Economic Journal* 5, no. 1 (1966): 42–63; Mahar Mangahas, "An Economic Analysis of the Diffusion of New Rice Varieties in Central Luzon" (Ph.D. diss., University of Chicago, 1970); Pedro R. Sandoval and Benjamin N. Gaon, "Agricultural Land Reform in the Philippines: Economic Aspects" (Los Banos, Laguna: Dept. of Agricultural Economics, College of Agriculture, University of the Philippines, 1971); Romana p. de los Reyes, Mahar Mangahas, and Francis J. Murray, "Land Reform and Agricultural Development in Nueva Ecija: Phase One," typescript (Ateneo de Manila, Institute of Philippine Culture, 1973).

3. Steven N. S. Cheung, "Private Property Rights and Sharecropping," *Journal of Political Economy* 76, no. 6 (1968): 1107–22.

4. Steven N. S. Cheung, "Transaction Costs, Risk Aversion and the Choice of Contractual Arrangement," *Journal of Law and Economics* 12, no. 1 (1969): 23–42.

5. L. Dean Hiebert, "Risk, Tenure, and Resource Allocation in Low Income Agriculture" (Ph.D. diss., University of Wisconsin, 1972).

6. P. K. Bardhan and T. N. Srinivasan, "Cropsharing Tenancy in Agriculture: A Theoretical and Empirical Analysis," *American Economic Review* 61, no. 1 (1971): 48–64

Table 6.1: Loci of Decisions as to Plant Variety and Fertilizer, Philippines,
1954/55, 1965, and 1971 (Percentages of total decisions made)

| | Choice of variety | Choice of fertilizer |
|---|---|---|
| Philippines, 1954/55, 3,255 tenant farms: | | |
| Tenants | 74% | 30% |
| Landlords | 15 | 10 |
| Joint | 7 | 7 |
| Unknown | 4 | 53 |
| Bulacan and Nueva Ecija, 1965, 112 share landlords: | | |
| Tenants | 33% | 32% |
| Landlords | 56 | 47 |
| Joint | 23 | 30 |
| Nueva Ecija, 1971, 34 share landlords: | | |
| Tenants | 38% | 37% |
| Landlords | 27 | 33 |
| Joint | 35 | 30 |
| 18 lessee landlords: | | |
| Tenants | 82% | 93% |
| Landlords | 6 | 7 |
| Joint | 12 | 0 |

*Sources:* Philippines: Horst von Oppenfeld, Judith von Oppenfeld, J. C. Sta.
Iglesia, and Pedro R. Sandoval, "Farm Management, Land Use, and Tenancy in the
Philippines," Central Experiment Station Bulletin no. 1 (Los Banos, 1957), p. 96;
Bulacan and Nueva Ecija, 1965: Enriqueta A. Bernal, "The Role of Landlords in
Philippine Agricultural Development: An Exploratory Study," mimeographed
(M.S. thesis, College of Agriculture, University of the Philippines, 1967), p. 66;
Nueva Ecija, 1971: Romana P. de los Reyes and Frank Lynch, "Reluctant Rebels:
Leasehold Converts in Nueva Ecija," *Philippine Sociological Review* 20, nos. 1–2
(1972): 19.

party will have certain preferences regarding the inputs to be applied to
the land, given a proposed contract characterized by a set of revenue-
and finance-sharing parameters. Obviously, the landlord owns the land,
the tenant owns his labor, and neither owns material inputs. Yet each
party will express his views as to how these resources ought to be
combined, and such statements are in the nature of an offer of his own
resources in exchange for that of the other.[7] The setting for this case
study is the Philippines, principally the province of Nueva Ecija in
Central Luzon. As much as possible, economic and socioanthropological research is used as a source of a priori judgments concerning the

7. This analytical symmetry is not meant to contradict the assertion that tenancy
involves an "asymmetric patron-client contract"; see Henry T. Lewis, *Ilocano Rice
Farmers: A Comparative Study of Two Philippine Barrios* (Honolulu: University of
Hawaii Press, 1971).

relationships that are to enter into the model of the landlord-tenant contract.

## THE FARMER'S UTILITY FUNCTION

In the first place, what constitutes a "realistic" farmer utility function? Consider table 6.2, which gives frequency rankings of various items that contribute to a "good life" mentioned most frequently by Nueva Ecija rice farmers. This evidence suggests two basic variables contributing to total farmer welfare: (1) consumption, interpreted as a means of raising the family's future income stream ("enough food and money for subsistence"; "job other than farming"; "money for farm expenses and equipment"; "bigger harvest"; "improvement of house"; and "education for children") and (2) wealth, a concept that is negative more often than not (a good life means "not being indebted"). Lessees and share tenants rank farm ownership as fourth or fifth, whereas owner-operators rank it as eighth; this clearly suggests a diminishing

Table 6.2: Rankings of Selected Items Constituting a Good Life Freely Mentioned by IPC/BAEcon Nueva Ecija Rice-Farmer Respondents, February 1971

| Average rank order | Selected item | Owner-operator (N = 114) | Lease-holder (N = 403) | Share tenant (N = 363) | Part owner (N = 66) | Lessee-share tenant (N = 40) |
|---|---|---|---|---|---|---|
| 1 | Enough food and money for subsistence | 1 (56)[a] | 1 (281) | 1 (247) | 1 (54) | 1 (26) |
| 2 | Education for children | 2 (46) | 8 (54) | 4 (94) | 2 (28) | 2 (22) |
| 3 | Job other than farming | 3 (35) | 3 (127) | 2 (125) | 6 (12) | 5 (8) |
| 4 | Not being indebted | 5 (26) | 2 (149) | 3 (109) | 5 (14) | 6 (7) |
| 5 | Money for farm expenses and equipment | 7 (14) | 5 (79) | 8 (44) | 3.5 (16) | 3.5 (13) |
| 6.5 | Owning a farm | 8 (9) | 4 (103) | 5 (75) | 7 (11) | 3.5 (13) |
| 6.5 | Bigger harvest | 4 (28) | 6 (63) | 6 (65) | 3.5 (16) | 8 (5) |
| 8 | Improvement of house | 6 (15) | 7 (56) | 7 (55) | 8 (5) | 7 (6) |

a. The figure in parentheses is the number of times an item was freely mentioned.

*Source:* De los Reyes and Lynch, "Reluctant Rebels," p. 73.

marginal utility of wealth. It might be noted that the data in table 6.2 in no way indicate that leisure is a variable of relevance to farmer welfare.

Given his income, the farmer can be considered to allocate it between consumption and saving so that he maximizes utility jointly from consumption during the income period and wealth at the end of the period. In figure 6.1, case 1 depicts allocation $E$ out of income $OY$ such that saving is positive and wealth is increased. The indifference curve, which has a horizontal portion indicating minimum permissible

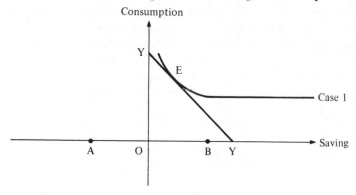

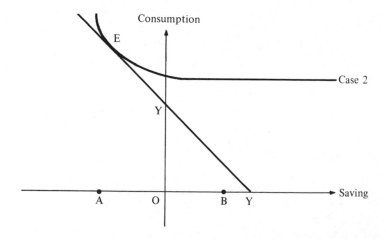

Fig. 6.1:  Allocation of Farm Income

consumption, is constructed with reference to a wealth axis. If the wealth axis point of origin is $A$, this means that $AO$ was initially (positive) wealth and that this was increased by the amount saved. If the point of origin is $B$, then $OB$ represents an original net indebtedness, which is somewhat reduced by the positive saving. In case 2, the income is too small for even the minimum consumption level, and dissaving occurs, either reducing original wealth or increasing the original level of indebtedness. Table 6.3 gives an indication of the difficulty farmers have in reducing their level of indebtedness over time.

Whatever the current level of consumption and wealth or indebtedness, it is clear that a larger income will make the farmer better off. The following sections proceed on this basis.

### THE REVENUE- AND FINANCE-SHARING SYSTEM

Table 6.4 gives an overview of the share-rental system under various rental rates. The rental ratio is applied to yield net of certain deductions. The *agad* (literally, "immediately") is a small portion of the produce which the farm family harvests for its own consumption, before the general harvesting with the hired workers takes place. Higher rental rates are seen to be partially compensated by a larger *agad* privilege. The "deductible operating expenses" include payments in kind for harvesting and threshing and repayments to both landlord and tenant for some of the expenses incurred. An interest rate is implicit in these repayments to the extent that the repayment value differs from the original cost of the inputs that are being repaid. It is well known that these interest rates are rather high. For example, in the 1972 wet season, mean interest rates on loans obtained by Nueva Ecija rice farmers were

Table 6.3: Credit Positions of Rice Farmers by Tenure Group, Nueva Ecija, November 1972 (In pesos)

| | *Owners* | *Leaseholders* | *Share tenants* |
|---|---|---|---|
| *Mean loan obtained in crop year* | 939.96 | 730.12 | 654.08 |
| *1972/73 wet season, all sources*[a] | (N = 38) | (N = 50) | (N = 48) |
| *Mean outstanding debt as of November* | 2,396.84 | 859.36 | 990.83 |
| *1972, all sources*[b] | (N = 59) | (N = 61) | (N = 65) |

a. Excluding those who did not borrow during the season.
b. Excluding those with no outstanding debt.

*Source:* IPC Pilot Survey.

Table 6.4: Product- and Cost-sharing Practices under Different Rental Rates, Bulacan and Nueva Ecija, 1965
(Columns 2–11 in 44-kg. sacks of palay per ha.)

| Sample size | Rental rate (%) (1) | Yield (2) | Agad (3) | Deductible operating expenses (4) | Produce subject to sharing (5)=(2) −(3)−(4) | Landlord share (6)=(5) ×(1) | Landlord operating expenses (7) | Overseer payment (8) | Net return to landlord (9)=(6) −(7)−(8) | Tenant's share (10)=(5) −(6) | Tenant's share plus agad (11)=(10) +(3) |
|---|---|---|---|---|---|---|---|---|---|---|---|
| 11 | 55 | 59.4 | 2.0 | 12.0 | 45.5 | 25.0 | 3.6 | 0.9 | 20.4 | 20.4 | 22.4 |
| 91 | 50 | 46.3 | 0.5 | 5.4 | 39.4 | 19.7 | 3.1 | 0.5 | 16.2 | 19.7 | 20.2 |
| 6 | 45 | 59.3 | 1.8 | 6.7[a] | 50.7 | 22.8 | 3.0 | 0.4 | 20.3 | 27.9 | 29.6[a] |
| 2 | 40 | 60.9 | | 3.3[a] | 57.5 | 23.0 | 0.5 | | 22.5 | 34.5 | 34.5[a] |
| 11 | 30 | 35.9 | | 3.3 | 32.6 | 9.8 | | | 9.8 | 22.8 | 22.8 |
| 4 | 25 | 55.1 | | 0.4[a] | 54.6 | 13.6 | | | 13.6 | 42.0 | 41.0[a] |

a. In these cases, harvesting expenses were borne solely by the tenant.

Source: Bernal, "Role of Landlords," p. 57.

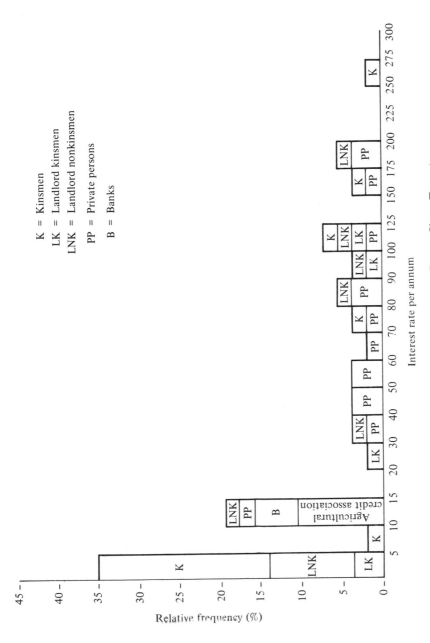

K = Kinsmen

LK = Landlord kinsmen

LNK = Landlord nonkinsmen

PP = Private persons

B = Banks

Fig. 6.2: Credit Sources and Interest Rates: Share Tenants

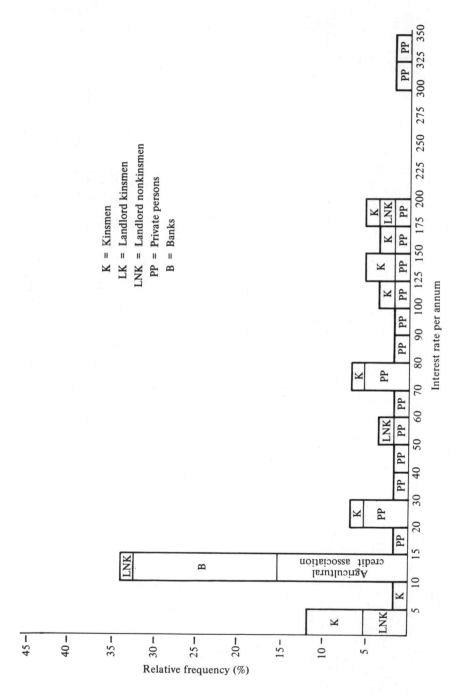

Fig. 6.3: Credit Sources and Interest Rates: Lessees

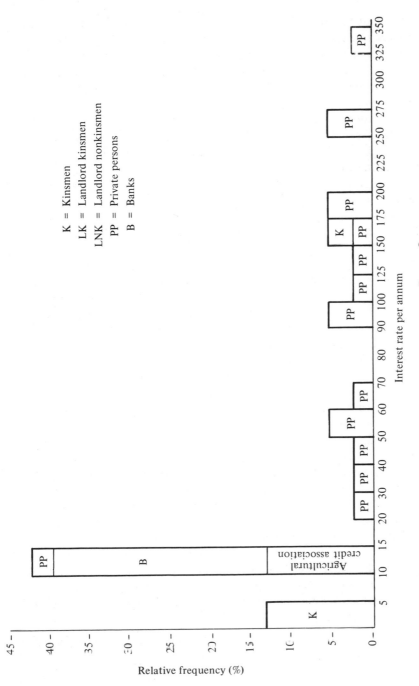

K   = Kinsmen
LK  = Landlord kinsmen
LNK = Landlord nonkinsmen
PP  = Private persons
B   = Banks

Fig. 6.4: Credit Sources and Interest Rates: Owners

61 percent for owner-operators, 54 percent for lessees, and 44 percent for share tenants.[8] The dispersion of interest rates is wide, however, ranging from 0 to over 200 percent. Relative frequency distributions for share tenants and lessees are charted in figures 6.2, 6.3, and 6.4.

As the rental rates decline, so do "deductible operating expenses" and "landlord operating expenses," suggesting that the magnitude of total landlord revenue declines with the rental rate. It should be noted that the last column, "tenants' share plus *agad*," is still gross of certain tenant expenses (weeding, land preparation, and the like) which are not among the tenant's portion of "deductible operating expenses."

In general, the data are not inconsistent with the thesis (1) that the tenancy contract consists of a *set* of parameters governing cost and revenue-sharing, and (2) that compensating changes can be made in parameters of the set such as not to disturb net incomes accruing to landlord and tenant. In column 9 of table 6.4, "net return to land-lord," the unusually low figure of 9.8 sacks is accounted for by the unusually low yield (35.9 sacks per hectare) attained by farmers in the category. In column 11, it is noted that the three largest figures are gross of harvesting expenses, whereas the three smaller figures are not.

A more detailed view of finance- and cost-sharing arrangements can be found in table 6.5. Some general points can be observed. First, in operations where the landlord shares in finance at all, the typical sharing rate is fifty-fifty. Part of the financial cost can be considered proportional to farm size (seeds, transplanting), part is proportional to production (all harvesting and postharvesting expenses), and part is "freely" variable (farm chemicals and fertilizer).

Second, in the majority of cases, the landlord's contribution is deductible from the gross before sharing of the product, that is, the contribution is in the nature of a loan rather than a bearing of the cost. An interest rate will be implicit in the agreed repayment rate (e.g., $X$ sacks of palay, or rice, per sack of fertilizer). The tenant's contribution is likewise deductible, at the same repayment rate as the landlord's, and therefore the tenant receives the same interest rate.

Third, where the tenant bears full financial responsibility his costs are *not* deducted from the gross before sharing of the product. The operations involved are mainly seedbed preparation, pulling of seedlings, land preparation, and weeding, which are labor-intensive and are functions primarily of the size of the farm.

8. De los Reyes, Mangahas, and Murray, "Land Reform and Agricultural Development."

Table 6.5: Frequency Distribution of Share Tenants Having a 50 Percent Rental Share System, by Landlord's Share in Financing, Nueva Ecija, November 1972 (N = 64)

| Operation | Landlord's share in financing (B) | | | | | | | | |
| --- | --- | --- | --- | --- | --- | --- | --- | --- | --- |
| | 100% | | 75% | | 50% | | 0% | | Not applicable[b] |
| | Deductible[a] | Non-deductible[a] | Deductible | Non-deductible | Deductible | Non-deductible | Deductible | Non-deductible | |
| Seed purchase | 12 | 2 | | | 43 | 2 | 2 | 3 | |
| Seedbed preparation | | | | | 1 | 5 | | 63 | |
| Pulling of seedlings | | | | | 10 | 2 | | 49 | |
| Land preparation | | | | | 3 | | | 59 | |
| Transplanting | 2 | 33[c] | | | 13 | 13 | 13 | 2 | 10 |
| Farm chemicals | | 1 | | | 21 | 17 | | 15 | 5 |
| Fertilizer | 1 | | | | 37 | 17 | | 3 | |
| Weeding | | 1 | | | 1 | 1 | | 62 | |
| Harvesting | | 1 | | | 27 | 4 | | 32[c] | |
| Threshing | | 1 | | | 54 | 7 | | 2 | |
| Hauling | | 1 | | | 15 | 32 | | 14 | 2 |
| Sack purchase | | | | | | 2 | | 3 | 59 |
| Irrigation | | | | | 8 | 10 | | 3 | 43 |

a. Deductibility means that the cost is subtracted from the product before the rental share is applied. Landlord and tenant contributions are equally deductible or nondeductible.

b. E.g., did not use fertilizer.

c. These cases of transplanting costs fully borne and nondeductible by landlords correspond to the cases of harvesting costs (on a wage basis) fully borne and nondeductible by tenants.

Source: IPC Pilot Survey.

MODELS OF THE TENANT AND THE LANDLORD

## The Share Tenant

Suppose the farmer's production function is

$$Q = Q(H, X, L_1), \tag{6.1}$$

where $H$ is the size of the farm in hectares, $X$ represents material inputs, and $L_1$ measures farmer labor applied on the farm. It will be convenient to assume that $Q$ is measured net of harvesting, threshing, and other similar costs which are paid directly from the produce and do not pose a financial or cost-sharing problem. Other production costs will be represented by $tH + PX$, where $t$ is the per hectare cost of seeds, land preparation, and the like, and $P$ is the price of $X$, both $t$ and $P$ being measured in units of the product.

Assume that the landlord finances a proportion, $b_1$, of $tH$ and another proportion, $b_2$, of $PX$. We have seen that $b_1$ refers to those farm operations or elements of $t$ that require cash payments; in order of magnitude, the range of $b_1$ is probably from 15 to 25 percent. On the other hand, $b_2$ is typically 50 percent. Further, assume that the entirety of the landlord's contribution is deductible from the gross, that is, it is merely a loan and is fully repayable, with some implicit interest, $i$. The total amount deductible is then $(1 + i)(b_1 tH + b_2 PX)$.

This is a somewhat monopolistic treatment of the credit open to a share tenant. Some share tenants borrow from relatives, some from private moneylenders, and a few from financial institutions. However, the great majority borrow from only one source,[9] and it may not be too unrealistic to assume that the share tenant cannot easily turn from one source to another in search of better credit terms.

On the tenant's part, we assume that his share in hectarage-linked expenses, $(1 - b_1)tH$, is not deductible from the gross. However, his

9. In Nueva Ecija, 85 percent of lessees and 87 percent of share tenants have only one source of credit. Share tenants' loans, distributed according to source, are: landlords, 47 percent; private moneylenders, 33 percent; kinsmen, 20 percent; and institutions, 14 percent. Lessees' loans are distributed as follows: landlords, 20 percent; private moneylenders, 45 percent; kinsmen, 19 percent; and institutions, 33 percent. See Romana P. de los Reyes and Frank Lynch, "Reluctant Rebels: Leasehold Converts in Nueva Ecija," *Philippine Sociological Review* 20, nos. 1–2 (1972): 35. In the 1972 wet season, the proportions of Nueva Ecija rice farmers who were totally self-financing were 27 percent for share tenants, 29 percent for lessees, and 42 percent for owner-operators (de los Reyes, Mangahas, and Murray, "Land Reform and Agricultural Development," table 12).

share in the cost of material inputs is deductible according to the same terms as the landlord, that is, $(1 + i)(1 - b_2)PX$ is deductible from the gross. Finally, assume that the tenant has an opportunity wage, such that his off-farm income is $w(L - L_1)$, where $w$ is the wage rate and $L$ is the total (fixed) amount of labor time the tenant has in the relevant period. We neglect any notion of variable leisure. If income from wage labor is considered less risky than that from farming, let $w$ be a wage rate incorporating an adjustment to compensate for the risk differential.

To summarize, the tenant's income from both farm and nonfarm activities is

$$C = (1 - r)[Q - (1 + i)(b_1 tH + b_2 PX) - (1 + i)(1 - b_2)PX]$$
$$- (1 - b_1)tH + i(1 - b_2)PX + w(L - L_1)$$
$$C = (1 - r)[Q - (1 + i)(b_1 tH + PX)] - (1 - b_1)tH$$
$$+ i(1 - b_2)PX + w(L - L_1), \qquad (6.2)$$

where $r$ is the landlord's rental share. We implicitly take tenant opportunity interest income to be zero. The set of parameters $r$, $i$, $b_1$, and $b_2$ constitutes the contractual arrangement between landlord and tenant. We assume that the tenant regards them as fixed and attempts to maximize $C$ with respect to $X$, $H$, and $L_1$.[10] His necessary conditions for an interior maximum are then

$$(1 - r)Q_X + i(1 - b_2)P = (1 - r)(1 + i)P \qquad (6.3)$$

$$(1 - r)Q_H = (1 - r)(1 + i)b_1 t + (1 - b_1)t \qquad (6.4)$$

$$(1 - r)Q_L = w, \qquad (6.5)$$

where $Q_X$, $Q_H$, and $Q_L$ are marginal products of material inputs, land, and labor respectively.[11]

Where his contribution is nondeductible (nonrepayable), the tenant's marginal revenue equals his revenue share times the marginal product. He earns an interest income on his share of the financing of material inputs due to its deductibility aspect. His marginal cost for material

10. It is not necessary that $C$ be positive. If it is negative, then there must be some automatic refinancing arrangement to allow the minimum consumption level. Cf. James N. Anderson, "Some Aspects of Land and Society in a Pangasinan Community," *Philippine Sociological Review* 10, nos. 1–2 (1962): 41–58.

11. Obtaining these conditions does not presuppose that the tenant is in complete control of $X$, $H$, and $L$. We may assume that he controls $L_1$, but of course he needs the landlord's consent regarding $H$ and, further, the landlord's financing regarding $X$. What these conditions do represent is a statement of the tenant's demands for $X$ and $H$ jointly with an offer of $L_1$ on his own part.

inputs depends on the rental rate and the rate of interest. However, his marginal cost of land depends also on the proportion he bears of the land-linked expenses.

In the common case $r = b_2$, then equation (6.3) reduces to $Q_X = P$, which is the same as the condition as it would appear to an owner-operator. Equation (6.4) indicates that the tenant has no intention of seeking to acquire land to the point where its marginal product becomes zero, since there are some expenses he bears that are distinctly related to farm size. According to equation (6.5), we expect the share tenant to spend more of his time on nonfarm activities than the owner-operator.

The effects of changes in $r$, $b_1$, $b_2$, and $i$ on the tenant's demands of $X$, $H$, and $L_1$ can be found in the usual way. Taking total differentials through equations (6.3) − (6.5) with respect to $r$ and solving, we find that the signs of $dX/dr$, $dH/dr$, and $dL_1/dr$ are indeterminate. Were it not for the interest income term in equation (6.3), $i(1 - b_2)P$, they would all be negative, on the assumption that the matrix of second derivatives of the production function is negative definite (see the appendix to this chapter). Since the interest income term cannot be very large in magnitude, we may judge that the effect of an increase in the rental share is indeed to lower the tenant's demands for material inputs, hectarage, and his own labor.

The signs of $dX/di$, $dH/di$, and $dL_1/di$ are likewise indeterminate. They are all negative, provided that $b_2 \geq r$, and, as we know that in general $r = b_2 = 1/2$, we expect that an increase in the interest rate will lower the tenant's demands for every input. The signs of $dX/db_1$, $dH/db_1$, and $dL/db_1$ are positive provided that $i/(1 + i) < r$. For $r = 1/2$, an increase in the proportion financed by the landlord of hectarage-linked expenses is generally encouraging to the tenant's demand for inputs, provided that the rate of interest is below 100 percent (per season), a condition that is usually satisfied.

We have the peculiar result that the signs of $dX/db_2$, $dH/db_2$, and $dL_1/db_2$ are all negative, i.e., the tenant will seek to apply less of every input when the landlord finances more of the material inputs. This result stems from the assumption that both the tenant's and the landlord's share in the cost of material inputs are fully deductible. The lower the tenant share, the less he stands to earn interest income through the repayment mechanism.

It may be readily observed that a number of features of the landlord–share tenant relationship are absent from the model. One such item is *agad*; also missing are any other fringe benefits received by the tenant which are not directly related to land, labor, or material inputs and which would not affect the marginal conditions expressed in equations (6.3)–(6.5) although they would affect the share tenant's total income. Such benefits include food loans (*rasyon*), gathering of fallen grains at the threshing floor, use of the farm land and home lot for secondary crops without charge, financing of some education of the tenants' children by the landlord, and assistance (which is a form of insurance) from the landlord in case of need for employment or in some emergency. There are, of course, some other duties and services expected of the tenant in return. The socioanthropological literature is replete with descriptions of the extra implications of the "patron-client" relationship which is the tenancy contract.[12]

### The Share Tenant's Landlord

We assume that the typical landlord has two sources of income, namely, his land and a fixed amount of financial wealth. He allocates his land entirely to share tenants but apportions his financial wealth partly to loans to his tenants and partly to some alternative carrying an opportunity earnings rate of $i_*$.

If income from the alternative use of funds is less risky, we assume that $i_*$ has been adjusted upward to compensate for the risk differential.[13] Assuming that his share tenants are more or less homogeneous, and that his land is likewise homogeneous,[14] the landlord divides his farm estate into equal-sized tenant farm plots and has identical contractual terms with each of his tenants. Then he maximizes his total income, which is

$$
G = \frac{E}{H} \left\{ \begin{array}{l} r\,[Q - (1 + i)\,(b_1 tH + PX)] + i\,(b_1 tH + b_2 PX) \\ + i_*\,[W - \dfrac{E}{H}\,(b_1 tH + b_2 PX)] \end{array} \right\}, \quad (6.6)
$$

where $E$ is the (given) size of his estate, and $W$ his (given) stock of

12. Cf. Marshall McLennan, "Land and Tenancy in the Central Luzon Plain," *Philippine Studies* 17, no. 4 (1969): 651–82.

13. The rate $i^*$ is the opportunity earnings rate adjusted to the riskiness of farm income. Suppose the risk-free institutional rate is 6 percent in six months (one season), and suppose the landlord expects to lose both interest and principal from a farming loan about once in ten seasons: he would then have to charge 18 percent in order to earn 6 percent on the average. Setting $10\% \,(0) + 90\% \,(1 + i^*) = 1.06$, then $i^* = 0.18$.

14. See Cheung, "Private Property Rights."

wealth. Maximizing $G$ is equivalent to maximizing $(G - i_*W)/E = N$, or income from land per hectare owned:

$$N = \{r [Q - (1 + i)(b_1tH + PX)] + (i - i_*) \\ (b_1tH + b_2PX)\}/H. \tag{6.7}$$

The landlord's function is to contribute land and finances to the farming operation. We assume, however, that he understands the relationship of finances to the underlying inputs and likewise understands the contribution of the inputs to the product, of which, after appropriate deductions, he is to receive a stipulated proportion. In particular, given the size of the farm allotted to a tenant, the landlord recognizes a one-to-one correspondence between his finances and the amount of material inputs to be applied, and the amount of finances offered is an expression of preference for a given amount of $X$ on the tenant farm. Indeed, the preference is often explicitly stated when a landlord contributes, say, fertilizer in kind. Maximizing $N$, therefore, with respect to $X$, $H$, and $L_1$ the landlord's necessary conditions are:

$$rQ_X + (i - i_*) b_2P = r (1 + i) P \tag{6.8}$$

$$rQ_H + (i - i_*) b_1t - r (1 + i) b_1t = N \tag{6.9}$$

$$rQ_L = 0. \tag{6.10}$$

The first condition equates the marginal return from a unit of $X$ to its marginal cost. The return has two sources: the marginal product of $X$ and the differential between the farm rate of interest and the opportunity rate of interest. (We assume the presence of capital market imperfections which maintain the differential.) Note that the income from the inherent differential induces the landlord to demand a greater amount of $X$ than, say, an owner-operator who had to borrow at interest rate $i$ in order to finance $X$. The left-hand side of equation (6.9) is the landlord's marginal net return per hectare allotted to one tenant if the allotment is fixed. To attain an optimum, the landlord must equate this to his net income per hectare of the entire estate, that is, if the net income is lower, he should raise the number of hectares per tenant by reducing the number of tenants. Finally, equation (6.10) states that the landlord's desire is that the tenant apply his labor to the farm up to the point of zero marginal product.

As in the case of the share tenant, we can consider the landlord in isolation and determine how he might respond to a change (dictated by the market) in one or another of the contractual parameters. The conclusions are as follows:

1. A reduction in the rental rate will lead to a reduction in his demand for $X$, in the farm size allotted per tenant, and in the amount of farm labor desired of the tenant, provided that the interest rate differential $(i - i_*)$ is not too large. (If the differential is large enough, he will attempt to obtain more of his income from the lending operation, where his advance is repaid before the share rental is applied, and less from the land rental per se.)

2. The effect of the interest rate is indeterminate. If $b_2 = r$, then the effect on $X$, $H$, and $L_1$ is nil; this serves as a first hypothesis. If $b_2 > r$, then there is a partial tendency for $X$ to increase but for $H$ to decrease; it is difficult to make a conclusion as to the general result when all three relations, equations (6.8)–(6.10), are taken into account.

3. The proportion of $b_1$ enters only condition (6.9). After the differentiation, we find that any change in $b_1$ will have no effect on the landlord's preferences regarding $X$, $H$, or $L_1$. Essentially this is due to the assumption that the size of the landlord's estate is fixed.

4. The effect of an increase in $b_2$ is to raise the landlord's demands for all inputs. By our assumptions, it simply implies a greater opportunity for the landlord to exploit the interest rate differential and to earn income from the lending operation.

## The Leaseholder

A leaseholder by definition pays a fixed rental of $R$ units of the product per hectare. We assume that the landlord may likewise share in the financing of the crop, charging a rate of interest. The interest rate and financing shares may differ, of course, from the share tenancy situation. Romana de los Reyes and Frank Lynch report, from the lessees' side: "Yet in one expectation (the sharing of farm expenses), lessees are much like the share tenants—they want the landlord to finance their farming." And from the landlords' side: "Contrary to the popular belief that landlord and lessees have no 'special relationship,' 61 percent of the landlord respondents who have lessees report that at least one of their lessees has asked to borrow money. Eight out of ten of the landlords so approached say that they have granted the loan, at least in part."[15]

15. De los Reyes and Lynch, "Reluctant Rebels," p. 19.

Given that the leaseholder likewise has an opportunity wage income, he will seek to maximize

$$
\begin{aligned}
D = Q &- RH - (1 + i)(b_1 tH + b_2 PX) - (1 - b_1) tH \\
&- (1 - b_2) PX + w(L - L_1) \\
D = Q &- (R + t) H - PX - i(b_1 tH + b_2 PX) + w(L - L_1)
\end{aligned}
\tag{6.11}
$$

with respect to $X$, $H$, and $L_1$. Since he has no specifically deductible expenses, he earns no implicit interest. (Clearly, there will be no change in the model if the financing is assumed to come from a nonlandlord.) His necessary conditions for a maximum are then as follows:

$$
Q_X = P(1 + ib_2)
\tag{6.12}
$$

$$
Q_H = R + t(1 + ib_1)
\tag{6.13}
$$

$$
Q_L = w
\tag{6.14}
$$

The total differentiation exercise indicates that the effects of $R$ and $i$ on $X$, $H$, and $L_1$ are all negative. (So also are the effects of $b_1$ and $b_2$, but this is somewhat artificial, since the leaseholder supposedly bears no interest cost on his own expenses.)

Comparing equations (6.12) and (6.3), we find after a little manipulation that, supposing $i$ and $b_2$ to be the same for leaseholder and share tenant, the share tenant's marginal product is equated to a lower marginal real cost than the leaseholder's; that is, other things being equal, the share tenant's demand for $X$ is greater. This holds regardless of the size of the rental share, $r$. If we compare equations (6.13) and (6.4), it is not clear to what extent a leaseholder's demand for land is different from a share tenant's, since the absolute value of $R$ is crucial to the comparison. Equations (6.14) and (6.5) suggest that, to a certain extent, at a given opportunity wage, the leaseholder will allocate more of his labor time to work on his own farm than the share tenant. However, if the systems described in (6.3)–(6.5) and (6.12)–(6.14) are compared, there is no clear indication of either the size or the direction of differences between a leaseholder and a share tenant with respect to the demands for material inputs, land, or own-labor.

The analysis is similar if the farmer is an "amortizing peasant," where the annual amortization per hectare is $R$.[16] The difference is

16. Presidential Decree No. 27 of October 1972 states that all share tenants and lessees are to be converted to amortizing owners who will pay 15 equal annual installments for land to be valued at 2.5 times the "normal" harvest, with interest of 6 percent per annum on remaining principal. Both land value and the amortization

that amortizations have a termination date. It would be interesting to bring in farmers' decisions regarding investments in farm improvements, and so on, all of which have been neglected here.

### The Leaseholder's Landlord

This type of landlord earns a total income of

$$\frac{E}{H}\left[RH + i\,(b_1tH + b_2PX)\right] + i^*\left[W - \frac{E}{H}\,(b_1tH + b_2PX)\right].$$

Clearly, the size of the individual leaseholder's farm will be of no importance to him. The landlord's finances will earn a constant marginal revenue in either farm lending or outside investing, and he will allocate as much revenue to his leaseholders as they will bear, if the interest rate differential is positive, or none at all if it is negative.[17] The analysis would, again, be similar for the amortization-receiving landlord, for the duration of the payment period.

### Bargaining between Share Landlord and Tenant

Given competition among landlords for tenants and among tenants for land and for financial resources, we may imagine demand or offer schedules represented by equations (6.3)–(6.5) and by (6.8)–(6.10), such that in the long run equilibrium contractual terms $r$, $b_1$, $b_2$, and $i$ are reached, consistent with the preferences and resources of both parties. Of course, when there are more parameters to the contract than inputs to be agreed upon, one expects many sets ($r$, $b_1$, $b_2$, $i$), characterized by compensating differences across parameters, each consistent with the equilibrium. Construction of a mathematical model

---

are thus stated in units of the product. The annual amortization implied is (intentionally) approximately one-fourth of the "normal" harvest, i.e., equal to the rental stipulated for land-reform lessees in R.A. 3844 (sec. 34), as amended by R.A. 6389 (sec. 5). See Jose Medina, Jr., "The Meaning and Intent of Presidential Decree No. 27," mimeographed (Paper presented at the Seminar-Workshop on Agrarian Reform, for College Instructors and Professors in the Bicol Region, Legaspi City, February 8, 1973).

17. On the determination of the distribution of contracts by tenure, there is some evidence that supports the "transactions cost" argument, though from the standpoint of the opportunity cost to the landlord. Lessee landlords have characteristics that would mark them as having higher opportunity costs, hence less time for supervision, than share landlords. The former are wealthier, have larger farms, which were acquired through inheritance rather than bought, have more tenants to oversee, are more involved in politics, more exposed to mass media, and take longer-distance trips. See de los Reyes and Lynch, "Reluctant Rebels," pp. 15–16.

representing the equilibrium process itself has not proved a simple task. At this point, some observations and judgments regarding equilibrium will be attempted.

First, we note that the demand schedules of both parties are dependent on the same underlying agricultural production function. This contrasts with the usual case, in which supply is based on production considerations whereas demand is based on consumption considerations. The theory would be simpler by far if the decision regarding a farm input could be made by one party with the complete acquiescence of the other. However, the theoretical implications of the simpler theory might be rather different and unrealistic. This is an important lesson to be drawn from the Bardhan-Srinivasan work.

Second, it would be more realistic to consider a contractual period that differs according to the input. Obviously, the amount of fertilizer to be applied can be decided afresh with every season; but it does not seem plausible for the farm size itself to be subject to modification as often as that. There is evidence, at least, that movement of tenants across landlords is rather infrequent.[18]

Shifts in various exogenous factors can be expected to upset the equilibrium. Land reform is a major factor of interest, the effect of which will depend on its conception and implementation. In the latter half of the sixties the strategy in the Philippines was to increase the proportion of leaseholders and decrease the proportion of share tenants. This, it was thought, would change the composition of the tenant group and hence the aggregate of the offers being made to landlords. At the same time, it would change the offers being made by landlords. The net effects are not yet clear. Published reports indicate that the most common share-rental rate has remained at fifty-fifty over the past fifteen years (see table 6.6). However, according to preliminary computations with Bureau of Agricultural Economics survey data, the mean ratio of rentals to *gross* output has been falling among share tenants: it was 40 percent in the 1969 wet season, 38 percent in the 1970 dry season, 35 percent in the 1970 wet season, and 31 percent in the 1971 dry season.

A suggestion of the recent state of equilibrium is also provided by a

18. Horst von Oppenfeld et al. reported that the average tenant had been operating the same farm for the past twelve years; see Horst von Oppenfeld, Judith von Oppenfeld, J. C. Sta. Iglesia, and Pedro R. Sandoval, "Farm Management, Land Use, and Tenancy in the Philippines," Central Experiment Station Bulletin no. 1 (Los Banos, 1957), p. 96.

Table 6.6: Relative Frequencies of Various Rental Shares, Philippines,
1956/55, 1965, and 1971 (In percents)

| Landlord's rental share | Philippines, 1954/55: 1,610 tenant farmers | Bulacan and Nueva Ecija, 1965: 112 landlords | Nueva Ecija, 1971: 32 share landlords |
|---|---|---|---|
| 25% | | 3% | |
| 30 | 2% | | |
| 33 | 4 | | |
| 35 | | 7 | |
| 40 | 5 | 3 | 3% |
| 45 | 4 | 3 | 19 |
| 50 | 76 | 72 | 67 |
| 55% | | 12 | |
| Other; n.a. | 9 | | 12 |
| Total | 100% | 100% | 100% |

Sources: Philippines, 1954/55: von Oppenfeld et al., "Farm Use, Land Use, and Tenancy," p. 99; Bulacan and Nueva Ecija, 1965: computed from data in Bernal, "Role of Landlords," p. 55; Nueva Ecija, 1971: de los Reyes and Lynch, "Reluctant Rebels," p. 16.

Table 6.7: Role Expectations of Landlords and Tenants,
Nueva Ecija, 1971

| Role expectations of ideal landlord | Average rank assigned | | | |
|---|---|---|---|---|
| | By share tenants | By share landlords | By lessees | By lessee landlords |
| Shares farm expenses | 1 | 4 | 2 | 1 |
| Provides fringe benefits | 2 | 1 | 7 | 3 |
| Extends credit | 3.5 | 3 | 6 | 6.5 |
| Is courteous or pleasant | 3.5 | 2 | 1 | 2 |
| Asks fair interest on loans | 5 | 6 | 5 | 5 |
| Has a good farming arrangement | 6 | 7.5 | 3 | 6.5 |
| Is solicitous or generally helpful | 7 | 7.5 | 8 | 8 |
| Is law abiding | 8 | 9 | 4 | 9 |
| Is paternalistic | | 5 | | 4 |

| Role expectations of ideal tenant | Average rank assigned | | | |
|---|---|---|---|---|
| | By share tenants | By share landlords | By lessees | By lessee landlords |
| Is industrious | 1 | 1 | 2 | 2 |
| Is honest, especially in complying with sharing agreement | 2 | 2 | 1 | 1 |
| Is courteous to superiors | 3 | 6 | 4 | 6 |
| Is a good subordinate | 4 | 5 | 6 | 5 |
| Has technical know-how | 5 | 3 | 3 | 3.5 |
| Is a good farmer in general | 6 | 4 | 5 | 3.5 |
| Is courteous to others in general | 7 | 7 | 7 | 7 |

Source: de los Reyes and Lynch, "Reluctant Rebels," tables 6, 7, 10, 11, and 12.

view of the "role expectations" tenants and landlords have both for themselves and for each other (see table 6.7). Congruence between rankings of role expectations would suggest an equilibrium situation. By this criterion, there appears to have been a disequilibrium situation among leaseholders, in contrast to an equilibrium situation among share tenants, in Nueva Ecija in 1971.[19]

## APPENDIX

Differentiating equations (6.3)–(6.5) with respect to $r$ gives

$$- Q_X + (1-r) Q_{XX} X_r + Q_{XH} H_r + Q_{XL} L_{1r} = - (1 + i) P$$
$$- Q_H + (1-r) Q_{HX} X_r + Q_{HH} H_r + Q_{HL} L_{1r} = - (1 + i) b_1 t$$
$$- Q_L + (1-r) Q_{LX} X_r + Q_{LH} H_r + Q_{LL} L_{1r} = 0,$$

where $X_r = dX/dr$, $H_r = dH/dr$, $L_{1r} = dL/dr$, and $Q_{ij} = dQ_i/dj$ for $i$, $j = X, H, L_1$. These three equations become

$$[q] \begin{bmatrix} X_r \\ H_r \\ L_{1r} \end{bmatrix} = \frac{1}{1-r} \begin{bmatrix} Q_X - (1 + i) P \\ Q_H - (1 + i) bt \\ Q_L \end{bmatrix} = \frac{1}{1-r} \begin{bmatrix} -\dfrac{i(1 - b_2) P}{1 - r} \\ \dfrac{(1 - b_1) t}{1 - r} \\ \dfrac{w}{1 - r} \end{bmatrix}$$

where $[q]$ is the matrix of second derivatives of the production function. For (6.3) – (6.5) to apply to a maximum, it is necessary that $[q]$ be negative definite, with negative determinant. We assume also that all cross-derivatives are positive (marginal products always rise as more of a different input is applied). Then

$$\det [q] \cdot X_r = - \frac{i(1 - b_2) P}{(1 - r)^2} \begin{vmatrix} Q_{HH} & Q_{HL} \\ Q_{LH} & Q_{LL} \end{vmatrix} - \frac{(1 - b_1) t}{(1 - r)^2} \begin{vmatrix} Q_{XH} & Q_{XL} \\ Q_{LH} & Q_{LL} \end{vmatrix}$$
$$+ \frac{w}{(1 - r)^2} \begin{vmatrix} Q_{XH} & Q_{XL} \\ Q_{HH} & Q_{HL} \end{vmatrix}.$$

The signs of the three right-hand side determinants are positive, negative, and positive, respectively. Hence $X_r$ is negative provided that $i(1 - b_2)P$ is small enough. Similarly, we obtain:

19. Cf. de los Reyes and Lynch, "Reluctant Rebels."

$$\det [q] \cdot H_r = \frac{i(1-b_2)P}{(1-r)^2} \begin{vmatrix} Q_{HX} & Q_{HL} \\ Q_{LX} & Q_{LL} \end{vmatrix} + \frac{(1-b_1)t}{(1-r)^2} \begin{vmatrix} Q_{XX} & Q_{XL} \\ Q_{LX} & Q_{LL} \end{vmatrix}$$
$$- \frac{w}{(1-r)^2} \begin{vmatrix} Q_{XX} & Q_{XL} \\ Q_{HX} & Q_{HL} \end{vmatrix}$$

$$\det [q] \cdot L_{1r} = - \frac{i(1-b_2)P}{(1-r)^2} \begin{vmatrix} Q_{HX} & Q_{HH} \\ Q_{LX} & Q_{LH} \end{vmatrix} - \frac{(1-b_1)t}{(1-r)^2} \begin{vmatrix} Q_{XX} & Q_{XH} \\ Q_{LX} & Q_{LH} \end{vmatrix}$$
$$+ \frac{w}{(1-r)^2} \begin{vmatrix} Q_{XX} & Q_{XH} \\ Q_{HX} & Q_{HH} \end{vmatrix}.$$

Writing $X_i = dX/di$, $H_i = dH/di$, $L_{11} = dL/di$, we have:

$$\det [q] \cdot X_i - \frac{b_2 - r}{1-r} P \begin{vmatrix} Q_{HH} & Q_{HL} \\ Q_{LH} & Q_{LL} \end{vmatrix} - b_1 t \begin{vmatrix} Q_{XH} & Q_{XL} \\ Q_{LH} & Q_{LL} \end{vmatrix}$$

$$\det [q] \cdot H_i = - \frac{b_2 - r}{1-r} P \begin{vmatrix} Q_{HX} & Q_{HL} \\ Q_{LX} & Q_{LL} \end{vmatrix} + b_1 t \begin{vmatrix} Q_{XX} & Q_{XL} \\ Q_{LX} & Q_{LL} \end{vmatrix}$$

$$\det [q] \cdot L_{1i} = \frac{b_2 - r}{1-r} P \begin{vmatrix} Q_{HX} & Q_{HH} \\ Q_{LX} & Q_{LH} \end{vmatrix} - b_1 t \begin{vmatrix} Q_{XX} & Q_{XH} \\ Q_{LX} & Q_{LH} \end{vmatrix}.$$

Writing $X_{b_1} = dX/db_1$, $H_{b_1} = dH/db_1$ and $L_{1b_1} = dL_1/db_1$, we have:

$$\det [q] \cdot X_{b_1} = - \left( 1 + i - \frac{1}{1-r} \right) t \begin{vmatrix} Q_{XH} & Q_{XL} \\ Q_{LH} & Q_{XL} \end{vmatrix}$$

$$\det [q] \cdot H_{b_1} = \left( 1 + i - \frac{1}{1-r} \right) t \begin{vmatrix} Q_{XX} & Q_{XL} \\ Q_{LX} & Q_{LL} \end{vmatrix}$$

$$\det [q] \cdot L_{1b_1} = - \left( 1 + i - \frac{1}{1-r} \right) t \begin{vmatrix} Q_{XX} & Q_{XH} \\ Q_{LX} & Q_{LH} \end{vmatrix}.$$

Writing $X_{b_2} = dX/db_2$, $H_{b_2} = dH/db_2$ and $L_{1b_2} = dL_1/db_2$, we have:

$$\det [q] \cdot X_{b_2} = \frac{iP}{1-r} \begin{vmatrix} Q_{HH} & Q_{HL} \\ Q_{LH} & Q_{LL} \end{vmatrix}$$

$$\det [q] \cdot H_{b_2} = - \frac{iP}{1-r} \begin{vmatrix} Q_{HX} & Q_{HL} \\ Q_{LX} & Q_{LL} \end{vmatrix}$$

$$\det [q] \cdot L_{1b_2} = \frac{iP}{1-r} \begin{vmatrix} Q_{HX} & Q_{HH} \\ Q_{LX} & Q_{LH} \end{vmatrix}.$$

PART III: GENERATING AND DIFFUSING NEW
AGRICULTURAL TECHNOLOGY

# 7

## Technology Transfer, Institutional Transfer, and Induced Technical and Institutional Change in Agricultural Development

VERNON W. RUTTAN

### PHASES OF TECHNOLOGY TRANSFER

The international diffusion of agricultural technology is not new. The classical studies by Carl O. Sauer and N. I. Vavilov, as well as more recent studies of agricultural origins and dispersals, indicate that the international and intercontinental diffusion of cultivated plants, domestic animals, hand tools, and husbandry practices was a major source of productivity growth in prehistory and in the classical civilizations.[1] The transfer of crops from the new continents to Europe after

The research on which this paper is based was supported by grants to the University of Minnesota Economic Development Center from the U.S. Agency for International Development (AID/csd-2815) and by the Rockefeller Foundation. The author is indebted to the members of the UM Trade and Development Workshop for helpful criticism of an earlier draft of this paper. Suggestions by Barbara Miller, Joseph Fitzharris, John Sanders, and Paul Schultz have been particularly helpful.

1. See Carl O. Sauer, *Agricultural Origins and Dispersals: The Domestication of Animals and Foodstuffs,* 2d ed. (Cambridge: Massachusetts Institute of Technology Press, 1969), pp. 113–34; N. I. Vavilov, *The Origin, Variation, Immunity, and Breeding of Cultivated Plants,* trans. from the Russian by K. Starr Chester, in *Chronica Botanica* 13, nos. 1–6 (1949–50). See also David R. Harris, "New Light on Plant Domestication and the Origins of Agriculture: A Review," *Geographical Review* 57 (1967): 90–107; Folke Dovring, "The Transformation of European Agriculture," in *The Cambridge Economic History of Europe,* vol. 6, *The Industrial Revolution and After,* Pt. 2, ed. H. J. Habakkuk and M. Postan (Cambridge: at the University Press, 1966), pp. 604–72; Ping-Ti Ho, "Early-Ripening Rice in Chinese History," *Economic History Review* 9, ser. 2 (1956): 100–18.

Table 7.1: Estimated Area Planted in High-Yielding Varieties (HYV) of Rice and Wheat in West, South, and Southeast Asia
(In thousands of acres)

| Country | Rice | | | | | Wheat | | | | |
|---|---|---|---|---|---|---|---|---|---|---|
| | 1966/67 | 1967/68 | 1968/69 | 1969/70 | 1970/71 | 1966/67 | 1967/68 | 1968/69 | 1969/70 | 1970/71 |
| Iran | ..[a] | ... | ... | ... | ... | | | 25 | 222 | 312 |
| Iraq | ... | ... | ... | ... | ... | | 16 | 103 | 482 | 309 |
| Turkey | ... | ... | ... | ... | ... | 1 | 420 | 1,444 | 1,343 | 1,184 |
| Afghanistan | ... | ... | ... | ... | ... | 5 | 54 | 302 | 361 | 574 |
| India | 2,195 | 4,408 | 6,625 | 10,729 | 13,593 | 1,270 | 7,270 | 11,844 | 12,133 | 14,559 |
| Nepal | | | 105 | 123 | 168 | 16 | 61 | 133 | 187 | 243 |
| Pakistan (East) | 1 | 166 | 382 | 652 | 1,137 | | | 20 | 22 | 24 |
| Pakistan (West) | | 10 | 761 | 1,239 | 1,548 | 250 | 2,365 | 5,900 | 6,626 | 7,288 |
| Burma | | 8 | 412 | 356 | 496 | ... | ... | ... | ... | ... |
| Ceylon | | | 17 | 65 | 73 | ... | ... | ... | ... | ... |
| Indonesia | | | 488 | 1,854 | 2,303 | ... | ... | ... | ... | ... |
| Korea | | | | | 7 | ... | ... | ... | ... | ... |
| Laos | 1 | 3 | 5 | 5 | 133 | ... | ... | ... | ... | ... |
| Malaysia | 104 | 157 | 225 | 238 | 327 | ... | ... | ... | ... | ... |
| Philippines | 204 | 1,733 | 2,500 | 3,346 | 3,868 | ... | ... | ... | ... | ... |
| Thailand | | | | | 400 | ... | ... | ... | ... | ... |
| Vietnam | | 1 | 100 | 498 | 1,240 | ... | ... | ... | ... | ... |
| Total | 2,505 | 6,486 | 11,620 | 19,105 | 25,293 | 1,542 | 10,186 | 19,771 | 21,376 | 24,493 |

a. Not applicable.

Source: Dana G. Dalrymple, Imports and Plantings of High-Yielding Varieties of Wheat and Rice in the Less Developed Nations, Foreign Economic Development Service Report no. 14 (Washington, D.C.: U.S. Department of Agriculture, in cooperation with the Agency for International Development, 1972), pp. 48, 49.

the discovery of America had a dramatic impact on European agriculture. The technological bases for the staple exports of many developing countries—cocoa in West Africa and rubber in Southeast Asia, for example—developed as a result of the international diffusion of crop varieties.

Before agricultural research and extension were institutionalized, this diffusion took place as a by-product of travel, exploration, and communication undertaken primarily for other purposes. Over a long gestation period—often lasting several decades and occasionally even centuries—exotic plants, animals, equipment, and husbandry techniques were gradually introduced and adapted to local conditions. In the nineteenth century the international diffusion process became more highly institutionalized. National governments established agencies to seek out and introduce exotic crop varieties and animal breeds deliberately.[2] Colonial governments and the great trading companies operating under their protection sought to introduce crops with export potential into new areas of cultivation. These efforts have, over time, had a substantial impact on the location of staple production and on international trading patterns in crops and animal products.

The most dramatic example of agricultural technology transfer during the last several decades has been the development and diffusion of new high-yielding varieties of rice, wheat, and maize in the tropics (table 7.1). This process involved more than the diffusion of crop varieties and the modification of husbandry practices. It involved a transfer of the capacity to invent a new, location-specific biological technology. It further involved the transfer of scientific ideas, the migration of individual scientists, and the establishment of relatively sophisticated research facilities.[3]

2. Nelson Klose, *America's Crop Heritage: The History of Foreign Plant Introduction by the Federal Government* (Ames: Iowa State College Press, 1950); also Wayne D. Rasmussen, "Diplomats and Plant Collectors: The South American Commission, 1817–1818," *Agricultural History* 29 (1955): 22–31; and Knowles A. Ryerson, "History and Significance of Foreign Plant Introduction Work of the United States Department of Agriculture," *Agricultural History* 7 (1933): 110–28.

3. E. C. Stakman, Richard Bradfield, and P. C. Mangelsdorf, *Campaigns against Hunger* (Cambridge: Belknap Press, 1967). At a more general level, this comment by Tom Burns is relevant: "The mechanism of technological transfer is one of agents, not agencies; of the movement of people among establishments, rather than of the routing of information through communication system" (Tom Burns, "Models, Images, and Myths," in *Factors in the Transfer of Technology,* ed. William H. Gruber and Donald G. Marquis [Cambridge: MIT Press, 1969], p. 12). See also Warren C. Scoville, "Minority Migrations and the Diffusion of Technology," *Journal of Economic History* 11 (1951): 347–60; Fritz E. Redlich, "Ideas—Their Migration in

## A TECHNOLOGY-TRANSFER TYPOLOGY[4]

It is analytically useful to distinguish three phases or levels of agricultural technology transfer: (1) materials transfer, (2) design transfer, and (3) capacity transfer.

*Material transfer* is characterized by the simple transfer or importation of new materials such as seeds, plants, animals, and machines, and the husbandry or management practices associated with these materials. Local adaptation through systematic selection of superior individuals or populations and the adaptation of husbandry and management practices is not highly institutionalized. The "naturalization" of plants and animals tends to occur primarily as a result of trial and error by farmers. The analogy in industrial technology transfer is the "turn key" plant.

*Design transfer* is characterized by the transfer of information in the form of blueprints, formulas, journals and books, and related software. During this process exotic plant materials, animal-breeding stock, or prototype machines may be imported for testing purposes, to obtain genetic materials, or in order to copy their designs. New plants and animals are subjected to systematic testing, propagation, and selection. Imported machines are tested and designs modified to adapt them to local ecological conditions or to different tasks.

*Capacity transfer* occurs primarily through the transfer of scientific and technical knowledge and capacity. The objective is to institutionalize local capacity for invention and innovation of a continuous stream of locally adapted technology. Increasingly, plant and animal varieties are developed locally to adapt them to local ecological conditions. Machine designs become less dependent on prototypes developed elsewhere. As local agricultural science and engineering capacity is strengthened, both biological and mechanical technologies are invented that are precisely adapted to the ecological conditions and factor endowments of the local economy.

An important element in the process of international capacity trans-

Space and Transmittal Over Time," *Kyklos* 6 (1953): 301–22; Robert Solo, "The Capacity to Assimilate an Advanced Technology," *American Economic Review* 56, papers and proceedings (1966): 91–97; Derek J. de S. Price, "The Structures of Publication in Science and Technology," in Gruber and Marquis, eds., *Factors in the Transfer of Technology*, pp. 91–104.

4. This typology was first outlined in Yujiro Hayami and Vernon W. Ruttan, *Agricultural Development: An International Perspective* (Baltimore: Johns Hopkins Press, 1971), pp. 174–82.

fer is the migration of individual scientists and the building of institutions with advanced research, development, and training capacity. In spite of advances in communications, diffusion of the concepts and crafts of agricultural science and engineering, and of science and culture generally, depends heavily on extended personal contact and association. The development of the new international agricultural institutes (CYMMIT, IRRI, CIAT, IITA, ICRESAT) and much of the institution-building effort of the international aid agencies can be viewed, and evaluated, in relation to the objective of speeding entrance of the less developed countries (LDCs) into the capacity transfer stage.

### Diffusion and Development of Sugar Cane Varieties[5]

The three phases of international transfer of agricultural technology outlined above can be illustrated by the history of the diffusion and development of sugar cane varieties (cultivars).

*Material transfer*

In nature the cane plant reproduces only asexually. The initial diffusion of sugar cane was based on the diffusion of planting materials (clones). Until the late 1700s commercial production was based entirely on two closely related species indigenous to India (*Saccharum sinense* and *S. barberi*). Sugar cane was cultivated in India as early as 400 B.C. Cane and the art of sugar making spread from India to China, Arabia, and the Mediterranean region very early. Sugar cane was introduced in Madeira and the Azores shortly after 1400. Columbus brought it to the New World on his second voyage. During the seventeenth century the Indian varieties were gradually displaced by a higher-yielding, thicker-stemmed variety from Southeast Asia (*S. officinarum*), which was the dominant commercial variety throughout the nineteenth century.

*Design transfer*

Procedures for the sexual reproduction of sugar cane were discovered independently in Java in 1887 and Barbados in 1888. It was discovered

---

5. This section is based on material developed by R. E. Evenson and reported in R. E. Evenson, J. P. Houck, Jr., and V. W. Ruttan, "Technical Change and Agricultural Trade: Three Examples—Sugar Cane, Bananas, and Rice," in *The Technology Factor in International Trade,* ed. Raymond Vernon (New York: Columbia University Press, 1970), pp. 415–80. See also J. J. Ochse, M. J. Soule, Jr., M. J. Dijkman, and C. Wehlburg, *Tropical and Sub-Tropical Agriculture,* 2 vols. (New York: Macmillan, 1961), pp. 1197–251.

that the cane plant can be induced to flower and produce seedlings under appropriate temperature and light control. Each new seedling produced by sexual reproduction becomes a potential new variety, since it can be reproduced asexually. The Java station (Proefstation Oost Java) was the first to develop a new variety of commercial significance. The relatively simple breeding methodology diffused rapidly. Important commercial varieties were developed at experiment stations in Hawaii, Barbados, India, and elsewhere. The varieties developed at the Java and Coimbatore (India) stations became particularly important sources of genetic materials throughout the world.

*Capacity transfer*

Breeding for disease resistance became a dominant concern, as many of the new varieties were found to be susceptible to local diseases and pests. In this effort the Java station played a leading role. In 1921 a new disease-resistant variety (P.O.J. 2878) was developed by crossing two species, a 118-chromosome, disease-resistant, thin-stemmed, wild cane (*S. spontaneum*) and a thick-stemmed, 80-chromosome cane (*S. officinarum*). Through a series of crosses and backcrosses, new interspecific hybrids were developed that incorporated the hardiness and disease resistance of the noncommercial species. Later the Coimbatore station developed a series of trihybrid canes by introducing a third species (*S. barberi*). This resulted in new varieties adapted specifically to the local climate, soil, and disease conditions.

The introduction of the new Java and Coimbatore interspecific hybrids was followed by rapid international transfer of the superior Java and Coimbatore genetic materials and breeding methods. It also set the stage for the development of more sophisticated breeding and agronomic research capacity directed toward the development of varieties and the design of crop-management practices suited to the specific soil, climate, disease, and related ecological characteristics of each major producing region. Genetic materials and research methods move freely and rapidly among regions. But almost every important sugar-cane–producing country now has the capacity to produce locally adapted varieties.

Where does the new "green revolution" cereals technology fit into the three-phase typology outlined above? In my judgment wheat, rice, and maize are just now entering the capacity transfer stage in most developing countries. The establishment of the new international research institutes has been instrumental in creating and transmitting new approaches to the design of higher-yielding grain varieties in the tropics.

They also represent an initial step in capacity transfer. It seems apparent that continuation of the momentum of the green revolution will require the development of experiment station capacity in each major ecological region for each crop of economic significance in the region.

### TECHNOLOGY TRANSFER AND INNOVATION

There are two bodies of literature on which we can draw in attempting to understand the phases of technology diffusion and transfer described in the previous section. There are several traditions of research on the diffusion of technical change—in the disciplines of anthropology, geography, sociology, and economics. There is also a more recent body of literature on induced innovation.

### Technology Transfer

There are substantial differences among the various disciplines on the diffusion of technical change.[6] The main focus of the work in anthropology, sociology, and geography has been on the impact of communication (or interaction) and of sociocultural resistance to innovation on diffusion over time and across space. The models of economists have focused primarily on how economic variables such as the profitability of innovation and the asset position of firms influence the rate of diffusion.[7] There has also emerged, in the recent literature, a concern with the feedback effects of technology diffusion on trade relationships.[8]

6. For a review of these several traditions see Elihu Katz, Herbert Hamilton, and Martin L. Levin, "Traditions of Research on the Diffusion of Innovation," *American Sociological Review* 28 (1963): 237–52; Everett M. Rogers, *Diffusion of Innovations* (New York: The Free Press of Glencoe, 1962); Allan Pred, "Postscript," in Torsten Hägerstrand, *Innovation Diffusion as a Spatial Process* (Chicago: University of Chicago Press, 1967), pp. 299–324; Everett M. Rogers, with F. Floyd Shoemaker, *Communication of Innovations: A Cross Cultural Approach,* 2d ed. (New York: The Free Press, 1971), pp. 44–97.

7. Zvi Griliches, "'Hybrid Corn': An Exploration in the Economics of Technological Change," *Economica* 25 (1957): 501–22; "Hybrid Corn and the Economics of Innovation," *Science* 132 (1960): 275–80; Edwin Mansfield, "Technical Change and the Rate of Imitation," *Economica* 29 (1961): 741–66; "The Speed of Response of Firms to New Techniques," *Quarterly Journal of Economics* 77 (1963): 291–311; "Size of Firm, Market Structure, and Innovation," *Journal of Political Economy* 71 (1963): 556–76; "Intrafirm Rates of Diffusion of an Innovation," *Review of Economics and Statistics* 45 (1963): 348–59; Edwin Mansfield, *The Economics of Technological Change* (New York: Norton, 1968); Lawrence Z. Brown, *Diffusion Processes and Location: A Conceptual Framework and Bibliography* (Philadelphia: Regional Science Research Institute, 1968).

8. Much of this work stems from the seminal article by Raymond Vernon, "International Investment and International Trade in the Product Cycle," *Quarterly*

In general, the diffusion literature provides more insight into the processes of material and design transfer than into the processes leading to capacity transfer. This is primarily because the attributes of the technology, the characteristics of the adopters, and the economic and social organization pattern are typically taken as given.[9] The typical assumptions of commercial availability and of direct transferability of the technology represent a critical limitation in adopting the models used in most diffusion research to understand the international diffusion of technology in situations where variations in ecological conditions and factor endowments severely restrict the diffusion or direct transfer of agricultural technology. An effective understanding of the process of capacity transfer must also include a perception of the process by which technical innovation is induced along an efficient path consistent with relative resource endowments and factor prices.

The study by Zvi Griliches of the diffusion of hybrid corn represents a rare attempt to incorporate the process of local adaptation into a diffusion model.[10] His study is relevant because the diffusion of hybrid

---

*Journal of Economics* 80 (1966): 190–207. See also the several articles in *The Technology Factor in International Trade,* ed. Raymond Vernon (New York: Columbia University Press, 1970). For a case study of the trade impact of diffusion of agricultural technology, see Yujiro Hayami and V. W. Ruttan, "Korean Rice, Taiwan Rice, and Japanese Agricultural Stagnation: An Economic Consequence of Colonialism," *Quarterly Journal of Economics* 84 (1970): 562–89.

9. This limitation has been of concern to some of the leaders in the field of diffusion research. Hägerstrand, in summarizing his work, points out: "In the models attention was directed to the processes of change, to how the distribution of $g_n$ generates the distribution of $g_{n+1}$. The location of the starting point of the diffusion process was stated among the assumptions. However, we observe that when agricultural indicators and agricultural elements are involved, the same small areas within the region seem repeatedly to be the starting points for new innovation. . . . The origin of such centers is a problem in itself" (Hägerstrand, *Innovation Diffusion*, p. 293).

10. Griliches, "Hybrid Corn." The Griliches study is also of interest because subsequent discussions helped to clarify the role of economic and sociocultural factors in the diffusion process. See Lowell Brandner and Murray A. Straus, "Congruence versus Profitability in the Diffusion of Hybrid Sorghum," *Rural Sociology* 24 (1959): 381–83; Zvi Griliches, "Congruence versus Profitability: A False Dichotomy," *Rural Sociology* 25 (1960): 354–56; A. Eugene Havens and Everett M. Rogers, "Adoption of Hybrid Corn: Profitability and the Interaction Effect," *Rural Sociology* 26 (1961): 109–14; Zvi Griliches, "Profitability versus Interaction: Another False Dichotomy," *Rural Sociology* 27 (1962): 327–30; Everett M. Rogers and A. Eugene Havens, "Rejoinder to Griliches' 'Another False Dichotomy,'" *Rural Sociology* 27 (1962): 330–32; Jarvis M. Babcock, "Adoption of Hybrid Corn: A Comment," *Rural Sociology* 27 (1962): 332–38; Gerald E. Klonglan and E. Walter Coward, Jr., "The Concept of Symbolic Adoption: A Suggested Interpretation," *Rural Sociology* 35 (1970): 77–83; Kenneth J. Arrow, "Classificatory Notes on the

corn among geographic areas, through the development of locally adapted varieties, is similar to my view of the process of international technology transfer in agriculture. He writes:

> Hybrid corn was the invention of a method of inventing, a method of breeding superior corn for specific locations. It was not a single invention immediately available everywhere. The actual breeding of adaptable hybrids had to be done separately for each area. Hence, besides the differences in the rate of adoption of hybrids by farmers . . . we have also to explain the lag in the development of adaptable hybrids for specific areas.[11]

The procedure employed by Griliches was to summarize the diffusion path by fitting an *S*-shaped logistic trend function to data on the percentage of corn area planted with hybrid seed in each maturity area. The logistic trend function is described by three parameters—an origin, a slope, and a ceiling. Griliches interpreted his results as indicating that differences among regions in both the rate (slope) and the level (ceiling) of acceptance are functions of the profitability of a shift from open-pollinated to hybrid corn. Variations in these two parameters among regions are thus explained in terms of farmers' profit-seeking behavior.

What makes the Griliches study particularly relevant to the problem of international technology transfer is that he incorporated into his model the behavior of public research institutions and private agricultural supply firms which make locally adapted hybrid seeds available to farmers. He attempted to explain variations in the date of origin, or of commercial availability, of hybrid corn by the size and density of the hybrid seed market, estimated from the size and density of corn production.

From this analysis Griliches drew the conclusion that the efforts of both the agricultural experiment stations and the commercial seed companies were guided by the expected return to research, development, and marketing costs. The particular merit of this model is that it incorporates the mechanism of local adaptation into the process of interregional transfer of agricultural technology. This mechanism is

Production and Transmission of Technological Knowledge," *American Economic Review* 59 (1969): 29–35. Arrow points out that "the economists are studying the demand for information by potential innovators and sociologists the problems in the supply of communication channels" (p. 293).

11. Griliches, "Hybrid Corn," *Economica*, p. 502.

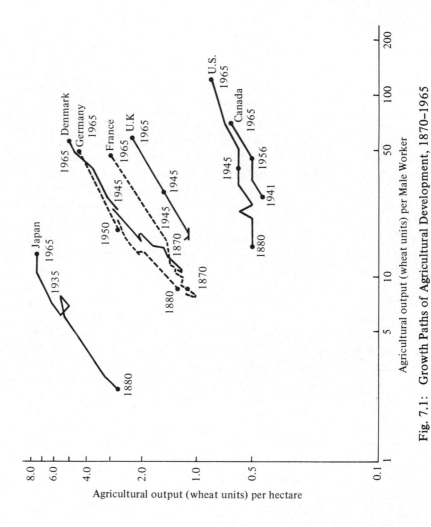

**Fig. 7.1: Growth Paths of Agricultural Development, 1870–1965**

based on the behavior of public research institutions and private agricultural supply firms. Modification of the model is needed, however, in applying it to the study of international technology transfer.[12]

## Induced Technical Change

Within the last decade the theoretical and empirical implications of relative resource endowments and factor prices on the "choice of technology" and on the direction of technical effort has undergone an extensive reevaluation.[13] The effect of the theoretical discussion has been a rehabilitation of the Hicksian view that relative factor prices affect not only the choice of existing technology but also the direction of technical effort and hence the direction of factor bias in the new production functions that become available to producers over time and among areas.[14]

The effect of empirical investigation has been to confirm that the alternative paths of technical change followed by countries with such diverse resource endowments as Japan, Denmark, and the United States (see figure 7.1) have been a response to relative factor prices which in turn represented reasonably accurate indicators of relative factor

12. In a recent article Robert E. Evenson and Yoav Kislev have succeeded in partitioning the contribution of international diffusion and indigenous research to the growth of yield of wheat and maize ("Research and Productivity in Wheat and Maize," *Journal of Political Economy* 81 [1973]: 1309–29).

13. In the 1950s and early 1960s discussion focused primarily on the "choice of technology" problem. See Amartya K. Sen, "The Choice of Agricultural Techniques in Underdeveloped Countries," *Economic Development and Cultural Change* 7 (1959): 279–85; idem, *Choice of Techniques: An Aspect of Planned Economic Development* (London: Basil Blackwell, 1960); W. E. G. Salter, *Productivity and Technical Change* (London: Cambridge University Press, 1960).

14. There are two major variants of the theory of induced innovation. In the Hicks-Ahmad version non-neutrality is induced by changes in relative factor prices. In the Kennedy-Samuelson version non-neutrality is induced by shifts in factor shares. The basic references are: J. R. Hicks, *The Theory of Wages* (London: Macmillan, 1932), pp. 124–25; Syed Ahmad, "On the Theory of Induced Invention," *Economic Journal* 76 (1966): 344–57; Charles Kennedy, "Induced Bias in Innovation and the Theory of Distribution," *Economic Journal* 74 (1964): 541–47; Paul A. Samuelson, "A Theory of Induced Innovation along Kennedy-Weiszäcker Lines," *Review of Economics and Statistics* 47 (1965): 343–65. These papers were followed by an extended discussion among Ahmad, Fellner, Kennedy, and Samuelson. For an excellent review and assessment of this literature, see Hans P. Binswanger, "Induced Innovation: A Critical Review of the Theory and Conclusions from New Evidence," University of Minnesota Department of Agricultural and Applied Economics Staff Paper p72–29 (St. Paul, Minnesota, December 1972).

endowments.[15] Studies in LDCs have demonstrated that institutionally determined biases in relative factor prices have induced patterns of technical change that have been inconsistent with relative resource endowments.[16]

A major implication of this research is that reliance on diffusion processes based primarily on materials and design transfer can, in the absence of the investment necessary to reach the *capacity transfer* level, severely bias the direction of technical change. Furthermore, the induced innovation perspective provides a useful guide to the design of a national research strategy in which experiment station capacity is developed to the fullest extent in those areas of biological technology which permit a nation to take advantage of unique environmental resources and in those areas of mechanical technology where resource endowments depart most sharply from the endowments in developed countries.

### The Transfer of High-Yielding Rice Varieties to the Tropics[17]

The transfer of the new high-yielding grain varieties from the temperate region to the tropics illustrates the processes of material, design, and capacity transfer. The prototype for the high-yielding, "fertilizer-consuming" rice varieties that have recently become available to producers in a number of tropical countries evolved in Japan, first as a result of selection by farmer "seedmen" and later under the stimulus

15. Yujiro Hayami and V. W. Ruttan, "Factor Prices and Technical Change in Agricultural Development: The United States and Japan, 1880–1960," *Journal of Political Economy* 78 (1970): 1115–41; William W. Wade, "Institutional Determinants of Technical Change and Agricultural Productivity Growth: Denmark, France and Great Britain, 1870–1965" (Ph.D. diss., University of Minnesota, June 1973); Hans P. Binswanger, "The Measurement of Biased Technical Change in the Many Factors Case: United States and Japanese Agriculture," University of Minnesota Department of Agricultural and Applied Economics Staff Paper p72–28 (St. Paul, Minnesota, December 1972).

16. John R. Sanders, "Agricultural Mechanization and Employment in Brazilian Agriculture, 1950–1971" (Ph.D. diss., University of Minnesota, June 1973); Harry W. Ayer and G. Edward Schuh, "Social Rates of Return and Other Aspects of Agricultural Research: The Case of Cotton Research in Sao Paulo, Brazil," *American Journal of Agricultural Economics* 54 (1972): 557–69; Hiromitsu Kaneda, "Mechanization, Industrialization and Technical Change in Rural West Pakistan" (Paper presented at the Twenty-eighth International Congress of Orientalists, Canberra, January 1971).

17. The material in this section is presented more completely in Yujiro Hayami, "Elements of Induced Innovation: A Historical Perspective for the Green Revolution," *Explorations in Economic History* 8 (1971): 445–72, and in Hayami and Ruttan, *Agricultural Development*, pp. 169–237.

of a concerted research effort by the national and prefectural experiment stations. In Japan the development and diffusion of the fertilizer-responsive varieties was closely associated with a decline in the price of fertilizer relative to the price of rice and the price of land.

In the 1920s a strenuous effort was made to transfer Japanese rice-production technology to Korea and Taiwan. The effort was spurred by the rapid rise in the price of rice in Japan during and after World War I. Under the Sanmai Zoshoku Keikaku (Rice Production Development Program) the Japanese government invested in irrigation and water control and in research and extension in order to develop and diffuse high-yielding rice varieties adapted to the local ecology of Korea and Taiwan.

In the case of Korea it was possible to achieve rapid expansion of rice production through the direct transfer of Japanese rice varieties (materials) and cultural practices (designs) under the stimulus of relatively low fertilizer prices and of administrative incentives. In Taiwan the problem was more difficult. It was not easy to adapt Japanese varieties to the more tropical environment. Research designed to improve the local varieties and to adapt Japanese varieties to the local environment had been initiated around 1900, shortly after the beginning of the Japanese occupation of Taiwan. It was not until the late 1920s, however, that well-adapted Ponlai varieties "developed by cross-breeding of Japanese varieties or between Japanese and traditional Taiwan (Chailai) varieties to have photo-sensitivities different from the original Japanese varieties"[18] became available for rapid diffusion. In spite of favorable resource endowments, resulting from heavy investment in irrigation development during the first two decades of the Japanese occupation and from relatively low fertilizer prices, the diffusion of high-yielding fertilizer-responsive varieties was delayed until local experiment station capacity for adaptive research had been established. It appears reasonable to interpret the transfer of Japanese rice-production technology as a response by the colonial government to a potential high pay-off (for Japan) from investment in research leading to an adjustment from a secular disequilibrium toward an equilibrium for the fertilizer/rice price ratios prevailing in the 1920s.

The question that remains is why the transfer of the high-yielding rice technology from Japan and Taiwan to South and Southeast Asia was delayed until the late 1960s. Why did rice yields in Southeast Asia

18. Fikichi Iso, *Horaimai danwa* [Discourse on the Ponlai rice] (Yamaguchi: Udokukai, 1964), pp. 18.

Table 7.2: Fertilizer/Rice Price Ratios and Rice Yields per Hectare
in Japan and in Selected Other Asian Countries, 1883–1962

| Country | Currency unit | Price of fertilizer per m. ton of nitrogen (1) | Price of rice per m. ton of milled rice (2) | Fertilizer/ rice price ratio (1)/(2) | Rice yield per hectare in m. ton of paddy (3) |
|---|---|---|---|---|---|
| Intercountry comparison | | | | | |
| 1963–65 | | | | | |
| India | rupee | 1,750 | 595[a] | 2.9 | 1.5 |
| | | | 723[b] | 2.4 | |
| Pakistan (East) | rupee | 1,632 | 780 | 2.1 | 1.7 |
| Philippines | peso | 1,048 | 530 | 2.0 | 1.3 |
| Thailand | U.S. dollar | 229 | 70 | 3.3 | 1.6 |
| Japan | 1,000 yen | 97 | 99 | 1.0 | 5.0 |
| 1955–57 | | | | | |
| India | rupee | 1,675 | 417[a] | 4.0 | 1.3 |
| | | | 505[b] | 3.3 | |
| Pakistan (East) | rupee | 1,322 | 511 | 2.6 | 1.4 |
| Philippines | peso | 962 | 352 | 2.7 | 1.1 |
| Thailand | U.S. dollar | 393 | 79 | 5.0 | 1.4 |
| Japan | 1,000 yen | 119 | 77 | 1.5 | 4.8 |
| Japan's time series | | | | | |
| 1958–62 | 1,000 yen | 100 | 85 | 1.2 | 4.9 |
| 1953–57 | 1,000 yen | 113 | 75 | 1.5 | 4.2 |
| 1933–37 | yen | 566 | 208 | 2.7 | 3.8 |
| 1923–27 | yen | 1,021 | 277 | 3.7 | 3.6 |
| 1913–17 | yen | 803 | 125 | 6.4 | 3.5 |
| 1903–07 | yen | 815 | 106 | 7.7 | 3.1 |
| 1893–97 | yen | 670 | 69 | 9.7 | 2.6 |
| 1883–87 | yen | 450 | 42 | 10.7 | n.a. |

a. Price in Sambalpur (Orissa).
b. Price in Bombay.

*Notes:* (1) Price paid by farmers. Intercountry data: average unit price of nitrogen contained in ammonium sulphate; 1963–65 data are the averages for 1962/63–1964/ 65; 1955–57 data are the data for 1956/57; government subsidies of 50 percent for 1963–65 and of 40 percent for 1955–57 are added to Pakistan's original data. Japan data: average unit price of nitrogen contained in commercial fertilizers. (2) Wholesale price at milled rice basis. Japan data are converted from brown rice basis to a milled rice basis assuming 10 percent for processing cost. (3) Japan data are converted from a brown rice basis to a milled rice basis using 0.8 for a conversion factor.

*Sources:* Intercountry data: FAO, *Production Yearbook,* various issues. Japan data: Kazushi Ohkawa et al., ed., *Long-term Economic Statistics of Japan,* vol. 9 (Tokyo: Tokyo Keizai Shimposha, 1966), pp. 202–03; Nobufumi Kayo, ed., *Nihon nogyo kisotokei* (Tokyo: Norin Suisangyo Seisankojokaigi, 1958), p. 514; Tokyo Keizai Shimposha, *Bukku Yoran* (Tokyo, 1967), p. 80; Institute of Developing Economies, *One Hundred Years of Agricultural Statistics in Japan* (Tokyo, 1969), p. 136.

increase so slowly in spite of substantial declines in the fertilizer/rice price ratio (table 7.2)? A partial explanation must be sought in the fact that public sector investment in the local experiment station capacity necessary to invent the locally adapted varieties was not initiated until the early 1960s. When such investment was made by the Ford and Rockefeller Foundations at the International Rice Research Institute, by the government of the Philippines at the Bureau of Plant Industry and the University of the Philippines, by the Indian Council of Agricultural Research, and by others, the rapid diffusion of capacity to develop locally adapted new varieties was facilitated by conceptual and methodological advance in breeding technique.[19] The first new varieties, such as IR-8, IR-5, and C4-63, diffused rapidly among farms in the regions where they were first released and beyond to other tropical rice-producing regions and countries. This has been followed by diffusion of the capacity to breed locally new varieties that are more precisely adapted to local ecological conditions. These new local varieties are now replacing the initial green revolution varieties.[20] The constraint on growth of output imposed by lack of fertilizer-responsive varieties is now being replaced by constraints imposed by limited investment in irrigation.[21]

I have described, in the case of rice, a situation where transfer of

19. Peter R. Jennings, "Plant Type as a Rice Breeding Objective," *Crop Science* 4 (1964):13–15; E. A. Jackson, "Tropical Rice: The Quest for High Yield," *Agricultural Science Review* 4 (1966): 21–26. The Jennings article represents the classic statement of the new crop-breeding strategy focusing on models of biologically efficient plant types.

20. The role of material transfers in the initial impact of the new grain varieties on production has been documented in a series of country papers prepared for the 1969 spring review at the U.S. Agency for International Development (AID). The material presented in the country papers has been summarized in Wayne A. Schutjer and E. Walter Coward, Jr., "Planning Agricultural Development—The Matter of Priorities," *Journal of Developing Areas* 6 (1971): 29–38. The contribution of material inputs is also emphasized in Wayne Schutjer and Dale Weigle, "The Contribution of Foreign Assistance to Agricultural Development," *American Journal of Agricultural Economics* 51 (1969): 788–97. The results obtained by Schutjer and Coward in the above-mentioned article do not reflect the significance of capacity transfer. It was only after the new production functions characterized by a higher response to material inputs were developed that the material transfer became profitable.

21. The environmental constraint on diffusion was anticipated at the time the new varieties were first being released. See S. C. Hsieh and V. W. Ruttan, "Environmental, Technological, and Institutional Factors in the Growth of Rice Production: Philippines, Thailand and Taiwan," *Food Research Institute Studies* 7, no. 3 (1967): 307–41.

the high-yielding rice technology to the tropics was delayed by an institutional lag in the development of research capacity. When that capacity emerged in the 1960s, the new varieties were sufficiently superior to the local varieties in many tropical areas that simple material and design transfer provided a powerful source of productivity growth in many areas. These stages are now being followed by the diffusion of the research capacity to provide locally adapted varieties and to protect the yield advances already made against depreciation.

### INSTITUTIONAL TRANSFER AND INNOVATION

Viewed from a historical perspective, the recent development of high-yielding varieties of wheat, rice, and maize in the tropics represented an institutional innovation[22] by national and international agencies whose aim was to make available, or obtain access to, the new income streams made possible by advances in the technology of plant breeding and fertilizer manufacture during the 1960s. It also appears that the technical changes embodied in the new high-yielding cereal varieties are biased toward saving an increasingly scarce factor (land) and using an increasingly abundant factor (fertilizer). In addition, these developments can be viewed as an attempt to evolve a science-based agriculture using material inputs produced by the industrial sector to augment an inelastic supply of (raw) land.

The process of institutional transfer and innovation has been an

22. There is usually a distinction, in the literature on institutional change, institutional development, and institution building, between institutions and organizations. *Institutions* are usually defined as the behavioral rules that govern patterns of action and relationships; *organizations* are the decision-making units that exercise control of resources. For some purposes more elaborate classifications are employed. Lance E. Davis and Douglass C. North, in *Institutional Change and American Economic Growth* (New York: Cambridge University Press, 1971), distinguish among (1) the institutional environment, "the set of fundamental political, social, and legal ground rules that establishes the basis for production, exchange and distribution" (p. 6); (2) the institutional arrangement, "an arrangement between economic units that governs the ways in which these units can cooperate and/or compete" (p.7); (3) the primary action group, "a decision-making unit whose decisions govern the process of arrangemental innovation" (p. 8); (4) the secondary action group, "a decision making unit that has been established by some change in the institutional arrangement to help effect the capture of income for the primary action group" (p. 8); and (5) institutional instruments, "documents or devices employed by action groups to effect the capture of income external to the existing arrangemental structures" (p. 9). In this chapter the term institutional innovation (or change, or development) is used to refer to a change in the actual or potential performance of existing or new organizations (households, firms, bureaus); in the relationships between an organization and its environment; or in the behavioral rules or possibilities that govern the patterns of action and relationships in the organizations' environment.

essential element in the process. Capacity transfer has depended on the successful institutionalization of public (or philanthropic) sector capacity to generate a continuous stream of new biological technology. Under modern conditions technology transfer is increasingly dependent on capacity transfer. Yet the literature on institutional transfer and innovation is, if anything, even more unsatisfactory than the literature on technology transfer and innovation.[23]

There are two bodies of literature that provide a limited basis on which to build an understanding of the processes involved in institutional transfer and innovation. One is the literature on institution building that has evolved out of an effort, primarily in the field of public administration, to provide technical assistance agencies with an effective methodology for external intervention aimed at inducing more effective institutional performance.[24] The second body of literature has grown out of efforts made by a number of economists and political scientists to develop models of bureaucratic behavior.[25]

23. Suggestions for the development of an endogenous or induced theory of institutional change have been made by T. W. Schultz, "Institutions and the Rising Economic Value of Man," *American Journal of Agricultural Economics* 50 (1968): 1113–22, and by Douglass C. North and Robert Paul Thomas, "An Economic Model of the Growth of the Western World," *Economic History Review,* 2d ser. 23, no. 1 (1970): 1–17. Schultz regards institutional innovation as a lagged response to the growth of productivity and the rising economic value of man associated with economic growth. North and Thomas regard technical change and productivity growth as a lagged response to institutional changes induced by long-run changes in relative factor and product prices and changes in the size of the market. Both regard institutional innovation as induced primarily from the demand side rather than the supply side.

24. The institution-building literature is largely a product of two major efforts: (1) The Interuniversity Research Program on Institution Building, which involved staff members from Indiana, Michigan State, and Syracuse universities and the University of Pittsburgh and was headquartered at the Graduate School of Public and International Affairs at Pittsburgh. The guiding concepts for this effort have been outlined in Milton J. Esman and Hans C. Blaise, "Institution Building Research—The Guiding Concepts," mimeographed (Pittsburgh: Graduate School of Public and International Affairs, University of Pittsburgh, 1966). (2) The Committee on Institutional Cooperation, Agency for International Development Rural Development Research Project, which involved staff members from the Universities of Wisconsin, Minnesota, Illinois, Missouri, Indiana, North Carolina, Ohio, Utah State, and Purdue. The objective of the project was to review and evaluate the results of AID-university cooperation in assisting the development of agricultural education and research institutions in developing countries. For a review and evaluation of the results achieved by the two research programs see William J. Siffin, "The Institution Building Perspective: Properties, Problems, and Promise," in *Institution Building: A Model for Applied Social Change,* ed. D. Woods Thomas et al. (Cambridge: Schenkman, 1972), pp. 113–48.

25. The seminal work in this body of literature is Anthony Downs, *An Economic Theory of Democracy* (New York: Harper, 1957), especially pp. 3–35. See also James

## The Institution-Building Perspective

The institution-building perspective involves an explicitly normative orientation toward social change. An "institution" is viewed as a package of behaviors and relationships that describe a particular organization and its interactions with its environment. The test of effective "institutionalization," in this perspective, is the normative impact of the organization on its setting. Thus the appropriate test of the institutionalization of experiment station capacity for rice research would consist in the impact of the new knowledge resulting from rice research on rice yields, the incomes of rice producers, or the price of rice to urban consumers.

This concern with the effectiveness of technical assistance has clearly exerted a substantial impact on the institution-building literature. There is a pervasive concern with the problem of transferring particular organizational forms from the developed to the developing nations, and with the institutionalization of capacity for technology transfer and innovation.[26]

At the same time the institution-building perspective has been criticized for not paying more explicit attention to the development of a typology by which organizations can be differentiated on the basis of both technology and environmental characteristics.[27] William Siffin argues, for example, that it is easier to institutionalize an organization whose operations are primarily concerned with a well-developed technology than an organization that is not technology centered. He points out that the relatively "closed-system" quality of many techno-

---

M. Buchanan and Gordon Tullock, *The Calculus of Consent* (Ann Arbor: University of Michigan Press, 1962); Mancur Olson, Jr., *The Logic of Collective Action: Public Goods and the Theory of Groups* (New York: Schocken Books, 1968); Anthony Downs, *Inside Bureaucracy* (Boston: Little, Brown, 1966); William A. Niskanen, Jr., *Bureaucracy and Representative Government* (Chicago: Aldine-Atherton, 1971).

26. In the more recent institution-building literature there is a good deal of rhetoric to the effect that technical assistance involves more than the simple transfer of resources, knowledge or institutions, and that emphasis should be placed on institution-building activities that have a greater experimental content. See, for example, Milton J. Esman and John D. Montgomery, "Systems Approaches to Technical Cooperation: The Role of Development Administration," *Public Administration Review* (1969): 507–39.

27. Siffin, "Institution Building Perspective," pp. 123–27. Siffin's perspective on the role of technology in institution building draws very heavily on James D. Thompson, *Organizations in Action* (New York: McGraw-Hill, 1967). Thompson's perspective can be summarized as follows: the design, structure, and behavior of organizations will vary systematically with (a) differences in technologies, and (b) variations in task environments.

logies means that the behaviors they require are quite particular to their operations—and not to the sociocultural system at large. On the other hand, where there is no closed-system technology, as in community development efforts, effective institutionalization may be exceedingly difficult to achieve.

From my perspective the major limitations of the institution-building literature are similar to the limitations of the literature on the diffusion of technology: (1) it is more relevant to the problems of material and design transfer than to capacity transfer, and (2) there is no model of the process by which institutional innovations are generated. In my judgment the most significant contribution of the research on institution building is the recent recognition of the close link between technical and institutional change. This opens up the possibility of developing models of organizational behavior induced by either technical innovation or institutional innovation.

## Models of Bureaucratic Behavior

The effort to model bureaucratic behavior has been primarily positive in orientation. It has represented an attempt to extend the microeconomic theory of the firm and of the consumer, to model the relationships between the public or semipublic organization (or bureau) and its environment, and to analyze the consequences of these relationships for public choice and for the generation of budgets and the supply of services or other output. The effect has been the development of an "economic" or "rational" theory of bureaucratic behavior as an alternative to the "organic" or "altruistic" model.[28]

The significance of this development is that it provides an approach to the modeling of the consequences of maximizing behavior on the budget and output performance of bureaus in response to variation in the several components of a bureau's environment—including the characteristics of the "markets" through which it (1) generates revenue, (2) acquires factors of production, and (3) distributes its output. A major positive implication of the formal models developed thus far is that, given the markets in which they operate, bureaus will be successful in capturing a relatively large share of the rents generated by their activities.[29] The rents captured by a bureau may be relatively low where

28. Downs, *Inside Bureaucracy*, pp. 81–84; Buchanan and Tullock, *Calculus of Consent*, pp. 11–39; Niskanen, *Bureaucracy*, pp. 36–42.

29. William A. Niskanen, "The Peculiar Economics of Bureaucracy," *American Economic Review* 58 (1968). 293–305.

the demand for its services is relatively elastic, or relatively high where the demands for its services are relatively inelastic. In general, the tests of the models on this point have been either synthetic or anecdotal.[30]

A second set of inferences deals with the mobilization of group behavior. Mancur Olson, in particular, has shown that in the "public goods" market there are severe constraints on the capacity to mobilize collective action.[31] A major implication of this second line of investigation is the importance of a proliferation of voluntary organizations— the source of demand for public services—around activities that generate private gains. It is further argued that the performance of the market for public services is improved by decentralization on the supply side.

The economic models of bureaucratic behavior and collective action provide preliminary insights into the role of economic factors in generating a supply of bureaucratic services—new knowledge of crop production practices, for example. In my judgment, however, the static nature of the models that have been discussed in the literature implies greater constraints on the capacity for collective action and on the bureaucratic response to economic incentives than is consistent with historical experience.[32] This failure stems, I believe, from a concentration on the short-run allocative and distributional implications of collective action and bureaucratic behavior and from a failure to explore more

30. For an exception see the analysis of the U.S. Food Stamp Program by W. Keith Bryant: "An Analysis of the Market for Food Stamps," *American Journal of Agricultural Economics* 54 (1972): 305–25; and "An Analysis of the Market for Food Stamps: Correction and Extension," *American Journal of Agricultural Economics* 54 (1972): 689–93.

31. "There are three separate but cumulative factors that keep larger groups from furthering their own interests. First, the larger the group, the smaller the fraction of the total group benefits any person acting in the group receives, and the less adequate the reward for any group oriented action and the further the group falls short of getting an optimal supply of the collective good, even if it should get some. Second, since the larger the group the smaller the share of the total benefits going to any individual, or to any (absolutely) small subset of members of the group, much less any single individual will gain enough from getting the collective good to bear the burden of providing even a small part of it. . . . Third, the larger the number of members in the group the greater the organization cost, and thus the higher the hurdle that must be jumped before any of the collective good can be obtained. For these reasons the larger the group the further it will fall short of providing an optimal supply of a collective good" (Olson, *Logic of Collective Action,* p. 48). See also Buchanan and Tullock, *Calculus of Consent,* pp. 43–62.

32. See, for example, Lance E. Davis and Douglass C. North, *Institutional Change and American Economic Growth* (Cambridge: at the University Press, 1971); and North and Thomas, "Economic Theory of the Growth of the Western World."

fully the dynamic implications of the potential gains from institutional innovation.

### Induced Institutional Change and Agricultural Productivity

It is possible to summarize the major implications of the institution-building and bureaucratic behavior literature for the process of institutional transfer and innovation.

Institutional transfer is clearly easier when the object is to institutionalize an organization whose operations are primarily concerned with applying a well-developed technology than an organization that is not technology centered. It is easier, for example, to institutionalize experiment station work or family planning than community development capacity. It also seems clear, from the induced innovation perspective, that the capacity of the technology to generate new income streams represents an important source of demand for institutional transfer.

The partitioning of the potential new income streams opened up through the transfer of a technology-centered institution represents a source of demand for institutional innovation. There is continuous pressure from within the institution (firm or bureau) to internalize the gains and to externalize the costs resulting from the transfer. There will also be continuous pressure from the external environment, from society, to externalize the gains and internalize the costs. The effect of the institutional changes induced by this process is to improve social efficiency by moving toward equalization of the private and social profitability of an activity. But the markets in which public sector institutions function are imperfect. Clearly there are limits to the capacity of voluntary associations to bring about sufficient equity in the distribution of power to simulate a "perfect" market for the allocation of institutional resources and products.

It is clear that we do not yet have available a fully articulated theory of induced institutional change, even though some of the elements of such a theory are available to us. It is possible, however, to illustrate the implications of the insights that are available to us from historical experience.

The Second Enclosure Movement in England represents a classic illustration. The issuance of the Enclosure Acts facilitated the conversion of communal pasture- and farmland into private farm units, thus encouraging the introduction of a more intensive, integrated, crop-livestock "new husbandry" system.[33] The acts can be viewed as an institutional innovation designed to exploit the new technical opportunities opened up by innovations in crop rotation utilizing the new fodder crops (turnip and clover), in response to rising food prices. Indeed, the long history of modernization of land tenure relationships, involving a shift from share tenure to lease tenure and owner-operator systems of cultivation in much of Western agriculture, can be explained, in part, as a shift in property rights designed to internalize the potential gains of innovative activity by individual farmers. Similarly the political and legislative history of farm price programs in the United States from the mid-1920s to the present can be viewed as a struggle between agricultural producers and consumers over the partitioning of the new income streams resulting from technical progress in agriculture.[34]

The close link between technical and institutional change is particularly apparent in the realization of the productivity gains resulting from the transfer of rice technology from Japan to Taiwan.[35] The essential technological and environmental elements for rapid development of the Taiwan rice economy were available by the mid-1920s. New and improved rice varieties had been introduced, and research and development institutions with the capacity for continuous improvements in varietal characteristics had been established. Much of the potential rice land was served by irrigation systems capable of delivering water to the land throughout the year. Technical inputs such as fertilizer were made available through economic integration with the Japanese economy. The rising demand for rice in Japan created incentives to increase the marketable surplus of rice in Taiwan.

Rice yields rose rapidly, by approximately 2.0 percent per year, between the mid-1920s and the late 1930s, when Japanese military efforts began to divert resources from development objectives. In spite of continued varietal development, it appears that the yield potential, under optimum environmental conditions, did not change significantly between the late 1920s and the mid-1960s. Yet rice yields rose rapidly

33. Peter C. Timmer, "The Turnip, the New Husbandry, and the English Agricultural Revolution," *Quarterly Journal of Economics* 83 (1969): 375–95.

34. Vernon W. Ruttan, "Agricultural Policy in an Affluent Society," *Journal of Farm Economics* 48 (1966): 1100–20.

35. The literature on which I draw in this section is reviewed in Hsieh and Ruttan, "Environmental, Technological, and Institutional Factors in the Growth of Rice Production," pp. 307–41. See also Yhi-min Ho, *Agricultural Development of Taiwan, 1903–1960* (Nashville, Tenn.: Vanderbilt University Press, 1966); Anthony Y. C. Koo, *The Role of Land Reform in Economic Development: A Case Study of Taiwan* (New York: Praeger, 1968).

between the early 1950s and the mid-1960s even though the technological and environmental factors affecting growth did not change significantly during this period. The rapid growth in rice output and productivity during the postwar period represents a response to institutional changes that facilitated the realization of the productivity potential inherent in the technical changes and resource investments of the pre-World War II period. The evolution of the farmers' associations into effective extension and marketing organizations and the improvement in incentives resulting from the land reform of 1949–52 were among the more significant institutional sources of continued productivity growth in Taiwan.

The innovative role of the Sino-American Joint Commission on Rural Reconstruction (JCRR) was a major factor in the implementation of the land reform program and the development of the farmers' associations and other institutional innovations in rural development.[36] Indeed the JCRR seems to have embodied much of (1) the institution-building wisdom suggesting the central role of a suitable technology around which to organize energies for institutional change, and (2) the analytical insight into the power of decentralized organization for effective collective action, derived from efforts to model bureaucratic behavior.

The cases presented in this section to illustrate the process of induced institutional change are clearly informed by the institution-building, bureaucratic behavior, and induced technical change models. They are, at least to me, intuitively plausible. Yet these illustrations, and the historical and analytical literature on which they are based, do not convey the same sense of conviction as the body of theoretical and empirical literature on induced technical change. The empirical literature on institutional behavior and innovation represents, at best, sophisticated storytelling informed by partial theoretical insights.[37]

There has been, for example, no successful effort to quantify the contribution of changes in land tenure institutions to economic growth in Taiwan or elsewhere that matches, in precision or conviction, existing research data measuring the contribution of technical change to factor

36. John D. Montgomery, Rufus B. Hughes, and Raymond H. Davis, *Rural Improvement and Political Development: The JCRR Model* (Washington, D.C.: American Society for Public Administration, 1966); T. H. Shen, *The Sino-American Joint Commission of Rural Reconstruction* (Ithaca, N. Y.: Cornell University Press, 1970).

37. For an attempt to rehabilitate the contribution of "storytelling" to the development of knowledge in economics, see Benjamin Ward, *What's Wrong With Economics* (New York: Basic Books, 1972), pp. 179–90.

augmentation or output. The formal analysis of land tenure systems, including the examples presented elsewhere in this volume, provides only limited insight into the sequence of tenure changes that have been associated with the transition from the premodern conservation systems of agriculture to the more modern industrial and science-based systems of agriculture.[38]

Our capacity to bring the tools of economics to bear on the process of institutional transfer and innovation, or on the interaction between technical and institutional change, remains rudimentary.

THE ROLE OF KNOWLEDGE IN TECHNICAL AND INSTITUTIONAL CHANGE

The search for an induced development model, in which technical and institutional change can be treated as endogenous to the development process, does not imply that agricultural development can be left to an "invisible hand" that directs either technical or institutional change along an efficient path determined by original resource endowments. On the contrary, the policies a country adopts with respect to the allocation of resources to technical and institutional innovation must be consistent with national physical and human resource endowments if they are to lead to an efficient growth path. Conversely, failure to achieve such consistency can sharply increase the real costs, or abort the possibility, of achieving sustained growth in the agricultural sector, or in the total economy.

At the same time, it seems clear to me that our understanding of the processes by which resources can be used to achieve effective technology transfer or innovation is significantly greater than our understanding of how to bring resources to bear on the problem of institution innovation and transfer. I would like, in this final section, to suggest that this is in part due to the development of a more rigorous conceptualization of the contribution of knowledge in the natural (i.e., biological and physical) sciences to technical change than of knowledge in the social sciences to the process of institutional change.

Economists have, in recent years, made substantial progress in measuring the contribution of advances in the natural sciences and

38. In addition to the other chapters in this book, see Steven N. S. Cheung, *The Theory of Share Tenancy* (Chicago: University of Chicago Press, 1969). For a review of the earlier literature see Vernon W. Ruttan, "Equity and Productivity Issues in Modern Agrarian Reform Legislation," in *Economic Problems of Agriculture in Industrial Societies,* ed. Ugo Papi and Charles Nunn (New York: Macmillan [St. Martin's Press], 1969), pp. 581–600.

technology to the growth of output.[39] The research and development system has been viewed as having a production function along the lines suggested in figure 7.2. The return to investment in the production of new knowledge has been evaluated in terms of its contribution to commodity and service output in agriculture or industry. The demand for new knowledge in the natural sciences and natural-science–based technology is viewed as derived from the demand for commodities and services. Increasingly sophisticated analytical efforts have been devoted to the formalization of research resource allocation and decision processes.

The same progress has not yet been made in conceptualizing the contribution of new knowledge in the social sciences and professions to the process of institutional change. In fact, institutional change has typically been treated as an evolutionary process only marginally responsive to the availability of new knowledge. It seems plausible to argue, however, that the demand for new knowledge in the social sciences is derived primarily from the potential contribution of new knowledge in the social sciences (and professions) to the process of institutional change.

This perspective opens up the possibility of measuring the returns to investment in social science capacity in terms of the contribution of social science knowledge to institutional change, or in terms of the new income streams made available to society through institutional changes resulting from new knowledge produced in the social sciences and professions. This perspective implies that a primary rationale for public investment in the development of capacity in the social sciences and professions is to produce institutional innovations that result in more efficient institutional performance. This means, for example, the development of market institutions that are more efficient in conveying information between producers and consumers and that reduce the resource costs of intersector commodity and service flows; the development of land tenure institutions that induce more efficient use of factors and embodied technology; and the development of credit institutions that are more efficient in linking and transfering credit between savers, central money markets, and borrowers.

An implication of this perspective is that the returns to public investment in social science research capacity—the contribution of social

39. See, for example, the papers in Walter L. Fishel, ed., *Resource Allocation in Agricultural Research* (Minneapolis: University of Minnesota Press, 1971). Also Evenson and Kislev, "Research and Productivity in Wheat and Maize."

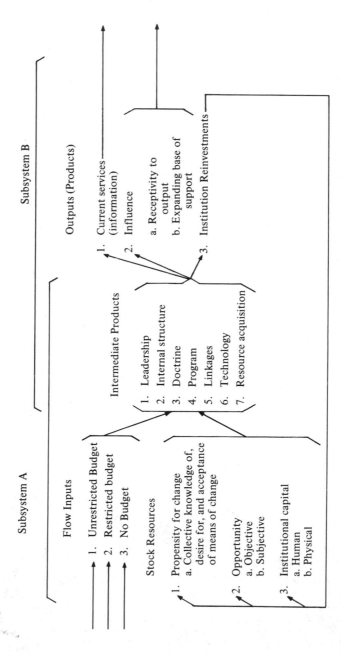

Fig. 7.2: Systems Model of Experiment Station Performance and Development (*Source:* The Agricultural Experiment Station: An Institutional Development Perspective," *Agricultural Science Review* 10 (1972): 11–16.)

science research to economic growth and development—can be enhanced if more explicit attention is devoted, in the allocation of social science resources, to the potential value of new knowledge in the social sciences to institutional change.

# 8

# Technology Generation in Agriculture

ROBERT EVENSON

Efficiency in food production is a central issue in contemporary development policy. Its importance in a world where millions of people live with the threat of malnutrition and starvation in times of adverse weather does not require emphasis. To the casual observer, it appears that food production in much of the world is subject to traditional technology which could not possibly be optimal. Surely the introduction of modern techniques of production to the developing economies would result in improved efficiency of production.

The lessons of much development experience have gradually led to the unhappy conclusion that this view has been wrong. Programs designed to transplant modern technology have continuously come up against the realization that the technology offered often had little or no advantage over the old and traditional methods, given the economic, soil, and climate conditions facing producers. Had this not been the case, the policies of the 1950s, which relied upon the existence of economically viable technology and were designed to transfer new l progressideas, to instilive values, and to improve the supply of modern inputs, might have met the high goals set for them.

The fact that so many development problems have not yielded to easy and inexpensive solutions is a hard reality. As the experience with various programs is now being assessed, the search for new understanding of the determinants of the discovery and diffusion of agricultural technology proceeds. A review of a number of studies directed toward that effort is presented in part 1 of this chapter. In part 2 a regional classification based on geoclimate factors is developed, and an analysis of cereal grain yield determination based on geoclimate regions is undertaken. Part 3 reports on an investigation of the determinants of productivity change in Indian agriculture since 1953. The final section of the chapter discusses policy issues.

1. THE ECONOMIC TREATMENT OF TECHNOLOGY
DISCOVERY AND DIFFUSION

## The Direct Inference Commodity Studies

Table 8.1 summarizes several studies that have related observed productivity gains in production of a particular commodity to the research expenditures that produced them. These studies reflect to a great extent the spirit of the cost-benefit literature. A benefit stream is measured, usually as a cost reduction directly attributable to a specific set of improved factors of production. The cost-benefit calculation is in some cases a by-product, in that the objective of several of the studies was to investigate the determinants of the adoption of the technology.

Table 8.1: Summary of Direct Inference Commodity Studies

| *Study* | *Country* | *Commodity* | *Time period* | *Ratio of benefit flow to adjusted costs*[a] | *Internal rate of return* |
|---|---|---|---|---|---|
| Griliches | U.S.A. | hybrid corn | 1940–55 | 7.0 | 35–40 |
| Griliches | U.S.A. | hybrid sorghum | 1940–57 | 3.6 | 20 |
| Peterson | U.S.A. | poultry | 1915–60 | —[b] | 21–25 |
| Ardito-Barletta | Mexico | wheat | 1943–63 | 7.5 | 90 |
| Ardito-Barletta | Mexico | corn | 1943–63 | 3.0 | 35 |
| Evenson | South Africa | sugarcane | 1945–62 | 2.47 | 40+ |
| Ayer | Brazil | cotton | 1924–67 | — | 77 |
| Hines | Peru | corn | 1954–67 | — | 35–40[c] 50–55[d] |

a. This not a benefit/cost ratio. It is the benefit flow as of the end period plus the accumulated benefits to that date converted to a flow at the same interest rate (usually 6 percent) divided by the accumulated costs also converted to a flow at the same interest rate.

b. Not calculated.

c. Returns to corn research only.

d. Returns to corn research plus cultivation "package."

*Sources:* Zvi Griliches, "Research Costs and Social Returns: Hybrid Corn and Related Innovations," *Journal of Political Economy* 66 (1958): 419–31; W. L. Peterson, "Returns to Poultry Research in the U.S." (Ph.D. diss., University of Chicago, 1966); N. Ardito-Barletta, "Costs and Social Returns of Agricultural Research in Mexico" (Ph.D diss., University of Chicago, 1970); R. Evenson, "International Transmission of Technology in Sugarcane Production," mimeographed (New Haven, Yale University, 1969); H. Ayer, "The Costs, Returns, and Effects of Agricultural Research in a Developing Country: The Case of Cotton Seed Research in Sao Paulo, Brazil" (Ph.D. diss., Purdue University, 1970); J. Hines, "The Utilization of Research for Development: Two Case Studies in Rural Modernization and Agriculture in Peru" (Ph.D. diss., Princeton University, 1972).

The classic study of hybrid corn by Zvi Griliches is the standard work here.[1] The consumer surplus basis for evaluating the benefits stream due to shift in cost and supply functions is developed in this study. Griliches also established procedures for dealing with certain definitional problems. He explicitly treated hybrid corn development not as a single "invention" but as a sequence of related inventions. This distinction has not always been made in studies of technology production.[2] In fact, the failure to do so has been one of the weaknesses of studies in this category. It is quite misleading to suggest that the cost-reducing improvements in these commodities can be attributed to a single invention or breakthrough. In reality they reflect the contribution of numerous researchers and of the institutions that organize and facilitate interactions between them.

The identification of the appropriate "costs" of technology production in these studies is not based on models of technology generation, either explicitly or implicitly. It is a straightforward identification of the "obvious" commodity-oriented research activity by agricultural experiment stations and by private firms. Most of the investigators adopt a conservative posture and give minimum estimates of cost-benefit ratios.

Overall, these studies support the policy proposition that too little investment in agricultural research is being made. All of the estimated rates of return are well above rates realized on more conventional investment. The studies of N. Ardito-Barletta, H. Ayer, and J. Hines are particularly important in this context.[3] Each is a careful study of specific research programs in Latin America. These estimated rates of return quite clearly establish the proposition that research programs in developing country settings can be highly productive.

Perhaps the major qualification that must be raised in connection with these studies is that they are studies of successful programs. It may

1. Zvi Griliches, "Research Costs and Social Returns: Hybrid Corn and Related Innovations," *Journal of Political Economy* 66 (1958): 419–31.
2. One of the few attempts to do so is reported in a paper by Y. Kislev and R. Evenson, "Investment in Agricultural Research and Extension: An International Survey," Growth Center Discussion Paper no. 141 (New Haven, Yale University, 1971).
3. See N. Ardito-Barletta, "Costs and Social Returns of Agricultural Research in Mexico" (Ph.D. diss., University of Chicago, 1970); H. Ayer, "The Costs, Returns, and Effects of Agricultural Research in a Developing Country: The Case of Cotton Seed Research in Sao Paulo, Brazil" (Ph.D. diss., Purdue University, 1970); and J. Hines, "The Utilization of Research for Development: Two Case Studies in Rural Modernization and Agriculture in Peru" (Ph.D. diss., Princeton University, 1972).

be that a national system inherently produces a mix of success and failures and that it is a priori impossible to predict which programs will be successes. The cost of the failures must accordingly be taken into account in the calculations as part of the cost of the successes. This problem is only partially met by the conservative posture of the studies. It should be noted, however, that most of the research programs evaluated in table 8.1 were quite broad in scope and that the evaluation did take into account the failures within the programs.

## Production Function Studies

The studies summarized in table 8.2 rely on indirect estimation to suggest a relationship between research activity and new technology. The specification utilized is generally some version of the following: Let equation (8.1) be an aggregate production function in a very general form.

$$Y = F(X_1 Q_1 T_1, X_i Q_i T_i, X_n Q_n T_n) \tag{8.1}$$

Conventionally measured factors of production are represented by $X_i$. In this specification they are augmented by two indexes, $Q_i$ and $T_i$. The $Q_i$ index measures those tangible dimensions of factor quality that are neglected in conventional measures. Changes in labor quality associated with schooling or in machine quality associated with different levels of horsepower are examples of measurable factor quality. The $T_i$ are indexes of factor-augmenting techniques and are not measurable in the foregoing sense.

Under the assumption that $F$ is homogeneous of degree 1, and that producers maximize profits, equation (8.2) shows the percentage rate of change in output ($\dot{Y} = [dY/dt]/Y$) as a weighted average of the percent rates of change in conventional factors, $\dot{X}_i$, measurable quality, $\dot{Q}_i$, and factor-augmenting technology, $\dot{T}_i$. The weights, $S_i$, are factor shares in total cost.

$$\dot{Y} = \sum_{i=1}^{n} S_i (\dot{X}_i + \dot{Q}_i + \dot{T}_i) \tag{8.2}$$

The natural "residual" rate of productivity change from this expression is:

$$\dot{P} = \dot{Y} - \sum_{i=1}^{n} S_i \dot{X}_i = \sum_{i=1}^{n} S_i (\dot{Q}_i + \dot{T}_i). \tag{8.3}$$

As the definition in equation (8.3) makes clear, productivity measure-

Table 8.2: Summary of Implicit Technology Generation Function Studies

| Study | Area, commodity, and time period | Estimated marginal: Output per research dollar | Internal rate of return (%) |
|---|---|---|---|
| Griliches | U.S.A., aggregate 1949–59 | $7 | —[a] |
| Latimer | U.S.A., aggregate 1949–59 | — | significant |
| Evenson, 1968 | U.S.A., aggregate 1949–59 | $10–12 | 47 |
| Khaldi | U.S.A., aggregate 1949–64 | not calculated, but high returns implied | |
| Tang | Japan, aggregate 1880–1938 | — | 35 |
| Ardito-Barletta | Mexico, crops 1943–63 | 2.9 | 45–93 |
| Peterson | U.S.A., poultry | 1.4 | 21 |
| Evenson, 1969 | South Africa, sugarcane 1945–58 | 15 | 40 |
| Evenson, 1969 | Australia, sugarcane 1945–58 | 35 | 50 |
| Evenson, 1969 | India, sugarcane 1945–58 | 40 | 60 |
| Hayami and Ruttan | International 1955–65 | not directly calculated, but high returns implied | |
| Kislev and Evenson | International 1955–68 Applied research in: | | |
| | LDCs[b] | — | 42 |
| | DCs[c] | — | 21 |
| | Scientific research related to agriculture in: | | |
| | LDCs | — | 60 |
| | DCs | — | 36 |

a. Not calculated.
b. Less developed countries.
c. Developed countries.

*Sources:* Zvi Griliches, "Research Expenditures, Education, and the Aggregate Agricultural Production Function," *American Economic Review* 54, no. 6 (1964): 961–74; Robert Latimer, "Some Economic Aspects of Agricultural Research and Extension in the U.S." (Ph.D. diss., Purdue University, 1964); R. Evenson, "The Contribution of Agricultural Research and Extension to Agricultural Production" (Ph.D. diss., University of Chicago, 1968), and "International Transmission of Technology in Sugarcane Production"; N. Khaldi, Ph.D. diss., Southern Methodist University; A. Tang, "Research and Education in Japanese Agricultural Development," *Economic Studies Quarterly*, 1963; Ardito-Barletta, "Agricultural Research in Mexico"; Peterson, "Returns to Poultry Research in the U.S."; Y. Hayami and V. Ruttan, *Agricultural Development: An International Perspective* (Baltimore: Johns Hopkins Press, 1972); Y. Kislev and R. Evenson, "Agricultural Research and Productivity: An International Analysis," mimeographed (New Haven, Yale University, 1973).

ments are, in principle, at least partially subject to explanation through proper quality measurement but are also composed of elements that can reasonably be viewed as the end products of directed efforts to acquire knowledge and to discover new or improved techniques of production. The growth-accounting literature of Griliches and others is addressed to the first point and will not be reviewed here.[4] The studies in table 8.2 have essentially been based on the second point.

Specifications usually are in terms of the determinants of productivity change. Measured productivity is regressed on measures of research, extension, and schooling. Alternatively, an aggregate production function is specified, and research, extension, and schooling variables are included as factors of production. In general, some time lag is incorporated into the specification to identify the relationship. That is, lagged research is specified as producing current productivity gains. This specification has been used to identify the time-shape of the research contributions as well as to handle at least partially the simultaneity problem arising from the fact that increased production may create a demand for more research. The timing of the latter relationship runs in the other direction, that is, current research investment responds to past production.

The studies in this group complement the earlier direct studies in two important ways. First, they are based on aggregate research programs and presumably measure the output of research programs of varying success and failure. Second, they provide some evidence for time-shape parameters. Further, the extension of this methodology to international data adds an important new dimension and lends support to the proposition that the experience of the United States is not unique.

Since calculations of internal rates of return are quite sensitive to alternative time-shape estimates, their reliability is questionable in those studies where relatively simple time lags were postulated, that is, Griliches, Latimer and Paarleburg, and the two international studies, Hayami and Ruttan, and Kislev and Evenson.[5] My 1968 study, which estimated an average time lag of six and a half years between research expenditure and realized productivity gain, is perhaps the most thorough estimate of the time shape. One aspect of interest in this study is the measured obsolescence or depreciation of research findings. The

4. But see Zvi Griliches, "Research Expenditures, Education, and the Aggregate Agricultural Production Function," *American Economic Review* 54, no. 6 (1964): 961–74.

5. For full references to these and other studies cited in this discussion, see the source note to table 8.2.

studies of the agricultural research-productivity relationship in the United States conclude that aggregate research has probably been as productive as the commodity research programs evaluated earlier.

The Hayami-Ruttan study represents an important pioneering effort. Even though the authors had available only a rough proxy variable for research activity, their study did reveal a systematic relationship between measured productivity change and research and extension type activities between countries, including a number of less developed countries (LDCs). The later work of Kislev and Evenson, based on more directly measured research activity, corroborated the Hayami-Ruttan results.

## Transfer and Information Specifications

The most recent developments in this field (summarized in table 8.3), have been addressed to two specification improvements. The first is the explicit treatment of errors and of information supply. This direction allows at least a potential improvement in the distinction between the economic contribution of extension and extension-type activities and research effort per se. From the work of Finis Welch, D. P. Chaudhri, and Richard Nelson and Edmund Phelps, we can note that at any point in time producers in a particular region will be making errors.[6] These errors can be divided into cost-minimizing errors, technique choice errors, and errors of human capital investment.[7]

The economic treatment of errors is slighted in much economic literature, usually as a casualty of the advantages of simplicity in model specification. It adds much to this field of study, however. The work cited above specified models in which a particular set of activities is devoted to error reduction. These activities can be viewed as part of an information market. That is, profit-maximizing producers demand information, because they perceive that they are making errors and that by acquiring information, in one of several forms, they will be able to process that information and, on balance, make decisions that will increase profits and reduce errors. The abilities to perceive errors,

6. F. Welch, "Education in Production," *Journal of Political Economy* 78 (1970): 35–39; D. P. Chaudhri, "Education and Agricultural Productivity in India" (Ph.D. diss., University of Delhi, 1968); and R. Nelson and E. S. Phelps, "Investment in Humans, Technological Diffusion, and Economic Growth," *American Economic Review* 56 (1966): 69–75.

7. Welch develops an allocative error concept which includes both cost-minimizing errors and technique choice errors. See Welch, "Education in Production."

to purchase information efficiently (the producers' time usually being the main price), and to process such information to make improved decisions are viewed by Welch as being heavily determined by schooling experience.

In a production setting where relevant new technology is not being discovered, production errors are induced only by product and factor

Table 8.3: Summary of Information and Transfer Studies

| *Study* | *Area* | *Conclusions* |
|---|---|---|
| Welch, 1972 | U.S.A. | One-third or more of the return to college education is attributable to research. |
| Welch, 1970 | U.S.A. | Research "accounts" for a significant portion of the productivity gains attributed to realized scale economies. |
| Evenson | U.S.A. | The marginal contribution of research and extension falls as the level of schooling rises. |
| Khaldi | U.S.A. | Estimated departures from cost minimization are positively related to research expenditures and negatively related to schooling. |
| Huffman | U.S.A. (corn belt) | Extension and schooling are substitutes in inducing optimal nitrogen fertilizer usage on hybrid corn. The marginal value of extension time is estimated to be $50 per hour of direct farmer contact. |
| Kislev and Evenson | International | The study specifies a transfer process between countries in similar climate regions.[a] |

a. The estimated "earnings stream" associated with a unit of research is:

| | *Direct contribution* | *Transfer facilitation* | *Contribution to others* |
|---|---|---|---|
| Wheat | 29,737 | 135,000 | 77,997 |
| Maize | 15,040 | 15,000 | 9,302 |

The cost of the research unit ranged from $40,000 in Asia and Latin America to $100,000 in North America and Northern Europe; see Kislev and Evenson, "Investment in Agricultural Research and Extension."

*Sources:* F. Welch, "Economies of Scale in U.S. Agriculture," mimeographed (New York, National Bureau of Economic Research, 1972), and "Education in Production," *Journal of Political Economy* 78 (1970): 35–39; R. Evenson, "Economic Aspects of the Organization of Agricultural Research," in *Resource Allocation in Agricultural Research,* ed. W. Fishel (Minneapolis, University of Minnesota, 1971); Khaldi, Ph.D. diss.; W. Huffman, "The Contribution of Education and Extension to Differential Rates of Change" (Ph.D. diss., University of Chicago, 1972); Y. Kislev and R. Evenson, "Research and Productivity in Wheat and Maize," *Journal of Development Economics,* forthcoming.

price changes. In such settings, as in many LDCs, the demand for information is low, and the information suppliers find an unreceptive audience. The introduction of real new techniques, factor quality improvements, or new factors that can substitute for old ones alters this situation. Producers demand information in varying forms and are willing to pay high prices in terms of their time and the cost of unsuccessful experiments. Information suppliers find a receptive and critical clientele. The economic value of schooling rises, making it a complement to technology generation. In equilibrium, however, information suppliers substitute for schooling-associated abilities, in that they partially process information and offer it in the form of recommended practices.

This substitute relationship between schooling and information supply was noted in one of my earlier studies.[8] A recent study by W. Huffman provides much better and more direct measures of the relationship. His estimate of the value of extension time (U.S. $50 per hour spent in direct contact with farmers) is one of the few to utilize this richer specification.[9] The study by N. Khaldi actually developed estimates of errors (departures from cost minimization) by state in American agriculture. These errors were then regressed on measures of research activity and schooling. The results support the basic model postulated here. Errors were positively related to technology generation and negatively related to schooling.[10]

Welch, treating measured scale economies as a particular kind of long-run error, reached a similar result. Scale errors were positively related to technology generation and negatively related to schooling. His paper raised an important issue in growth accounting. It shows that much of the growth attributed to scale economies by Griliches can be reattributed to technology-generating and error-reducing activities.[11]

The second specification advance of recent years is based on technology transfer or technology borrowing. Technology transfer was

8. R. Evenson, "Economic Aspects of the Organization of Agricultural Research," in *Resource Allocation in Agricultural Research,* ed. W. Fishel (Minneapolis: University of Minnesota Press, 1971).

9. W. Huffman, "The Contribution of Education and Extension to Differential Rates of Change" (Ph.D. diss., University of Chicago, 1972).

10. See N. Khaldi's Ph.D. dissertation, prepared for Southern Methodist University.

11. See F. Welch, "Economies of Scale in U.S. Agriculture," mimeographed (New York, National Bureau of Economic Research, 1972); and Zvi Griliches, "Research Expenditures, Education, and the Aggregate Agricultural Production Function," *American Economic Review* 54 (1964).

indirectly faced in the aggregate production function studies based on cross-section data. In an early study, R. Latimer and D. Paarleburg concluded that research results were so pervasive that one could not identify the research effort with state cross-section data.[12] The successful efforts of several investigators utilizing cross-section data diverted attention from the issue for a time.

It is, of course, an important issue, not only from the point of view of the identification of the research-productivity relationship, but from a policy viewpoint as well. If one region or country can simply borrow new technology at a relatively low cost, an efficient national development strategy will be based on facilitating such borrowing. If, on the other hand, the transfer of technology is not easy or low in cost, it may be more efficient for a developing country to generate its own technology. The "externalities" inherent in the transfer process are important and obvious.

A paper by J. Houck, Vernon Ruttan, and myself deals with technology transfer in the context of a case study of technical change in three commodities.[13] A formal treatment has been developed by Yoav Kislev and myself along the following lines.[14] Techniques of production are postulated to have a degree of specificity to biological and economic conditions. That is, a particular technique is superior to all others only when certain conditions obtain. A particular crop variety, for example, is generally superior to alternative varieties only under a small range of conditions. The wheat and rice varieties now widely heralded as triggering a "green revolution" in parts of the world are only partial (and temporary) exceptions to this rule. The historical experience in sugarcane variety development[15] has been compared to the green revolution experience in wheat and rice in this context. As with the first interspecific sugarcane hybrids, which created a green revolution in the 1920s and 1930s, the widespread planting of a single variety is a temporary phenomenon. It is the relatively easy to develop, improved varieties that have more climate-specific characteristics.

12. Robert Latimer and Don Paarleburg, "Geographic Distribution of Research Costs and Benefits," *Journal of Farm Economics* 47 (1965): 234–41.

13. J. Houck, V. Ruttan, and R. Evenson, "Technical Change and Agricultural Trade: Three Case Studies, Sugar, Bananas, and Rice," in *The Technology Factor in International Trade,* ed. Raymond Vernon (New York: National Bureau of Economic Research, 1970).

14. Y. Kislev and R. Evenson, "Research and Productivity in Wheat and Maize," *Journal of Development Economics,* forthcoming.

15. R. Evenson, "International Transmission of Technology in Sugarcane Production," mimeographed (New Haven, Yale University, 1969).

The Kislev-Evenson formulation utilized an international system of regions based on climate factors.[16] The system was such that several wheat-producing countries were included in the same climate region. Technology-generating activity in each country and in each region was measured by the number of internationally abstracted publications that were attributable to particular commodities (wheat and maize in this case). The basic transfer specifications were:

$$P_i(t) = A_i + b\,R_i(t) + c\,[1 - \alpha\,EXP^{-PR_i(t)}]\,BR_i(t) + Z(t) \qquad (8.4)$$

$$P_i(t) = A_i + b'R_i(t) + c\,[1 + \alpha'EXP^{-PR_i(t)}]\,BR_i(t) + Z(t) \qquad (8.5)$$

Equation (8.4) specifies exponential interaction terms between indigenous research activity, $R_i(t)$ (measured as some distributed lag of research publications in time $t$ and previous periods), and the stock of "borrowable" research, $BR_i(t)$, defined similarly to $R_i(t)$, except that it is research activity in other countries in the same climate region. Equation (8.5) specifies a logistic interaction.[17]

Table 8.3 includes a summary of the economic implications of the estimates of equation (8.5). The results are presented in terms of the estimated marginal income stream generated by one unit of research activity in a typical country.[18] The specification divides this into three additive components: (a) the direct earnings stream associated with the indigenous research activity, (b) the transfer acceleration (the borrowing-from-others effect) income stream from the interaction term, and (c) the average contribution to *other* countries in the region that are in a position to borrow from this country. These estimated income streams are priced at different levels in different parts of the world. The price in Latin America and South Asia is approximately U.S. $40,000. In North America and Northern Europe the price is $100,000, and in a few African countries it runs to $200,000, largely because of the very limited supply of indigenous scientific talent. Even at the highest research supply prices, the income streams justify their purchase prices, and at the lower price levels these earnings streams represent the kinds

16. The regions were based on the work of Juan Papadakis reported in his "Agricultural Climates of the World" (Buenos Aires: J. Papadakis, 1952).

17. This term implies that as indigenous research is increased from year to year a standard logistic-type curve traces out the proportion of the borrowable research actually borrowed.

18. In this study, a research unit is defined as that research which produces an internationally abstracted, commodity-oriented publication.

of low-cost earnings streams that Theodore Schultz and others have argued must provide the basis for rapid development.[19]

A final note on the Kislev-Evenson results: Even though the estimated return to transfer-acceierating research is high, the same study estimated that the transfer between countries, where no indigenous research was undertaken, was effectively zero, i.e., $1/(1 + \alpha')$ in equation (8.5). Costless transfer apparently does not exist. Even the extension activity undertaken in countries that did not do research (substantial in some cases under technical aid programs) did not effect transfer.

## 2. RESEARCH AND PRODUCTIVITY IN CEREAL GRAIN PRODUCTION: A GEOCLIMATE REGIONAL ANALYSIS

One of the directions taken in the studies of the contribution of research in recent years has been to incorporate geoclimate data into the specification. A study done in 1973 by Kislev and myself focused on the transfer of wheat and maize research findings between geoclimate regions. A strong complementarity between indigenous research findings and transferred or borrowed research findings *within* a geoclimate region was identified, and it was concluded that relatively little in the way of research findings transfer occurred between regions.[20] This suggests that an analysis in which the geoclimate region is the unit of observation might allow an improved estimate of the relationship between research activity and economic performance.

In particular, this approach avoids the problem of research "pervasiveness." If complex transfer processes govern the relationship of research to productivity within a region, but not between regions, a model based on regional observations might reveal the gross relationship with more reliability. The transfer mechanism, of course, cannot be investigated, but other features, especially the contribution of the more basic sciences, can be identified.

In this section an analysis of cereal grain productivity is undertaken utilizing geoclimate regional observations. An extensive climate classification, based primarily on the work of J. Papadakis, will be used.[21]

19. T. W. Schultz, *Transforming Traditional Agriculture* (New Haven: Yale University Press, 1964).
20. Y. Kislev and R. Evenson, "Agricultural Research and Productivity: An International Analysis," mimeographed (New Haven, Yale University, 1973).
21. Papadakis, "Agricultural Climates of the World."

Table 8.4: Geoclimate Region Research in Cereal Grain Production

| Region | Adjusted number of sub-regions | LDC share of sub-regions (%) | Publications (1942–70) per adjusted subregion | | | | | Total cereals pub. per subregion | Ratio of basic fo crop pub. | Cereal grain yields | | |
|---|---|---|---|---|---|---|---|---|---|---|---|---|
| | | | Wheat | Barley | Maize | Sorghum | Rice | | | 1950–51 (kg./ha.) | 1966–67 (kg./ha.) | Ratio |
| 1. Tropical zone | ... | ... | ... | ... | ... | ... | ... | 48.3 | 0.90 | 11.00 | 13.79 | 1.253 |
| 1.1. Humid equatorial | 15.91 | 100 | ...[a] | ... | 30.2 | 11.6 | 111.8 | 51.6 | 1.06 | 11.92 | 14.33 | 1.20 |
| 1.2. Humid tropical | 5.00 | 86 | ... | ... | 15.1 | 2.1 | 121.7 | 28.1 | .32 | 16.98 | 24.62 | 1.45 |
| 1.3. Dry equatorial | 4.06 | 100 | 1.5 | 0.2 | 4.7 | 1.1 | 22.5 | 8.2 | 1.53 | 10.61 | 14.53 | 1.37 |
| 1.4. Hot equatorial | 10.22 | 95 | ... | ... | 19.3 | 13.6 | 224.5 | 68.7 | .96 | 10.57 | 13.58 | 1.28 |
| 1.5. Semiarid equatorial | 6.35 | 100 | .0 | ... | 4.1 | 32.2 | 8.6 | 8.6 | .65 | 8.46 | 10.69 | 1.26 |
| 1.7. Humid tierra | 16.19 | 100 | 20.4 | 20.4 | 30.6 | 26.0 | 20.8 | 24.1 | .85 | 12.38 | 12.91 | 1.04 |
| 1.8. Dry tierra | 2.06 | 100 | ... | ... | 42.4 | ... | 18.1 | 52.8 | .50 | 14.49 | 10.11 | .70 |
| 1.9. Cool winter tropical | 5.58 | 86 | ... | ... | 18.5 | 87.4 | 353.1 | 144.9 | 1.00 | 10.39 | 13.77 | 1.33 |
| 2. Tierra fria zone | ... | ... | ... | ... | ... | ... | ... | 52.1 | .62 | 7.93 | 12.84 | 1.619 |
| 2.1. Tropical highlands | 8.72 | 100 | 8.0 | 6.7 | 132.9 | 28.2 | ... | 52.1 | .62 | 7.93 | 12.84 | 1.619 |
| 3. Desert zone | ... | ... | ... | ... | ... | ... | ... | 15.6 | 2.69 | 9.22 | 12.05 | 1.307 |
| 3.1. Hot tropical | 3.00 | 100 | .0 | ... | ... | ... | 4.5 | 2.3 | .22 | 28.28 | 31.86 | 1.13 |
| 3.2. Hot subtropical | 16.94 | 100 | 20.9 | 11.8 | 2.0 | ... | 6.7 | 15.8 | .76 | 8.99 | 11.80 | 1.31 |
| 3.7. Continental | 4.00 | 60 | 1.4 | 1.6 | .0 | .0 | 93.5 | 24.5 | 6.26 | 9.98 | 11.83 | 1.19 |
| 4. Subtropical zone | ... | ... | ... | ... | ... | ... | ... | 54.9 | 1.18 | 6.83 | 9.01 | 1.320 |
| 4.1. Humid | 9.22 | 75 | 30.4 | 4.7 | 51.6 | 1.6 | 63.0 | 28.4 | 1.20 | 12.50 | 15.65 | 1.25 |
| 4.2. Monsoon | 6.91 | 66 | 116.6 | 128.1 | 69.7 | 144.9 | 52.0 | 102.7 | 1.31 | 6.41 | 8.16 | 1.27 |
| 4.3. Hot | 6.05 | 100 | 105.7 | 46.7 | 47.6 | 156.8 | 6.6 | 68.7 | .99 | 5.21 | 7.41 | 1.42 |
| 4.4. Semiarid | 2.00 | 100 | ... | ... | 10.0 | 5.0 | ... | 7.5 | .80 | 14.21 | 17.93 | 1.26 |
| 5. Pampean zone | ... | ... | ... | ... | ... | ... | ... | 97.3 | 1.23 | 13.61 | 16.73 | 1.229 |
| 5.1. Pampean | 4.53 | 20 | 99.5 | 99.0 | 168.4 | 36.6 | ... | 97.3 | 1.23 | 13.61 | 16.73 | 1.23 |

|  | | | | | | | | | | | | |
|---|---|---|---|---|---|---|---|---|---|---|---|---|
| *6. Mediterranean zone* | ... | ... | ... | ... | ... | ... | ... | 39.6 | 1.95 | 10.14 | 13.03 | 1.284 |
| 6.1. Subtropical | 18.68 | 45 | 72.9 | 71.3 | 33.5 | 11.7 | 104.9 | 55.4 | 2.59 | 10.38 | 13.10 | 1.26 |
| 6.2. Marine | 7.24 | 25 | 14.0 | 2.2 | 34.4 | 12.0 | .0 | 16.8 | .80 | 9.20 | 13.32 | 1.45 |
| 6.5. Temperate | 11.27 | 17 | 77.3 | 18.9 | 45.5 | 4.0 | 23.5 | 37.4 | 1.90 | 11.93 | 15.86 | 1.33 |
| 6.7. Continental | 19.68 | 30 | 67.0 | 27.7 | 133.4 | 8.3 | 1.6 | 47.5 | 1.41 | 10.79 | 14.48 | 1.34 |
| 6.8. Subtrop. semiarid | 14.26 | 50 | 46.9 | 22.8 | 21.3 | 6.0 | ... | 26.7 | 1.68 | 8.64 | 9.75 | 1.13 |
| 6.9. Contin. semiarid | 4.61 | 66 | 4.6 | 3.0 | 9.0 | 1.0 | ... | 5.8 | .20 | 6.16 | 6.48 | 1.05 |
| *7. Marine zone* | ... | ... | ... | ... | ... | ... | ... | 120.1 | 2.02 | 17.01 | 28.13 | 1.654 |
| 7.1. Warm | 2.00 | 00 | 11.5 | 5.4 | ... | ... | ... | 8.4 | 2.00 | 25.13 | 35.48 | 1.41 |
| 7.2. Cool | 6.81 | 00 | 78.9 | 236.3 | 92.9 | ... | ... | 136.1 | 3.10 | 22.12 | 34.82 | 1.57 |
| 7.6. Cool temperate | 21.71 | 03 | 97.1 | 145.8 | 158.9 | 20.3 | ... | 120.3 | 1.75 | 18.44 | 28.86 | 1.57 |
| 7.7. Cold temperate | 8.00 | 00 | 90.6 | 144.8 | 187.9 | ... | ... | 133.9 | 1.46 | 9.62 | 20.79 | 2.16 |
| *8. Humid continental zone* | ... | ... | ... | ... | ... | ... | ... | 256.2 | 2.79 | 19.61 | 34.02 | 1.735 |
| 8.1. Warm | 7.62 | 00 | 152.4 | 151.2 | 450.5 | 92.2 | 417.0 | 254.3 | 4.60 | 24.43 | 42.54 | 1.74 |
| 8.2. Semiwarm | 12.16 | 00 | 164.3 | 124.1 | 703.0 | 283.5 | 622.3 | 291.5 | 1.50 | 18.77 | 33.55 | 1.79 |
| 8.3. Cold | 2.00 | 00 | 52.0 | 17.0 | ... | ... | ... | 34.5 | .63 | 7.98 | 11.90 | 1.49 |
| *9. Steppe zone* | ... | ... | ... | ... | ... | ... | ... | 357.9 | 1.35 | 11.57 | 18.26 | 1.578 |
| 9.2. Semiwarm | 12.92 | 00 | 606.5 | 346.6 | 818.6 | 304.2 | 24.7 | 450.3 | 1.10 | 12.29 | 21.14 | 1.68 |
| 9.3. Cold | 7.28 | 00 | 636.4 | 348.5 | 111.9 | 12.0 | ... | 382.3 | 1.75 | 10.11 | 14.82 | 1.47 |
| 9.4. Temperate | 4.34 | 00 | 38.2 | 35.5 | ... | ... | ... | 36.9 | 1.96 | 11.85 | 17.36 | 1.47 |

a. Not applicable.

*Notes:* Subregions are defined as $n(1 - d) + d$ where $n$ is the number of individual countries in the region, and

$$d = \sum_{i=1}^{n} A_i - \bar{A} / (2A_i - 2)\bar{A}.$$

$A_i$ is the acreage of the crop in country $i$. The term $d = 0$, when all countries in the region have the same acreage, approaches 1 as acreage in the region is concentrated in one country.

Cereal grain yields are computed by simply totaling cereal production of the different grains without price weighting. While prices vary considerably by country, international prices per kilogram are approximately the same for all cereals.

*Source:* Publications data from Kislev and Evenson, "Investment in Agricultural Research and Extension."

Thirty-three geoclimate regions of the world were defined. Table 8.4 provides data on research and economic performance for each of the regions. This particular climate system is oriented to agricultural production somewhat more directly than some of the more standard systems used by geographers. It is closely related, however, to other systems.

Table 8.4 provides three basic categories of information. The adjusted number of subregions indicates the size of the region, where size is defined in such a way as to reflect the extent and diversity of problems. Subregions are distinct geographic units within the region for each major crop. For example, in region 1.1, the humid equatorial tropical region, there are 15.91 subregions. Portions of twenty-two countries are actually located in the region. None produces significant amounts of wheat or barley; almost all produce some rice. The adjustment is made to take into account the variable size of subregions, and to scale the subregions into regions of standardized size.

The number of internationally abstracted publications from 1942 to 1970, *per adjusted subregion,* is an indicator of research intensity. It is a kind of "research per problem" measure. The proper deflator for research is a very difficult problem. One could use research per acre, or research per farm, and for some purposes these would be acceptable. Fundamentally, however, the geoclimate information provides the best basis for deflation. The third main category of data in the table is the reported levels of food grain yields and the ratio of yields in the late 1960s to yields in the early 1950s.

One feature of table 8.4 that bears mention is the high correlation of region with level of development. Of the 129 (unadjusted) subregions in the tropical, tierra fria, desert, and subtropical climate zones, only 6 were developed country regions. In fact, only the Mediterranean climate regions encompass both developed and less developed countries.

The differences in the relative levels of research activity show up quite clearly. The humid continental and steppe climate zones, for example, report from five to seven times as many research findings per subregion as the less developed regions. A number of less developed regions have conducted virtually no research at all over the period.

The developed country regions (zones 7, 8, and 9) quite clearly have higher average yields of cereal grains than most of the less developed regions. These regions have also realized the highest rate of increase in yields from 1950/51 to 1966/67.

An analysis of the determinants of yield per hectare is developed as follows. First, the production function is specified as being divisible into a biological process and a mechanical process:

$$Q = f[f_b(X_b), f_m(X_m)],$$ (8.6)

where $Q$ is output; $X_b$ are biological inputs, plants, fertilizer, and climate factors; $X_m$ are mechanical inputs, implements, mechanical and animal power, and human labor.

The basic determination of output per unit of land is based heavily on the biological process. Nonetheless the mechanical process is important, of course. It represents the performance of tasks by alternative means. The incentives for performing the tasks of seed-bed preparation, seeding, cultivating, and harvesting are such that the marginal effects on yield levels are slight. The major impact of advances in mechanical technology shows up in lower production costs achieved by economizing on labor and changing the scale of operation.

Yield levels are changed largely through improvements in the biological subprocess. Fertilizer, water use, pesticides, and plant varieties are the primary determinants of yield. Agronomic practices regarding the timing of operations are part of this biological process. An analysis of changes in yields over time would depend basically on changes in the biological inputs, including agronomic practices. The regression analysis reported in table 8.5 is based on a biological process specification:

$$Q_{it} = D_i H_{it}^{a_1} F_{it}^{a_2} R_{it}^{a_3 + \sigma_4} (B_{it}),$$ (8.7)

where:

$Q_{it}$ = output in kilograms for region $i$, time $t$

$H_{it}$ = hectares of land, region $i$, time $t$

$F_{it}$ = fertilizer per cropped acre, region $i$, time $t$

$R_{it}$ = technological research, the cumulative number of publications from 1942 to time $t$ (a 6-year distributed lag was applied to inclusion); this is crop-specific agronomic and plant breeding research

$B_{it}$ = fundamental research in plant physiology, plant pathology, and soil science; computed as with $R_{it}$, except that it is not crop specific

$D_i$ = regional dummy variables.

Regression results based on this specification are reported in table 8.5. The model was applied to the five major food grains separately. An aggregate cereals regression was also created by summing results

Table 8.5: Regression Analysis: Geoclimate Yield Determination

| Regression number: | 1 | 2 | 3 | 4 | 5 | 6 |
|---|---|---|---|---|---|---|
| Dependent variable | Wheat | Barley | LN (output) Maize | Sorghum | Rice | All cereals |
| $R^2$ | 0.996 | 0.991 | 0.998 | 0.997 | 0.997 | 0.990 |
| LN (acres) | .917 | 1.050 | .865 | .912 | .985 | 1.20 |
|  | (.020) | (.02) | (.016) | (.019) | (.025) | (.015) |
| LN (fert/ha.)[a] | .037 | .054 | .033 | −.014 | .018 | .037 |
|  | (.007) | (.011) | (.007) | (.019 ) | (.008) | (.006) |
| LN (rec/SR)[b] | .087 | .009 | .115 | .115 | .033 | .056 |
|  | (.005) | (.005) | (.005) | (.014) | (.008) | (.005) |
| LN (Res/SR) | .00005 | .00008 | .00012 | .00034 | −.000006 | .00005 |
| *PB[c] | (.000004) | (.00001) | (.00001) | (.00004) | (.000004) | (.000004) |

a. A price-weighted average of nitrogen, phosphorus, and potash application per cropped acre; not a crop-specific measure.

b. Publications summed from 1942 to year of observation per subregion in the regions.

c. Publications in plant physiology, plant pathology, and soil science.

Observations are from the period 1948–68 for regions with significant production. Regressions were weighted by acreage.

Regional dummy variables were included in all regressions. This has the effect of converting all variables to deviations from mean values.

for the individual grains. In all cases, only observations with significant production of the grain or grains in question were included in the regressions. All regressions were weighted by the acreage of the grain in question. All regressions included regional dummy variables, which effectively converts all observations to deviations from regional means. These differences in yield levels by region do not determine the relationship between output and the research activity.

The regression results themselves are rather extraordinary. Given the fact that fertilizer use is not a crop-specific measure, it is surprising that it contributes to explanation in four of the five crop regressions. Land is of course the major determinant of production. The research variables indicate that research activity is an important determinant of cereal grain output. Not only has crop-specific, applied agronomic, and plant-breeding research contributed to output, but the more basic plant physiology, pathology, and soil science research has contributed as well.

These estimates suggest that the research associated with one publication, costing approximately $100,000, generates or produces an income stream in each future year of approximately the following values:[22]

22. The marginal products computations were based on geometric means. Cereal grains were valued at U.S. $75 per metric ton.

|  | *Annual income stream* | *Internal rate of*<br>*return (percent)* |
|---|---|---|
| Wheat | $620,000 | 49 |
| Barley | 58,000 | 10 |
| Maize | 337,000 | 34 |
| Sorghum | 275,000 | 30 |
| Rice | 150,000 | 20 |
| All cereals<br>  (applied research) | 123,000 | 18 |
| All cereals<br>  (basic research) | 180,000 | 22 |

These income streams are realized with a time lag. An average lag of five years is specified in the estimation procedure and in the internal rates of return reported. It is quite likely that the actual lag is greater for basic research. The finding that basic research generates an income stream of roughly the same magnitude as applied research, while somewhat tentative, is an important result.

3. RESEARCH, EXTENSION, AND AGGREGATE AGRICULTURAL
PRODUCTIVITY IN A MAJOR DEVELOPING COUNTRY:
THE CASE OF INDIA

The studies of specific commodity-oriented research programs reviewed above in section 1 indicated that research could be productive in less developed settings. In this section of the chapter we will take a closer look at the contribution of research and extension in a major developing country. India has undertaken significant research activity in the past twenty-five years. It is a large and geographically varied country. Its research investment has been very unevenly distributed among regions. As the following analysis shows, its economic performance has varied regionally as well.

### Measured Productivity Growth

Table 8.6 reports rates of growth of total factor productivity by state and for all India (see also figure 8.1). The major details of the table's construction are as follows: (1) The output series is a price-weighted Laspeyres index of the quantity of agricultural commodities produced. (2) The input series is computed as a factor share-weighted index (of the Divisia type) of rates of input growth (see table 8.7 for factor shares). (3) Input growth rates were calculated on an annual basis for

Table 8.6: Growth in Agricultural Output and Inputs in Selected
Indian States, 1953/54 to 1970/71

| | Period I 1953–56 to | Period I 1958–61 | Period II 1958–61 to | Period II 1963–65 | Period III 1963–65 to | Period III 1969–71 |
|---|---|---|---|---|---|---|
| **Andhra Pradesh** | | | | | | |
| Annual output growth | | 2.42 | | 2.63 | | -0.24 |
| Annual input growth | | 1.57 | | 2.52 | | 1.29 |
| Traditional inputs | 1.48 | | 1.09 | | .18 | |
| Modern inputs | .09 | | 1.41 | | 1.11 | |
| Residual productivity growth | | .85 | | .11 | | -1.05 |
| **Assam** | | | | | | |
| Annual output growth | | 1.22 | | 1.48 | | 5.45 |
| Annual input growth | | 3.49 | | 1.66 | | 1.47 |
| Traditional inputs | 3.02 | | 1.55 | | 1.40 | |
| Modern inputs | .47 | | .11 | | .07 | |
| Residual productivity growth | | -2.27 | | -.18 | | 3.98 |
| **Bihar** | | | | | | |
| Annual output growth | | 3.43 | | 2.36 | | 1.57 |
| Annual input growth | | 2.03 | | 2.04 | | 2.39 |
| Traditional inputs | 1.83 | | 1.68 | | 1.58 | |
| Modern inputs | .20 | | .36 | | .81 | |
| Residual productivity growth | | 1.40 | | .32 | | -.82 |
| **Gujarat** | | | | | | |
| Annual output growth | | 3.00 | | 4.71 | | 7.13 |
| Annual input growth | | 2.26 | | 1.90 | | 2.35 |
| Traditional inputs | 1.83 | | 1.16 | | 1.62 | |
| Modern inputs | .43 | | .74 | | .73 | |
| Residual productivity growth | | .74 | | 2.81 | | 4.78 |
| **Haryana** | | | | | | |
| Annual output growth | | 4.73 | | 1.23 | | 20.40 |
| Annual input growth | | 2.32 | | 1.93 | | 4.30 |
| Traditional inputs | 1.15 | | .48 | | 2.60 | |
| Modern inputs | 1.37 | | 1.45 | | 1.70 | |
| Residual productivity growth | | 2.41 | | -.70 | | 16.10 |
| **Kerala** | | | | | | |
| Annual output growth | | 3.00 | | 1.30 | | 2.15 |
| Annual input growth | | 1.03 | | 2.55 | | 2.82 |
| Traditional inputs | 1.8 | | 1.20 | | 1.63 | |
| Modern inputs | .85 | | 1.35 | | 1.19 | |
| Residual productivity growth | | 1.97 | | -1.25 | | - .67 |
| **Madhya Pradesh** | | | | | | |
| Annual output growth | | 4.45 | | .76 | | .30 |
| Annual input growth | | 2.44 | | .71 | | 1.82 |
| Traditional inputs | 2.17 | | .44 | | .95 | |
| Modern inputs | .27 | | .27 | | .87 | |
| Residual productivity growth | | 2.01 | | .05 | | -1.52 |
| **Maharashtra** | | | | | | |
| Annual output growth | | 3.59 | | .85 | | .08 |
| Annual input growth | | 1.48 | | 1.78 | | 2.21 |

Table 8.6 *(Continued)*

| | Period I | | Period II | | Period III | |
| --- | --- | --- | --- | --- | --- | --- |
| | 1953 –56 | *to* 1958 –61 | 1958 –61 | *to* 1963 –65 | 1963 –65 | *to* 1969 –71 |
| Traditional inputs | 1.36 | | 1.34 | | 1.46 | |
| Modern inputs | .22 | | .44 | | .75 | |
| Residual productivity growth | | 2.11 | | –.93 | | –2.13 |
| *Mysore* | | | | | | |
| Annual output growth | | 3.97 | | 2.96 | | 1.93 |
| Annual input growth | | 2.94 | | 2.27 | | 1.66 |
| Traditional inputs | 2.79 | | .75 | | .28 | |
| Modern inputs | .15 | | 1.52 | | 1.34 | |
| Residual productivity growth | | 1.03 | | .69 | | .27 |
| *Orissa* | | | | | | |
| Annual output growth | | .88 | | 4.80 | | 3.15 |
| Annual input growth | | 2.22 | | 2.87 | | 1.85 |
| Traditional inputs | 2.21 | | 2.86 | | 1.68 | |
| Modern inputs | .01 | | .01 | | .17 | |
| Residual productivity growth | | –1.34 | | 1.93 | | 1.30 |
| *Punjab* | | | | | | |
| Annual output growth | | 4.73 | | 3.60 | | 19.20 |
| Annual input growth | | 2.32 | | 3.08 | | 5.80 |
| Traditional inputs | 1.32 | | 1.28 | | 2.64 | |
| Modern inputs | 1.00 | | 1.80 | | 3.16 | |
| Residual productivity growth | | 2.41 | | .52 | | 13.40 |
| *Rajasthan* | | | | | | |
| Annual output growth | | 3.51 | | .06 | | 13.6 |
| Annual input growth | | 3.42 | | 1.05 | | .95 |
| Traditional inputs | 3.40 | | .92 | | .23 | |
| Modern inputs | .02 | | .13 | | .72 | |
| Residual productivity growth | | .09 | | –.99 | | 12.7 |
| *Tamil Nadu* | | | | | | |
| Annual output growth | | 4.48 | | 1.77 | | 3.08 |
| Annual input growth | | 2.99 | | 3.26 | | 2.47 |
| Traditional inputs | 2.91 | | 1.26 | | 1.04 | |
| Modern inputs | .08 | | 2.00 | | 1.43 | |
| Residual productivity growth | | 1.49 | | –1.43 | | .61 |
| *Uttar Pradesh* | | | | | | |
| Annual output growth | | 1.87 | | 2.47 | | 4.87 |
| Annual input growth | | 1.44 | | 1.81 | | 1.96 |
| Traditional inputs | 1.06 | | 1.13 | | .76 | |
| Modern inputs | .38 | | .68 | | 1.20 | |
| Residual productivity growth | | .43 | | .66 | | 1.93 |
| *West Bengal* | | | | | | |
| Annual output growth | | .36 | | 4.66 | | 2.18 |
| Annual input growth | | 2.48 | | 1.99 | | 2.54 |
| Traditional inputs | 2.37 | | 1.56 | | 2.49 | |
| Modern inputs | .11 | | .13 | | .05 | |
| Residual productivity growth | | –2.12 | | 2.67 | | –.36 |

Table 8.6*(Continued)*

| All India | Period I 1953 to 1958 −56 to −61 | Period II 1958 to 1963 −61 to −65 | Period III 1963 to 1969 −65 to −71 |
|---|---|---|---|
| Annual output growth | 3.01 | 2.25 | 4.44 |
| Annual input growth | 2.20 | 1.92 | 2.13 |
| Traditional inputs | 1.91 | 1.18 | 1.16 |
| Modern inputs | .29 | .74 | .97 |
| Residual productivity growth | .81 | .33 | 2.31 |

Table 8.7: Estimated Factor Shares, Indian State Agricultural Production, 1960 and 1971

| Area | Year | Land | Labor | Animal Power | Imple- ments | Pump- sets | Trac- tors | Ferti- lizer |
|---|---|---|---|---|---|---|---|---|
| Andhra Pradesh | 1960 | .336 | .451 | .127 | .012 | .061 | .003 | .010 |
| | 1971 | .307 | .407 | .088 | .008 | .158 | .008 | .024 |
| Assam | 1960 | .186 | .683 | .124 | .006 | —a | .001 | — |
| | 1971 | .316 | .570 | .102 | .009 | — | .001 | .002 |
| Bihar | 1960 | .265 | .569 | .138 | .010 | .001 | .002 | .003 |
| | 1971 | .353 | .510 | .095 | .013 | .008 | .006 | .014 |
| Gujarat | 1960 | .329 | .574 | .079 | .009 | .003 | .002 | .003 |
| | 1971 | .373 | .539 | .055 | .006 | .008 | .005 | .015 |
| Haryana | 1960 | .335 | .516 | .125 | .010 | .004 | .009 | .002 |
| | 1971 | .379 | .530 | .040 | .007 | .016 | .010 | .020 |
| Kerala | 1960 | .301 | .595 | .077 | .007 | .005 | — | .014 |
| | 1971 | .394 | .478 | .053 | .005 | .044 | .001 | .024 |
| Madhya Pradesh | 1960 | .343 | .457 | .158 | .016 | .023 | .001 | .002 |
| | 1971 | .423 | .425 | .114 | .012 | .015 | .001 | .007 |
| Maharashtra | 1960 | .385 | .441 | .155 | .011 | .002 | .001 | .004 |
| | 1971 | .412 | .453 | .096 | .007 | .013 | .003 | .016 |
| Mysore | 1960 | .378 | .501 | .092 | .012 | .009 | .002 | .006 |
| | 1971 | .412 | .380 | .060 | .009 | .020 | .034 | .027 |
| Orissa | 1960 | .535 | .319 | .135 | .005 | — | — | .002 |
| | 1971 | .640 | .197 | .082 | .008 | .001 | — | .004 |
| Punjab | 1960 | .373 | .430 | .151 | .020 | .007 | .011 | .003 |
| | 1971 | .369 | .489 | .045 | .012 | .015 | .029 | .043 |
| Rajasthan | 1960 | .466 | .430 | .089 | .010 | .002 | .001 | .001 |
| | 1971 | .565 | .342 | .062 | .008 | .013 | .002 | .007 |
| Tamil Nadu | 1960 | .257 | .497 | .140 | .016 | .074 | .002 | .015 |
| | 1971 | .301 | .443 | .095 | .009 | .095 | .003 | .053 |
| Uttar Pradesh | 1960 | .308 | .479 | .185 | .017 | .001 | .014 | .001 |
| | 1971 | .382 | .404 | .135 | .012 | .006 | .036 | .025 |
| West Bengal | 1960 | .255 | .589 | .137 | .012 | — | — | .006 |
| | 1971 | .345 | .525 | .105 | .007 | .003 | .005 | .011 |

a. Not applicable.

land, fertilizer, pump-sets, and tractors (after 1960). For animal power and implements the growth rates were based on livestock census data

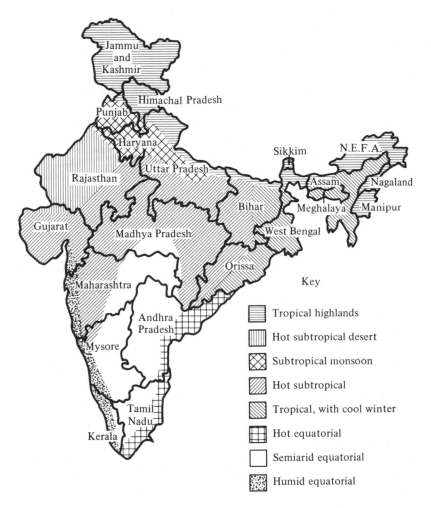

Fig. 8.1: Indian Climate Zones

for five-year intervals. The labor input growth rate was calculated as a constant rate between the 1951, 1961, and 1971 censuses. (4) Factor shares were computed for 1961, 1966, and 1971 and applied to periods I, II, and III.

In table 8.6, the total input growth rate is disaggregated into the contribution of traditional inputs, i.e., land (including canal irrigation), labor, and animal power, and of modern inputs, i.e., fertilizer, tractors, and pump-set irrigation. The productivity growth rate is measured as a residual. It is simply the difference between the growth rate of output and the growth rate of inputs. Each input is priced, in computing the shares, at market prices (or the best estimates of market price available). All labor is priced at hired-labor wage rates. Different wage rates for males and females for each state were used, and National Sample Survey data on the number of days worked per year were utilized to obtain the labor shares. Market prices are used on the assumption that they approximate marginal products well.

Factor-share data (table 8.7) show a general decline in the labor shares in all states except the Punjab, Haryana, and Maharashtra. It is interesting to note that wages rose significantly in these states over time. The share of animal power declined in all states and the share of all of the modern inputs rose significantly in all states.

The contrast between the three periods in table 8.6 is quite significant. In period I (the 1950s) all states except West Bengal, Assam, and Orissa recorded residual productivity growth of respectable proportions. (The negative results in West Bengal and Orissa were offset in period II, suggesting that they were probably due to weather effects.) The measured contribution to growth of the modern inputs was relatively low in most states.

Period II is characterized by an increased contribution of modern inputs in most states, but the relatively even regional pattern displayed in period I disappears: 6 of the 15 states have a decline in productivity and 2 have negligible positive growth.

Period III shows the effects of the exceptional performance of the states of Haryana, Punjab, Rajasthan, and Gujarat. The dominant feature of these data is the increasing regional disparity over time. Individual state indexes showed actual declines over the period in Bihar and West Bengal, and no increase in Assam, Kerala, Maharashtra, and Andhra Pradesh. Punjab, Haryana, and Gujarat, on the other hand, had productivity increases of approximately 5 percent during the period. The all-India index of productivity rose from a base of 100 in

Table 8.8: Indian Agricultural Research Expenditures, 1950–68
(Millions of constant 1968 rupees)[a]

| Year | Crop research | Livestock research | Specialty crops[b] | Total | Research spending as a percent of value of agric. production |
|------|---------------|--------------------|--------------------|-------|-------------------------------------------------------------|
| 1950 | 34.9  | 10.6 | 6.3  | 51.8  | .07 |
| 1951 | 35.7  | 11.1 | 6.5  | 53.3  | .07 |
| 1952 | 37.2  | 11.5 | 6.7  | 55.4  | .07 |
| 1953 | 38.1  | 12.6 | 6.9  | 57.6  | .07 |
| 1954 | 39.4  | 14.5 | 8.4  | 62.3  | .08 |
| 1955 | 45.0  | 18.5 | 8.8  | 72.3  | .09 |
| 1956 | 48.6  | 19.7 | 9.8  | 78.1  | .10 |
| 1957 | 52.3  | 21.1 | 10.1 | 83.5  | .10 |
| 1958 | 57.1  | 22.4 | 10.5 | 90.0  | .10 |
| 1959 | 61.3  | 23.8 | 10.8 | 95.9  | .11 |
| 1960 | 71.8  | 25.0 | 11.0 | 107.8 | .12 |
| 1961 | 74.5  | 26.4 | 11.1 | 112.0 | .12 |
| 1962 | 90.0  | 27.8 | 11.1 | 128.9 | .14 |
| 1963 | 94.5  | 28.0 | 11.1 | 133.6 | .14 |
| 1964 | 100.8 | 29.1 | 11.5 | 141.4 | .14 |
| 1965 | 108.0 | 30.0 | 11.5 | 149.5 | .17 |
| 1966 | 119.9 | 30.0 | 11.5 | 161.4 | .18 |
| 1967 | 127.3 | 30.0 | 11.5 | 168.8 | .17 |
| 1968 | 135.6 | 30.0 | 11.5 | 177.1 | .17 |

a. The exchange rate in 1968 was Rs. 7.5 = U.S. $1.
b. Includes coconuts, tea, arecanut, lac, and jute. Other crops included in crop research.

1952–55 to 117 in 1971. The comparable index of land productivity (aggregate yield of crops per hectare) stood at 141 in 1971.

Before analyzing the determinants of productivity change in Indian agriculture, we should look at some information on the research system in India.[23] In table 8.8, time-series data on research investment in constant 1968 rupees are presented. By international standards, research expenditures of only 0.2 percent of the value of production are relatively low. This is roughly in line with other developing countries but far below the 1 percent that many developed countries have consistently spent over the past thirty or forty years.[24] It should be noted, however, that India purchases considerably more scientist man-years with its budget than most other countries.

23. Data are from R. Mohan, D. Jha, and R. Evenson, "The Indian Agricultural Research System," *Economic and Political Weekly* (Bombay), March 1973.
24. See Kislev and Evenson, "Investment in Agricultural Research and Extension."

Table 8.9: Crop-Related Research Expenditures by States, 1953–68

| | Total expenditures (millions of constant 1968 Rs.) | | | | Expenditures per community development block | | | |
|---|---|---|---|---|---|---|---|---|
| Area | 1953 | 1958 | 1963 | 1968 | 1953 | 1958 | 1963 | 1968 |
| Andhra Pradesh | 3.53 | 4,40 | 5.69 | 9.29 | 7.9 | 9.0 | 12.8 | 20.9 |
| Assam | 1.19 | 1.22 | 1.22 | 1.28 | 7.4 | 7.6 | 7.6 | 8.0 |
| Bihar | 3.00 | 4.50 | 5.48 | 5.48 | 5.2 | 7.8 | 9.5 | 9.5 |
| Gujarat | 1.80 | 3.20 | 4.75 | 9.00 | 8.0 | 14.3 | 21.1 | 50.1 |
| Haryana | 1.20 | 1.88 | 3.49 | 4.96 | 14.6 | 22.9 | 42.5 | 60.5 |
| Kerala | 0.50 | 0.73 | 1.28 | 1.80 | 3.5 | 5.1 | 9.0 | 12.6 |
| Madhya Pradesh | 1.61 | 1.71 | 3.90 | 5.95 | 3.9 | 4.1 | 9.3 | 14.3 |
| Maharashtra | 1.76 | 4.26 | 5.93 | 13.90 | 4.2 | 10.0 | 13.0 | 32.7 |
| Mysore | 3.28 | 4.37 | 4.50 | 7.20 | 12.2 | 16.3 | 16.8 | 26.8 |
| Orissa | 2.45 | 2.45 | 5.48 | 5.83 | 8.0 | 8.0 | 17.8 | 19.0 |
| Punjab | 2.04 | 3.20 | 5.94 | 8.45 | 17.6 | 27.6 | 51.2 | 72.8 |
| Rajasthan | 1.13 | 1.66 | 7.35 | 7.40 | 4.9 | 7.2 | 31.6 | 31.9 |
| Tamil Nadu | 5.62 | 7.00 | 9.07 | 9.19 | 15.0 | 18.7 | 24.2 | 26.1 |
| Uttar Pradesh | 4.44 | 5.91 | 14.52 | 17.12 | 4.9 | 6.6 | 16.2 | 19.1 |
| West Bengal | 1.00 | 2.31 | 3.64 | 3.64 | 2.9 | 6.8 | 10.7 | 10.7 |
| Delhi | 5.80 | 8.90 | 12.90 | 24.51 | —a | — | — | — |

a. Not available.

Table 8.9 presents annual expenditures (in constant 1968 rupees) for selected years by state and for the Indian Agricultural Research Institute in New Delhi. These are expenditures for major crop research only. Special crop research expenditures (arecanut, lac, tea, jute, and coconut) are not included in these figures. The research expenditures include both state and central government funds. State university systems as well as state government organizations are included; private research and development expenditures are not included.

Table 8.10: Commodity-Oriented Indian Agricultural Research Publications
Abstracted in International Abstracting Journals, 1948–68

| | Rice | Barley and wheat | Maize | Millets | Sugar | Cotton | Phyto-pathology | Soils | All crops | Livestock |
|---|---|---|---|---|---|---|---|---|---|---|
| 1. Publications | | | | | | | | | | |
| 1948–54 | 258 | 61 | 53 | 86 | 255 | 357 | 292 | 123 | 1,564 | 512 |
| 1955–61 | 274 | 170 | 70 | 139 | 245 | 394 | 450 | 189 | 1,962 | 607 |
| 1962–68 | 517 | 253 | 101 | 264 | 259 | 435 | 1,050 | 331 | 3,456 | 1,094 |
| 2. Publications per billion Rs. of commodity value | | | | | | | | | | |
| 1948–54 | 1.5 | 1.1 | 3.7 | 1.2 | 5.0 | 14.1 | — | — | 2.9 | — |
| 1955–61 | 1.2 | 1.9 | 3.4 | 1.5 | 3.8 | 14.6 | — | — | 2.7 | — |
| 1962–68 | 2.3 | 3.0 | 4.1 | 3.3 | 2.9 | 12.2 | — | — | 4.5 | — |

Source: See notes to table 8.11.

India's rural area is divided into "community development blocks." The blocks are the basic extension and community development administrative units, and each has approximately the same number of farms. In table 8.9, research expenditure is divided by the number of blocks in each area. By this measure, for example, Punjab's research is three times more intensive than that of Andhra Pradesh, even though total expenditures are roughly equal in the two states.

Table 8.10 utilizes publication counts to provide further data on the direction of research work in India. The data reveal a gradual shift away from the commercial crops, sugar and cotton, and toward food grains.

## Productivity and Research

This section turns to a statistical analysis of the effect of agricultural research on productivity in India. The framework of the analysis is the following functional relation:

$$P = f \text{ (research, extension, weather, time, region)}, \qquad (8.8)$$

where $P$ stands for state productivity level and research is introduced with a five-year lag (see notes to table 8.11 for definitions of variables).

Productivity in states is affected by research done both in the states themselves and in other states of similar climate. The geoclimatic regional classification of Papadakis was used to facilitate the analysis of the transfer (borrowing) of knowledge between states. Four regions were defined (see figure 8.1). An exponential borrowing function was assumed and the stock of borrowed knowledge was defined as

$$B = R(1 - \alpha^{-\cdot 01S}) = R - \alpha Re^{\cdot 01S}, \qquad (8.9)$$

where $S$ is intrastate research and $R$ is research done in the geoclimate region to which the state belongs.

In the absence of state data on extension expenditures or workers, an index measuring the intensity of extension work was constructed. Extension programs in India have been developed in stages. The index of extension intensity is the weighted average stage in the state, with the weights 0.25 for stage I, 0.75 for stage II, and 0.25 for stage III.

Weather was represented in the analysis by a drought years dummy variable. Other dummies stood for time (periods 1953–59, 1969–71) and regions (Northwest).

Regression estimates are presented in table 8.11. The regressions

Table 8.11: State Productivity Analysis: 15 Indian States, 1953–71

|  | *Reg. 1* | *Reg. 2* | *Reg. 3* |
|---|---|---|---|
| $R^2$ | 0.549 | 0.575 | 0.587 |
| Constant | 96.930 | 102.350 | 104.230 |
| State research ($S$) | .050 | .049 | .030 |
|  | (4.85) | (4.84) | (2.50) |
| Regional research ($R$) | .004 | .017 | .011 |
|  | (4.00) | (5.12) | (2.74) |
| $Re^{-.01s}$ |  | −.402 | −.499 |
|  |  | (4.09) | (4.84) |
| ($R + S$) extension |  |  | $1.7 \times 10^{-5}$ |
|  |  |  | (2.83) |
| Drought | −16.640 | −17.700 | −17.700 |
|  | (9.96) | (10.73) | (10.79) |
| Period: 1953–59 | −2.130 | −2.170 | −2.810 |
|  | (1.05) | (1.16) | (1.51) |
| Period: 1964–71 | −3.730 | −.620 | −.470 |
|  | (2.14) | (.30) | (.23) |
| Region: Northwest | 3.530 | 3.410 | 5.500 |
|  | (1.76) | (1.73) | (2.64) |

*Notes:* Observations are on 15 states for the 1953 to 1971 period. The dependent variable is the state productivity index. The independent variables are as follows:

State research ($S$): Indigenous state research expenditures, cumulated from 1953 to $t$ and deflated by the 1960 value of resources devoted to agricultural production in the state. The 1953 research stock was assumed to be five times the 1953 expenditures. A distributed lag over a ten year period was used to cumulate new research.

Regional research ($R$): Cumulated research expenditures of research programs conducted outside the state but within the same major geoclimate region, deflated by the state research deflators. India was divided into four geoclimate regions on the basis of the classification of Papadakis ("Agricultural Climates of the World").

Extension: A measure of the maturity of the extension program in the state: (.25 × stage I blocks + .75 × stage II blocks + .25 stage III blocks)/total blocks.

Drought: Dummy for drought years, i.e., years in which production dropped more than 10 percent below trend.

Period: Dummy variable for average annual number of publications in the agricultural sciences for the 1960–65 period, which were abstracted in Indian Sciences Abstracts (R. Mohan, D. Jha, and R. Evenson, "The Indian Agricultural Research System," *Economic and Political Weekly* [Bombay], March 1973).

Region: Dummy for the Northwest Region.

show positive and significant research coefficients, including a borrowing element and a research-extension interaction effect. Drought and region dummies have the expected sign.

In all of the regressions reported in table 8.11 a variable measuring the extent of irrigation acreage, i.e., net irrigated acreage relative to net sown acreage, was included. In all cases it was negative and insignificant.

## The Returns to Research Investment

The regression estimates of table 8.11 allow estimates of the marginal contribution of investment in research and in the extension system. Table 8.12 provides such estimates based on parameters estimated from regressions 1, 2, and 3 in table 8.11. The estimated contribution based on regression 3 is most defensible, in my view. It can be interpreted as follows. If the research variable measuring state research were increased by 1,000 rupees, productivity would be higher and the economic value of the higher level of productivity would be 7,900 rupees (6,600 + 1,300). According to the underlying model it would remain at the higher level, hence the 7,900 rupees is not a "once-for-all" gain; instead it represents a stream of gains of 7,900 rupees each year into the future.

From an investment perspective, the current research variable reflects investment in the past. Consequently there is a lag between the investment and the stream of returns. It is *not* appropriate therefore to conclude that the ratio 7,900/1,000 reflects a 790 percent rate of return. We do not have an explicit estimate of the time lag between investment and the realization of results for India. The specified lag in the model is an average five years, i.e., a rupee spent in year *t* will contribute to production over a ten-year period; thus the average lag will be five years. A study of this lag structure in the United States estimated the average lag to be six and a half years. Applying a lag of six and a half years to the

Table 8.12: Estimated Income Stream Generated by an Investment of
Rs. 1,000 (1968)

| Calculated from Table 8.11 | State research | Regional research outside state | Extension |
|---|---|---|---|
| Reg. 1 | 10,650 | 3,100 | — |
| Reg. 2 | 10,880[a] | 1,340 | — |
| Reg. 3 | 6,660[a] + 1,300[b] | 800 | 175[c] |

a. This can be divided into a direct contribution (10,500 in regression 2, 6,460 in regression 3) and a "borrowing" contribution (340 in regression 2; 140 in regression 3).

b. This is the part of the contribution that interacts with extension.

c. Calculated from the coefficient in regression 3, table 8.9, which implies an income stream of Rs. 27,600 associated with a one-unit change in the extension variable *EI*.

$EXT = 100 (.25 \, SI + .75 \, S2 + S3)$/blocks where $S1$, $S2$, and $S3$ are the numbers of stage I, II, and III blocks. In a typical state, if one district were to introduce its research program one year earlier, the index would increase by 1.25. It is estimated that the cost of doing so would be roughly Rs. 200,000.

7,900/1,000 ratio yields an "internal" rate of return of 42 percent to investment in state-based research.

In table 8.12, the separation of the sum of $7,900 into two parts is arbitrarily based on the interaction of research with extension. If extension activity were zero, the income stream from research investment would be reduced to 6,600 rupees. The marginal income stream generated by a 1,000-rupee investment is not 1,300 rupees, however. It is 175 rupees and probably is realized with very little lag. It might legitimately be regarded as a 17.5 percent rate of return, quite modest compared to the return on research.

When one state invests in research, other states in the region will benefit. We estimate that a 1,000-rupee increase in research investment in the region generates an income stream in the average state in the region of 800 rupees (for regression 3). This suggests that purely regional institutions, such as the Indian Agricultural Research Institute in New Delhi, are probably contributing a little less than the state programs. (The 800 rupees is for each state in the region, and each of the four regions in India includes approximately four states).

These results have significance beyond these estimates. They show that a country that is in some ways underdeveloped can build technology-discovery institutions capable of producing substantial income streams. The estimates derived for India compare favorably with estimates reported for developed countries.

### 4. RESEARCH POLICY ISSUES

The studies under review in this chapter as well as the new evidence reported here have as a common feature the estimation of extraordinarily high rates of return to investment in agricultural research. These results hold for developing as well as developed countries, and in international comparisons as well. On the face of it, it would appear that the appropriate policy for most developing countries is to expand their agricultural research systems as fast as supply conditions for scientists will permit.

In fact, few countries are doing so. Furthermore, the international aid agencies are not aggressively fostering such policies. Extension, credit, and related programs still tend to have higher priority. After twenty years of development experience, we have yet to see a really first-rate agricultural research center (comparable to the best United States agricultural experiment stations) emerge in a developing country. And now, with the development of the international centers such as the International Rice Research Institute, indigenous research centers are likely to receive little international support. Of course, some less developed countries have expanded their research efforts, but certainly not in the aggressive manner called for by the rates of return implied by past evidence. It is difficult to believe that many countries could not have efficiently pursued policies over the past twenty years that would have resulted in higher-quality research systems double their present size.

It may be, of course, that the evidence for such a policy is not as strong as these studies indicate. Surely, it is appropriate to review critically the models utilized and to analyze sources of bias in the results. Critics have, in fact, pointed out a number of possible sources of bias. Two bear mentioning here. The substitution of a measure of research activity for a measure of research output in the productivity relationship creates an "errors in variables" problem. This source of bias should serve to lower the estimated research effect. However, the results obtained from studies using alternative definitions of research suggest that this is not generally serious.

The second issue is causality. Does research generate productivity or vice versa? The level of research investment is presumably endogenously determined in a system including a demand function for research. It may be that the use of single-equation methods fails to identify the technology-generating function as claimed by the investigators. Two points deserve mention in this context. First, the demand for research is probably related more directly to production than to what we have called productivity. Productivity is the outcome of the research activity. Second, the time relationships are generally in opposite directions. The demand for research investment at time $t$ is related to expectations based on previous production experience. Technology generation from research investment in time $t$ will clearly be distributed into the future. The studies cited in this chapter have utilized this property to claim identification of a technology-generating function.

The real issues do not lie with these econometric matters. Fundamentally, skepticism of these results is based on a conviction that "simple" models and econometric specifications cannot really capture the important characteristics of something as complex as research activity. Scientists themselves cultivate the supposition that activities are not subject to analysis. The process of discovery is painted as mysterious and subject to accidental "flashes of insight." This elitist view of science is probably quite in error.

Economists have been able to model production processes, consumer behavior, and other activities that are complex. It seems quite likely that the next few years will see considerable progress in this direction, progress that will enhance our understanding of not only inventive activity but economic growth as well. Working with a colleague, Y. Kislev, I applied a search model to research activity.[25] This approach shows some promise and has some relevance to the outcome of particular research programs, notably sugarcane.[26]

More promising for the present are models of selective reproduction. By and large, economists have not systematically explored the potential for utilizing both genetic and economic information to understand plant and animal improvement based on inherited characteristics. A plant (or animal) can be viewed as a set of characteristics, $x_1, x_2, \ldots x_n$, which are partially determined by inheritance and partially by environment. The economic value of the plant (or animal) can be expressed in terms of "shadow" prices for the characteristics (i.e., $V = \sum P_i x_i$). Geneticists can predict "heritability" for a considerable number of characteristics. That is, for a given "selection intensity" in the parent population, the mean of the characteristic in the progeny can be predicted. For example, if only those beef cattle in a parent herd with a ratio of loin eye diameter to weight at least one standard deviation above the mean are selected for reproduction, the characteristics of the progeny can be predicted with some confidence. Loin eye diameter of the progeny will be increased, and other characteristics may be increased or decreased, depending on the heritability coefficients. Heritability coefficients are estimated from controlled experiments for traits that do not have simple dominant-recessive determination.

We have oversimplified the matter greatly, but given cost functions for selection and the heritability matrix, a rather straightforward economic problem can be set up. The conditions for maximizing $V$ subject to the selection cost and heritability constraints are straightforward. One can also derive the economic value of better heritability coefficients from such a model. The extension to $n$ reproductive cycles

25. Y. Kislev and R. Evenson, *Agricultural Research and Productivity* (New Haven: Yale University Press, 1975).
26. Evenson, "International Transmission of Technology."

calls for more elaborate heritability data, but again this is quite within the realm of possibility.

This model in its full development will show economic growth ($dV$) as determined by economic conditions (measured by shadow prices), technical factors, such as the length of the reproductive cycle and the age of the parent stock, selection activity, and heritability measurement. It represents some of the potential for investigating the growth process in economic terms.

As the level of sophistication rises, the quality of evidence will become "harder" and presumably it will have more policy impact. Nonetheless, it remains a puzzle why such large apparent gains from research have gone unrealized. Hayami and Ruttan have pursued this question partially by investigating "induced institutional response." Their work appears to overstate the "invisible hand" aspects, in view of the existing misallocation of research resources. It does, however, represent an important avenue for further research. The question partially is pursued to some extent in the international survey undertaken by Kislev and myself.[27] It shows that commodity-oriented research is positively related to commodity production and export performance, as well as to the level of per capita income. This is not a real test of the hypothesis that managers of public sector research programs are optimizing, given the economic conditions facing them. The issue of optimum research investment requires a great deal of information that we are only beginning to assemble. Matters of efficient size of experiment station and efficient interaction with graduate teaching as well as factors peculiar to particular fields of science have to be brought to bear in a full-blown, efficient strategy. The lack of the "fine tuning" information, however, should not deter countries from moving aggressively to exploit the growth potential in agricultural research.

27. Kislev and Evenson, "Investment in Agricultural Research and Extension."

# 9

## Agricultural Research Organization in Economic Development: A Review of the Japanese Experience

YUJIRO HAYAMI AND SABURO YAMADA

In recent years a new consensus has been emerging that research on agricultural science and technology is the critical factor in transforming agriculture into a dynamic sector of the economy. Analysis of the economic organization of agricultural research is thus required for the effective design of agricultural development. The historical experience of Japan, where a program of agricultural development was consciously undertaken during the late nineteenth century, offers insight on the search for a socially optimal organization of agricultural research in the course of economic development.

As Theodore Schultz has pointed out, research is an economic activity that uses scarce resources in order to produce something of value.[1] In this respect there is no difference between research and the production of ordinary goods and services traded in the marketplace. However, both the special attributes of the end product of research and the unique characteristics of agriculture require a distinct mode of organization in order efficiently to supply an agricultural research product. In fact, the agricultural research organizations that now exist, though they vary among countries, are distinctly different not only from

This study was supported in part by a grant from the Rockefeller Foundation to the University of Minnesota Economic Development Center. Suggestions and comments from Kenzo Henmi, Mahar Mangahas, Takashi Negishi, Vernon Ruttan, Theodore Schultz, and Jeffrey Williamson are gratefully acknowledged.
1. T. W. Schultz, "The Allocation of Resources to Research," in *Resource Allocation in Agricultural Research,* ed. W. L. Fishel (Minneapolis: University of Minnesota Press, 1971), pp. 90–120.

organizations that produce ordinary goods and services but also from industrial research organizations.

In this chapter, we will attempt to analyze such organizational aspects of agricultural research within the framework of the theory of public goods and industrial organization. First, we will identify the distinct organizational features of agricultural research, taking the present Japanese system as an example. Second, we will discuss in theoretical terms the prerequisites for a socially optimal system of agricultural research. Third, we will trace the historical evolution of agricultural research organization in Japan and try to evaluate the Japanese system in terms of efficiency criteria. Finally, we will discuss the general implications of the Japanese experience for economic development.

### 1. THE PRESENT PATTERN OF AGRICULTURAL RESEARCH IN JAPAN

One of the major characteristics of the present pattern of agricultural research in Japan is that it is dominated by public research conducted mainly in agricultural experiment stations under the auspices of national and prefectural governments. The public-private mix in research in agricultural science and technology is shown in table 9.1. In terms of the volume of research expenditures as well as the number of people involved, about 60 percent of agricultural research is conducted at governmental institutions and nearly 40 percent at universities; the private sector's share is only 3 percent.

Table 9.1: Composition of Research Expenditures and Staff in Japan, 1972
(In percents)

| | *Research expenditures*[a] | | *Research staff* | |
|---|---|---|---|---|
| | *Agriculture*[b] | *Nonagriculture*[c] | *Agriculture*[b] | *Nonagriculture*[c] |
| Universities[d] | 35 | 14 | 40 | 24 |
| Public research: | | | | |
| National government | 17 | 4 | 17 | 3 |
| Local government | 44 | 2 | 40 | 2 |
| Private research | 4 | 80 | 3 | 71 |
| Total | 100 | 100 | 100 | 100 |

a. Including both current and capital expenditures.
b. Including forestry and fishery research.
c. Excluding medical research.
d. Including both public and private universities.

*Source:* Bureau of Statistics, Office of the Prime Minister, *Kagaku gijutsu kenkyu chosa hokoku* [Report on the survey of research and development in Japan] (Tokyo, 1972), pp. 62, 150, 166.

Such a structure is in marked contrast to the organizational pattern of industrial research in Japan, as shown in table 9.1, and is also distinctly different from the organizational pattern of agricultural research in the United States, where private firms account for roughly half of agricultural research expenditures.[2]

Another distinctive aspect of agricultural research organization in Japan is that agricultural experiment stations are organized separately from education and extension programs. This represents a sharp contrast with the U.S. land-grant college system, characterized by the trinity of education, research, and extension. In Japan agricultural experiment stations operate under the jurisdiction of the Ministry of Agriculture and Forestry, whereas colleges and faculties of agriculture in universities are under the Ministry of Education. No formal linkage between experiment stations and universities has been established.

Extension programs, which are carried out by the prefectural extension services, are also separate from the experiment stations. However, because both the prefectural experiment stations and the prefectural extension services are under the agricultural departments of the prefectural governments, they operate in close cooperation. In many cases senior extension specialists are stationed in the experiment stations working as contact points.

Another organizational characteristic of Japanese agricultural research is the division of labor between the national and the prefectural experiment stations. National experiment stations under the administration of the Agricultural, Forestry, and Fishery Technology Commission within the Ministry of Agriculture and Forestry include: the Central Agricultural Experiment Station at Konosu; six regional agricultural experiment stations (Hokkaido, Tohoku, Hokuriku, Tokai-Kinki, Chugoku, Shikoku, and Kyushu); six specialized experiment stations (horticulture, tea, sericulture, livestock, veterinary science, and agricultural engineering); a station for forestry; and nine stations for fishery. Under the same administration are the National Research Institute of Agricultural Science, which is engaged in more basic research in the natural science side of agriculture; the National Research Institute of Agriculture, concerned primarily with social science aspects; the Food Research Institute for research on food nutrition, chemistry, and processing; the Plant Virus Research Institute; the

2. Yujiro Hayami and V. W. Ruttan, *Agricultural Development: An International Perspective* (Baltimore: Johns Hopkins Press, 1971), p. 144.

Radiation Crop-Breeding Farm; and the newly established Tropical Agriculture Research Center. In addition, there are the Farm Mechanization Research Institute and the Beet Research Institute, which have semipublic status. Finally under the auspices of the forty-six prefectural governments, more than three hundred agricultural experiment stations and research institutes (including those for fishery and forestry research) are operated.

There is a division of labor between the national and local experiment stations, although the division is rather rough and there are considerable overlaps. The national stations place emphasis on research projects that produce results applicable over wider regions, whereas the prefectural stations tend to concentrate on research of local significance. In consequence there is a tendency for the former to engage in the more basic end of the research spectrum and the latter in the applied end.

Such a division of labor is reflected in the difference between the national stations and the prefectural stations in the average scale of operation, as shown in table 9.2. The scale is larger in the universities and the national experiment stations, which conduct more basic research, than in the prefectural stations, which place more emphasis on applied research.

Table 9.2: Scale of Agricultural Research in Universities and in National
and Local Government Institutions, 1972
(In 100 millions of yen)

| | *Universities* | *Government research institutions* | |
| --- | --- | --- | --- |
| | | *National* | *Local* |
| Number of institutions[a] | 63 | 30 | 336 |
| Number of researchers:[a] | | | |
| Mean per institution | 114 | 104 | 22 |
| Total | 7,174 | 3,127 | 7,290 |
| Research expenditures:[a] | | | |
| Per institution | 543 | 543 | 126 |
| | (2,049)[b] | (2,049) | (475) |
| Per worker | 4.8 | 5.2 | 5.8 |
| | (18.1) | (19.6) | (21.9) |
| Total | 342 | 163 | 424 |
| | (129) | (62) | (160) |

a. Including forestry and fishery research.
b. Figures in parentheses are millions of U.S. dollars converted at the rate of 265 yen per dollar.

*Source:* Same as table 9.1.

## 2. REQUIREMENTS FOR EFFICIENT ORGANIZATION OF AGRICULTURAL RESEARCH

Agricultural research is an activity that produces information, either embodied in material inputs or not, contributing to an increase in agricultural output for a given level of conventional inputs. It is an activity aimed at producing an input for agricultural production. The socially optimal system of agricultural research is determined by the attributes of the research product, the form of the research production function, and the industrial organization of agriculture that determines the structure of demand for the research product.

### Attributes of the Research Product

New information or knowledge resulting from research is typically endowed with the attributes of a "public good," in the Samuelson-Musgrave definition; it is characterized by (1) *nonrivalness,* or jointness, in supply and utilization, and (2) *nonexcludability,* or external economies.[3] The first attribute implies that the good is equally available to all. The second implies that it is impossible for private producers to appropriate through market pricing the full social benefits arising directly from the production (and consumption) of the good; in short, it is difficult to exclude from the utilization of the good those who do not pay for it. A socially optimal level of supply of such a good cannot be expected if its supply is left to private firms.

Nonrivalness is an essential attribute of information. The use of information about a new farming practice (contour ploughing, for example) by a farmer is not hindered by the adoption of the same practice by other farmers. There is no capacity limit for its utilization.

Nonexcludability, in contrast, is not a natural attribute of information but rather is determined by institutional arrangements. In fact, patent laws are the institutional arrangement that make a certain kind of information (called an "invention") excludable, thereby creating profit incentives for private creative activities. Also, it is the common practice of big firms to keep secret the know-how that they have pro-

---

3. P. A. Samuelson, "The Pure Theory of Public Expenditure," *Review of Economics and Statistics* 36 (1954): 387–89; "Diagrammatic Exposition of a Theory of Public Expenditures," *Review of Economic Statistics* 37 (1955): 350–56; and "Aspects of Public Expenditure Theories," *Review of Economics and Statistics* 40 (1958): 332–38. R. A. Musgrave, *The Theory of Public Finance* (New York: McGraw-Hill, 1959).

duced. However, present institutional arrangements are such that the information produced from basic research is nonexcludable. This is the reason why basic scientific research is conducted primarily at non-profit institutions.[4]

A unique aspect of agricultural research, particularly that focusing on biological technology, is that even the products of research at the applied end are characterized by nonexcludability. Protection by patent laws is either unavailable or insufficient. The nature of agricultural production to be conducted in an open space makes it difficult to keep the know-how secret. Moreover, for small-scale farmers, the potential gains from secret know-how are hardly sufficient to repay the cost of producing it.

It is no wonder that private research activities in agriculture have been directed primarily toward developing mechanical technology for which patent protection is established. Since it is difficult for private firms to capture the social benefits rising out of research on the biological technology of agriculture, an optimal supply of biological research products cannot be expected without the participation of public agencies. Thus, it is understandable that the private sector share in agricultural research is so small in Japan, where research efforts have been directed primarily toward developing biological technology because of the conditions of factor endowments.[5]

As mentioned above, the *noncompetitive* character of information implies that it is equally available to all. However, it does not follow that it has the same utility to all. The utility of the information produced from agricultural research tends to be limited to specific locations, because its utility depends on its contribution to agricultural production, which is by nature highly location specific or constrained by local ecologies.[6] Although the basic principles and methods (e.g., plant type concepts and the method of artificial crossbreeding) are more widely applicable, the technologies of actual farm use (e.g., improved seed varieties) are limited to specific ecological conditions. If the final product of agricultural research is intended primarily for the joint

4. R. R. Nelson, "The Simple Economics of Basic Scientific Research," *Journal of Political Economy* 67 (1959): 297–306.

5. For a discussion of the contrast in the development of biological and mechanical technologies in Japanese and U.S. agriculture, see Hayami and Ruttan, *Agricultural Development,* pp. 111–35.

6. This aspect was emphasized in A. H. Moseman, *Building Agricultural Research Systems in the Developing Nations* (New York: Agricultural Development Council, 1970); and in Hayami and Ruttan, *Agricultural Development.*

consumption of local people, it should be more appropriate as well as more effective for local government to take charge of its supply. Agricultural research at the applied end of the spectrum resembles local police work, rather than national defense. It works more efficiently in a decentralized system to satisfy local demand.

### Research Resources and the Research Production Function

Research uses scarce resources to produce useful information. Among those resources human capital in the form of competent research workers represents the critical limiting factor.[7] The supply of this form of human capital is highly inelastic, at least in the short run. In order to increase the supply of this factor, institutions of advanced education and training have to be expanded, but this cannot be accomplished in a short period of time.[8] The agricultural research capacity at a given point in time is a function of the historical accumulation of agricultural scientists and technicians. In organizing agricultural research, highest priority must be placed on economizing on the use of this critical limiting factor.

It appears that the form of the production function of agricultural research is conditioned by the fact that it includes scientific research personnel as a critical factor. It has been conjectured that agricultural research is characterized by scale economies;[9] a study made by Robert Evenson gives empirical support to this hypothesis.[10]

It is likely that scale economies are an attribute of the production function of research in general. To some extent research facilities and equipment can be utilized more efficiently in larger-scale operations. More importantly, the productivity of scientists increases through mutual interaction. It is a basic feature of intellectual activity that new ideas are generated by mutual stimulation among the participants in that activity. In the research production function of an individual scientist, his colleagues are included as an input with positive marginal product. This production externality among individual scientists is a

7. This point was emphasized by Schultz in "Allocation of Resources to Research."

8. The supply of this form of human capital in a specific field, such as agricultural science, may be more elastic since it is possible to draw scientists away from neighboring disciplines, such as biology and engineering. Yet, the possibility of such transfers is limited.

9. T. W. Schultz, *Transforming Traditional Agriculture* (New Haven: Yale University Press, 1964), pp. 150–52.

10. R. E. Evenson, "Economic Aspects of Organization of Agricultural Research," in Fishel, *Resource Allocation,* pp. 163–82.

primary reason for scale economies in the "aggregate" research production function.

Production externality exists not only among scientists of the same discipline but also among the different disciplines of science. Advances in other disciplines increase the possibility of breakthroughs in agricultural science (e.g., the application of radioactive elements to crop-breeding). As T. W. Schultz has asserted, "the comparative advantage of an agricultural experiment station associated with a major research-oriented university is clearly large,"[11] because such an organizational setup makes it easier to capture benefits arising from production externality among the different disciplines of science. This is particularly important in basic research.

Another important attribute of the research production function is that it has a stochastic form. Research is, by nature, characterized by risk and uncertainty. Success in a research project is like hitting a "successful oil well." Any number of dry holes may be bored before the successful one is found. As Richard Nelson has pointed out, this stochastic nature of the research production function, which is especially strong in the case of basic research, contributes to the "failure of the market" in attaining optimum resource allocation over time:

> The very large variance of the profit probability distribution from a basic research project will tend to cause a risk-avoiding firm, without the economic resources to spread the risk by running a number of basic-research projects at once, to value a basic-research project at significantly less than its expected profit, and hence . . . at less than its social value.[12]

Public investment is needed to correct such market failures.

## The Industrial Organization of Agriculture

The "public good" attributes of the agricultural research product together with production externalities and the stochastic nature of the research production function make public support of agricultural research socially desirable. It does not necessarily follow, however, that agricultural research should be conducted in governmental institutions financed by tax revenue. The social benefit produced by agricultural research can be measured as the sum of increases in consumers'

11. Schultz, "Allocation of Resources to Research," p. 114.
12. Nelson, "Simple Economics of Basic Scientific Research," p. 304.

and producers' surpluses due to the downward shift in the supply function of an agricultural product. If the benefit consists primarily of producers' surplus, agricultural research may be left to the cooperative activities of agricultural producers (i.e., to the activities of such institutions as farm bureaus and agricultural cooperatives).

The share of producers' surplus in the social benefit from research depends on (1) the organization of the industry that uses the product of the research as an input, and (2) the price elasticity of demand for the product of that industry. Assuming profit maximization by firms, under a monopolistic structure of industry, the lower the demand elasticity the larger will be the producers' share of the gains.

The organization of agricultural production, with a large number of small producers who have no power to impose monopolistic pricing, is unique in its proximity to perfect competition. Also, most agricultural commodities, except those intended for export, are characterized by low price elasticity of demand. As a result, a major share of the social benefit produced by research tends to go to consumers. In such a situation the cost of agricultural research should be borne by the general public. The predominance of public institutions in agricultural research in Japan can be justified on this ground.

### Information Linkage with Agricultural Producers

Because the products of agricultural research are not subject to market pricing, the allocation of given research resources among different research projects must be based on research administrators' and scientists' perceptions of the potential demand of farmers for various techniques that may be developed. The process of interaction among farmers, research administrators, and scientists, which leads research in a socially desirable direction, has been explained elsewhere.[13] It is clear that the allocation of resources among different research projects can be more efficient when there are close information linkages between farmers and research administrators and staff.

In this respect a decentralized system is more effective in research resource allocation, because in this type of system agricultural scientists can better perceive the needs of farmers, while working more closely with them. Lobbying by farmers' associations can work as an effective channel of information, especially in a decentralized system.

One important information link with farmers is through extension

13. Hayami and Ruttan, *Agricultural Development*, pp. 56–59.

programs. Close association between research and extension is desirable not only in terms of the effectiveness of extension programs but also in terms of efficient research resource allocation.

### Requirements for Efficient Organization of Agricultural Research

From the above discussion we can specify the conditions for a socially efficient organization of agricultural research as follows:

1. Public support is critical for attaining the socially optimal level of agricultural research activity because of the nonrivalness and nonexcludability characteristic of the product of agricultural research, in addition to production externalities and the stochastic nature of research. The need for public support is reinforced by the small scale of farm firms, which have little ability to capture sufficient gains from research to cover its cost.

2. Financing agricultural research from tax revenue is justified on the ground that the major gains from research are transferred to consumers in the form of consumers' surplus, because of the competitive structure of the agricultural industry and the low price elasticity of demand for farm products. Research on agricultural commodities of high demand elasticity, typically those for export, might be left to the cooperative support of farmers.

3. The location-specific nature of agricultural technology requires decentralization of agricultural research, whereas the scale economies that characterize the production of knowledge or information give the advantage to a large centralized operation. Balancing these conflicting requirements is a critical problem in the design of an efficient agricultural research organizational pattern. A major consideration in this respect is how to economize on the use of the critical limiting factor, that is, scientists and technicians.

4. Production externalities—specifically, interdependence among the different disciplines of science—makes linkages between agricultural research and research in other disciplines a critical element in agricultural research organization. Association of an agricultural experiment station with "research-oriented universities" is desirable for this reason.

5. Because the allocation of resources among various research projects is not based on market prices, it is critical to develop information channels through which research administrators and scientists can assess the demand of farmers for their research products. A decentralized system has the advantage in establishing more accurate in-

formation channels. The close association of research with extension can contribute to efficient research resource allocation.

## 2. THE EVOLUTION OF AGRICULTURAL RESEARCH ORGANIZATION IN JAPAN

In this section we will attempt to review the historical process of evolution of Japanese agricultural research organization in terms of the criteria specified in the previous section.[14]

### Quantitative Aspects of Agricultural Growth

Before sketching the history of agricultural research, we will quickly review the quantitative aspects of agricultural growth in Japan. The trends in agricultural output, inputs, and productivity are shown in figure 9.1.

For the period 1880–1965 total output, input, and productivity in Japanese agriculture show upward growth trends, except for the period of devastation due to World War II. For the period as a whole, total output more than tripled. Inputs of the two primary factors, labor and land, changed relatively slowly; labor declined by 15 percent during the prewar period and by 25 percent during the decade from 1955 to 1965, which saw extremely rapid economic growth; land increased by only 30 percent for the period as a whole. To a large extent the changes in labor and land have canceled each other out, as far as growth in total input (aggregate of all conventional inputs by factor share weights) is concerned. Capital grew relatively slowly in the prewar years and started to expand at a rapid pace in the postwar period. The growth rates of current nonfarm inputs, particularly fertilizers, have been much higher than those of other inputs.

Overall, total input for the whole period grew at an annual compound

14. The historical sketch in this section draws heavily on Hayami and Ruttan, *Agricultural Development,* pp. 153–63. Useful references are: Toshio Furushima, ed., *Nogaku* [Agricultural science], Nihon kagaku gijutsushi taikei [A comprehensive history of science and technology in Japan], vols. 22 and 23 (Tokyo: Daiichi Hoki Shuppan, 1967, 1970); Nogyo Hattatsushi Chosakai, ed., *Nihon nogyo hattatsushi* [The history of agricultural development in Japan], 10 vols. (Tokyo: Chuo-Koronsha, 1953–58); Takekazu Ogura, ed., *Agricultural Development in Modern Japan* (Tokyo: Fuji Publishing Co., 1963); Yukihiko Saito, *Nihon nogakushi* [The history of agricultural science in Japan], 2 vols. (Tokyo: National Research Institute of Agriculture, 1968, 1971).

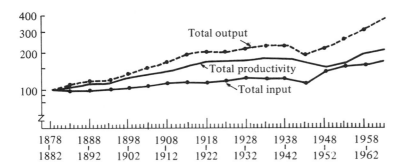

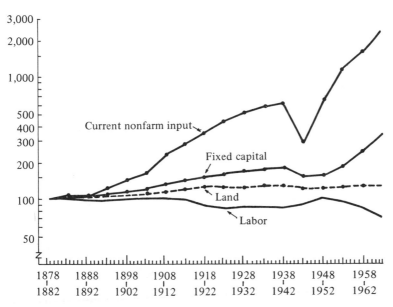

Fig. 9.1: Trends in the Indices of Output, Inputs, and Productivity in Agriculture (1878–82 = 100, five-year averages, semi-log scale) *Source:* Saburo Yamada and Yujiro Hayami, *Growth Rates of Japanese Agriculture, 1880–1965* (Paper presented at the conference on Agricultural Growth in Japan, Korea, Taiwan, and the Philippines, sponsored by the University of Hawaii East-West Center Food Institute and the University of Minnesota Economic Development Center, held at Honolulu, Hawaii, February 1973).

growth rate of 0.7 percent, while total output grew at 1.6 percent. Consequently, total productivity more than doubled, with a growth rate of nearly 0.9 percent per year. This implies that more than half of the growth in agricultural output is left unexplained by the growth in inputs. In terms of total output and productivity trends, three major phases are distinct: (1) relatively rapid growth up to the late 1910s, (2) relative stagnation in the interwar period, and (3) a growth spurt in the post-World War II period.

In the following historical sketch we will try to assess how such quantitative growth patterns were related to the evolution of agricultural research.

## National Government Initiatives

From the beginning of modern economic history in Japan with the Meiji Restoration (1868), research on agricultural science and technology has been conducted almost exclusively in governmental institutions. The national government initially attempted to develop agriculture through direct importation of foreign farm machinery, plants, and livestock.

In order to exhibit large-scale farm machinery imported from England and the United States, the Farm Machinery Exhibition Yard was established in 1871 in Tsukiji, Tokyo. The operations of the machines were demonstrated at the Naito Shinjuku Agricultural Experimental Station, set up in 1872. The government also tried to transplant foreign plants and livestock. The Mita Botanical Experiment Yard (1874), the Shimozawa Sheep Farm (1875), the Kobe Olive Farm (1879), and the Harima Grape Farm (1880) represent such efforts.

Institutions of advanced agricultural education were established by the government: the Komaba Agricultural School (1877), which was later redesignated the University of Tokyo College of Agriculture, and the Sapporo Agricultural School (1875), which was designed to develop Hokkaido, the last frontier of Japan. Instructors for the Komaba School were invited from Britain and for the Sapporo School from the United States, and the curriculum was along the Anglo-American pattern of large-scale mechanized farming.

Such early trials of direct "technology borrowing" represented one example of the broad effort of Meiji Japan to catch up with Western technology. Unlike the case of industry, however, this attempt was largely unsuccessful.[15] The factor endowments and the scale of Japanese farming (about one hectare per farm) were simply incompatible with large-scale machinery of the Anglo-American type. In most cases the efforts to transplant foreign plants and livestock proved also unsuccessful because of differences in ecological conditions.

The Meiji government quickly perceived these failures and redirected agricultural development strategy toward the search for a modern technology consistent with the factor endowments and ecological conditions of Japanese agriculture. In 1881, when the contracts of the British agricultural instructors at the Komaba School expired, they were replaced by German scientists. Thereafter the curriculum of agricultural education in Japan was reorganized to place primary emphasis on German agricultural chemistry and soil science in the Liebig tradition. The display and demonstration of Western machinery, plants, and livestock were largely discontinued during the 1880s.

In 1885 the newly founded Ministry of Agriculture and Commerce (1881) established the Itinerant Instructor System, under which instructors traveled throughout the country holding agricultural extension meetings. In contrast with the earlier emphasis on the direct transplant of Western technology, the itinerant instruction system was designed to expand use of the best seed varieties already developed by Japanese farmers and the most productive cultivation practices for the production of Japan's traditional staple crops, such as rice and barley. Not only the graduates of the Komaba School but also veteran farmers (*rōnō*) were employed as itinerant instructors in order to combine the best practical farming experience with the new scientific knowledge of the inexperienced college graduates.

In order to provide better information for the itinerant instructors' lectures, the Experiment Farm for Staple Cereals and Vegetables was set up in 1885; this project was later strengthened, and in 1893 it was redesignated the National Agricultural Experiment Station, with six regional branch stations in the nation. The itinerant instruction system was subsequently absorbed into the program of the National Agricultural Experiment Station. Meanwhile, the national government encouraged the prefectural governments to set up local experiment stations. However, only a few prefectures had established experiment

15. There were some exceptional cases. For example, large-scale farming technology was successfully transplanted in the upland area of Hokkaido. However, the impact of such cases was but limited.

stations before the Law Providing State Subsidies for Prefectural Agricultural Experiment Stations was enacted in 1899.

Thus the development of the agricultural experiment station system in Japan was from its beginning characterized by strong initiatives from the national government. This contrasts sharply with the experience of Western Europe. In England the famous Rothamsted Experimental Station was established (1843) and financed personally by a country gentleman, John Lawes. The Edinburgh Laboratory (founded in 1842) was supported by the Agricultural Chemistry Association of Scotland, a voluntary agricultural society. In France the first agricultural experiment station was established personally (in 1834) by Jean Boussingaullt, on his estate at Bechelbrom. Even in Germany the movement was basically private; the first experiment station, established at Möckern, Saxony, was publicly supported, but it was set up in response to an initiative by the Saxon farmers, whose draft charter for the station was legalized by the Saxon government.

Why was the government of Meiji Japan (its leaders primarily from the ex-samurai class) clearly determined from the very beginning of modern economic growth to take responsibility for conducting agricultural research? Part of the answer appears to lie in the fact that the "public good" characteristics of agricultural research were particularly evident in Japan.

The basic unit of agricultural production in Japan was the dwarf-sized family farm of only about one hectare of arable land, used primarily in field crop production (more than half of the value produced at the farm coming from rice). Needless to say, individual farms were too small to take any advantage whatsoever of the scale economies inherent in research. They were also too small to have any monopolistic power enabling them to internalize the gains from research and thus cover its cost.

Because land was the factor limiting the expansion of agricultural production, farmers demanded technology that would make possible savings in land. Major emphasis was placed on research aimed at developing biological technology, such as the improvement of seed varieties. There was no incentive for private firms to conduct biological research since there was no institutional arrangement to internalize the gains from it. Furthermore, because of the low price elasticity of demand for staple food crops, the major products of Japanese agriculture, the gains from agricultural research were primarily transferred to consumers in the form of consumers' surplus.

In such a situation the need for public support of agricultural research was obvious. But why did the national government rather than the local governments take the initiative? Why was it not left to the cooperative activity of farm producers, especially in the case of export crops?

The answer must be sought in the basic approach of Meiji Japan to economic development, that is, "exploiting agriculture for industrialization." When Japan opened her doors to foreign countries shortly before the Meiji Restoration, the country was in danger of being colonized by the Western powers. The national slogan then was to "build a wealthy nation and a strong army" (*fukoku kyohei*). To attain this goal it was considered necessary to "develop industries and promote enterprises" (*shokusan kogyo*).

In a predominantly rural state such as Meiji Japan, industrialization must be financed from the agricultural surplus. Government revenue for industrial development was derived from agriculture in the form of a land tax. The foreign exchange needed for the import of capital goods was earned from the export of primary products.

In a sense the establishment of the National Agricultural Experiment Station in 1893 was an attempt to counteract the agitation for the reduction of the newly established land tax. The *Konoronsaku* (*A Treatise on the Strategy of Agricultural Development*), which was drafted in 1891 by the Agricultural Science Association and which had an immediate impact on the establishment of the National Agricultural Experiment Station, denied the argument for a land-tax reduction on the basis that it would contribute only to the welfare of landlords and would not benefit the large number of tenant farmers.[16] It advocated "more positive measures to develop agriculture, such as agricultural schools, experiment stations, itinerant lectures, and agricultural societies" to reduce the burden of farmers.[17]

More fundamentally, an increase in the food supply for the growing urban industrial population was critical for industrialization. If the food supply had not kept up with the growth in urban demand, the price of food would have risen. In the early stage of development, characterized by a high Engel coefficient, the rise in food prices would have resulted in a significant rise in the cost of living and in the wage

16. Reprinted in Ministry of Agriculture and Forestry, ed., *Meiji zenki kannojiseki shuroku* [A compilation of measures to encourage agriculture], vol. 2 (Tokyo: Dainihon Nokai, 1939), pp. 1765–79.

17. Ibid., pp. 1766–67.

rate, which would have reduced profits and thereby depressed industrial capital accumulation.[18]

Given industrial development as a national goal, it was natural for the national government to undertake measures, including agricultural research, to develop agriculture, leading to an increased supply of food, a critical wage good for industrial development. Furthermore, because foreign exchange set the ceiling for capital good imports, it was rational for the government to support out of tax revenue research on such export products as tea and silk, even though the gains from research on export commodities characterized by high demand elasticity might have been captured by producers in the form of producers' surplus.

### Linkage with Extension and Education

The linkage between agricultural research and extension has traditionally been strong in Japan. As mentioned previously, the Experiment Farm for Staple Cereals and Vegetables was designed to provide relevant data for itinerant instructors, and the itinerant extension programs were absorbed into the National Agricultural Experiment Station. Later, as the prefectural experiment station network was established, the extension programs were transferred to the prefectural stations. When agricultural associations, which were organized under the Agricultural Association Law (1899) into a pyramidal structure with the Imperial Agricultural Association on the top and village associations on the bottom, began to develop active extension programs with the help of government subsidies, their extension workers were trained in the Agricultural Training Centers attached to the prefectural experiment stations.

In contrast, no formal linkage has been established between research at the agricultural experiment stations and at institutions of higher education. This was against the expectation of the pioneers of agricultural science in the Meiji period. In the *Treatise on the Strategy of Agricultural Development* they wrote:

> It is advantageous that agricultural experiment stations and the itinerant instruction system be combined. . . . It is advantageous that the agricultural experiment stations belong to agricultural colleges. . . . It is highly effective for students to observe projects

18. For an appraisal of agricultural policy in Japan from this point of view, see Yujiro Hayami, "Rice Policy in Japan's Economic Development," *American Journal of Agricultural Economics* 54 (1972): 19–31.

in the experiment stations. The results of experiments are useful for colleges, and the education in colleges is also useful to the experiment stations. . . . Agricultural associations should encourage study by students and should encourage farmers to use the established results of experiments.[19]

It appears that they had in mind an image of the trinity of research, extension, and education, supported by agricultural associations, a system similar to the U.S. system. Contrary to their expectation, the National Agricultural Experiment Station was established independent from the Komaba School, and the system of national and prefectural experiment stations was developed separately from the institutions of advanced agricultural education.

Evolution of such a system may be explained in terms of (1) the strong (and hasty) demand of government for experiment stations to produce practical results immediately useful for farmers, and (2) the fact that basic research at the university level was not very useful in producing practical techniques in the Meiji period.

In the initial stage the staff members of the agricultural colleges or agricultural faculties of the universities were engaged primarily in the study of principles and theories developed abroad. Although a few distinguished research results, such as the artificial crossbreeding of wheat by Kizo Amari, were produced, they were not immediately applicable to actual farming. A more productive approach in the short run was to exploit the potential of indigenous farming practices by simple scientific tests and demonstrations.

The initial research conducted at the Experiment Farm for Staple Crops and Vegetables and at the National Agricultural Experiment Station was primarily at the applied end of the research spectrum. The major projects were simple field experiments comparing the various varieties of seeds or various husbandry techniques (for example, check-row planting of rice seedlings versus irregular planting). Facilities, personnel, and, above all, the state of knowledge did not permit research to go beyond simple comparative experiments.

Nevertheless, such experiments provided a basis for the rapid growth of agricultural productivity during the later years of the Meiji period. This was because of the existence of substantial indigenous technological potential which could be further tested, developed, and refined at the new experiment stations, combined with a strong propensity to

19. *Meiji zenki,* pp. 1778–79.

innovate among farmers, with whom the research workers interacted effectively. During the three hundred years of the Tokugawa period, which preceded the Meiji Restoration, farmers were subject to the strong constraints of feudalism. Personal behavior and economic activity were highly structured within a hierarchical system of social organization. Farmers were bound to their land and were, in general, not allowed to leave their village except for occasional pilgrimages to, for example, the Ise Grand Shrine. Nor were they free to choose what crops to plant or what varieties of seeds to sow. Furthermore barriers dividing the nation into feudal estates actively discouraged communication. In many cases, feudal lords prohibited the export of improved seeds or cultural methods from their territories. Under such conditions, diffusion of superior seeds and husbandry techniques from one region to another was severely limited. Although the Tokugawa period was characterized by significant growth in agricultural productivity, Japanese agriculture entered the Meiji period with a substantial backlog of unexploited indigenous technology.

With the reforms of the Meiji Restoration such feudal restraints were removed. Farmers were free to choose what crops to plant, what seeds to sow, and what techniques to practice. Nationwide communication was facilitated with the introduction of modern postal service and railroads. The cost of the diffusion of information about new technology was greatly reduced. The land-tax reform, which granted a fee-simple title to the farmers and transformed a feudal share-crop tax to a fixed-rate cash tax, increased the farmers' incentive to innovate. The farmers, especially those of the *gono* class (landlords who personally farm part of their holdings), responded vigorously to such new opportunities. They voluntarily formed agricultural societies called *nodankai* (agricultural discussion society) and *hinshukokankai* (seed-exchange society) and searched for higher payoff techniques. Such rice production practices as the use of salt water in seed selection, improved preparation and management of nursery beds, and check-row planting were discovered by farmers and propagated by the itinerant instructors, sometimes enforced by the sabers of the police. The major improved varieties of seeds, up to the end of the 1920s, were also the result of selections by veteran farmers. For example, the *Shinriki* variety, which was more widely diffused in the western half of Japan than any other single variety that has since been propagated, was selected in 1877 by Jujiro Maruo, a farmer in Hyogo Prefecture (the variety was called Shinriki, meaning "the Power of God," by the farmers, who were surprised by its high yield). The *Kameno-o* variety, which was propagated widely and which contributed greatly to stabilizing the rice yield in northern Japan, was selected in 1893 by Kameji Abe, a farmer in Yamagata Prefecture. The development and diffusion of these rono varieties took place in the western part of Japan, which includes the country's most agriculturally advanced regions (Kinki and Northern Kyushu). Then this process was transmitted to the relatively backward eastern part of Japan.[20]

Experiment station research was successful in testing and refining the results of farmer innovations. The rono techniques (i.e., veteran farmers' techniques) were based on experiences in the specific localities where they were originated. They tended to be location specific and to require modification when transferred to other localities. Simple comparative tests effectively screened the rono techniques and varieties, thereby reducing greatly the cost of technical information for farmers. Slight modification or adaptations of indigenous techniques on the basis of experimental tests often gave them universal applicability. A good example is the technique of rice-seed sorting in salt water. Jikei Yokoi, who later became a prominent leader of agriculture and agricultural science in Japan, observed this technique practiced by farmers when he was a young instructor at a vocational agricultural school in Fukuoka Prefecture. After he perfected the technique and it was subjected to repeated tests at the National Agricultural Experiment Station, it was propagated throughout Japan. It is interesting that a person like Yokoi, who throughout his life advocated very strongly the superiority of modern agricultural science over the rono knowledge, contributed to the propagation of a rono technique.

Given the backlog of indigenous technological potential and the innovative attitude of farmers on the one hand, and the infant state of university education and research on the other, it may have been more effective in terms of the contribution to agricultural productivity growth to organize experiment station and extension services in close association, sacrificing the linkage between experiment station and university. Also, the loose formal linkage between experiment station and university did not pose a serious problem during the Meiji period when the scale of the agricultural research-education-extension com-

20. For this process, see Yujiro Hayami and Saburo Yamada, "Technological Progress in Agriculture," in *Economic Growth: The Japanese Experience since the Meiji Era,* ed. Lawrence Klein and Kazushi Ohkawa (Homewood, Ill.: Richard Irwin, 1968), pp. 135–61.

plex was small. Since the key personnel in experiment stations, extension services, and agricultural colleges were all graduates of either the Komaba School or the Sapporo School, interaction among experiment stations and agricultural colleges on an ad hoc basis, primarily through personal contact, probably was adequate.

## Centralization versus Decentralization

It appears that the evolution of an agricultural research organization system in Japan has been determined by the search for a workable balance between the conflicting merits of centralization and decentralization in agricultural research organization, within the constraints set by research resources.

Pioneers of agricultural science in Japan seem to have recognized the fact that agricultural technology is highly location specific and that in order to produce practical results for farmers agricultural research must be conducted in various ecological regions. They also appear to have recognized the need for coordination of central and local experiment stations. In the *Treatise on the Strategy of Agricultural Development* they proposed to establish (1) one central experiment station in Tokyo, (2) five regional stations, and (3) one or more prefectural station in each prefecture.[21]

The network of a National Agricultural Experiment Station with headquarters in Nishigahara, Tokyo, and six regional branch stations represents the realization of this proposal. However, Atsushi Sawano, the first director of the National Experiment Station and one of the five committee members who drafted the *Treatise*, considered the system vastly insufficient. He remarked that the existing pattern of "regional breakdowns [is] not sufficient [to deal with] the variations in soil and climate. If additional funds are available, another forty-five stations should be established."[22] Local political groups also lobbied at the national Diet, and the number of branch stations was increased from six to nine in 1895.

However, resource limitations severely restricted activities at the experiment stations. The staff of the National Experiment Station, including branch stations, initially consisted of only 20 researchers and 7 technicians; it was increased to 30 and 15, respectively, in 1899. Experiments were always handicapped by inadequate facilities and insuf-

---

21. *Meiji zenki*, p. 1774.
22. Cited in Saito, *Nihon nogakushi*, p. 121.

ficient logistical support.[23] Under such conditions it was hardly possible to conduct more basic research, beyond the simple tests and demonstrations mentioned above.

Meanwhile, the backlog of indigenous technological potential was gradually exhausted as it was exploited. It began to seem necessary for research institutions to recharge the declining potential by conducting more sophisticated and basic research. The prefectural experiment stations, the establishment of which was accelerated in 1899 by the State Subsidy Law for Prefectural Agricultural Experiment Stations, gradually accepted responsibility for conducting the more applied research tests and demonstrations. Rapid expansion of such local research and experimentation is reflected in the increase in the prefectural governments' share of agricultural research expenditures, as shown in table 9.3.

In response to the establishment of the network of prefectural experiment stations, the National Agricultural Experiment Station reduced its branch stations from nine to three in 1903. The intention was to exploit scale economies in more basic research by concentrating research resources in a smaller number of stations. In the next year, for the first time, the National Experiment Station launched an original crop-breeding program, at the Kinai branch. The object of this project was to develop new rice varieties by artificial crossbreeding based on the Mendelian principles rediscovered in 1900. It took almost two decades before new varieties of major practical significance were developed, though the project contributed greatly to the accumulation of experience and knowledge. Another project was started in 1905 at the Rikuu branch, to improve rice varieties by pure-line selection. This approach brought quicker practical results. Thereafter in the Taisho era (1912–25), the main crop-breeding efforts were directed toward pure-line selection.

Rice breeding by the method of pure-line selection represented the final stage of exploitation of the indigenous technological potential embodied in the rono varieties. As the purity of those varieties was improved the potential was exhausted.[24] The exploitation and consequent exhaustion of indigenous potential became evident in the 1910s before more basic research, represented by the crossbreeding

23. Ibid., pp. 126–34, 161–64.
24. Takamine Matsuo, *Suito hinshu kairyo shijo no shomondai* [Problems in the history of rice variety improvement], Nogyo Hattatsushi Chosakai Data Paper 42, mimeographed (Tokyo, 1951).

Table 9.3: Composition of Agricultural Research Expenditures by
National and Prefectural Governments

|  | *Expenditures in thousands of yen (1934–36 prices)* | | | *Percentage compositions* | |
|  | *Total* | *National*[a] | *Prefectural* | *National*[a] | *Prefectural* |
|---|---|---|---|---|---|
| 1897 | 616 | 367 | 249[b] | 60 | 40[b] |
| 1902 | 2,044 | 930 | 1,114[b] | 46 | 55[b] |
| 1907 | 2,032 | 718 | 1,314[b] | 35 | 65[b] |
| 1912 | 3,044 | 822 | 2,222[b] | 27 | 73[b] |
| 1918 | 2,521 | 849 | 1,672[b] | 34 | 66[b] |
| 1923 | 5,385 | 1,286 | 4,099[b] | 24 | 76[b] |
| 1927 | 6,561 | 1,251 | 5,310[b] | 19 | 81[b] |
| 1932 | 8,196 | 1,686 | 6,510[b] | 21 | 79[b] |
| 1955 | 9,478 | 4,190 | 5,288[c] | 44 | 56[c] |
| 1960 | 12,300 | 4,661 | 7,639[c] | 38 | 62[c] |
| 1965 | 38,814 | 12,257 | 26,557[a] | 32 | 68[a] |
| 1970 | 60,093 | 17,257 | 42,836[a] | 29 | 71[a] |

a. Five-year averages ending with the years shown, except the 1918 and 1923
figures, which are five-year averages ending in 1917 and 1922 respectively.

b. Single-year figures for the years shown.

c. Estimates. Changes in percentage composition between 1951–55 and 1956–60
were assumed to be the same as those between 1956–60 and 1961–65; the percentage
composition in 1958 was applied for 1956–60.

*Sources:* National government expenditures: Ministry of Agriculture and Forestry,
*Norinsho yosan kessan hennenshi* [Annual budget and expenditure accounts of the
Ministry of Agriculture and Forestry], 1954; Ministry of Agriculture and Forestry,
*Norinsho yosansho* [Annual budget of the Ministry of Agriculture and Forestry],
various issues; and Agriculture, Forestry, and Fishery Research Council, *Todofuken
norinsuisan kankei shikenkenkyu kikan no gaiyo* [Outline of agriculture, forestry, and
fishery research institutions in prefectures], 1963–72.

Local government expenditures: Ministry of Agriculture and Forestry (formerly
the Ministry of Agriculture and Commerce), *Norinsho tokei hyo* [Statistical yearbook
of the Ministry of Agriculture and Forestry], various issues; Nogyo Gijutsu Kyokai,
*Todofuken nogyo-kankei shikenjo yoran* [Outline of agricultural experiment stations
in prefectures], 1959; and *Todofuken norinsuisan kankei shikenkenkyu kikan no gaiyo*
[Outline of Agriculture, Forestry and Fishery Research Institutions in Prefectures],
1963–72.

Deflator: The general price index from Kazushi Ohkawa et al., eds., *Estimates of
Long-term Economic Statistics of Japan since 1868,* vol. 8 (Tokyo: Toyo Keizai
Shinposha, 1967): 134; and the implicit deflator in Economic Planning Agency, *An-
nual Report of National Income Statistics,* 1972, pp. 24–29.

project, began to produce major breakthroughs. The rate of increase
in rice yield began to decelerate, and Japanese agriculture entered a
stagnation phase during the interwar period.

Meanwhile, not only the National Experiment Station but also the
prefectural stations began crossbreeding projects. However, those

projects were handicapped by lack of coordination and by research resource limitations. Under such circumstances, the nationwide co-ordinated crop-breeding program, called the Assigned Experiment System (formally, the System of Experimentation Assigned by the Ministry of Agriculture and Forestry) was established, first for wheat (1926), next for rice (1927), and in subsequent years for other crops and livestock.

Under the Assigned Experiment System the national experiment stations were given responsibility for conducting crossbreeding through the selection of the first several filial generations. The regional stations, in each of eight regions, conducted further selections so as to achieve adaptation to regional ecological conditions. The varieties selected at the regional stations were then sent to prefectural stations to be tested for acceptability in specific localities. The varieties developed by this system were called *Norin* (an acronym for the Ministry of Agriculture and Forestry) varieties.

This system was outstandingly successful, as demonstrated by the fact that the Mexican dwarf wheat that is revolutionizing Mexican and Indo-Pakistani agriculture was based on the Norin no. 10 wheat variety. The Norin numbered varieties were developed and successively re-placed older varieties in the latter half of the 1930s. If the supply of fertilizer and other agricultural inputs had not been restricted due to the diversion of resources for military purposes during World War II, the second epoch of agricultural productivity growth in Japan would probably have begun in the late 1930s, instead of after the war.

The Assigned Experiment System was an institutional innovation that economized on the use of research resources—above all, knowledge and experience—while satisfying the requirement for location-specific agricultural research. The system has evolved in such a way that not only the national experiment stations but also the prefectural experi-ment stations themselves now conduct crossbreeding from the first step of artificial crossing. This change reflects an increase in the capacity of prefectural stations due to accumulation of knowledge and experi-ence, which has enabled the prefectural stations to conduct research more specifically designed to satisfy local demand.

A continuous stream of new knowledge or information from scientific research, which contributes to the production of goods and services, is one of the critical factors underlying the dynamism of a modern economy. Information is typically endowed with "public good" characteristics, and public investment in research is required in order to allocate resources to research at a socially optimal level.

Public good characteristics are especially strong for the products of agricultural research because of the competitive economic structure of agriculture, with its large number of small producers. Without government awareness of the social productivity of agricultural research, and without effective government leadership, investment in agricultural research can hardly be expected. This seems to be a basic reason why agriculture has remained a stagnant sector in many developing countries.

The perception of the social need for agricultural research, and government initiative in organizing it, seems to be one of the keys to understanding the achievement of agricultural growth in Japan despite the very unfavorable endowment of land relative to labor. However, it appears that there was gross underinvestment in agricultural research even in Japan. For example, if much larger resources had been allocated to agricultural research in the earlier days of modern economic growth, the interwar stagnation of Japanese agriculture might have been avoided or reduced considerably. Public planners and policy makers should be constantly reminded that there is a tendency to underestimate the returns to research because of uncertainty and the long gestation period.

At any rate, the resources allocated to agricultural research are likely to be less than optimal and their scarcity is accordingly high. The extremely high rate of social returns from agricultural research estimated in a number of case studies indicates that there is underinvestment in agricultural research even in the United States, despite vigorous public support of agricultural research.[25] Efficient allocation of given resources among different research enterprises thus becomes more important.

The conflict between the need for location specificity and scale economies poses a critical problem in the allocation of scarce research resources. The Assigned Experiment System in Japan represents a successful attempt to solve this problem. Such organizational innova-

25. Those studies are summarized in W. L. Peterson, "The Returns to Investment in Agricultural Research in the United States," in Fishel, ed., *Resource Allocation*, pp. 139–62; and W. L. Peterson and Yujiro Hayami, *Technical Change in Agriculture*, mimeographed (St. Paul: University of Minnesota Department of Agricultural and Applied Economics, 1972).

tions should be promoted in developing countries highly constrained by research resources, especially by the endowment of experienced research and technical staff.

Interaction among research administrators, scientists, and farmers is of critical importance in order to direct research resources to the production of information useful to farmers. At the same time, the interaction of agricultural scientists with those in neighboring disciplines is the source of research productivity. The close association of agricultural experiment stations with extension programs and agricultural associations in Japan probably contributed to increased responsiveness of agricultural research to farmers' needs.

However, this system was established at a sacrifice of the formal linkage of experiment stations with universities. This part of the Japanese experience may represent a bad example which should not be followed by developing countries. Today the frontier of agricultural science is far more advanced than it was in the Meiji period. Highly advanced specialized research, together with an interdisciplinary approach, seems necessary for the transfer of technology developed in advanced countries to developing countries. For this purpose, close linkage between experiment stations and universities is required.[26]

Close linkage between experiment stations and universities, however, should not be established at a sacrifice of the responsiveness of agricultural research to the needs of farmers. How to establish a close association between experiment stations and universities while promoting active interaction among farmers and research workers, either directly or through extension agents, remains a major unsolved problem in organizing agricultural research for agricultural development.

26. Unfortunately, however, in most developing countries the university–experiment station linkage has followed the Japanese rather than the American pattern.

# PART IV: AGRICULTURAL SECTOR PERFORMANCE

# 10

## Special Problems of Policy Making in a
## Technologically Heterogeneous Agriculture:
## Colombia

R. A. BERRY

Much discussion of economic policy—whether for industry, agriculture, or some other sector—proceeds on the implicit assumption of a high level of homogeneity across productive units in each sector and arrives, partly as a result, at fairly straightforward policy conclusions.[1] Or, in respect to policies by definition specific to a subsector (such as research on a given product, marketing of a product, and so on) the homogeneity assumption may be made with respect to the productive units in that subsector. In such a situation agricultural policy would involve principally: making available the appropriate amount of credit to the sector; facilitating capital formation (and possibly capital transfer to other sectors); allocating public capital efficiently within the agricultural sector; generating and disseminating new productive technologies; planning for a smooth transfer of human resources from agriculture to nonagriculture, a transfer more effectively carried out to the extent that the persons moving are appropriately prepared educationally and otherwise for the nonagricultural sector; and finally (in part related to the last point) inducing smooth growth of agricultural output so as to avoid the sharp fluctuations in agricultural income that might result from output fluctuations, given the usually low income elasticity of demand. Granted that awkward problems may arise even in such a context, I would contend that effective policy making is much more complicated

Valuable comments from Michael Lipton and Wayne Thirsk have steered me away from a number of confusions and ambiguities; they bear no responsibility for those that remain.

1. For example, more credit or better vocational training.

and difficult in the highly heterogeneous[2] agricultural sector of a
country like Colombia. No country, of course, either has or is assumed
to have fully homogeneous productive units in each subsector; there
are inevitably differences among farms by size; different products are
vulnerable in different ways to price fluctuations, and so on. And the
"slow growth" character of agriculture, especially during the later
stages of economic development, creates adjustment problems that
have attracted much attention from agricultural economists. While the
differences that form the topic of this chapter may tend to be ones of
degree rather than of kind, they are nonetheless striking and worthy of
special attention.

Before turning to them, a brief description of some of the dominant
features of Colombia's agriculture will be useful.

COLOMBIAN AGRICULTURE

Important characteristics of Colombian agriculture, some of them
closely related to the policy problems to be discussed, include the
following:

1. Considerable diversity in type of agriculture, defined primarily by
product. Production of coffee for export constitutes one important
subsector; coffee has long been Colombia's major crop and major foreign exchange earner. During the first half of the twentieth century its
contribution to total foreign exchange earnings ranged between 25
percent (just after the turn of the century, when gold exports were still
quite important) and 65 percent; the usual range was 40–55 percent;
since the rapid growth of minor exports, especially during the sixties,
this figure is now consistently below 50 percent. Livestock farming tends
to constitute another somewhat separate and certainly different activity; most cattle (the dominant animal) are raised on large farms, with
"extensive" methods, by owners who are usually fully or partially
absentee. This is a relatively capital-intensive form of production,
with a low labor/capital ratio. Since World War II, so-called commercial crop agriculture has expanded rapidly; it involves the modern,

2. In a previous draft of this essay, Colombia's agriculture was described as
dualistic. As pointed out to me by Michael Lipton, that term probably confuses more
than it clarifies, so its use has been dropped here. Although I would argue (somewhat speculatively) that parts of the sector are characterized by a number of the
features usually associated with dualistic models, such features are not at the heart
of this discussion, so given the considerable ambiguity of meaning that now sur-
rounds the term it seemed best to eschew its use.

technified production of such items as sugar, rice, cotton, barley, and a few others. Here, too, many of the producers are partially absentee, although most take a reasonably active hand in the management of the farm; they tend to be interested in new technologies and relatively well stocked with modern machinery. Finally, there is a large residual subsector often termed subsistence or traditional crop farming; it involves smaller-scale producers of food crops, partly for home consumption and partly for sale in the towns and cities.[3] This subsector is quite heterogeneous in itself, but it is useful to compare it with the other three cited.

Gradations and combinations of these ideal types exist, of course, but mixtures are by no means widespread, partly because the last-cited category is distinguished from the large-scale livestock farm and the commercial farm by its smallness; coffee is sometimes mixed with cattle and other crops, but in the heart of the coffee zone diversification is limited—it has proven elusive even when pushed by public agencies. During the postwar period the size of the coffee sector has not changed dramatically, although it underwent some growth with the rising coffee prices of the late forties and early fifties. Livestock production has also grown only gradually, being replaced in some zones by commercial crop farming and appearing in new, more distant regions. The residual category too has been fairly static. Thus, commercial crop farming has been the only dynamic subsector.

2. Growth of agricultural output has, over the long run, been relatively slow—around 3 percent a year for the last four decades—commensurate with a moderate rate of overall economic growth and a relatively low income elasticity of demand for agricultural products. The fortuitous rise in coffee prices in the late forties and early fifties turned agriculture into a sort of leading sector, but only for a decade. Technology was relatively stagnant till the postwar period; since then there appears to have been a small to middling technological gain, judging from the measured "residual" after growth of land, labor, and capital are taken into account.[4] Food consumption remains far from adequate in important segments of the population, especially in the rural areas.

3. There is, of course, a spectrum in terms of size also, but much land is in the livestock and commercial subsectors and perhaps a majority of people are in the "residual" subsector.

4. As discussed in U.S. Department of Agriculture, *Agricultural Productivity in Colombia,* Foreign Agricultural Economic Report no. 66 (Washington, D.C.: Government Printing Office, 1970), and in R. Albert Berry, *The Development of the Agricultural Sector in Colombia,* forthcoming, chap. 2.

3. Since World War II a substantial share of output growth has come from the commercial crop subsector. Of a total increase of about 95 percent between 1950 and 1970, about one-third was attributable to that subsector,[5] which at the start of the period accounted for perhaps 10 percent of total agricultural output.[6]

4. Given the quality of the available natural resources, Colombia's agricultural productivity appears to compare unfavorably with many other countries. Fertilizer usage remains quite limited, low-productivity technologies are widespread, and absentee ownership is common. Although small farms as a group appear to be relatively efficient when compared to large ones, they could not be called productive in absolute terms or in relation to their potential; better infrastructure, technical conditions, markets, and so on are prerequisites for realization of this potential.

5. Colombian agriculture is highly heterogeneous in the sense that widely varying factor proportions are often used in the production of a given item. Technologies range from quite traditional ones focusing on the hoe (and not too long ago on the digging stick), to the use of large machines—tractors, combines, and so on. The labor/land ratio varies tremendously with size, labor productivity rising several-fold and land productivity falling substantially[7] (see table 10.6 below). These

5. See Berry, *Agricultural Sector in Colombia,* chap. 2.

6. This depends partly, of course, on exactly how it is defined. Both these absolute shares and the increase in the commercial sector share are probably biased upward somewhat by the use of value of output rather than value added figures and by the failure to take account of the greater foreign exchange costs of the commercial sector. Correcting for these aspects (i.e., measuring the share of value added with imputed input costs measured at an estimated equilibrium exchange rate), the figures would be about 9 percent in 1950 and about 17 percent in 1967 (instead of 10 percent and 20 percent respectively). The use of value of output figures thus biases the estimated increase in the share of commercial agriculture upward a little but not dramatically.

7. Some writers on dualism tend to define it in terms of a bimodal distribution of farms by size or by type of technology used. Some evidence might be found in Colombia for the latter phenomenon; for example, while a substantial number of farms use tractors and a substantial number use human labor exclusively, only a small group uses either horses or oxen as a source of power. When, as in this case, a technology that has characterized a certain stage of development in many parts of the world is missing, the term bimodal may be applicable. But in terms of such quantifiable indicators as farm size, output, and the like, there is no tendency to bimodalism. (This is true also for the industrial sector, the commerce sector, and so on.) Often the idea underlying the term dualism seems to be wide dispersion of farm sizes, output levels, and—of more interest—factor proportions, both in the aggregate and in the production of specific products. This, as indicated above, is the type of heterogeneity that forms the topic of the present discussion.

Table 10.1: Relative Social Efficiency and Implicit Returns to Capital
by Farm Size with Varying Assumptions re the Opportunity
Cost of Labor

| | Case 1 | | Case 2 | | Case 3 | |
|---|---|---|---|---|---|---|
| | Opportunity cost of Non-white-collar labor: 1,400 white-collar labor: 8,000 | | Opportunity cost of Non-white-collar labor: 700 White-collar labor: 8,000 | | Opportunity cost of all labor: 0 | |
| *Farm size (ha.)* | *Coefficient of efficiency* | *Implicit social rate of return to capital* | *Coefficient of efficiency* | *Implicit social rate of return to capital* | *Coefficient of efficiency* | *Implicit social rate of return to capital* |
| 0–3 | .85 | 5.69 | 1.16 | 20.48 | 1.73 | 35.3 |
| 3–5 | 1.00 | 11.84 | 1.30 | 24.11 | 1.79 | 36.4 |
| 5–10 | 1.14 | 15.92 | 1.36 | 24.45 | 1.62 | 33.0 |
| 10–50 | 1.10 | 14.05 | 1.46 | 19.04 | 1.21 | 25.0 |
| 50–500 | 0.98 | 11.46 | 0.87 | 13.27 | 0.78 | 16.0 |
| >500 | 1.00 | 11.82 | 0.81 | 12.47 | 0.89 | 14.0 |
| Total | 1.01 | 11.98 | 1.01 | 15.82 | 1.00 | 20.4 |

*Note:* Labor is assumed to be homogeneous except for employed white-collar workers; product prices are assumed to equal marginal social benefit.

*Source:* Berry, "Land Distribution," p. 33.

factor productivity–farm size relationships exist in most if not all countries but are substantially more marked in Colombia than in agricultural sectors that appear less heterogeneous, such as those of the United States and Japan.

6. Attempts to assess static efficiency of resource utilization by farm size have suggested—for most plausible assumptions about the social opportunity cost of factors—that fairly small farms come out ahead of larger ones[8] (see table 10.1). Where average market prices (in the case of capital, the average rate of return) are assumed to measure true opportunity costs, middle-sized farms (5–50 hectares) appear to be a trifle more efficient than either smaller ones or larger ones, but the differences

8. See R. Albert Berry, "Land Distribution, Income Distribution, and the Productive Efficiency of Colombian Agriculture," in *Food Research Institute Studies,* forthcoming. The use of alternative shadow prices for foreign exchange tends to favor the smaller farms (from which most of the coffee comes) in terms of these average efficiency estimates. In terms of marginal efficiency, however, the picture is different, since the coffee quota is easily satisfied, whereas the agricultural exports and import substitutes from larger farms (sugar, rice, cotton, etc.) have more elastic demands. The large-scale sector does, of course, use more imported inputs, a fact not taken into account in the estimates in table 10.1. Several combinations of shadow prices did not significantly alter the relative efficiency estimates of the farm size groups, however (see the study just cited).

are not striking. There is certainly no evidence of increasing returns to scale as a general phenomenon. Thus, if labor is overpriced (or capital underpriced) in the market, or if the objective function assigns any weight to income distribution, the smaller farms have higher social efficiency than the larger ones; their value added per unit of resource used seems to be at least as great as that on the larger farms, and a much higher share of the income generated goes to low-income earners, either small-scale landowners or wage earners.

7. Government policy, while not easy to summarize without fear of overgeneralization, has clearly had output growth as its main objective;[9] modernization, primarily in the sense of mechanization, has been considered the key to raising output. Credit has been continuously and easily available for mechanization, machinery prices have been subsidized (via the overvalued exchange rate), and extension and research efforts have focused on the commercial crop subsector. Coffee policy has, naturally enough, not focused on output increases, because of the state of the world coffee market (although there now seems to be some danger of a new overproduction, with the development of the sun-grown high-yield varieties); livestock producers have always been favored by relatively easy access to credit, but other policies have had little success in this sector, and research and extension efforts have been limited. Little attention has been given to the smaller farmers; the agrarian reform program of the sixties did mark a new direction, and although its effects are generally agreed to have been small quantitatively and dubious qualitatively, it may be an interesting portent for the future. For the most part the agrarian reform, small-scale supervised credit, community action, and so on have been thought of as social programs rather than economically paying investments, reflecting the general assumption that small-scale farmers are inefficient and have

9. Albert Hirschman has argued that the relative emphasis on output as opposed to distribution, or social justice, has varied over time. The latter first received serious consideration under Alfonso Lopez in the thirties, output regaining top priority in the forties and fifties and distribution (or perhaps more the relief of social tensions related to the *violence* that plagued much of rural Colombia, especially through the late forties and early fifties) coming to the fore again in the sixties and being institutionalized in the Agrarian Reform Institute (INCORA). (Albert O. Hirschman, *Journeys toward Progress* [New York: Twentieth Century Fund, 1963], chap. 2.) In retrospect, INCORA has achieved little (if any) income redistribution. (For a critique, see, for example, Herman Felstehausen, "Agrarian Reform: Colombia," in *Land Reform in Latin America: Issues and Cases,* ed. Peter Dorner [Madison, Wisc.: Land Economics, 1971]). Whether this is because it was not a serious objective or because it is technically very difficult is open to debate; I would incline toward the former view.

little potential relative to their larger counterparts. Wide-ranging agrarian reform would, it is argued, create a risk situation for many large farmers and would prejudice output growth. Existing small-farm programs still have many wrinkles to be ironed out, which is not surprising in view of the relatively low quality, until recently at least, of most public institutions dealing with agriculture, and given the widespread doubts as to the potential and efficiency of small farmers.[10]

Table 10.2: Growth of Crops on Small and Large Farms, 1960 and 1966

*Percent of harvested area on:*

| Crop | Farms of ≤ 5 ha. 1960 | Farms of < 5 ha. 1st semester, 1966 | Farms of ≥ 50 ha. 1960 | Farms of ≥ 50 ha. 1st semester, 1966 | Plots of ≤ 5 ha. 1960 | Plots of ≥ 50 ha. 1960 |
|---|---|---|---|---|---|---|
| Perennials: | | | | | | |
| Coffee | 21.6 | 18.7 | 20.8 | 22.0 | 48.4 | 8.0 |
| Cacao | 16.5 | 15.0 | 29.4 | 29.8 | 63.5 | 3.8 |
| Bananas (export) | 13.6 | 13.8 | 43.8 | 40.6 | 52.8 | 25.6 |
| Platanos | 21.8 | 19.9 | 24.2 | 28.5 | 78.2 | 1.6 |
| Sugar | 18.4 | 15.7 | 40.0 | 40.7 | 51.9 | 25.6 |
| Annuals—relatively modern technology | | | | | | |
| Barley | 21.2 | 31.3 | 39.1 | 41.8 | 44.6 | 23.6 |
| Cotton | 8.3[a] | 2.2 | 50.7[a] | 85.3 | | |
| Rice | 7.1 | 6.7 | 66.7 | 68.0 | 29.1 | 32.3 |
| Sesame | 22.2 | 22.5 | 36.3 | 44.0 | 35.1 | 16.6 |
| Annuals—traditional technology | | | | | | |
| Beans | 24.2 | 25.5 | 29.3 | 31.7 | 64.8 | 9.5 |
| Corn | 26.6 | 24.6 | 31.2 | 36.9 | 61.7 | 7.6 |
| Potatoes | 31.8 | 39.9 | 19.9 | 20.1 | 67.4 | 4.2 |
| Tobacco | 41.0 | 37.8 | 10.2 | 21.8 | 84.8 | 1.6 |
| Wheat | 30.6 | 33.7 | 16.9 | 24.7 | 64.9 | 5.7 |
| Yuca | 24.7 | 19.8 | 24.2 | 35.2 | 87.7 | 0.8 |

a. The cotton information refers only to the interior of the country; probably large farms are somewhat more important on the coast. Because of the different base, the 1960 and 1966 figures cannot be compared in this case.

*Source:* Berry, "Land Distribution," p. 37. For all crops but cotton the 1960 figures are from DANE, *Denso agropecuario: Resumen general, segunda parte.* For cotton, see Instituto de Fomento Algodonero, *Colombia, su. desarrollo agricola: Algodon y oleaginosos, 1961–1962* (Bogota, 1966). For 1966 all figures are based on U.S. Department of Agriculture, *Agricultural Productivity in Colombia,* pp. 24–26.

10. The ancient but never well understood distinction between technical efficiency and economic efficiency has tended to escape most policy makers, as noted by Wayne

8. Much evidence on the Colombian economy as a whole suggests serious factor market imperfections; these are undoubtedly important causes of the heterogeneity of factor proportions and technologies. Colombian data on land and labor productivity by farm size (see table 10.6) indicate a roughly twentyfold difference in factor proportions between the smallest size category shown and the largest.[11] While some of this differential would be consistent with perfect factor markets,[12] one of this magnitude could hardly be explained thus. (Differences in the product composition of output by farm size are suggested in table 10.2.) Factor shares differ tremendously by farm size, as indicated in table 10.3. The suggestion that accessibility to credit varies significantly

Table 10.3: Functional Distribution of Labor and Capital by Farm Size

| Farm size (ha.) | Paid blue (1) | Paid white-collar and technical (2) | Total paid (3) | Total labor (4) | Capital (5) | Total labor (6) | Capital (7) |
|---|---|---|---|---|---|---|---|
| <1/2 | 9.4 | | 9.4 | 54.7 | 45.4 | 67.7 | 32.3 |
| 1/2–1 | 14.4 | | 14.4 | 57.2 | 42.8 | 71.6 | 28.4 |
| 1–2 | 20.7 | | 20.7 | 60.2 | 39.8 | 71.8 | 28.2 |
| 2–3 | 21.3 | | 21.3 | 60.6 | 39.4 | 68.6 | 31.4 |
| 3–4 | 21.9 | | 21.9 | 60.9 | 39.1 | 66.7 | 33.3 |
| 4–5 | 22.2 | | 22.2 | 61.2 | 38.8 | 65.0 | 35.0 |
| 5–10 | 22.6 | | 22.6 | 51.7 | 48.3 | 57.4 | 42.6 |
| 10–20 | 23.0 | 2.5 | 25.5 | 43.9 | 56.1 | 49.2 | 50.8 |
| 20–30 | 25.7 | 2.6 | 28.3 | 42.8 | 57.2 | 42.7 | 57.3 |
| 30–40 | 26.1 | 7.6 | 33.7 | 45.3 | 56.7 | 39.3 | 60.7 |
| 40–50 | 25.8 | 8.0 | 33.8 | 43.7 | 56.3 | 36.5 | 63.5 |
| 50–100 | 22.0 | 8.1 | 30.1 | 37.3 | 62.7 | 30.1 | 69.9 |
| 100–200 | 17.3 | 6.9 | 24.2 | 28.2 | 71.8 | 21.9 | 78.1 |
| 200–500 | 13.0 | 10.0 | 23.0 | 26.3 | 73.7 | 15.7 | 84.3 |
| 500–1,000 | 9.8 | 10.0 | 19.8 | 20.5 | 79.5 | 12.4 | 87.6 |
| 1,000–2,500 | 8.3 | 9.3 | 17.6 | 18.0 | 82.0 | 9.2 | 90.8 |
| >2,500 | 3.9 | 6.0 | 9.9 | 10.0 | 90.0 | 5.1 | 94.9 |
| Total | 18.2 | 5.0 | 23.2 | 33.3 | 66.7 | 37.9 | 62.1 |

*Distribution A* spans columns (1)–(5); *Distribution B* spans columns (6)–(7).

*Source:* Berry, "Land Distribution," table A-1, p. 22. Columns 1–5 are based on the paid labor distribution of the "best" estimate (estimate A) from table A-1, and on the assumption that for farm sizes where producer income is less than 2,800 pesos (twice the average salary), half is labor income and half capital income. Distribution B is based on the assumption that the imputed wage level for a given farm size equals 1,400 times the efficiency coefficient corresponding to that farm size.

Thirsk. Otherwise such relevant criteria as the output/capital ratio would have received much more attention.

11. The former using one-quarter of labor inputs and the latter one-quarter of combined land and capital inputs.

12. Farms of different sizes may specialize in products which, at a given relative factor price, use quite different factor proportions.

Table 10.4: Caja Agraria Credit/Value of Output by Farm Size

| Farm size (ha.) | Value of 1960 output (millions of 1971 pesos) (1) | Number of loans (2) | Farms (3) | Number of loans/ farm (4) | Value of loans (5) | Ratio of value of loans to value of output (6)=(5)/(1) |
|---|---|---|---|---|---|---|
| <2 | 2,114 | | | | | |
| | } 3119 | } 115,000 | } 606,423 | } .190 | } 376.30 | } 12.06 |
| 2–3 | 1,005 | | | | | |
| 3–4 | 996 | | | | | |
| | } 1695 | } 70,000 | } 150,182 | } .466 | } 302.10 | } 17.82 |
| 4–5 | 699 | | | | | |
| 5–10 | 3,004 | 75,000 | 169,145 | .443 | 407,26 | 13.56 |
| 10–20 | 3,224 | 46,000 | 114,231 | .403 | 383.35 | 11.89 |
| 20–30 | 1,575 | | | | | |
| | | } 25,000 | } 70,549 | } .354 | } 314,06 | } 11.44 |
| 30–40 | 1,170 | | | | | |
| 40–50 | 866 | 5,000 | 16,240 | .308 | 105.30 | 12.16 |
| 50–100 | 2,815 | 9,318 | 39,990 | .233 | 277.60 | 9.86 |
| 100–200 | 2,635 | 6,351 | 22,317 | .285 | 279.81 | 10.62 |
| 200–500 | 3,143 | 4,500 | 13,693 | .329 | 374.26 | 11.91 |
| 500–1,000 | 1,898 | 1,300 | 4,142 | .314 | 383.41 | 20.20 |
| 1,000–2,500 | 1,536 | | | | | |
| | | } 401 | } 2,761 | } .145 | } 269.79 | } 18.57 |
| ≥2,500 | 1,453 | | | | | |

*Sources:* Output figures are from Berry, "Land Distribution." The credit figures are from Berry, *Development of the Agricultural Sector in Colombia,* app. table A-79; distribution of credit by farm size, based on the distribution by patrimony, was estimated by the author. The estimates are quite crude, since the methodology was indirect.

by farm size is implicit in the roughly calculated distribution of Caja Agraria credit by size, shown in table 10.4. Although the Caja is the "small farmer" credit agency, the figures suggest little relationship between size and the ratio of Caja credit to the value of output. Were commercial banks included, the ratio of total institutional credit to value of output would show a strong positive relation to size, over at least part of the range.

### THE COMPLEXITIES

The added difficulties of policy making in a heterogeneous context may, I believe, be categorized as follows: (1) since income distribution is almost certain to be bad, the likelihood of *perceived* conflict between the goals of output growth and income redistribution is higher than in the homogeneous farm model cited earlier; (2) moderately different policy packages may lead to quite different results and/or moderately different conditions or economic structures may call for substantially different policies; (3) the heterogeneity of productive units is likely to imply a greater variance of response on the part of different units to any given policy (e.g., technological advance); (4) heterogeneity also implies conflict among pressure groups representing different subgroups of people involved in agriculture; (5) market imperfections are likely to be important and widespread, implying that policy making must take place in the complicated context of the second best; it is not generally possible to use observed factor prices as indicators of opportunity cost (e.g., in benefit-cost studies); (6) different levels of uncertainty are likely to be attached to different agricultural strategies, with some of the potentially more productive strategies being perceived as greater risks by decision makers and therefore reduced in priority; (7) finally, certain popular economic intuitions based on one or another logical fallacy seem to create more problems in heterogeneous systems than in relatively homogeneous ones, that is, superficially plausible points of view are more frequently incorrect and dangerous.

GOAL CONFLICT

Typical goals of an agricultural sector—or, better, goals of the economy to which the sector can contribute—are output growth, improvement in income distribution, and expansion of exports. Multiplicity of goals

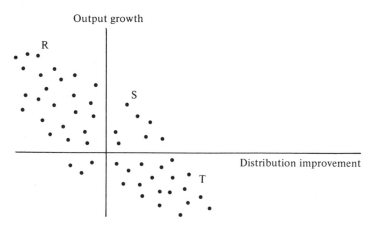

Fig. 10.1

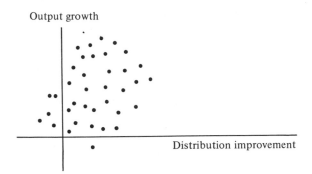

**Fig. 10.2**

is problematic when policy packages effective in the achievement of one goal either do not contribute to the achievement of others or in fact work against them. Such a situation, illustrated in figure 10.1, is compared with its opposite, figure 10.2. Dots are feasible policy packages; points along the northeast frontier, such as *R*, *S*, and *T*, are undominated packages, among which, if policy making were efficient, the selection would be made. In fact it is unlikely that decision making is this agile, so the package chosen is likely to be somewhere inside the frontier. In the case shown in figure 10.1, the wide range of possible goal combinations means at best (that is, when decision makers are aware of all the alternatives) that the decision is likely to be a hard one, and at worst (where only some of the feasible alternatives are perceived) that a package which implies a quite unsatisfactory level of one of the goal variables could be chosen. Where most policies that advance one goal satisfactorily advance the other one too, as in figure 10.2, problems are clearly much reduced. It has been increasingly argued of late that the same policies that would maximize the rate of growth would also improve the distribution of income (as in figure 10.2) not just in the long run[13] but in the short run as well.[14] Such a conclusion would at least be suggested by the probably higher average productivity on small farms than on large ones.

13. As would be implicit in the observation that income distribution usually improves in the later stages of development.

14. See, for example, Gustav Ranis, "Some Observations on the Economic Framework for Optimum L.D.C. Utilization of Technology," mimeographed (New Haven, Yale Economic Growth Center Discussion Paper no. 152, 1972).

But the fact that, when all options are considered and all the economics understood, little conflict exists by no means clears the way. Consider the following hypothesis. With a homogeneous sector, output and distribution under optimal (frontier) policies will not be in much potential conflict, nor will conflict be perceived. In contrast, with a heterogeneous sector, although under optimal policies the two goals will be substantially complementary, especially in the long run, conflict will be perceived. It will be perceived because the larger, more capital-intensive producers—whose opinion will prevail because of greater articulation and pressure group power—consider their technology superior to the more traditional, labor-intensive technology. They intuitively define efficiency as the developed countries do, by high *labor* productivity, and by what will raise their particular profits[15] (rather than maximize sectoral output).[16] This dogma may receive support from foreign advisers and foreign-trained nationals whose perception of relative efficiency is based on countries with different factor endowments. The upshot is that no one will be even aware of the high capital productivity of small farms, and programs directed at them will be defined as "social" rather than "economic."[17] When a large-farm technology cannot easily compete at existing factor prices, those prices will frequently be changed (e.g., machinery imports will be subsidized); the technology will then be competitive at existing market prices. Well-

15. That is, they support technologies in which, because of farm size, high labor cost, and low capital cost, they have a comparative advantage.

16. No theory of conspiracy or immorality is required to predict that this group will, like almost all groups, simply assume that what is good for them is good for the country.

17. The overall economic superiority of small farms cannot be taken as demonstrated either, of course. What is interesting is the few people who even argue this case.

Savings rates are alleged to be higher on the large farms; limited evidence from Colombia supports this. (See my *Agricultural Sector in Colombia,* chap. 3.) But this fact does not per se imply higher total savings in a large-farm system, with its complement of landless workers and subsistence farmers. The marginal propensity to save as a function of income may be the relevant factor; even more limited information gives no evidence of this propensity's increasing with income. Further, as noted to me by Michael Lipton, the savings of small farms may be related to low-cost investment goods (produced with their own labor) while that of large farms involves socially expensive imports. This appears generally to be true in Colombia.

Lack of responsiveness to technological change is also attributed to the small farms—an unconvincing claim when they still register higher static efficiency than the large ones.

While it is not our concern to discuss these issues in detail here, it must be remembered that the large question at issue remains imperfectly understood and quite unresolved.

trained economists may catch some of this mispricing, but it is totally unrealistic to expect many decision makers to do so, especially when the conclusion that the modern is inefficient is counterintuitive to them. The above sequence depends in part on unequal distribution of "pressure," or political power, and on the subtler inequality of input into the formation of the conventional wisdom as to what is efficient and what is not. These two inequalities are likely to reflect rather closely the distribution of income. In table 10.5, Colombia's agricultural income distribution (column 1) is compared to that of several other countries; the top 5 percent of the earners probably receive almost twice as much as the comparable group in the United States and more than twice as much as in Sweden and the Netherlands. Countries with relatively dualistic agricultural sectors—Mexico and, increasingly, Puerto Rico—have quite skewed distributions also, although less so than Colombia, according to the figures in table 10.5.[18] When the top 5 percent earns, on an average, thirty times as much as the bottom 20 percent, the existence of the sort of political-cultural phenomenon described above is not hard to understand.

Without going any further, it is evident already that policy conflict will be perceived, and a number of special problems (see below) will emerge. But at least one major complication must be added. Even an objective outsider to this issue would typically find it easier to formulate a policy (research, extension, marketing, and so on) to raise large-farm productivity; little information is available on the microstructure of small-scale farming in Colombia, nor on the precise behavior patterns of the farmers. Without that, policy formation tends to be (and has been over the few recent years when attempts have been made) groping in the dark. There is no reason to believe that a fine package does not

18. It must be remembered that the estimates of column 1 were generated by a different methodology from almost all of the others, that is, they are based on agricultural output figures, rather than sample survey income figures. There are a number of reasons for believing that samples tend to underestimate the skewness of income distribution, but there are also reasons to believe that column 1 does so; certainly it underestimates the total income of the top group since it does not include nonagricultural income, of which absentee landlords, for example, have a lot. But it also underestimates the income of the lower groups, so exactly how the figures would change with the inclusion of other types of income is not clear.

Alternative estimates to the basic or best estimate of column 1 are given in the source cited; it is clear that, unless the information from the other countries involves severe underestimation in the top 5 or 10 percent, none has as high a share of income going to that top small group as does Columbia; but caution is always warranted in such comparisons, and my familiarity with the sources for the other countries is limited.

Table 10.5: Distribution of Income Generated in Agriculture in Colombia and Selected Developing and Developed Countries (In percents)

| Decile | Colombia | | U.S.A. | | Puerto Rico[a] | | Mexico[b] | | Sweden | Netherlands |
|---|---|---|---|---|---|---|---|---|---|---|
| | Agricultural personal income 1960[c] | Rural family income 1965 | Rural farm families, money income 1960 | Farm families, money income 1960–62 | Rural family income 1953 | 1963 | Rural family income 1963 | Agricultural family income 1963 | Rural family income 1959 | Rural family income 1954 |
| | (1) | (2) | (3) | (4) | (5) | (6) | (7) | (8) | (9) | (10) |
| 1 | 2.24 ⎱ | ⎱ | ⎱ 3.0 | ⎱ 5.4 | 3.1 ⎱ 7.8 | 2.8 ⎱ 6.7 | 2.8 | ⎱ 4.4 | ⎱ 5.7 | ⎱ 11.0 |
| 2 | 2.87 ⎰ | ⎰ 19–26 | ⎰ | ⎰ | 4.7 ⎰ | 3.9 ⎰ | 3.9 | ⎰ | ⎰ | ⎰ |
| 3 | 3.34 ⎱ 16.3 | ⎰ | ⎱ 8.8 | ⎱ 9.5 | ⎱ 12.3 | ⎱ 10.4 | ⎱ 8.5 | ⎱ 7.5 | ⎱ | ⎱ |
| 4 | 3.73 ⎰ | ⎰ | ⎰ | ⎰ | ⎰ | ⎰ | ⎰ | ⎰ | ⎰ 27.1 | ⎰ 33.0 |
| 5 | 4.21 ⎰ | ⎰ | ⎱ 15.3 | ⎱ 15.3 | ⎱ 16.3 | ⎱ 13.6 | ⎱ 12.8 | ⎱ 10.8 | ⎰ | ⎰ |
| 6 | 4.68 | 5–7 | ⎰ | ⎰ | ⎰ | ⎰ | ⎰ | ⎰ | ⎰ | ⎰ |
| 7 | 5.78 | 7–10 | ⎱ 24.0 | ⎱ 22.6 | ⎱ 22.6 | ⎱ 19.5 | ⎱ 19.5 | ⎱ 17.6 | ⎱ 24.3 | ⎱ 21.5 |
| 8 | 7.90 | 10–13 | ⎰ | ⎰ | ⎰ | ⎰ | ⎰ | ⎰ | ⎰ | ⎰ |
| 9 | 12.77 ⎱ 65.25 | 13–15 ⎱ 50–55 | ⎱ 48.9 | ⎱ 47.4 | 12.9 ⎱ 41.0 | 14.1 ⎱ 49.9 | 15.4 ⎱ 54.1 | 16.7 ⎱ 59.6 | ⎱ 39.9 | ⎱ 34.5 |
| 10 | 52.48 ⎰ | 37–38 ⎰ | ⎰ | ⎰ | 28.1 ⎰ | 35.8 ⎰ | 38.7 ⎰ | 42.9 ⎰ | ⎰ | ⎰ |
| Top 5% | ≈41.5 | ≈25 | —d | 20.5 | 18.5 | 24.5 | 25.8 | 29.1 | 14.5 | 12.4 |
| Gini Coefficient | 0.58 | — | 0.46 | — | .32 | .41 | .47 | .58 | .36 | .22 |

a. Agriculture includes forestry and fisheries.
b. Includes forestry, hunting, and livestock.
c. The data refer to agricultural income only, and to the national accounts concept of income, i.e., appreciation of assets is excluded.
d. Not available.

*Sources and Methods:*

Column 1 is from Berry, "Land Distribution, Income Distribution and the Productive Efficiency of Colombian Agriculture."
Column 2 is based on the information presented in Asociacion Colombiana de Facultades de Medecina y Ministerio de Salud Publica, *Estudio de recursos humanos para la salud y educacion medica en colombia: Metodos y resultados* (Bogota, 1969), and Ascofame and Ministerio de Salud, *Estudio de recursos humanos para la salud y educacion: Investigacion nacional de morbilidad: La muestra* (Bogota, 1968). (These data are presented in Urrego M. German, *Distribucion del ingreso rural colombiano comparada con la distribucion urbana*, Instituto Colombiano Agropecuario, Boletin de Investigacion no. 18 [Bogota, December 1971], p. 126.) This column differs in concept from column 1, so the striking difference in results does not indicate any necessary inconsistency between the two data sources. The rural labor force—for which column 2 gives the income distribution—while it includes primarily people in the agricultural sector, includes also anyone else living outside towns of 1,500 people and up; more important, this population excludes many high income earners from agriculture who live in towns and cities. So the fact that column 1 indicates a very high concentration of the income generated in agriculture is not inconsistent with the fact that column 2 indicates a substantially lesser degree of concentration in the distribution of rural income. It should be noted that a number of observers have questioned the validity of the Ministry of Health-Ascofame figures, especially in the light of the fact that the study was not undertaken primarily to collect such data; the focus, rather, was on health statistics. Further, the highest income category was open ended, making it very difficult to guess at the average income of the people falling within it; the lowest income category is also a wide one, and there is substantial uncertainty also as to the average income and its distribution within that category. The estimates of column 2 are subject to question also because a substantial share (about one-sixth) of all farm families did not record an income, but rather fell in the category "don't know". To take these uncertainties partially into account, some range of estimates has been given in column 2.

Column 3 is from David H. Boyne, "Changes in the Income Distribution in Agriculture," *Journal of Farm Economics* 47 (1969): 1222; the data come originally from U.S. Bureau of the Census, *Trends in the Income of Families and Persons in the United States: 1947–1960*, Technical Paper no. 8 (Washington, D.C.: Government Printing Office, 1963), pp. 152–61. Rural farm families consist of farm managers, most of the farm laborers and foremen, and a group of part-time farmers whose primary occupation is something other than farming. This group corresponds quite closely to the "farmer and farm manager" group, whose quintile income distribution was almost identical in 1960 to that shown here for the rural farm families.

Column 4 is from Richard Weisskoff, *Income Distribution and Economic Growth: An International Comparison* (Ph.D. diss., Harvard University, 1969), p. 158, and originally from Jeannette Fitzwilliams, "A Size Distribution of Income in 1963," *Survey of Current Business* 44, no. 4 (1964): 3–11. This is quite similar to the 1960 distribution reproduced in column 3 except for the substantially

Table 10.5, Sources (*Continued*)

higher share of the bottom quintile; in the same source as that used for column 4, an estimate for the period 1957–59 indicates an even higher share (6.2 percent) for the bottom 20 percent. Possibly column 4 takes into account non-money income, although it seems hardly likely that this factor alone could account for the wide spread between the two figures over a full quintile.

Columns 5 and 6 are from Weisskoff, *Income Distribution*, p. 132. They come originally from reports of the Puerto Rico Department of Labor in 1953 and 1963 respectively. One aspect of the strikingly small share of the bottom quintile in the U.S. case is probably the inclusion of many part-time retired farmers—individuals who are essentially living on their wealth. In a less developed country, such individuals would probably be living with their sons and would not appear as separate families. (This hypothesis could be tested if information were available on the average family size for the various income categories.)

Columns 7 and 8 are from Weisskoff, *Income Distribution*, pp. 147 and 183 respectively. The original source was Banco de Mexico SA, Oficina de Estudios Sobre Proyecciones Agricolas, *Encuesta sobre ingresos y gastos familiares en Mexico, 1963* (Mexico DF, 1966). A comparison of columns 7 and 8 supports the point made earlier in connection with Colombia, that the agricultural distribution tends to be more unequal than the rural income distribution. The difference in Mexico is not so great as to imply, however, that this conceptual difference would explain the full difference in the distributions shown in columns 1 and 2 for Colombia; both Mexican distributions refer to families, while those for Colombia differ in this respect also. Weisskoff does present separate series for families and individuals in the case of Mexican agriculture; that for individuals shows less inequality than that for families. This could suggest perhaps that none of the difference between columns 1 and 2 can be explained in this way. Reported distributions for Argentina over 1958–61 tend to indicate a somewhat greater share of income going to the top 5 percent than in Mexico, and about the same for the top 10 percent; on the other hand, the share going to the bottom 20 percent is somewhat greater than in Mexico.

Columns 9 and 10 are from Weisskoff, *Income Distribution*, p. 161, and originally from Simon Kuznets, "Quantitative Aspects of the Economic Growth of Nations, VIII: Distribution of Income by Size," *Economic Development and Cultural Change* 11, no. 2, pt. 2 (1963).

exist, but no one knows many of its ingredients. Further, as discussed below, it may be that the complementarity, while eventually high, is less striking in the short run; this is perhaps especially true with respect to the income distribution and export goals, given the advantages of relatively large quantities, quality control, and so on, in the modern trading world. Hence the ironic state of affairs where in some underlying sense conflict is probably at a minimum but in the perception of the typical policy maker it is nearer the maximum.[19]

An added complication in a heterogeneous agricultural system is related to the presence and extent of a landless rural proletariat; the welfare of this group may be related in a complicated way to the steps taken vis-à-vis both small farms and large ones. An agrarian reform can, for example, either raise or lower the demand for this labor, depending on the circumstances.[20] If the labor-displacing effect of a policy package favoring small farms is greater than that of a package favoring large farms, then the distribution effect of the former may be worse in some income ranges and better in other ranges. With a homogeneous sector, the effects of a given policy on labor demand are easier to ascertain, since they do not involve weighing off different effects within various subgroups.

The greater range of policy options meriting consideration in a heterogeneous sector normally does (and should) lead to greater specialization among public institutions dealing with the sector; rel-

19. Perhaps the only fairly obvious policy would be one involving land redistribution. The best vehicle to achieve this—considered recently in Colombia—would probably be a tax system raising costs to large farmers. This would both give those farms an incentive to raise productivity and encourage some to sell to more efficient smaller farmers. The transfer, occurring through the marketplace, would involve less (and different) trauma than that usually surrounding agrarian reform. (For details see R. Albert Berry, "Presumptive Income Tax on Agricultural Land: The Case of Colombia," *National Tax Journal* 25, no. 2 [1972]: 169–81.) But the fate of this proposal, made at various times in Colombia—including the 1969 Musgrave Commission Report—is instructive. Despite its being, in this author's opinion at least, one of the best possible agricultural policies vis-à-vis both output and distribution, it has in fact received even shorter shrift than agrarian reform and (at present) a small-farm technological change policy. The comparison with agrarian reform is instructive. Though generalization is dangerous, there appears to be little evidence that much real wealth transfer has occurred (in some cases landholders have been paid excessive prices, according to rumor) or that any distributional improvement has occurred. Was this policy more feasible (though still not very feasible) than the land tax in part because powerful groups saw it is easier to evade?

20. See R. Albert Berry, "Land Reform and the Agricultural Income Distribution," *Pakistan Development Review* 11, no. 1 (1971): 30–44.

evant here is the specialization between those institutions or branches of institutions focusing their attention on the larger scale commercial farmer, and those focusing on the smaller-scale and usually more traditional subsistence-type farmer. This separation tends to parallel two broad agricultural policy strategies, a fact that usually impedes effective integration between the two. At best such complementarity as these two wings of policy may have will be hard to take advantage of; at worst, a sort of bureaucratic warfare may result. This conflict is probably not as far advanced in Colombia as in some other countries. The Colombian Ministry of Agriculture has traditionally focused its attention on the larger-scale farms, and the weight of opinion in the relatively new Instituto Colombiano Agropecuario (ICA) seems also to have leaned in that direction. The Caja Agraria, despite its presumed orientation toward the smaller farm, has tended to focus on what may more accurately be categorized as medium-sized farms, has favored mechanization, and has probably often thought of its small-farm programs more as social than as economic ones. This is not to belittle its substantial contributions as a credit agency; but it has never systematically argued that the small farmer has high potential. The agency that might be expected to reflect that point of view is INCORA (the Agrarian Reform Institute). But, while INCORA has pursued the goal of land redistribution within very limited political constraints, a number of aspects of its policy, especially during the earlier years, seemed to reflect the traditional point of view that size and modern technology are necessary for high productivity, that the typical small farmer must be told what to do, and so on. During the last few years, a branch of thinking has developed within INCORA—including a number of sociologists—to the effect that the agency must become a much more dynamic social force, must learn how to work much better with small-scale farmers, and must focus more on the social development of those farmers, with a view to turning them into an independent political force. This point of view has, however, never attained power in INCORA.

While the potential bureaucratic conflict cited above has not been severe in Colombia to date, it will probably become more so as information on the relative efficiency of small farmers becomes available, and as the political need to direct more attention to them becomes obvious. In the absence of an articulate institutional proponent of a policy emphasizing the smaller farmers, the belief that output and redistribution of income are in conflict is not surprising. With even a mild opening up of the system, it is possible that politicians will begin to raise banners in favor of less traditional strategies.

## NONROBUSTNESS OF POLICY

The depth of understanding required to achieve a given degree of success[21] in a relatively homogeneous agricultural sector appears to be substantially less than in a technologically heterogeneous one. For many policies (e.g., credit) such sectors tend to not be characterized by situations in which total benefits are very sensitive to small differences in the level of the instrumental variable. Overinvestment in one particular line lowers its marginal productivity, but less, I will argue, than tends to be the case in a heterogeneous agricultural sector. Coupled with a fairly smooth (probably quadratic) relationship between the level of a policy variable and the total resulting benefits is likely to be a low dispersion frequency distribution of benefits accruing to the various productive units, for a given level of the policy variable. For example, while one would expect that a machinery credit policy would imply greater benefits for some farmers than for others, because, for instance, they dedicate a greater share of their land to mechanized crops, one would also expect a substantial clustering—across different farms—of the variable "benefits per acre" and would not expect to find many farmers harmed by the policy (see figures 10.3 and 10.4). An increase in the level of credit would tend to shift the whole frequency distribution to the right, with only a few farms not being benefited.

In the case of other policies, benefits may be, or appear to be, more sensitive to the level of policy variables when farms are all similar; thus, one mechanical innovation might be totally irrelevant (no farms would use it) whereas another (say, less capital intensive) might be widely applied. In a technologically heterogeneous sector, almost any innovation is likely to be adopted by some farmers. Homogeneity, in these cases, means that many conceivable innovations or instruments would have zero input; but this fact tends to focus research and investinent on the range where an impact will be felt, rather than to imply that many investments have no effect. It does not necessarily or generally mean that the range of payoffs of different seriously considered policies is

21. That is, to raise the objective function to a given percent of the feasible maximum.

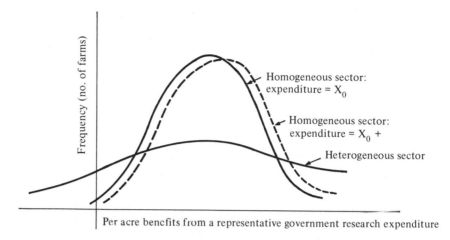

Per acre benefits from a representative government research expenditure

Fig. 10.3

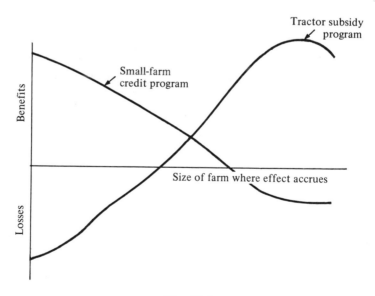

Fig. 10.4

great.[22] In the heterogeneous case, on the other hand, the fact that almost any innovation will be adopted by some may give the misleading impression that almost any innovation will pay off socially; but one that raises the private benefits to a socially inefficient subset of farmers may have no social benefits or even a negative effect.

Overall, therefore, it is arguable that homogeneity and the relatively perfect markets probably associated with it simplify the technical task of policy makers; the same is true on the political side. Usually a package that generates income increases for a good majority of the producing units will avert political problems; wide dispersion of benefits is important unless political power is extremely unequal. Political and economic considerations are more likely to be complementary in a homogeneous agriculture. If, for example, more credit is made available it would probably reach and benefit all subsectors; discrimination among groups—which would create invidious comparisons, strong feelings, and criticisms—is unlikely to be desirable on efficiency grounds, nor is it likely to occur; in a dualistic economy, on the other hand, it is likely to occur in favor of large farms (see below).

In a heterogeneous agriculture, the needs of different groups—even groups producing the same crop—are substantially different. Consider two farms producing corn, one with an isoquant lying fully within the capital-intensive range and facing a low capital price relative to that of labor, the other with an isoquant lying fully within the labor-intensive range and facing a high capital price relative to that of labor. Given their factor market situations, labor-saving technological change will raise profitability of the large farm;[23] the opposite is true for smaller farms. The former will increase the competitiveness of the large farms and thus have negative (rather than, say, neutral) effects on the small farms. With respect to credit, marketing, and other needs, programs for small and large farms are likely to be sufficiently different that they are handled by different agencies; thus, with policy defined at subsector levels, discussion may surround small-farm credit, rather than farm

22. Since most programs, such as multiplication of a new seed, application of a new spray, or whatever, must in any case be expanded gradually, it is often possible to trace out a benefits curve; serious errors are unlikely when such a procedure is possible. Of course, some capital investments are once and for all, and for these a complete estimate of the benefits must be made in advance. But in the other cases, being able to assume that benefits are a simple function of the level of the policy variable does simplify the planning.

23. At least until general equilibrium effects on the price of the product are taken into account.

credit, and the lack of mutual interest across the subsectors becomes transparent. Because their input structures are quite different, price subsidy and improved access programs that help the large farmer (machinery, air spraying) will not help the small one; rather, via the competitive relation between subsectors, they will often hurt him.[24] Mutuality of interest exists on occasion too, of course, but it does not obviously dominate; hence, the wide dispersion of the frequency distribution of gains (or losses) resulting from a given policy, as shown in figure 10.4.

That this heterogeneity[25] creates political problems and complicates decision making is obvious; that it is related to nonrobustness of policy is less so. Here it is useful to focus on the time element. Viewing the future positively, successful development will bring a decrease in Colombia's agricultural labor force, an increase in average farm size, and a substitution of other factors for labor. Mechanization will eventually be applied on all mechanizable farms. Labor-intensive technologies that are productive at present will become less and less so, as they become inconsistent with the economy's factor proportions. There is therefore (hopefully) a limit to the payoff period for investment in improving labor-intensive-technology agriculture. How long this potential payoff period will last depends on the overall rate of growth of the economy, which in turn depends in part on the relative success of labor-intensive technologies in the early stages of development of the nonagricultural sector. Generation and encouragement of technologies substantially different from those that will at a later stage be the most efficient appears to be going against the tide; but such policies may be required to produce the development that will eventually make them passé.

Consider figure 10.5, with points $L$ and $S$ corresponding to the factor combinations chosen by large and small farms, respectively. Their relative factor prices explain their different factor proportions; were

24. The policy of importing tractors at low cost will obviously have no direct relevance for the majority of farmers; to a few it will have an indirect positive effect via the opportunity to rent the service, and to some it will have an indirect negative effect as, for example, their previous landowners—on opting to cultivate with machinery—eject them from the land they have been sharecropping or renting. And wide differences in technology often imply that a new seed is relevant only for some farms; for example, only some producers may be able to use modern seeds requiring a lot of water and heavy fertilizer application.

25. The difference from what I am calling homogeneous agriculture is, of course, one of degree; producers of a given crop will also wrangle with producers of other crops for subsidized resources, and so on. But here there is an added dimension of heterogeneity, which divides the producers of given items.

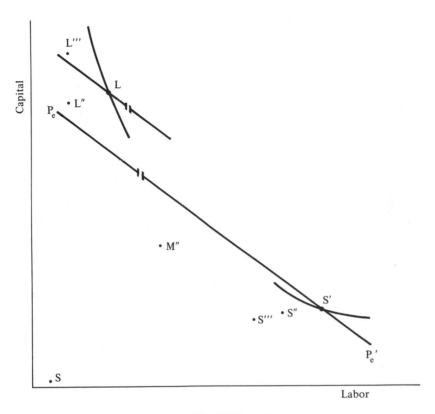

Fig. 10.5

factor markets perfect, the factor price ratio would be $P_e P_e'$. For simplicity, let point $S'$ represent the input/output combination of that number of $S$ farms which would produce the same output as one $L$ farm. As indicated by the fact that $P_e P_e'$ through $S'$ passes below $L$, the small farms are more efficient, judged in relation to the equilibrium factor price.[26] Compare now two alternative technological improvements, each obtainable by a given research expenditure, one benefiting the large farms ($L''$), the other the small farms ($S''$); unless $L''$ is far below $L$, technology $S''$ will in the short run be superior to $L''$ (judged

26. If there are intermediate technologies that lie below the straight line $LS'$, it would of course be more efficient if all the resources were used by firms with such technologies (e.g., $M$). But the factor market imperfections prevent their use, and the analysis of optimal technological change certainly cannot assume this fact away.

at equilibrium factor prices). As the capital/labor ratio rises, the slope of the equilibrium factor price line will gradually increase, and $S''$ will become relatively less efficient compared to $L''$. The move to $S''$ is preferable if the rate of increase in the overall capital/labor ratio falls below a certain level—a level at which the two improvements are equally beneficial, $S''$ providing greater short-run gains and smaller long-run gains. More realistically, one should think of a gradual improvement of technology but the basic argument remains the same.[27]

If one conceives of technological change as "free," or "automatic," the above comparison is of less interest, since under a fairly wide range of conditions it is better to have both improvements than one.[28] In fact, however, the development and dispersion of relevant technological improvement for the small farmer has definite costs (this is probably less true for the large farmer), given the lack of understanding of what constitutes an improvement for him. Correspondingly, technological improvement is desirable only if the benefits exceed these costs. Small-farm technological improvement is the more desirable (1) the lower the costs, and (2) the longer the payoff period and the greater the payoff per period. Measurement of payoff is complex. Consider a small-farm improvement (e.g., $S'''$) which has considerable short-run payoff and whose existence is *the* source of growth (with rising $K/L$ and $P_L/P_K$) that eventually renders it obsolete. Now, it would be invalid to measure the contribution of $S'''$ by the benefits accrued over the period of its application, since no subsequent growth would have occurred without it either. Benefits are measured by the discounted difference between the future income flow with application of this technique and without it, taking account, therefore, of the indirect as well as the direct effects. In an extreme opposite case, the small-farm technology might again be applied over a short period, but because the new large-farm techno- logy is socially productive and contributes to an increase in $K/L$; short-lived application would then be associated with a relatively low payoff. When the majority of agricultural resources are in the large-

27. To ascertain which improvement raises national income more, it is necessary also to take into account the relative amount of resources currently used by farms with each technology and the probable extent of substitution of one type for the other when the first becomes more efficient. The discussion in the text refers to the simple case where an equal amount of resources is used in each and no substitution occurs when one technology is improved.

28. There are cases, however, in which a new large-farm technology will be adopted but will not raise agricultural output; this would occur if the change were from $L$ to $L''$, the latter activity being more profitable to the large farm (given his factor prices) but a less efficient use of resources for the economy as a whole.

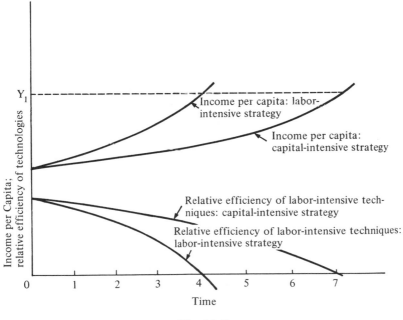

**Fig. 10.6**

farm sector (as in the United States) the latter result is more probable; in India it would seem quite implausible. For an intermediate country, characterized by a high degree of technological heterogeneity, there is no strong presumption in either direction; the expected payoff of the two quite different strategies may be similar, but ex post one might be much better since it may promote sufficient growth to generate a sort of take-off, while the other does not. Or relatively small exogenous factors (e.g., an increase in the price of inputs) may render one of the improvements superior. Were the sector homogeneous, the generation of a new technology $M''$ would be the logical objective, since it would have positive implications over a considerable range of relative prices, that is, over a considerable range of "sequences of events" endogenous and exogenous to the sector. But this technology is irrelevant in the case portrayed since it is high cost for both sets of farms.[29] Failing this

29. The above discussion is oversimplified into the dualistic mold eschewed at the beginning of this chapter, but the results are qualitatively the same when there is a whole series of subgroups, each with somewhat differing factor prices, but with greater proportions of farms toward the two ends of the spectrum than in the

middle way, one might hope for a balanced emphasis between large and small. It has been rather persuasively argued, however, that a simultaneous improvement of both small farms and large-farm technology is very difficult, if not impossible, when political, institutional, and technical constraints are all taken into account.[30] I will return to this question below.

The variability of a given policy's effects across mildly different situations is portrayed in figure 10.6; if quite successful labor-intensive technologies are introduced fairly quickly, then their payoff period will be up to, say, $T = 4$, with their relative efficiency high at $T = 0$ and gradually falling to $T = 4$, at which time they are presumably replaced by more capital-intensive techniques. A less growth-promoting capital-intensive strategy[31] would lengthen (say, to $T = 7$) the period during which the labor-intensive techniques would be more efficient (at equilibrium factor prices), since the economy's emergence from its current low $K/L$ state would be delayed. In other words, it would take the economy longer to reach a per capita income $Y_1$ which, for simplicity, we may treat as the dividing line between a low capital/labor and a high capital/labor condition. The potential gains from a labor-intensive strategy depend, clearly, on how far the existing income level $K/L$ is from that corresponding to $Y_1$, and on the country's relative capacity in designing and applying one of the strategies vis-à-vis the other. In economies

---

"homogeneous" case. Another oversimplification is the failure to consider the impact of factor prices and technological change or the distribution of resources between the two subsectors, but inclusion of this complexity does not alter my general conclusions.

30. See, for example, Don Kanel, "The Role of Land Tenure in the Modernization of Agriculture," mimeographed (Paper presented at the Purdue Workshop on Small Farm Agriculture in Developing Nations, November 1972).

31. It must be remembered that by "capital-intensive strategy" is meant a strategy in which a high share of the total capital stock is employed in conjunction with a small number of workers; the rest of the labor force, of course, works with very little capital (or is unemployed), so more highly labor-intensive techniques may exist in one part of this economy than in the one where a "labor-intensive strategy" is pursued. But, given the low policy priority such technologies receive, they are likely to be unproductive compared to their potential. The differences between the two systems, then, are as follows. (1) The economy where the labor-intensive strategy is pursued will be characterized by less variance in factor proportions across different productive units; this tends to imply greater overall efficiency of resource use. (2) That same economy strives especially to improve those technologies whose factor proportions correspond somewhat more closely to the existing factor endowment; a given increase in the total factor productivity of an activity raises national income more when the factor proportions of that activity correspond to those of the economy than where this is not the case.

that are overwhelmingly agricultural[32]—India, Pakistan, or Guatemala could be cases in point—it seems almost a foregone conclusion that successful development must involve labor-intensive technologies which advance both agricultural output and employment; this is the more obvious the greater the weight given to the employment and distribution goals. The arguments against wholesale mechanization seem overwhelming, since it appears inconceivable that the rest of the economy, starting from so small a base, could generate employment opportunities rapidly enough to substitute for a labor-intensive policy in agriculture. The agricultural sectors of these economies, though characterized by a wide range of observed factor proportions, tend to have a concentration of resources near one end of the spectrum; the output contribution of the smaller-scale traditional subsector tends to be high and the vast majority of the labor force is located there.[33] For countries having currently a high percentage of the labor force in traditional agriculture and high average labor/capital or labor/natural resources ratios in the economy as a whole, it may be presumed that attempts to introduce highly capital-intensive techniques will frequently fail in the market and will even more frequently lower national income;[34] their potential negative impact would in general be greater the higher the country's labor/resources ratio. At the other end of the spectrum—the developed countries—where heterogeneity has tended to diminish, technological

32. And where a vast majority of the agricultural labor force works on quite small farms. In India, as of the early fifties, perhaps 25 percent of the labor force worked on farms smaller than five acres and 50 percent on farms smaller than ten acres (see table 10.6; note that these estimates are based on only five regions and may therefore be somewhat biased).

33. The seriousness of the "heterogeneity" discussed here is a function of the tendency of productive units to be found near the two ends of the technological spectrum. Consider the figure below.

System A, while factor proportions cover the same range, is less heterogeneous than system B since a small proportion of the labor force is found working in units with extreme factor proportions. Frequency distributions of firms or output would of course have different shapes than those for labor; one system could have a higher share of the labor force near the extremes while another had a higher share of output produced by units near one extreme. Thus it may not be obvious which one should be defined as more heterogeneous. In any case, the definition would involve both the proportion of factors and the proportion of output associated with productive units whose factor proportions are toward the two extremes of the distribution.

34. They will not always fail, of course, because: (1) they may in some cases dominate labor-intensive techniques; and (2) pressure toward the generation or perpetuation of market imperfections that increase the market competitiveness of the technique will arise and, for reasons discussed earlier, will sometimes be successful in "saving" the technique.

change of a capital-intensifying type is not only beneficial with respect to output but is likely to imply a fairly widespread distribution of the benefits. The in-between case—and Colombia would seem to fall in this category—is the difficult one;[35] the theoretically attractive inter-

35. Table 10.6 compares relevant data in Colombia with a poorer less dualistic country (India) and with richer less dualistic countries—the United States as an example of the land-intensive case and Japan as an example of the labor-intensive case. Column 4 suggests that the top decile of workers (i.e., the 10 percent working on the largest farms) have a labor productivity level perhaps six times as high as the bottom 20 percent; land productivity on the former farms is about half as high as on the latter, so the labor/land ratio is about one-twelfth as high. For the limited sample of five Indian states included in the figures in columns 11, 12, and 13, it is seen that labor per acre (expressed in labor days) for the category 0–2.5 acres is only slightly over twice as high as that for the category 50 acres and up. (These size classes may correspond roughly to the bottom 20 percent of the labor force and the top 10 percent, though there are no data here permitting more than a rough guess that this is the case.) And labor productivity is only a little over 50 percent higher on the latter farms than on the former, while land productivity is about a third lower. The 2:1 ratio for labor productivity across the size range cited is also approximately that implicit in Rao's figures for Telangara in India (see source note to table 10.6). Although comparisons with the Colombian data are difficult because of the lack of information on distribution of labor by farm size for the country as a whole, the use of labor-days rather than labor force, and other data differences, even the rough picture painted indicates rather clearly the lesser degree of heterogeneity in India.

As may be expected, the Japanese data indicate a substantial homogeneity across farm sizes, with labor productivity in 1952–54 only about 50 percent higher in the largest category shown in table 10.6 (with 10 percent of the labor force) than in the smallest one (with 16 percent of the labor force); the differential was about 66 percent in 1959–61. As of 1959–61 the labor/land ratio was less than 50 percent higher in the smallest category. Since the farm size range is small (only from a category less than about 1.25 acres to a top category of about 5 acres and up), comparisons with other countries are hard to interpret; in fact the ratios appear at first glance, and taking into account the serious data limitations, to be not far out of line with those for India over the same range; the total range in India is, of course, much greater.

There is considerable information on input/input and output/input relationships with farm size in Japan based on individual farm studies. One hypothesis is that much of the relative constancy across size categories may be due to the homogeneity of output: rice is very much the dominating crop. (See, for example, Dan Maxwell Etherington, *Structural Changes in Peasant Agriculture: A Comparative Study of Indian and Japanese Farm Data* [M. Sci. thesis, Cornell University, February 1962].)

The comparison with the United States is of considerable interest, in view of the fact that that country has a perhaps above average degree of inequality in land distribution, given its level of development. Once again, the divergences are substantially smaller than in Colombia, where the labor productivity of the 10 percent of workers on the largest farms is about twice as high as that of the 20 percent on the smallest farms; land and buildings productivity (measured by value) is about 70 percent as high on the former as on the latter; thus the "labor/value of land and buildings" ratio is about one-third as high on the larger farms. Table 10.7 sum-

mediate route is, in practice, much less feasible than one might expect. It is not inconceivable that rapid expansion of the nonagricultural sector would create enough jobs to induce a decrease in the agricultural labor force and thus prevent the potentially serious employment and income distribution results of labor-displacing technological change; in such a case the payoff to improvements in labor-intensive technologies would be relatively small. For a given combination of "potential technologies" there will be a critical income level (or capital/labor ratio) below which it pays to focus on improving traditional agriculture and above which it does not; although this "one or the other" way of describing the alternatives is extreme, I will argue below that political conditions make them to some extent incompatible; where this is not the case,[36] the risks of policy making become substantially less. If the country is still below this critical level, the result of encouraging capital-intensive techniques will (by definition) be negative; switching to a labor-intensive strategy will also be harder, having begun with the other approach,[37] so extrication from this box may be difficult. The negative effect of such a policy could be greatest for a country with income not far below the critical level, since the social inefficiency of the capital-intensive technology would then be less likely to lead to market failure and the excision of the inefficiency; but this is not clear. If a large-farm push does provide a stimulus to growth and helps to "get the country over the line"—stimulating rural to urban migration with the accompanying advances in health, education and so on—it may have a substantial positive impact.

Two aspects of the situation under discussion warrant further comment. It has been assumed above that technological change is factor proportion specific, in both the short and the long run. Thus, an improvement in a capital-intensive technique (e.g., a better machine) will not be beneficial to farmers operating outside a certain $K/L$ range. The less valid this assumption, the less important is the precise type of technological change that occurs, and the less sensitive the economy's development to the $K/L$ range where the technological effect is focused.

marizes differences as measured by the percent of the agricultural labor force that works in conjunction with the top 10 and 20 percent of the land (by acreage or value, according to data availability).

36. For example, a political system different from the common type described below.

37. Both because public sector services will be focused on the larger farms, and because the political difficulties of removing advantages once conceded are substantial.

Table 10.6: Land Productivity, Labor Productivity, and the Labor/Land Ratio by Farm Size for Selected Countries

Colombia, 1960 (In thousands of 1960 pesos)

| Farm size (ha.) | Value added/ effective hectare[a] (1) | Value added/ worker (2) | Workers/ effective hectare (3) | Percent of Resources: Of labor force (4) | Of land and capital by value (5) |
|---|---|---|---|---|---|
| 0–3 | 0.75 | 1.67 | 0.450 | 26.0 | 6.9 |
| 3–5 | 0.79 | 2.08 | 0.380 | 11.2 | 3.5 |
| 5–10 | 0.73 | 2.71 | 0.270 | 15.0 | 6.7 |
| 10–50 | 0.57 | 3.47 | 0.160 | 25.9 | 19.7 |
| 50–500 | 0.38 | 6.18 | 0.060 | 17.6 | 37.0 |
| >500 | 0.35 | 15.07 | 0.023 | 4.5 | 26.2 |
| Total | 0.48 | 3.71 | 0.130 | 100.0 | 100.0 |

Table 10.6 (Continued)
India (In rupees)

| Size of holding (acres) | Gross value of output/operated area (1950–51) (6) | Gross value of output/agricultural population (7) | Percent of resources: Agricultural population[b] (8) | Area operated (9) |
|---|---|---|---|---|
| 0–5 | 287 | 200 | 43.0 | 16.8 |
| 5–10 | 236 | 309 | 26.9 | 19.6 |
| 10–15 | 167 | 352 | 10.6 | 12.6 |
| 15–20 | 153 | 428 | 6.8 | 10.7 |
| 20–25 | 140 | 479 | 3.7 | 7.0 |
| 25–30 | 137 | 576 | 2.6 | 6.1 |
| 30–40 | 127 | 701 | 2.6 | 7.9 |
| 40–50 | 134 | 928 | 1.3 | 4.9 |
| >50 | 131 | 1350 | 2.5 | 14.4 |
| Total | 185 | | 100.0 | 100.0 |

| Size of holding (acres) | Gross output/area — Unweighted average of indices for eight states:[c] mid-fifties (10) | Gross output/area — Unweighted average for five states:[c] mid-fifties (11) | Index of labor-days/acre: five states (12) | Index of gross output/labor-days: five states (13) | Percent of resources — Labor-days: five states (13a) | Percent of resources — Area, five states (13b) |
|---|---|---|---|---|---|---|
| 0– 2.5 | 11.93 ⎱ 115.5 | 123.8 ⎱ 120.2 | 156.6 ⎱ 140.2 | 79.0 | 11.40 | 6.5 |
| 2.5– 5.0 | 111.2 ⎰ | 116.6 ⎰ | 123.8 ⎰ | 94.2 | 14.15 | 10.2 |
| 5.0– 7.5 | 101.0 ⎱ 1.0 | 107.2 ⎱ 1.0 | 109.2 ⎱ 1.0 | 98.2 | 12.96 | 10.6 |
| 7.5–10.0 | 99.7 ⎰ | 100.8 ⎰ | 95.6 ⎰ | 105.4 | 10.28 | 9.6 |
| 10–15 | 83.8 | 84.7 | 81.7 | 103.7 | 11.53 | 12.6 |
| 15–20 | 81.8 | 77.5 | 77.8 | 99.6 | 9.31 | 10.7 |
| 20–25 | 77.1 | 78.1 | 71.2 | 109.7 | 5.57 | 7.0 |
| 25–50 | ≈75.0 | 77.7 | 69.5 | 111.8 | 14.70 | 18.9 |
| >50 | 70.6 | 80.0 | 62.4 | 128.2 | 10.07 | 14.4 |

Table 10.6 (Continued)
Japan (In yen)

| Farm size (tan)[a] | Value added/tan | | Labor hours/tan | | Value added/ (yen per hour) | | Labor hours (1960) | Percent of resources | |
| | | | | | | | | Land (1960) | Number of farm households (in thousands) (1960) |
| | 1952–54 (14) | 1959–61 (15) | 1952–54 (16) | 1959–61 (17) | 1952–54 (18) | 1959–61 (19) | (20) | (21) | (22) |
|---|---|---|---|---|---|---|---|---|---|
| <5 | 13.0 | 15.6 | 428.6 | 339.0 | 303 | 460 | 15.70 | 14.54 | 1266 |
| 5–10 | 14.8 | 16.7 | 433.7 | 356.4 | 341 | 468 | 33.92 | 29.87 | 991 |
| 10–15 | 13.9 | 16.6 | 344.8 | 316.4 | 403 | 525 | 27.10 | 26.88 | 907 |
| 15–20 | 13.6 | 16.8 | 305.3 | 274.3 | 445 | 612 | 13.43 | 15.37 | 1001 |
| >20 | 13.7 | 16.3 | 268.7 | 232.2 | 509 | 701 | 9.85 | 13.42 | 404 |

Table 10.6 (*Continued*)

United States, 1964 (In dollars)

| Farm size (acres) | Value added/ acre of pro- ductive land (23) | Value added/ value of land and buildings[e] (24) | Value added/ persons working (25) | Value added/ man-hours (26) | Percent of resources | |
| --- | --- | --- | --- | --- | --- | --- |
| | | | | | Labor (27) | Value of land and buildings (28) |
| <10 | 733 | .153 | 3,811 | 3.73 | 2.78 | 1.64 |
| 10– 49 | 704 | .108 | 3,016 | 3.06 | 9.25 | 6.37 |
| 50– 99 | 346 | .112 | 3,050 | 3.13 | 10.52 | 7.13 |
| 100–139 | 317 | .126 | 3,502 | 3.46 | 8.40 | 5.60 |
| 140–179 | 309 | .129 | 3,980 | 3.82 | 9.46 | 6.81 |
| 180–219 | 304 | .131 | 4,385 | 4.14 | 6.73 | 5.16 |
| 220–259 | 303 | .130 | 4,925 | 4.62 | 6.18 | 5.35 |
| 260–379 | 280 | .125 | 5,524 | 5.11 | 12.23 | 12.12 |
| 380–499 | 251 | .119 | 6,036 | 5.51 | 7.23 | 8.14 |
| 500–699 | 223 | .111 | 6,421 | 5.79 | 6.57 | 8.29 |
| 700–999 | 194 | .110 | 6,901 | 6.12 | 5.26 | 7.07 |
| >1,000 | 67 | .087 | 7,573 | 6.13 | 15.39 | 26.20 |

a  An effective hectare was defined by the value of an average hectare in farms of 4–5 hectares. The absolute numbers in this column and in column 3 are therefore not meaningful.

b. Landless families are included in the bottom size category.

c. States are listed in sources and methodology.

d. One tan equals .245 acres or .10 hectare.

e. Excluding farm dwellings.

*Sources and Methods:*

The data for Colombia come from Berry, "Land Distribution." As discussed in that source, there are many data weaknesses, so that the figures are not precise indicators of what they purport to measure; there is little doubt, however, that the comparisons with the other countries in terms of factor proportion variation by size, and the distribution of resources by farm size, the matters of prime interest here, are valid ones; for further discussion and alternative estimates for Colombia, see the reference.

Columns 6–9 are calculated on the basis of figures presented by D. Narain in *Distribution of the Marketed Surplus of Agricultural*

Table 10.6, Sources (Continued)

*Produce by Size of Holding in India, 1950–51* (New Delhi: Asia Publishing House, 1961), statistical App. tables 1 and 7 (ii), pp. 39, 44. The measure of land used in columns 4 and 9 includes nonagricultural lands, but this inclusion is "felt to be factually unimportant." In column 7, figures for the agricultural population are used rather than the agricultural labor force, since the latter were not available in that source; it is probably not too far-fetched to assume relative constancy of the labor force/population ratio. I have been unable to find any source presenting the distribution of the labor force by size of farm for India as a whole. For the same practical reason gross value of output data are used rather than value added—the latter data are not available in this study.

Column 10 is based on an unweighted average of gross output/acre indexes (with the category 5–10 acres equal to one) in eight states or regions: Uttar Pradesh, Punjab, West Bengal, Andhra, Madras, Madhya Pradesh, Bombay, and Telangara. The data were originally presented in H. Hanumantha Rao, *Agricultural Production Functions, Costs, and Returns in India,* Studies in Economic Growth no. 5 (Bombay and New York: Asia Publishing House, 1965). I am unaware how representative this selection of states is; the possible unrepresentativeness, plus our inability to weight the indices for the different states, creates an unknown bias with respect to the country as a whole.

The data of Column 11 are taken from Lawrence J. Lau and Pan A. Yotopoulos, "A Test for Relative Efficiency and Application to Indian Agriculture," *American Economic Review* 61, no. 1 (1971): 109. The original source, as for the data in column 10, is: Government of India, Ministry of Food and Agriculture, *Studies in the Economics of Farm Management* (New Delhi, 1957–62). The calculations presented here are somewhat less precise than those of column 10 and include fewer states, but they are presented because the underlying data are the same as for column 12, which shows figures on the labor/land ratio, and it is important to base an output/land and a labor/land series on the same data. It is not clear by what criterion the authors divided the farms by size, since only an "average acres per farm" was presented for each category, rather than the range of sizes to which that average corresponded. For columns 11 and 12 cultivable rather than total land is the unit—the latter was used in column 10 also in the all-India data. In the Lau and Yotopoulos data, labor is given in terms of labor days employed, another difference from the all-India data. The states included are West Bengal, Madras, the Punjab, Uttar Pradesh, and Madhya Pradesh.

Columns 14 through 17 are from Hiromitsu Kaneda, "Sources and Rates of Productivity Gains in Japanese Agriculture, as Compared with the U.S. Experience," *Journal of Farm Economics* 49, no. 5 (1967): 1448. Columns 18 and 19 are calculated on the basis of the previous ones. The estimate in column 21 is based on Ministry of Agriculture and Forestry, *Agricultural Statistics,* as reproduced in Taheo Misawa, "An Analysis of Part-Time Farming in the Postwar Period," in Kazushi Ohkawa, Bruce F. Johnston, and Hiromitsu Kaneda, *Agriculture and Economic Growth: Japan's Experience* (Tokyo: University of Tokyo Press, 1969), p. 251. Hokkaido and Okinawa are excluded from these figures. Column 20 estimates the distribution of labor hours, using the data from columns 21 and 17.

Columns 23–26 are from R. Albert Berry, "Farm Size and Factor Productivity in U.S. Agriculture," mimeographed (1972). The original data are from the U.S. Agricultural Census of 1964 and other material published by the U.S. Department of Agriculture.

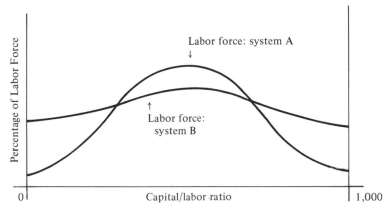

Fig. 10.7

If a new labor-intensive technology could be modified in a capital-using direction gradually and over a considerable $K/L$ range, there would be less danger in sinking large sums into the development of such technologies. Much seed improvement, for example, fits the category of general applicability.[38] But the proportion of all change that is rather factor proportion specific seems high enough to imply the difficulties discussed above.

Even if each new technique were factor proportion specific, it might be argued that any research process will tend to generate new techniques appropriate to a wide range of factor proportions, given the many components of technological change. This argument would be more convincing were it not so frequently the case that the bulk of the research effort is geared toward a certain set of farms (be they the large ones or the small ones); feedback comes from them, and modifications are effected to their specifications.

To summarize, in the situation described it is possible, perhaps probable, that over a fairly narrow income range the effect of a large-farm technology policy will vary from considerably negative to considerably positive. The need to appraise just where the country is along this spectrum thus takes on special importance, since a relatively small

38. Though probably less than one would suspect, since many varieties are of varying usefulness according to the way the soil is cultivated, the amount of fertilizer applied, whether they are grown with other crops, and so on.

Table 10.7: Indicators of Variation in Factor Proportions

| | *Percent of labor used on those largest farms encompassing: X% of land*[a] | | *Percent of land or land and buildings held by those largest farms with top X% of land* | | | | | |
| --- | --- | --- | --- | --- | --- | --- | --- | --- |
| | *X = 10* | *X = 20* | *X = 10* | | | *X = 20* | | |
| | | | *Land* | *Land by value* | *Land and capital* | *Land* | *Land by value* | *Land and capital* |
| Colombia (1960) | 0.87[b]–4.4[c] | 3.12[b]–9.59[c] | 81.14 | 67.64 | 69.52 | 89.3 | 79.3 | 80.6 |
| United States (1964) | ≈ 5.0[c] | ≈ 11.1[d] | 63.9 | | 38.07[d] | 74.9 | | 53.30[e] |
| India (mid 1950s) | ≈ 6.0 | ≈ 14.1 | | | | | | |
| Japan (1960) | ≈ 7.3 | ≈ 15.5 | 26.54 | | | 43.21 | | |

a. That is, with farms ranked by size (acres), the group in question is made up of as many farms as must be included, starting from the largest, in order to encompass $X$ percent of all the land.

b. Best estimate.

c. The alternative estimates of land and capital distribution were used in such combinations as to provide what are very much upper limit estimates. The chance that the true values are this high is almost nil.

d. Interpolation in an end category necessary but possible error unlikely to be greater than 0.5 percentage points.

e. Land and buildings only; dwellings excluded.

error in judgment could imply a quite inferior policy. In Colombia, most government policies have focused on the modern producers, who also happen to be the larger, better educated, and more powerful ones; witness the relative attention given to mechanization as opposed to the improvement of hand tools, the research and extension work on varieties produced on the large farms relative to such home consumption items as yuca, platanos, and so on. Relatively little experience with and confidence in policies designed to raise the efficiency and the capital stock of the smaller farmer has been built up. It is an open question how long it would take to streamline the provision of public services complementary to the small farmers,[39] that is, to attain the technical information, the appropriate institutional structures, and the positive attitude on the part of the bureaucracy needed to make their

39. More precisely, it is not clear how costly various levels of efficiency achieved within various periods of time would be. Successful experiences with small-farm–oriented policies such as those in Japan and Taiwan do not, without extensive probing into their histories, yield a great deal of relevant evidence; their success has usually been observed after they have been long in operation.

intervention productive. Given Colombia's current growth rate,[40] and rapid rural to urban migration, a small-farm policy might have to pay off quickly to be useful at all; the risks involved in pursuing the opposite policy are probably lower, now that the country appears to have reached a level of nondependence on agriculture such that, even if an error were made in agricultural policy, overall growth would still occur; as long as this happens, rising $K/L$ will eventually make the capital-intensive technologies relevant.[41]

PROBLEMS OF THE SECOND BEST

Whenever market imperfections are present, the policy complexities associated with second-best situations appear. Presumably the wide range of technologies[42] observed in Colombian agriculture is related to imperfections in both the labor market and the capital market.[43] The foreign exchange market has often been in disequilibrium, with substantial overvaluation of the currency and underpricing of imports to those individuals and firms who can get them. Such a set of imperfections tends to imply that benefits are a complex and unstable function of a given policy—a nonrobustness similar to that discussed in the previous section. Consider, for example, a product of modern, relatively capital-intensive, large-scale agriculture that is fairly close to the margin of exportability; social infrastructure investments that would lower its cost are under consideration. Assuming a relatively

40. An average of over 6 percent for six years.

41. One reason one might anticipate greater efficiency from a large-farm policy is the possibly higher savings rate out of income generated; even if there were no reason to believe that the marginal propensity to save was an increasing function of income and farm size, it might be argued that the greater transferability of savings generated on large farms to other sectors or productive units could constitute a significant advantage, especially as the economy shifts more and more from its agrarian base to other sectors. But this argument is difficult to evaluate in any empirical or practical sense; in a given case such funds might go to undesirably capital-intensive investments.

42. Wide in the sense of the degree of variance in factor proportions, with substantial shares of all productive units being fairly close to the two ends of the spectrum.

43. One might speculate as to whether the problems discussed here would be present if the wide range of factor proportions were due not so much to market imperfections as to a linear or almost linear isoquant; one question of interest would then be: Would the impact of specific policies on farms using different technologies along a more or less linear isoquant tend to be similar, or at least more so than if the isoquant were more curved? There is no obvious answer to this question.

inflexible foreign trade policy,[44] then, for a small effort along the line in question, leading to a cost decrease insufficient to push the product into the export category, there is little or no payoff.[45] But if the product is exported, substantial gains accrue, given the productivity of foreign exchange. The relationship between the value of the variable and net benefits from the policy is at least a polynomial of the third degree. In Colombia a number of products grown primarily in the larger-scale commercial sector typically have prices in the range where with an equilibrium exchange rate the domestic price would be roughly competitive with the world price, but in the presence of an overvalued exchange rate it is not.

An example of particular interest in Colombia is mechanization. Subsidized by an unbalanced exchange rate and low-interest credit (less now than before) and used on large farms, whose average efficiency has been on the low side,[46] it seems to have all the marks of an unproductive, distribution-worsening phenomenon. Yet closer examination reveals that mechanization has not generally led to direct labor displacement, as it has in some Asiatic countries, since it is associated with a switch from usually extensive cattle raising to crop production. The direct impact, before reactions brought about through output increases and relative price changes are taken into account, is both to increase the productivity of the farms in question and to raise labor inputs.[47] In this case the imperfections in the capital or land market that prevent the large farmers from renting their land to more productive small ones provide the base for the a priori implausible result that potentially labor-saving machinery might actually be labor using.

### SPECIAL POLITICAL AND ADMINISTRATIVE PROBLEMS

In the heterogeneous system under discussion there may develop

44. This might or might not include export subsidies designed to offset the disadvantageous effect of the overvaluation of the currency. The losses associated with the overvaluation can, of course, be offset by a sufficiently agile subsidy policy. This is not normally a way out, though; subsidy policy will often labor under constraints similar to those facing exchange rate policy.

45. In fact, the impact on income distribution is negative where, for example, small farms are as efficient producers as large ones, so that there is no output advantage vis-à-vis a different investment.

46. Note though that no separate efficiency calculation has been made for these mechanized farms, as opposed to large, nonmechanized farms. They may not compare unfavorably to small farms in average efficiency.

47. See Wayne Thirsk, *The Economics of Farm Mechanization in Colombia* (Ph.D. diss., Yale University, 1972).

considerable divergence of opinion on policy, fueled in part by the existence of pressure groups representing distinct subsets of the agricultural population, such as the large farmers, possibly the small farmers, and (not too likely) the landless proletariat. The most powerful associations will tend to be made up of large farmers and to favor their interests. If there is organized support for a small-farmer program, it may come from the small farmers themselves (this depends upon the country and has not by and large been the case in Colombia), from technocrats with no particular ax to grind, or from a variety of other sources.[48] Especially where the distribution of the benefits of public policy among groups of farmers is the issue, large-farm agriculture is sure to be well represented and to create obstacles to the application of an integrated small-farm strategy; the compromise process whereby a few components of a well-planned program are lost may reduce the potential payoff quite disproportionately, given the apparent advantages of "package programs" involving a big push, with simultaneous increases in availability of modern inputs, credit to buy them, improved markets in which to sell them, and so on.[49] The greater political power behind a large-farm program, and the correspondingly lower likelihood of its being dismembered at the legislative or administrative level, constitutes an advantage.

### ECONOMIC INTUITIONS

Among people who make decisions on agricultural policy are a few with some background in and understanding of economics, others with professional expertise in agronomy, engineering, or other disciplines, and many with lower levels of formal training. Since in fact policy tends to be made at all levels, the attitudes of many persons on the various issues of agricultural policy are likely to be relevant to one degree or another. Policy making is at best a complicated thing and it should be no surprise that people who have not had the chance or the occasion to think through the larger context of agricultural policy suffer under some erroneous assumptions. One such difficulty in any economic system is the failure to grasp the concept of opportunity cost.

48. Some members of the urban elite may support such a policy because of a wish to see rural-to-urban migration slowed down by inducing more people to stay in the country, and the presumption that to do this it is necessary to throw some sops to the small-scale farmer.
49. The presence of foreign aid for such programs can help to alleviate this problem.

Another is the fallacy of composition in one context or another; when what is good for the economic system as a whole is not a blown-up version of what is good for the individual family, the layman's intuition will be weak.[50] Since there tend to be subtler issues in heterogeneous than in homogeneous economies, the field for such errors is broadened. It is both true and plausible in the aggregate that the objective of an economic system is to raise labor productivity (the same as raising income per capita) and that one way to do this is by raising the capital/labor ratio. In a homogeneous system, increasing capital intensity in all productive units is desirable. But in a heterogeneous system, with some highly capital-intensive units (low capital productivity and high labor productivity), the idea that these are in some sense more efficient than less capital-intensive ones, and that efforts should be bent to increasing their labor productivity, is a disastrous error of intuition. Since capital is likely to be the scarcer resource of the two, capital productivity is likely to be a better indicator of efficiency than is labor productivity; since the two productivities are usually inversely related across firms, those with high labor productivity are likely to be low in overall efficiency. Whether this conceptual error be due to the fallacy of composition or to the association of capital intensity and modernity with economic development, few decision makers—even those who are relatively well trained in economics—seem to avoid it fully; few capture fully the meaning of factor proportions and factor productivities under technological heterogeneity. In terms of the mistaken policies to which it can lead, this is probably the most serious error afflicting popular thinking on the issues under discussion.

The intuitive denial of economic constraints, which is implicit in the failure to recognize opportunity costs, frequently shows up in another unhappy chain of reasoning. Most people have some concept of poverty as immoral, feeling that it is in some sense "wrong" for anybody to be expected to live below a certain standard of living; this standard, since it has no basis in any absolute reality but rather is generated out of comparisons with observed living conditions in the society, varies widely from country to country. A frequent offshoot is the idea that "no one should be expected to make a living off a farm of less than $X$ acres." That the goal specified may not be achievable for all

---

50. For example, the case of public attitudes in the Great Depression, when the idea was popular that because private family spending obviously had to be curtailed public spending also needed to be curtailed (a view not limited, of course, to the layman).

is not normally borne in mind by proponents of this view; they simply define optimal policy to be "moving as far as possible toward this goal," that is, pushing as many people as possible over the line. In a context of, say, agrarian reform, this could imply redistributing such land as is available to as many people as one can, giving each his "morally defined" minimum of $X$ hectares. Over time, hopefully, more and more people will be given land. The alternative of giving everyone the same amount of land—whatever amount is implicit in the policy of equal distribution—is not articulated, and it is seldom accepted that it would be the more equitable policy. In short, when te cohnstraint tends to evolve out of moral or social considerations, somewhat independently of economic limitations, it often suffers from internal contradiction. At the same time, the moral approach has great popular appeal; the policy is never phrased as "we promise 10 percent of you an adequate land base," but rather as, "we promise an adequate land base; no one will have to farm on less than $X$ hectares."

Another widespread misunderstanding is the assumption that economic efficiency is in some sense measured by total income. Thus it is concluded that, as long as it generates more profits, a large farm is more efficient than a small one even if its output/input ratio is lower. In Colombia it seems clear that the total income of a farm is negatively related to the efficiency of resource utilization on it.

## AN OVERVIEW

Among the policy complexities discussed above, some are more serious than others and some are more definitely and generally present than others. Perhaps the biggest open question is whether large-farm and small-farm programs are in fact mutually exclusive or close to it, either for technical or for political and administrative reasons. Comparisons of small-farm and large-farm programs often take for granted that the programs are competitive, not only in the sense that resources expended in one cannot be expended in the other, but also in the sense that the presence of one will directly worsen the situation of the nontarget group. As a general proposition, however, this is not obvious. Programs initiated with large farmers may generate both direct and indirect trickle-down benefits to small farmers. Direct complementarity is exemplified where fairly large- (or more likely middle-) scale farmers act as intermediaries with respect to credit which the banking system finds it too risky to grant directly to small farmers; or large-scale farmers may be the first adopters of new varieties, which are then picked up by minifundistas (small farmers) to the mutual benefit of all. More indirectly and less obviously, it could even be argued that the long-run welfare of today's small farmer is increased by his being pushed or squeezed out by the large farmer and having to migrate to the city, where he benefits from the greater long-run opportunities for own advancement, for education of his children, and so on.

Historical comparisons, at least as perceived by some students, augur somewhat against the possibility of successful small-farm programs where large farmers are powerful. Summing up perceptively, Don Kanel notes:

1) The large farms of many countries are the historical result of various processes (feudalism, conquest, etc.) which have little to do with strictly economic viability of different sizes of farms. That is, their size is not due to competition between farms in factor and product markets but is due to other causes. However, since such farms exist, they are available to assume a new modernizing role in introducing new technology, infrastructure and processing. On the eve of rapid economic development such farms are owned by the elite.

2) In European development in the XIX century, urbanization and attractive opportunities in industry, commerce, politics and education drew the elite (as well as new classes) to nonagricultural opportunities, leaving agriculture to the peasants. Absentee ownership is particularly deadening to incentives and initiatives when owners lose interest but continue their ownership. The Western European land reforms from the French Revolution on facilitated transfer of ownership from inactive to active managers, though these transfers were also accomplished by voluntary sales. The underlying rationale for the transition was: a) economies of size achievable on family farms, and b) greater attractiveness of nonagricultural opportunities for wealth and entrepreneurial ability.

3) Development opportunities in the L.D.C.'s in the XX century (and particularly the "green revolution") may have a different balance of underlying factors. At a time when nonagricultural opportunities are still limited, the green revolution has brought sudden and dramatic increases in income. On larger farms, the income of the landowner can be increased by mechanization, by displacement of tenants and hired workers, and by active management.

4) In addition, at a time when government agencies, cooperatives and private marketing firms serving small farmers are poorly developed, actively managed large farms can assume the role of providing services and infrastructure, and can expand aggressively into new markets as opportunities develop.

5) Under these circumstances, with attractive income opportunities in agriculture and active management on large farms, private operators of large farms will be making crucial decisions about how agriculture is to be modernized. Development is more likely to proceed along a capital intensive, labor saving path, increasing the employment problem and concentrating the benefits of development in a few hands. These patterns are directly opposed to the requirements of a situation characterized by much more rapid population growth and more deficient employment opportunities in industry than those which characterized XIX century European development.[51]

By way of policy prescription Kanel argues as follows:

Under these conditions, the creation of development opportunities for smaller farms may depend on wholesale land reforms which abolish large farms. Then there are no alternatives to developing technology and institutions which serve small farmers. [Carl H.] Gotsch argues for this as one possible solution (the other being cooperative farming) in contrasting use of tubewells in Pakistan and Bangladesh.[52] In the latter case small farms were predominant, and cooperative or joint ownership arrangements had to be and were worked out to make possible the use of tubewells. On the other hand, in Pakistan, tubewells were predominantly installed by larger farmers. In a similar manner, Clark describes the rebuilding of the marketing system in Bolivia after the land reform. Before the reform the landowner transferred the bulk of the marketable surplus from his hacienda to his own warehouse in town. After the reform new market towns and itinerant truckers appeared to assume the marketing functions.[53]

. . . Danish agriculture of the 1870's was a dualistic agriculture with a much more unequal land ownership distribution than the

51. Kanel, "Role of Land Tenure," pp. 2–4.
52. Carl H. Gotsch, "Technical Change and the Distribution of Income in Rural Areas," *American Journal of Agricultural Economics* 54, no. 2 (1972): 326–41.
53. Kanel, "Role of Land Tenure," p. 12.

Indian Punjab and probably the Pakistani Punjab, but less unequal than much of Latin America. If the difference between Denmark and present L.D.C.'s was a greater presence of attractive nonagricultural opportunities in XIX century Europe, then not much can be done about it. . . . But it should be the purpose of research to ascertain what the possibilities are.[54]

Kanel's arguments are persuasive and discouraging. But many questions remain to be solved. The increasing fear of agrarian uprisings and the increasingly vocal character of the agriculturally disadvantaged could be promising factors, as could the decrease in the relative power of agricultural interests in government as the sector gradually declines in relative economic importance. Since many of the modern commercial farmers have important nonagricultural interests, the loss of some agricultural income from not entirely having their way in respect of agricultural policy might not be very traumatic. Shrewd policy choices may help to minimize the conflicts and emphasize the complementaries between the two types of agriculture.

Possibly, too, my perception of Colombia's current state is shortsighted, having been generated at this particular juncture, only a couple of decades after technologically modern farming burst on the scene and just at the time some pressures are being mounted in favor of the small farmer, but before the resulting attention to his problems has begun to bear fruit. If ten years from now they have borne fruit, I, or someone else, will undoubtedly find numerous complementaries to replace the conflicts emphasized here. All that will remain of these arguments will be the fact that, because the political constellation delayed attention to the minifundista for several decades after the technological take-off of modern large-scale farming, his standard of living remained low longer than it needed to. This (obviously) strikes me as optimistic; I would guess that, if the small farmer is out of the woods in ten years, the explanation will be the development of non-agriculture, and the associated rural-urban migration.

54. Kanel, "Role of Land Tenure."

# 11

Measurement of the Direct and Indirect
Employment Effects of Agricultural Growth
with Technical Change

RAJ KRISHNA

It is now widely accepted that accelerated economic growth need not, by itself, solve the unemployment problems of densely populated countries.[1] Even in agriculture, which must carry the whole labor force which cannot find nonagricultural employment, it is likely that government policies with respect to prices, farm-size structure, trade, taxation, technology, and investment may not allow the full absorption of the farm labor force in spite of the availability of the new high-yield technology.[2] It is also generally agreed that growth does not necessarily improve the distribution of income and wealth. Apart from these weak, negative assertions, however, professional economists can currently offer very little empirically verified wisdom about what happens

I am grateful to Narain Sinha, K. L. Sharma, and Asha Hada for computational assistance.

1. For documentation, see Erik Thorbecke, "Unemployment and Underemployment in the Developing World," mimeographed (New York, Columbia University, 1970).

2. W. Arthur Lewis, "The Causes of Unemployment in Less Developed Countries and Some Research Topics," *International Labour Review* 101 (1970): 547–54; Robert D. Shaw, "The Employment Implications of the Green Revolution," *Development Digest* 9 (1971): 88–97; Bruce F. Johnston and John Cownie, "The Seed-Fertilizer Revolution and the Labor Force Absorption Problem," Food Research Institute Studies, mimeographed (Stanford, 1969); Thorbecke, "Unemployment and Underemployment"; Walter P. Falcon, "Agricultural Employment in Less Developed Countries: General Situation, Research, Approaches, and Policy Palliatives," mimeographed (Washington, D.C., IBRD, 1971); Shlomo Reutlinger et al., "Agricultural Development in Relation to the Employment Problem," mimeographed (Washington, D.C., IBRD, 1971).

to distribution and employment when the growth of production accelerates, particularly in the agricultural sector.

Considerable time and resources would be required to fill the vast knowledge gap in this area. In this chapter I shall attack only a couple of unsolved problems that arise when we try to measure the direct and indirect employment effects of the green revolution.

I shall first present a brief review of some recent attempts to project the employment effects of technical change in agriculture. The review will show that the methodology used in all these studies (with one exception) can measure only the *direct* employment effects of farm innovation. The essence of the method is measurement of the change in the labor coefficient per hectare produced by technical change. But technical change comprises many simultaneous changes in water availability, cropping intensity, seed varieties, fertilizer use, and the degree of mechanization of each individual operation. Therefore, we face the problem of decomposing the total observed change in the labor input per hectare in crop production into the separate contribution of each of these changes. In order to solve this problem, an algebraic expression that separates the employment effects of disaggregated technical changes will be developed, and its use will be illustrated with Punjab wheat and rice data. This decomposition equation enables us to grade each individual technical change according to the magnitude of its positive or negative direct employment effect and to identify the combinations of changes that produce a positive or negative employment effect. In particular, the equation can be used to measure the true employment effect of tractorization. This is especially important because at present, in the absence of a technique for separating different employment effects, many effects that are really due to other changes are attributed to tractorization.

As regards indirect effects, the available literature mentions only the various chains of causation triggered by technical change.[3] But since no method has been developed for classifying and measuring the different indirect effects, the net change in employment caused by technical change remains a matter of inconclusive verbal controversy. Therefore, in the third section of the chapter, I use an adaptation of the basic input-output model for measuring the total indirect effects as well as each separate indirect effect. The different indirect effects are rigorously classified for the purpose of measurement.

3. See Ronald G. Ridker, "Agricultural Mechanization in South Asia," *Development Digest* 9 (1971): 108–13.

Finally the use of this model in projecting the net employment effects of assumed changes in coefficients is illustrated with a condensed two-sector version of the 77 × 77 coefficient matrix and national accounts of India for 1964–65.

## 1. MEASUREMENT OF THE DIRECT EMPLOYMENT EFFECTS OF INNOVATION

Many attempts have been made recently to project the direct effects of the new technology on farm employment. The basic procedure in these studies is (1) to compute from field data the coefficients of labor input per hectare for each crop as it is grown with traditional and with improved techniques, (2) to project the area in each crop, and the proportion of the area under each technique, and (3) to compute the aggregate labor input by multiplying the projected area in each crop-technique category by the relevant labor coefficient and then adding up the results.

Using this procedure, the *Provisional Indicative World Plan for Agricultural Development* (IWP), prepared by the Food and Agriculture Organization (FAO), predicted that in Asia and the Far East greater intensity of land use and higher yields would increase the number of labor days per farm family per annum by 15 percent, from 227 in 1962 to 261 in 1985. Therefore, farm employment would increase, in spite of an increase in the agricultural population from 583 million to 880 million. Explaining the method used, the IWP says:

> Labour requirements per hectare were estimated crop by crop for each of six countries (Ceylon, India, Pakistan, Philippines, Thailand and West Malaysia). Distinctions were made between irrigated and non-irrigated land and in certain other cases where labour requirements were known to be different, e.g. between broadcast and transplanted rice. Labour requirements per hectare (1962 and 1985) were then multiplied by the number of hectares in each category in 1962 and the IWP proposals for 1985.[4]

The analysis is restricted to employment in crop production and the development of land and water resources. The coefficients used are admittedly based on very meager evidence. And the projections assume a substantial increase in multiple cropping, and the achievement of

4. FAO, *Provisional Indicative World Plan for Agricultural Development* (Rome: FAO, 1970), 2: 658.

projected yields. It is also assumed that the technical innovations adopted will not displace labor.

In another study, conducted by John Cownie, Bruce F. Johnston, and Bart Duff, the 1985 farm labor force in West Pakistan is projected as the total labor force *minus* the nonfarm labor force which is assumed to grow 4.5 percent per annum. A coefficient of 0.08 man-years per acre is assumed for the tractor area. Bullock area employment is then computed simply as the difference between the total agricultural labor force and the tractor area employment.[5]

Martin H. Billings and Arjan Singh, after calculating for the Punjab and Maharashtra, India, the demand for farm labor with alternative techniques, concluded that in the Punjab the demand will decline by 17 percent, while in Maharashtra it will increase by 4 percent by 1983/84.[6] The basic methodology, again, involves the calculation of labor requirements per acre for each crop under different technological assumptions, and the multiplication of the projected area in each crop/technique by the changing coefficients.

S. V. Sethuraman has computed the direct farm employment coefficient of high-yielding varieties of wheat and rice in India as 0.208 man-years per acre *without mechanization* (1 man-year equals 240 man-days). He is perhaps the only writer who has also tried to put together some estimates of the indirect employment that may be generated by the additional production of inputs, consumption goods, and investment goods demanded by farmers. This adds up to about 0.256 man-years per acre, he figures. Thus, the total employment potential is estimated as 0.464 man-years per acre in high-yielding wheat and rice.[7]

All these studies have brought into focus the many complications involved in measuring the employment effects of technical change. In the first place, each individual operation required for crop production can be performed with many alternative techniques requiring varying proportions of labor and capital per unit of land. Thus seedbed preparation, irrigation, cultivation, harvesting, and threshing operations

5. John Cownie, Bruce F. Johnston, and Bart Duff, "The Quantitative Impact of the Seed-Fertilizer Revolution in West Pakistan: An Exploratory Study," *Food Research Institute Studies* 9 (1970): 43–55.

6. Martin H. Billings and Arjan Singh, "The Effect of Technology on Farm Employment in India," *Development Digest* 9 (1971): 98–107.

7. S. V. Sethuraman, "A Note on the Implications of Agricultural Development for Employment and Investment in the Indian Economy," mimeographed (New Delhi, USAID, 1971).

may be mechanized separately or in various possible combinations. And the change in the total labor input per hectare in a given crop will depend on the extent to which some or all of these operations are mechanized. To project employment, therefore, the assumed technological changes have to be disaggregated into specific changes in individual operations.

Second, the labor input is likely to be approximately proportionate to output in some operations, such as threshing, and to area in other operations, such as ploughing and irrigation. Let us call these output-oriented operations and area-oriented operations respectively. The change in the labor coefficient per hectare for area-oriented operations can be measured directly if the necessary technological data are available. But in measuring the change in the labor coefficient per hectare for output-oriented operations it is necessary to project not only the area but also the output per hectare. Thus, yield projection becomes a necessary part of the methodology of employment projection. And the extent to which mechanization changes the labor input for area-oriented operations and output-oriented operations has to be measured separately.

The third complication relates to the effects of irrigation and the increase in the intensity of cropping. Irrigation may increase yield without increasing the cropping intensity; or the cropping intensity may increase, due to the introduction of short-duration varieties and mechanized ploughing, with the same water availability; or increases in water availability and cropping intensity may occur together. The quantitative effect on employment per hectare will be different in each case.

Finally, changes in the crop mix alone will change the labor coefficient per hectare in crop production as a whole, because the coefficient is different for each crop. But in reality crop-mix changes accompany all the other technological changes mentioned above.

Thus, even a change in the direct labor input per hectare in crop production is the result of a large number of simultaneous changes in the input mix and the output mix. In order to discover how the net change in this coefficient can be determined, let us derive the algebraic expression for it, assuming that varietal improvements, increased fertilizer application, irrigation development, cropping intensity increases, mechanization, and crop-mix changes occur at the same time.

Consider first the derivation of the total labor input per (cropped) hectare in a single crop. The effects of changes in the cropping intensity and cropping pattern will be introduced later. Assuming that one hectare is planted with a given crop, let:

$w$ = the proportion of one hectare that is irrigated

$h$ = the proportion of irrigated area in the high-yielding variety

$y$ = basic yield per hectare on unirrigated area (old variety without chemical fertilizer)

$m_1 y$ = yield per hectare on irrigated area (old variety without chemical fertilizer)

$m_2 y$ = yield per hectare on irrigated area (high-yielding variety with chemical fertilizer)

$t$ = proportion of area ploughed by tractor

$w_w$ = proportion of area irrigated with wells

$w_c$ = proportion of area irrigated with canals

$w_p$ = proportion of area irrigated with pumps

$s$ = proportion of output mechanically threshed

$u_a$ = labor per hectare ploughed by bullocks

$u_a'$ = labor per hectare ploughed by tractors

$u_{ww}$ = labor per hectare irrigated with wells

$u_{wc}$ = labor per hectare irrigated with canals

$u_{wp}$ = labor per hectare irrigated with pumps

$u_w$ = labor per hectare irrigated with wells/canals/pumps, 1968–69.

$u_w'$ = labor per hectare irrigated with wells/canals/pumps, 1973–74

$u_h$ = labor per kilogram threshed by bullocks

$u_h'$ = labor per kilogram mechanically threshed

$u_m$ = labor per hectare in interculture

$y^*$ = total yield per hectare

$u_i$ = total labor per hectare in crop $i$

With this notation, the rainfed area (in a single hectare) is $(1 - w)$, the irrigated area (old variety) is $w(1 - h)$, and the irrigated area (new variety) is $wh$. The yields in these three subsectors being $y$, $m_1 y$, and $m_2 y$, the total yield, $y^*$, will be:

$$y^* = wh\,(m_2 y) + w\,(1 - h)\,(m_1 y) + (1 - w)\,y. \qquad (11.1)$$

And the total labor input is:

$$\begin{aligned} u_i = tu_a' + (1 - t)\,u_a + w u_w \\ + sy^* u_h' + (1 - s)\,y^* u_h + u_m \end{aligned} \qquad (11.2)$$

where

$$u_w = w_w u_{ww} + w_c u_{wc} + w_p u_{wp} \qquad (11.2')$$

Substituting the value of $y^*$ and $u_w$ in equation (11.2), we can write the total labor input as a function of the seven variable proportions $w$, $w_w$, $w_c$, $w_p$, $h$, $t$, and $s$. The first four proportions represent the progress of irrigation, and $h$, $t$, and $s$ represent the progress of varietal improvement, tractor ploughing, pumping, and mechanical threshing respectively.[8] The basic yield $y$, the yield multipliers $m_1$ and $m_2$, and the eight labor coefficients for specific operations will enter the expression for $u_i$ as technological constants.

Now, we are interested in the change in $u_i = (\Delta u_i)$ between two periods produced by given discrete changes in the seven proportions $\Delta w$, $\Delta w_w$, $\Delta w_c$, $\Delta w_p$, $\Delta h$, $\Delta s$, and $\Delta t$. Since the expression for $\Delta u_i$ using algebraic symbols for all the variables and constants is tediously long, I will write it out in a simpler form after substituting the numerical values of the eleven technological constants. The values of these constants pertain to wheat cultivation in the Punjab in 1968–69 (see table 11.1). The utmost care has been taken to see that the technological constants represent the labor time required for each *separate* operation under assumed conditions.

Using these values we have:

$$
\begin{aligned}
\Delta u_i = \ & 271.38\,(\Delta w) + 57.83\,(\Delta h) \\
& - 75.12\,(\Delta t) + 32.99\,(\Delta w_p) \\
& + 49.42\,(\Delta w_c) + 197.68\,(\Delta w_w) \\
& - 176.46\,(\Delta s) \\
& + 115.66\,(\Delta h)\,(\Delta w) - 69.78\,(\Delta h)\,(\Delta s) \\
& + 98.84\,(\Delta w)\,(\Delta w_c) + 395.37\,(\Delta w)\,(\Delta w_w) \\
& - 65.98\,(\Delta w_p)\,(\Delta w) - 140.19\,(\Delta w)\,(\Delta s) \\
& - 138.55\,(\Delta h)\,(\Delta s)\,(\Delta w).
\end{aligned}
\tag{11.3}
$$

The first five terms of this expression can be clearly identified as:
1. the (positive) irrigation effect,
2. the (positive) variety effect,
3. the (negative) tractor-ploughing effect,
4. the (negative) pumping effect, and
5. the (negative) threshing effect.

The last five terms include the positive interaction effect of irrigation and varietal improvement and six other negative interaction effects.

Assuming, for illustration, the values of $w$, $w_w$, $w_c$, $h$, $w_p$, $t$, and $s$ to be

---

8. It is assumed that chemical fertilizer use is confined to the irrigated area in the new variety, that interculture labor input does not change, and that harvesting is not mechanized.

Table 11.1: Assumed Technological Constants for Wheat, Punjab, 1968–69

| Symbol | Description | Unit | Value |
|---|---|---|---|
| $y$ | Basic yield per hectare on unirrigated area (old variety without chemical fertilizer) | Kg./ha. | 728.536[a] |
| $m_1$ | Ratio of yield per hectare on irrigated area (old variety) to basic yield $y$ | Ratio | 1.662[b] |
| $m_2$ | Ratio of yield per hectare on irrigated area (new variety) to basic yield $y$ | Ratio | 2.974[c] |
| $u_a$ | Labor per hectare ploughed by bullocks | Man-hours/ha. | 93.898[d] |
| $u_a'$ | Labor per hectare ploughed by tractors | Man-hours/ha. | 18.780[e] |
| $u_{ww}$ | Labor per hectare irrigated with wells | Man-hours/ha. | 395.369 |
| $u_{wc}$ | Labor per hectare irrigated with canals | Man-hours/ha. | 98.842 |
| $u_{wp}$ | Labor per hectare irrigated with pumps | Man-hours/ha. | 65.977 |
| $u_w$ | Labor per hectare irrigated 1968–69 | Man-hours/ha. | 156.190[f] |
| $u_w'$ | Labor per hectare irrigated 1973–74 | Man-hours/ha. | 87.018[g] |
| $u_h$ | Labor per kilogram threshed by bullocks | Man-hours/kg. | 0.194[h] |
| $u_h'$ | Labor per kilogram threshed mechanically | Man-hours/kg. | 0.048[i] |
| $u_m$ | Labor per hectare in interculture | Man-hours/ha. | 239.687[j] |

a. 650 pounds per acre of rainfed area in 1947/48–1951/52. There were no high-yielding varieties, and little chemical fertilizer was used in this period.

b. 1,080 pounds per acre of irrigated area, divided by 650 pounds; 1947/48–1951/52; without high-yielding varieties and chemical fertilizer.

c. Wheat yield in the Punjab in 1968/69 (2,167 kg./ha.) divided by basic yield $y$ (728.536 kg./ha.). The yield in this subsector is the result of the use of the high-yielding variety with chemical fertilizer.

d. Ploughing, planting, and sowing.

e. One-fifth of $u_a$.

f, g. Bunding and irrigation. In 1968/69, 54 percent of irrigated land in the Punjab was irrigated by canals, 22 percent by wells, and 24 percent by pumps. The labor coefficients for these three modes of irrigating wheat are 40, 160, and 26.7 hours per acre respectively. (The pump coefficient is one-sixth of the well irrigation coefficient.) See Martin H. Billings and Arjan Singh, "Agricultural and Technological Change in Maharashtra," mimeographed (New Delhi: USAID, 1971). Therefore, using the equation (11.2'), the 1968/69 coefficient is computed as 156.190 hours per hectare. For 1973/74, the coefficient is computed similarly, assuming that the canal area ratio remains the same, the pump area ratio rises to 0.45, and the well area ratio falls to 0.01.

h. Harvesting, threshing, and winnowing. Inderjit Singh's figure for hours per acre is converted into hours per kilogram, using his yield (1,200 kg./ha.).

i. One-fourth of $u_h$.

j. Hoeing and fertilizer application. It is assumed that technical changes do not affect this coefficient.

*Sources*: $y$ and $m_1$: Directorate of Economics and Statistics, Ministry of Food and Agriculture, Government of India, *Quinquennial Average Yield per Acre of Principal Crops in India, 1947/48 to 1951/52* (New Delhi, 1956); $m_2$: Directorate of Economics and Statistics, Ministry of Food and Agriculture, Government of India, *Indian Agriculture in Brief* (New Delhi, 1970); $u_a$, $u_w$, $u_{ww}$, $u_{wc}$, $u_{wp}$, $u_h$, and $u_m$: Inderjit Singh et al., *Field Crop Technology in the Punjab India*; $u_a'$, $u_w'$, $u_h'$: Billings and Singh, "Agricultural and Technological Change in Maharashtra."

the same as those assumed by Billings and Singh for the Punjab for the interval from 1968/69 to 1973/74 (see table 11.2), the total change in the labor input turns out to be −91.61 hours per hectare, from 555.67 hours in 1968/69 to 464.06 hours in 1973/74. This figure is decomposed into the five separate effects and their interactions in table 11.3. The table shows that the positive irrigation and variety effects are roughly equal; the largest negative effect is due to the mechanization of threshing; the second largest negative effect is due to the shift from well irrigation with bullocks to power pumping. The tractor-ploughing effect is relatively small.

These results are of course due to the particular values of the constants and variables relevant to this study. With different data on initial conditions, technological constants, and rates of technical change in other areas and situations, different results will be obtained.

Table 11.2: Assumed Changes in Proportions Reflecting Technical Change
in Punjab Wheat Cultivation Between 1968/69 and 1973/74

| Symbol | Description | Proportion in 1968/69 | Proportion in 1973/74 | Increase |
|--------|-------------|-----------------------|-----------------------|----------|
| $w$ | Proportion of one hectare irrigated | 0.50 | 0.56 | 0.06 |
| $w_w$ | Proportion of area irrigated with wells | .22 | .01 | −.21 |
| $w_c$ | Proportion of area irrigated with canals | .54 | .54 | .00 |
| $h$ | Proportion of irrigated area in the high-yield variety | .50 | .80 | .30 |
| $t$ | Proportion of area ploughed by tractor | .03 | .10 | .07 |
| $w_p$ | Proportion of area irrigated by pumps | .24 | .45 | .21 |
| $s$ | Proportion of output mechanically threshed | .50 | .90 | .40 |

*Source:* Billings and Singh, "Farm mechanization and the Green Revolution."

Table 11.3: Analysis of the Change in the Total Labor Input per
Hectare in Wheat, Punjab, 1968/69 to 1973/74

| *Effect* | *Man-hours/ha.* |
|----------|-----------------|
| 1. Irrigation effect | +16.28 |
| 2. Variety effect | +17.35 |
| 3. Tractor-ploughing effect | − 5.26 |
| 4. Irrigation technology effect | −34.59 |
| 5. Threshing effect | −70.58 |
| 6. Interaction effect of irrigation and varietal improvement | + 2.08 |
| 7. Negative interaction effects | −16.89 |
| Total | −91.61 |

## 2. DIRECT EMPLOYMENT EFFECTS: MANY CROPS

So far we have discussed the change in the labor coefficient per hectare
of a single crop. But if $u_i$ and $\Delta u_i$ are computed for all the crops of a
region according to equations (11.2) and (11.3), the variation in the
employment coefficient per hectare in crop production as a whole
can also be projected. Let

$c$ = cropping intensity,

$r_i$ = proportion of the gross cropped area in crop $i$, and

$u$ = labor per hectare (net) in total crop production.

Then the gross area in crop $i$ is $cr_i$ for every hectare of net area in all
crops. Since $u_i$ is the labor input per (gross) hectare in crop $i$, the total
employment per (net) hectare will be:

$$u = c \sum_i u_i \, r_i \qquad (11.4)$$

and the change in $u$ will be:

$$\Delta u = c \sum_i (r_i \, \Delta u_i + u_i \, \Delta r_i + \Delta r_i \, \Delta u_i)$$
$$+ \Delta c \sum_i (r_i u_i + r_i \, \Delta u_i + u_i \, \Delta r_i + \Delta r_i \, \Delta u_i). \qquad (11.5)$$

We can regroup the terms in this equation into:

the technology effect:   $c \sum_i r_i \, \Delta u_i,$

the crop-mix effect:   $c \sum_i u_i \, \Delta r_i,$

the intensity effect:   $\Delta c \sum_i r_i \, u_i,$

and their interactions.

The analysis of $\Delta u$ according to equation (11.5) for all crops is not
attempted here.[9] However, for the two-crop (wheat and rice) subsector
of Punjab agriculture we can see how the technology effect, the crop-
mix effect, and the intensity effect can be separated.

Calculations for rice similar to those for wheat shown in tables
11.1, 11.2, and 11.3 show the initial (1968/69) labor input in the Punjab to be 969.74 and the later (1973/74) input to be 946.31 hours
per hectare.[10] Thus the decrease in the labor input turns out to be
23.43 hours per hectare.

9. A project to collect and process the required data is contemplated.
10. The coefficient is high because of the large number of irrigation operations
required in rice cultivation in the Punjab.

Table 11.4: Separation of Technology, Crop-Mix, and Intensity
Effects on Labor per Hectare (Net) in Wheat and Rice
(combined), Punjab, 1968/69 to 1973/74

| *Effect* | *Man-hours/ha.* |
|---|---|
| Technology | −108.54 |
| Crop mix | + 16.71 |
| Intensity | + 27.98 |
| Interactions | −  0.22 |
| Total | − 64.07 |

Let subscripts 1 and 2 denote wheat and rice, and assume that the cropping intensity increases from 1.345 to 1.390, and that $r_i$ decreases from 0.84 to 0.81.[11] Then the two-crop version of equation (11.4)[12] gives the total labor input in both crops as 836.48 hours per hectare in 1968/69 and 772.41 hours per hectare in 1973/74. The decrease[13] of 64.07 hours per hectare has been broken down in table 11.4. The table shows that with the given data for wheat and rice cultivation in the Punjab the negative technology effect is not offset by the positive crop-mix and intensity effects.

### 3. TRACTORIZATION

At this stage we can conveniently consider the direct employment effect of tractorization. In section 1 only the effect of tractor ploughing was isolated. But it is well known that the tractor is used not only for seedbed preparation but also for "wheelwork": pumping, threshing, and transport. It has also been emphasized in recent work that tractors are directly responsible for increasing the cropping intensity.[14] Therefore, in measuring the total direct employment effect of tractorization it is necessary to know the extent to which each operation is tractorized and the contribution of the tractor to the increase in the intensity of cropping. It is, of course, wrong to assume, as some research workers

11. Martin H. Billings and Arjan Singh, "Farm Mechanization and the Green Revolution," mimeographed (New Delhi, USAID, 1970).

12. $u = c(u_1 r_1 + u_2 r_2)$      (11.4′)

13. $\Delta u = c(r_1 \Delta u_1 + r_2 \Delta u_2)$    technology    (11.5′)
$+ c(u_1 \Delta r_1 + u_2 \Delta r_2)$    crop-mix
$+ \Delta c(u_1 r_1 + u_2 r_2)$    intensity
$+ c(\Delta u_1 \Delta r_1 + \Delta u_2 \Delta r_2)$
$+ \Delta c(u_1 \Delta r_1 + u_2 \Delta r_2)$ } interactions.
$+ \Delta c(r_1 \Delta u_1 + r_2 \Delta u_2)$
$+ \Delta c(\Delta r_1 \Delta u_1 + \Delta r_2 \Delta u_2)$

14. Ridker, "Agricultural Mechanization in South Asia"; Sapre, 1969.

have done,[15] that the entire increase in cropping intensity is due to tractors, for irrigated nontractorized farms frequently have a higher intensity of cropping than tractorized farms; nor can we assume that the tractor is used to do all the pumping everywhere.[16] Only more detailed field investigations can reveal the extent to which the tractor is used for various purposes. If the required proportions are known, however, the total effect of tractorization can be computed.

Let us suppose, for example, that ploughing and threshing are entirely tractorized, and that half of the pumping is done with the tractor. Then the total tractor effect on employment in wheat cultivation, according to table 11.3, will be:

$$[- 5.26 - 70.58 + .5 \, (6.93)] = -72.38 \text{ hours per hectare.}$$

The total tractor effect on employment in rice cultivation can be computed from a similar analytical table for rice[17] as:

$$[- 4.10 - (.5)\,(45.28)] = -26.74 \text{ hours per hectare.}$$

The change in the labor coefficient for each crop can now be broken down into the tractor effect and the nontractor effect.

$$\Delta u_1 = \Delta u_1^t + \Delta u_1^n = -72.38 - 19.23 = -91.61 \text{ hours.}$$
$$\Delta u_2 = \Delta u_2^t + \Delta u_2^n = -26.74 + 3.31 = -23.43 \text{ hours.}$$

Rewriting equation (11.4) we have:

$$u = r_1 \, (u_1^t + u_1^n) + r_2 \, (u_2 + u_2^n), \tag{11.4'}$$

and rewriting (11.5') we have:

$$\begin{aligned}
\Delta u = &\, c \, [r_1 \, (\Delta u_1^t + \Delta u_1^n) + r_2 \, (\Delta u_2^t + \Delta u_2^n)] \\
&+ c \, [u_1 \, \Delta r_1 + u_2 \, \Delta r_2] \\
&+ \Delta c \, [r_1 u_1 + r_2 u_2] \\
&+ \text{interactions.}
\end{aligned} \tag{11.5'}$$

If we attribute half of the $\Delta c$ to the tractor the total tractor effect in the two-crop economy is:

15. E.g., C. H. H. Rao, 1972.

16. In his careful study of tractor farms in a district of Maharashtra, India, Sapre observed that only 21 out of 76 farmers having tractors used the tractor for irrigation because the cost of irrigation with oil engines using crude oil was 60 to 70 percent lower than the cost with tractors using diesel fuel. He has also noted that only 54 percent of the increase in the double-cropped area can be attributed to tractors (Sapre, 1969).

17. Omitted here to save space.

Table 11.5: Separation of the Tractor Effect on Labor per
Hectare (net) in Wheat and Rice (combined), Punjab,
1968–69 to 1973/74

| *Effect* | *Man-hours/ha.* |
|---|---|
| Tractor technology[a] | −73.54 |
| Other technology | −21.01 |
| Crop mix | +16.71 |
| (Nontractor) intensity | +13.99 |
| Interactions | − 0.22 |
| Total | −64.07 |

a. See equation 11.6.

$$c\,[r_1\,\Delta u_1^i + r_2\,\Delta u_2^i] + \tfrac{1}{2}\,\Delta c\,[r_1 u_1 + r_2 u_2]. \qquad (11.6)$$

The total change ($-64.07$ hours) which was decomposed in table 11.4 can now be redistributed so as to isolate the tractor effect (see table 11.5).

The importance of the decomposition equations developed in this and the foregoing sections lies in the fact that they enable us to measure correctly the separate (marginal) employment effect of each technical change as well as the total effect of any combination of particular changes, such as those associated with tractorization in a single-crop or a multicrop economy.

The unit of measurement in all these equations and illustrative computations has been man-hours per hectare of gross area for each crop and per hectare of net area in multicrop equations. By multiplying the projected total net crop area in any region by the labor coefficients estimated by these equations, total farm employment in the region can be projected and analyzed. Thus these equations can also serve as projection models.

These projections are obviously critical if policy makers concerned about the employment effects of technical changes are to regulate the relative rates of diffusion of different innovations by means of appropriate pricing or other policies.

In choice models what we really need are social benefit/cost ratios of different "baskets" of innovations. But so far benefit/cost calculations have been distorted by the failure to disaggregate technical change and its effects on labor use and labor cost in different situations.[18]

It is hoped that the methodology presented here will remedy this

18. The World Bank studies on the basis of which substantial loans have been given to India to finance tractor loans to farmers are an example.

deficiency and lay the basis for more reliable calculations of the costs and benefits of farm innovations.

## 4. MEASUREMENT OF INDIRECT EFFECTS

Ronald Ridker has presented a fairly complete list of the various indirect employment effects in his survey of recent work on the mechanization of agriculture. Logically the nonfarm effects can be grouped into additional demands for (1) nonfarm current inputs (fertilizer, pesticides, transport, marketing, repairing services, etc.), (2) nonfarm consumption goods, and (3) nonfarm investment goods (construction, equipment, etc.). There are also induced (4) input, (5) consumption, and (6) investment demands on the farm sector itself. All these effects on demand (output) and the corresponding employment effects are recognized in the literature, but since no method has been developed for measuring them it is impossible to say whether or not the initial employment effects (assuming them to be negative) are offset by the indirect positive effects. And the direction of the net change in employment due to technical change remains uncertain. Fortunately the input-output technique can be adapted to measure all the indirect effects.

## 5. THE MODEL FOR MEASURING INDIRECT EFFECTS

There are at least three reasons for resorting to input-output economics for the measurement of the indirect employment effects of agricultural growth accompanied by technical changes. First, indirect effects are, by definition, macro effects external to, or occurring outside of, the sector in which primary technical change takes place. Therefore, we can measure them only with a macro model.

Second, change in a major sector like agriculture, which accounts for half or more of the national product and of employment in many developing economies, must affect all the important aggregate magnitudes in the economy, namely, income, consumption, investment, and employment. Initial changes in these macro magnitudes will in turn change aggregate magnitudes in the agricultural sector. Therefore, there can be no separate submodel of the determination of agricultural employment alone. Any model that determines farm employment must also determine all important macro variables at the same time. And even if the focus is on the projection of farm employment, the use of a macro model is indispensable.

Third, macro data *are* available in the form of national accounts and intersectoral transactions. In theoretical models production and demand relations may be specified in presumably more realistic linear or nonlinear forms, but multisectoral production, exchange, and demand data are available in a form that permits only fixed coefficient specifications. However, this limitation can be overcome in two well-known ways. Sensitivity analysis can be used to study the effects of changing production and demand coefficients over specified ranges; and more satisfactory submodels can be used to project parts of the data which are fed into the basic input-output model exogenously.

These improvements will require more work in the future. In this chapter I demonstrate only the applicability of an input-output model to measurement and separation of the direct and indirect employment effects of growth and technical change in the farm sector.

In the open Leontief model, if the final demand vector, $D$, and the input-output coefficient matrix, $A$, are given, the equilibrium output vector, $X$, is computed as:

$$X = A^*D \qquad (11.7)$$

where $A^* = (I - A)^{-1}$. If the employment-output coefficient vector $U$ is also given, employment required in each sector to produce $D$ is given by the vector:

$$L^d = \hat{U}D, \qquad (11.8)$$

where $\hat{U}$ is the diagonal matrix of the elements of $U$. The total direct plus indirect employment in each sector is

$$L = \hat{U}X = \hat{U}A^*D, \qquad (11.9)$$

and the aggregate employment is

$$N = U'X = U'A^*D. \qquad (11.10)$$

The sectorwise *indirect* employment is

$$L - L^d = \hat{U}(X - D), \qquad (11.11)$$

and the total indirect employment is

$$N - N^d = U'(X - D). \qquad (11.12)$$

Abstracting from its composition, gross value added in each sector, defined as the difference between its gross output and its purchases from other sectors, is

$$V = (I - \widehat{A'i})\, X. \qquad (11.13)$$

Since final demand is

$$D = (I - A)\, X, \qquad (11.14)$$

aggregate value added and the aggregate final demand are equal:

$$i'D = i'V. \qquad (11.15)$$

Now, when we wish to isolate the output and employment effects of growth with innovation in one sector, we should specify the elements of our data that are supposed to change exogenously.

A growth rate for the output of the innovating sector $j$ must be specified. If growth is accompanied by innovation, the material input vector $A_j$ and the labor input element $j$ in vector $U$ must change. The change in $A_j$ will also change the ratio of gross value added to gross output, $v_j$.

The gross value added may be divided into wages and gross profit.[19] A profitable innovation will at least increase the share of gross profit in gross output. If the share of wages also increases, the ratio of gross value added to gross output will increase. If, however, the innovation displaces labor, the share of wages will fall; if the increase in the share of profits is more than the decrease in the share of wages, the share of gross value added in gross output will increase; and if the increase in the share of profit is less than the decrease in the share of wages the share of value added in output will decrease. Thus workers as well as owners, or owners alone, will have greater gross income available to spend.

Some assumptions are necessary about the distribution of this additional spending between the output of different sectors. We can then predict the new (comparative static) equilibrium values of the variables of the system—output, income, final demand, and employment—in the innovating sector, other sectors, and the economy as a whole. These new values will reflect the sectoral as well as the economywide "multiplier" effects of an exogenously given rate of growth in sector $j$, accompanied by technical change.

19. All quantities are valued at constant base-year prices.

The logic of the procedure may be clearly illustrated with a two-sector example. Let the first sector be agriculture and the second non-agriculture. Then, in any period,

$$X_1 = a_{11} X_1 + a_{12} X_2 + D_1, \tag{11.16}$$

$$X_2 = a_{21} X_1 + a_{22} X_2 + D_2, \tag{11.17}$$

$$V_1 = (1 - a_{11} - a_{21}) X_1, \tag{11.18}$$

$$V_2 = (1 - a_{12} - a_{22}) X_2, \text{ and} \tag{11.19}$$

$$N = u_1 X_1 + u_2 X_2. \tag{11.20}$$

It is, of course, implied by these relations that

$$V_1 + V_2 = D_1 + D_2. \tag{11.21}$$

Given $D_1$, $D_2$, and the coefficients $a_{ij}$ and $u_j$, the five relations (11.16) to (11.20) determine $X_1$, $X_2$, $V_1$, $V_2$, and $N$. But, alternatively, we can specify $X_1$ and $D_1$ exogenously[20] and determine $X_2$, $D_2$, $V_1$, $V_2$, and $N$. In analyzing the effects of growth in $X_1$, with technical change, this specification is more appropriate.

Let us assume a growth rate $g$ in agricultural output $X_1$. Innovations in the farm sector change $a_{11}$, $a_{21}$, and $u_1$. The coefficients of the non-farm sector, $a_{12}$, $a_{22}$, and $u_2$, remain unchanged. Then, in the second period, we have the following:[21]

$$X_1^1 = (1 + g) X_1^0. \tag{11.22}$$

$$V_1^1 = (1 - a_{11}^1 - a_{21}^1) X_1^1 = (1 - a_{11}^1 - a_{21}^1) (1 + g) X_1^0. \tag{11.23}$$

$$\Delta V_1 = [(1 + g) (1 - a_{11}^1 - a_{21}^1) - (1 - a_{11}^0 - a_{21}^0)] X_1^0. \tag{11.24}$$

For the demand effects of increased income in sector 1 and of the secondary increase in the income of sector 2 we can specify:

$$\Delta D_1 = m_{11} \Delta V_1 + m_{12} \Delta V_2, \tag{11.25}$$

where $m_{11}$ and $m_{12}$ are marginal propensities to spend income originating in sectors 1 and 2 on the output of sector 1. Then:

$$D_1^1 = D_1^0 + m_{11} \Delta V_1 + m_{12} (1 - a_{12} - a_{22}) (X_2^1 - X_2^0). \tag{11.26}$$

Implicitly, since there are only two sectors,

20. Only a part of $D$ is exogenous. See below.
21. The initial values have superscript 0 and the second-period values have superscript 1.

$$D_2^1 = D_2^0 + (1 - m_{11})\,\Delta V_1$$
$$+ (1 - m_{12})\,(1 - a_{12} - a_{22})\,(X_2^1 - X_2^0). \qquad (11.27)$$

The new equilibrium value $X_2^1$ is given by the second-period version of equation (11.16):

$$(1 - a_{11}^1)\,(1 + g)\,X_1^0 = a_{12}^1\,X_2^1 + D_1^0 + m_{11}\,\Delta V_1$$
$$+ m_{12}\,(1 - a_{12} - a_{22})\,(X_2^1 - X_2^0). \qquad (11.16')$$

Here $\Delta V_1$ is known from equation (11.24); and all quantities other than $X_2^1$ are constants. Given $X_1^1$, $V_1^1$, $D_1^1$, and $X_2^1$ from equations (11.22), (11.23), (11.26), and (11.16') respectively, equations (11.17), (11.19), and (11.20) for the second period will determine $D_2$, $V_2$, and $N$.

It should be noted that in equations (11.25) and (11.26) only a part of the increase in final demand is exogenous, that is, the part directly due to the increase in output and income in that sector ($m_{11}\,\Delta V_1$). The other part, due to the induced increase in output (income) in sector 2, remains endogenous because the model itself determines $X_2^1$ and its income and demand effects.

In the empirical exercise presented below in section 6, three variations of the above model have been tried: (1) technical change takes place in the farm sector (i.e., $a_{11}$, $a_{21}$, $v_{11}$, and $u_1$ change)[22] without growth; (2) growth occurs without technical change; and (3) growth occurs with technical change. The three variations give us, respectively, the pure "substitution effect" of technical change, the pure "scale effect" of growth, and the net total effect (substitution effect *plus* scale effect) of growth with technical change on employment.

Since we are assuming that technical change initially displaces labor, the substitution effect on employment is negative. The pure scale effect is, of course, positive. And the net total effect turns out to be positive but smaller than the pure scale effect.

## 6. AN EMPIRICAL ILLUSTRATION

Table 11.6 provides basic data for an empirical illustration. These data include the $X$, $V$, $D$, and $L$ vectors for India in the base year 1964/65, and the coefficients $A$, $U$, $v$, and $m$. The 77 × 77 input-output table of the Indian Statistical Institute for that year has been condensed into

22. Here $v$ is the ratio of gross value added to gross output:
$$v_1 = (1 - a_{11} - a_{21}).$$
$$v_2 = (1 - a_{12} - a_{22}).$$

Table 11.6: Basic Data, India, 1964/65

| Variable | Unit | Value | Coefficient | Value |
|---|---|---|---|---|
| $X_1$ | | 8,990.7 | $a_{11}$ | 0.124395 |
| $X_2$ | 10 millions | 19,229.7 | $a_{12}$ | 0.108358 |
| | of rupees | | | |
| $V_1$ | at 1960/61 | 7,377.0 | $a_{21}$ | 0.055090 |
| | prices | | | |
| $V_2$ | | 10,832.1 | $a_{22}$ | 0.328341 |
| $D_1$ | | 5,788.6 | $v_{22}$ | 0.820515 |
| $D_2$ | | 12,420.5 | $v_2$ | 0.563301 |
| $L_1$ | 10 millions | 6.0238 | $u_1$ | 0.000670 |
| $L_2$ | of man-years | 2.1153 | $u_2$ | 0.000110 |
| | | | $m_{11}$ | 0.458700 |
| | | | $m_{12}$ | 0.332200 |

*Source:* Computed from tables in M. R. Saluja, "Structure of Indian Economy: Inter-industry Flows and Pattern of Final Demand, 1964–65," *Sankhya,* ser. B, 30 (1968): 97–122.

a two-sector table by grouping sectors into a composite farm sector and a composite nonfarm sector to get $X$, $V$, $D$, and $v$. The derivation of $L$ and $U$ is explained in appendix A and that of $m$ in appendix B. The growth rate of agricultural output assumed in two of the three variations of the exercise is 5 percent. Technical change is reflected in changes in the coefficient vectors (elements) relating to sector 1 in $A$, $U$, and $v$. The method used to compute these changes requires some explanation. Field studies of the effects of the new technology in some areas of India furnish data on each item in the cost of cultivation per acre of a few crops in these areas. The data distinguish between samples of farmers using new technology and farmers sticking to the traditional technology. Since the region and the crop year are the same for each body of data, and prices may therefore be assumed to be the same, the cost structure of the traditional and progressive farmers may be assumed to differ primarily due to technical change.

The items of cost for each class of farmers are grouped as follows:

1. material input from agriculture, including expenditure on seed and animal labor,
2. material input from nonagriculture, including chemical fertilizer, pesticides, cost of irrigation, and use of equipment,[23]
3. the cost of human labor, including family and hired labor, and

23. Depreciation of equipment is included here because wear and tear on farm equipment is real nonfarm input. Farmers make no specific provision for depreciation which can properly be included in gross value added.

4. the return to capital, including the rent of land, interest, and net profit.

Profit is calculated as gross output *minus* the total of all other costs per acre. The sum of items 3 and 4 is value added. The percentage changes in the material input from agriculture, the material input from non-agriculture, labor cost, return to capital, value added, and gross output per acre, caused by technical change have been computed from the subtotals of these items for traditional and progressive farmers. By dividing the percentage change in each input by the percentage change in output we get the elasticity of each input with respect to output. When output increases by 0.05 input $i$ is supposed to increase by (0.05) $e_i$, where $e_i$ is the elasticity of input $i$ with respect to output. Thus we get the new input levels due to 5 percent growth in the output of the base period, accompanied by technical change, and compute the new coefficients in $A$, $U$, and $v$.

The cost data were available in the required detail and separately for traditional and innovating farmers for only wheat, rice, and maize in two areas of India (see appendix C). The elasticities computed from each available body of data have been averaged, and the average elasticities have been used to compute the changes in $A$, $U$, and $v$. Ideally, of course, we ought to have data on changes in the cost structure of every product caused by technical change, representative of the whole country, and on the proportion of the output of every product affected by technical change. But in the absence of these data we use the average of the elasticities computed from whatever cost data we have.[24] Implicitly this procedure assumes that input changes of the order indicated by these average elasticities take place over the whole gross cropped area as output grows.

The results of the computations for each variation of the exercise are shown in table 11.7. The growth rates of each of the quantities $X_1$, $X_2$, $(X_1 + X_2)$, $V_1$, $V_2$, $(V_1 + V_2)$, $D_1$, $D_2$, $(D_1 + D_2)$, $L_1$, $L_2$, and $(L_1 + L_2)$ are also shown.

It can be seen from table 11.7 that, in the case of technical change without growth, agricultural employment falls by 4 percent, in proportion to the decline in the employment coefficient. But total employment declines by only 2.6 percent because of the induced growth of 1 percent in the nonagricultural sector.

24. Work is in progress to compile more observations on the effect of technical change on the input structure in different parts of India.

Table 11.7: Projected Effects of Technological Change and/or 5 Percent Agricultural Growth, India

| Variable | Unit | Initial (1964/65) | Innovation without growth | | 5 % farm output growth without innovation | | 5 % farm output growth with innovation | |
|---|---|---|---|---|---|---|---|---|
| | | | Projected value | Growth rate | Projected value | Growth rate | Projected value | Growth rate |
| $X_1$ | | 8,990.7 | 8,990.7 | 0.0000 | 9,440.23 | 0.0500 | 9,440.23 | 0.0500 |
| $X_2$ | | 19,229.7 | 19,427.4 | .0103 | 19,989.17 | .0395 | 20,213.00 | .0511 |
| $X_1 + X_2$ | | 28,220.4 | 28,418.1 | .0070 | 29,429.40 | .0428 | 29,653.24 | .0508 |
| $V_1$ | 10 millions of rupees at 1960/61 prices | 7,377.0 | 7,349.49 | −.0037 | 7,745.85 | .0500 | 7,716.96 | .0461 |
| $V_2$ | | 10,832.1 | 10,943.47 | .0103 | 11,259.92 | .0395 | 11,386.00 | .0511 |
| $V_1 + V_2$ | | 18,209.1 | 18,292.96 | .0046 | 19,005.77 | .0428 | 19,102.97 | .0491 |
| $D_1$ | | 5,788.6 | 5,817.56 | .0050 | 6,099.93 | .0538 | 6,128.56 | .0587 |
| $D_1 + D_2$ | | 12,420.5 | 12,475.40 | .0044 | 12,905.84 | .0391 | 12,974.40 | .0446 |
| | | 18,209.1 | 18,292.96 | .0046 | 19,005.77 | .0437 | 19,102.97 | .0491 |
| $L_1$ | | 6.4373 | 6.1766 | −.0405 | 6.7592 | .0500 | 6.4854 | .0475 |
| $L_2$ | 10 millions of man-years | 2.6537 | 2.6809 | .0103 | 2.7585 | .0395 | 2.7893 | .0511 |
| $L_1 + L_2$ | | 9.0911 | 8.8575 | −.0257 | 9.5177 | .0469 | 9.2748 | .0202 |

In the second case, agricultural growth without innovation, the main result is that 5 percent growth in agricultural output is consistent with 3.95 percent growth in nonagricultural output. Changes in sectoral employment are of the same order, and therefore aggregate employment increases by 4.7 percent.

When agricultural growth occurs with technical change, 5 percent growth in agricultural output induces a slightly higher—5.11 percent—growth in the nonagricultural sector. Employment in the nonagricultural sector also grows by 5.11 percent, but labor displacement causes farm employment to grow less than 1 percent, and therefore growth in aggregate employment is only 2 percent.

This result implies that, if the labor force is growing at a rate exceeding 2 percent, unemployment will increase in spite of the fact that farm output growth is 5 percent and induced nonagricultural growth is even higher. Thus when labor-displacing technical changes are taking place in agriculture, growth in employment, due to direct as well as induced output growth, may not always be sufficient to absorb the whole increase in the labor force. This conclusion is in sharp contrast with the usual theoretical expectation that the immediate negative employment effect of labor-displacing technical change in a sector will be more than offset by the positive indirect employment effects of output growth in this and other sectors. Whether or not this theoretical expectation proves valid depends on the particular constellation of the relevant parameters: the growth rate, the changes in input coefficients, and the marginal propensities to spend out of sectoral incomes.

The particular result of the present exercise is subject to the limitations of available data on these coefficients and propensities. However, it shows that the indirect employment effects *can* be computed, and that even when they are taken into account total employment growth *can* fall short of labor force growth.

### AN ANALYSIS OF EMPLOYMENT GROWTH

We can also decompose the total (direct and indirect) employment growth into the separate contributions of the different causes mentioned above.

Denoting intermediate demand $R = X - D$, employment in the second period is

$$L_1^1 + L_2^1$$
$$= u_1^1 X_1^1 + u_2 X_2^1$$
$$= u_1^1 D_1^1 + u_1^1 R_1^1 + u_2 D_2^1 + u_2 R_2^1, \tag{11.28}$$

and in the base period,

$$L_1^0 + L_2^0 = u_1^0 D_1^0 + u_1^0 R_1^0 + u_2 D_2^0 + u_2 R_2^0. \tag{11.29}$$

Therefore,

$$\Delta(L_1 + L_2)$$
$$= (L_1^1 + L_2^1) - (L_1^0 + L_2^0)$$
$$= u_1^0 (\Delta D_1) + (\Delta u_1) D_1^0 + (\Delta u_1)(\Delta D_1) + u_1^0 (\Delta R_1)$$
$$+ (\Delta u_1) R_1^0 + (\Delta u_1)(\Delta R_1) + u_2 (\Delta D_2) + u_2 (\Delta R_2)$$
$$= (\Delta u_1) X_1^1 + u_1^0 (\Delta D_1) + u_1^0 (\Delta R_1) + u_2 (\Delta D_2) + u_2 (\Delta R_2). \tag{11.30}$$

The terms in the last equation can be identified and named as five economically important effects:

1. the pure labor displacement effect: $(\Delta u_1)(X_1^1)$,
2. the farm final demand effect: $u_1^0 (\Delta D_1)$,
3. the farm input demand effect: $u_1^0 (\Delta R_1)$,
4. the nonfarm final demand effect: $u_2 (\Delta D_2)$, and
5. the nonfarm input demand effect: $u_2 (\Delta R_2)$.

It should be noted that these five effects cover all the major negative and positive effects that growth and technical change in the farm sector may generate. The grouping of terms in equation (11.30) enables us to measure them separately.

Using the results of the last case in table 11.7 (5 percent farm output growth with innovation), the total employment increase, 1,837,970 man-years, can be decomposed as in table 11.8.

Table 11.8: Decomposition of Total Employment Growth Due to 5 Percent Farm Output Growth with Technical Change, India (Base, 196/465)

| Effect | Man-years | Percent |
|---|---|---|
| 1. Pure labor displacement effect | −2,737,760 | −148.90 |
| 2. Farm input demand effect | 784,490 | 42.70 |
| 3. Farm final demand effect | 2,434,180 | 132.40 |
| 4. Nonfarm final demand effect | 764,390 | 41.60 |
| 5. Nonfarm input demand effect | 592,580 | 32.20 |
| Total | 1,837,970 | 100.00 |

The negative labor displacement effect is counterbalanced by positive effects of which the strongest is the agricultural final demand effect; the next strongest is the agricultural input demand effect; and next in order are the nonfarm final demand and input demand effects.

This ordering of effects is, of course, partly due to the assumed marginal propensities to spend. The propensities to spend on agricultural output are much higher than the propensities to spend on nonfarm output; therefore, the farm final demand effect is very large. The relative magnitude of input and final demand coefficients also causes the two final demand effects to be relatively larger than the two input demand effects.

In summary, while recent studies of the employment effects of innovation and growth in agriculture have tried to measure only direct effects, the input-output technique can be used to measure the indirect as well as the direct employment effects and to separate the negative labor displacement effect and each of the positive effects, namely, those due to additional final and input demands of the growing sector and the additional final and input demands induced in other sectors.

Thus, verbal arguments about the positive and negative employment effects of agricultural growth accompanied by labor-displacing technical change can be clinched. And the aggregate as well as the separate employment effects of any growth-technology-demand mix can be computed. With one set of assumptions, based on Indian data, it turns out to be quite possible that, even after all the positive effects counterbalancing the initial negative effects of technical change on employment are taken into account, aggregate employment growth may fail to keep pace with the growth of the labor force, and unemployment may continue to increase. The normal expectation of growth with innovation producing full employment turns out to be contingent on a number of conditions that a developing economy may not fulfill.

The policy implications of these results are obvious. If policy makers do not want unemployment to increase they should establish, with appropriate measures, a growth-innovation-demand mix that can be shown, with actual computations, to be capable of increasing employment at a rate higher than the growth rate of the labor force.

The methodology for projecting the various employment effects of *any* given mix has been developed and illustrated with the currently available data. The task now is to use it for actual projections with more broadly based and reliable data.

## APPENDIX A:
## THE COMPUTATION OF EMPLOYMENT IN THE BASE YEAR, AND LABOR-OUTPUT COEFFICIENTS

Labor-output coefficients are calculated for each sector of the Indian Statistical Institute input-output table for 1964/65 (at 1960/61 prices) from data derived from the following sources.

For fifteen industrial sectors the total employment is divided by the value of gross output given in India, Central Statistical Organization, *Annual Survey of Industries* (*ASI*) (Calcutta, 1965). The definitions of these sectors correspond very closely to the definitions of *ASI* sectors.

For the nonagricultural sectors not included in the *ASI*, and for agricultural sectors other than crop production, the figures on employment and gross output have been taken from a variety of other sources.

For the crop production sectors, "food grains" and "other agriculture" labor days per acre were calculated separately for the individual crops (wheat, rice, pulses, jowar, ragi, gram, maize, and bajra) from data given in India, Directorate of Economics and Statistics, *Studies in the Economics of Farm Management* for various crop years. Labor per acre is multiplied by the gross cropped area in each crop in 1964/65 given in India, Economic and Statistical Adviser to the Ministry of Food and Agriculture, *Area, Production, and Yield of Principal Crops in India, 1950–51 to 1968–69*, to estimate total employment in each crop.

The value of gross output of each crop is available in India, Department of Statistics, Central Statistical Organization, *Brochure on Revised Estimates of the National Product, 1960–61 to 1965–66* (New Delhi: Government of India Press, 1967). The labor-output coefficient is therefore computed by dividing the total estimated employment in man-days by the gross output of 1964/65 in 1961 prices. The man-days are divided by 250 to estimate man-years of full employment. A man-year has been treated as equal to 250 man-days because in the industrial sector covered by the *ASI* the average number of days of work per person turns out to be 250 days.

The aggregate labor output ratio for all the crops for which separate labor/land ratios are available is applied to other crops for which such ratios are not available.

## APPENDIX B:
## A CALCULATION OF PROPENSITIES TO SPEND

The model requires marginal propensities to spend on the output of each of the two sectors out of gross income generated in each of the two sectors ($m_{11}$ and $m_{12}$).

The total expenditure is divided into only two parts: consumption and investment. The total marginal propensities to spend on agricultural output out of agricultural income and nonagricultural income are computed as:

$$m_{11} = s_1 [(a_{11}/(a_{11} + a_{21})] + (1 - s_1) d_{11}$$

and

$$m_{12} = s_2 [(a_{12}/(a_{12} + a_{22})] + (1 - s_2) d_{12},$$

where $s_1$ and $s_2$ are the savings rates of the two sectors, $d_{11}$ and $d_{12}$ are marginal propensities to spend on agricultural goods out of the total consumption expenditures of the agricultural and nonagricultural sectors respectively, and $a_{ij}$ are the input-output coefficients.

Rural and urban savings rates for 1962/63 (available in the *Reserve Bank of India Bulletin* for March 1965) are treated as marginal propensities to spend on investment out of agricultural and nonagricultural income respectively; 1962/63 is the last year for which separate rural and urban savings rates are available in the Reserve Bank data.

Investment expenditure is broken up into expenditures on agricultural and on nonagricultural output, on the assumption that the proportion of each in the total investment expenditure is the same as the proportion of expenditures on current inputs to the total material input. Thus $a_{11}/(a_{11} + a_{21})$ and $a_{12}/(a_{21} + a_{22})$ are the proportions spent on agricultural output out of the investment expenditure of the agricultural and nonagricultural sectors respectively. This is a strong assumption, but in the absence of precise data there is no better alternative.

The proportion of income not spent on investment is regarded as spent on consumption. Data from the Indian *National Sample Survey* on rural and urban consumption expenditures in 1963/64 are used to break up the consumption expenditure of the agricultural and nonagricultural sectors into expenditures on agricultural and on nonagricultural output. Expenditures on food grains, milk, and milk products are assumed to be expenditures on agricultural output. The remainder of the consumption expenditures is assumed to be spent on nonagricultural output.

The basic coefficients derived from the above sources are as follows:

$$s_1 = 0.0339 \qquad d_{11} = 0.4505$$
$$s_2 = 0.1502 \qquad d_{12} = 0.3471$$

Since there are only two sectors, $m_{21} = 1 - m_{11}$ and $m_{22} = 1 - m_{12}$.

## APPENDIX C: CHANGES IN THE COMPOSITION OF THE INPUT VECTOR DUE TO TECHNICAL CHANGE

|  | Wheat | | Wheat | | Paddy | | Maize | |
|---|---|---|---|---|---|---|---|---|
|  | $T^a$ | $M^b$ | T | M | T | M | T | M |
|  | (1) | (2) | (3) | (4) | (5) | (6) | (7) | (8) |
| Material input from agriculture | 0.25 | 0.11 | 0.22 | 0.11 | 0.17 | 0.05 | 0.15 | 0.05 |
| Material input from nonagriculture | .04 | .06 | .02 | .20 | .05 | .11 | .05 | .09 |
| Return to human labor | .14 | .07 | .22 | .15 | .20 | .06 | .36 | .10 |
| Return to capital | .57 | .76 | .54 | .54 | .58 | .78 | .44 | .75 |
| Nonprofit | .08 | .04 | —$^c$ | — | .06 | .02 | .03 | .02 |
| Profit | .49 | .72 | — | — | .52 | .76 | .41 | .73 |
| Gross output | 1.00 | 1.00 | 1.00 | 1.00 | 1.00 | 1.00 | 1.00 | 1.00 |

a. Traditional technique.
b. Modern technique.
c. Not available.

*Sources:* For wheat (cols. 1 and 2), paddy, and maize (all Utter Pradesh data): S. P. Dhondyal, "Cost and Effectiveness of Modern Technology on Farm Production and Farm Income," *Indian Journal of Agricultural Economics*, April-June 1968.

For wheat (cols. 3 and 4, Punjab data): Bhagat Singh, "Economics of Tractor Cultivation: A Case Study," *Indian Journal of Agricultural Economics*, January-March 1968.

PART V: AGRICULTURE, GROWTH, AND TRADE

# 12

## Agriculture and Economic Development in the Open Economy

HLA MYINT

The customary approach to the role of agriculture in economic development is formulated in terms of the "contributions" the agricultural sector can make or the "functions" it can perform during the process of economic development. Thus it is generally accepted that agricultural development can promote the economic development of the under-developed countries in four distinct ways: (i) by increasing the supply of food available for domestic consumption and releasing the labor needed for industrial employment; (ii) by enlarging the size of the domestic market for the manufacturing sector; (iii) by increasing the supply of domestic savings; and (iv) by providing the foreign exchange earned by agricultural exports.

This chapter is concerned with the open-economy implications of the role of agriculture in economic development. It attempts to clarify the customary approach to the subject and examine it critically from the standpoint of international trade theory. Section 1 begins by distinguishing the two possible interpretations of the terms "contributions" and "functions" of the agricultural sector. It then describes the model of the "semi-open" economy—a hybrid between the closed and the open economy—which underlies much of the writings on the role of agriculture in economic development. Sections 2 and 3 are explicitly concerned with the economic policies designed to increase the agricultural sector's capacity to contribute to economic development; they discuss the degree of compatibility of the policies designed to promote all four of the agricultural sector's "standard" functions. The chapter concludes with a discussion of the conflict between the policy of trying to increase the agricultural sector's contribution to domestic savings and the need to give adequate incentives to the farmers.

## 1. CLOSED, OPEN, AND SEMI-OPEN ECONOMIES

The terms "contributions" and "functions," as related to the agricultural sector, may be interpreted in two ways. First, they may be taken to mean the voluntary contributions or the spontaneous functions of the agricultural sector reflecting its interrelationship with the rest of the economy during the long-term process of economic development. Second, they may be interpreted as the compulsory contributions that can be exacted from the agricultural sector or the functions it can be made to perform by deliberate policy. This can be illustrated for each of the four types of contribution mentioned above. For example: (i) the agricultural sector may be said to make a contribution in the voluntary sense to the domestic food supply if a rise in agricultural productivity spontaneously lowers the free market price of food. On the other hand, it can be *made* to contribute to the domestic food supply by, say, imposing price controls on the food sold to the workers in the manufacturing sector. (ii) Similarly, the agricultural sector can spontaneously increase the size of the domestic market if the farmers freely decide to spend their incomes on domestically manufactured goods in preference to imports; but the agricultural sector can also be made to contribute to the size of the domestic market by import restrictions, that is, by being treated as the captive market of the protected manufacturing industry. (iii) The agricultural sector can voluntarily contribute to the supply of domestic savings if these savings flow out freely, induced by the higher returns to investment in the manufacturing sector; on the other hand, savings can be squeezed out of the agricultural sector by taxation or by deliberately turning the terms of trade against agricultural products. (iv) The same distinction can be applied to the agricultural sector's contribution to the foreign exchange supply.

Existing literature on the role of agriculture in economic development has two aims: first, to provide a broad historical perspective on the role of agriculture in economic development, and, second, to try to draw historical lessons from the experiences of the advanced countries during "the early stages of economic development," with the purpose of applying these lessons to the present-day underdeveloped countries. Writers who are especially concerned with the second aim[1]

1. These include W. H. Nicholls, "The Place of Agriculture in Economic De-

tend to move freely between description of the role the agricultural sector has actually played in the history of the advanced countries and prescription of the policies the present-day underdeveloped countries should follow in order to enable the agricultural sector to increase its contributions to economic development. Thus the distinction between the voluntary and the compulsory contributions of the agricultural sector gets blurred, if ever it is recognized. In this chapter I shall try to keep these two meanings distinct, as far as possible. I am concerned here, not so much with the agricultural sector's role in the secular or longer-term pattern of structural changes accompanying economic development, but rather with the more immediate issues of development theory and development policy in the shorter or the medium run. I will therefore find it convenient to use the terms "contributions" or "functions" of the agricultural sector mainly in the compulsory sense, that is, to refer to what the agricultural sector can be made to do by means of deliberate policy.

A further ambiguity in the existing writings on the role of agriculture in economic development arises from the common practice of treating the four contributions of the agricultural sector, namely, those to (i) the domestic food supply, (ii) the size of the domestic market, (iii) the supply of domestic savings, and (iv) the supply of foreign exchange, on the same footing. This obscures the important point that the first three of these are based on *internal* relations within the domestic economy—more specifically, on the relations between the domestic agricultural and the domestic manufacturing sectors, defined in terms of the closed-economy model. In contrast, the fourth introduces an *external* trading relationship between the domestic economy and the rest of the world and brings the analysis into the open-economy setting.

These relations can be clearly sorted out if we accept the formal distinction between the closed economy and the open economy. If we accept the closed-economy model, then we exclude (iv) by definition and the three remaining internal relations can be fitted together into a consistent framework. If, on the other hand, we adopt the open-

velopment," in *Economic Development with Special Reference to East Asia*, ed. K. Berill (New York: St. Martin's Press, 1964); B. F. Johnston and J. W. Mellor, "The Role of Agriculture in Economic Development," *American Economic Review* 51, no. 4 (1961): 566–93; and H. J. Habakkuk, "Historical Experience in Economic Development," in *Problems of Economic Development*, ed. E. A. G. Robinson (London: MacMillan, 1965). S. Kuznets seems to put a greater emphasis on the quantitative aspects of the historical perspective than on the historical lessons; see his "Economic Growth and the Contribution of Agriculture," *International Journal of Agrarian Affairs* 3, no. 2 (1961).

economy model by introducing the external trading relation (iv), then we should allow the general equilibrium principle of comparative advantage to override the partial view of the role of agriculture defined in terms of the closed economy.

Thus (i) in the closed economy, the agricultural sector serves the obvious and vital function of supplying the domestic food requirements. But in the open economy it is no longer obvious why even an underdeveloped country with a dense and rapidly growing population should try to reach self-sufficiency in food. If the country has a comparative advantage in nonfood agricultural products, it could more efficiently feed its population by exporting these products and importing food. (ii) In a two-sector model of the closed economy, a rise in the income and the spending power of the agricultural sector is necessary for enlarging the size of the domestic market of the manufacturing sector. But in the open economy it is no longer necessary for the two sectors to grow in a "balanced" way.[2] Normally, the country would gain from specialization, that is, by increasing the output of one sector and reducing the output of the other, according to the direction of its comparative advantage. (iii) In a closed economy, assuming a low-income elasticity of demand for agricultural products, we may expect the agricultural sector to release spontaneously a growing proportion of its labor and savings to the manufacturing sector as productivity and income rise in the country. But in the open economy the amount of resources that can be profitably employed in the agricultural sector is no longer limited by the domestic demand for food but will depend also on the external demand for agricultural exports, both food and nonfood. Thus the free movement of resources between the agricultural and the manufacturing sectors in response to the changing conditions of demand and comparative advantage may be in either direction. The agricultural sector can, however, be made to contribute to the one-way traffic of resources from itself to the manufacturing sector by a deliberate policy of extracting the "agricultural surplus."

The formal distinction between the closed- and the open-economy models has been largely disregarded in the existing literature. Instead, those economists who wish to draw historical lessons attach a greater importance to the distinction between the earlier and the later stages

2. See J. Sheahan, "International Specialization and the Concept of Balanced Growth," *Quarterly Journal of Economics* 72, no. 1 (1958): 181–97 and also the "Comment" by Ronald Findlay, in the same journal, 73, no. 2 (1959): 339–45.

of economic development. They believe that in the early stages of economic development agriculture plays a more important role in promoting economic development than is usually suggested by the standard international trade theory, and that this is particulary true for large, densely populated underdeveloped countries such as India which are experiencing rapid population growth.

The first historical lesson they draw is clearly stated by the economic historian H. J. Habakkuk, writing mainly on the early stages of development of the European countries:

> The implication of historical experience . . . is not that export sectors did not still have an important role in economic development but only that they are unlikely to promote vigorous economic growth without extensive changes in agrarian structure. . . . All the successful nineteenth century industrializations were accompanied in their early stages by an increase in agricultural output and . . . there are no cases where unresponsiveness of domestic agriculture was made good by imports of agricultural products. . . . This coincidence of successful development and agrarian improvement does not seem to be accidental. For agrarian improvement performed functions which could not have been performed by imports of food even if these had been made available on very favourable terms.[3]

These functions of agrarian improvement are of course what I have listed as the four contributions of the agricultural sector. Writing from a European perspective, Habakkuk stresses the agricultural sector's contribution to the labor supply available for industrial employment. On the other hand, the agricultural economists, with their eye on the present-day underdeveloped countries where labor is abundant and food is scarce, stress the agricultural sector's contribution to the domestic food supply. Thus W. H. Nicholls emphasizes "the almost universal importance of having a substantial and reliable food surplus for launching and sustaining economic growth."[4] However, as I indicated at the outset, I shall follow the agricultural economists and define the four standard contributions of the agricultural sector as

3. Habakkuk, "Historical Experience in Economic Development," pp. 122–23.
4. William H. Nicholls, "An 'Agricultural Surplus' as a Factor in Economic Development in Agrarian Economies," *Journal of Political Economy* 71, no. 1 (1963): 1–29.

consisting in its contributions to (i) the domestic food supply, (ii) the size of the domestic market, (iii) the supply of domestic savings and (iv) the supply of foreign exchange.

As we have seen, in formal terms (i), (ii) and (iii) describe the internal relations between the agricultural and the manufacturing sectors within a two-sector model of the closed economy, whereas (iv) breaks down the isolation of the closed economy and brings the analysis into an open-economy setting. In arguing that agricultural development is especially important in the early stages of economic development because it can make all four of these contributions at the same time, the agricultural economists are faced with the problem of constructing a model that combines the features of both the closed economy and the open economy. That is to say, the model must have some international trade based on agricultural exports so that the agricultural sector's contribution to the foreign exchange earnings can be included in the "standard" list. At the same time, instead of being a thorough-going open economy, it must be only a semi-open economy: that is to say, a large part of the domestic economy must remain insulated from the impact of foreign trade and comparative costs so that the agricultural sector's contribution to the domestic food supply, to the size of the domestic market, and to the domestic supply of savings can be treated as though we were still in a closed-economy model.

It is fair to say that few writers on the role of agriculture in economic development have systematically considered the formal problem of constructing a semi-open economy. However, we may try to construct such a model by piecing together their scattered remarks on the reasons why a large part of the domestic economy of a country in the early stages of development would remain insulated from the impact of foreign trade.

First, there is an implicit identification of agricultural exports as the exports from the plantation sector and identification of domestic food production with peasant farming, reinforced by the belief that plantation exports tend to create a "dualistic" economic structure. In this view, the semi-open economy is another aspect of export dualism. There is no need to go at great length into the familiar arguments about dualism. Insofar as dualism is attributed to the lack of "linkages," the limitations of the concept of linkages in an open-economy setting will be discussed in section 3 below. As for the argument that dualism is attributable to the deliberate policy of the colonial governments in the past of encouraging plantation exports at the expense of peasant agriculture, this does not appear to be an inevitable or inherent economic characteristic of the countries in question at the early stages of development.[5] Further, the correction of dualism in this sense by the present-day governments of the underdeveloped countries need not necessarily mean a policy of domestic self-sufficiency in food; the peasant sector, when properly encouraged, may develop a comparative advantage in some line of nonfood agricultural export.

Second, even leaving aside policy-induced dualism, there is a possibility that in the early stages of development a large part of the domestic economy would remain spontaneously free from the impact of foreign trade because of "traditional agrarian structures unfavorable to the transmission of the impulses derived from foreign trade,"[6] or simply because of the underdevelopment of the internal network of marketing, transport, and communications. This concept of the insulated or semi-open economy may be contrasted with the thoroughgoing open economy of the standard international trade theory. The standard theory, by assuming the "perfect competition" model of the domestic economy, takes it for granted that a country already possesses a fully developed internal economic framework when it is first opened to international trade and can therefore effectively respond and adjust to the external economic impulses by means of appropriate changes involving the entire domestic economy as a general equilibrium system. In fact, in a realistic historical setting, when a country at the early stages of development is opened to international trade it is likely to remain a semi-open economy with a large part of its domestic economy insulated from the impact of foreign trade because of the lack of the internal economic mechanisms necessary to respond in a comprehensive manner to the external economic forces. In such a situation, it may be argued that domestic agricultural development has a special role to play which is not recognized by the standard trade theory: namely, to involve all of the domestic economy in the process of economic transformation and thus contribute to the development of the internal framework the existence of which is taken for granted in the standard trade theory.

In order to construct a hybrid model of the semi-open economy, a number of restrictive assumptions have to be imposed to minimize the effect of foreign trade on the domestic economy. To begin with, agri-

5. For example, British colonial administration in West Africa prohibited the plantation system in order to protect peasant agriculture.
6. Habakkuk, "Historical Experience in Economic Development," p. 122.

cultural exports have to be treated as being autonomously given and constant. As we shall see later, pessimism about the world market demand for nonfood agricultural exports plays an important part in the argument for increasing domestic self-sufficiency in food in the underdeveloped countries. Even without export pessimism, however, the assumptions required for the construction of the semi-open economy virtually rule out any possibility of expanding exports. The model implies that there is no interaction between the agricultural exports and the rest of the agricultural sector (and hence the rest of the domestic economy) either through the pattern of foreign exchange expenditure on imports or through the allocation of resources between agricultural exports and domestic food production. The agricultural sector is supposed to pass on its "contribution" of foreign exchange earnings to the manufacturing sector to pay for the latter's imports of capital goods and food, without any effect on the domestic agricultural output: the incentive effect on the farmers of the opportunity or the lack of opportunity to import cheap consumer goods is ignored in the model. It is also assumed that agricultural exports require specific kinds of natural resources and therefore cannot be expanded once these special resources have been fully employed. On the other hand, it is assumed that domestic food production can be increased by agricultural improvements making use of the nonspecialized resources that are in abundant supply and may actually be underutilized. This permits domestic food production to be expanded without reducing agricultural exports. Assuming the value of the nonfood agricultural exports to be given and constant, the only way the agricultural sector can increase its foreign exchange contributions is to cut down food imports.

The exponents of the customary approach to the role of agriculture in economic development have not explicitly formulated or consciously used the semi-open economy model I have pieced together; but the main ingredients in their thinking fall into place when we adopt the model as our frame of reference. The question is how useful this framework is in studying the role of agriculture in the present-day underdeveloped countries.

Prima facie, the semi-open economy model is more plausible when applied to a large, densely populated country, such as India, with a low ratio of foreign trade to total domestic product, than in reference to the more populous class of underdeveloped countries that have high ratios of foreign trade to national income, either because of their more favorable resource endowments or simply because of their small size. But there is a basic logical weakness in the argument that a country should increase its food production for domestic consumption just because a large part of its domestic economy is spontaneously insulated from the world market forces owing to its "traditional agrarian structure" and the underdevelopment of its internal network of marketing, transport, and communications. For the potential comparative advantage of the unorganized traditional sector may lie in the direction of peasant exports or in small-scale, labor-intensive manufactured products either for domestic consumption or for export. Moreover, the semi-open economy model, by identifying agricultural exports almost entirely with plantation exports, serves to underplay the historical lessons that can be drawn from the peasant export economies, notably in Southeast Asia and West Africa. This has resulted in three serious weaknesses.

First, there is the general assumption that the internal economic framework of a country in the early stages of development can be developed only by encouraging some form of domestic economic activity as opposed to export activity. But in the actual experiences of the peasant export economies it was the expansion in peasant export production that drew the resources of the subsistence sector into the money economy and laid the foundations of the internal economic framework. Thus there seems to be a two-way relationship: domestic agricultural development may improve the internal economic framework and enable a country to participate more effectively in international trade. But the development of peasant export production may also encourage the growth of the internal economic framework and domestic agricultural development. In the open-economy setting, the extent of these possible interactions must ultimately depend on whether or not the resources are being used according to the potential comparative advantage of a country. If this essential condition is not fulfilled, then the encouragement of a domestically oriented economic activity as such need not lead to the development of the internal framework. On the contrary, it may even retard it. This may be illustrated by the "new dualism" which has been introduced into the economic structure of many underdeveloped countries as a consequence of their policy of encouraging domestic industrialization. Such policies have frequently led to the provision of the scarce capital funds, foreign exchange, and public economic services such as transport and power on excessively favorable terms to the modern industrial sector and on excessively unfavorable terms to the traditional agricultural sector. The result has been to aggravate the dualism between the two sectors, and to undermine the cohesiveness of the internal economic framework.[7]

Second, the semi-open economy model ignores the incentive effect of imports on agricultural production. Historically, there has been an intimate connection between the expansion of exports and imports. It was the growth of new desires and the incentive to acquire cheap imported consumer goods that induced peasants to bring new unused land into export production. It should be noted that the transition from the "vent for surplus" phase of export expansion to the modern phase of scientific agriculture and intensive farming does not diminish the need to provide adequate economic incentives to the peasant farmers. If anything, the incentive problem is intensified, for now the farmers have to be provided with the opportunity to purchase not only cheap consumer goods but also cheap farm inputs, notably fertilizer and farm equipment, to induce them to adopt the improved agricultural methods. The crucial question is whether the domestic manufacturing sectors of the underdeveloped countries can provide these products at prices comparable to the world market prices of the imports.

Third, the semi-open economy model is based on a distinction between the scarce and specific natural resources required for export production and the abundant, unspecialized resources that can be used for domestic food product. This distinction is strongest for the mining exports. For plantation exports, it is not so much the differences in natural resources as the economies of large-scale production that may give the advantage to the plantation system of export production. But the distinction is extremely artificial when applied to peasant exports. In peasant economies, not excepting densely populated countries like India, peasant producers have been generally observed to respond to relative price change by flexibly reallocating their resources between subsistence production and cash crops, including export crops. The distinction between the two types of resources, those for export and those for domestic production, becomes even more questionable when we turn to a setting of technical changes as illustrated by the "green revolution" taking place in a number of Asian and Latin American countries. Here the characteristic effect is not only to

7. For a fuller discussion of this see Hla Myint, "Dualism in the Internal Integration of the Underdeveloped Economies," *Banca Nazionale del Lavoro Quarterly Review* (June 1970) reprinted in his *Economic Theory and the Underdeveloped Countries* (New York: Oxford University Press, 1971).

raise the productivity and output of food grains but also to encourage multiple cropping on a given plot of land. This means that the problem of crop diversification is introduced early in the process of agricultural development, both by the technical considerations on the supply side and by the prospect of saturating the domestic market for food grains.[8] It is therefore unrealistic to suggest, as some writers tend to do, that the underdeveloped countries should concentrate "at the early stages of development" on increasing domestic food production and should consider the problem of crop diversification and agricultural exports only after they have achieved a domestic food surplus.

## 2. FOOD SELF-SUFFICIENCY AND COMPARATIVE ADVANTAGE

In this section and the one that follows, I will be concerned with the policy implications of the semi-open economy model and the customary approach to the role of agriculture in economic development in terms of its four "standard" contributions. Now if we interpret the term "contributions" explicitly as what the agricultural sector can be made to contribute by means of deliberate policy, the customary approach may be regarded as the advocacy of development policies that aim to increase simultaneously the agricultural sector's capacity to make all four of its standard contributions, namely, contributions to (i) the domestic food supply; (ii) the size of the domestic market; (iii) the supply of domestic savings, and (iv) the supply of foreign exchange. Our problem is to examine how far these policies are mutually consistent with each other.

In terms of the standard international trade theory, an underdeveloped country can have a comparative advantage either in food production or in nonfood products. Which way the comparative advantage will lie is an empirical question: with given international demand, it depends on the individual circumstances of the country, particularly on its factor endowments and the production functions in food and nonfood products. If a country has a comparative advantage in food, it will export food under free trade and the agricultural sector can then contribute both to its domestic food supply and to its foreign exchange earnings, that is, policies promoting agricultural sector contributions (i) and (iv) will be consistent. If, on the other hand, the country has a comparative advantage in nonfood production policies,

8. See Shigeru Ishikawa, *Agricultural Development Strategies in Asia* (Asian Development Bank, 1970).

promoting (i) and (iv) would be inconsistent. Since resources are assumed to be fully employed and nonspecific, domestic food production can be increased only by reducing exports, and the lack of comparative advantage in food production means that a policy of increasing domestic self-sufficiency in food would save less foreign exchange than the resources withdrawn could have earned in export production.

There are a number of food-exporting underdeveloped countries, for example, the rice-exporting countries of Southeast Asia, where the agricultural sector fulfills both functions (i) and (iv). But the agricultural economists are not concerned with these countries. They are concerned with the food-deficit countries, which at present are exporting nonfood products on the basis of their existing comparative advantage. Economists argue that these food-deficit countries, irrespective of their factor endowments, have a *potential* comparative advantage in food production because of the characteristic features of their domestic economy "in the early stages of development"; and that this potential advantage from increasing domestic food production is greatest for densely populated countries such as India, where the rapidly growing population generates an increasing drain on foreign exchange which cannot be met by expanding nonfood agricultural exports. Thus, by means of appropriate agricultural development policies the agricultural sector can be made to increase its contribution to the foreign exchange supply, by cutting down on its food imports.

As I have already noted, agricultural economists have tried to bypass the standard proposition that domestic food self-sufficiency could be increased only at the expense of agricultural exports by introducing a special assumption, namely, that the specific natural resources required for export production are scarce and fully employed, whereas appropriate agricultural development policies can increase food supply by making use of the abundant nonspecialized resources that are underemployed. That is to say, the domestic food supply can be increased without reducing export production.

This, however, crucially depends on the possibility of increasing agricultural productivity by the introduction of improved techniques. Here the agricultural economists appeal to the historical lesson to be learned from Japan in her early stages of development, and also from the more recent experiences of Taiwan. The lesson they draw has two points: first, that even poor Asian countries starting from a typical situation of backward agriculture and with population densities much higher than most underdeveloped countries can successfully and rapidly increase their domestic food supply, provided the appropriate agricultural development policies are pursued; and, second, that the pattern of appropriate agricultural development is indicated by or can be "induced" by the initial economic conditions of the countries concerned.[9] Thus they argue that the Japanese agricultural development, characterized by the use of higher-yielding seeds and intensive application of fertilizer, was "induced" by the initial conditions of a technically backward peasant agriculture combined with intense population pressure on land. This directed government agricultural research into the biological and chemical fields, resulting in land-saving and labor-using agricultural innovations. They contrast this with the different pattern of agricultural development in the newly settled countries of the temperate zone, notably the United States, where the initial conditions of abundant land and labor scarcity induced a series of labor-saving innovations in the form of the progressive mechanization of agriculture. They put forward the Japanese pattern of induced agricultural innovations as the appropriate path of agricultural development for the densely populated underdeveloped countries currently suffering from a growing food deficit.

Their argument may be summarized as follows.[10] (a) In these countries with a technically backward peasant agriculture combined with an intense and growing population pressure on land, there is a vast pool of underutilized labor which can be used to increase agricultural output in two ways: first, by a more intensive application of labor to land, and, second, by using the underemployed labor to construct the simpler forms of agricultural capital, such as minor irrigation and drainage works, hand-dug wells, improved farm roads, and so on, which in their appropriate location can greatly increase the productivity of land. (b) This potential for increasing agricultural productivity remains untapped at present because of the scarcity of certain strategic inputs: notably, technical knowledge concerning the improved agricultural methods for peasant farmers, suitably trained personnel for agricultural research and extension, and improved physical inputs, that is, high-yielding seeds and fertilizer. (c) Because of the constraints imposed by the scarcity of these strategic inputs, which are complementary with the abundant factors, the employment of the abundant factors has been

9. See Yujiro Hayami and Vernon W. Ruttan, *Agricultural Development: An International Perspective* (Baltimore: Johns Hopkins Press, 1971), pt. 3.

10. This summary relies heavily on John W. Mellor, "The Process of Agricultural Development in Low-Income Countries," *Journal of Farm Economics*, August 1962.

pushed to the point of very low marginal returns in the conditions of
stagnant technology. This accentuates the problem of the underutili-
zation of the abundant factors, which affects the use of both labor and
land. For instance, given the very low returns available, there are no
economic incentives to use the abundant factors more intensively, for
instance, by multiple cropping on the same piece of land. (d) In this
situation, if the government could be induced to adopt appropriate
agricultural development policies which break the constraints imposed
by the scarcity of the strategic inputs by introducing land-saving and
labor-using agricultural innovations (or by taking advantage of the
backlog of known improved methods) a vast increase in agricultural
output would be obtainable in return for modest injections of capital
into the agricultural sector.

This argument for expanding domestic food production based on the
unused potential for increasing agricultural productivity is then reinforced by the agricultural economists' pessimism concerning the world
market demand for nonfood agricultural exports. The advocates of
domestic industrialization tend to be pessimistic about the world market
demand for all primary products including food (on the grounds of low
income elasticity of demand). On the other hand, the agricultural economists believe that, so long as the food-deficit countries are going
through a phase of rapid population growth, there is certain to be an
expansion in the domestic demand for food. So their export pessimism
is selective and is confined only to nonfood agricultural exports.

With this summary in mind, we may now make a number of comments on the case for increasing self-sufficiency in food in the underdeveloped countries. First, we must question the assumption that
advances in the seed and fertilizer technological methods generally
enable the underdeveloped countries to increase their food production
in large quantities in return for modest investments of capital. B. F.
Johnston and J. W. Mellor elaborated this assumption in terms of what
they call "Phase II," during which the expansion of agriculture is
supposed to take place "based on labor-intensive, capital-saving
techniques, relying heavily on technological innovations."[11] But S.
Ishikawa, after detailed studies of the agricultural conditions in a
number of Asian countries, has pointed out that the success of the seed
and fertilizer technology crucially depends on a fully developed system
of irrigation and flood control and that in many underdeveloped countries the provision of these facilities necessary to sustain the green

11. Johnston and Mellor, "Role of Agriculture," sec. 3.

revolution would entail very heavy capital investment.[12] Thus, depending on the climate and resource endowments of the countries concerned, the Johnston and Mellor "Phase II" in agricultural development may be very short or even nonexistent. The need to provide expensive irrigation facilities would then greatly reduce the potential comparative advantage in food production claimed for some underdeveloped countries. This would also reduce the contribution to the supply of domestic savings expected from the agricultural sector.

Second, we may briefly compare the agricultural economists' model of induced agricultural development with the familiar Heckscher-Ohlin theory of international trade based on factor endowments. Insofar as we can apply the simple Heckscher-Ohlin model to the underdeveloped countries, the argument would run as follows. Assume two factors, land and labor, and assume that food is a more land-intensive product than the nonfood exports. In that case, we should expect a food-deficit country with abundant land, say, Chile, to gain more from a policy of increasing domestic self-sufficiency in food than a food-deficit country with land scarcity, say, India. This would seem to conflict with the drift of the agricultural economists' argument. It may be noted, however, that both approaches are based on the factor-proportions analysis. The Heckscher-Ohlin theory seeks to take advantage of the initial factor endowments through an appropriate pattern of international trade, assuming techniques of production to be constant. The agricultural economists seek to take advantage of the initial factor endowments through an appropriate pattern of induced technical changes in agriculture. The trade approach assumes that it would be easier for the underdeveloped countries to allow the market forces to take advantage of the existing production possibilities rather than to rely on government policy to induce the appropriate technical changes. On the other hand, the agricultural economists assume that in the early stages of development it would be more difficult for the underdeveloped countries to develop a competitive labor-intensive line of exports, which would probably mean manufactured exports, than to use their abundant labor supply in increasing food output for the domestic market.

Third, we may consider the demand factors. The agricultural economists' selective pessimism concerning the world market demand for nonfood agricultural exports been has reiterated by W. Arthur Lewis, who writes:

12. Shigeru Ishikawa, *Economic Development in Asian Perspective* (Tokyo: Kinokuniya, 1967), chaps. 2 and 4.

Between 1955 and 1965 world trade in agricultural products grew 54 per cent, while tropical trade in agricultural products grew only by 44 per cent. There was booming demand for cereals, livestock products, feeding stuffs and fruit while the tropics were pushing tea, cocoa, coffee, sugar and rubber, for which the demand is sluggish.[13]

Lewis attributes the unfavorable world market situation for the non-food agricultural exports to the new expanding supplies of these products from the tropical African countries. He argues that the comparative advantages of these African countries in this type of export lies, not in their higher productivity in these nonfood crops compared with the Latin American and Asian countries, but in their lower productivity in food production. Thus "a price of commercial crops in terms of food which may repel the Brazilian farmer may attract the African farmer because of his lower opportunity costs."[14] On this basis, he puts forward the theory that the terms of trade between the manufactured products produced by the advanced countries and the nonfood agricultural products produced by the underdeveloped countries are determined not by the demand and supply for these products but by the relative productivities of labor in food production in the advanced and the underdeveloped countries. According to this theory, so long as their labor productivity in food remains constant, the underdeveloped countries cannot benefit by increasing their labor productivity in nonfood agricultural exports, since this will merely be passed on to the consumers in the form of lower export prices, without raising domestic real wages. The underdeveloped countries can benefit only by raising their labor productivity in food production: this will raise the opportunity cost of labor employed in the nonfood agricultural exports and raise their prices relative to the price of the manufactured imports. This theory suggests that a rise in labor productivity in food production would not only contribute to the domestic food supply and the supply of foreign exchange by reducing imports; it would also contribute to the country's foreign exchange supply by improving the country's terms of trade.

Although Lewis summarily dismisses "marginal utility" and the demand factors as the long-term determinants of the terms of trade,[15] his theory seems nevertheless to have been based on the assumption

13. W. Arthur Lewis, *Aspects of Tropical Trade, 1883–1965,* Wiksell Lectures (Stockholm: Almquist and Wiksell, 1969), p. 14.

14. Ibid., p. 15.

15. Ibid., p. 17.

that, in the longer run, demand for food usually remains buoyant, presumably because of population growth.[16] Without this buoyant domestic demand for food, an increase in food productivity per worker may be more than counterbalanced by the reduction in the price of food, so that the per worker wage would fall as a consequence of a rise in food productivity. This would reduce the opportunity cost of labor for nonfood exports. Thus a country with a faster growth in labor productivity in food, using Lewis's line of reasoning, would turn its terms of trade against itself, which is exactly the opposite of his conclusion. But what is more likely to happen is that a country with a faster growth in food productivity would develop into a food exporter instead of remaining a food producer for only the domestic market. At this point it may be asked whether the present buoyant condition of world market demand for food is not due largely to the existence of so many food-deficit countries demanding such large quantities of food imports and whether these buoyant demand conditions would continue if all the current food-deficit countries were to succeed in achieving domestic food self-sufficiency or turning themselves into food-exporting countries. Further, Lewis's method of trying to determine the price of exports in terms of the *domestic* opportunity cost of labor is plausible only for goods that are not internationally traded. We may accept the fact that people in the service industries in different countries tend to be paid, not by the quality or quantity of the services they perform, but by the opportunity cost of their labor in the alternative domestic uses. But this is precisely because services are not internationally tradable. In considering the prices of internationally traded goods, however, we cannot avoid taking into account the world market demand and supply of the exportable goods in addition to the domestic opportunity costs of labor.

Finally, we must be cautious in drawing conclusions about the appropriate trade policies for individual underdeveloped countries from the aggregate statistical trends presented by Lewis. A somewhat different perspective is obtained when we look at the world market demand prospects for the nonfood agricultural exports from the standpoint of individual underdeveloped countries, in terms of each country's share of the world market for particular products and the substitution possibilities between a country's export product and rival products on a broader definition of the concept of the "commodity." Empirical

16. Ibid., p. 26.

studies along these lines have suggested a more optimistic view of the possibilities of expanding nonfood agricultural exports from the underdeveloped countries.[17]

Similarly, the overall price trends in sugar and rubber between 1880 and 1960, which Lewis presents as the leading examples of the case where growth in productivity in nonfood exports has failed to benefit the producing countries, do not bring out the contrasting experiences of the individual countries that have specialized in these products. For instance, Lewis's argument does not explain why a country such as Malaysia which specializes in rubber exports should have a distinctly higher standard of living than neighboring countries like Thailand and Burma which export rice. In spite of the green revolution, a country such as Malaysia may still benefit from continuing to specialize in export products such as rubber and palm oil rather than attempting to attain self-sufficiency in rice.[18]

To summarize, the agricultural economists' general assumption that all food-deficit underdeveloped countries, irrespective of their factor endowments, are likely to have a potential comparative advantage in increasing domestic food production cannot be accepted without a detailed study of the individual circumstances of each country. Their general presumption, while plausible in the case of a large, densely populated country like India, becomes less plausible when extended to the more numerous smaller export economies, such as Malaysia. If a country does *not* have a potential comparative advantage in domestic food production, then policies aimed at increasing agricultural sector contributions (i) to the domestic food supply and (iv) to the foreign exchange supply would be inconsistent. Contributions (i) and (iv) would be compatible only if we could accept, on empirical grounds, that a particular undeveloped country had a potential comparative advantage in food production.[19] For the sake of simplifying the argument, I will adopt this assumption in the remainder of this chapter.

17. See Ian Little, Tibor Scitovsky, and Maurice Scott, *Industry and Trade in Some Developing Countries* (New York: Oxford University Press, 1970), chap. 7; also Barend A. de Vries, *The Exporting Experience of Developing Countries* (IBRD, 1967).
18. See Hla Myint, *Southeast Asia's Economy: Development Policies in the 1970's* (1972), chap. 2.
19. We are here concerned with the minimum condition of compatibility between (i) and (iv) based on the *direction* of potential comparative advantage. Albert Berry has pointed out that, even if a country has a comparative advantage in food production, a policy of artificially encouraging domestic self-sufficiency in food beyond the *extent* of comparative advantage would still lead to inefficient use of resources.

### 3. ARE AGRICULTURE'S FOUR "FUNCTIONS" MUTUALLY COMPATIBLE?

Given that appropriate agricultural development policies can increase agricultural sector contributions (i) and (iv), what about its other contributions: (ii) to the size of the domestic market, and (iii) to the supply of domestic savings? It is frequently assumed in a tacit way that (ii) and (iii) would follow more or less automatically from the fulfillment of (i) and (iv). But in the open-economy setting this would not necessarily be true, and we are faced with a number of difficulties arising from the attempt to extend the relationships defined in terms of the closed-economy model to the open economy.

Most agricultural economists take it for granted that a rise in agricultural productivity would tend to increase the size of the domestic market of the manufacturing sector in two ways. First, a rise in the total income of the agricultural sector would raise the purchasing power of the farmers. Second, the expansion of domestic food production (identified with peasant farming) relative to nonfood agricultural exports (identified with plantations) would result in a more equal income distribution and thus, out of a given increase in total income, more would be spent on manufactured goods. But in the open-economy setting there is no automatic or invariable relationship between increased spending by the agricultural sector and the creation of a larger domestic market for the manufacturing sector. The farmers may prefer to spend the foreign exchange saved from import substitution in food on imported manufactured goods. Thus an increase in domestic self-sufficiency in food can spontaneously increase the size of the domestic market only to the extent that domestically manufactured products are competitive with imports. Beyond this point, determined by comparative costs, the agricultural sector can be made to contribute to the size of the domestic market only by restricting imports and by giving tariff protection to domestically manufactured goods. Thus we must ask whether the agricultural economists who emphasize the importance of the agricultural sector's contribution to the size of the domestic market are willing to accept a policy of protecting domestic manufacturing industry to promote this aim.

A further conflict arises between the agricultural sector's function (ii) of enlarging the size of the domestic market by increased spending and its function (iii) of increasing the supply of domestic savings. Johnston and Mellor recognize the existence of this conflict and put a greater emphasis on (iii), that is, on "the capital contribution of agriculture in the early stages of structural transformation."[20]

A policy of making the agricultural sector increase its contribution to the size of the domestic market beyond the point dictated by comparative costs, by giving tariff protection to domestic manufacturing industry, implies the encouragement of the domestic manufacturing sector at the expense of the agricultural sector. In theory, this policy, which for convenience I shall call policy (ii), can be distinguished from policy (iii), whose aim is to raise the agricultural sector's contribution to the supply of domestic savings above the voluntary savings of the farmers. Policy (iii) is not concerned with encouraging the manufacturing sector, as such, at the expense of agriculture; it is concerned with increasing the supply of domestic savings and the rate of capital accumulation at the expense of present consumption in both sectors. Thus while policy (ii) can be fulfilled by putting a tariff solely on imports, policy (iii) requires the imposition of a uniform tax or "revenue tariff" on both imported and domestically manufactured consumer goods. In theory, the savings extracted from the agricultural sector by policy (iii) need not be used only for industrial investment but may be reinvested in the agricultural sector. But in practice, in underdeveloped countries, the bulk of the savings squeezed out of the agricultural sector is devoted to investment in the manufacturing sector. Thus we shall here concern ourselves mainly with the realistic case where the agricultural sector's contribution to the supply of domestic savings is to be interpreted as the compulsory savings extracted from this sector for the purpose of increasing investment in the manufacturing sector.

Given this interpretation, there is a serious conflict between policies designed to promote agricultural sector functions (i) and (iv) on the one hand and policies designed to promote functions (ii) and (iii) on the other. In order to enable an underdeveloped country to realize its potential comparative advantage in food production, it would be necessary to subsidize the agricultural sector to some degree. That is to say, the agricultural sector would have to be cast in the role of a net recipient of resources rather than a net donor of resources. This implies that the farmers should not be compelled to pay more than the world market prices for the domestically manufactured products. On the other hand, the policies designed to increase the size of the domestic market of the manufacturing sector, by tariff protection and the compulsory extraction of agricultural savings for industrial investment, imply that

20. Johnston and Mellor, "Role of Agriculture," p. 581.

the agricultural sector would be cast in the role of a net donor of resources.

The agricultural economists fall into two groups in the way they react to this dilemma. On the one hand, there are some writers, notably W. H. Nicholls and T. W. Schultz, who unequivocally advocate policies to promote agricultural sector functions (i) and (iv) while rejecting policies for promoting domestic industrialization denoted by agricultural sector functions (ii) and (iii).[21] This is a logically consistent approach which will be supported in the course of my analysis. On the other hand, other writers, notably Johnston and Mellor, emphasize the complementary relations between the agricultural and the manufacturing sectors and thus advocate all the policies designed to promote the four "standard" functions of agriculture simultaneously. Thus they conclude their influential 1961 paper as follows:

> We part company with those who draw the inference that agricultural development should precede or take priority over industrial expansion. . . . It is our contention that "balanced growth" is needed in the sense of simultaneous efforts to promote agricultural and industrial development. We recognize that there are severe limitations on the capacity of an underdeveloped country to do everything at once. But it is precisely this consideration which underscores the importance of developing agriculture in such a way as to both minimise its demand on resources most needed for industrial development and maximise its net contribution required for general growth.[22]

There are several weaknesses in this approach. First, as for the complementary relations between the agricultural and the manufacturing sectors, the earlier hope that industrial expansion, by drawing away a significant amount of labor from agriculture, would relieve the presure on land and facilitate agricultural improvements has not been fulfilled. In most underdeveloped countries, the employment-creating capacity of industrial expansion has been small and the migration of labor from agriculture to industry induced by the higher wages in the latter has merely converted rural disguised unemployment into the more serious problem of open unemployment in the big cities. Thus, the

21. Nicholls, "Agricultural Surplus"; T. W. Schultz, "Comment" on J. W. Mellor's paper "Toward a Theory of Agricultural Development," in *Agricultural Development and Economic Growth*, ed. H. M. Southworth and B. F. Johnston (Ithaca, N.Y.: Cornell University Press, 1967), p. 63.
22. Johnston and Mellor, "Role of Agriculture," pp. 59–91.

theory of the complementary relations between industry and agriculture has to be based mainly on the existence of the technical "linkages" between the two sectors. It is accordingly claimed that industrial expansion would encourage agricultural development by creating the demand for domestically produced raw materials, while agricultural expansion, with the spread of the green revolution, would encourage industrial development by creating the demand for locally manufactured farm inputs, particularly fertilizers and farm equipment. In the open-economy setting, however, this theory of mutual interactions between the agricultural and the manufacturing sectors through linkages needs to be treated with great caution. This is so because the linkages are conceived purely in terms of the technically given and fixed coefficients of production and do not take into account the relative costs and prices of the domestically produced products and the imported products.

Consider, for instance, the argument that the encouragement of the domestic textile industry by protection would create the demand for domestically grown cotton. In order to take advantage of this linkage, the country must either have unused land suitable for cotton cultivation or otherwise have a potential comparative advantage in cotton growing. But if this is true it would be more economical to encourage cotton growing for export directly, by subsidies and by improving the transport and marketing facilities, instead of encouraging it indirectly, by setting up a textile industry under protection. Conversely, if the country does not have a comparative advantage in textile manufactures, the domestic cotton growers would not benefit from the linkages. Judging from the results of Pakistan's attempt to encourage cotton and jute manufactures by keeping down the price of domestic raw cotton and jute, the farmers are more likely to suffer from the existence of "backward linkages" from an inefficient manufacturing industry.[23] Turning now to the linkages created by the agricultural sector's demand for manufactured inputs, the fact that the green revolution would increase the demand for, say, chemical fertilizers does not necessarily mean that the underdeveloped countries could then set up a fertilizer industry on an economical basis. In fact, as Johnston himself has recently pointed out, in collaboration with P. Kilby, technological advances, particularly in nitrogen fertilizer, have drastically reduced the costs of production for

23. See Hla Myint, "International Trade and the Developing Countries," in *International Economic Relations,* ed. Paul A. Samuelson (New York: St. Martin's Press, 1969), pp. 15–34; also Little, Scitovsky, and Scott, *Industry and Trade,* p. 74.

the new type of large-scale plants which have a maximum capacity well beyond the requirements of any single underdeveloped country. They conclude that "an individual underdeveloped country is probably misallocating its scarce capital resources if it immediately attempts to realize the linkages that become possible with rising usage of chemical fertilizer."[24]

In addition to the linkages argument based on the complementary interrelationships on the demand side, economists who wish to combine agricultural and industrial development have also tried to soften the competitive claims of the two sectors on the available scarce resources. This is done by trying to draw a sharp distinction between the abundant resources required mainly in agricultural development and the scarce capital and foreign exchange resources required especially for industrial development. Thus it is argued that the agricultural sector's demand for the scarce resources most needed for industrial development can be minimized by encouraging a labor-using and capital-saving pattern of agricultural development. This is of course another aspect of the semi-open economy model. Previously, it was argued that domestic food production could be expanded without reducing export production. Now it is argued that agricultural expansion can take place without reducing industrial expansion. We have already come across two important considerations that undermine this convenient supposition. First, as Ishikawa has pointed out, the success of the seed and fertilizer technology crucially depends on a high standard of irrigation and flood control, and in many underdeveloped countries the provision of these facilities would require very heavy capital investment. Second, if the Johnston-Kilby analysis is correct, the underdeveloped countries would need to import, in the short and medium terms at least, large quantities of chemical fertilizer if their agricultural development is not to be handicapped by the higher costs of the domestically produced fertilizer. Thus even a "labor-using" and "capital-saving" pattern of agricultural development may generate a very considerable demand on the scarce resources required for industrial development.

If this is accepted we cannot ultimately avoid the problem of choice between giving priority to industrial development or to agricultural development. We can either regard the manufacturing sector as the "infant industry" sector which should be subsidized to realize the

24. B. F. Johnston and P. Kilby, "*Agricultural Strategies, Rural-Urban Interactions, and the Expansion of Income Opportunities,* mimeographed (November 1971), p. 148.

potential comparative advantage in manufacturing, or alternatively, we can regard the agricultural sector as the infant industry sector which should be subsidized to realize its potential comparative advantage in food production. Here it turns out that, in the light of the modern formulation of the infant industry argument, the agricultural sector's claim to be treated as the infant sector is much stronger than the traditional claim made for the manufacturing sector.

The traditional infant industry argument suffers a number of defects. First, it was applied exclusively to manufacturing industry presumably on the ground that there is no scope for "learning by doing" in agriculture. This assumption has now been shattered by the green revolution. Second, it was formulated as an argument for granting tariff protection rather than subsidies. International trade theorists have now shown that a "domestic distortion" should be cured by applying a subsidy directly at the source of the distortion in the allocation of resources within the domestic economy, and not by a tariff duty on imports, which would introduce a new source of distortion. Thus from the standpoint of trade theory, tariff protection and import restrictions as such, whether applied in favor of the manufacturing sector or the agricultural sector, would be undesirable. The significance of this argument has been enhanced by the green revolution, which makes it technically possible for some of the food-deficit underdeveloped countries to attain domestic self-sufficiency in food. For example, the food-deficit countries of Southeast Asia, notably Malaysia and the Philippines, are now increasingly tempted to achieve the national goal of food self-sufficiency, not only by giving subsidies but also by introducing protection and restrictions on food imports. Third, the traditional infant industry argument contended that temporary protection during the period of infancy should be given to a new industry provided it had a genuine prospect of lowering its costs and becoming internationally competitive after the initial period. It has now been shown that the mere fact that a new industry would pass through an initial period of losses is not a sufficient argument for giving it special encouragement. For, if its future profits were genuinely high enough to more than compensate for the initial losses, private investors would not be deterred from entering the industry, provided that there was a capital market to advance loans to tide them over the initial losses. Thus, in order to make a case for giving a subsidy to a particular type of investment, it must be shown that it yields social benefits and "external economies" which are not appropriable by the private investor, who would therefore not enter into this particular type of economic activity in the absence of special encouragement.[25]

In this modern version of the argument, agriculture has a stronger claim to be treated as an "infant industry" on three counts. First, in most underdeveloped countries, the capital market in the agricultural sector is notoriously underdeveloped compared with the capital market in the manufacturing sector. As a rule, a peasant farmer is less able to obtain loans, to take the risks of trying out new methods, and generally to take the long-range view than is a businessman starting a new industry.[26] Second, agricultural technology is more location specific than industrial technology, and thus research work to adapt new agricultural discoveries to local farming conditions is likely to yield higher social returns. Third, since the peasant farmers are generally likely to be more ignorant than the industrialists about the existing improved methods of production, educational and extension services in the agricultural sector are likely to yield greater social returns. The pioneering farmer who experiments with a new method and popularizes it in his district is likely to generate external economies and should be encouraged by subsidies.

My analysis showing the conflict between the policies designed to promote agricultural sector functions (i) and (iv) on the one hand and the policies designed to promote functions (ii) and (iii) on the other is based on the assumption that the savings extracted from the agricultural sector are used to the benefit of the industrial sector. This makes the effects of policies (ii) and (iii) very similar. In either case the farmers are made to pay a higher-than-world-market price for domestically manufactured products, and thus the agricultural sector is made to increase its contributions to the size of the domestic market and the supply of domestic savings. In theory, however, it is possible to combine policies (i), (iv), and (iii) by interpreting (iii) purely as a policy aimed at increasing the agricultural sector's contribution to savings and capital accumulation as such. To simplify exposition I will adopt the unrealistic assumption that the savings extracted from the agricultural sector are ploughed back into agricultural development in the form of subsidies

25. Harry G. Johnson, "Optimal Trade Intervention in the Presence of Domestic Distortions," in *Trade, Growth and the Balance of Payments*, ed. Richard E. Caves, Peter B. Kenen, and Harry G. Johnson (Chicago: Rand McNally, 1965), pp. 3–34.

26. See Little, Scitovsky, and Scott, *Industry and Trade*, p. 120, for a similar argument.

and capital investment. This would have the effect of making the farmers pay more for their purchase of manufactured consumer goods, whether imported or domestically produced, while making them pay less for the farm inputs which would be let in duty free or would be subsidized. How far such a policy would promote agricultural development depends on the relative importance of the two types of inputs or investable resources: (a) those that can be provided only by the government by increasing taxation and saving, and (b) those that can be provided by the farmers for themselves, if they are given adequate economic incentives in the form of cheap consumer goods. The second type of input or investable resources consists mainly of the underutilized labor of the farmers and their families which can be used in the creation of the simpler forms of agricultural capital, particularly small-scale land improvement and irrigation works. In most underdeveloped countries the potential contribution to agricultural capital formation from this source is likely to be at least as important as government investment in large-scale agricultural projects. Even in purely quantitative terms, the small additions to agricultural capital made by millions of peasant farmers may add up to a very large aggregate capital formation. But what is more important is that, qualitatively, this type of capital formation is likely to be highly productive, because it is undertaken in the light of intimate knowledge of local conditions. The agricultural economists have argued that the "strategic inputs" to be provided by the government would mobilize the abundant resources to be provided by the farmers. In practice, however, in many underdeveloped countries, the large-scale irrigation works provided by the government have frequently not been fully or effectively used because of the lack of small-scale irrigation works, for example, the ditches connecting the water supply to the individual plots. Thus, once the large-scale irrigation or highway works have been constructed, the provision of adequate economic incentives to the farmers to undertake small-scale irrigation works, farm roads, and the like has a vital role to play in "filling in the corners" of the agricultural sector's capital structure and raising the effectiveness of the whole productive framework.[27]

27. It is theoretically possible to try to mobilize the farmers' investable resources by giving subsidies to small-scale investment projects instead of offering economic incentives in the form of cheaper consumer goods (See Ishikawa, *Economic Development*, pp. 137–55). But in practice it may not be easy to administer such a subsidy effectively, in view of the somewhat inefficient administrative machinery in the rural areas in many underdeveloped countries.

Finally, in order to obtain a reasonable perspective on the agricultural sector's role in contributing to the supply of savings, it is necessary to take into account the possibility of obtaining external capital funds to supplement domestic savings. Even leaving aside international aid, the present-day underdeveloped countries have better access to the international capital market than is suggested by the analogy with the countries at "the early stages of development." They do not suffer from any special handicap in obtaining long-term loans for investment in social overhead capital from the World Bank, the regional development banks, and other international financial institutions. The chief obstacle has been their limited capacity to absorb capital on commercial terms, and this lack of absorptive capacity will not be cured by trying to squeeze more savings out of the agricultural sector. The underdeveloped countries can also attract private foreign investment into the manufacturing sector. The trouble here is that they tend to offer tax concessions and protection to the wrong type of foreign investment, generally the "sophisticated" manufacturing industries producing consumer durables for which the size of their domestic market is usually too small, while discouraging on nationalistic grounds foreign investment in the traditional, or labor-intensive, manufacturing industries where they may have a comparative advantage. In either case the agricultural sector is made to contribute to the cost of these policies.

To summarize, the customary approach to the role of agriculture in economic development suffers from not clearly distinguishing whether the contributions of the agricultural sector are to be interpreted in a voluntary or a compulsory sense. If we interpret the contributions in the compulsory sense of the term, then the practice of emphasizing all the four standard contributions of agriculture implies the advocacy of policies designed to increase the agricultural sector's capacity to make all four contributions at the same time. With this interpretation, there is a conflict between policies aimed at promoting agricultural sector functions (i) and (iv) if an underdeveloped country does not have a comparative advantage in food production. Even assuming functions (i) and (iv) to be compatible, there is a serious conflict between policies designed to promote (i) and (iv) on the one hand and those designed to promote (ii) and (iii) on the other, on the realistic and commonly adopted assumption that the savings extracted from the agricultural sector are appropriated for industrial investment. Finally, there is a conflict between the need to give adequate economic incentives to the farmer to adopt the improved agricultural methods and the desire to squeeze as much savings as possible out of the agricultural sector. This conflict may be eased by taking into account the possibility of obtaining external capital funds to supplement domestic savings.

# 13

---

## Agriculture in Two Types of Open Economies

JOHN C. H. FEI AND GUSTAV RANIS

A full examination of the role of the agricultural sector in development has to be undertaken in a historically and typologically sensitive context. That is to say, the "ideal" developmental role of agriculture will differ depending on the historical phase of development in which a country finds itself, as well as on the particular type of developing country we are concerned with.

In Simon Kuznets's view, colonialism as a long epoch of growth ultimately gives way—if a country is successful—to a long epoch of modern growth.[1] During the past decades, longer in the case of Latin America, most less developed countries (hereafter LDCs) can be said to have been attempting a transition growth from the first to the second epoch. Moreover, that transition process itself can be further demarcated as containing a number of subphases, and the role of the agricultural sector will depend on just where the country finds itself in this historical perspective.

We must recall that the contemporary developing world is not a homogeneous mass but contains several types of "families." There exists, for example, a family of large, labor-surplus, natural-resource-poor economies (India and China), in which the domestic orientation—or closed-economy characteristics—dominate. There is another family of small, labor-surplus, natural-resource-poor economies (Taiwan, Korea, and historical Japan), in which foreign trade necessarily plays an important role. There is a family of small natural-resource-rich countries (for example, the Philippines, Malaysia, much of Latin America), in which trade again is important. Finally, there are develop-

1. Simon Kuznets, *Modern Economic Growth: Rate, Structure, and Spread* (New Haven: Yale University Press, 1966).

ing countries (e.g., in Africa, south of the Sahara) that are still strug-
gling with the construction of the infrastructure prerequisites (human
and physical) for attempted transition to modern growth. In each of
these the role of the agricultural sector over time can be expected to be
quite different.

In the case of the large (relatively closed) labor-surplus economy,
such as India, a balanced growth process with respect to the simultaneous "modernization" of agriculture and industry is inevitable. The
role of the agricultural sector here is to supply wage goods, manpower,
savings, and a market, in order to foster, over time, the expansion of the
nonagricultural sector. This is the central focus of the closed, dualistic
economy models which will not be elaborated on here.[2] Similarly, we
shall not, in this chapter, deal with the African type, in which the
establishment of infrastructure and the expansion of directly productive
capacity must proceed side by side, for some time to come, in the
context of a relatively more plentiful supply of land and a large urban
services sector.

In this chapter, rather, we shall concentrate on the role of the agricultural sector in only two types of developing countries, namely, in
the open economies of the labor-surplus, natural-resource-poor variety
and in the open economies of the natural-resource-rich type. Section
1 will deal with the former, as exemplified by the cases of Korea, Taiwan,
and historical Japan. Section 2 will deal with the latter, as exemplified
by much of Latin America. Finally, a brief summary of our conclusions
is presented in section 3.

## 1. THE NATURAL-RESOURCE-POOR OPEN ECONOMIES

The role of the agricultural sector in the course of the transition growth
of postwar Korea and Taiwan may be thought of as part of an evolutionary process as the economy moved through two subphases of
growth, first import and then export substitution. Both economies,
and Japan (if in a somewhat milder form) at an earlier time, exhibited
common characteristics, as can be explained in part by their family

2. See, however, Arthur Lewis, "Development with Unlimited Supplies of Labor,"
*Manchester School of Economics and Social Studies* 22 (1954); John C. H. Fei and
Gustav Ranis, *Development of the Labor Surplus Economy: Theory and Policy*
(Homewood, Ill.: Richard D. Irwin, 1964). Also, B. F. Johnston and J. W. Mellor,
"Agriculture in Economic Development," *American Economic Review* 51 (1961):
566–93.

affinity in respect to certain basic economic and geographic characteristics or initial conditions, and in part by their common colonial heritage. Taking the case of Taiwan as an example, these particular typological characteristics include (1) open dualism characterized by the coexistence of a large food-producing agricultural sector, a small externally oriented agricultural export sector (mainly sugar), and a small nonagricultural sector; (2) a situation of labor surplus, that is, an excess supply of labor at given institutionally determined wages, especially in traditional agriculture; (3) a shortage of natural resources, that is, land and exportable raw materials for the long run; (4) a relatively favorable rural infrastructure as a consequence of the rural emphasis of Japanese colonial rule; and (5) a relatively favorable human resources endowment traceable once again partly to Japanese colonial education policy and partly to the postwar influx of entrepreneurial talent from the mainland.

These background conditions gave Taiwan a peculiar set of initial conditions to fuel transition growth, admittedly shared by relatively few contemporary LDCs. As a small economy Taiwan's relatively favorable human resources could ultimately reveal themselves in terms of a changing pattern of comparative advantage in trade. But an examination of the transitional growth path which permitted an ever greater participation of the country's total human resource endowment, as the economy moved from a land-intensive to a labor-intensive basis of production and exports, is likely to be most instructive.

Central here is the crucial role of agricultural productivity increases facilitated by the aforementioned favorable inherited rural infrastructure, plus land reform. This point is best illustrated by tracing the economic flows between food-producing, internally oriented agriculture; cash-crop–producing, export-oriented agriculture; nonagriculture; and the foreign sector. We can only briefly (and roughly) sketch these, with the help of figure 13.1.

During Taiwan's import substitution subphase, 1950–59, foreign exchange was allocated increasingly to capital goods imports and away from consumer goods imports (line 1) in order to build up domestic import-substituting industrial capacity. As a consequence, imported consumer goods as a fraction of domestic output of such goods can be seen to decline (line 2). This is import substitution in the domestic market sense. Moreover, consumer goods imports of course become a declining fraction of total imports. This is import substitution in the

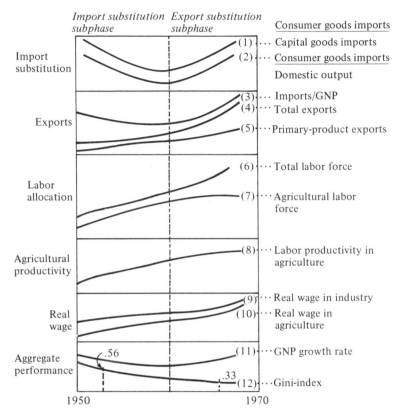

Fig. 13.1:  Taiwan

foreign exchange allocation sense. Both lines 1 and 2 follow a *U*-shaped pattern, indicating that primary import substitution came to a close by the end of the fifties.

Import substitution is thus an internally oriented growth phase, with the country utilizing directly interventionist policies, via the distortion of a number of factor and commodity markets. This can be seen through the gradual decline of foreign trade as a fraction of gross national product (GNP) in line 3. From the export data, moreover, we note that during the import-substitution subphase Taiwan retains her essentially colonial characteristics in that primary product exports account for over 80 percent of total exports. Traditional exports, in other words, finance the import substitution process once foreign exchange earnings are diverted from colonial to developmental purposes (lines 4 and 5).

During the export substitution subphase (1960–70), on the other hand, we note that the importance of the primary-product exports in the total declines dramatically, so that by about 1970 such exports account for about 20 percent of a total which is itself growing at rates of more than 30 percent a year (lines 4 and 5). What lies behind this pronounced export substitution phenomenon is the replacement of natural resources by other primary factors of production, mainly labor and entrepreneurship, as the major source of value added in production and trade. During this period of increased external orientation, the imports/GNP ratio rose, and by the end of the sixties it had climbed back up to the 40 percent level (line 3).

In a small labor-surplus economy like Taiwan full advantage of the opportunities of international trade could thus be taken. Once entrepreneurial capacity had matured sufficiently, it was possible to combine it with the large supply of unskilled labor to penetrate international markets for labor-intensive consumer goods. The data indicate (lines 6 and 7) that the total labor force employed in the agricultural sector increased slightly during the import substitution subphase while the fraction employed in all of agriculture declined slowly. However, in the export substitution subphase the labor reallocation process accelerated, more than doubling (from 3 to 6.5 percent annually), with the agricultural labor force declining not only in percentage terms but absolutely by the end of the sixties.

The historical importance of import substitution, in terms of both entrepreneurial maturation and agricultural infrastructure preparation, is that of a period of preconditioning. The preparation for successful transition to export substitution requires marked productivity increase in the food-producing agricultural sector, in the sense that this represents a major source of investment finance,[3] a source of labor supply maintained at a low wage, and a continuously expanding market for the new industrial consumer goods (line 8). Our data also indicate that the real wage (lines 9 and 10) increased only very modestly during the import substitution subphase, and more markedly in the course of export substitution, especially toward the end of the sixties. The two

3. Accounting for close to 30 percent of the total during the period 1952–54 to 1967–69.

factors that account for the relative wage stability, namely, expansion of agricultural productivity and the existence of surplus labor in the agricultural sector, have major growth- and distribution-theoretic implications. Moreover, the often encountered widening of the inter-sectoral wage gap seems to have been avoided. By the end of the sixties the real wage began to increase more rapidly, heralding the end of the labor surplus condition and taking Taiwan toward the modern growth epoch in which the export base is shifting away from unskilled labor and toward skill- and technology-intensive commodities.[4]

We can then more explicitly raise the question as to the role of the agricultural sector in this historical perspective. Clearly this role can be examined only by differentiating between the role of export-oriented primary-product agriculture and that of domestically oriented food-producing agriculture. The role of the export-oriented primary-product agricultural sector will be seen to be especially crucial in the import substitution subphase, that of the domestically oriented food-producing agricultural sector becoming relatively more crucial in the export substitution subphase.

Export-oriented primary-product agriculture plays three essential roles in the import substitution subphase, providing foreign exchange, domestic finance, and markets. First, and most obvious, exports from, say, sugar provide the foreign exchange earnings that are used for the importation of the capital goods and raw materials needed to build up new capacity in the import-substituting industries.[5] Second, profits of the primary-product export sector represent a major source of savings to finance industrial capital accumulation.[6] To implement this import-substitution strategy a particular policy package that serves to transfer these export-related profits to the new industrial entrepreneur-ial class is resorted to. This package consists of inflation, budget de-ficits, overvalued exchange rates, strong protection, and low interest rates, among other things. The profits of the industrial entrepreneurs

4. While considerations of space preclude further elaboration, the above summary is based on conclusions that can be deduced theoretically. (See John C. H. Fei and Gustav Ranis, "A Model of Growth and Employment in the Open Dualistic Economy: The Cases of Korea and Taiwan," *Journal of Development Studies,* forthcoming).

5. This is in contrast to the colonial epoch, when the foreign exchange proceeds flowing from these exports were used for the expansion of the primary-product ex-port base itself and/or the importation of consumer goods to satisfy workers' demands for necessities and capitalists' demands for luxuries.

6. Again, in contrast to the colonial epoch, when such savings could be repatriated to the mother country whenever it suited the "global calculations."

are thus partly of a windfall nature because of the fact that profits are transferred to them via the policy-caused distortion of relative factor and commodity prices. The income of the primary-product export sector, moreover, continues to constitute an important source of purchasing power, but now as a market for the expanding import-substituting consumer goods industries. The existence of such a visible and protected domestic market is essential for a time to reduce uncertainty and to permit the maturation of a relatively inexperienced indigenous entrepreneurial class.

In Taiwan the import substitution subphase also witnessed a very rapid expansion of agricultural productivity in the domestically oriented food-producing agricultural sector. Here again the system was favored by the colonial heritage of fifty years of rural infrastructure creation, both physical (especially in irrigation) and organizational (especially the farmers' associations) which proved indispensable for the achievement of a sustained agricultural productivity increase.[7] But postindependence governments complemented this by (1) land reform, (2) price policies favorable to agriculture, and (3) increased fertilizer and new seed input combinations, as well as other measures. The result was a sustained expansion of agricultural labor productivity during the import substitution subphase, not only contributing to fairly sustained overall growth, but also providing the foundation for the emergence of the export substitution subphase during the sixties. For it is through the expansion of agricultural productivity that enough of the labor force can be released at only slightly rising wages, being fed via the wages fund in the form of the food surplus simultaneously being generated. This freeing of labor by a domestically produced food surplus also represents a financial phenomenon in that in this way agricultural savings are mobilized to finance capital accumulation in the nonagricultural sector. Once domestic entrepreneurs have matured sufficiently they are in a position to take advantage of the plentiful cheap labor supply by restructuring output and penetrating foreign markets via the exportation of labor-intensive industrial commodities. This process, of course, also continues to be supported by the export of the still-large primary-product agricultural sector, even as the relative importance of industrial exports continues to grow.

7. Other members of the same family of countries may have to spend considerable resources and energy during the import substitution subphase to construct an equally high level of physical and organizational infrastructure. This is true even of Korea, for example, whose rural sector received substantially less attention and resources than Taiwan's during the Japanese colonial period.

Viewed in this historical perspective, the agricultural sector's role in the labor-surplus open economy is thus a very important one. In the long run, when all is said and done, it is likely that a natural-resource- or land-poor country like Taiwan will ultimately be an importer of food, with the agricultural sector not playing as prominent a role. In fact, in spite of the technological spurt provided by the green revolution in the early sixties, the rate of increase of agricultural productivity began to slow down by the end of the decade. With the "mopping up" of Taiwan's labor surplus having by then been completed, and with a condition of unskilled labor shortage now prevailing, it is likely that agriculture, acting like any normal homogeneous sector—that is, like part of the input/output structure of the mature economy—will become increasingly oriented toward greater capital intensity, via tractorization and the like, to avoid too strong a rise in the commercialized agricultural, and industrial, wage levels. But what is nevertheless crucial is that, in the course of the transition period, agriculture played its crucial historical role to the hilt—moreover, that without its central contribution the rest of the success story depicted above would not have been possible.

## 2. THE NATURAL-RESOURCE-RICH OPEN ECONOMIES

Another type of developing country, which stands in contrast to the above, is represented by many of the small or moderately sized natural-resource-rich countries of Latin America[8] and Southeast Asia (such as the Philippines, Thailand, and Malaysia). The attempt at transition to modern growth in this type of economy may be viewed as a prolonged case of import substitution. For example, the observable growth pattern of a "typical" Latin American country (e.g., Brazil or Chile) for the period 1930–70 may be portrayed by the time series presented in figure 13.2. We shall use a simple theoretical framework to sort out the essential relations among them.

As previously, we must again distinguish between two agricultural sectors: the domestically oriented, food-producing agricultural sector and the export-oriented, primary-product agricultural sector. These two sectors exist side by side with a substantial nonagricultural sector. Let us use the term "enclave" to encompass both the commercialized sectors, that is, the primary-product export sector and the nonagri-

8. There the attempted transition started much earlier, in response to the great depression of the 1930s.

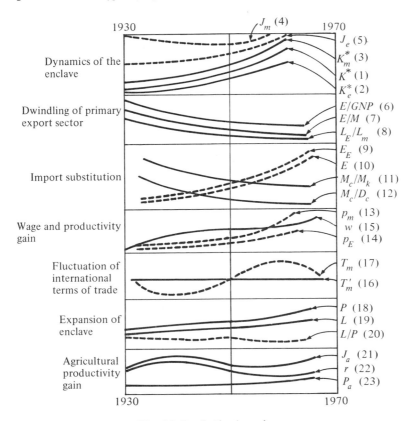

Fig. 13.2: Latin America

cultural sector, in contrast to the subsistence agricultural hinterland. The term enclave thus refers to the fact that these are the more dynamic, capitalistic sectors, while the food-producing, subsistence agricultural sector is relatively stagnant and noncommercialized. We shall assume that the output of the primary-product sector is entirely exported and that the output of the nonagricultural sector is entirely consumed at home.

Concentrating first on the enclave, we shall assume that labor and capital are used as inputs in both sectors. When the total capital stock and labor force are given, the production possibilities and allocation of resources in the enclave are given by the Edgeworth box $OL_1B_1K_1$ in figure 13.3. The commercial orientation of the enclave justifies the assumption that resources in the enclave are employed efficiently, or neo-

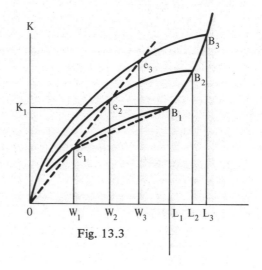

Fig. 13.3

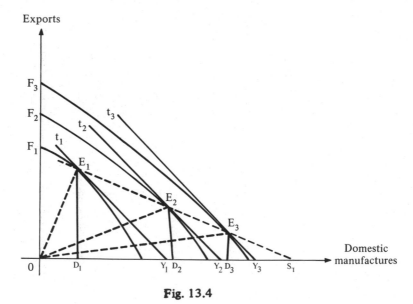

Fig. 13.4

classically, so that resource allocation between the two sectors is given by the contract curve $Oe_1B_1$. The same argument also permits us to generate the production frontier (i.e., the $F_1$-curve) in figure 13.4.

The dynamics of this enclave have two dimensions. First, there is the observable phenomenon of capital deepening, that is, capital per head ($K^*$) in the enclave increases through time (see line 1 in figure 13.2). Second, innovations occur in both enclave sectors as depicted by lines 4 and 5 in figure 13.2, showing the intensity of innovation for the industry subsector, $J_m$ (line 4), and for the primary-product export subsector, $J_e$ (line 5). In figure 13.3 the observed capital deepening is indicated by the locus of factor endowment points $B_1$, $B_2$, $B_3$, and so on. This leads to the shifting of the contract curve ($Oe_1B_1$, $Oe_2B_2$, $Oe_3 B_3$) and the expansion of the production frontier ($F_1$, $F_2$, $F_3$ curves) in figure 13.4. When innovation occurs at the same time, we may assume, for simplicity's sake, that innovations in both subsectors are neutral, leaving the production contours and the contract curve unchanged. However, the expansion of the production frontier ($F_1$, $F_2$, $F_3$) is now assumed to summarize both the capital-deepening and the innovation effects.

A crucial feature affecting the operation of this open economy is the international terms of trade facing the primary-product exporting subsector. There are two dimensions to this phenomenon: the long-term trend, $T_m'$ (line 16 in figure 13.2), and fluctuations around that trend, $T_m$ (line 17). While these two characteristics, which have given occasion to a good deal of literature in connection with Latin American and other development,[9] should be analyzed separately, we shall concentrate here only on the trend by assuming constancy in the international terms of trade. Any actually observed increase or decrease could be treated in a similar fashion.

In figure 13.4 these constant international terms of trade are indicated by the parallel lines $t_1$, $t_2$, and $t_3$. This establishes the production equilibrium points $E_1$, $E_2$, and $E_3$ on the production frontier and the corresponding allocation points $e_1$, $e_2$, and $e_3$ on the contract curve of

9. On the secular trend, see, for example, R. Prebisch, "Commercial Policy in the Underdeveloped Countries," *American Economic Review* 44 (1959): 251–73; and on the fluctuations around that trend see B. F. Massell, "Export Concentration and Export Earnings," *American Economic Review* 54 (1964): 47–63, and also W. C. Brainard and R. N. Cooper, "Uncertainty and Diversification in International Trade," *Studies in Agricutlural Economics, Trade, and Development* 8, no. 3 (1968).

figure 13.3. Referring to the latter, we see that the constant input ratio[10] in the industrial sector (slope of $Oe_1$) is larger than that of the primary-product export sector (slope of $B_1e_1$), reflecting the fact that the output of the industrial sector is relatively more capital using than that of the primary-product export sector.[11] Thus, with constant terms of trade, a capital deepening for the enclave as a whole constitutes capital deepening for both component producton sectors, $K_e^*$ and $K_m^*$, as shown in lines 2 and 3 of figure 13.2.

Referring once again to the production frontier (figure 13.4), the equilibrium points $E_1$, $E_2$, and $E_3$ thus trace out the Rybczynski line, which indicates that the country is becoming more specialized in the production of the capital-intensive (i.e., domestic manufacturing) goods at the expense of the primary-product sector. This conclusion is reflected by the reality of Latin America in at least three ways. First, there is evidence of an increasingly internal orientation, in the sense that trade (exports as a fraction of enclave GNP) declines through time. This expected time pattern is shown in line 6. In the frontier map (figure 13.4), the enclave GNP is measured by $OY_1$, $OY_2$, and $OY_3$ while imports are $D_1Y_1$, $D_2Y_2$, and $D_3Y_3$. Second is the observed phenomenon of a relative dwindling of the primary export sector in an output sense, and third is a similar dwindling in a labor reallocation sense. In the production frontier of figure 13.4, the ratio of the value added of the two sectors is given by the slope of the radial lines ($OE_1$, $OE_2$, $OE_3$). In figure 13.3, the labor force allocated to the domestic industrial sector is alternatively $OW_1$, $OW_2$, $OW_3$, while the total enclave labor force is $OL_1$, $OL_2$, $OL_3$. The relative dwindling of the primary export sector in these two senses is shown by lines 7 and 8 in figure 13.2.

It is often asserted that transition growth in the typical Latin American country constitutes a prolonged process of import substitution. It should be recognized that this notion is relative to the fact that, throughout the transition period, the exports of Latin America remain dominated by primary-product exports. While line 10 indicates total exports, $E$, line 9 shows primary-product exports ($E_E$), which indicates that the ratio of the two remains approximately constant. The so-called export substitution phenomenon, so outstanding a feature of Taiwanese growth, simply has not as yet occurred in the span of the thirty or forty years of attempted transition in Latin America.

10. Under assumptions of constant returns to scale and following the Stolper-Samuelson theorem.

11. By empirical observation. Land is assumed to be encompassed by "technology change" in the latter sector.

In other words, the process of import substitution has continued on the strength of the fuel provided by the primary-product export base, as also was the case in Taiwan in that phase. Lines 11 and 12 again present us with the empirical sense of import substitution, that is, in the foreign exchange allocation sense (line 11) and in the domestic market sense (line 12). Given the gradual dwindling of the primary-product export sector, this prolonged process of import substitution is, moreover, showing signs of terminating in the long run. The prolongation of import substitution in Latin America, relative to Taiwan, is due to the favorable natural resource basis in primary-product agriculture and is reflected by the high innovation intensity (line 5) which summarizes the natural resource potential. However, as in Taiwan, there exists a long-run tendency toward termination of the import-substitution phase; in the process of continued capital deepening, termination occurs at $S_T$ in figure 13.4, where the Rybczynski line intercepts the horizontal axis. The empirical counterpart of this phenomenon is the gradual running out of import substitution possibilities for primary or consumer goods and increased emphasis on backward linkage import substitution (capital goods, processing, etc.) en route gradually to termination in the long run.

Meanwhile, the dynamics of the enclave, reflecting capital deepening and innovation, lead to a continuous increase of labor productivity in both production sectors ($p_m$, $p_E$) as well as an increase in the real wage ($w$), as shown in lines 13, 14, and 15. The source of these gains should be carefully explained. In the absence of innovations, and if only capital deepening takes place in the enclave, both labor productivities and the real wage remain constant through time.[12] The constant real wage is shown in figure 13.5 by the horizontal line passing through $w_1$, the magnitude of the constant real wage in terms of industrial goods (i.e., the real wage shown is the marginal physical product for the industrial subsector of the enclave). If innovation takes place, the marginal product rises in proportion to innovation intensity, as shown by the increasingly higher horizontal wage lines passing through $w_1$, $w_2$, and $w_3$.

In figure 13.2, notice that a vertical line has been drawn demarcating the existence of two hypothetical subphases during this prolonged period of import substitution. It may be assumed that $J_m$ (enclave

12. This follows directly from the Stolper-Samuelson theory of factor price equalization. For constant international terms of trade, the productive equilibrium points ($E_1$, $E_2$, $E_3$) in figure 13.4 lead to the allocation equilibrium points ($e_1$, $e_2$, $e_3$) which fall on a straight line (figure 13.3). This imposes a constancy of the input ratios in both industries and hence a constancy in the productivity of labor and the real wage.

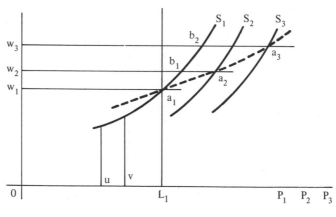

Fig. 13.5

innovational intensity) is falling in the first subphase and rising in the second subphase. If that were the case empirically (as indicated by line 4), then, under constant international terms of trade, we would predict that the real wage and labor productivity would rise more rapidly in the first than in the second subphase. If not, the reverse obtains.[13] In short, in the open economy, under our assumptions, capital deepening is irrelevant to productivity and wage behavior.

Up to now we have discussed only performance within the enclave. Our attention will now shift to the relationship between the enclave and the traditional agricultural hinterland, which is still an important sector, even in countries that have been in transition for several decades. In figure 13.5, suppose the total population is indicated by $OP_1$. We can then postulate a supply curve of labor to the enclave as denoted by the curve $S_1$. This curve indicates the amount of labor that will be supplied to the enclave at each level of real wage (in terms of industrial goods). The allocation of the economy's total labor force between the enclave and the traditional agricultural sector is then indicated by the equilibrium point $a_1$ where the supply curve intersects the horizontal line through $w_1$. This point determines the size of the labor force allocated to the enclave $(OL_1)$, and those remaining in the traditional agricultural sector $(P_1L_1)$.

13. In the Taiwan case discussed above, the two subphases depicted constituted observed phenomena. In the present instance such phasing is only for hypothetical analytical purposes, at least at this stage. We have not as yet examined the behavior of $J_m$ over time in individual countries belonging to this family.

What lies behind the supply curve of labor ($S_1$) is a subject that has been exhaustively discussed in the development literature relevant to the dualistic economy. For example, Arthur Lewis postulated the existence of such a curve and developed his thesis of an "unlimited supply curve of labor" based on it.[14] What lies behind this supply curve are such factors as (1) population size and (2) the state of agricultural technology. Once the economy's total population and the state of the arts in agriculture are given, the curve is determined. The fact that the curve as depicted in figure 13.5 is rising is due to the fact that, as more labor is allocated out of the agricultural sector (e.g., from $u$ to $v$), there results a shrinkage of the agricultural labor force. Given a constant state of agricultural technology, this would cause a shrinkage of the per capita supply of agricultural output. This will, in turn, lead to a worsening of the industrial sector's terms of trade, and if the agricultural real wage, in terms of agricultural goods, prevailing in the hinterland is institutionally fixed, then the industrial real wage in terms of industrial goods will rise as a consequence.[15]

The supply curve may be shown to shift through time, from $S_1$ to $S_2$, $S_3$, and so on, indicating an improvement in agricultural technology, that is, in the agricultural supply condition. This, in turn, leads to the shifting of the equilibrium position tracing out the locus $a_1$, $a_2$, $a_3$, in figure 13.5. Thus, through time, we can determine the proportion of the labor force still active in food-producing agriculture and the proportion allocated to the enclave. The observable empirical reality of a typical Latin American country, of course, is that the total population or labor force ($P$) is itself expanding (see figure 13.2, line 18) while the labor force in the traditional agricultural sector ($L$) is expanding more slowly (line 19). As a result, the proportion of the total labor force engaged in traditional agriculture ($L/P$) declines over time (line 20).

Thus we see that the expansion of the commercialized enclave sector, relative to the rest of the economy, depends, in the first instance, on the rapidity with which the supply curve shifts up. Once we admit the possibility of population growth proceeding at the same time, the net

14. To Lewis, the supply curve has a long horizontal portion depicting the "unlimitedness" of the labor supply over a substantial range (Lewis, "Development with Unlimited Supplies of Labor"). See also Fei and Ranis, *Development of the Labor Surplus Economy*.

15. The extent to which the supply curve will rise depends upon the strength of the law of diminishing returns to labor in the agricultural sector. In the (unlikely) event that there is completely redundant labor in that sector, there will be no rise at all, since its removal and reallocation would not occasion any diminution of agricultural output.

shift of the supply curve will depend on the relative strength of Malthusian pressures and the intensity of innovation in the agricultural sector. This is indicated by means of the "struggle" between agricultural innovation ($J_a$) in line 21 and population growth ($r$) in line 22. The net effect of these two forces determines the path of agricultural labor productivity ($p_a$) in line 23.

With respect to the rate of population growth (line 22) we may accept the real world conclusion drawn by Kuznets that it is likely to accelerate during the early subphase of transition (for fertility as well as mortality reasons) and to decelerate later on. The agricultural innovation intensity (line 21) is shown to lie normally (but not always) above the population growth rate curve (line 22). Unless the innovation rate exceeds the population growth rate, there can be no shift of the labor supply curve. In the razor's edge case, when innovation is just strong enough to equal population growth, development will proceed along the same supply curve, that is, through equilibrium points $a_1$, $b_1$, and $b_2$. There results, to be sure, some labor force reallocation to the enclave, the rapidity of which depends on the rate of innovation intensity in the enclave.[16]

The role of the agricultural sector in the development of a country of the open, natural-resources-rich type must thus be broken down again into that of the traditional agricultural sector and that of the primary-export-oriented agricultural sector. The significance of the former is that it is only through a fast enough rate of technology change in agriculture, able to more than compensate for population growth, that a sustained shift of the center of gravity of the economy to the commercialized enclave can be effected. The often referred to "stagnation" of the traditional agricultural sector in Latin America can thus be seen to be responsible for the slow expansion of the enclave labor force and the general inability in most cases to shift from land-intensive to labor-intensive industrial exports (i.e., from import to export substitution).

The strength of the primary-product export sector relative to that of the industrial sector, on the other hand, determines the allocation of labor force and output between primary-product exports and domestic industry. The role of the enclave agricultural subsector then is to provide the fuel, consistently and over long periods of time, to keep import substitution going. In the absence of a relatively favorable and

16. This can be understood as people being "pulled" out of subsistence agriculture, with agricultural labor productivity rising along a given supply curve.

diversified natural resource base and relatively good demand conditions abroad, there is much less pressure than in the family of open labor-surplus economies to shift into a new pattern or subphase of transition.

### 3. SUMMARY

For the two types of LDCs considered in this chapter, the underlying differences in the initial conditions with respect to the abundance of natural and human resources substantially delimit the systems' growth potential. The relatively labor-abundant open economy has little choice but to shift away from a growth pattern based on primary-product exports to one based on unskilled labor and (later) skilled labor, capital, technology, and so on. In contrast, for the relatively natural-resource-rich open economy, the observed fact is that such a shift has not yet taken place and that such countries in the main continue to rely on the export of the services of land as their main source of comparative advantage.

We have noted that the natural-resource-poor type of open economy ultimately tries to shift its major source of developmental fuel from land-intensive to unskilled-labor-intensive goods. The policy stages required to make this move from import to export substitution are by no means politically easy; vested interests in the protected industrial sector will be loath to give up windfall profits, while civil servants are equally loath to give up the power that comes with direct controls. But the necessity is at hand to utilize the limited bounty of both agricultural sectors in order to put the economy into a position from which to move forward into its next subphase, en route to economic maturity.

The natural-resource-rich or Latin American type of economy, on the other hand, has a somewhat different prognosis. It can afford to prolong import substitution substantially, even taking it into backward linkage areas that are more and more costly in terms of capital and technology. There is some question as to the final termination of this prolongation process and of the likelihood of occurrence of a new subphase of growth (e.g., export substitution, or something else). Our theory does not answer that, but it does suggest what factors are likely to be relevant; namely, the termination of the import substitution process is likely to be indefinitely postponed as long as, externally, the economy does not experience a worsening trend in its international terms of trade and, internally, the primary-product export supply does not run into severe natural resources bottlenecks. In that case, import substitution prolongation will take place because, essentially, the society can "afford" it.

Consequently, looking toward the future, we see less pressure here for the modernization of the food-producing agricultural hinterland as well. If such modernization of the agricultural sector does in fact occur, then the new growth subphase that emerges is likely to be a type of export substitution that may combine natural resources with both labor and capital. For example, both labor-intensive industrial exports and the processing of primary goods for export may play a role. What may be in store for some Latin American cases or Malaysia, for example, countries that do not have a labor surplus, is a path approaching the New Zealand case over time; and in a country like the Philippines, which does have a substantial surplus of unskilled labor ready to be utilized, the future path may combine features of Taiwan and New Zealand.

# 14

## The Political Economy of Rice Production
## and Trade in Asia

C. PETER TIMMER AND WALTER P. FALCON

Economists have generally viewed the importance of rice in Asia in two widely different manners. Asian development specialists, accustomed to two-sector models, have thought of rice as the key wage good whose price is determined in competitive markets. Commodity specialists, by contrast, have known it as a political commodity, on whose domestic price governments rise and fall, and whose trade is so conditioned by special deals and constraints that "the international price of rice" has little meaning. The result has been that the commodity specialists, buried in the vastly contradictory political and economic data, felt an economic model of the Asian rice economy was impossible; the development specialists were frequently not aware of the necessity.

In this chapter, we attempt to build a preliminary empirical model from diverse national data for rice. The ultimate function of this model is to explain the magnitude, direction, and price of international rice flows. These variables are the crux of the matter; a model that can explain them will explain other important variables along the way.

After reviewing some of the national production, consumption, price, and trade statistics that have made the problem appear so perplexing, we use a traditional, neoclassical economic model to explain certain

This essay is the first working paper of a twenty-seven month project to study the political economy of rice in Asia under funding provided by the United States Agency for International Development, contract no. CM-ASIA-C-73-39. The views expressed are not necessarily those of the sponsoring agency.

We have received helpful comments from William Jones, Bruce Johnston, Raj Krishna, Scott Pearson, Vernon Ruttan, and Lance Taylor, and from participants at an Agricultural Development Council Seminar on Trade organized by George Tolley. The usual disclaimers apply.

differences among these magnitudes. The results, documented by some surprisingly good statistical relationships, show that varying production levels are well explained by an analysis of covariance production functions containing area harvested and fertilizer applications as continuous arguments. Relative fertilizer applications, in turn, depend to a large degree on the price of rice relative to fertilizer. These relationships extend the search for the "cause" of production and trade levels beyond the confines of neoclassical economics. We therefore introduce a political economy model to provide a framework for explaining national differences in rice policies. In the last section of the chapter we illustrate the approach by using Indonesia as a case study.

## 1. THE INTERNATIONAL RICE ECONOMY IN PERSPECTIVE

Table 14.1 provides an array of statistics that describe the quantitative role of rice in Asia. Per capita domestic disappearance levels (approximately equal to direct personal consumption except in regions where significant quantities are used for animal feed) are remarkably different for similarly situated countries and remarkably similar for vastly different ones. The levels in Laos, the Khmer Republic (Cambodia), Thailand, and Burma are nearly double the West Malaysia level. And yet Japan and Indonesia have almost identical per capita consumption. China, India, and the Philippines have similar but significantly lower levels, reflecting alternative sources of carbohydrates in these diets.

The yield data show a fairly continuous distribution from a low of 1.70 metric tons per hectare in Burma to a high of 5.64 tons in Japan. The three highest yields occur in Japan, South Korea, and Taiwan, which have some of the poorest soils among these Asian countries. The success of these countries derives from greater environmental control, especially of water; from differential use of inputs, such as fertilizers and high-yielding varieties; and from temperate patterns of rainfall and sunshine.[1]

Of all the contrasts among countries, however, perhaps the most

1. For a fuller discussion of the impact of environmental factors see S. C. Hsieh and Vernon Ruttan, "Environmental, Technological, and Institutional Factors in the Growth of Rice Production: Philippines, Thailand and Taiwan," *Food Research Institute Studies* 7, no. 3 (1967): 307–42; and Randolph Barker and Mahar Mangahas, "Environmental and Other Factors Influencing the Performance of New High Yielding Varieties of Wheat and Rice in Asia," reprinted in *Current Papers from the Department of Agricultural Economics, International Rice Research Institute* (Los Banos: Rice Policy Conference, May 1971).

striking is in prices. The differences in national prices, shown in table 14.2, are so substantial that they would not be affected greatly by

Table 14.1: Comparative Country Data on Rice, 1970

| Country | Production (1,000 metric tons, rough) | Area (1,000 ha.) | Yield (tons per ha.) | Domestic disappearance per capita (kg. milled rice) | Proportion of area in new varieties |
|---|---|---|---|---|---|
| Burma | 8,162 | 4,809 | 1.70 | 174.1[a] | 4.0 |
| Ceylon | 1,616 | 611 | 2.65 | 124.5 | 4.5 |
| China, Mainland | 102,000 | —[b] | 3.05 | 88.4 | — |
| India | 63,672 | 37,432 | 1.70 | 77.7 | 14.7 |
| Indonesia | 17,529 | 8,186 | 2.14 | 104.3 | 11.3 |
| Japan | 16,479 | 2,923 | 5.64 | 102.9 | — |
| Cambodia | 3,814 | 2,399 | 1.59 | 265.2[a, c] | — |
| Korea, South | 5,476 | 1,209 | 4.55 | 139.1 | — |
| Laos | 916 | 670 | 1.37 | 215.2[a] | 7.0 |
| Malaysia, West | 1,429 | 525 | 2.72 | 130.1 | 24.5 |
| Pakistan | 20,014 | 11,416 | 1.75 | 115.8 | 41.7[d] |
| Philippines | 5,343 | 3,113 | 1.72 | 93.3 | 50.3 |
| Taiwan | 3,226 | 776 | 4.16 | 149.8 | — |
| Thailand | 13,270 | 6,727 | 1.97 | 218.5[a] | 2.1 |
| Vietnam, North | 5,000 | 2,500 | 2.0 | 156.7 | — |
| Vietnam, South | 5,716 | 2,510 | 2.28 | 238.1[a] | 19.3 |
| United States | 3,758 | 734 | 5.12 | 3.9 | — |

a. Domestic disappearance levels for the delta countries of Indochina include very substantial amounts of rice used as animal feed. For estimates of magnitudes for the Mekong Delta in South Vietnam, see Richard J. Foote, "Supply and Utilization Tables for Rice and Implications for Policy and Research: Final Report" (Saigon: United States, Agency for International Development, December-January 1971–72).

b. Not available.

c. 1969–71 average.

d. West Pakistan only.

*Sources:* Data for area, production, and yield for all countries except Mainland China from Food and Agriculture Organization (FAO), *Production Yearbook 1971.* Mainland China yield from United States Department of Agriculture, *World Agriculture Production and Trade, Statistical Report* (Washington, D.C.: Government Printing Office, December 1971). Per capita consumption is calculated from production milled at 66 2/3 percent, plus or minus net trade from FAO, *Trade Yearbook 1971;* population from United Nations, *Demographic Yearbook,* and idem, *Monthly Bulletin of Statistics,* November 1972. Change of stocks for the United States, Japan, and the Philippines included; data for change of stocks from United States Department of Agriculture, *Foreign Agriculture,* (Washington, D.C.: Government Printing Office, February 1972), August 30, 1971. Proportion planted in high-yielding varieties from United States Department of Agriculture, *Imports and Plantings of High-Yielding Varieties of Wheat and Rice in the Less Developed Nations,* (Washington, D.C.: Government Printing Office, Feb. 1972).

adjustments for inappropriate exchange rates or differences in quality
and variety. Japan's price was nearly double South Korea's, the next
highest price; nearly triple the prices in Taiwan and Ceylon; and seven
times the Thai and Indonesian prices.

The ratio of rice price to fertilizer price, partly because it circumvents
exchange rate problems and partly because of the element of input price,
is a truer reflection of the price climate facing farmers. These ratios for
1970 are also shown in table 14.2 and the differences are even more
pronounced than those for rice prices alone. Not only did Thai and
Burmese farmers receive low prices for their rice, but they paid high
prices for their fertilizer. This rice-to-fertilizer price ratio plays an

Table 14.2: Comparative Price Data for Fertilizer and Rice

| Country | Paddy price to producers (U.S. cents per kg.) | Price of fertilizer nutrients to producers (U.S. cents per kg.) | Ratio of paddy price to fertilizer price | Paddy yield in 1970 (m. tons per ha.) |
|---|---|---|---|---|
| Japan | 30.7 | 21.5[a] | 1.428 | 5.64 |
| South Korea | 18.4 | 19.1 | 0.963 | 4.55 |
| Taiwan | 11.7[a] | 26.2[a] | 0.447 | 4.16 |
| Malaysia | 8.8 | 20.3[b] | 0.433 | 2.72 |
| Ceylon | 11.3 | 15.8 | 0.715 | 2.64 |
| Indonesia | 4.5 | 15.2 | 0.296 | 2.14 |
| Thailand | 4.5[a, c] | 14.3–50.0[d] | 0.315–0.090 | 1.97 |
| Philippines | 7.0[e] | 17.3[e] | 0.405 | 1.72 |
| Burma | 3.1[f] | 25.1[g] | 0.124 | 1.70 |

a. Average for 1969/70 and 1970/71.

b. Calculated from *Padi Farming in West Malaysia,* Department of Agriculture,
March 1972.

c. Calculated from the price of #2 paddy in Bangkok multiplied by 0.9 to get a
producer price.

d. The fertilizer price is a price for ammonium phosphate in 1967. The lower price
assumes both the nitrogen and $P_2O_5$ content contribute to increasing output; the
higher price assumes only the nitrogen content is effective. All other fertilizer prices
are for the nitrogen content of urea.

e. The producer price of paddy was P0.45 per kilogram and the nutrient cost of
fertilizer was P1.111 per kilogram. The "fluctuating free exchange rate" of P6.43 =
$1.00 was used for the conversion.

f. Figure for 1965. Trade reports indicate the paddy to fertilizer ratio improved by
1970, so a figure of 0.20 was used in the analysis.

g. Figure for 1969/70 only.

*Sources:* Paddy prices for South Korea, Indonesia, and the Philippines and the
fertilizer nutrient price for Indonesia are from *Viewpoints on Rice Policy in Asia* (Los
Banos: International Rice Research Institute, 1971). All other prices are from FAO,
*Production Yearbook 1971.* In all cases attempts have been made to approximate
prices actually faced by producers.

important role in the analysis in section 2, below, where it turns out to be a critical factor in explaining indirectly the patterns of international trade in rice.

What are these trade patterns, and how have they changed? Figure 14.1 documents the major exporting and importing countries in 1970 (shown as circles and squares, respectively). The width of the arrows indicates the size of the trade flows. Two striking patterns are apparent. First, the traditional Asian exporters (Thailand, Burma, Khmer Republic, Taiwan) were the main suppliers of the traditional Asian importers (Ceylon, India, Hongkong, Malaysia, Singapore, Philippines). Perhaps surprisingly, China was also a major supplier in this market. The second striking feature was the large volume of exports of United States rice to Asia. South Korea, South Vietnam, and Indonesia received the greater part of their rice imports from the United States under extremely favorable concessional terms. Indeed, the United

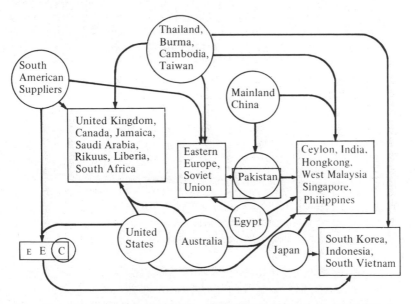

Fig. 14.1 Origins and Destinations of World Rice Exports, 1970 (Circles indicate exporters; squares, importers) *Source:* James W. Willis, *Review of World Rice Markets and Major Suppliers*, United States Department of Agriculture, Economic Research Service, report no. 246 (Washington, D.C., August 1972).

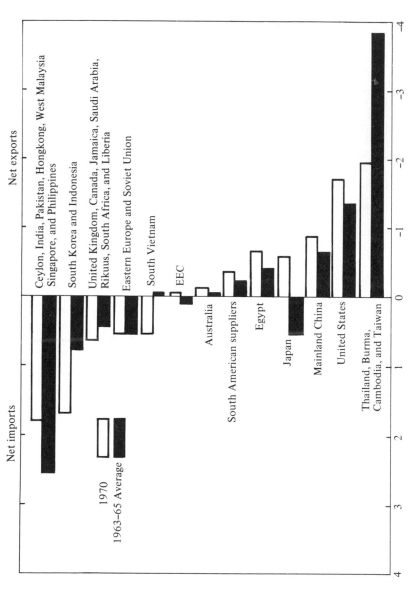

Fig. 14.2: Net Exports and Imports of Rice in 1970, Compared with the 1963–65 Average (Million metric tons of milled rice) *Source:* Food and Agriculture Organization, *Trade Yearbook* (Rome, 1969, 1970, 1971).

States exported more than 60 percent of its rice crop, all of it under some type of direct or indirect trade subsidy program. Relative to production, the United States exports more rice than any other farm commodity.

Changes in rice trade patterns over time have also been dramatic. Especially important is the ratio of trade to production. This ratio has become so small that for the 1969–71 period only about 7 million tons of milled rice moved annually in international trade, amounting to a mere 3.5 percent of world production. Figure 14.2 shows the major recent changes in the composition of the market. The share of the traditional East Asian suppliers has been considerably reduced, with the United States, China, and other less developed countries increasing their share of a slightly smaller absolute total. The importing countries also showed impressive changes: South Vietnam changed from an exporter to a major importer, South Korea increased its imports, and the Philippines changed (temporarily) from importer to exporter.[2] Similarly, Japan went from the world's largest importer to a large exporter over a four-year period.

In quantitative terms, the largest reduction in imports occurred in India, Pakistan, Ceylon, Malaysia, the Philippines, and the other traditional Asian importers, largely as a result of the green revolution. Whereas in the twenty-year period from 1934 to 1953 production of rice grew by only 0.7 percent annually in these Asian countries, between 1964 and 1970 the annual growth in production was 5 percent—a substantially higher rate. Such growth had a profound impact on the internal markets for rice in these countries and on the international market as well.

After the green revolution in the late 1960s international prices began a strong downward trend. Indeed, figure 14.3 shows that until mid-1972 prices declined by about 30 percent in each succeeding year. The price of Thai white export rice (15 percent brokens) was $220 per metric ton in February 1968, but only $90 in March 1972. Beginning in July 1972, however, prices soared and by September they had increased by 50 percent. These price movements mirror two aspects of the world rice market: successive downward movements reflecting the sensitivity of international prices to long-run technological change, and the recent rapid rise resulting from the razor-thin nature of the short-run rice market, a function of production instability due to weather condi-

2. The move from net importer to net exporter occurred in 1968 for the Philippines and is not apparent from the data in figure 14.2.

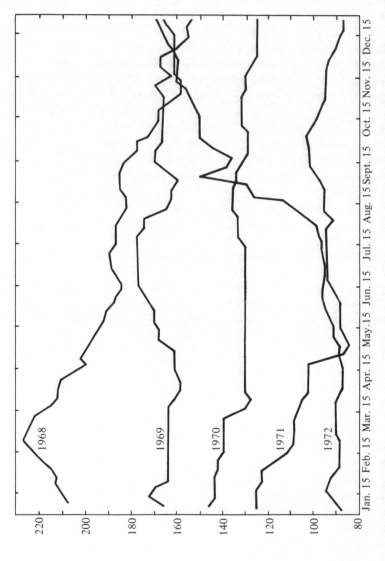

Fig. 14.3:  Price of Thai White Export Rice, 15 Percent Brokens, 1968–72 (Dollars per metric ton) *Source:* United States Department of Agriculture, Marketing Service (SF), *Rice Market News*, various issues.

tions and the very small percentage of trade relative to production. When broad areas suffer drought or flood, as in 1972, the international rice market is ill equipped to respond quickly with increased supplies; this lack of responsiveness in turn causes substantial price instability.

Two aspects of market differentiation deserve special mention. Concessional sales comprise a large and growing proportion of the market. The largest concessional supplier has been the United States, whose exports in this category have more than doubled since 1965, totaling 1.2 million tons in 1970.[3] Japan also entered this side of the market in a major way, beginning in 1969. Japanese rice, together with American and Italian concessional components, accounts for nearly one-third of total rice exports. Since much of this concessional rice has moved at extremely favorable terms, the market effect has been dramatic. Even with a clause specifying "usual marketing requirements" in most concessional agreements, the traditional exporters have been understandably upset by this type of competition. Arrangements whereby a rice "loan" is to be repaid in kind after thirty years complicate the concept of *an* international price for rice.

The market is also differentiated by the types of rice traded internationally. The longer-grain *Indica* varieties constitute much of the rice moving commercially, the remainder being the rounder, more glutinous *Japonica* types. Extra-long-grain scented rices, preferred by certain Middle East importers, are relatively unimportant in quantitative terms. Broadly speaking, round-grain rice is preferred in Japan, Korea, and Taiwan, whereas long-grain varieties are preferred in most other countries. Such taste preferences tend to constrain the movements of rice among countries. On the other hand, much rice is traded on government account, and at times consumer preferences are subordinated to other objectives. The Sino-Ceylon barter agreements in which rice has been exchanged for rubber appear to be one example of this phenomenon.

The very small international market for rice is thus made even smaller by government-to-government concessional sales and varietal differentiation. In turn, the leverage effects of relatively minor swings in production on international prices are substantial. For this reason almost all national governments insulate their domestic rice economy from the international market by enacting licensing arrangements for importing or exporting, or frequently by reserving such trade solely for govern-

3. See James W. Willis, *Review of World Rice Markets and Major Suppliers*, United States Department of Agriculture, Economic Research Service, Report no. 246 (Washington, D.C.: Government Printing Office, August 1972).

ment account. Consequently, the international price for rice need not bear any resemblance to national prices. On the other hand, these national prices—for rice and for inputs used in rice production—are a substantial determinant of international trade.

## 2. RICE PRICES, PRODUCTION, AND TRADE IN ASIA

Explaining international trade in rice, and the prices at which it is traded, is the goal of our model of the Southeast Asian rice economy.[4] As a first step in this process, we estimate a cross-section production function for rice for the years 1962 to 1970. Later we intend a similar treatment for consumption, but for the present analysis we take it as given.[5] A standard Cobb-Douglas production function containing rice area harvested and total fertilizer nutrients applied, with separate intercepts for each country, adequately explains the widely different levels of rice production in the nine countries examined (i.e., Japan, Burma, Thailand, Indonesia, Philippines, Malaysia, Taiwan, Ceylon, and South Korea).

The area devoted to rice culture in any country is a long-run policy variable, especially in terms of irrigation investment, but it has limited flexibility in the short run. Thus, for a given area, the emphasis must be on the factors that affect output in the short run, such as fertilizer. Holding other things constant, the level of fertilizer application determines yields. But what determines the level of fertilizer application? Much of the agricultural development literature talks of farmer knowledge, environmental factors, effectiveness of the extension service,

4. Our model builds on the earlier work of E. Roy Canterbery and Hans Bickel ("The Green Revolution and the World Rice Market," *American Journal of Agricultural Economics* 53, no. 2 [1971]: 285–94), and on that of Virach Arromdee ("Economics of Rice Trade among Countries of Southeast Asia" [Ph.D. diss., University of Minnesota, 1970]). Both the approach and the results, however, are substantially different. Other appraisals of trade are given in J. Norman Efferson, "Current Developments in Rice Production and Trade in Asia," *Rice Journal,* August 1968; and United States Department of Agriculture, Economic Research Service, *World Demand for Grain in 1980, with Emphasis on Trade by the Less Developed Countries,* report no. 75 (Washington, D.C.: Government Printing Office, December 1971).

5. Assuming that consumption is fixed is not quite as arbitrary as it might seem. The price used in our analysis is the price of paddy relative to the nutrient content of fertilizer. The rice price can be held constant while varying the price of fertilizer, thus leaving the nominal price to the consumer unaffected. On the other hand, the policy implications of varying rice versus fertilizer prices are quite different, and the next stage is to include consumption in the analysis.

and so on, but a factor that is frequently taken for granted is fertilizer price. At least for our sample of countries, the intensity of fertilizer application is highly correlated with the price of rice relative to fertilizer. Since yields depend on fertilizer application, they also depend, via the production function, on the relative price ratio. What is needed initially, therefore, is an empirical estimate of the aggregate fertilizer-yield relationship for this sample of countries.

In the Cobb-Douglas, log-linear form usually assumed for this type of analysis, the critical parameter is the elasticity of output with respect to fertilizer: $\beta$ in our notation. From a production function of the general form

$$Q = AH^\alpha F^\beta,$$

where $Q$ represents rice production, $H$ is area harvested, and $F$ is fertilizer application, the relationship between output ($Q$) and the ratio of rice price to fertilizer price to the farmer ($P$) is of the form

$$Q = (A\beta H^\alpha P^\beta)^{\frac{1}{1-\beta}}.$$

The elasticity of $Q$ with respect to $P$ is $\beta/(1 - \beta)$.

The results of several alternative ways of estimating the value of $\beta$ (the coefficient attached to $F$ or $F/H$) are presented in table 14.3. All six equations were run on the same set of data: rice production, area harvested, and total fertilizer nutrients applied *to all crops* for each country for each of the nine years from 1962 to 1970. The major criticism that can be levied against these data is that no attempt was made to determine amounts of fertilizer actually used on rice. For equations 1, 5, and 6 in table 14.3 the implicit assumption is that all countries used a constant proportion of the fertilizer on rice. For equations 2, 3, and 4, the assumption is less restrictive: the proportion of total fertilizer applied to rice can vary from country to country but must still be constant over time for each country.

For those accustomed to supply analysis for a single country's time series data, the results must look surprisingly good. The reason, of course, is the much greater range of variation in both dependent and independent variables achieved by pooling the cross-section of countries. In view of the underlying nature of these data, the consistently reasonable magnitudes of the estimated parameters and their high statistical significance are very reassuring.

Equation 1 is the two-factor production function in its simplest form.

Table 14.3: Rice Production Functions, 1962–70

*Variables and coefficients*

| Equation number | $R^2$ | Dependent | $A_0$ | $A_i$ | F | $F_i$ | H | F/H |
|---|---|---|---|---|---|---|---|---|
| 1 | 0.9372 | Q | −1.049 (−3.2) | — | 0.251 (12.4) | — | 0.867 (32.56) | — |
| 2 | 0.9952 | Q | −2.377 (−2.6) | * | 0.123 (4.9) | — | 1.202 (10.1) | — |
| 3 | 0.9973 | Q | −3.769 (−2.8) | * | 0.028 (0.8) | * | 1.473 (9.8) | — |
| 4 | 0.9955 | Q | −2.413 (−2.7) | * | 0.109 (4.3) | * | 1.222 (10.4) | — |
| 5 | 0.6641 | Q/H | 0.035 (0.5) | — | — | — | — | 0.206 (12.5) |
| 6 | 0.7077 | Q/H | −1.049 (−3.2) | — | — | — | 0.118 (3.4) | 0.251 (12.4) |

*Country-Specific coefficients[a]

| Country | Equation 2 $A_i$ | Equation 3 $A_i$ | Equation 3 $F_i$ | Equation 4 $A_i$ | Equation 4 $F_i$ |
|---|---|---|---|---|---|
| Japan | 0.627 (4.0) | −5.561 (−2.0) | 0.467 (2.4) | −1.929 (−1.5) | |
| South Korea | 0.779 (3.4) | −0.542 (−0.4) | 0.157 (1.5) | −1.494 (−1.3) | 0.181 (2.0) |
| Taiwan | 0.865 (3.3) | −2.481 (−1.5) | 0.333 (2.5) | −1.301 (−1.2) | |
| Malaysia | 0.736 (2.3) | 3.070 (2.4) | −0.134 (−1.5) | 0.809 (2.6) | |
| Ceylon | 0.468 (1.6) | −2.943 (−1.7) | 0.370 (2.6) | 0.537 (1.9) | |
| Indonesia | −0.273 (−3.9) | −0.496 (−0.6) | 0.028 (0.4) | −0.248 (−3.5) | |
| Thailand | −0.191 (−3.7) | −1.345 (−2.8) | 0.111 (2.3) | (−0.176) (−3.4) | |
| Philippines | −0.369 (−3.8) | −3.570 (−4.7) | 0.301 (4.4) | (−0.329) (−3.4) | |

a. A separate intercept for Burma was dropped from Equations 3, 4, and 5 to avoid a singular matrix. Its effect is included in $A_0$.

*Note:* All functions were estimated in double logarithmic form. Thus both the dependent and independent variables shown are logarithms. Numbers in parentheses are *t*-statistics. There are 81 observations (9 countries for 9 years).

The fertilizer coefficient, $\beta$, is 0.251, significant at any reasonable level. The acreage coefficient is 0.867, also highly significant. The sum of these coefficients is 1.119, which seems to indicate a surprising degree of scale economies; however this probably reflects variables omitted from the equation, plus the use of high-yielding irrigation projects as a means of expanding acreage. Equation 6, although in per hectare form, is identical to equation 1. The coefficient attached to $H$, 0.118, reflects the "leftover" scale economies when the other variables are divided by $H$. Equation 4 is a yield function estimated directly. Even without an independent coefficient for $H$, the value of $\beta$ is 0.206, sufficiently close to the first value of 0.251 to be reassuring.

Equation 2 reports the results of ·a partial analysis-of-covariance specification, with each country permitted a separate intercept value. All countries have the same fertilizer response coefficient in this specification. Total production rather than yield is the dependent variable, for reasons of convenience: the results are not affected, as equations 1 and 6 show. The results are very much as would be predicted by the "management bias" literature.[6] The area coefficient rises—and use is negatively correlated with "management" (i.e., wih the capital inputs that seem to accompany "good management"). The fertilizer coefficient is cut almost exactly in half. Fertilizer use is highly correlated with other output-raising *but excluded* variables. Of course, "management" is only one of these variables, and the separate intercept terms serve as a proxy for all of them. In particular, differences among countries in labor use, irrigation facilities, and sunlight are captured largely by the equation 2 covariance country intercepts shown in table 14.3.

The relationship between the "biased" value of $\beta$ from equation 1, 0.251, and the "unbiased" value from equation 2, 0.123, is essentially the relationship between long-run and short-run adjustment coefficients. In the long run the response to a change in fertilizer application is greater than in the short run because all the other output-changing inputs correlated with fertilizer use have time to change as well. In the short run, holding all these things constant (in the country-specific intercept), the "pure" response to fertilizer is much lower—in fact, half.

Equations 3 and 4 test the legitimacy of pooling the nine countries' data in the first place. Equation 3 introduces separate slope coefficients for fertilizer (but not for harvested area) for each country along with the separate intercepts of equation 2. The improvement in explanatory power, from an $R^2$ of 0.995 to 0.997, is very small but significant. In-

6. See Zvi Griliches, "Specification Bias in Estimates of Production Functions," *Journal of Farm Economics* 39, no. 1 (1957): 8–20; Irving Hock, "Estimation of Production Function Parameters Combining Time-Series and Cross-Section Data," *Econometrica* 30, no. 1 (1962): 34–53; Yair Mundlak, "Empirical Production Function Free of Management Bias," *Journal of Farm Economics* 43, no. 1 (1961): 44–56; C. Peter Timmer, "On Measuring Technical Efficiency," *Food Research Institute Studies* 9, no. 2 (1970): 91–171.

donesia, Malaysia, and Burma seem to have smaller fertilizer response coefficients than indicated in equation 2, while Japan, Taiwan, Ceylon, and the Philippines have larger coefficients. However, a number of both slope and intercept coefficients are insignificant, and equation 3 does not provide a satisfactory explanation of similarities and differences among countries.

A much more satisfactory explanation is achieved in equation 4, which introduces a single slope-modifying coefficient for the three temperate countries in our sample: Japan, South Korea, and Taiwan. Although none of these countries has significant slope or intercept differences from the overall sample when introduced individually (not shown in table 14.3), a single slope modifier for the three countries taken together is significant. This significance, however, is at the expense of the significance of the separate intercept terms, and the improvement in explanatory power from equation 2 to equation 4 (0.9952 to 0.9955) is not significant. Thus the separate intercept terms of equation 2 do an adequate job of explaining the production differences between countries. Still, there is evidence that the fertilizer response coefficient is not constant across countries. In particular, the three temperate countries seem to have a response coefficient of about 0.30, while the remaining countries' coefficient is about 0.11. But the production simulation runs with values of 0.25 and 0.125 will give a satisfactory picture for the issues at hand. The smaller coefficient is more likely to give reasonable results because response to fertilizer change is mostly a short-run phenomenon.

Yields, therefore, depend on fertilizer application. We should have expected no less. The next question, and clearly the critical one for this stage of the analysis, is whether fertilizer applications depend on the ratio of rice prices to fertilizer prices. There is sufficient evidence to believe that a given group of farmers in a particular country will probably respond to fertilizer price changes over time. But our question is different. Do farmers in different countries, when faced by different price ratios at a given point of time, use correspondingly different fertilizer levels? If they do, then the implications are that both the farmers and the basic rice production functions for this region are from a single universe.

That prices do matter is best seen in figure 14.4, which plots the relative price of rice to fertilizer in 1970 for our sample of countries against the 1970 level of fertilizer application per hectare. The ordinary least squares estimate of this relationship shows that an increase in the

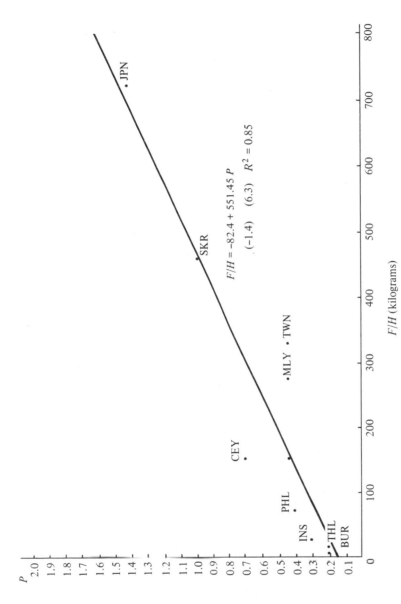

Fig. 14.4: Relationship of Relative Price of Rice to Fertilizer ($P$) and to Fertilizer Application per Hectare ($F/H$)

price ratio of 0.1 leads to an extra 55 kilograms of nutrients per hectare.[7] The startling statistic from this regression, however, is clearly the $R^2$ of 0.85. This says that 85 percent of the variation in fertilizer application per hectare observed in these nine Southeast and East Asian countries in 1970 was accounted for by the different price ratios of rice to fertilizer faced by their farmers. It seems that prices may be more important in the development process than many of us realized.[8]

Given that rice production depends on fertilizer applications, which in turn depend on rice to fertilizer price ratios, the last step is to calculate directly the impact of the price ratio on rice production. With this relationship established, the price ratio can be varied parametrically to observe the level of rice production in each country as a function of the price ratio. By subtracting a fixed level of consumption, an implied level of trade in rice is generated, also as a function of the price ratio.

We must first solve a technical calibration problem with interesting economic ramifications. Recall that in figure 14.4 about 15 percent of the variation in $F/H$ was *not* accounted for by the different price ratios. Since it is desirable in the parametric variation of price ratios to have each country start from its actual 1970 values, some adjustments must be made to those countries that do not exactly fit the relationship.

Even when the intercepts for each country have been adjusted so that they exactly fit the yield-fertilizer relationship (and equation 2 closely approximates this), it may be that the implied optimal price ratio, $P^*$, at the observed fertilizer level, $F$, may not be the same as the observed price ratio, $P$. While most of the difference is likely to be due to accumulating errors in measurement, variable definition, and so on, we might suspect that there should be some relationship between $F^*$, the optimal level of fertilizer application, and $F$, especially with respect to the degree of development of a particular country. As it turns out, the

7. At the mean values of $F/H$ and $P$, the elasticity of $F/H$ with respect to $P$ is 1.36. This value compares very favorably with a value calculated by C. S. Shih for the 1930–37 period in Taiwan (quoted by T. H. Lee, "Government Interference in the Rice Market in Taiwan," in *Viewpoints on Rice Policy in Asia* [Los Banos: International Rice Research Institute, 1971]). The Taiwan elasticity, calculated from more micro-level data than that of our study, was 1.3682. The results are also consistent with those of Pal Yong Moon for Korea and Randolph Barker for the Philippines; see Moon, "Farm Producer Response to Price Changes: The Case of Korean Farmers," Working Paper no. 7216 (Seoul, Korea Development Institute, 1972); and Barker, "Annual Research Review: Agricultural Economics," mimeographed (Los Banos, International Rice Research Institute, February 1973).

8. An alternative explanation is possible. Perhaps only developed countries can afford high prices of rice relative to fertilizer.

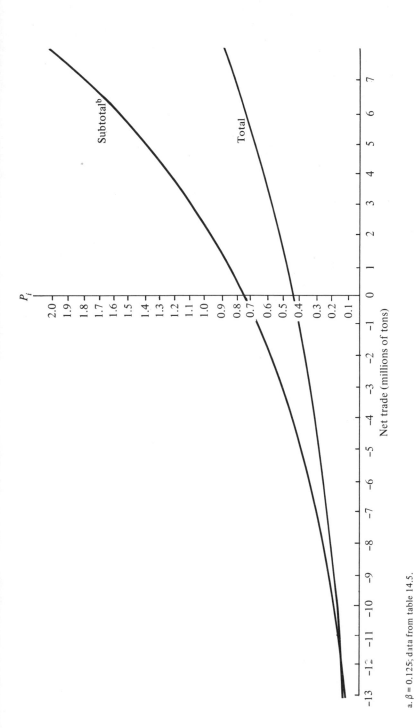

$P_i$

2.0
1.9
1.8
1.7
1.6
1.5
1.4
1.3
1.2
1.1
1.0
0.9
0.8
0.7
0.6
0.5
0.4
0.3
0.2
0.1

-13 -12 -11 -10 -9 -8 -7 -6 -5 -4 -3 -2 -1 0 1 2 3 4 5 6 7

Net trade (millions of tons)

Subtotal[b]

Total

a. $\beta = 0.125$; data from table 14.5.
b. Subtotal excludes Thailand and Burma.

Fig. 14.5:  Net Trade in Rice as a Function of Price[a] ($P$)

ratio of $F/F^*$ is roughly indicative, with a number of sizable exceptions, of what might be thought of a priori as the "degree of agricultural development."[9]

The functional relationship between rice production and the ratio of rice price to fertilizer price was used to determine the effect of varying the price ratio parametrically. It is possible to insert the equation estimated in figure 14.5 directly into the production function of equation 2 (with some calibrating), but the resulting simulation equation is not very different from the one derived in the appendix, and it would be based on only one year's data (in figure 14.5). We have chosen to use the derived relationship in the rest of our analysis.

The production-price ratio simulations, the results of which are reported in tables 14.4 and 14.5, ask a slightly different question than standard supply response models. Instead of asking what the supply response would be if the price were varied a given amount, we are asking what production (and production minus assumed consumption equals trade) would be if the farmers in all the countries in the sample were presented with a given price ratio. This price ratio is varied from 0.1 to 2.0; thus for any given level (between 0.2 and 1.43) some countries are in reality above and others below the simulation price ratio.

Table 14.4 reports the result of the simulations with $\beta$, the elasticity of output with respect to fertilizer, equal to 0.25. As argued earlier, this value for $\beta$ might be a reasonable approximation when all output-affecting factors have had to reach new equilibrium values and might also be a more appropriate value for the temperate countries. This long-run process of reaching new equilibrium values is similar conceptually to the meta-response function outlined by Yujiro Hayami

---

9. The ratios are as follows: Japan, 0.72; South Korea, 0.82; Taiwan, 1.41; Malaysia, 1.88; Ceylon, 0.66; Indonesia, 0.38; Thailand, 0.28; Burma, 0.12; and Philippines, 0.85. This ratio is clearly sensitive to whether or not all the fertilizer consumption observed was actually used on rice. The improbably high value for Malaysia almost certainly occurs because only about 10 to 20 percent (by very rough calculations) of total fertilizer consumption is used on rice. This would lower Malaysia's value to 0.19–0.38, somewhat lower than might be expected but clearly closer to reality than the value of 1.88.

The other troublesome value is that for Taiwan. No obvious reason appears to explain why the value is significantly greater than one. Perhaps the forced fertilizer-rice barter system was very effective in extracting some of the producer's surplus from the farmers, or a large volume of fertilizer was used on vegetable crops. We expect to complete further work on this general topic, and to establish time series on fertilizer prices which will permit a more straightforward estimation of some of the equations presented in this section.

Table 14.4: Net Trade in Rice at Different Assumed Ratios of Rice to Fertilizer Prices
(1,000 metric tons)

| $P_i$ | Japan | South Korea | Taiwan | Malaysia | Ceylon | Indonesia | Thailand | Burma | Philippines | Subtotal, excluding Burma and Thailand | Total |
|---|---|---|---|---|---|---|---|---|---|---|---|
| 0.1 | -9,079 | -3,488 | -1,222 | -745 | -1,365 | -6,192 | -1,711 | -966 | -2,056 | -24,147 | -26,824 |
| 0.2 | -7,314 | -2,828 | -714 | -517 | -1,146 | -3,037 | 1,028 | 717 | -1,181 | -16,737 | -14,992 |
| 0.3 | -6,079 | -2,364 | -358 | -357 | -992 | -824 | 2,949 | 1,898 | -567 | -11,538 | -6,691 |
| 0.4 | -5,091 | -1,995 | -74 | -229 | -869 | 938 | 4,478 | 2,838 | -79 | -7,399 | -83 |
| 0.5 | -4,259 | -1,684 | 165 | -122 | -765 | 2,425 | 5,769 | 3,632 | 334 | -3,906 | 5,495 |
| 0.6 | -3,531 | -1,412 | 375 | -27 | -675 | 3,726 | 6,898 | 4,326 | 695 | -849 | 10,375 |
| 0.7 | -2,881 | -1,168 | 562 | 57 | -594 | 4,889 | 7,908 | 4,946 | 1,017 | 1,882 | 14,736 |
| 0.8 | -2,289 | -947 | 732 | 133 | -520 | 5,946 | 8,825 | 5,510 | 1,310 | 4,365 | 18,700 |
| 0.9 | -1,746 | -743 | 889 | 204 | -453 | 6,918 | 9,669 | 6,029 | 1,580 | 6,649 | 22,347 |
| 1.0 | -1,241 | -554 | 1,034 | 269 | -390 | 8,720 | 10,452 | 6,510 | 1,830 | 8,768 | 25,730 |
| 1.1 | -769 | -377 | 1,170 | 330 | -331 | 8,664 | 11,185 | 6,961 | 2,064 | 10,751 | 28,897 |
| 1.2 | -324 | -211 | 1,298 | 388 | -276 | 9,458 | 11,874 | 7,385 | 2,285 | 12,618 | 31,877 |
| 1.3 | 96 | -54 | 1,419 | 442 | -223 | 10,210 | 12,526 | 7,786 | 2,493 | 13,383 | 33,695 |
| 1.4 | 495 | 95 | 1,534 | 494 | -174 | 10,924 | 13,146 | 8,166 | 2,691 | 16,059 | 37,371 |
| 1.5 | 876 | 238 | 1,643 | 543 | -126 | 11,604 | 13,737 | 8,530 | 2,880 | 17,658 | 39,925 |
| 1.6 | 1,240 | 375 | 1,748 | 590 | -81 | 12,255 | 14,302 | 8,877 | 3,060 | 19,187 | 42,366 |
| 1.7 | 1,589 | 505 | 1,848 | 635 | -38 | 12,879 | 14,844 | 9,210 | 3,234 | 20,652 | 44,706 |
| 1.8 | 1,925 | 631 | 1,945 | 679 | 4 | 13,480 | 15,365 | 9,530 | 3,400 | 22,064 | 46,959 |
| 1.9 | 2,248 | 752 | 2,038 | 720 | 44 | 14,058 | 15,867 | 9,839 | 3,561 | 23,421 | 49,127 |
| 2.0 | 2,561 | 869 | 2,128 | 761 | 83 | 14,617 | 16,352 | 10,137 | 3,716 | 24,735 | 51,224 |
| 1970 net trade (actual) | 611 | -554 | 50 | -195 | -594 | -800 | 1,024 | 719 | -80 | -1,562 | 181 |

Notes: Positive levels are exports; negative levels are imports. The values in this table were generated from the $Q = f(P)$ equation derived in the appendix, using a value of $\beta = 0.25$. Thus the base was equation 1 of table 14.3.

Table 14.5: Net Trade in Rice at Different Assumed Ratios of Rice to Fertilizer Prices (1,000 metric tons)

| $P_i$ | Japan | South Korea | Taiwan | Malaysia | Ceylon | Indonesia | Thailand | Burma | Philippines | Subtotal, excluding Burma and Thailand | Total |
|---|---|---|---|---|---|---|---|---|---|---|---|
| 0.1 | -4,607 | -2,092 | -575 | -464 | -987 | -3,367 | -242 | -61 | -1,043 | -13,135 | -13,438 |
| 0.2 | -3,435 | -1,682 | -304 | -343 | -859 | -1,809 | 1,007 | 708 | -587 | -9,019 | -7,304 |
| 0.3 | -2,693 | -1,423 | -133 | -267 | -779 | -824 | 1,797 | 1,194 | -298 | -6,417 | -3,426 |
| 0.4 | -2,140 | -1,230 | -5 | -210 | -719 | -90 | 2,386 | 1,556 | -83 | -4,477 | -535 |
| 0.5 | -1,696 | -1,074 | 98 | -164 | -670 | 501 | 2,860 | 1,847 | 89 | -2,916 | 1,791 |
| 0.6 | -1,322 | -943 | 184 | -126 | -630 | 998 | 3,259 | 2,093 | 235 | -1,604 | 3,748 |
| 0.7 | -998 | -830 | 259 | -92 | -595 | 1,428 | 3,604 | 2,305 | 361 | -467 | 5,442 |
| 0.8 | -712 | -730 | 325 | -6 | -563 | 1,809 | 3,910 | 2,493 | 473 | 539 | 6,942 |
| 0.9 | -454 | -640 | 385 | -36 | -535 | 2,150 | 4,184 | 2,661 | 573 | 1,443 | 8,288 |
| 1.0 | -221 | -558 | 439 | -12 | -510 | 2,461 | 4,433 | 2,815 | 664 | 2,263 | 9,511 |
| 1.1 | -6 | -483 | 488 | 10 | -487 | 2,746 | 4,662 | 2,955 | 747 | 3,015 | 10,632 |
| 1.2 | 191 | -414 | 534 | 30 | -465 | 3,009 | 4,873 | 3,085 | 824 | 3,710 | 11,668 |
| 1.3 | 377 | -349 | 577 | 49 | -445 | 3,255 | 5,070 | 3,206 | 896 | 4,360 | 12,636 |
| 1.4 | 550 | -289 | 617 | 67 | -426 | 3,485 | 5,254 | 3,320 | 963 | 4,967 | 13,541 |
| 1.5 | 712 | -232 | 654 | 84 | -409 | 3,701 | 5,428 | 3,426 | 1,027 | 5,537 | 14,391 |
| 1.6 | 866 | -178 | 690 | 99 | -392 | 3,905 | 5,591 | 3,527 | 1,086 | 6,076 | 14,108 |
| 1.7 | 1,012 | -128 | 723 | 114 | -376 | 4,098 | 5,746 | 3,622 | 1,143 | 6,586 | 15,954 |
| 1.8 | 1,150 | -79 | 755 | 129 | -361 | 4,282 | 5,894 | 3,713 | 1,197 | 7,073 | 16,680 |
| 1.9 | 1,282 | -33 | 786 | 142 | -347 | 4,457 | 6,035 | 3,800 | 1,248 | 7,535 | 17,370 |
| 2.0 | 1,408 | 11 | 815 | 155 | -333 | 4,625 | 6,169 | 3,882 | 1,297 | 7,978 | 18,029 |
| 1970 net trade (actual) | 611 | -554 | 50 | -195 | -594 | -800 | 1,024 | 719 | -80 | -1,562 | 181 |

Notes: Positive levels are exports; negative levels are imports. The values in this table were generated from the $Q = f(P)$ equation derived in the appendix, using a value of $\beta = 0.125$. Thus the base was equation 2 from table 14.3.

and Vernon Ruttan.[10] Although much needs to be studied about the nature and timing of price-induced shifts in the production function, our results are broadly consistent with their hypothesis. In this longer-run perspective, therefore, the vast export surpluses generated at the higher price ratios are not so surprising. These results give some hint, perhaps, of regional potential for rice production. No other significance should be attached to table 14.4.

Table 14.5, however, seems considerably more realistic, on both theoretical and empirical grounds. By assuming $\beta = 0.125$, the more satisfactory short-run estimate of fertilizer response from equation 2, we reduce the changes in production response to price ratio changes by half. Still, the latent supply response in these Asian rice-producing countries is very substantial. In 1970, actual net trade for these nine countries was 181,000 metric tons, which would occur according to the simulation model if all farmers in these countries faced a relative price of rice to fertilizer of only 0.43. Five of the nine countries had price ratios at or above this level. Merely raising the price ratio to 0.5, still only half or less than the level in Japan and South Korea, raises the total export surplus in the region to nearly 1.8 million tons, ten times the actual level in 1970. The leverage effect is obviously very great.

A good deal of the rapid response comes from the two major exporting countries with exceptionally low price ratios, Burma and Thailand. Raising their price ratios from 0.2 to 0.4 increases their export surplus from 1.7 million tons to over 3.9 million tons. Because their increases totally dominate what is happening in all the other countries, it is interesting to look at a subtotal that excludes Burma and Thailand.

The remaining seven countries in our sample had a net rice trade deficit in 1970 of nearly 1.6 million tons. This level would have been achieved at an average price ratio for all seven countries of about 0.6, substantially higher than the level of 0.43 implicit in the actual net trade figure for the region in total. Yet figure 14.5 shows that even this traditionally deficit group of countries might reach self-sufficiency in rice rather quickly under the assumptions of the model if they presented their farmers with a price ratio of about 0.75. This ratio is still lower than the actual level for Japan and South Korea.

Figure 14.6 shows the results of table 14.5 further disaggregated to the country level. This figure graphically demonstrates the point that

10. See Yujiro Hayami and Vernon Ruttan, *Agricultural Development: An International Perspective* (Baltimore: Johns Hopkins Press, 1971), pp. 82 ff.

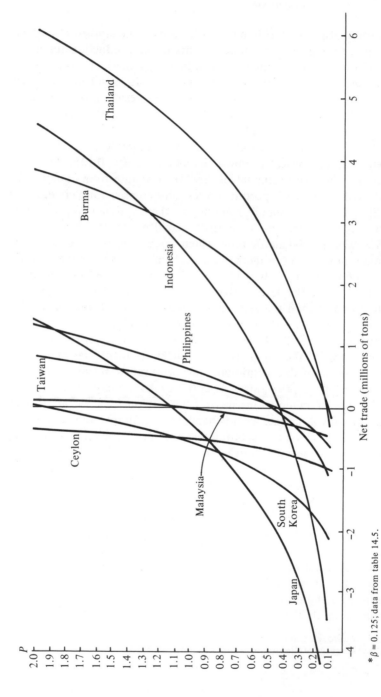

**Fig. 14.6: Net Trade in Rice as a Function of Price,* by Country**

*β = 0.125; data from table 14.5.

self-sufficiency is not an absolute. At the level of relative prices prevailing in Burma and Thailand, no other country in the sample is self-sufficient in rice. At Japan's price ratio, all countries except South Korea and Ceylon become self-sufficient. For these two countries, self-sufficiency will almost certainly require shifting the supply function rather than moving along it. Self-sufficiency for Malaysia would probably prove very expensive on the basis of price policy alone—a lesson that does not seem to be lost on Malaysia's leaders. Indonesia and the Philippines, however, seem very close to self-sufficiency even without major functional shifts. A price ratio of less than 0.5 would probably put them over the mark.

One last question is appealing. If this sample of countries were to strive for regional self-sufficiency, what would the resulting production and trade patterns look like? From figure 14.5 we find that the equilibrium price ratio would be about 0.42, and from figure 14.6 we can discover what each country's net trade would be like at this level. Table 14.6 compares an impressionistic trade matrix resulting from these individual country flows with the actual movements of rice in 1970. Somewhat more rice is moved around in total in the projected pattern than was actually shipped in 1970. Further, by producing in accord with regional comparative advantage, the apparent costs of production for the entire nine countries would be reduced by more than 30 percent, prior to transport charges.

Reducing the overall impact of table 14.6 to a few statistics is impossible, but the general impression is plain. Japan shifts from being the third largest exporter in the region to the largest importer. Both Thailand and Burma more than double their exports, partly at Japan's expense and partly because of the greater volume of trade occasioned by more reliance on comparative advantage in allocating production. Indonesia shifts from the largest importer to a minor exporter, almost the mirror image of Japan's implied transformation. The Philippines, Malaysia, and Ceylon are relatively unaffected except by fairly minor shifts in sources of imports (necessitated by the assumption of gross as well as net regional self-sufficiency).

Clearly, the relative price of rice to fertilizer, as it varies from country to country in this region, has a major impact on the structure of production and trade, and probably also on consumption though we have no evidence yet. But the causes of the great diversity observed among these economies are not yet understood; the problem has simply been pushed back one stage. Our first-stage explanation falls squarely within

Table 14.6: Rice Trade in 1970, Simulated and Actual
(1,000 tons)

| Importers | Exporters | | | | | | | | | | |
|---|---|---|---|---|---|---|---|---|---|---|---|
| | JPN | SKR | TWN | MLY | CEY | INS | THL | BUR | PHL | ROW | Total |
| JPN | | | | | | | 2,000 (18) | 950 | (1) | | 2,000 (19) |
| SKR | (332) | | | | | | 260 (4) | | (218) | | 1,210 (554) |
| TWN | | | | | | | (5) | | | | 0 (5) |
| MLY | | | | | 50 | 190 | (119) | (1) | (75) | | 240 (195) |
| CEY | | | | | | | (23) | 700 (250) | (321) | | 700 (594) |
| INS | (151) | | | | | | (140) | (20) | (489) | | 0 (800) |
| THL | | | | | | | | | | | 0 (0) |
| BUR | | | | | | | | | | | 0 (0) |
| PHL | | (50) | | | 100 | | | (30) | | | 100 (80) |
| ROW | (147) | | | | | | (715) | (418) | | | 0 (1,280) |
| Total | 0 (630) | 0 (0) | 0 (50) | 0 (0) | 0 (0) | 150 (0) | 2,450 (1,024) | 1,650 (719) | 0 (0) | 0 (1,104) | 4,250 (3,527) |

*Notes:* Actual flows are shown in parentheses. Simulated flows are based on a "no-net-trade" price of 0.42, with actual shipments roughly allocated on the basis of distance and historical trade preferences. Abbreviations: JPN, Japan; SKR, South Korea; TWN, Taiwan; MLY, Malaysia; CEY, Ceylon; INS, Indonesia; THL, Thailand; BUR, Burma; PHL, Philippines; ROW, rest of world.

the traditional purview of economists. The second stage requires paying more attention to political factors. For this reason we outline in the next section a political economy model designed to explain cross-country variations in rice policy, especially with respect to prices.

### 3. A POLITICAL ECONOMY FRAMEWORK

The framework we develop here builds on Jan Tinbergen's theoretical analysis of economic policy.[11] He noted that governments attempt to reach certain objectives by using policy instruments at their disposal. However, the use of these policy instruments is constrained by economic and political relationships (e.g., demand elasticities, availability

11. See Jan Tinbergen, *Economic Policy: Principles and Design* (Amsterdam: North Holland, 1956).

of funds, laws and institutions, personnel, political matters, and so on.)

This intersecting framework of objectives, policies, and constraints fits easily into the language (and in the appendix into the algebra) of linear programming. Although the optimizing capability of programming is only hinted at in this paper, and indeed may not be realizable empirically, there is a good deal to be learned just by framing each country's policies within a general context of objectives, policies, and constraints. For this approach to yield new insights, however, it is important that the *system* be general. That is, the variables should be the same, but different countries should then have varying coefficients attached to these variables. The intent of this framework is, therefore, to provide a general system in which each country's policies can be analyzed.

What then are some of the general aspects of the system? Policies are the activities available to government planners that can help the country achieve its objectives. These in turn contribute to fulfilling the broadly defined goals of the society. Each policy requires some effort to implement and the total effort must be finite. If a simple budget expenditure is required to operate the policy, the constraint on this input would be the feasible budget allocation. The framework thus requires that each policy have an associated vector of implementing inputs which are in limited supply. Since such inputs as government personnel and revenue will serve alternative policies, the necessity to choose an "efficient" set of policies relative to the objectives is obvious.

The objective function completes the framework. If each policy had only one objective, then defining the objective function would be relatively easy conceptually. But the very heart of the difficulty in making economic policy decisions is the interaction of policies and objectives. Thus each policy may make some contribution, either positive or negative, to several objectives although it will remain true that many policies are designed to meet particular objectives.

In our preliminary review of rice policies by country, we have identified eight broad areas of objectives that nations generally pursue:

1. income generation for farms
2. welfare protection for consumers (including maintenance of a low-cost wage good)
3. generation of government revenue (at local and/or national levels)
4. generation of foreign exchange (through exports or through reduced imports)

5. reduced reliance on foreign markets for basic foodstuffs (self-sufficiency)
6. price stability
7. regional development (and equity)
8. provision of adequate nutrition.

Despite what appear to be an endless variety of rice policies in force in different Asian countries, designed to achieve their own unique weightings of these objectives, the basic policy choices in fact are relatively limited:

1. farm production programs (either intensification or diversification)
2. consumer programs (including rice subsidies or subsidies for rice substitutes)
3. domestic marketing investments
4. concessional foreign trade (including exchange rate biases)
5. direct taxation or other forms of fiscal transfers
6. price controls, including
   a. floor price
   b. ceiling price
   c. buffer stock as stabilizer
7. physical controls, including rationing and nonprice collections.

Objectives come free; implementing policies requires resources, and these resources have opportunity costs. It is thus necessary to identify the inputs required for policy implementation and to determine the maximum amount of these inputs available, that is, the economic, technical, and political constraints on policy implementation.

The list of constraints is likely to be longer than the lists of policies and objectives. This is especially so given the political constraints that are also necessary to make any model realistic. At the same time, there is an inherent circularity among coefficients, constraints, and efficiency in policy making. We follow a conceptual course now common in linear programming analyses of firms, that is, we assume the decision maker is rational and then search for the constraints that cause the model to explain his behavior accurately. We assume, as a starting point, that policy makers are rational and efficient. Political and economic constraints are then added to the model until actual policies are explained. The rationality or efficiency of policies can then be examined by asking how hard it would be to break constraints, or whether the constraints are real or merely perceived.

Our preliminary list of constraints includes the following:

1. production technology and domestic supply parameters
2. consumption structure and domestic demand parameters
3. international market structure and supply-demand parameters relative to the country in question (e.g., the price effect of entering the world market as a buyer or seller)
4. availability of foreign assistance, both in the short run as food aid (e.g., rice and wheat) and in the longer run as research inputs (e.g., new varieties from the Rice Research Institute)
5. government administrative capacity (and effectiveness of field workers)
6. domestic market and foreign trade prospects for alternative crops
7. state of development of the basic marketing system for both inputs and outputs
8. government budget that can be committed to rice policy (which may depend on the effectiveness of the policies in the current or previous periods)
9. political factors, such as ability to change prices, use of the price program for patronage and corruption, and the role of vested interests.

To what purpose is this framework directed? In the short run, its descriptive powers are substantial. But a longer-run goal will be to use the model's potential for answering questions about the future course of rice policies in Asia. As productive technology, demand patterns, bureaucracies, and political forces change (i.e., as the constraints change), how will individual governments respond? This framework should help us make predictions. Objectives are likely to evolve over time as well, as a society perceives new possibilities and achieves old goals, and the model may help to explain how this evolution will take place.

Thus the framework has both static and dynamic potential. In the static case it should help predict the types of policies a country will use in the face of a given set of objectives and constraints. It should help identify policies that are inefficient relative to objectives and constraints. In a dynamic context the framework is designed to examine what happens as constraints change. In particular, one policy option might be investment in raising the level of a constraint (e.g., development of the marketing system). Breaking a constraint may permit using an old policy more intensively, or it may open a whole new set of policy options. Finally, the model may reveal dynamic patterns in the process whereby objectives and constraints interact to form operative policies.

### 4. PRELIMINARY APPLICATIONS OF THE POLITICAL ECONOMY MODEL

At least two different approaches exist to implementing this political economy framework for Asian rice policy. Table 14.7 shows how it might be used to make rough comparisons across countries with respect to policies and objectives. Conjectural as it is, Table 14.7 shows at a glance some of the most striking differences among these countries' rice policies and what they hope to achieve from them. At an aggregate level, however, this approach quickly exhibits diminishing returns.

The second approach is to build from the country level toward international comparisons. This requires detailed country studies by national experts who understand how rice policy gets formulated.[12]

We have attempted this approach for Indonesia, more as an example of how the model works than as an accurate description of how Indonesia works. The effort is strictly verbal. No quantification is attempted because our knowledge of Indonesia's economic interactions is too sparse, and because the political framework, when expressed in full mathematical rigor as in the appendix, is merely a subset of relationships that make up a total economy.

Short of this, however, much can be learned just by thinking about the formulation of Indonesia's rice policy as it was influenced by objectives and constraints. Table 14.7 has already provided some general picture of how we view Indonesia's objectives and what some of its broad implementing policies are. What are the constraints that account for this pattern? In particular, what factors account for the price policies that have been used?

Reference to table 14.2 will show that Indonesia's rice to fertilizer price ratio is among the lowest in Asia—only Burma and Thailand are lower. The earlier simulation results noted that a relatively small increase in this price ratio would leave Indonesia self-sufficient in rice, and self-sufficiency was the leading stated objective of the country's First Five-Year Plan which drew to a close in March 1974. From the point of view of the model, the important question must be why price policy was not used to achieve self-sufficiency. The answer lies in the "real" objectives of Indonesian rice policy and the constraints that prevent them all from being fully satisfied.

12. Six of these country studies are planned as a part of the overall project.

Table 14.7: Rice Policy Objectives in Selected Asian Countries

| | Japan | South Korea | Taiwan | Malaysia | Ceylon | Indonesia | Thailand | Philippines | Burma |
|---|---|---|---|---|---|---|---|---|---|
| **Objectives[a]** | | | | | | | | | |
| Farm income | 0.7 | 0.2 | 0.1 | 0.7 | 0.1 | 0.15 | 0.1 | 0.2 | |
| Consumer welfare | 0.2 | 0.3 | 0.1 | 0.1 | 0.8 | 0.3 | 0.2 | 0.4 | |
| Government revenue | | | 0.2 | 0.1 | | 0.1 | 0.5 | | |
| Foreign exchange | | 0.1 | 0.2 | | | 0.1 | 0.2 | | |
| Self-sufficiency | 0.1 | 0.1 | 0.2 | | 0.1 | 0.1 | | 0.2 | |
| Nutrition | | | | | | 0.05 | | | |
| Price stability | | 0.3 | 0.2 | 0.1 | | 0.3 | | 0.2 | |
| Looking inward | | | | | | | | | 1.0(?) |
| Overall weight[b] | 5 | 5 | 4 | 6 | 9 | 10 | 7 | 8 | ? |
| **Policies[c]** | | | | | | | | | |
| Production intensification | +− | ++ | +++ | +++ | ++ | ++ | ++ | ++ | |
| Consumer subsidies | + | | | +− | ++ | | | | |
| Marketing investment | | + | + | | | | + | ++ | |
| Concessional foreign trade | | | | | | | | | |
| Exports | ++ | ++ | | + | + | ++ | ++ | | |
| Imports | + | ++ | | | | +++ | | | |
| Taxation | +++ | ++ | ++ | | | | ++++ | | |
| Floor price | | | | ++ | ++ | +++ | ++ | +++ | |
| Ceiling price | | | | | ++ | ++ | ++ | +++ | |
| Buffer stock | + | + | ++ | ++ | ++ | | | + | |
| Physical controls or rationing | | + | ++ | | +++ | + | | | |

a. Each country's objectives are scaled so that its total adds up to one.
b. "Overall weight" is a rough judgment as to the importance of rice policy relative to the overall national policy set. The scale is from 0 to 10.
c. Each country receives a total of 10 plusses or minuses. A combination of a plus and a minus for the same policy indicates that a country has two programs operating in opposite directions.

Sources: include Viewpoints on Rice Policy in Asia (Los Banos: International Rice Research Institute, 1971), FAO's National Rice Policy 1970, and good a deal of conjecture.

The difference between objectives and constraints in a programming context is fuzzy. The customary distinction is that objectives are something that makes one continuously better off as more is available, whereas constraints "must" not be broken; however, staying below the constraint level does not make one better off. It is possible, of course, that some objective may also be constrained to be more than a certain minimum. In such a case the item is both an objective and a constraint.

This view of the relationship between objectives and constraints forces us to give relatively little weight (0.1 out of 1.0) to achieving self-sufficiency per se, although this was clearly the major stated objective in the Indonesian Five-Year Plan. It is not possible to relegate the other factors in the decision-making process—farm income, consumer welfare, government revenue, nutrition, and price stability—to the constraint ledger because they are not "unbreakable." Achieving more of any one of them makes the country better off. So the important problem is to define the relative rates of trade-off among these objectives, and this is attempted in a rough manner in table 14.7. It is our judgment that price stability and consumer welfare dominate all other objectives. In our view, they account for 60 percent of total rice policy objectives. Also, some minimum degree of price stability might be treated as a constraint.

The policy set used to achieve these objectives is also crudely outlined in table 14.7.[13] The constraints that interact with the objectives to produce this policy set derive mostly from two sources: the government's capability, both administrative and financial, to carry out programs, and the state of the international market for rice, especially in the region near Indonesia.

Administrative capability affects the performance of two major government programs: the BIMAS rice intensification program operated primarily by a secretariat drawn from the Ministry of Agriculture and its extension service, and the price stabilization program (consisting of a floor price, ceiling price, physical rice ration distributions, and a buffer stock) operated by BULOG.[14]

The effectiveness of the BIMAS staff limits the rate at which the supply function for rice can be shifted out. If the package of seeds,

13. A more detailed discussion can be found in Saleh Afiff and C. Peter Timmer, "Rice Policy in Indonesia," *Food Research Institute Studies* 10, no. 2 (1971): 131–159.

14. BIMAS is the Indonesian acronym for Bimingan Masaal, meaning mass guidance. BULOG is the acronym for Badan Urusan Logistic, or Food Logistics Board.

credit, fertilizer, pesticides, and irrigation water is not available to the farmer, he retains his traditional way of doing things. Even if it is available (and this alone requires massive government efforts), the farmer may need some help in understanding the requirements and benefits of the new technology. Thus self-sufficiency from shifting the supply function is constrained by these factors.

Why then is self-sufficiency not achieved by moving up the short-run supply curve? Here the BULOG effectiveness constraint is felt, especially as the organization's capability interacts with conditions in the world rice market. In 1970 and 1971 rice was a cheap commodity in Southeast Asia. Quotations for delivery out of Singapore, Rangoon, and Bangkok ranged as low as $75 per ton for rice similar in quality to that eaten by most Indonesians. The availability of this low-cost rice served as an effective constraint on the consumer price level of rice in Indonesia, even though all international trade in rice was conducted by BULOG on government account. Because of the many thousands of miles of coastline in Indonesia, the smuggling potential is so great that the internal price of rice could not be much higher (only enough to cover transportation, profit, and risks) than the price for Thai, Burmese, or Chinese rice. This is an administrative constraint in a broader sense, because customs officials would simply have been unable to keep cheaper rice out of the country if the domestic price had been set too high. It is no coincidence then that Indonesia's internal rice to fertilizer price ratio was low, but not as low as Burma's and Thailand's. These two countries supplied most of the low-cost rice available in 1970 and 1971.[15] The price policies of these two countries were thus a major constraint on any Indonesian attempt at self-sufficiency via price policies.

While the international market constraint adequately explains the consumer ceiling price level, it does not fully explain the level of the floor price to farmers. The spread between the two was designed to encourage private trade to play a major role in purchasing and storing rice from harvest to consumption, but this is not a logical necessity. It was done partly for ideological reasons, i.e., it was thought the private sector should handle the bulk of marketing activities, but also because BULOG was incapable of handling more than a small fraction of the

15. Students of Indonesian economic history might ask why the constraint did not work both ways. Prior to 1969 Indonesia had historically maintained its rice prices well below world prices. The answer is that some rice probably did get exported illegally, but shipping significant quantities of rice out would have been much harder than getting it in, especially since the government controlled most of the rice mills.

marketed surplus. If the floor price had been set higher, or the ceiling price lower, BULOG's limited capacity to buy and sell quantities would not have been sufficient to guarantee the price of rice—a key commodity in the government's price stabilization program. The price policy was thus designed, to a considerable extent, in terms of what BULOG could defend. The program was successful, however, in removing some of the extreme seasonal price fluctuations, to the benefit of both producers and consumers. Farmers received higher harvest prices and consumers paid lower preharvest prices. But the government could not encourage farmers to move further up their supply curves through an even higher rice price because BULOG was incapable of defending it. And financial considerations prevented lowering the fertilizer price through an increased subsidy. Indeed, all efforts were aimed at finding ways to *reduce* the subsidy, thus increasing the price of fertilizer to the farmer. This has not happened so far, however.

Constraints change. As international rice prices soared in 1972 and 1973, Indonesia's rice policy was severely buffeted. The urban price ceiling was exceeded by more than 100 percent as BULOG's buffer stock ran out and imports were not sufficient to make up the shortage from a poor domestic crop (and procurement). This much is history. The fact that the government did not fall during the rice crisis partly explains why price stabilization and consumer welfare are made objectives rather than constraints in the model. They in fact *appeared* as constraints to government policy makers until they were broken, thus transforming them into objectives with high payoffs.

The interesting question, of course, is what happens now. The critical external constraint, the international rice price, has drastically changed. And although BULOG may be little better prepared to defend a floor price, its task has been greatly transformed by the external situation. The central question is whether the government will try to enforce a floor price sufficiently higher than before to both challenge BULOG and provide a real incentive to farmers to increase production, or whether it will be content with an "easy" floor price target that will not change the situation. The floor price has already been raised by 30 percent, but market prices will probably not dip that far in the immediate future except in very isolated areas. A real commitment to self-sufficiency and producer welfare would probably require well over a 50 percent (rather than a 30 percent) increase. This higher level would surely press hard against BULOG's administrative capacity. But unless that happens, self-sufficiency appears unlikely. That such low weights have been placed on self-sufficiency and farmer income in table 14.7 indicates our own doubts that the policies necessary to achieve self-sufficiency will be forthcoming in the near future, even though the new constraints now mean it might be feasible.

To understand rice policy in Asia is to understand much about the economics and politics of the region. Following completion of the various country studies, it should be possible to write with greater precision about the forces that affect production, marketing, consumption, and international trade in rice. Even at this preliminary stage, however, we believe several important conclusions emerge.

First, the international rice market is imperfect in several important senses. In particular, variations in price, trade barriers, and the concessional nature of much of the trade result in substantial distortions of resource use. This variation in prices across countries also indicates the need for a closer look at the price assumptions in two-sector development models.

Second, *given* a set of policy-determined national prices, a simple aggregate production function that combines cross-section and time-series data appears to provide a crude but useful tool for examining the effect of prices on production, consumption, and trade. Prices are a major determinant of fertilizer use via the short-run production function. They also play a longer-run role in shifting the short-run production function, that is, in inducing movement along the meta-production function. This process is little understood but is likely to be important in determining future patterns of regional and world trade in rice.

Finally, to understand how the prices are established among countries requires a heavy infusion of political economy. We believe there is much to be gained from a formal framework that emphasizes objectives, constraints, and implementing policies. Even if the formal system is never solved, we are convinced that comparing countries in this consistent manner will help explain the diversity of policies that are used and will provide some basis for suggesting alternative policy approaches.

## APPENDIX

The political economy framework can be specified in a standard linear programming framework, as follows:

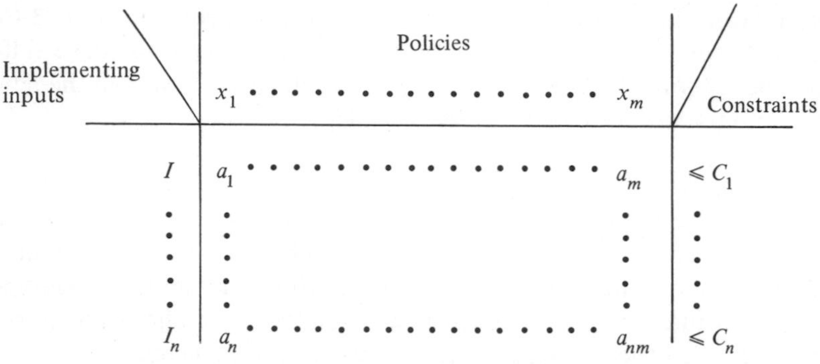

Fig. 14A

The various $x_j$ are policies available to government planners, to be implemented in greater or lesser degree, that can help the country achieve its goals. Each policy $x_j$ requires a vector of implementing inputs, $I_i$, and the coefficient matrix $a_{ij}$ tells how much of each input is required for a "unit of output" of $x_j$. The definition of a unit of ouptut of $x_j$ must be in terms that translate more or less directly into variables in the "real" economy. The linkages between the political economy and the real economy are likely to be extremely complex. The difficulties involved in their full specification stand as the major obstacle to a formal implementation of the political economy programming model.

Since no input necessary to implement policies is available in un-limited quantities (otherwise it is conceptually trivial), the standard row constraints of linear programming hold in the political economy framework as well:

$$\sum_{i}^{m} a_{ij} X_j \leq C_i,$$

where $X_j$ is the level of operation of policy $x_j$. Certain constraints will be policy specific. In those cases only one $a_{ij}$ in row $i$ will be non-zero.

The objective function completes the framework. If each policy were uni-objective it would be possible to define the objective function as

$$\text{Max} \sum_{j}^{m} P_j X_j,$$

where $P_j$ is the weight the government attaches to each objective generated by policy *j*. In this world, if the government wants to save foreign exchange, then policy $x_j$ does exactly (and only) that.

Realism requires, however, that the interaction among policies and objectives be recognized, so the objective function should be defined as

$$\text{Max} \sum_{k}^{n} P_k W_k,$$

where $P_k$ continues to be the weight the government attaches to each objective,[16] but now $W_k$ is the sum of all the contributions to objective *k* from all the policies $X_j$:

$$W_k = \sum_{j}^{m} b_{kj} X_j.$$

The net effect of this is to introduce a second coefficient matrix, $b_{kj}$, that determines the unit contribution of policy $x_j$ to objective $W_k$.[17] If policies are in fact uni-objective, then $b_{kj}$ is a diagonal matrix. To the extent that policies are designed to have single objectives but in fact have small spillover effects—positive and negative—on other objectives, the off-diagonal terms will tend to be small. The resulting overall objective function can now be written, in matrix notation, as follows:

$$\text{Max } PbX',$$

where *P* is a row vector ($1 \times s$), *b* is a matrix ($s \times m$), and *X* is a row vector ($1 \times m$).

Seven sets of variables must be identified:

*W* = the sum of contributions to each objective from all policies
*P* = the weight given each objective
*x* = the policies
*I* = the implementing inputs
*C* = the constraints
*a* = the coefficients relating policies to constraints
*b* = the coefficients relating contribution of policies to objectives.

Of these, only three are country specific: *P*, *C*, and *b*. The rest will be general to the model. The set of national objectives from rice policy (but *not* the weights), the policies to achieve these objectives (but not the levels, which are the "answer" to the problem), the set of inputs,

16. It is useful to normalize $P_k$ so that $\Sigma_k^s P_k = 1$.
17. We are indebted to Martin Abel for suggesting the importance of the $b_{kj}$ matrix.

and the input-output coefficients attached to each policy (the $a_{ij}$, but not the level of the constraint applied to each input) are general to the model. What must be determined on a country-by-country basis are the weights each country attaches to each objective (in the general set), the level of constraint attached to each input,[18] and the extent to which each policy contributes to various objectives (the $b_{kj}$ matrix). This latter matrix may well be fairly similar for all countries, especially if there is a tendency for it to be diagonal.

The general aspects of the system are spelled out informally in section 3 of the text along with a rough specification of some of the country-specific aspects for Indonesia. These rough country specifications are very helpful in forming a basis for comparisons of rice policies from country to country, and a series of country studies is planned in this context. More formal implementation of the political economy model awaits, as its relegation to an appendix indicates, much more detailed quantitative knowledge of the structure and mechanisms of both the real economy and the political economy of the countries in question.

18. Clearly it is also possible to set the constraint levels equal for all countries and vary $a_{ij}$.

PART VI: COMPARATIVE STUDIES

# 15

## Agriculture in the Economic Growth of the East European Socialist Countries

Z. KOZLOWSKI

The achievement of two goals has persistently been proclaimed as the basic principle of agricultural policy of all communist regimes in East Europe: the socialist reconstruction of agriculture and increased agricultural output. Although the implementation of this policy has undergone numerous changes and twists, some of great practical and theoretical significance, the fact remains that there has been an underlying hard core which has shaped what one may term the pattern of agricultural growth in East European communist countries. It seems worthwhile to attempt to identify and discuss this, in view of the effect it has on tens of millions of human beings, both their everyday lot and their life perspectives, particularly given that this experience has already spread over almost a quarter of a century and is most likely to go on for several more decades to come.

Also, it indisputedly has a lasting theoretical value for many others since it is bound to affect the thinking of all those dissatisfied with existing imperfect conditions in agriculture anywhere in the world.

No claim is made to novelty or originality with regard to the many observations discussed in this chapter which have already been formulated on various occasions, particularly by students of Soviet agriculture.

What justifies their repetition—whenever this is the case—is, I believe, the new context, which allows hypotheses to be regarded as confirmed fact through the mere accumulation of experience over time and because of their corroboration in different social and geographical conditions. It is our new perspective at the present moment that widens the horizon in relation to the past and gives a new dimension to old problems.

411

### THE RELEVANCE OF THE SOCIALIST GROWTH STRATEGY

The pattern of agricultural growth as embodied in over two decades of experience in East European countries (and to some extent also in over half a century in the Soviet Union) reveals some general characteristics, despite the fact that it has undergone alterations in various time periods, and that it bears in particular countries the imprint of specific economic and social conditions prevailing there.

If one takes a bird's-eye view of the development of agriculture in East European communist countries, a number of tendencies become apparent. First, in all these countries the general trend of agricultural output is an upward one (see table 15.1).[1] On the one hand, this trend is strong enough to be discernible even in per capita figures and in indices of marketed agricultural produce per capita among the non-agricultural population. On the other hand, however, it is not strong enough to preclude considerable fluctuations and downward movements in particular years or over periods of several years. Whereas the former are normally the result of variable weather conditions, the latter are usually coupled with variations and turns in agricultural policy. All in all the growth trend of agricultural output is far from solid. Its weakness is particularly noticeable in the all-too-frequent shortages of food supplies that have become a permanent feature of socialist economies.[2]

The agricultural problem of the socialist countries is one of a shortage of agricultural output in relation to the demand for it. The wide discrepancy between the long-term growth rates of agriculture and of industry is such that it constitutes an intrinsic imbalance in the general process of economic growth. Industrial expansion is undoubtedly very

1. In 1966 most countries achieved a record growth rate (for East Germany and Poland the peak year was 1965). The level of food production per capita increased further in 1968. Since then, however, it has stagnated.

2. An illuminating illustration of this situation can be observed in Poland, where 1972 was marked by an exceptionally high rate of increase in livestock production. Despite this a gap seemed to exist in the meat market as reflected on the one hand in official statistics and on the other in the experience of the consumer. The statistics indicate a record increase in the supply of pork, exceeding even the 11 percent target figure. Hence the press and mass media were making triumphant noises. The consumer did not, however, find that much improvement in the shops. The usual shortages of various sorts of meat, particularly those in the lower price brackets, persisted. See J. Musialowski, "Trudne nasze miesne sprawy," *Glos Pracy,* August 24, 1972. Of course, if shortages persist at such a time there can be no doubt that they must have been significantly more acute at any other previous time, particularly because exports of animal products used to run at a much higher rate than they now do.

Table 15.1: Growth of Agricultural Production in East European
Countries, 1960–71 (Preceding year = 100)

|  | *1960* | *1961* | *1962* | *1963* | *1964* | *1965* | *1966* | *1967* | *1968* | *1969* | *1970* | *1971* |
|---|---|---|---|---|---|---|---|---|---|---|---|---|
| Bulgaria | 103 | 96 | 104 | 102 | 112 | 102 | 115 | 103 | 93 | 104 | 105 | 102 |
| Czechoslo-vakia | 105 | 100 | 92 | 107 | 103 | 96 | 111 | 106 | 105 | 102 | 101 | 103 |
| East Germany | 109 | 88 | 99 | 107 | 104 | 108 | 104 | 106 | 101 | 93 | 104 | 99 |
| Hungary | 94 | 100 | 103 | 106 | 106 | 95 | 108 | 104 | 100 | 107 | 95 | 110 |
| Rumania | 102 | 105 | 92 | 104 | 106 | 107 | 114 | 102 | 97 | 103 | 95 | 118 |
| Poland | 105 | 110 | 92 | 104 | 101 | 108 | 105 | 102 | 104 | 95 | 102 | 104 |
| Soviet Union | 102 | 102 | 101 | 92 | 105 | 102 | 109 | 102 | 105 | 96 | 109 | 100 |
| Yugoslavia | 87 | 94 | 105 | 109 | 103 | 95 | 125 | 98 | 96 | 112 | 88 | 114 |

*Source:* Główny Urzad Statystyczny, *Rocznik statystyczny 1972* (Warsaw, 1972),
p. 654, table 74.

rapid and so is the process of urbanization. As a result there is an
accelerated increase in the demand for food and agricultural output.
A special factor is at work here, attributable to the particular pattern
of industrialization characteristic of communist countries, namely,
their neglect of the light consumer goods industries for the sake of a
speedier growth of heavy capital goods industries. Owing to the constraint imposed on the expansion of consumer goods industries, their
output grows rather slowly and their produce is consequently rather
expensive in relation to both foodstuffs and wages. Hence the demand
for industrial consumer goods is harnessed and eventually diverted
toward food.[3] The income elasticity of food demand is relatively high
due to the low income level, but the adopted pattern of industrializa-

3. The main characteristics of the Soviet growth pattern and its implications for
agriculture have already been described by many authors. See, for example, the
following:
The [Soviet] government policy, carried out through the collective farms, of . . .
keeping the income of the agricultural population low, facilitated Soviet economic growth. The low incomes of the peasants . . . coupled with the high prices
of manufactured consumer goods, resulted in a diminished demand for manufactured consumer goods. Thus, the Soviet government could (1) curtail investment
in consumer goods industries and center most of the investment in capital goods
industries, thus increasing the growth of strategic sectors of industry, (2) assign a
higher proportion of the manufactured consumer goods to meet the demand of
the industrial labour force, compensating to some extent for the decrease of food
consumption, and (3) keep the output of manufactured consumer goods limited
in the absence of capital investment in those industries, as well as shift labour to
employment in construction, mining, and other capital goods industries [Arcadius
Kahan, "The Collective Farm System in Russia: Some Aspects of Its Contribution to Soviet Economic Development," *Agriculture in Economic Development,*
ed. Carl Eicher and Lawrence Witt (New York: McGraw-Hill, 1964), pp. 263–64].

tion in communist countries boosts the demand for food and agricultural output even further. At the same time, the communist pattern of industrialization contains an inherent check on the growth of agricultural output. This once again springs from the special priority given to capital growth. This priority is interpreted as economizing on everything that does not directly enhance the productive capacity of industry. Among other things it implies economizing on those industries that produce supplies for agriculture such as agricultural machines, chemicals, and so on.

Thus an outstanding feature of communist agricultural growth is what has long since come to be known in communist literature as "agriculture lagging behind industry." The slogan is merely a description of the apparent gap between the accelerated growth of the demand for agricultural output and its retarded and unstable increase rate resulting from the communist growth pattern.[4]

4. It may seem difficult to support this contention with statistics, despite the fact that any observer of the realities existing in communist countries can be in no doubt with regard to its truthfulness. Indeed, looking at the basic figures illustrating the growth rates of agricultural output in communist countries for the last decade and the standard of food consumption there, one finds the figures most impressive. For example the annual compound growth rate of gross agricultural production in East Europe and the Soviet Union for 1959–69, as calculated by the Food and Agriculture Organisation (FAO), amounts to 3.1 percent in terms of total and 2.0 percent in terms of per capita production (FAO, *Agricultural Commodity Projections 1970–1980* [Rome, 1971], 1:13, table 1). These figures seem to be more favorable than those in any other geographical area distinguished in FAO publications. (See tables 15.2 and 15.3.)

Leaving aside the question of the truthfulness of communist statistics, one has to accept that in terms of both consumption per capita and the rate of the improvement of the diet these figures are most satisfactory. Dietary improvement is best illustrated by the increase in the animal protein content of the diet in the Soviet Union and Eastern Europe. Between 1962 and 1970 this increase amounted to 10.5 grams per person per day, i.e., a 33 percent rise, as compared with an increase of only 6.7 grams per day (15.9 percent) in West European countries, and only 5.4 grams (8 percent) in North America. There is no doubt that the communist countries are catching up with the West in terms of food consumption. How then is it possible to reconcile these data with my basic contention?

In another publication of the same FAO series (*Agricultural Commodities: Projections for 1975 and 1985* [Rome, 1967] 1:34, table 5), the following estimates of the growth rates (percent per year compound) of the total demand for food in the period 1965–1975 are made:

East Europe and Soviet Union 2.0–2.3%
West Europe 1.1–1.4%

(The estimates attribute 50–57 percent and 42–52 percent of these growth rates in demand for food to the population increase in each area respectively.)

On the surface of it, a 2.0–2.9 percent rate of growth of demand for food in communist countries as compared with the 3.1 percent growth of total agricultural

For political reasons the communist regimes cannot afford to close this gap through price increases. Higher food prices would result in a reduction of the purchasing power of the population, particularly among the lower income groups. Planned indices of the growth of real incomes, which are unimpressive even with the food prices kept low, would have to be considerably reduced. Thus the preferred course has always been to have higher personal income targets in the plans, even if they are known to be unfeasible, rather than lower, more realistic ones that might have a psychologically depressing effect on the public.

Communist literature, needless to say, has never been inclined to give a true explanation of the celebrated phenomenon of the lagging of agriculture. In the stage before collectivization this lag is interpreted as a justification for the call for collectivization of agriculture as the only means of overcoming the alleged inability of private farming (said to be inherent in the nature of private agriculture) to expand in step with industrialization. After collectivization it is forgotten.

This main feature of the socialist pattern of agricultural growth is linked directly with the cornerstone of the communist theory of economic growth, represented by the tenet that the basic condition for economic growth is that the industries producing capital goods expand faster than those producing consumer goods.

As is widely known, this doctrine has its origin in the so-called Marxist law of extended reproduction and is based on Marx's breakdown of the economy into departments 1 and 2, representing capital

---

production would seem to ensure full equilibrium in the food market. (The slight difference in the periods to which the two rates refer—1959–69 in the case of output and 1965–75 in the case of demand—can, I believe, be disregarded.)

Finally, it may be relevant to give three randomly chosen quotations from East European sources confirming the observation in question:

"The specific character of agriculture in Czechoslovakia conditions . . . rests in the lagging development of production and [on the other hand] demand for foodstuffs and agricultural raw materials constantly exceeding their supply" (Jaromir Havlicek and Vladimir Jenicek, "Model of the Long-term Development of Czechoslovak Agriculture," *Czechoslovak Economic Papers* no. 11 [Prague: Academia, 1969], p. 83). These two authors from the Research Institute of Economic Planning in Prague, who set out to present in the above article a long-term planning model for the Czechoslovak economy, therefore conclude: "For this reason even the prognostic model has acquired the character of a supply model, whose main purpose it is to ascertain the productive potential, the prerequisites conditioning it, and also its efficiency" (ibid.).

The third quotation concerns Yugoslavia: "Demand for food has been expanding faster (6.4 percent per annum) than agricultural supply (5 percent per annum) throughout the postwar period" (E. E. Ian Hamilton, *Yugoslavia: Patterns of Economic Activity* [G. Bell and Sons, 1968], p. 158).

Table 15.2: Growth of Agricultural Production by Major Country
Groups, 1959–69

| Annual compound growth rate of agricultural production, 1959–69 | Soviet Union and East Europe | De-veloped market eco-nomies | Developing countries | | | | |
|---|---|---|---|---|---|---|---|
| | | | Aggre-gate | Latin America | Africa | Near East | Asia and Far East |
| Total | 3.1 | 2.5 | 2.9 | 3.3 | 2.4 | 2.9 | 2.9 |
| Per capita | 2.0 | 1.2 | 0.3 | 0.4 | 0.1 | 0.2 | 0.3 |

*Source:* Food and Agriculture Organisation (FAO), *Agricultural Commodity Projections 1970–1980* (Rome, 1971), 1:13, table 1.

Table 15.3: Trends in Available Food Supplies, 1960s
(In calories and protein per capita)

| Group of countries | Energy (calories) | | | Protein (grams) | | | Animal protein (grams) | | |
|---|---|---|---|---|---|---|---|---|---|
| | 1962 | 1965 | 1970 | 1962 | 1965 | 1970 | 1962 | 1965 | 1970 |
| Soviet Union and East Europe | 3,014 | 3,132 | 3,181 | 82.9 | 90.5 | 92.9 | 30.4 | 35.8 | 40.9 |
| West Europe | 2,949 | 2,997 | 3,051 | 86.6 | 86.3 | 88.6 | 42.0 | 45.3 | 48.7 |
| North America | 3,090 | 3,166 | 3,261 | 91.2 | 94.0 | 96.6 | 64.0 | 66.4 | 69.7 |

*Source:* See source note to table 15.2.

goods and consumer goods respectively.[5] This law was derived by Marx in a specific context and given some specific interpretations. These referred to the problem of the business cycle and its causes. Marx believed he had explained, through his analysis of the conditions of extended reproduction, why business cycles are inherent in the nature of capitalism. The gist of his argument is the requirement of strict equilibria between all the numerous segments and spheres of the economy as a prerequisite for smooth balanced growth of the economy as a whole. Of these numerous equilibria, that between departments 1 and 2 is only one, though the one of greatest importance. Marx argues that the nature of capitalist production is such that the balance between departments 1 and 2 is bound to be cyclically destroyed due to the workings of the market forces inherent in the capitalist system. In order to eliminate the business cycle, a fully planned economy would have to be established to replace the erratic market forces, with the task of seeing to it that the myriads of equilibria are constantly maintained everywhere in the economy. Marx's analysis seemed to imply

5. Karl Marx, *Das Kapital* (Hamburg: O. Meissner, 1867–94), vol. 2, pt. 3.

that under certain conditions (including the assumption of no technological progress) economic growth would require that department 1 should expand faster than department 2 in order for equilibrium to be maintained in the process of growth. However, this simplified theoretical model, apparently meant by its author to serve merely as an analytical tool, has been taken literally by Soviet planners and its implications have been proclaimed as constituting the fundamental law of development in any socialist economy.

The fallacy of this claim has already been exposed in economic literature, and this makes any further deliberations on the subject unnecessary.[6] There is one point, however, which seems worth touching upon in the context of our discussion. It concerns the consequences of such a growth model (one is tempted to call it the Stalinist model[7] as it has shaped the pattern of economic development in all communist countries since the time of Stalin's five-year plans) on agricultural growth in communist countries. In other words, leaving aside the problem of the validity of the law of extended reproduction,[8] I will consider the question of its practical consequences for agriculture when implemented as a principle of real-life economic policy.[9] The point is that this growth model is bound to produce (in the way explained above) a persistent shortage of agricultural supply in respect to demand in the course of economic growth. Unfortunately it is diffi-

6. See E. Domar, *Essays in the Theory of Economic Growth* (London: Oxford University Press, 1957), pp. 223–61; P. J. D. Wiles, *The Political Economy of Communism* (Oxford: Basil Blackwell, 1962), pp. 272–300; J. R. Hicks, *Capital and Growth* (Oxford: Clarendon Press, 1965), pt. 3.

7. "The low priority of agriculture was, of course, inherent in the nature of Stalinist industrialization. . . . Therefore the relative neglect of the needs of farming and especially of the peasants was no accidental [phenomenon]" (Alec Nove, "Peasant and Officials," in *Soviet and East European Agriculture*, ed. J. F. Karcz [Berkeley: University of California Press, 1967], p. 66).

8. Recent communist literature maintains that Stalin's strategy of degradation of agriculture was based on a false interpretation of Marx. See for example S. Felbur, *Problemy wzrostu produkcji rolniczej w Polsce* (Warsaw: Państwowe Wydawn Naukowe, 1972), pp. 31–37. The author asserts that Marx's schemata imply a requirement for a rather balanced approach to agriculture and industry as a condition for harmonious growth.

9. An attempt to find a reflection of this policy in statistics is presented in Lubo Sire, *Economic Revolution in Eastern Europe* (Longmans, 1969), chap. 2: "The Western countries have been investing comparatively more in agriculture than communist countries. . . . While the U.S. committed almost 3 per cent of its fixed 'productive' investment per 1 per cent of agricultural contribution to the national income, the U.S.S.R. comes very near to spending as little as 1 per cent of fixed 'productive' investment per 1 per cent of agricultural contribution of the national income" (p. 10).

cult to assess to what extent the Stalinist growth model and its consequences have been an inescapable feature of communist economic development, that is, how deeply inherent it is in the nature and goals of communism itself, or to what extent it represents a temporary, transient, subjective Stalinist aim which could easily be abandoned without changing the nature and goals of communism.

One might deliberate about Stalin's motives in advancing Marx's law of extended reproduction to the high place it has held in communist economic teaching. The fact is that he believed it to be a means of maximizing economic growth in the long run, and hence to be a guarantee of overtaking the most advanced capitalist countries in terms of the level of economic development, that is, per capita production in the shortest possible time. The pursuit of this goal was the principal and unquestionable aim of the communist movement. It seemed logical that the key to its achievement was the strictest possible implementation of Marx's law of extended reproduction in the practice of socialist planning. Communism accepted the above theory not only as an explanation of the instability of capitalist economic development but also as a straightforward guideline for socialism which would cure it of the capitalist ills and allow it to exercise all the advantages it was believed to have over capitalism, the main one being the ability to grow rapidly in a stable manner.

Of course Marx's schemata do not specify the extent to which department 1 has to expand faster than department 2. Therefore, when Stalin began to implement Marx's theory in planning he had to determine this detail himself. He settled for giving maximum possible priority to heavy industry at the expense of every other sector of the economy not directly contributing to the growth of productive capacity.[10] The aim was to increase productive capacity at the maximum possible rate. This meant producing the greatest possible number of machines capable of producing machines, in order to produce even more machines. No question was ever raised as to the limits of the priority given to the production of means of production. The only rule was the more the better. It also seemed that one did not need to bother about the possible negative effect of this policy and its harmful consequences on the current standard of living, namely, a fall which could

10. Probably the first interpretation of Marx's schemata as implying a massive contribution of agriculture to industrialization was given by E. Preobrazhenskiv, *Novaya ekonomika, cpyt teoreticheskovo analiza sovietskovo khozyaystva,* 1 (Moscow: Kommunistischeskaîa Akademiia, Sektsiîa Ekonomiki, 1926): 130–32; English trans. by Brian Pearce, *The New Economics* (Oxford: Clarendon Press, 1966).

result in a reduction of the productivity of labor and, in the end, cause a slowing down of the rate of growth in relation with what could be achieved with a more balanced approach to the expansion of departments 1 and 2. Communist indoctrination was supposed to take adequate care of the morale of the populace. The latter's isolation from the outside world and the ruthless suppression of dissent were supposed to protect it against any defeatist ideas that might emanate from abroad or arise spontaneously from inside.

There is no doubt that the Stalinist pattern of economic growth was successful in producing rapid rates of expansion of productive capacity, though at the cost of an extremely low standard of living and un imaginable hardships and sacrifices for the peoples subjected to it. The point that an even higher rate of growth at a much lower cost in terms of sacrifices could have been obtained if there had been less imbalance between departments 1 and 2 is immaterial, since it has not been understood in communist countries. For the entire Stalinist era and long afterward it has been commonly accepted in the communist movement that the rate of economic growth is the single main criterion of superiority of one socioeconomic system over the other. This belief rested on the persuasive suggestion that a country with a higher growth rate must in time overtake one with a lower growth rate in terms of the level of economic attainment. The time factor was usually overlooked in these considerations. The sacrifice of the well-being of contemporary generations for the sake of the future was taken for granted. The general public has been unaware of the real effect the race with advanced capitalist countries for the achievement of faster growth would have on their standard of living. It was deluded by the chance of eventually achieving the highest level of economic development, in the belief that this would not come too late and would be tantamount to a record standard of living then. Thus two factors contributed to the establishment of the Stalinist pattern of growth in communist countries: its ruthless enforcement by the states concerned, and the more or less general compliance with it by a public deceived as to its costs and objectives.

### THE PREFERENCE FOR COLLECTIVIZATION

However significant the above-mentioned implications of the general pattern of economic growth as practiced by communist countries, they are not the sole determinant of the pattern of agricultural growth.

Communist beliefs regarding the objectives of agricultural policy and communist ideas concerning forms of ownership in farming constitute another set of factors determining the specific features of this pattern. In particular these include (1) communist hostility toward capitalist forms of farming; (2) the unfriendly attitude toward peasant and small private holdings; and (3) the belief in the necessity of subordinating agriculture—like the rest of the economy—to far-reaching forms of government and party control and supervision.

In the context of communist hostility toward capitalist ownership in farming, two problems seem to have a bearing on the role of agriculture in the process of economic growth. The first is the impact of the land reforms,[11] and the second is the effects of the policy of suppression carried out in relation to the remnants of larger holdings which, being below the reform ceiling, had not been broken up. This policy applies also to all well-to-do farms that exhibit a particularly strong growth potential. Basically, land reforms exercise their impact on agricultural growth in two ways: economic and sociopolitical. In theory the economic effect of land reforms on agricultural growth is by no means unambiguous. It has sometimes been suggested that the effect might be unfavorable, and particularly harmful to the industrialization program whose success is the crucial condition for sustained growth. This argument is based mainly on the assumption that the large landed property, whose break-up is the essence of the land reform, is much more market oriented than the family holdings which benefit from the reform and which take over from the former the task of supplying the economy with agricultural produce. The point is that the proportion of marketed agricultural output is bound to fall in the wake of the land reform.

The experience of East European communist countries seems to demonstrate convincingly the erroneous nature of this sort of reasoning. Not only did land reforms not hamper the provision of food

11. "In Eastern Europe as a whole, land reforms affected almost a quarter of all land used for agriculture and forestry. The state kept about half of the confiscated land. Large-estate farming disappeared completely (except on state farms), and most of the land was given to small peasants. After completion of the reforms, small and subsistence farm units accounted for two-fifths or more of all land in Bulgaria and Hungary and about a quarter of private acreage in Poland and Czechoslovakia. Medium-large and large peasant farms were important only in Czechoslovakia, where they comprised about half of total private land, and in Poland, where they comprised a third. Their share of total private holdings in Bulgaria and Hungary was one-fifth and one-fourth respectively" (Nicolas Spulber, *The Economics of Communist Eastern Europe* [New York, 1957], p. 245).

for the increasing urban population in the course of industrialization but they made it possible for this process to take place simultaneously with an improvement in the standard of consumption of the rural population as well. This experience is undoubtedly one of the most valuable lessons to be learned from the strategy of agricultural growth of the communist countries. It shows that land reform itself can, in a relatively short period of time, result in such an increase of total agricultural output that despite the fall of the proportion marketed the absolute volume of the latter may still increase. The rise in agricultural output is stimulated by the economically more rational combination of factors of production brought about by the more equal distribution of land in agriculture resulting from the land reform.

Before the reform the basic drawback of the prevailing pattern of land ownership and labor utilization was that, on the one hand, the bulk of the labor was employed on farms whose labor/land ratio was too high to secure high levels of labor productivity and that, on the other hand, the bulk of the land was occupied by farms whose labor/land ratio was too low to achieve a high level of land productivity.

On tiny, dwarfish holdings the labor force cannot be fully utilized economically. Land is intensively cultivated to the point of near zero marginal returns. On the other hand, in the large capitalist farms labor is hired only to the point determined by profit considerations, and land is cultivated somewhat less intensively than the amount of available agricultural labor would require if the aim were the maximization of output rather than profit from the existing amount of land and labor available in the economy as a whole.

Land reform to a large extent removes both of the above drawbacks. The breaking up of the biggest holdings and the transfer of most of their land to the smallest farms rationalizes the labor/land ratio in the farms benefiting from the reform. All in all, both labor and land productivity rise. On the one hand the broken up plots are worked to produce more per unit of land, and on the other hand the small farmers who acquire land increase the productivity of their labor input. (The rise in land productivity does not necessarily mean higher yields per unit of land, but rather a more intensive pattern of land usage and a higher degree of conversion of crops into animal products.) Consequently agriculture produces more after the land reform than before, though it may sometimes take a while for the transient difficulties that unavoidably accompany the management of the reform itself to be overcome. In the end, however, the increase in agricultural output resulting from the new pattern of land distribution makes it possible for the farmers both to eat better and also to market more, to support the rising standard of consumption among the urban population whose incomes rise due to industrialization.

It has sometimes been feared that the elimination of large-scale farming would destroy the most advanced centers of agricultural progress and annihilate the very fine stock of know-how accumulated there, particularly with regard to the cultivation of some highly demanding plants and their varieties and the breeding of especially valuable animals. In this way the land reform was supposed to have an adverse effect on agricultural growth. The experience of East European countries proves all such fears to be exaggerated.

The noneconomic, mainly sociological effects of the land reform on agricultural growth are even more significant.[12] One cannot overestimate the beneficial effects of the eradication of the landed class on the social status of the peasantry. It radically weakens the barriers between the peasantry, as the lowest social stratum, and the rest of society. Although the fact that the peasantry remains at the bottom of the social ladder of course cannot be changed, the ladder itself gets shorter, even if only temporarily. The philosophy that justified the old pattern of social stratification, with its inequalities and privileges, disappears, and by the same token a belief in greater equality and better chances for all takes root, whether it corresponds to reality or not. A new psychological mood emerges among the peasantry, and particularly its younger generation. All this contributes to greater dynamism and entrepreneurship among the farming population. This change is further assisted by some indirect effects of other reforms. Thanks to industrialization, new career opportunities are open to those young people who want to leave farming. Education becomes more accessible, and farm education attracts more pupils who will eventually make their contribution to agricultural growth. The most gifted individuals find their way to positions previously unattainable, and this in itself marks an improvement in the degree of utilization of the nation's stock

12. "The conception of a break with the past can be a powerful stimulus in national life. Because land systems are deeply rooted in custom and tradition, and preservative of social attitudes hostile to change, and because the cultivators of the land are at the bottom of the social hierarchy, the decision to carry out a land reform crystallizes the determination to break with the past in an irrevocable way. That decision may well be one of the strategic factors in development" (Doreen Warriner, "Land Reform and Economic Development," in Eicher and Witt, *Agriculture in Economic Development*, p. 280).

of talent and obviously has a beneficial effect on the growth of the economy. On the whole the land reform speeds up the growth of the economy not only in a direct manner by stimulating agricultural growth, but also by making an indirect contribution to faster growth of the nonagricultural sectors of the economy.[13]

An entirely different role seems to be performed by the communist policy of "containing capitalist elements in agriculture," which follows the land reform. The policy is deliberately aimed at retarding the growth of the wealthier farmers, that is, all those prosperous entrepreneurs who exploit existing opportunities for their own good and that of the economy. This policy is carried out under the assumption that such farms pose a threat to the socialist order of the country.

The containment of capitalist elements in agriculture takes a variety of forms, depending on the time and place of its application. The most common ones are: the imposition of land ceilings to farm holdings through a prohibition of the purchase of land, the imposition of a limit on the number of hired hands, the prohibition of the purchase of some types of equipment (e.g., tractors), steeply progressive tax levies, and discrimination in provision of agricultural supplies. Often special types of discrimination are added—for example, barring higher education to the children of wealthier farmers and the like.

The harm done to agriculture through state persecution of these so-called capitalist elements cannot be exaggerated. Though the number of farms falling in that category may be relatively small, their share in aggregate agricultural output and particularly in the output marketed is very great. For one thing, they farm a higher proportion of agricul-

---

13. The beneficial effects of the land reforms in Eastern Europe may be regarded as opposite to the results of the capitalist changes they underwent about a century ago. "In Eastern Europe capitalism worsened the lot of the peasant. . . . To regulate production by profit maximization is probably the worst thing that can happen to an overpopulated economy, for that would increase unwanted leisure while diminishing the national product" (Nicolas Georgescu-Roegen, "Economic Theory and Agrarian Economics," *Oxford Economic Papers* 12 [1960]: 34). The two opposite effects are, in fact, based on the same economics.
Interesting though highly controversial theoretical considerations of possible effects of land reforms on agricultural output and growth are presented by V. M. Dandekar. Of particular interest is his point that, "for various technological considerations, it seems that even in agriculture, in order to realize maximum output from given amounts of resources, the production unit has to be of an optimum size," from which the author derives the conclusion that "the argument leads inevitably to a structure composed of large production units managed not on capitalist principles, but for collective good" (V. M. Dandekar, "Economic Theory and Agrarian Reform," *Oxford Economic Papers* 14 [1962]: 69–79).

tural land than is suggested in terms of mere numbers; they also represent the most proficient, productive, and dynamic elements in agriculture. Moreover, such anticapitalist policies, even if directed in theory only against a small section of the farming population, in reality assume much wider proportions. Restrictions designed to impede the expansion of the economically strongest units only will in fact affect to various degrees a much greater number of farms. In effect a crucial part of agriculture is paralyzed as a result of deliberate efforts to prevent some of the farms from turning capitalist and to hamper the growth of those that cannot be anything but capitalist. It is a paradoxical affair, since the produce of all farms is badly needed by the economy and the services of the best ones cannot be replaced.

However, of even greater importance than the hostility of the communist state to capitalist elements in agriculture is its unfriendly attitude toward peasant farming in general. Communism is ideologically opposed to private ownership of the means of production, and this applies to ownership of small plots of land by small private farmers no less than to capitalists. First, all small private holdings are a denial of, and a challenge to, the collectivist philosophy and ethics of communism because of the spirit of individualism, entrepreneurship, and private initiative on which they are based and which they nurture. For this reason, small private farming is classified in Marxist-Leninist theory as half-related to capitalism,[14] despite the admission that because of the way the small farmer earns his living the other half of his soul gravitates toward the working class. It is implied, therefore, that the private farmer, with the possible exception of the smallest ones, is by nature a dubious ally of the ruling socialist order. He may, in certain circumstances, tend to side with capitalism in the political struggle between the socialist state and the remnants of capitalism in society.

Second, communist economic doctrine strongly argues that the system of small private farming is extremely backward and inefficient. It is a tenet of Marxism that the emergence of large-scale capitalist production is a natural outcome of the historical process of economic progress; as for the small private farm, it represents a remnant of

14. "In the official attitudes of Communist governments workers as a group are in general idealized as opposed to farmers. These attitudes are reinforced by the schools and mass media, as well as by the disadvantaged position of the farmer in a nation placing emphasis on industrial growth. There then naturally arises an antipathy and contempt with regard to farming as a way of life or even as an occupation" (Joel M. Halpern, "Farming as a Way of Life: Yugoslav Peasant Attitudes," in Karcz, *Soviet and East European Agriculture,* p. 361).

precapitalist modes of production and is a stumbling-block in the way of socialist agricultural growth. Communist economic theory believes fanatically in the superiority of large-scale production in agriculture and aims to transform small-scale private farming into large-scale socialist enterprise.[15]

The innate aversion to private peasant farming determines another of the peculiarities of the pattern of agricultural growth as experienced in the communist countries of Eastern Europe. It produces the persistent endeavor to eliminate all private farms and to replace them with collective ones. There is little doubt, at present, that this doctrinally motivated pursuit has made its own contribution to the retardation of agricultural growth in most, if not all, countries concerned.

### EFFICIENCY PROBLEMS OF COLLECTIVE AGRICULTURE

Although the aim of collectivization was to obtain a more efficient organization of agriculture in terms of increased productivity and higher growth rates of output, the results of this operation hardly match the expectations. The amalgamated large-scale collective farms undoubtedly create more favorable potential conditions for crop production. However, for the new potentialities to materialize a number of requirements must be met. For example, a new type of heavier technical equipment is demanded, as is qualified management expert in both agricultural and economic matters.[16] In reality the communist economies, subjected to the specific pattern of growth, are anything but suited to meeting any such requirements, particularly insofar as technology and industrial supplies for agriculture are concerned. Moreover, the farmers' mood and attitude—since they have been collectivized under pressure—is rather nonconducive to high attainments.

15. "The collectivization of agriculture to some extent reflected the naive Marxian view that the efficiencies of large-scale organization were as applicable to agriculture as to industry; it was primarily aimed at destroying the independent peasantry which remained the chief potential threat to the Soviet regime" (W. H. Nicholls, "The Place of Agriculture in Economic Development," in Eicher and Witt, *Agriculture in Economic Development,* p. 28).

16. According to the Albanian minister of agriculture ("Rruga e partise," no. 3 [1971], pp. 23–31), collective farms are lagging behind state farms because "they can no longer be administered by their members and elected management. They need an administrative and scientific apparatus to take care of the plan, research, finance, etc.: simple book-keeping is not sufficient" (reprinted in *Abstract of Soviet and East European Statistics (ABSEES),* pt. 2, [1971]: 1–140).

Animal husbandry on the collective farms lacks even the potential superiority that exists, in theory at least, in crop production. Experience shows that the size of a particular plot has no bearing on the scale and productivity of livestock production. Hence the collective farms have no particular advantage here over the small private plots.[17] Rather, the opposite is the case.

The former private farmers already have the necessary buildings in their yards, whereas the collective farms are short of capital and materials to erect new ones for this purpose.[18] Besides, animal farming is a labor-consuming activity. The farmer's family has an excess of labor which is most conveniently utilized in looking after the animals in their private yards. As a result, it is the tiny private plots of the members of the collectives that manage to run relatively large animal farms, despite the smallness of the plots,[19] and not the collective enterprises with their vast fields. These lack adequate facilities and have difficulty in getting their members, and particularly their families, to work hard for the collectives.

The tensions and conflicts of interest that tend to arise between the collective enterprise and the members' private plots over the question of animal husbandry are the more astounding in view of the fact that the two seem to be linked by some natural complementarity. On the one hand, in order to be able to develop livestock production, the collective enterprises would require members to be willing to supply more labor. Also, private plots produce relatively great amounts of manure, for which collective fields are starving.[20] On the other hand,

17. "While the limitations of the collective farming system are considerable even in achieving efficient grain production, they may prove to be insurmountable in achieving efficient livestock production" (Nicholls, "Place of Agriculture in Economic Development," p. 24).

18. "Attempts were made to introduce collectivized animal husbandry. The capital costs of construction were of course considerable, and the problem was accentuated by widespread shortages of materials. Nor was it easy to avoid the spread of tuberculosis or brucellosis under those circumstances. In many instances, livestock suffered from a shortage of stalls" (J. Karcz, "Comparative Study of Transformation of Agriculture in Centrally Planned Economics: The Soviet Union, Eastern Europe, and Mainland China," in *The Role of Agriculture in Economic Development,* ed. E. Thorbecke [New York: National Bureau of Economic Research, 1969], p. 246).

19. In Hungary, for instance, the share of private plots in the market produce of agriculture in 1971 was as follows: milk, meat, and poultry, 30 percent; eggs, 35 percent; fruit and vegetables, 25 percent (Istvan Szalo, president of the National Council of Producers' Cooperatives, in *Nepszabadsag,* March 30, 1972, pp. 1–3).

20. The following observation by J. M. Montias suggests that, although this specific conflict of interests may seem of minor importance, one must not dismiss it too easily. He writes, with reference to Rumania: "the transformation of private into col-

the expansion of animal farms on the private plots requires large amounts of fodder which must, at least partially, come from collective crops.[21] This clash of interests which arises in practice in Eastern European agriculture is far from being resolved and does not help the growth of agricultural output.

The tensions and clashes between the two partners of collectivized farms manifestly demonstrate the failure of the underlying ideology. The most striking proof is that in the procurement of some vital agricultural foodstuffs for the population the actually microscopic private plots play a role several times larger than their share in the stock of land, capital, or industrial supplies would indicate. Contrary to original theoretical suppositions, which envisaged them as tiny vegetable gardens of no serious economic significance either to the farmer or to the country as a whole, the latter could not do without their output. Also, the members of collective farms derive almost as much income from their plots as from the collective farms themselves.[22] The small plots have in a sense turned into the private farms they once replaced, although they are much smaller in size.

The overall result of collectivization in terms of its effect on factor combination in agriculture is, therefore, opposite to that of the land reform. Once again the overall stock of agricultural land has been split into two parts: one farmed in the form of large and the other in the

---

lective farms failed to raise the average application of natural fertilizers on the collectives, which, if anything, applied them even more sparingly than before. . . . Overall performance in crop output would have been better if a sharp reduction had not occurred in the application of organic fertilizers, especially to soils planted with cereals. Since animal herds increased during the period, the potential supply of these fertilizers should not have declined. It is probable that collectivization as such, or apprehensions of it, affected the use—or nonuse—of this valuable resource" (J. M. Montias, *Economic Development in Communist Rumania* [Cambridge: MIT Press, 1967], pp. 110, 112–13).

21. "Some kolkhozniki complain that they do not receive fodder or meadows to make hay for their private livestock" (Selskoye Khozaystvo, July 20, 1971, p. 3, reported in *ABSEES* 2, no. 2 [1971]: 71). Note also the following observation by Alec Nove: "Voprosy ekonomiki showed that restrictions on the private plot are counterproductive, since all additional difficulties in getting fodder compel the peasants to devote more time to a smaller number of private livestock" (Alec Nove, "Peasant and Officials," in Karcz, *Soviet and East European Agriculture,* p. 61).

22. "In Georgia the proceeds from the private plots constituted more than 50 percent and from the collective farms only 25 percent of all farmers' earnings" (A. Teriayeva, *Voprosy Ekonomiki,* 1972, no. 5, p. 71). N. Jasny estimated that in 1958 the collective farms provided the peasants with only a quarter of their incomes, the other three-quarters coming from their private plots. For the East European countries those figures are undoubtedly exaggerated.

form of small productive units. Once again the former exhibits low indices of land productivity and the latter low levels of labor productivity. The overall productivity of land and labor is below what it could be under an alternative pattern of land distribution which ensured in all productive units a land/labor ratio closer to the overall average in the respective localities.[23]

There can be no doubt that collectivization has so far not succeeded in rooting out the private proprietor's mentality in its members and in replacing it with the collectivist mentality required by the ruling socialist order. The members of the collectives are as strongly attached to their private plots as they once were to their private farms, and their indifference toward the collective farm is so striking that there can be no question as to whether it will ever be regarded by the farm population as anything but alien. The collective farms seem to have nothing in them that would tend to integrate the communities of one-time private farmers into socialist brotherhoods cemented by internal solidarity and loyalty, and which would induce their members to place the common, collective interest above the private interest. The only case in which anything like group solidarity would emerge is when the particular group's interest clashed with that of another group, the state, or society at large.

One must not overlook another crucial characteristic of the collectivist system, namely, that it does very little in fact to reduce economic inequalities not attributable to qualifications and quality of work. Even ignoring the fact that the distribution of income within particular collective farms is far from the principle "to each according to his work," the differences and disparities in the earnings of members of different collectives are to such an extent determined by factors like quantity of land per member, land quality, climate, size of local market, economic development of the region, the amount of capital goods owned by the collective, and so on, that they fully resemble the differences and disparities existing in private agriculture.[24]

23. "Suppose these plot farms were increased to no more than ten acres and suppose small hand (garden-type) tractors and complementary machines and equipment were made available: total agricultural production in the Soviet Union would rise sharply and chiefly of those farm products that are at present in short supply" (T. W. Schultz, *Transforming Traditional Agriculture* [New Haven: Yale University Press, 1964], p. 113).

24. "Studies in the three Baltic republics where land has been evaluated according to a point system showed that differences in profit rates between farms were about two thirds due to objective factors (differences in land and equipment) rather than subjective. But the predominant objective factor is differences in the supply of fixed

Contrary to the egalitarian philosophy behind the collectivization reform, collectives are poor and rich for the same reasons that private farms are, namely, whether they possess more or less land and capital, whether they are more or less advantageously located, and so on.[25] All this is in striking contrast to the socialist ideas on which they are based.

The communist countries of East Europe have traveled a long way along the collectivization route, through numerous trials and errors, since the Soviet Union first embarked on it almost half a century ago, and, though reluctantly, they learned a few lessons from those experiences. They have therefore been able to avoid some of the most disastrous failures of the Soviet Union in agriculture. Despite this the lessons are undoubtedly far from complete. The all-too-frequent and numerous turns and changes in agricultural policies bear witness to this. To mention only the main ones, one could cite, for example, the dissolution of the Machine Tractor Stations (MTS), the fluctuation in policies toward private plots, the imposition and abolition of compulsory deliveries, the invention of the day's work unit and the experiments to abandon it, and, last but not least, the total abandonment of the collectivization programs in Poland and Yugoslavia with no clear prospect for their reintroduction at any definite time in the future.

True, the Polish and Yugoslav cases, apart from some possible politi-

---

and working capital which explain 50–60 percent of all profit rate variations. Differences in land quality explain 10–25 percent of variations. But in 70–80 percent of cases farms with better capital equipment and labour supply are those that have better-quality land and/or are better situated (proxmiity to sales and supply points)" (M. Bronstein, *Voprosy Ekonomiki,* 1972, no. 4, pp. 75–85). Similar observations are made by the same author in *Voprosy Ekonomiki,* 1970, no. 9, pp. 44–53, and also by A. Kotechenkov, V. Sevasmyanov, and N. Turischev in ibid., 1970, no. 8, pp. 68–75.

25. M. Kozlov presents the following correlation between the volume of capital per unit of land and the profitability rates in the collective farms of Smolensk oblast in 1968:

| Capital per unit of land (in rubles per hectare) | Number of farms | Profitability rate (%) |
|---|---|---|
| 174.9–250.4 | 33 | 12.9 |
| 250.9–291.9 | 52 | 15.5 |
| 292.1–351.0 | 88 | 19.2 |
| 351.9–424.6 | 52 | 24.9 |
| 425.6–662.3 | 33 | 37.6 |
| Total | 238 | 22.1 |

*Source:* M. Kozlov, *Voprosy Ekonomiki* 1971, no. 12, p. 39.

cal considerations, seem to be explained basically by a combination of two major factors: (1) the abundance of labor in agriculture, and (2) the high natural rate of population growth. Not only do the two countries in question have an adequate supply of labor in industry but industry seems to be incapable of absorbing all of it.[26] In these circumstances collectivization would only aggravate the problem of disguised unemployment which, at least in Poland, exists in both the agricultural and nonagricultural sectors of the economy.

In East Germany and Czechoslovakia the situation is entirely different, and a very special and specific factor enters into the picture. These two most industrially advanced countries of the East European bloc have long experienced a labor shortage in industry and thus they had an additional motive for collectivization, aiming in this way at speeding up the transfer of labor to industry while minimizing the possible adverse effect of a rapid fall in the number of people employed in agriculture on its output and growth.

How successful collectivization is as a means for achieving such aims would be difficult to assess on the basis of these two cases alone. It is obvious that their agricultural growth is not at all impressive. Hence it must remain doubtful whether collectivization of agriculture could be regarded as an efficient economic policy instrument for ac-

26. See, for example, the following discussion:
  If we really want to speed up the rate of increase of real wages we must limit the decline of the absolute level of agricultural employment (which during the late decade, 1961–1970, had been diminishing at 1 percent per annum) to a rate that would make it possible to reduce (and even a fraction of a percent counts in this context) the hitherto rapid increase of employment outside agriculture.
  In all types of industrial and commercial businesses, in the services, and particularly in various offices there is excessive employment which finds its expression in the poor utilization of the labor force. In a sense one could speak of a zero marginal productivity of a considerable proportion of employees in the nonagricultural sector. I believe that in these conditions the transfer of labor from agriculture not only does not contribute to the growth of national income but actually diminishes the rate of wage-rate increases [W. Herer, "Rolnicza bariera wzrostu plac," in *Dyskusja o polityee rolnej PRL,* ed. J. Rasiński (Warsaw: Państwowe Wydawn, Rolnicze i Leśne, 1971–72), p. 163].
  See also the following:
  Surplus labor in agriculture can be estimated to amount to 1.5–2.2 million people, or 26–38 percent of the total agricultural labor force. This is, however, only a potential surplus. Practical conditions for its utilization will emerge in the course of the socialist reconstruction of agriculture. On the other hand they also depend on the ability of industry and the nonagricultural sector at large to absorb the above surplus. . . . The Polish farmer has the lowest relative productivity in comparison with both the European socialist and advanced capitalist countries [Felbur, *Problemy wzrostu producji rolniczej w Polsce,* pp. 129–30].

celerating the transfer of labor from agriculture to industry at a relatively advanced stage of industrial development.[27]

All in all, in the light of East European experience, one must remain skeptical about the value of collectivization in accelerating agricultural growth. Certainly, the effect in the short and medium run has been rather negative. What it will be in the much longer run can only be a matter for speculation.

State control, being one of the major canons of the communist creed, is closely connected with the belief in the overriding importance of economic planning, particularly insofar as the achievement of smooth and uninterrupted growth is concerned. But the striving for all-embracing state control of agriculture stems from a number of special characteristics attributed to it. Agriculture is believed to be of a particularly volatile nature. It is viewed as a combination of elements in which spontaneity is inherent: (1) biological and climatic forces, (2) the instability of peasants, and (3) market forces. The integration of agriculture into the economic system of communist planned growth is therefore said to require some special measures to harness all these forces and subordinate them to the control of the state.

This control covers three major areas: production, marketing, and income distribution. It is worth emphasizing that, at one time, state intervention in production went so far as the issue of exact directives to particular farms regarding what, where, when, and how much to produce and also by what means and methods. There is no doubt, and even communist leaders have been outspoken on this subject, that most of the petty regulations and interventions concerning the organization of productive processes in particular agricultural enterprises have proved to be absurd and extremely harmful. By now such excesses have been abandoned; the general tendency in all managerial and planning reforms in agriculture successively introduced in various East European countries have been to relax this type of restrictions gradually, though only up to a point.[28]

27. There is no doubt, however, that labor shortages persisting in the collective farms are to a large extent responsible for the major problems continuously plaguing agriculture in these countries, as is for instance apparent from an article in *Einheit,* 1971, no. 5, pp. 551–60. The article complains that there is a tendency to reduce the cultivation of labor-intensive crops and animal husbandry on collective farms. Many collective farms find it difficult to keep cultivation within the specified limits. There is a general reluctance to engage in multishift work, as farms claim that they do not have the necessary labor force for one full shift, let alone more. See *ABSEES* 2, pt. 2 (1971): 179.

28. See, for example, the following assessment of Polish failure:

On the other hand there should be little doubt that all the extensive and detailed planning of agricultural production is in some sense of little real importance. Normally the planners try to anticipate what would be done by farmers anyway. Thus they envisage the production of the same crops and rearing of the same animals that would in any case have occurred. Usually they prescribe the use of methods that are in common practice, at times ones that are more or less dictated by nature. This safeguards agriculture from the extreme wastes that might result from major errors in planning. Thus, it appears that there are some natural limits to the nonsense of this purely bureaucratic activity.

How negligible is the real influence of central directives on the development of agricultural production can be seen from a comparison of the major trends in the composition of planned agricultural output with similar trends which automatically take place in market economies. One would be unable to detect in East European countries any difference from what would have to be expected under the circumstances without planning.[29]

Another proof of the virtual impotence of the planning of agricultural output is the instability of agricultural growth and the all-too-wide

---

The situation may seem paradoxical but for years there has been no discernible sign of a production policy relevant to the natural and socioeconomic conditions of our agriculture.

The production policy, implying a concerted action corresponding to the objective conditions of agricultural development, has been replaced by fragmentary programs. There are plenty of them. The grain program, the seed program, the fertilizer program, the drainage program, the ensilage program, the drier program, the building program, and the like.

All these programs have been either mutually contradictory or uncoordinated, to say the least. As a result they are inefficient and wasteful. The implementation of some of them with no regard to an overall agricultural production policy has been harmful to social needs. The grain program set against the growth of pig production serves as a prime example [J. Rasiński, "O rozwoju polskiego rolnietwa i polityce rolnej dyskusyjnie," *Polityka,* 1971, no. 8].

29. A rather unusual exemplification of this generalization can be found in the following observation regarding Rumania. "The output of agricultural products requiring a long production cycle—fruits, grapes, and beef—has lagged seriously behind that of short-cycle products like annual crops, pork and eggs, particularly in the last decade. An identical phenomenon would have been observed in a free market system, ceteris paribus, if the interest rates paid by farmers on bank credits had risen steeply. In the Rumanian context, the shortening of the average production cycle of farm produce, which seems especially marked since the onset of the last collectivization campaign, may represent the farmers' response to the increased risk and uncertainty of tying up resources in slow-maturing investments (for example in fruit trees, vineyards, and large-horned cattle)" (Montias, *Economic Development in Communist Rumania,* pp. 101–02).

amplitude of its fluctuations, mentioned at the beginning of this chapter. East European planning of agricultural growth has manifestly failed to fulfill the basic task of stabilizing growth through the elimination, or at least moderation, of excessive and destructive fluctuations.

However, the most serious failure of production planning is related to technological progress. The basic reason for the relative backwardness of agricultural technology in most East European countries is the extreme shortage of modern industrial inputs and machines due to the underdevelopment of the industries supplying agriculture. But there are also specific obstacles inherent in the system of generating and promoting technological progress in agriculture. This task is entirely assigned to a bureaucratic machine of state institutions in which there is little room for genuine innovation and entrepreneurship and which are not exposed to any competition. The lack of pressure from the market and its weakness hinder the transmission of any spontaneous inspirations and feedbacks from farmers to industry. A few Polish examples may serve as cases in point. In the 1950s Polish planners were caught by surprise when the results of an agricultural census revealed a strong drive on the part of the peasants to replace the traditional iron-rimmed wheels of their horse-driven carts with used car tires. It turned out that this tiny innovation was of major economic importance to the farmer since it helped to increase considerably the effective hauling power of the existing horse population. Surveys carried out *ex post* indicated that transporting products to and from the fields and to and from the towns had been taking up about 50 percent of the farmer's working day. But tires continued to be practically unobtainable in the shops and warehouses. The only source of supply remained the black market.

Another aspect is revealed by the recent case of fertilizers. For years they had been in short supply. In the late 1960s it was decided to solve the problem abruptly through huge investments in fertilizer plants. Very shortly, as a result of the large scale of the change compressed into too short a span of time, an excess fertilizer supply developed and the productivity of fertilizer dropped considerably. It is becoming evident that at least some of the money could have been spent much more efficiently on some other technological improvements, and that a bigger increase of agricultural output could have been obtained with the same resources.[30]

30. Nakonieezny, "Wiecej kultury na kilogram nawozów," *Zycie Gospodarcze,* 1971, no. 11. Also Herer, "Rolnicza bariera wzrostu plac."

To cite another, more recent example, for a number of years it had been assumed that the basic harvesting machine on private farms should be the sheaf-binder, and production plans had been geared accordingly. Last year harvesting was particularly difficult because of heavy rains and sheaf-binders proved to be of little use. Farmers were looking for combine harvesters. Whole villages were literally fighting for the chance of getting hold of those few that were in the possession of the so-called agricultural circles.[31] It turns out that it is the peasant himself who must rectify the planners' errors in anticipating the lines of technological development. It is no wonder considerable delay and waste are caused.

All this is not to say that central planning and management of agriculture have had no success at all as far as the growth of agricultural output is concerned. Suffice it to point to the common feature in all communist countries of the impressively fast growth of the output of technical crops, exceeding considerably the average rates of increase of agricultural output. This rapid expansion of the output of raw materials for industry is a matter of deliberate state policies embodied in agricultural production plans and originates from these plans. However, and this is most instructive, in order to achieve this success the plans do not rely mainly on administrative directives (as in other cases) but rather make wide use of material incentives; in other words, the plans act chiefly through market forces and especially through the basic one—prices and profitability.[32] Plan directives appear here as a camouflage of the real economic forces behind them, namely, strong market incentives that stimulate growth. Of course the latter are manipulated by the plans but they reflect the existence of a demand, which in order to induce a corresponding supply must find its expression in an adequate level of profitability in a way similar to that which would operate in a free, unplanned market economy.

The control of agricultural production is not an aim in itself. In fact

31. A.Woś, "Wnioski z doświadczeń," *Zycie Gospodarcze,* October 9, 1972.
32. "Experience has proved that direct intervention through administrative directives in farming does not result in a strengthening of the role of the central plan in agricultural growth but, to the contrary, weakens it. . . . Experience has also proved that the transmission of the centrally planned tasks through the market, that is, through the price system and really free contracting, constitutes the most effective way of subordinating agriculture to those tasks" (Herer, "Rolnicza bariera wzrostu plac," pp. 155–15). According to Kahan, "the relatively high prices for cotton and tea turned out to be more conducive to raising output than the method originally applied," that is, administrative directives (see "Collective Farm System in Russia," p. 262).

it is merely a means of controlling and determining agricultural procurements. Production processes are interfered with only because they predetermine the latter in terms of both quantity and composition. On the other hand, the control of the agricultural market is a vital element of the communist pattern of economic growth in general. The absolute necessity of this control is an unavoidable consequence of the drive to maximize the rate of growth of industrial productive capacity at the expense of industries not contributing directly to this expansion, which include also industries producing agricultural supplies. The check on the growth of agricultural output resulting from this policy and its permanent shortage in relation to demand makes it practically impossible for the communist countries to leave the agricultural market to itself. For the conditions of permanent imbalance between supply and demand prevailing in the agricultural market tend to force up agricultural prices and incomes, produce inflation, and thus distort the planned pattern of income distribution between agriculture and industry, ultimately threatening the adopted pattern of growth and its tempo. Thus the aim of the control of the agricultural market is, in fact, a dual one: to extract from agriculture as large a volume of procurements as possible, and to keep down agricultural prices. The task is certainly formidable in view of the circumstances described.

The difficulty of the problem explains the numerous experiments, the variety of methods, and the multitude of changes that have taken place in the pursuit of a solution to it. The application of various forms of extraction of procurements from agricultural farms at a low price has been an outstanding feature of state-farm relations in all communist countries. Compulsory deliveries, taxation in kind, sharing by MTS in the farm output, remuneration in kind for their services, so-called planned contraction of agricultural produce—all these methods have contained strong, though sometimes slightly disguised, elements of coercion.

At this point it is tempting to compare the communist technique of controlling income distribution between agriculture and industry, represented by the above measures, with that exemplified by the known Japanese growth pattern, which depended on both the preservation of private, small-scale farming in a free market and the imposition of an extremely high level of taxation on peasant holdings. In this latter method fiscal measures instead of market intervention are employed to make agriculture contribute to the costs of industrialization.

Does this comparison offer any firm conclusions regarding the relative effectiveness of the two alternative methods? The high efficiency of the Japanese strategy of growth is commonly appreciated.[33] The disastrous, in many respects, results of the communist practices are also widely recognized. Despite this striking difference in the general evaluation of the two examples, however, one must be cautious not to stretch the comparison too far because of the enormous differences between the countries involved. This is not to say that the comparison with Japan does not offer well substantiated arguments against the East European approach.

It appears that the methods employed there to control the agricultural market and the distribution of income between agriculture and industry owe some of their characteristics to the fact that they originated under Stalin and reflect to a large extent his preference (if not predilection) for brute force and drastic measures, particularly in dealing with peasants. These methods represent one of his personal imprints on communist development which outlived him for several years.

It is no wonder that, having learned their lesson, all communist countries seem to be engaged in a process of experimenting with new methods of agricultural market and income regulations. By and large they seem to depend on a switch from direct market control to more market freedom coupled with more extensive use of fiscal policies. Hence compulsory deliveries, which used to be proclaimed as an inherent, permanent feature of planned relations between the socialist state and the agricultural sector, have come to be portrayed as a transient phenomenon justified by particularly difficult conditions of a certain (rather early) stage of economic development and ultimately have been abandoned. The same applies to the dissolution of MTS and the like. Thus the question also arises to what extent the authorities will be prepared to accept some relief of the farmers' burden as far as their contribution to the national accumulation fund for industrialization is concerned.

### OPERATION OF STATE-OWNED FARMS

Another aspect of direct state control over agriculture finds its expression in the role of state-owned farms. Their most immediate task is to

---

33. "The experience of Japan shows that . . . government can have spectacular effects on the output of peasants . . . and that agriculture, far from lagging behind other sectors, and acting as a brake on the rest of the economy, can be turned into a leader" (W. Arthur Lewis, *Theory of Economic Growth,* 8th ed. [London: Allen and Unwin, 1965], p. 279).

contribute to the speedier growth of agricultural output and above all to give the state a commanding hold over agriculture to be used directly in support of its current policies and particularly for intervention in the market.

However, among the various tasks assigned by communist doctrine to state ownership in agriculture the widest is to serve as a model and paragon of fully socialist agricultural enterprises. Collective ownership as opposed to state ownership is regarded as representing a lower level of socialization. Hence the ultimate aim for all collective farms is to become, in the unspecified future, state owned, and so to bring about the dissolution of the separate class of members of farm collectives. State-owned farms are, therefore, supposed to establish themselves as the most efficient farming units employing the most modern and advanced technology and pioneering the most progressive methods of management and production.

The existence of such units in agriculture is vital for agricultural growth. A number of agricultural productive processes and techniques find the necessary or most suitable conditions only in enterprises of the size common in the state sector. In addition to their large scale of production, the technology on state-owned farms is usually superior to that of the collective farm sector (and of private farms, wherever they exist) and so too are the qualifications of the executive staff, a large percentage of whom are graduates of specialized agricultural curricula.

In the light of the East European experience it may be doubted, however, whether these enterprises meet the expectations attached to them or are as efficient as they should be (see table 15.4). There is no question that, in general, they fulfill their main task of contributing greatly to the procurement of foodstuffs and agricultural raw materials.

Table 15.4: Profitability of Livestock Production in
Soviet Collective and State Farms

| | Collective farms | | State farms | |
| | 1962–65 | 1966–69 | 1962–65 | 1966–69 |
|---|---|---|---|---|
| Overall profitability (%) | −5.0 | 5.2 | −1.8 | −3.0 |
| Unit costs (in rubles per 100 kg. of production) | | | | |
| Milk | 14.24 | 16.57 | 16.89 | 17.34 |
| Beef | 107.76 | 111.05 | 113.47 | 119.38 |
| Pork | 119.29 | 118.58 | 129.50 | 107.59 |
| Wool | 279.13 | 373.82 | 319.12 | 348.58 |
| Eggs | 84.41 | 72.64 | 85.09 | 66.94 |

*Source:* V. Desatov, *Voprosy Ekonomiki* 1971, no. 5, p. 51.

Their share in the market product of agriculture exceeds the percentage of the land they hold. They are more specialized, sometimes in unique lines of production, and they achieve higher labor productivity than the rest of agriculture.

On the other hand, however, one must point out the following three facts. First, state farms enjoy special privileges in capital equipment, priorities in obtaining industrial inputs, better remuneration, more favorable working conditions, and so on. Second, their costs of production are rather high.[34] Third, as far as their managerial, organizational, and productive achievements are concerned, these are inferior to what is obtained in large-scale capitalist farms elsewhere. They certainly are much lower than what can be regarded as worldwide records of agricultural progress in any of the areas one might wish to consider and also lower than what has become standard in the top class of modern, large-scale farming in any Western country.

The privileges and priorities enjoyed by state farms regarding equipment and industrial inputs are of particular importance because of the overall shortage of machinery, tools, building materials, chemicals, fodder, and the like. Priorities for state farms are given at the expense of supplying the other types of farms with adequate amounts of all these things.

When considering the high unit cost of production in state farms (as shown by communist surveys) one has to remember that, in addition, land and capital goods are either excluded from cost calculations or are not fully reflected in them. The main reason for these costs of production exceeding those in collective or private peasant holdings is the extremely low remuneration for labor in the latter together with the inefficiencies in management and organization of production processes in the former.[35]

34. Naum Jasny's analysis led him to conclude that "farms owned by the Soviet State were unable to produce even at high, or even very high, costs" ("Production Costs and Prices in Soviet Agriculture," in Karcz, *Soviet and East European Agriculture,* p. 245).

A more recent, quite sophisticated study of the profitability of production in state farms in Poland produced the following conclusion: "Under the assumption of the present rate of growth, the achievement of full profitability by state farms before 1985 is impossible if they are to bear the full cost of all inputs and to receive no subsidies" (T. Rychlik, "System ekonomiczny, PGR—czy potrzebna reforma?" in Rasiński, *Dyskusja o polityee rolnej PRL,* pt. 1, p. 225).

35. Below is a rough idea of the discrepancy in question: "Given the fact that in 1965 the collective farm man-day was valued at about 90 per cent of the state farm

With regard to labor remuneration in agriculture it should be noticed that the discrepancy between the earnings of a state-farm worker and those of his collective or private farm counterpart would be even greater than it now appears if one were to take into account the more intensive efforts of the latter, the greater unpleasantness of his work, and the lower social status he has (by and large) to put up with.

In this respect the relations seem to resemble very closely similar ones of the precommunist era. At that time also peasants had to compete with large-scale capitalist farms by lowering their costs of production per unit of output, mainly through accepting extremely low rates of remuneration for family labor. The same takes place under communism. Despite all the advantages given to state farms, they appear to be unable to raise their labor productivity far enough above that of the alternative sectors to offset the higher remuneration they pay for labor per unit of work, despite its being lower than in industry.

The unique feature of state-farm economics as compared with that of the other sectors is the attempt to substitute capital and industrial input for labor as far as possible. As a result, the productivity of capital is extremely low. Compared with Western large-scale capitalist farms, state-owned farms in Eastern Europe are backward in all respects: they are poorly organized, slow in adopting new technology and techniques, less enterprising, and generally less dynamic.

---

man-day and that the number of man-days worked in a collective farm is about two-thirds of the state farm man-days per year, the yearly wage income of the collective farmers from the socialized sector amounted to about 60 per cent of such income of the state farm workers" (Kassof, *Prospects for Soviet Society*, p. 289). Similar figures relating to Hungary are presented by Janos Laszlo, "Polityka con productów rolnych na Wegrzech," *Economista* (Warsaw), 1966, no. 1, pp. 196–203.

In this context it is also worthwhile to take a closer look at some of T. Rychlik's observations regarding the comparative costs of production in peasant farms and state farms in Poland. "When comparing the two it is usual to emphasize," he writes, "that state farms receive subsidies, do not pay the full rates of capital depreciation, pay only minimal taxes, are exempt from low-priced compulsory deliveries, do not have to invest from their own funds, and even then make only a small profit, en masse, that is, on the average. On the other hand, private farms which do not enjoy any of these privileges are profitable and have no problems." He sets out to rectify this allegedly "idealized" picture. Among the arguments put forward is the following: "In private farms a considerable part of overhead costs takes the form of unpaid labor. The peasant's time devoted to management and to maintenance of links with the outside world is not valued in cost calculations. The latter, it has been found, involves 75 days per year on average. State farms have to pay for all these functions, albeit they spend less time per hectare to carry them out" (Rasiński, *Dyskusja o polityee rolnej PRL*, pt. 2, pp. 220–22).

AN APPRAISAL OF OUTPUT RESULTS

Taking an overview, I would like to stress once again the double nature of the experience of agricultural growth in East European communist countries.

The general functions performed by agriculture in the process of economic growth in the form of supplies of food, raw materials, unskilled labor, and contributions to the capital accumulation fund are, of course, as essential for the growth of communist economies as for any other economies. The distinctive marks of agricultural growth in communist countries depend on the specific methods employed in securing the above services of agriculture to economic growth.

On the one hand, there is no doubt that these countries have managed to gear the economies toward a model of sustained growth in which agricultural growth is an intrinsic element. Relations between agriculture and the economy at large are modeled in such a way as to make agriculture an integral part of it. There is a rising level of agricultural output, ensuring in general a rising standard of food consumption by both the rural and the urban populations and also an increasing supply of agricultural raw materials for industry. There is continuous flow of labor to nonagricultural sectors of the economy, and the proportion of the population involved in agriculture is declining relative to the overall population and in most countries also in absolute terms. Increasing numbers of qualified specialists are being absorbed, the standard of education of the labor force is rising, and new methods of production and technological progress in general are being continuously adopted. The market for industrial supplies and capital equipment is expanding.

On the other hand, although agriculture is growing, it persists in being the weakest link in the expanding economy. Its growth rate is too slow and its instability too great to secure equilibrium between the supply and demand for foodstuffs. There is an excess of coercion and administrative control in the relationship between the state and agriculture, which hampers the development of entrepreneurship and personal initiative. The economic position and social status of the farmer are low and are further undermined by an unfavorable economic policy. In these circumstances the movement out of agriculture is predominantly made up of its best elements: the brightest and most dynamic individuals.

Because of the dual effects of the policies regarding agricultural growth, their evaluation cannot be expressed in unequivocal terms. In absolute terms the fact that agriculture does participate in the sustained growth of the economy is crucial, despite the numerous problems that have troubled it in the course of development. At the same time, when assessing the results in relative terms, that is, in terms of relations between achievements and needs, realities and possibilities, results and costs, we must draw different conclusions. It is in view of the latter criteria that the East European pattern of agricultural growth must be regarded as unsatisfactory.

However, even when considering the phenomenon of agricultural growth in absolute terms one must not overlook the fact that the countries concerned were far from being economically underdeveloped when they undertook industrialization; they were also far from being over-populated, though at the same time they enjoyed an abundance of semiskilled labor in agriculture. In combination, the above factors determined a pretty high level of intensity of agricultural production at the outset of the industrialization program. It was, however, a special type of intensity, depending to a very small extent on industrial inputs but utilizing huge amounts of labor inputs per hectare, as well as all other sorts of inputs of agricultural origin, like animal power, manure, and so on. In conjunction with a well-developed market (local and national), an adequate money and credit system, and not too poor a system of basic education, these conditions created a favorable foundation for agricultural growth. The complexity of the above conditions contained natural potential for agricultural growth of a self-sustained nature.[36]

Thus, when the East European communist regimes began their industrialization drives their agricultures provided well-developed bases for such undertakings. The respective agricultural sectors possessed an inherent capacity for growth founded primarily on internal resources. Only the two then most industrialized East European countries—Czechoslovakia and East Germany—represent possible exceptions. This capacity to grow on internal resources was strong enough to

36. It is worthwhile to point out the regularity in the differential growth rates of agricultural output in East European countries. By and large high rates are achieved by the least industrialized ones (Bulgaria, Rumania) and low rates by the most industrialized ones (East Germany and Czechoslovakia). The differences are very considerable. It seems logical to attribute them to the fact that, whereas the growth potential of agriculture in the "agricultural" countries could be utilized without significant industrial support, the lack of this support in the industrialized countries frustrated agricultural growth to a much greater extent (see table 15.5).

Table 15.5: Growth Rate of Agricultural Output and Size of the
Agricultural Sector

| Country | Growth rate of agricultural production, 1956/60–1966/70 | Share of agriculture in national income in 1968 (current prices) | Prewar agricultural employment (as % of total) |
|---|---|---|---|
| Bulgaria | 4.5 | 26.2 | 80.0 (1934) |
| Rumania | 3.7 | 25.5 | 78.2 (1930) |
| Poland | 2.8 | 21.0 | 70.3 (1931) |
| Hungary | 2.2 | 24.2 | 53.0 (1930) |
| Czechoslovakia | 2.0 | 11.5 | 38.3 (1930) |
| East Germany | 1.4 | 13.7 | 29.2 (1945) |
| Soviet Union | 3.1 | 21.4 | 50.2 (1939) |

*Source:* Left column: FAO, *The State of Food and Agriculture 1971* (Rome, 1971), p. 53. Center column: GUS, *Rocznik statystyczny 1970* (Warsaw, 1970), p. 600, table 26. Right column: *Rocznik statystyczny 1967* (Warsaw, 1967), p. 626, table 33.

withstand all the errors of the official doctrinaire agricultural policy and to bear fruit despite the lack of necessary support from outside, that is, from the industrial sector.

It is to the credit of the communist countries of Eastern Europe that they apparently did take advantage of this potential, to some extent at least. Also, they no doubt enhanced this potential by means of their land reforms and by spreading primary education to the rural population.

Several factors contributed to the marked difference in the growth of East European agriculture as against that of the Soviet Union two or three decades earlier. First of all, the former had already achieved a higher level in their secular process of growth. Second, they were parts of generally more advanced economies. Third, the communist parties of Eastern Europe were well advised by the Russians themselves to avoid at least some of the errors and most harmful experiments in agriculture that they themselves recognized.[37] Finally, Stalin's death in the rather early stages of communist rule in Eastern Europe and Khrushchev's denunciation of Stalin's "great mistakes" in agricultural policy saved them from having to follow all such policies to their disastrous ends. It was probably for these reasons that the East European communists have managed not to hamper the growth of agriculture to such

37. A publication by the Bulgarian Academy of Science finds it worth emphasizing that the fact "that the Bulgarian Communist Party has never resorted to nationalization of land" bears witness to the creativeness in adaptation of Marxist-Leninist principles to the specific conditions of the country (*Social and Economic Development of Bulgaria 1944–1964* [Sofia: Foreign Languages Press, 1964], p. 84).

an extent as did the Soviet Union. Since 1954–56 all East European countries have demonstrated some greater concern for agriculture and have been manifestly much more careful in all their dealings with it.[38]

In the light of statistics it looks as if a 3 percent annual growth rate of agricultural output characterizes the long-run trend in these countries. There have been some attempts in Poland to interpret this rate as the feasible maximum that is determined by the nature of agriculture itself and particularly by the all important role of biological factors in its growth.[39]

Allegedly comparisons with the past and present experience of Western countries ought to prove this point. Neither of these comparisons, however, seems relevant. The actual position of Western countries is such that, due to the high level of food consumption already obtained, the income elasticity of the demand for food and agricultural produce is at present generally low (much lower than in the less affluent East European countries). This in itself acts as a successful brake on agricultural growth in the West. There is no strength in the argument that the actual rates of agricultural growth in the West should reflect in any respect an inherent inability of agriculture to grow faster. As far as the past (mainly the nineteenth century) is concerned, reference to it seems irrelevant if only because the pace of technological progress was then so much slower than it is at present. Hence it would be odd to accept the growth rates experienced in the past as representative of the present-

38. This approach in Rumania has been stressed by Montias: "All in all, the orderly and relatively mild character of the Rumanian collectivization campaign of 1958 to 1962 contrasts happily with the Soviet experience of the early 1930's and even with Rumania's earlier attempts to dragoon farmers into collectives in the early 1950's. The facilities given to the GAP's to buy cattle from members, instead of confiscating it outright, helped to mollify recalcitrant joiners" (Montias, *Economic Development in Communist Rumania*, pp. 96–97).

Karcz makes the following generalization: "Agricultural trends in Eastern Europe after World War II did not follow a uniform pattern. The Soviet example of a massive collectivization drive was not repeated. For the most part, gradual collectivization of individual peasant holdings did not begin until 1949 in the aftermath of the Yugoslav schism. . . . In East European countries, collectivization was gradual and non-violent, although various forms of compulsion were frequently employed" (*Soviet and East European Agriculture*, preface, p. xv).

39. "Data referring to the last two decades (marked by the highest rates of growth of agricultural production in human history) indicate that, not excluding countries in which socioeconomic conditions are most conducive to the growth of agricultural output per hectare, nowhere in Europe does the annual rate of growth reach 4 percent . . . It seems that at the present stage of technological development . . . the rate of growth of agricultural production cannot exceed in the long run 3–3.5 percent, under European conditions" (Herer, *Procesy wzrostu w rolnictwie*, pp. 188, 194). In some earlier publications the author put the figure in question at 2–3 percent.

day maximum. Rather, one would be justified in expecting some direct link between the speed of technological advance in a given historical period and the maximum rate of growth of agricultural output physically attainable in that period. From this point of view comparisons between actual growth rates of agricultural output in East European countries and those experienced many decades ago by industrializing capitalist countries seem to prove that, on the contrary, the maximum rates of agricultural growth achieved currently in communist countries are most likely far below what is determined by technological factors. They rather prove the point that it is the economic system itself that puts a ceiling on these growth rates at a considerably lower level than that corresponding to the capacity of modern agriculture.

A question arises as to whether the communist system can be expected to be able to overcome the inherent imbalance between agriculture and the economy at large in the process of economic growth and assume a growth pattern ensuring continuous equilibrium between demand and supply of agricultural products. Most likely it would require a change in both trends concerned: an acceleration of the long-run growth rate of agricultural output and a deceleration of the rate of expansion of the demand for agricultural produce. One should not overlook the intrinsic forces that magnify the income elasticity for food in communist economies. On the one hand they result from the discrimination against light consumer industries which leads to high prices of industrial consumer goods in relation to food. On the other, they are a natural consequence of the basic philosophy of the system, which tends to diminish the public's propensity to save and hence to increase its propensity to consume, by eliminating any outlets to private investment.

It is obvious that some of these forces, particularly those springing from the philosophy of the system, cannot be expected to be easily eliminated or mitigated without affecting the nature of the system itself. Their role may, however, not be the most crucial one in the context of our problem. Can one then expect the communist system to change the priorities embodied in its growth pattern in favor of light consumer industries and those supplying agricultural inputs, in order to achieve both some diversion of demand from foodstuffs to industrial consumer goods and an acceleration of the growth of agricultural output?

There seems to be no straightforward deductive answer to this question. Essentially it remains to be answered in the light of practical experience. However, the following reasoning warns against optimism.

The main cause for the hitherto prevailing imbalances in the communist pattern of growth has been the drive for maximizing growth rates in order to achieve supremacy as soon as possible over the capitalist system and to prove in this way the superiority of communism.

The problem is, however, that everything seems to indicate that the operative efficiency of communism, that is, its system of management of the economy, is somewhat lower than that of its rival. Hence the communist system seems to be incapable of surpassing capitalism— as it has dedicated itself to doing—on the basis of a better, more efficient use of resources. Moreover, since the absolute level of economic development of communist countries is still far below that of the advanced capitalist West, the former cannot expect to catch up with the latter in the normal way. Communism may find it necessary, therefore, to continue to concentrate on the expansion of productive capacity at the expense of the standard of living of the current generations for the sake of surpassing capitalism in the future. In these circumstances nothing but minor transient fluctuations in the general pattern of growth of communist countries can be expected until they reach quite a high level of disposable income per capita.

Though it is impossible to foretell future developments exactly, I am inclined to presume that in the near future the communist countries are rather unlikely to give in entirely to the demands of their peoples for a living standard comparable to that of the West—certainly not to the extent of seeing the messianic mission of surpassing capitalism in terms of productive potential fade away as the gap between the growth rates of the two systems closes. My anticipation is rather that having had, under popular pressure, to redress slightly the basic imbalance of their growth pattern communist countries will go on with their attempt first to catch up with Western countries and then to overtake them in terms of productive capacity by applying the old policies in a slightly less extreme form.

Should this be so, the basic feature of agricultural growth hitherto prevalent in the communist pattern of growth, that is, its lagging behind industry, will remain for as long as can be foreseen.

### THE FUTURE OF AGRICULTURAL SYSTEMS

The next question regards the prospects for change in the structure of agriculture itself. To any observer not incurably dogmatic but willing to learn from real life, there is one obvious lesson to be drawn from the agricultural experience of all East European countries, namely, that the main reason for their troubles has been the mistaken communist attitude toward the peasant: the lack of appreciation for his role, potential, and capacity in contributing to the growth of the economy. All the communist parties of Eastern Europe have in fact proven themselves to be only too willing to try to "do it" without the peasant's wholehearted cooperation. The waste of a substantial margin of the peasant's potential is certainly a crucial factor that has hampered East European agricultural growth.[40] Most important is probably the waste of all that potential which lies in the initiative, dedication, and enthusiasm of millions of small farm owners.[41] It has become apparent that these are invaluable virtues in terms of their effect on agricultural performance. There is no compensation for their loss in transferring decisions to bureaucratic managers of collective and state-owned farms, even if these managers are better educated and qualified and have at their disposal the advantages of large-scale production and modern technology.[42] The effectiveness and tempo of agricultural growth seem

40. At this point one is tempted to level at the communist policies the criticism once made by W. H. Nicholls with regard to advocates of unbalanced growth to the effect that "by seriously underestimating the time, effort, and resources required to bring about drastic structural changes . . . they overlook (and often even deprecate) the short run potentialities of raising agricultural output with given supplies of land and labour and existing small scale farming units" (Nicholls, "Place of Agriculture in Economic Development," p. 16).

41. It is, therefore, difficult to accept the view expressed by Jacek Romanowski regarding the Polish peasant: "For historical, social, economic, and political reasons, the Polish peasant is a bulwark of willfulness, disrespect for outside authority, ignorance, and poverty. This is not true of all peasants and in all regions of Poland, but it nevertheless is more often true than not" (in Karcz, *Soviet and East European Agriculture*, p. 433). It is no wonder that Romanowski's prediction that "Poland's peasant economy seems to have its days numbered" has been proven wrong by events.

On the contrary, Polish economists seem to be coming more and more to believe in the great adaptability of the Polish peasant to the requirements of modern farming. According to F. Tomczak, for instance, the experience of Polish agriculture after 1956 has brought about a revolution in the outlook regarding the role of peasant farming in a socialist system. It has become evident that this type of farming is capable of developing alongside the rest of the economy, contributing to its growth and posing no threat to the predominance of socialism in the country as a whole. At the same time it also undergoes a gradual transformation and adapts itself to socialism ("Indywidualna gospodarka w rolnictwie Polski Ludowej," *Zycie Gospodarcze,* August 20, 1972).

42. Recently two economists have written that they "suspect" the main reason for the "poor performance of socialized agriculture in the Soviet Union and Eastern Europe" to be "the peculiar difficulties of supervising farm operations" (M. B. Bradley and M. G. Clark, "Supervision and Efficiency in Socialized Agriculture,"

to depend largely on the extent to which a country understands how to stimulate and utilize the growth potential of the numerous farm producers instead of trying to frustrate them by putting agriculture into a straightjacket of hostile ideological dogmas.

There are signs that this realization has already dawned upon most communist rulers. Indeed, the fact that two communist countries, Yugoslavia and Poland, went so far as to abandon their collectivization attempts altogether and have committed themselves to maintaining private farming as the main form of agricultural production for an indefinite period seems to prove this.[43] Further, the Soviet Union's tolerance of the Yugoslav and particularly the Polish deviations from strict orthodoxy raises the suspicion that the Russian rulers themselves may have been infected by the truth.

In Poland events appear to have gone so far as to make the rulers understand the harmful effects on agriculture as a whole of the anticapitalist measures directed against well-to-do farmers. More and more of these measures are being dropped and laws on which they have been founded repealed.

Many symptoms suggest that the obstinacy and doggedness that once reigned in communist agricultural doctrine and policy have faded already and are in fact in the process of evaporating.[44] It seems as if a tacit understanding was reached between the communist countries to exclude agricultural policy from among those policies they agreed to keep uniform throughout the bloc. As a result, agricultural policy has obviously lost the all-important ideological significance it held not long ago and instead has gained the right to greater flexibility in particular

---

*Soviet Studies* 23, no. 3 [1972]: 465–73). The difficulties of supervision are obviously only a consequence of the lack of the farmers' genuine interest in their work.

43. According to H. Cholaj, for the foreseeable future private farming in Polish agriculture is indispensable. The need to avoid a drop in agricultural output makes it impossible to determine the span of time it would take to socialize Polish agriculture. The period will certainly be much longer than elsewhere. It is also impossible to define at present which of the various existing types of agricultural enterprises would play the decisive role in the future process of socialization ("Kilka problemów spoleczno-ekonomicznej rekonstrukeji wsi polskiej," *Nowe Drogi*, 1970, no. 11, pp. 12–26).

44. According to J. F. Karcz, "there is no reason to think that progress elsewhere in Eastern Europe will be continuous. But the process of reform, once it is introduced, often develops a logic of its own. As time goes on, official attitudes towards agriculture and the peasants may well be altered. The recent shifts in Soviet agricultural policies and in the underlying attitudes of the Soviet leadership may perhaps be considered as a first, even though modest, step in this direction" (*Soviet and East European Agriculture*, preface, p. xvi). See also Arcadius Kahan's conclusions:

countries. For several years now there have been significant changes and reforms undertaken in one communist country after another. Russia herself since Khruschev has pointed the way with some major examples.

There is, however, practically no chance for the Soviet Union or any other East European country that has brought to completion the Stalinist reconstruction of agriculture to try to go back. The countries concerned have most certainly passed the point of no return in this respect. Their search for improvements in agricultural efficiency will have to be made within the existing constraints imposed by the monopoly of collective and state ownership.[45] There is, however, no reason to doubt the existence of a vast scope for possible progress— even within these constraints—should pragmatism prevail in place of ideological dogma.[46] In the end no economic organization is ideal, nor can any one be deemed absolutely inefficient. Efficiency is in itself a relative concept difficult to measure accurately. It is also not necessarily the only or even the main consideration in the evaluation of a social system's performance. Any economy has a multitude of aims, among which the growth and efficiency of agriculture are only part of a rather broad complex. Hence, even if Soviet agriculture proves incapable of solving its so-called grain problem (the lack of self-sufficiency in grain production), importing grain from the United States or elsewhere will

---

"It seems certain that the Soviet policy-makers have finally learned the lessons of the past, when disastrous results followed rigid adherence to dogmatic principles and antiquated organizational methods, or when the mechanical, indiscriminate application of half-developed schemes based upon limited experience led to frequent and destructive organizational shake-ups" (Kahan, "Agriculture," p. 272).

45. "Russia is unlikely to go back to individual farming. The gap between the private and the collectivized lands is, therefore, likely to be narrowed only after a very long haul" ("Russia's Miserable Harvest," editorial in *The Times* [London], November 10, 1972).

46. Here is an extremely optimistic view regarding the Soviet Union: "A number of the conditions for catching up with Western Europe and America undoubtedly exist in the Soviet Union. There is no shortage of competent and trained scientific personnel, hence there is general awareness and specific knowledge of the basic techniques and their application to Soviet conditions; there is at last a real effort to supply capital goods and current industrial inputs in quantities commensurate to the task in hand; and finally there is a determination to pay the full price—perhaps even a very high price—to make the production of most or all agricultural commodities economically attractive at the high current cost levels. This means that there is enormous room for future improvement, and in many cases only a relatively narrow threshold to pass before this potential can be fully exploited in practice" (Erich Strauss, *Soviet Agriculture in Perspective: A Study of Its Successes and Failures* [London: Allen and Unwin, 1969], pp. 299, 300).

always present itself as a simpler and more acceptable solution than far-reaching reforms involving substantial changes in the communist system of agricultural organization that are bound to have undesirable ideological overtones.[47] The same applies to a greater or lesser extent to all East European countries with a Soviet-type agriculture, though their position is understandably much more difficult because of their relative lack of natural resources, compared with the Soviet Union. But the highly industrialized countries like East Germany and Czechoslovakia can afford to make up their agricultural deficiencies by importing foodstuffs in exchange for industrial goods.

As for Poland and Yugoslavia, it is difficult to foresee whether and when they will feel compelled to fall strictly back in line with their communist partners. With regard to the former one may venture to predict that this is not likely to happen before the 1980s, since only by then can the crucial demographic conditions which at present are rather unfavorable be expected to become favorable for a new collectivization drive.[48]

47. A controversy on this subject between K. Bush and A. Kahan seems to have been solved in a way that proves the latter's rather more flexible guesses correct. "Strategically, the USSR cannot afford to be dependent upon the West for staple foodstuffs. Economically, the Soviet gold reserves are, according to the best Western estimates, down to less than 2 billion dollars' worth, and the USSR is finding it increasingly difficult to export enough to the developed nations in order to pay for the equipment and technology which she so urgently needs. Politically, the Soviet Union can hardly proclaim, with any conviction, the superiority of socialist agriculture to her own subjects and to underdeveloped nations whose greatest enemy is hunger, when it must import grain from the West. The new leaders must, therefore, solve the "grain problem" where their predecessors have failed" (Keith Bush, Harry E. Walters, and Richard W. Judy, "Soviet Agricultural Output by 1970," comment 2, in Karcz, *Soviet and East European Agriculture,* p. 353).

"The decision to purchase large quantities of grain from abroad is a major departure from traditional policies and one that may well be repeated in the future. This deviation does not invalidate the long-run goals of self-sufficiency or even surplus in grain production. But it indicates that Soviet policy-makers may in the future be more realistic and less autarky-motivated. It may lead, political conditions permitting, toward a re-examination not only of foreign-trade policy, but more fundamentally to a shift to specialization in areas of production where the USSR possesses a comparative advantage. That this realization is a slow, piecemeal process for a generation brought up on ideas of the virtue of autarky is reflected in the long time it took to give up the idea of growing oranges in the Soviet Union at greenhouse costs. But at least there are now precedents for the more rational alternative" (Kassof, *Prospects for Soviet Society,* p. 270).

48. "After 1980 the rate of increase of the labor force will abruptly decline from over 1.5 million in the period 1971–75 and 1.2–1.5 million in the period 1976–80 to about 600–800 thousand in the quinquennium 1980–85" Herer, in Rasiński, *Dyskusja o polityee rolnej PRL,* pt. 2, p. 164).

It seems, however, that as far as the communist agricultural doctrine at large is concerned it will draw some important lessons from the East European experience and will rid itself of those dogmas which have been exposed and discredited by this experience. This fact, in turn, is certain to have an effect on developments in the third-world countries and particularly on their policies regarding the role of agriculture in economic growth.

# 16

## Peasant Families and the Agrarian Community in the Process of Economic Development

SHIGERU ISHIKAWA

The purpose of this chapter is to attempt to construct a positive socio-economic model of contemporary agricultural society in Asia capable of describing (1) the state of market economy underdevelopment within that society, and the reasons for this; (2) processes by which this state changes in the direction of a more developed market economy; and (3) some of the issues that are closely related to the above changes. This attempt will be made on the basis of an empirical examination of agricultural societies in prewar Japan, precommunist China, and some other countries of Asia.

The principal concern underlying this study may be stated as follows: In contemporary discussions of the developing nations, it is often said that the market economy is still underdeveloped in their economies. The fact of market economy underdevelopment, however, is in many cases not satisfactorily incorporated into the conceptual framework used for analysis of the state of economic underdevelopment. Theories of economic development often lack explanations of the mechanism of the rise and development of the market economy. Moreover, in policy discussions of economic development, market economy under-development is not given proper emphasis as an issue, nor is it effectively tackled. This is true particularly in studies of the agricultural sector of the developing economies.

There are of course exceptions to the above remarks, among which

I am indebted to Yukihiko Kiyokawa and Tsuneo Ishikawa for useful comments on an earlier draft of this paper. I am also grateful to Mataji Umemura and Hiroshi Fukazawa for informing me of some useful source materials. Finally, I would like to thank John Fei for his detailed comments, which, however, were not received in time for me to take them into consideration in writing this final version.

the contributions of Hla Myint are particularly noteworthy.[1] His well-known "vent-for-surplus" model not only represents a model of economic development for those countries where both land and labor are initially underutilized; it also constitutes a model for the rise and development of a market economy in such places. This is indicated by two components of the vent-for-surplus model. The first component pertains to the process by which the hitherto isolated nonmarket economy (what he calls the "subsistence economy") is opened up for the money or wage economy. This process is explained by "new wants" (i.e., a shift in the tastes and preferences) of the residents of the subsistence economy aroused by contact with novel commodities and ways of life from the outside world. The second component is related to the process by which the residents' subsistence activities proportionately decrease while their cash-earning activities increase. This is explained in terms of normal economic behavior on the part of the residents, who allocate resources between these two activities according to their utility maximization calculus. Hence, the persistence of active demand and improvements in transport and communications is the major explanatory factor in the process, until the point is reached where surplus land finally ceases to exist.

The policy implications of this vent-for-surplus model are indicated most straightforwardly by what he calls the continuation of the "colonial policy" adopted by the independent government, namely, export promotion and the provision of improved transport and communications networks. As Myint himself admits, this model and its policy implications have clear-cut limitations in their applicability to the rise and development of the market economy in densely populated economies. Even in relation to those countries with surplus land and surplus labor, they are not fully relevant to the phase in which market economy development tends to accompany a productivity increase in the economy. Hence, there remains the task of improving the model for purposes of generalization.[2]

1. Hla Myint, *The Economics of the Developing Countries* (London: Hutchinson, 1964), chaps. 2, 3, and 4; and Myint, *Economic Theory and the Underdeveloped Countries* (London: Oxford University Press, 1971), chaps. 5, 13, and 14.
2. Myint's own attempt to generalize can be found in his discussion of economic dualism in the developing countries; he argues that it is brought about by inappropriate government economic policies which result in unequal access to the scarce economic resources by the "modern" and "traditional" sectors (Myint, *Economic Theory*, chaps. 13 and esp. 14). His policy recommendation is an economic integration of the two sectors by correcting these misguided economic policies.

One clue to this generalization task can be found through observation of the agricultural society in densely populated countries. Such observations indicate that it is not necessarily valid to consider the rise and development of the market economy simply on the basis of a division of the economic activities of people in the agricultural society into cash-earning and subsistence activities. Essentially, this dichotomy emerges when these activities are observed from the point of view of their relations with the world outside the agricultural society. From the point of view of interpersonal relations within the agricultural society, they are found to consist not only of activities of the market economy type and those of the closed, self-contained type (i.e., subsistence activities) but also of customary, community-type activities. Also, these community-type activities are often found to be firmly grounded in the deep-rooted desire of the people forming the agricultural society jointly to secure at least a minimum subsistence level of living. It follows that the rise and development of the market economy involves critical reappraisals of these community-type activities under changing external conditions, reappraisals that are often discontinuous and irreversible. Moreover, it is quite likely that activities of the market economy type, in relation to the outside world, are sometimes identical to those that are community-type activities, when viewed from within the agricultural society. Hence, a study focusing on these community-type activities may be useful for the purpose of generalization, and perhaps also in clarifying the relationship between market economy development and productivity increases within the agricultural society, and other related issues.

In the socioeconomic model of the agricultural society I am trying to construct here, my focus will thus be on community-type activities and their interrelations with the other categories of activities of the people in the agricultural sector. In section 1, I shall identify and elucidate some of the observable characteristics of agricultural society in contemporary Asia as a set of stylized facts, and on the basis of this I will clarify the principal variables that enter into this model. Two sets of issues that will be examined by means of this model will be specified. In sections 2 and 3, I will study the first such set of issues: the processes by which community-type activities are preferred by some or all of the people and, further, are established as an objective institution in some specific aspect of the agricultural society, under given states of other variables. Section 2 is specifically devoted to empirical studies of agricultural societies in Asia, with the aim of pointing out concrete forms of community-type activities and their economic characteristics. Section 4 will be devoted to a preliminary study of the second set of issues: the mechanisms by which (1) community-type activities tend to shift to market-economy-type activities and (2) the productivity and income distribution of the people in the agricultural society tend to change as variables related to the extra-agricultural economy change.

## 1. STYLIZED FACTS OF THE AGRICULTURAL SOCIETY

Let me begin by presenting a set of stylized facts of contemporary agricultural society in Asia. These facts either seem to be agreed on by most observers without reference to empirical evidence, or are supported by evidence that will be presented in later sections. They are summarized in the following four items.

*The agricultural society is already entangled with the market economy, but the market economy remains more or less underdeveloped.* This underdevelopment has two different aspects: one is the relationship of the agricultural society with the outside economy through the market, and the other is the place of market-economy-type activities in the total economic activities of the agricultural society. In the former sense, underdevelopment is measured by the extent of the activities that are exposed to the outside market economy. In the latter sense, it is measured by the relative magnitude of market-type activities vis-à-vis the community-type activities and closed, self-contained-type activities. As was stated in my preliminary remarks, market-type activities defined in relation to the outside economy and those activities viewed within the agricultural economy as being market type do not necessarily correspond with each other. One such example may be shown in figure 16.1.[3] This suggests that these two measures are both important and that, while the former is a commonly accepted measure, the latter should always be considered as well.

The reader should be cautioned that the separation of total economic activities into the various types of either aspect should be made, at least initially, by separating the economic activities of the agricultural society into a few specific categories such as product disposal, land use, and labor use. The relative magnitudes of these classifications of activities vary greatly among these different categories. When each

3. For an application of this general diagram to economic activities in production disposal in prewar Japan, see note 16.

| Classification assigned by the agricultural society | Classification in relation to the outside economy |
|---|---|
| Market-economy-type activities | Market-economy-type activities |
| Community-type activities | (Closed, self-contained-type activities) |
| Closed, self-contained-type activities | |

*Note:* This diagram shows how an individual activity classified in the left-hand column as any of the three types of activities can be reclassified in the right-hand column.

Fig. 16.1: Correspondence of Types of Economic Activities in the Agricultural Society from Two Viewpoints

of these categories is further separated into more specific divisions, such as the landlord-tenant relationship and the employer-employee relationship, cases may be found in which only one specific type of activity exists. Hence, to derive a measure of the market economy development of the society as whole, some kind of aggregation is necessary.

Naturally, the market economy development of an agricultural society is dependent on the degree of market economy development and the degree of productive force development in the outside economy. These two factors together determine the size of the exogenous market opportunities available to the agricultural society. But the actual response to these exogenous market opportunities and, hence, market economy development in the agricultural society seem to be conditioned by factors within the agricultural society, which will be described below.

*Agricultural society consists of families that can be grouped into distinct economic classes.* An economic class here is defined as a group of families whose "permanent" income position is significantly differentiable from that of other families. The families in the society are further differentiable according to a number of more detailed economic criteria, e.g., the amount of land under their ownership or tenureship, the amount of land under their management, the type of land management (such as self-cultivation and cultivation with the aid of a non-family labor force), and the type of employer-employee relations. These criteria are sometimes essential for the analysis. It is only by the above class differentiation, however, that a comparable economic class pattern can be derived.

As one such economic class, it is possible to single out a significant number of families whose permanent income position barely assures them a minimum subsistence level of existence (hereafter MSL). While the families not included in the MSL class may be further differentiable into a host of classes, it is sometimes convenient to lump them together as a single, non-MSL class.

*There are at least two distinct features of MSL families: (a) Their income and consumption are at or even somewhat below MSL, and (b) there are uncertainties about their ability to maintain MSL. Moreover, the content and magnitude of both the MSL class and these uncertainties tend to vary according to the degree to which the agricultural society is entangled with the market economy.* To elaborate, the concept of MSL must first be described. Generally, MSL not only denotes the minimum amount of the means necessary for reproducing or maintaining a physiological human being, e.g., food, housing, clothes, and health and sanitary services; it also includes a minimum amount of the means necessary for acquiring human capabilities in a socioeconomic sense, such as culture, general education, and vocational training. Of those, the MSL components of a socioeconomic nature are particularly sensitive to the development of the market economy, since it brings about increasing competition among individuals; and, in order simply to survive such competition, more diversified and larger components of a socioeconomic nature are required. This is the case even with the components of a physiological nature, though to a lesser extent.

It should also be noted that the concept of MSL thus defined is a long-run concept. In the short run, it may be possible to fall below this long-run MSL without serious harm. However, if such a situation persists, the human being deteriorates physiologically due to the resulting malnutrition, and he is unable to compete socially and economically.[4]

4. In Myrdal's new system of "circular causation," which purports to explain contemporary underdevelopment, the concept of standards of living is used to derive one of the crucial determinants of underdevelopment. It seems that the specific standard of living he conceived there is one that is persistently below the long-run MSL (G. Myrdal, *Asian Drama* [New York: Pantheon, 1968], app. 3). In Harvey Leibenstein's theory of underemployment, a peculiar functional relationship between the wage or income level and labor productivity seems to be particularly concerned with the domain in which the actual standard of living is, in a sense, somewhere between the long-run MSL and the point below which even the short-run standard of living cannot be reduced (Harvey Leibenstein, *Economic Backwardness and Economic Growth* [New York: John Wiley and Sons, 1957], chap. 6).

This situation is equivalent to what was referred to earlier as the state where income and consumption are somewhat below MSL.[5]

Uncertainty about maintaining MSL is traditionally a result of harvest fluctuations and such unexpected contingencies as disease, death, and social and political disorders. With progressive entanglement of the agricultural society in the market economy, additional uncertainties are caused by unforeseeable changes in the product and factor market conditions and by the possibilities of unemployment, debt, and the loss of the sources of livelihood. Since the resulting uncertainties are usually considerable, MSL families essentially act as risk averters in making decisions on production and income expenditures.

Behind these states of MSL and the uncertainties surrounding them there is generally a low level of productive force development in the agricultural society, and of available market opportunities coming from the outside economy. Productive force here is a comprehensive concept whose determining factors are population, labor force, natural resources, capital, and technology. A convenient measure of it is the "permanent" per capita output. The states of MSL and its uncertainties are also dependent on the principle of income distribution accepted in the agricultural society, the outcome of which is partly reflected in the existing economic classes described above.

*Market-economy-type activities, community-type activities, and closed, self-contained-type activities, which together constitute the total economic activities in specific aspects of the agricultural society, are each carried out on the basis of specific institutions regarding interfamily relations. Each of these institutions or their particular combination is established as a result of the interaction of the institutional preferences of both MSL and non-MSL families.* The institutions behind these three types of activity are here designated "market relations," "community relations," and "closed-family economy," respectively. First, these concepts must be defined. The concept of market relations may be more readily described by referring to the concept of an "agrarian community." The agrarian community here denotes a territorial group organized spontaneously and nearly permanently by families residing in the same locality of the agricultural region, a group in which the member families are mutually interdependent by virtue of customary rules governing each member's obligations and privileges in every aspect of economic activity, with the collective purpose of securing

5. Of the many survey and research reports indicating that this state of affairs really exists, I will cite only three: V. M. Dandekar and Nilakantha Rath, "Poverty in India," pts. 1 and 2, *Economic and Political Weekly*, January 2, 1971, and January

every member's welfare. That the families are subject to such customary rules means that the independent decision-making power of these families is transferred to the agrarian community. This agrarian community is a pure and extreme concept, since in historical examples of agrarian communities at least some aspects of economic activity seem to have been left to individual families' discretion. Furthermore, with the rise and development of the outside market economy, the agrarian community becomes entangled with it and gradually transforms itself into a distinctly mixed type of agricultural society. Yet some of the essential principles of the agrarian community continue to be in operation in certain economic activities of the agricultural society: there are still instances of collective decision making through customary rules and with the aim of collective welfare. The institution based on these principles is what I have termed "community relations."

"Market relations" signifies the institution by which families residing in the agricultural society are mutually interdependent through the market, while maintaining their position as independent decision makers seeking to attain maximum individual welfare. When this institution is chosen in specific economic activities of the agricultural society, the families in the agricultural society are liable to be connected to outside economic units through the market related to these economic activities.

The closed-family economy is an institution in which every family is independent and isolated from the others. In terms of the purpose of our discussion, however, this is not very important as an institutional alternative. For, in historical context, this institution is most often chosen passively and as an appendage to either community or market relations, although this does not deny the fact that the relative magnitude of activities under the closed-family economy is sometimes quite large.

9, 1971; S. S. Madalgi, "Foodgrains Demand Projections: 1964–65 to 1975–76," *Reserve Bank of India Bulletin*, January 1967; and Madalgi, "Poverty in India," *Economic and Political Weekly*, February 20, 1971. These reports deal with the issue of mass poverty in India, which has recently come to the fore again against the background of both a possible increase in income differentials among people brought about by the green revolution and a possible long-term decline in the real consumption level of the lower income brackets. A cursory review of these reports (aided partly by the statistics provided in Government of India, Cabinet Secretariat, *The National Sample Survey, Sixteenth Round, July 1960-August 1961, No. 138, Tables with Notes on Consumer Expenditure* (Delhi, 1969), suggests that the MSL families in rural India in 1960–61 corresponded to the consumer class of 13–15 rupees (in terms of average monthly per capita consumption) and below, and the proportion of the rural population comprised by these families was as high as 38 percent. A somewhat different interpretation of the source's statistics suggests that the MSL families correspond to the consumer class of 15–18 rupees and below, and that they constitute 50 percent of the rural population.

Both community relations and market relations as institutions have many different patterns. As we shall see shortly, the economic and even social positions of individual families which are implied in community relations vary greatly depending on whether the original agrarian community was established as a hierarchical society, a caste society, or a society of equal status. Market relations sometimes resemble the competitive market. More often, however, various imperfections prevail in the market, at least partly as a result of the existence of the economic classes previously described. The pattern of the community relations that have been superseded by market relations is also responsible in part for the form of the latter.

### Principal Variables of the Socioeconomic Model

The above discussion of the four stylized facts of contemporary agricultural society in Asia can be summarized by listing the principal variables (or sets of variables) involved in the socioeconomic model I intend to construct. These variables may be described as follows:[6]

A. Variables pertaining to the internal agricultural society:
   1. The structure of the constituent families in terms of their relative "permanent" income positions (measured by the proportion of MSL to non-MSL families).
   2. Institutions relating to interfamily relations (market relations, community relations, the closed family economy, or their various combinations).
   3. The productive force of the society (determined by the levels

---

6. There are two important qualifications to the above discussion of the stylized facts and, hence, to this list of variables. First, I ignored political power, taxation, and other economic policies which the government enforces in relation to the agricultural economy and which must play an important role in this socioeconomic model. The role of these factors in traditional societies is discussed by John Hicks, who characterizes a primitive nonmarket organization as a mixture of "customary economy" and "command economy" and discusses the interaction between the two (Hicks, *A Theory of Economic History* [Oxford: Clarendon Press, 1969]). The customary economy is a concept essentially the same as my concept of the agrarian community, and the command economy is a concept relating to the above relationship in which political power and taxation are imposed upon communities from above. Therefore, in terms of Hicks's concepts, we ignore the command economy aspect of the traditional agricultural society. (Hicks's discussion, however, seems to lack an analysis of the process by which the customary economy or community relations are preferred by the residents and brought to an objective institution.) Next, in the agricultural society many important functions of community relations are carried out by the family system in various forms (see W. Arthur Lewis, *Theory of Economic Growth* [London: George Allen & Unwin, 1955], pp. 113–20). This and related issues are largely omitted from consideration here.

of population, labor force, natural resources, capital, and technology, and measured in terms of per capita "permanent" output).

B.   Variables pertaining to the external agricultural society:

1. The degree of market economy development in the outside economy (measured by the degree of development of such factors as the network of distribution facilities, transport and communications, and financial organizations).

2. The productive force of the external economy.

It is assumed that all families have a common behavior pattern aiming at maximizing individual welfare.

It should be noted immediately that variable A2 on this list indicates the establishment of particular institutions regarding interfamily relations. The degree of market economy development within the agricultural society is implicitly determined once these institutions are established, but the process of establishment of these institutions is not yet clarified. Therefore, while all the variables in the list may be combined to indicate broadly a cross-section socioeconomic picture of the agricultural society (on the condition that the institutions are already established without inconsistency with the other variables), in terms of the aim of my socioeconomic model they are not satisfactory. Only when the process of establishment of these institutions is clarified and related to the above variables will my socioeconomic model be complete.

The task of the remainder of this chapter can now be specified: (1) to study the mechanism by which particular institutions of interfamily relations tend to be established in some or all aspects of the activities of the agricultural society, under given states of all other variables, and (2) to explore in a preliminary way the mechanism by which a particular institution (A2) and, side by side with it, the ratio of MSL to non-MSL families (A1) and the productive force of the agricultural society (A3) tend to change with changes in the given states of market economy development and productive force in the outside economy.[7]

7. Some characteristics of this peculiarly formulated socioeconomic model are indicated here. First, this is a model describing the society's choice of a particular institution of interfamily relations from among certain alternatives. It requires initially description of the preferences for particular institutions by different member families, whose views may or may not be identical. It then requires description of the agreement or compromise that should be reached among these families in order for the society to be able to determine the particular institution. Second, we assume that, under any institution, families' economic activities would be carried on efficiently

2. THE AGRARIAN COMMUNITY AND COMMUNITY RELATIONS IN ASIA

In this section and the following, I will be discussing the first of the two problems specified immediately above. As a preliminary step, let

---

according to the individual welfare maximization objective and under the constraints of (a) the objective conditions described by variables Al, A3, B1, and B2 and (b) particular principles working in the particular institution. Third, an individual family's preference for a particular institution is dependent on their comparison of the welfare gains that may accrue to them under different institutions. Fourth, this individual family's preference is likely to change from time to time due to changes in objective conditions. Yet the society's determination of a particular institution may not change as often, so that conflict among families may increase due to increasing divergence among the individual families' preferences. The above characteristics of my model contrast with those of more orthodox models also dealing with social institutions, such as those discussed in P. K. Bardhan and T. N. Srinivasan, "Cropsharing Tenancy in Agriculture: A Theoretical and Empirical Analysis," *American Economic Review* 61, no. 1 (1971): 48–64; Steven N. S. Cheung, *The Theory of Share Tenancy, with Special Application to Asian Agriculture and the First Phase of Taiwan Land Reform* (Chicago: University of Chicago Press, 1969); and C. H. Hanumantha Rao, "Uncertainty, Entrepreneurship, and Sharecropping in India," *Journal of Political Economy* 79, no. 3 (1971): 578–95. This type of model is essentially based upon the framework of analysis inherent in the question: How is the subjective equilibrium of individual families attained in the realm of ordinary farm economic activities? Here, however, certain alternative institutions are given under which specific activities are carried on (such as sharecropping tenancy or wage employment for the laborers' families, and direct management of land or rental to sharecroppers' families). Families can freely choose among these alternative institutions, or among the various combinations of them, and their resources are allocated accordingly. Their criterion in making this choice is maximization of their welfare. (The previously cited Myint case, in which choices between cash-earning activities and subsistence activities were made by families, is an example of such a choice.) The differing states of subjective equilibrium among the different families (such as laborers and landlords) are coordinated by the market mechanism (e.g., by the parametric functions of land rent and wage rate), and are thus brought to the objective equilibrium. This framework may be used to describe either the rise or the decline of a particular institution, but this is confined to the situation in which alternative institutions under question are freely chosen individually. In fact, these alternative institutions are not what I am examining; in terms of my definitions, they are simply alternative subinstitutions under market relations, or in the situation where market relations are already dominant in the society. Finally, a comment is in order regarding the third characteristic of my model. This arises from the assumption that the families comprising the society are fundamentally individualistic, and that, although they pursue the goal of collective welfare within the context of community relations, they do so because they judge that it serves their individual long-term interests. Perhaps this is too strong an assumption. As is postulated by A. K. Sen in reference to the labor supply of the altruistic member families of socialist cooperatives (Sen, "Peasants and Dualism with or without Surplus Labour," *Journal of Political Economy* 74 [1966]: 425–50), the welfare function of member families in the context of community relations has, as independent variables, not only their own individual welfare but also other families' welfare. This is likely to be the case when community relations are long established and stabilized. Yet, this latter assumption complicates the model and I will not follow it here.

us examine some empirical data on community relations, both historically and on a country-by-country basis. This is necessary because our
knowledge of community relations from the economic point of view is
still very slight, and, in order to enlarge it, it is essential to examine
concrete forms that vary significantly among countries and, for each
country, among historical periods. Empirical findings on these matters,
however, are still only tentative. What is presented below is confined
mainly to studies of prewar Japan and precommunist China, and some
preliminary findings on India and some other Asian countries.

Analyses of empirical data on community relations are hard to
conduct without also considering concurrent studies on market relations, which tend to manifest themselves in close connection with community relations. In this section, therefore, I will refer to market relations also, insofar as it is necessary.

### Prewar Japan

Historically, the unit of the agrarian community in Japan seems to
have been a village constituted by an extended family or a modification
thereof—a special type of quasi-kinship group. In this village, there
was a hereditary main family (*honke*, or *oyakata*), subordinated to
which were kinship branch families (*shinzoku bunke*), servant branch
families (*kokata bunke*), and servants (*kokata*). As a specific form of
this subordination, the servants of the branch families customarily
participated in the cultivation of lands under the direct management
of the main family, either as corvée laborers or as domestic helpers.
In return, they were assured a means of maintaining their livelihood.[8]

With the gradual development of the outside market economy,
these subordinate families slowly acquired a semi-independent position.[9] The main families found it more advantageous to reduce the extent of direct management. Thus, first the kinship branch families and

8. The most authoritative literature on sociological studies of the agrarian community in Japan is found in Kizaemon Ariga, *Nihon kazoku seido to kosaku seido*
[The family system and tenancy system in Japan] (Tokyo: Kawade Shobo, 1948).

9. As a very rudimentary step in which the subordinate position of the MSL families shifts toward an independent one, the servants or servant families in mediaeval
Japan were allowed by their masters to reclaim small plots of wasteland for their
private use, in their free time. These plots of land, called *homachi* or *shingai*, constituted a form of precautionary savings for MSL families. With the development of
the nearby market towns, and also as the remaining wasteland began disappearing,
monetary savings gradually took the place of homachi or shingai as a form of precautionary savings. Yet the words homachi and shingai continue to be used for such
savings (Ariga, pp. 407–14).

then the servant branch families were each allotted part of the main family's land or were permitted to rent parts of such land, with the result that the economic position of the subordinate families was strengthened. Yet their independence was by no means complete. There remained the customary practice of offering labor services: the branch families would help the main family with its farm operations and domestic affairs, and in return they would receive from the main family various forms of assistance in maintaining their livelihood. Moreover, with regard to tenants, while the form of rent was fixed in kind, since the payment was subject to reduction according to crop conditions, the tenancy system was in a sense similar to an ordinary sharecropping arrangement. Thus, the traditional form of community relations in Japan was both socially and economically hierarchical. Yet mutual exchanges of assistance also occurred among small families of equal status; of these practices, labor exchanges (*yui*) and mutual financing groups (*tanomoshi-kō*) are the main examples. These mutual aid practices should also be considered a traditional characteristic of community relations in Japan.

In the early eighteenth century in the regions near large administrative, commercial, and transportation centers and where commercial crops were widely raised, a new type of village began appearing, in which the economic positions of the branch families and the servants were substantially raised, and the social and political influence of the main families accordingly declined. In some of these regions, a landlord-tenant relationship of a modern, contractual type had already emerged.[10] A major landmark in the shift from community relations to market relations, however, appears to be what is called in Japan the widespread retardation of the "landlords' direct management of their own lands" (*jinushi-tezukuri*), which took place during the 1900s and the 1910s. This was an important event because the direct management of lands by the landlords (or by the main families in each village) with the aid of a few permanently hired laborers (or the traditional servants) was the economic basis of one of the traditional community relations patterns in Japanese agricultural society, although the size of landholdings was already small as 3–5 hectares on the average. These landlords also played a central role in disseminating new technology in agricultural production throughout the Meiji era (1868–1911). Thereafter, it is generally believed that the traditional landlords were largely

10. Toshio Furushima, *Nippon nōgyō-shi* [A history of agriculture in Japan] (Tokyo: Iwanami Shoten, 1956), chap. 7.

replaced by, or transformed themselves into, so-called parasitic land-lords, who owned lands simply in order to rent them out, and landlord-tenant relations in the market economy sense began to prevail, with intermittent tenant disputes. In the interwar period, the proportion of medium-sized, peasant-owned farms steadily increased, and this class of peasants came to play a role as the major agent of technological progress in agriculture in cooperation with the government experiment stations, which were only then set up nationally.[11]

It is, however, a remarkable feature of Japan's agricultural society that, even after the market economy and productivity outside the agricultural society had become fairly well developed, some elements of community relations remained in operation and even generated a dynamic force for raising agricultural productivity and, with it, the income level of the majority of farm families. In this connection, partic-ularly noteworthy are the functions and the nature of the agricultural practices associations (*nōji-jikko-kumiai*) and other similar associa-tions—generically designated minor cooperatives (*nōka-ko-kumiai*). These associations were established all over Japan by the early 1920s, each within the boundary of an individual natural village (*buraku* or *shūraku*) which had been part of the administrative villages or towns since the enforcement of the modern municipality system in 1889.[12] The functions of the minor cooperatives were various but generally fell into three categories: (1) joint purchases of current production means and joint marketing of farm products; (2) joint purchase and joint utilization of farm machinery and equipment, such as pump-sets with electric and oil motors, rice-milling and rice-hulling equipment, and even cultivators; and (3) joint farm operation. A review of a number of survey reports on the activities of these minor cooperatives suggests that each of these three categories of functions was already playing an indispensable role in maintaining and

11. Shigeru Ishikawa and Kazushi Ohkawa, "Significance of Japan's Experience: Technological Changes in Agricultural Production and Changes in Agrarian Struc-ture," in *Agriculture and Economic Development: Structural Readjustment in Asian Perspective,* ed. Shigeru Ishikawa (Tokyo: Japan Economic Research Center, 1972).

12. The minor cooperatives began to be established in 1896, and their number increased especially rapidly in the 1920s, when almost every natural village in the country appears to have been covered by at least one minor cooperative. A good account of the minor cooperatives is found in Kuraichi Ogura, "Activities of Minor Cooperatives and Agricultural Associations," in *Nippon nōgyō hattatsu-shi: Meiji-iko ni-okeru* [A history of agricultural development in Japan since the Meiji era], ed. Nōgyō Hattatsu-shi Chōsakai, vol. 8 (Tokyo: Chūō-Kōron-sha, 1956).

accelerating the economic activities of families in Japan's agricultural society in the interwar period.[13]

Especially interesting among those functions are the first two categories, which played the explicit role of protecting the member families from monopolistic and monopsonistic "exploitation" by urban merchants. It also appears that the institutional factor responsible for the spread of the minor cooperatives and their activities was in many cases community relations patterns that were similar to those in operation in traditional agricultural society. While the system of jinushi-tezukuri had already disappeared, the former landlords were among the promoters of the minor cooperatives in each buraku, calling for joint activities aimed at collective welfare.[14] Thus, the hierarchical society principle remained in operation in these new organizations. Yet the principle of mutual help also worked, as the majority of families in a buraku responded to these calls and have, moreover, made an effort to maintain the same organization even up until the present.[15] There were also cases in which it is not clear whether the factor responsible for the spread of minor cooperatives and their activities was community or market relations. These cases seem to occur in regions where a market economy had developed earlier and, accordingly, the hierarchical society principle was no longer operating significantly. Yet the mutual help principle seems to have remained even in these regions; it is likely that the emergence of active minor cooperatives was due mainly to the operation of this principle.[16]

13. Of these survey reports particularly useful is Teikoku-Nōkai, *Rōryoku chōsei yori mitaru buraku nōgyō-dantai no bunseki* [An analysis of agricultural organizations in natural villages from the viewpoint of readjustment of labor use] (Tokyo: Teikoku-Nōkai, 1941).

14. See the survey report on the natural village called Tsukabori in Asahi Village, Akita Prefecture, in ibid.

15. The Japanese Ministry of Agriculture and Forestry made an interesting survey in 1970 on the economic and social aspects of shūraku or buraku all over Japan; see Japanese Government, Ministry of Agriculture and Forestry, *Nōgyō Shūraku chōsa hōkokusho* [Report on the survey of agricultural shūraku] (Tokyo, 1972). The survey reveals that the number of shūraku in the country in 1970 was 142,699, of which 128,825 were established before the Meiji Restoration. The proportion of shūraku in which a minor cooperative was organized within the boundary of each respective shūraku was 69.7 percent and the proportion of shūraku in which there was no minor cooperative was 6.6 percent. Moreover, in 92.7 percent of the shūraku in the country (excluding Hokkaido), public road repair was done jointly by the constituent families, and in 53.1 percent of the shūraku all the constituent families were obliged to participate directly in joint work on public road repair.

16. See especially the survey report on the natural village called Nakano in Obie

The relationship between the minor cooperatives, on the one hand, and the agricultural associations and industrial (agricultural) cooperatives, on the other, should also be noted. The latter two organizations are often said to have been the main organizational apparatus of Japanese agricultural development since the turn of this century. Both had hierarchical national networks reaching down to individual administrative villages. The former performed the powerful function of spreading new technologies and improved practices in agricultural production all over Japan. The latter also played an important role in improving farm economic conditions through four categories of cooperative activities: credit, purchasing, marketing, and production.[17] The organizations were in a sense authoritarian and commanding, even in the case of the industrial (agricultural) cooperatives. These organizational set-ups, however, may be considered a rational response (in the market economy sense) of the governments at all levels to the changing conditions of agriculture and the national economy.[18] It is important to note that the activities of these two organizations were in fact strengthened by making the minor cooperatives their *de facto* subordinate organs.

### Precommunist China

Leaving aside the period prior to the Sung dynasty (960–1127), in which the socioeconomic structure of agriculture is not clear, the traditional unit of the agrarian community in China seems to have been a village constituted by a single clan (*sung-tzu*) or more.[19] The clan was a kinship group consisting of families with a common ancestor or a com-

---

Village, Okayama Prefecture, in Teikoku-Nōkai, *Rōryoku chōsei yori mitaru buraku nōgyō-dantai no bunseki*. This peculiar correspondence of activities based on community relations within agricultural society to activities classified as market type can be illustrated by applying to figure 16.1 a specific aspect of the activities of the agricultural society: product disposal.

17. Takekazu Ogura, ed., *Agricultural Development in Modern Japan* (Tokyo: Japan FAO Association, 1963), pp. 246–48.

18. In this possible alternative interpretation, I have in mind that part of the Hayami-Ruttan induced innovation model which is used to explain the behavior of public sector organizations (Yujiro Hayami and Vernon W. Ruttan, *Agricultural Development: An International Perspective* (Baltimore: Johns Hopkins Press, 1971).

19. C. K. Yang, *Chinese Communist Society: The Family and the Village* (Cambridge: MIT Press, 1959); Gennosuke Amano, *Shina nōgyō keizai ron* [Studies on China's agricultural economy] (Tokyo: Chūō-Kōron-sha, 1940); Tatsumi Makino, *Shina kazoku kenkyū* [Studies on the Chinese family] (Tokyo: Seikatsu-sha, 1944).

mon original settler, and bearing the same family name. The member families held their own assets and ran their family economies almost independently. The equal-inheritance system of bequest among male children prevented the income and wealth positions of the member families from becoming excessively differentiated. The clan, however, performed important functions in sustaining the economic life of its member families in at least two respects: (1) through the formation, management, and maintenance of clan assets (*tsu-ch'an*) on the basis of which the clan supported, and extended assistance to, the production activities of member families (in particular, clan land was rented to member families by parceling it into pieces of equal size), made expenditures on education of the children of member families, and gave relief to distressed families; (2) through the operation of cooperative works such as irrigation, water conservation and road building and of police, defense, and other social activities. Labor exchange and other forms of mutual help were also practiced among families within the clan. The administration of clan affairs was conducted by an elders' council consisting of the eldest males among the families with the longest history. Hence, in the traditional Chinese agrarian community, the social and economic positions of member families tended to be broadly equal, and there was no hierarchical principle working, such as there was in Japan.

However, the above description of the agrarian community is to some degree an abstraction from the historically recorded agricultural society. The actual agricultural society had long since been penetrated by the outside market economy, which seems to have developed prematurely, considering the general productivity level of the economy. There were, of course, significant regional differences in this penetration, and those between northern and southern China were especially marked.[20]

20. The fact that the external market economy penetrated China's agricultural society significantly was recognized only recently, when the results of extensive surveys on northern Chinese village customs made by Japanese researchers with the South Manchurian Railway Company gradually became known. See especially Chūgoku Nōson Kankō Chōsa Kankō-kai, *Chūgoku nōson kankō chōsa* [Investigations of rural customs in China], vols. 1–6 (Tokyo: Iwanami Bookstore, 1952–58). "[Because of rich source materials provided by these survey results] it has now become almost irrelevant to argue that China's village and clan system are a self-contained framework which prevents the residents from acting in accordance with economic rationality. Also, it has now become irrelevant to attempt to explain thereby the stagnation of China's economy" (Yuji Muramatsu, *Chūgoku keizai no shakai*

With regard to the development of commodity markets in rural China, we can benefit from a study made by William Skinner on the spatial system of standard and higher-level markets in China.[21] His study indicated that, by the period immediately prior to the establishment of the People's Republic of China, the market economy had developed in the agricultural regions of China to the extent where these regions were completely covered by contiguous standard marketing areas, numbering some 58,000. The modal case of such standard marketing areas, each comprising eighteen natural villages surrounding one market town, was of a size which put the most disadvantaged villager within easy walking distance (4.5 kilometers) of town, was 53 square kilometers in area, and included nearly 8,000 persons. These standard markets were connected first with the intermediate market, whose servicing area was theoretically 44 to 72 villages, and then through it to the central market. Traditional change in the marketing structure consisted of a proliferation of these markets on the landscape. In the stage of modern change that took place in the first half of this century under the impact of treaty ports and modern transport facilities, standard markets were extinguished and engulfed by the higher-level marketing systems in the environs of most of the cities served by steamer or railroad. A question remains whether the emergence and proliferation of the standard markets in the period of traditional change was brought about by the internal force of the agricultural society or by the penetration of the outside market economy. (Skinner seems to present a model of intensification of the marketing system along the former line.) It is evident, however, that through this marketing system the peasants' products flowed upward and the imported merchandise and goods produced outside the agricultural society flowed downward.

The specific ways in which factor markets developed side by side with the above development of commodity markets should also be noted. One important characteristic especially marked in the coastal regions was that, for the wealthier class of families, commodities, land, and loans were essentially alternative objects of asset holding for the same purpose of making money, and markets were developed to the point where choice among these alternatives became meaningful and effec-

---

*taisei* [The social structure of the Chinese economy] [Tokyo: Keizai Shimposha, 1949], p. 228).

21. C. William Skinner, "Marketing and Social Structure in Rural China," *Journal of Asian Studies* 24 (1964): 3–44, 195–228; concluded in vol. 25 (1965), pp. 363–400.

tive.[22] To elaborate, in the case of the land market, the purchase and sale of private lands seem to have been easy and frequent in China as compared to other countries in Asia, at least partly because land was a form of near-money to be mortgaged or sold depending upon the need for cash. Despite varying forms of rent arrangements, inclusive of share rent, a common feature of the market for rental land was that the landlords did not supply capital and credit to their tenants, nor did they intervene in the tenant's management of the land. Also, tenants' and landlords' agreements were short-lived, and landlords frequently changed tenants.[23] A remarkable characteristic of the labor market in China's agricultural society was the lack of personal connections among the individuals concerned. Hence, the mobility of peasants as seasonal or long-term emigrants was potentially large for family members who could not obtain jobs enabling them to sustain a livelihood within their village.[24]

These characteristics may suggest that the traditional agrarian community in China had already largely disintegrated in the precommunist period. There are some additional pieces of evidence supporting this suggestion. In many instances, the economic activities of the clan seem to have been either sharply reduced or discontinued, and the clan itself was small or nonexistent. This was especially the case in northern China, where frequent invasions by non-Han races resulted in earlier destruction of the original communities. Even in southern China, where the clan activities remained in operation and clan lands occupied a significant proportion of total land in many villages, there were cases where, as was indicated in Chen Han-shen's survey of the villages of the Pearl River delta, the management of these clan lands was under the control of a few wealthy families of the clan, who aimed simply at increasing their own profits.[25]

It is also true, however, that in many other instances community relations patterns were found in operation. One such pattern was the practice of exchanging labor, draft animals, and farm implements, which seems to have been fairly widespread in northern China, although

22. Muramatsu, *Chūgoku keizai,* pp. 283–93.

23. Raymond H. Meyers, *The Chinese Peasant Economy: Agricultural Development in Hopei and Shantung, 1890–1949* (Cambridge: Harvard University Press, 1970), pp. 227–29; and Yang, *Chinese Communist Society,* p. 229.

24. Yang, *Chinese Communist Society,* chap. 4.

25. Chen Han-Seng, *Agrarian Problems in Southernmost China* (published for Lingnan University, Canton, by Kelly & Walsh, Shanghai, Hong Kong, Singapore, 1936), chap. 2.

the participants in the exchange comprised only a small number of the families residing in the same villages. When the Chinese Communist Party launched a campaign to increase production in the Shensi-Hansu-Ninghsia Border Region in 1943, it conducted an extensive survey on the various forms of labor exchange practices then existing and made the survey results the basis for formulating their policy of organizing "mutual-aid teams" and "production cooperatives" as a main pillar of the compaign.[26] On the other hand, cases where clan land still played an important role in raising the economic standard of member families of the clan were also found.[27]

It should also be stressed that the development of the market economy in precommunist China by no means implied an accompanying improvement in agricultural productivity and in the farm economy in all classes. An expansion of market relations without a parallel increase in the productive force of the society tended to result in the failure of part of the families in the agricultural society to obtain land to rent, or employment opportunities, in order to sustain their minimum standard of living; hence, there were numerous cases of starvation and death in years of widespread bad crops and ensuing famine.[28]

## India and Other Asian Countries

As for the social and economic structure of the traditional village in India, which also seems to have been the basic unit of the agrarian community, there are still many unknowns even for the period immediately prior to British rule. The following may be said broadly, though at the risk of underestimating regional variations and of overemphasizing the communal nature of the structure.

26. H. G. Schurmann, *Ideology and Organization in Communist China* (Berkeley and Los Angeles: University of California Press, 1966), pp. 416–25; and Shih Ching-tang, *Chung-kuo nung-yeh ho-tso-hua yung-tung shih-liao* [Historical materials on the agricultural cooperative movement in China] (Peking: San-lien Shu-tien, 1962), pp. 67–69.

27. Yang, *Chinese Communist Society,* pp. 41–43.

28. Walter H. Mallory gives a classic account of this in his *China: Land of Famine* (New York: American Geographical Society, 1928). William Hinton's *Fanshen: A Documentary of Revolution in a Chinese Village* (1966; Japanese translation by Y. Kato et al. published through Heibonsha, Tokyo, 1972), which is a unique report on the land reform that was engineered by the Chinese communists in a village in the northern province of Shansi, also gives a vivid account of precommunist days in the same village. One can see in it many stories of extreme poverty, starvation, and death, and of the sale and purchase human beings, caused by the penetration of the market even into the realm of family relations, because of an extremely low level of productivity.

Before British rule a village was typically composed of cultivators, artisans (functionaries), and laborers (untouchables), each group being distinct both within the caste structure and in terms of the functions of the integral village economy. All land within the boundary of the village was owned by the village as a nonalienable community asset; this land was in some cases jointly cultivated by the cultivator families and in other cases parceled out, mainly to the cultivator families for self-cultivation and partly to the artisans as homesteads. Between the cultivators and the artisans (the blacksmith, carpenter, potter, barber, washerman, weaver, and so on), there was in operation a hereditary system of cooperation called *jajimani*; between the cultivators and laborers there was also a hereditary relationship of masters and clients. Most of the income accruing to individual families in each group was customarily determined as a share of the entire product.[29] Thus, it may be said that in the traditional community in India a hierarchical principle similar to the Japanese type was in operation not among the individual member families but between the cultivator group, on the one hand, and the artisan and laborer groups, on the other. An equality principle reminiscent of the Chinese was accordingly operative within the group, especially among the cultivator families.

The actual process by which this traditional agricultural society came to be entangled in the market economy was subtle in many respects. It is evident, however, that the major landmark in the process was a series of land revenue settlements imposed by the British colonial government, beginning toward the end of the eighteenth century. These settlements, on the one hand, created land tenure systems which, though modern in the Western sense, contradicted existing patterns of community relations by conferring exclusive ownership of a particular

29. With regard to the socioeconomic structure of pre-British agricultural society, the most controversial issue has been whether or not agricultural laborers existed as a class. One school of historians argues that there was no such class, although there was a small number of menials serving the Brahmans; agricultural laborers were a phenomenon that developed during the British colonial period due to the destruction of the village communities and the accumulation of rural indebtedness, both of which resulted in the alienation from land of a vast number of cultivators. See for instance, Kamal Kumar Ghose, *Agricultural Laborers in India* (Calcutta: Indian Publications, 1969). One very detailed and rigorous study has been published, providing evidence that there were significant numbers of laborers in the early nineteenth century all over the Madras Presidency; see Dharma Kumar, *Land and Caste in South India: Agricultural Labor in the Madras Presidency during the Nineteenth Century* (Cambridge: at the University Press, 1965).

land area on those with whom the colonial authority made the land revenue settlement for that area. On the other hand the settlements, by introducing at least in the earlier stage a rigid and exorbitantly high tax rate, compelled the new landowners to abandon their land and thus accelerated the transformation of land into a commodity. The activities of moneylenders and traders played important roles in this process only in later stages, especially after the opening of the Suez Canal. Since India became independent, government policies aimed at deliberate industrialization and land reform have been bringing India into a new stage in which the speed of market economy penetration is significantly high but its process seems peculiarly complex.[30]

With regard to the current state of community relations in India's agricultural society, I will refer here to the cases of only two villages in Mysore State surveyed by Scarlett Epstein in 1954–56.[31] Before 1939 these two villages, which are close together, were on similar dry land and had similar socioeconomic conditions. Then canal irrigation was introduced. In the first village the land was watered from the canal, and this, together with the construction of a new sugar refinery in a nearby town, created a new opportunity for developing agricultural production, mainly by raising sugarcane. The land of the second village could not be watered from the canal for topographical reasons; but the villagers were able to extend their activities to include secondary and tertiary services for the neighboring villages and towns.

Epstein's survey indicates that, while in the second village the jajimani system disappeared almost completely, in the first village it persisted. Apart from the potter and the goldsmith, all artisans had a hereditary relationship with the cultivators; they were paid annually, in a quantity of grain that had not varied since 1939, for doing certain defined jobs throughout the year; for any extra work they were paid in

30. In a sense, land reform legislation in India since independence has aimed at recovering various privileges which nonowners of land had once possessed but were deprived of by British colonial policies; see Walter C. Neale, *Economic Change in Rural India: Land Tenure and Reform in Uttar Pradesh, 1800–1955* (New Haven: Yale University Press, 1962). Existing landowners have tended to forestall and evade this land reform by selling their land, by dispersing ownership among their relatives, or by evicting the existing tenants and engaging in direct management themselves. On this trend and for an attempt to characterize the socioeconomic structure of Indian agricultural society which is emerging as a result of the land reform, see P. C. Joshi, "Agrarian Social Structure and Social Change, June 1971," mimeographed (New Delhi, Institute of Economic Growth, 1971).

31. T. Scarlett Epstein, *Economic Development and Social Change in South India* (Manchester: Manchester University Press, 1962).

cash. The hereditary relationship between untouchables and cultivators no longer existed in the second village. It remained, however, in the first village, a situation that was preferred both by untouchables and by cultivators to straightforward competition. This relationship put the client untouchable under an obligation to provide labor for his patron (a cultivator family determined by heredity), whenever the latter required it. In return, the client was paid wages at the general rate for hired labor in the village. Moreover, the patron families were obliged to provide at least a minimum of subsistence to the client families. To quote Epstein, the patron families "know full well what it is like when their clients squat outside the house begging for food, broadcasting their [patron's] meanness to the whole village."

As for other Asian countries, only a few words are in order here. In the agricultural societies of Java, the relative weight of community relations has been large and they have been similar in type to those of Japan.[32] In the recently opened areas in other Southeast Asian countries, such as the Philippines, Thailand, and Malaysia, it appears that traditionally the most important unit for mutual security and elementary labor exchange was a small group of relatives. Villagewide community relations, if any, appear to have been very weak.[33] However this does not seem to have been the outcome of market economy relations superseding community relations. In some of these areas (such as in Central Luzon and the Central Plain of Thailand), the proportion of peasant output directed to export was substantial and the activities of traditional moneylenders were extensive. Yet market economy development did not go as far as the commercialization of cultivable

32. See, for instance, Clifford Geertz, *Agricultural Involution: The Process of Ecological Change in Indonesia* (Berkeley and Los Angeles: University of California Press, 1963). The concept of the *sawah* ecosystem which is in operation in inner Indonesia (Java) and in what Geertz calls "agricultural involution" is applicable here.

33. Recently, the contributions of Japanese geographers, anthropologists, and political scientists on the basis of field studies in these countries have been increasing. See, for example, Akira Takahashi, *Land and Peasant in Central Luzon: Socio-Economic Structure of a Bulacan Village* (Tokyo: Institute of Developing Economies, 1969); Toru Yano, "Economic Life of Rural Villages in Southern Thailand: An Observation in a Thai-Islam Community," *Tōnan Ajia Kenkyū* [Southeast Asian studies] 8, no. 4 (1971): 442–88; Koichi Mizuno, "Family cycle and village structure," *Soshioroji* [sociology], October 1971; and Kenzo Horii, "Land Tenure System of the Malay Padi Farmer: The Case Study of Kampong Sungei, Bujor, Kedah State," *Ajia Keizai* [Asian Economics], October 1971. I myself was struck, on an inspection tour in Central Luzon, by the lack of a feeling of collective welfare among the villagers; see Shigeru Ishikawa, *Strategies of Agricultural Development in Asia: Case Studies of the Philippines and Thailand* (Manila: Asian Development Bank, 1970).

land. (It is only in the postwar years that cultivated land has been extensively commercialized, resulting in the emergence of income differentials among peasant families.) In general, the relative position of the closed-family economy was quite strong in these countries, though in export production areas market economy relations were in the process of replacing closed-family relations.

## Implications of Empirical Studies

Three important conclusions can be derived from the above data, insofar as community relations are concerned. First, although the essential components or community relations are as they were described in section 1 and are common to the countries surveyed above, the specific pattern or form of community relations varies greatly among them, and so do the causes of the transformation of community relations and/or the speed of their replacement by market relations. These variations are summarized in table 16.1. Second, these differences seem to be explainable partly by cultural and historical factors, which determined the relative prevalence of the hierarchical-society principle and the egalitarian principle. They are also explainable in terms of differences in the development of the outside economy and its productive force.

Third, the modes of operation of these various forms suggest that community relations manifest themselves in a number of working principles, which are itemized below, and that the retardation of community relations is in fact the gradual replacement of these principles by the corresponding market economy principles.

1. A community principle of employment and income distribution. This principle promises all member MSL families in the community "full" employment, with an income not less than MSL. It seems to work most effectively in the hierarchical societies.

2. A community principle of bringing about economies of scale. This principle is exhibited when the formation of common assets for production purposes, or joint cultivation or other farm operations, are accomplished at least partly through cooperation among member families. The increase in production capacity thus obtained for the agricultural society tends to exercise, though indirectly, a function similar to that of principle 1.

3. A community principle of protection against monopolistic and monopsonistic "exploitation" by urban merchants. This principle

Table 16.1: Specific Forms of Community Relations by
Country and by Phases

| | *More traditional phase* | *More modern phase* |
|---|---|---|
| Japan | Land is occupied and managed directly by the major families. The subordinate families provide corvée labor and in return are assured MSL. | With increasing penetration by the market economy, the subordinate families become independent. Common asset formation and joint farm operation come to occupy the central place in community relations. During the interwar period, joint measures against "exploitation" by urban merchants are taken. |
| China | Common assets for production, education, and consumption are maintained by the socially equal and economically nearly independent families in the clan. Some farm operations are performed jointly by the clan. | With increasing penetration by the market economy, income and wealth differentials among families increase and "exploitative" relations appear among them. Clan assets decrease. Farm operations are performed jointly only among neighboring families. |
| India | A village is comprised of cultivators, artisans, and laborers, each a hereditary category. Between the former two groups the jajimani system is in operation. The first and the last are in a master-client relationship. To each group certain shares of produce are assured. | With market economy penetration the jajimani system and the master-client relation are gradually replaced by contractual transactions, though in many places at least part of the above system and relation is still in operation. Income differentials among these groups and with the cultivator group increase. |

seems to be found only in the activities of the minor cooperatives in Japan, insofar as empirical studies are concerned. It plays the role of increasing the real income of the society, in a context of increasing penetration by the market economy.

4. A community principle of mutual relief in emergencies. The most positive form of this principle is seen in the formation and maintenance of common assets for consumption purposes, as security against uncertainties in maintaining MSL.

### 3. AN ECONOMIC ANALYSIS OF COMMUNITY RELATIONS

This section, focusing on the mechanism by which community relations are established as an institution under given states of the other variables listed in section 1, will examine the following question: Why and how is each of the four working principles of community relations adhered to in the agricultural society under such states, instead of the corresponding principles of market economy relations? I shall concentrate on the first two principles, namely, the community principle of employment and income distribution, and the community principle of bringing about economies of scale. This is because, once the mechanisms regarding the first two principles are made clear, those regarding the remaining two are not very difficult to understand.

The analysis of the mechanism in question will be made by assessing the following three elements: (1) The preference of MSL families for either the community or market relations principle, (2) the preference of non-MSL families for either the community or market relations principle, and (3) the society's determination of a particular principle.

We should bear in mind that the mechanism in question is a real issue only when both community and market relations are known to families in the agricultural society and, moreover, when both are considered by them to be real and effective alternatives. If either of them is not known or, even when it is known, if one of them is long established and stabilized as an institution, the following analysis is not very meaningful.

## The Concept of Structural Disequilibrium

Before going into the main discussion, let me introduce the concept of "structural disequilibrium." This concept is intended to refer to the particular combination of objective conditions of agricultural society (A3, B1, and B2 on the list in section 1) which characterizes most of the agricultural societies in which MSL families constitute a dominant class. The introduction of this concept will, therefore, greatly facilitate our main discussion.

Structural disequilibrium here is defined as the state in which, due to (1) the constraint imposed on the labor supply schedule of the family members by the existence of MSL, or the wage inflexibility in the schedule below MSL (an aspect of the state of variable A3), (2) the relative scarcity of land, capital, and technological knowledge within the agricultural society (an aspect of the state of variable A3), and (3) the limited employment opportunities offered by the outside economy (a combined state of variables B1 and B2), the competitive market determination of employment would leave part of the labor force in the agricultural society either unemployed or underemployed, except in the case to be mentioned shortly. Under the given technological conditions, this state of structural disequilibrium can be resolved only if the endowments of land and capital are increased in a certain relation to the labor force, or if exogenous employment opportunities are increased to a certain extent.

To elaborate the concept of structural disequilibrium, a somewhat formal and simplified presentation is in order. In an economy consisting solely of the agricultural societies represented in figure 16.2, there are only two classes of families, laborers and landlords, and only two factors of production, land and labor. Land, the supply of which is fixed at $\bar{L}$, is exclusively owned and managed by landlords. Labor is exclusively supplied by laborers, and the quantity of labor ($N$) is measured by the number of laborers, when each of them works for the number of hours per day or the number of days per month that is considered socially normal. Rewards for labor, or wages ($w$), are determined for the unit of such $N$. The curve $ACG$ represents the aggregate supply curve of the economy. The reason why this curve takes this particular shape is as follows. First, the laborers' family is not willing to supply labor unless for each unit of $N$ it is paid a level of $w$ that is not less than MSL until all working members of the family obtain work opportunity with reward $\bar{W}$. Thus there emerges a reward or wage inflexibility in the domain below MSL, and this is reflected in section $AC$ of the aggregate labor supply curve, which is parallel to the horizontal axis. Second, section $AC$ ends at point $C$ when all laborers in the economy are employed at this MSL level of wages. Section $CG$ is forward rising because laborers are willing to work longer than what is considered socially normal only when the level of $w$ is increased correspondingly.[34] Curves $mm$ and $aa$ represent the aggregate marginal

34. It still is not easy to make a realistic assumption about the labor supply function of the families that entertain a serious concern for maintaining MSL. Under our assumption, the concepts of $N$ and of *MSL* wages or reward may be somewhat awkward in that they are based on the notion that there are, in the given society, many families in which the number of work hours per day per laborer or the number of work days per month per laborer is considered socially normal. However, this notion is essentially equivalent to the notion that there is in such a society an MSL wage or reward per person per day or per month that is socially accepted. The latter notion must imply a certain number of hours or days in which a person is expected to work in return for the MSL wage or reward. Also, it seems possible to cite actual examples of either of these notions existing in agricultural regions in the developing countries.

Meanwhile, the labor supply function in figure 16.2 may be re-interpreted in two alternative ways. (In these alternatives, the horizontal axis should be read in terms of

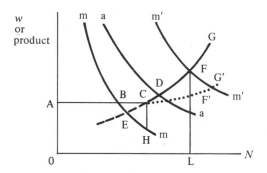

Fig. 16.2:   Society's Determination of Employment and Rewards (Wages) in Different Institutions in the Static Context

and average productivity curves of labor in the economy with the use of land $\bar{L}$. Under the condition of a competitive market economy, curve *mm* turns out to be the aggregate demand curve for labor.

Now, under competitive market conditions, the landlords, acting as surplus maximizers, would determine the employment of labor (*N*) at point *B* where the marginal productivity of labor is equal to wages (*w*) that are identical to MSL. This results in involuntary unemployment corresponding to distance *BC*.[35] In the same competitive market condition, this unemployment would disappear only when, due to an

the hours worked and the vertical axis in terms of hourly wages or reward). The first is to rely on A. K. Sen's assumption of the labor supply function of the peasant family, as presented in his "Labour Allocation in a Collective Enterprise," *Review of Economic Studies* 33 (1966): 361–71. The shape of this function is identical to ours, although its derivation is entirely different. It should be noted that Sen's labor supply function seems to be the maximum attainable in the effort to reflect the MSL phenomenon in the neoclassical framework. The other alternative is to rely on the labor supply function of Harvey Leibenstein and Paul Wonnacott (see Leibenstein's *Economic Backwardness and Economic Growth,* chap. 7; and Paul Wonnacott, "Disguised and Overt Unemployment in Underdeveloped Economies," *Quarterly Journal of Economics* 76, no. 2 [1962]: 279–97). This is based on the former's theory of a wage-productivity relationship which is essentially a physiological interpretation of labor supply as a function of per-worker wages. When this alternative is chosen, the shape of our labor supply schedule must be modified as far as section *AC* is concerned. However, the essential conclusions derivable in that case as to the issues of the determination of employment and wages either under competitive market conditions or under community relations are the same as those to be presented in this section.

35. This conclusion is the same as that derived by Wonnacott under the same competitive conditions (see "Labour Allocation in a Collective Enterprise") but is different from Leibenstein's (*Economic Backwardness and Economic Growth*).

increase in the supply of land, curve *mm* shifts sufficiently upward to cross curve *ACG* somewhere in section *CG*. An example of this case is shown by curve *m'm'*. Thus, structural disequilibrium in this economy is defined as a state in which the aggregate marginal productivity curve of labor *mm* crosses the aggregate supply curve of labor *ACG* somewhere in section *AC* (excepting point *C*), regardless of whether or not the economy is actually operating under competitive market conditions.

The definition of structural disequilibrium should be modified somewhat in an agricultural society the economic and social structures of which are more complex than, or different from, those posited above. (1) When the agricultural society is surrounded by a nonagricultural economy and establishes market-economy relations, the aggregate demand curve of labor (*mm*) should be shifted eastward to the extent that corresponds to the market opportunities (especially the employment opportunities) offered by the nonagricultural economy. (In the static context we are here assuming, the magnitude of the market opportunities available to the agricultural society is considered to be measurable with reasonable certainty.) If this new curve *mm* crosses the aggregate labor supply curve *ACG* somewhere in section *AC*, the agricultural society is still under structural disequilibrium. (2) When the agricultural society consists simply of landlords and tenants, structural disequilibrium should be redefined as a state in which a competitive land-rent market would result in part of the tenants being left with no land to rent, because of rent inflexibility in the domain above a certain rate the payment of which would leave the tenants simply an MSL income. The essential content of this state is the same as that of the above simplified model, and it can be indicated by using figure 16.2. (3) When the agricultural society consists solely of owner-cultivator families, a possibility arises in which the above definition should be changed. If the families are altruistic and communistic, involuntary unemployment arises only when the aggregate *average* productivity curve of labor, *aa*, crosses curve *ACG* in section *AC*, and the definition of structural disequilibrium should accordingly be changed.[36] When the relationship between family members is individualistic, such as in China,[37] the above definition need not be changed. (4)

36. The principle behind the determination of labor supply in this case is similar, though not identical, to that of the community principle of employment.
37. See note 28, above.

When the society consists of landlords, owner-cultivators, owner-cum-tenant cultivators, owner-cum-tenant cultivators who are also occasionally laborers, tenants and laborers, the aggregate marginal productivity curve of labor in the above definition should be redrawn excluding the productive capacity that is obtainable by self-cultivation of owned lands, and the aggregate supply curve of labor should be redrawn excluding the portion that corresponds to the labor supply for the self-cultivation of owned lands. The amount of labor supply for self-cultivation of own lands differs for the two types of families described above.

## The Community Principle of Employment

Turning now to the main discussion, let us look first at the mechanism regarding the community principle of employment and income distribution.[38] The alternative principle is a market principle of employment and income distribution, which is identical to the familiar marginal-productivity principle under perfect market conditions. In situations where market imperfections are expected to exist, the market principle is accordingly modified, also in familiar ways. For the sake of simplicity, I will assume an agricultural society consisting simply of landless laborers and landlords.[39] The implication is that the former represent MSL families and the latter non-MSL families. The discussion can be extended without loss of generality to other types of agrarian communities. In this extension it is necessary only to keep in mind the above discussion of the states of structural equilibrium and disequilibrium in different types of agricultural societies, and to extend the scope of the MSL and non-MSL families as follows: we will classify those families who own land but whose income from self-cultivation is not sufficient to maintain MSL, and those who rely on the cultivation of rented-in lands as the major means of maintaining MSL, as MSL families, and will classify the rest of the families as non-MSL families.

38. In theoretical discussions of the developing economies, those that incorporate this community principle in the framework are not rare. Typical examples are W. Arthur Lewis, "Development with Unlimited Supplies of Labour," *The Manchester School* 12 (1954): 139–91; and John C. H. Fei and Gustav Ranis, *Development of the Labor Surplus Economy: Theory and Policy* (Homewood, Ill.: Richard D. Irwin, 1964). However, in these discussions, the process in which this principle is established does not seem to have been studied.

39. The relationship between the cultivators' families in the caste system is similar to this relationship between landlords and landless laborers.

## The Preference of Laborers (MSL families)

Laborers' preferences tend to differ according to whether or not the economy is in structural disequilibrium. Under the condition of structural disequilibrium, regardless of whether or not the agricultural society is surrounded by the outside market economy, laborers are most likely to prefer employment based on the community principle of employment (hereafter called "community-employment"). This is evident for three reasons. (1) The concept of structural disequilibrium indicates by definition that, when the agricultural society is in that condition, the market principle of employment (hereafter called "market-employment") results in unemployment of some laborers, involving the ultimate danger of starvation or social failure. For each individual laborer family, this means that it faces uncertainty about maintaining MSL, with a probability equal to the ratio of $BC$ to $AC$ in figure 16.2. (2) Community-employment is by definition a social institution that averts such unemployment with certainty. Figure 16.2 assures all individual families "full" employment with the MSL reward at point $C$. (The reason why point $D$ is not chosen is explained by the effort of landlords to minimize the sacrifice of their surplus, even under the pattern of community relations to be described later.) (3) The MSL families can safely be assumed to be risk averters.[40]

In a situation where structural disequilibrium has already been overcome, laborers are very likely to prefer market-employment. This can be explained by referring to the economy of figure 16.2 and assuming the economy's aggregate marginal productivity curve of labor to be curve $m'm'$. First, it is certain that under such conditions the market principle would determine the employment of laborers at point $F$, with wages corresponding to $FL$. Second, the community principle would result in employment that is between the minimum point $C$ with MSL wages and the maximum point $F$ but with average wages $FL$, for the following reasons: (1) Community-employment at point $C$ represents the case where the aggregate marginal productivity curve of labor

40. In the discussions of the uncertainties in this and the next sections, those of a short-term nature are left aside because short-term fluctuations were abstracted in defining both the aggregate marginal productivity curve of labor and the aggregate labor supply curve. Also, even with regard to the uncertainties involved in employment and in other opportunities of a rather long-range nature, I shall in the remaining part of this section refrain from repeating the discussion relating to them. I shall take up this problem again in the next section in the more complicated dynamic context.

derivable on the basis of the productive force of the agricultural
society itself is such that it crosses curve *ACG* somewhere in section
*AC*. (2) The opposite, extreme case is that where the economy consists
solely of the agricultural society and curve *m'm'* represents the agricultural society's marginal labor productivity curve based on its own
productive force. Community-employment would then make curve
*ACG* the marginal labor cost curve to the landlords, while curve *ACG'*
would correspond to the average labor cost curve. Community-employment is determined at point *F'* with reward corresponding to *F'L*.

## The Preference of Landlords (Non-MSL Families)

The landlords' preference tends to vary also according to whether or
not the economy is in structural disequilibrium, but in a manner
opposite to the case of the MSL families. Under structural disequilibrium, the landlords tend to prefer market-employment to community-
employment. Community-employment would certainly force them to
sacrifice at least part of the surplus that would accrue to them under
market-employment. In figure 16.2 the amount of this sacrifice is shown
by area *BCH*. However, the landlords may worry about the possible
consequences of market-employment and the resulting unemployment
of laborers, such as social and political disturbances in the agricultural
society, and instability in making available the required volume of
employment at the required time. Therefore, it is likely that the landlords will also prefer community-employment.

In a situation where structural disequilibrium has already been
overcome, the landlords would prefer community-employment to the
market principle. The reason for this has already been indicated in the
previous discussion about the preference of the laborers under the
same condition.

## The Society's Determination of a Particular Institution

The process by which the community principle of employment or its
alternative, the market principle, is established as a result of the interaction of the preferences of laborers and landlords is not easy to explain. This process is entirely different from the one in which market
equilibrium for a commodity or a factor is attained as a result of
transactions among different parties. In the process leading to market
equilibrium, (1) individual preferences are expressed as a schedule
relating the desirable volumes of transaction to the market prices; (2)
individuals have freedom to choose between participation and non-

participation in transactions; (3) transactions are made by peaceful agreement, and market equilibrium is attained as a particular relation between the market price and the quantity of goods or factors exchanged; (4) transactions in the market confer an "all-round advantage" to all individuals participating in transactions.[41] In contrast, in the process of establishment of an institution, (1) individual preferences are expressed as a simple ordering of the alternative institutions; (2) individuals have in general no freedom to decline to participate in the process of determining a particular institution; (3) interaction of different individuals' preferences takes the form of agreement about a particular institution when their preferences happen to be identical, while in other cases it takes the form of compromise (through bargain or threat) or coercion; and (4) the institution thus established is often advantageous to some individuals, but disadvantageous to others.

While an adequate analysis of the present subject thus requires a new theory on this entirely new issue,[42] some conclusions about the subject may be derived on the basis of the above remarks.

First, my analysis of the preferences for a particular principle by both MSL and non-MSL families indicates that these preferences tend in general to be conflicting both in the state of structural disequilibrium and in the state of structural equilibrium. This implies that the institutions related to employment are in general not determined on the basis of agreement among the parties. Compromise and coercion tend easily to enter into the process of their determination. A typical example of compromise is given in the above-mentioned survey by Epstein: a blacksmith, one of the functionary families in Wangela, wanted to sever all his traditional obligations and instead to establish relations on a purely cash basis, but upon a village council's decision against it he abandoned his "preference," for to defy the village council's decision meant to him that he would have to get out of the village.[43]

41. I am of course not arguing that the market transaction is the institution for providing every individual participant satisfaction in the most fundamental sense. Even in the case of Pareto's optimum attained as a result of transactions in the perfect market, the income differential among families as the initial condition is not likely to be fundamentally changed, and this is the income differential which resulted in the present study in the distinction between the MSL and non-MSL families. We are here interested only in the analytical characteristics of the process of attaining market equilibrium itself.

42. Some insights are provided by János Kornai, *Anti-Equilibrium* (Amsterdam: North Holland Publishing Company, 1971); and Yasuaki Murakami, Hisao Kumagaya, and Shumpei Kumon, *Keizai taisei* [Economic systems] (Tokyo: Iwanami Bookstore, 1973).

43. Epstein, *Economic Development and Social Change in South India*, pp. 37–38.

Second, the preferences for the community principle expressed by
MSL and non-MSL families in a state of structural disequilibrium tend
to coincide when the non-MSL families are concerned about the social
and political stability of the agricultural society, as seen in India and,
especially, in Japan.

Third, in the case where the community principle is hard to establish
in the agricultural society, the market principle of employment tends to
prevail, regardless of whether or not the agricultural society is in structural disequilibrium. Even in this situation, however, it is possible that
the community principle will still be adhered to within a section of the
agricultural society if either compromise or agreement is attainable
within that range. Many examples of this were seen in the empirical
studies described in section 2.

### The Community Principle of Bringing about Scale Economies

Let us now turn to the next community principle, that regarding the
realization of the economies of scale. There are three preliminary
points to be made. First, this community principle manifests itself in
the following three forms:

a. *Technological scale economies:* When community ownership of
   such productive assets as irrigation facilities, common lands and
   forests, farm machinery and equipment, and common warehouses and work places is combined with joint cultivation and
   other productive activities of the community type, economies of
   scale in a technological sense are likely to become obtainable.
   Even without joint productive activities, an individual and al-
   ternating use of these common assets by member families is likely
   to bring about the same effect. Indivisibility of inputs is not
   confined to these capital assets. It is also seen in the use of human
   and animal labor in such operations as irrigation, sowing,
   fertilization, and interculture, which require at least a few units of
   laborers and/or animals in combination, and in such operations
   as transplanting, weeding, and harvesting, which require a much
   larger number of human laborers due to the time limitations on
   these operations.[44] Thus, joint cultivation of the community type
   is also likely to bring about scale economies.

b. *Managerial or organizational scale economies:* In a labor-intensive

44. Shih, *Chung-kuo nung-yeh ho-tso-hua yung-tung shih-liao;* and Heiriki Watana-
be, "A Few Observations on Agricultural Labor in North China," *Pao-Kao Chang-
p'ien* [Institute of Rural Economy, Peking University], vol. 1 (June 1943).

and small-scale agricultural production system, expansion in farm size tends to be accompanied by diseconomies of scale in a managerial sense. Yet it is also true that the expansion of the size of joint productive activities tends to economize on the use of managerial skills and leadership, which are also indivisible in a technical sense. The resulting economies of scale are especially marked in the spread of improved methods of cultivation, such as was exhibited in prewar Japan.

c. *Financial scale economies:* This is defined as the capability of purchasing expensive ("lumpy") productive assets which can be obtained only by organizing small family units, under conditions of undeveloped or underdeveloped capital markets. These financial scale economies are a prerequisite for community owner-ship of most assets, which are available only in the market. A typical example of financial scale economies is the activities of the minor cooperatives in Japan.

The role of these scale economies in the context of contemporary agricultural society is most clearly understood in that they help to overcome structural disequilibrium. To refer again to figure 16.2, it can be explained by their effect of shifting curves *mm* and *aa* upward, when this shift is hard to attain by any other means.

Second, a few words are necessary regarding the market economy alternative to the community principle of realizing scale economies. This alternative is not as distinct as in the case of the market principle of employment, the alternative to the community principle of employ-ment. Logically, most of the scale economies listed above should be obtainable in the market to even a larger extent. For instance, it should be possible for individual families to organize themselves into coopera-tives or similar joint schemes from individualistic motivation (rational behavior in the market economy sense) and thereby to purchase jointly the same productive assets as were listed above or to engage in joint economic activities that are similar to the above. The rental service of firms owning farm machinery and equipment, which has recently come into vogue in some countries of Asia, is one means for small families to obtain technical scale economies without having financial scale economies. More generally, well-developed labor and capital markets play decisive roles with regard to these scale economies.[45] In providing these scale economies, public investments (e.g., on irrigation works)

45. Lewis, *Theory of Economic Growth,* pp. 76–77.

and current government expenditures (e.g., on extension work) are
capable of acting as able assistants to the market, if the pressure
mechanism in Hirschman's sense is working effectively. However, in
stages where the outside market economy is not yet sufficiently developed, and particularly where it is not accompanied by a well-
developed productive force in the economy, the effective choice is
likely to be simply between the community principle of bringing about
scale economies and private individual efforts to obtain them.

Third, the community principle of bringing about scale economies
seems to have originated in egalitarian agrarian communities or, in
hierarchical communities, among families with equal status (according
to the mutual-help principle), in contrast to the community principle of
employment, which seems to have originated in the hierarchical relationship among families in hierarchical communities. For this reason,
and also because even in more recent times the small cultivators seem
to be most interested in community ownership of assets and in joint
economic activities of the community type, the community principle
regarding scale economies can most conveniently be studied in an
agricultural society that consists solely of owner-cultivators. There is
no reason, of course, why landless laborers and landlords should not be
interested in some of these joint activities, although the range of
common assets and joint productive activities that potentially benefit
each of these classes may be limited. Therefore, in the following discussion of this community principle I shall take into consideration all
families in the agricultural society, although my emphasis is on the
MSL and non-MSL cultivators, and MSL and non-MSL families are
designated by these two terms respectively.

## The Preference of the MSL Cultivators

The MSL cultivators tend to prefer the community principle of scale
economies, regardless of whether the agricultural society is in structural disequilibrium or not. This preference is particularly strong in the
case where the community principle of employment is not in operation.
For, in this case, acquisition of the economies of large scale is likely to
be the only means of avoiding starvation and social failure.

The emergence of exogenous market opportunities for obtaining
scale economies may tend to weaken this preference. Yet, as long as
the capital market remains underdeveloped, the very low income and
wealth position of the MSL cultivators prevents them from benefiting
adequately from these opportunities. Hence, the community principle

may be preferred as strongly as before, as a means of realizing financial scale economies.

## The Preference of the Non-MSL Cultivators

In the stage in which exogenous market opportunities for obtaining scale economies have not yet emerged, the preference of non-MSL cultivators for the community principle of scale economies is likely to be determined by a comparison of the net gains accruing from relying upon community-type productive assets and activities with the net gains from having and using similar productive assets by themselves and engaging in activities of their own. Net gains here stands for the gross gains accruing from scale economies in each mode of holding and using assets and engaging in economic activities minus the losses incurred in obtaining these gross gains. The gross gains from scale economies tend to be greater in community schemes than in individual schemes, insofar as the non-MSL cultivators can benefit from scale economies through joint cultivation as well as other joint productive activities in the community schemes, whereas in the individual schemes they can benefit only from scale economies resulting from indivisible productive assets. The main form of losses is each cultivator's mandatory contribution to the community schemes, or alternatively his private expenditure for bringing the individual schemes into being. Where the economy is in structural disequilibrium, the possible losses incurred through the political and social instability of the agricultural society that is likely to arise when the MSL cultivators are deprived of the chance to organize community schemes should be also taken into account. Thus, when the net gains from participating in community schemes are found to be greater than those from the individual schemes, the former tends to be preferred. With the emergence of exogenous market opportunities for obtaining scale economies, the net gains that would be secured from the individual schemes by utilizing these market opportunities tend to be larger than before.

## The Society's Determination of a Particular Institution

These considerations indicate that the attitudes of MSL and non-MSL families toward the community principle of bringing about scale economies do not tend to be as divergent and contradictory as in the case of the community principle of employment. Since a major possible source of divergence here is the non-MSL families' calculation of comparative net gains from adhering to this principle and from individually utilizing market opportunities for obtaining scale economies, when the outside market economy is not sufficiently developed, the possibility is great that their preferences will converge. Their preferences tend to diverge only in the later stages of market economy development. This explains the changing importance of clan assets for productive purposes in China. Yet, even in the latter case, if the non-MSL families are seriously concerned with the social and political stability of the agricultural society, the preferences of MSL and non-MSL families tend to converge. This seems to have been the case in Japan in the interwar period.

Finally, even when the community principle is retarded on a village-wide scale, the principle may remain in operation on a smaller scale among some or all of the MSL families. However, the community principle working on a small scale is most often confined to joint culti-vation of one kind or another, since in such cases the MSL families lack sufficient funds to purchase farm machinery and equipment, and there is no institutional foundation for undertaking such labor-inten-sive projects as irrigation. Hence, scale economy effects are not then very significant.

## 4. THE SHIFT TO MARKET RELATIONS

Let us turn now to the issue of the mechanism by which community relations in the agricultural society and, side by side with this, the class structure and the productive force in the agricultural society undergo certain changes under the impact of changes in the nonagricultural economy. Change in the nonagricultural economy will be analyzed here by separating the state of that economy into (1) the state of the market economy, and (2) the state of the productive force, although in the last section these two aspects are dealt with in combination, and as such the state of development of the nonagricultural economy is as-sumed to be given.

From the empirical evidence in section 2 on community relations in certain countries of Asia, we have already obtained a host of broad facts relating to this mechanism. Some of them (relating to Japan and China only) are summarized in table 16.2. From these, the following findings may be derived:

a.  The shift from community relations to market relations tends to proceed with a certain regularity. It begins in the aspect of the

Table 16.2: Specific Steps in the Shift from Community Relations to
Market Relations: Japan and China

*Japan*

| | |
|---|---|
| Product disposal | Sale of produce by individual families developed since around 1700. (In the interwar period, joint sale of a community type emerged.) |

Land use — Occupation and direct management of land by main families

→ Self-cultivation
- Direct management by main family on a smaller scale
- Self-cultivation by independent peasants→

↘ Cultivation by tenants
- Commercialized landlords →
- (Community-type tenancy)

Labor use — Corvée labor by subordinate families →
- ↗ Self-employment by independent peasants and tenants→
- → Hired-labor in the market→
- ↘ (Employment through personal relations and joint operations) →

Producers of capital goods — (Self-supply under management by main families) → Self-supply or market purchase
- By individual families→
- (By joint construction or joint purchase) →

*China*

| | |
|---|---|
| Product disposal | Sale of produce by individual families already developed in the tenth century. In early twentieth century new commercial crops were introduced for export. |

Land use — (Owned and operated by independent families)
- → Self-cultivation by peasants→
- ↘ Cultivation by tenants with landlords commercialized→

(Aided by clan assets) → (Decreased weight of clan lands)

Labor use —
- Self-employment by independent families→ → Self-employment by peasants
- Hired labor in the market
- (Aided by joint operations) → (Labor exchange continues)

Producers of capital goods —
- Self-supply by independent families→ Self-supply or purchase by individual peasants→
- (Joint construction of clan assets) → (Decreased importance of clan assets)

*Notes:* Parentheses indicate community-type activities and arrows indicate the direction of shifts. Arrows extending to the right margin indicate relations continuing up to the recent past.

economic activities of the agricultural society related to product
disposal. In the land and labor use aspects, the shift begins in a
later stage and tends to proceed evenly.

b. There are two contrasting types of shifts to market relations:
one is the Japanese type, in which the shift is accompanied by a
general improvement of the social and economic position of the
MSL families relative to the non-MSL families, and the other is
the pattern of China and India, in which the shift is accompanied
by an absolute worsening of the economic position of the MSL
families. Underlying these contrasting types is probably a tendency for productivity development in the agricultural sector to
be more significant in the latter type.

c. There is also a possibility that community relations may be
reactivated in the context of the development of the outside
market economy and may then promote the improvement of
both the economic position of the MSL families and the productive force of the agricultural society, as was observable in Japan
during the interwar period.

With regard to the second of these findings, we recall that the development of the market economy and of the productive force in the
nonagricultural sector was disparate both in China and India in modern
times. Only in Japan did they proceed side by side. This poses the
question whether or not this is related to the different rates of development of the market economy and the productive force inside the
agricultural society.

To study these findings and this question further in terms of the
mechanism described above is ideally the subject of this section, which
presents the "dynamic" aspect of my socioeconomic model. However,
we are not yet at a stage where it is possible to present the mechanism
in analytical terms. What I can do here is mainly to refer to more
detailed empirical data relating to a few specific points at issue in this
section and thereby to increase our empirical knowledge with regard
to the working of the above mechanism.

### Retardation of the Community Principle of Employment

The first point is related to the process of retardation of the community
principle of employment, as a specific aspect of the shift from community relations to market relations. Specifically, I will take up the
Japanese phenomenon of the general decline of "the landlords' direct

management of their own lands" (jinushi-tezukuri), which, as was discussed in section 2, took place during the 1900s and the 1910s. In terms of table 16.2, I will go into more detail regarding the columns for land and labor use in Japan.

The initial change that caused this shift was the expansion of labor demand in urban industrial centers, which seems to have begun around the turn of this century and which was especially rapid during World War I. The immediate effect of this change was the disappearance of structural disequilibrium in the economy, inclusive of the agricultural society. For example, in Saga Prefecture, which is located near the industrial center of northern Kyushu, the number of persons economically active in agriculture began decreasing in 1899, and the decrease rate was especially rapid after 1912. This resulted in the outflow of nearly half of the agricultural labor force by 1920. The number of farm households began decreasing around 1900, but the total decrease by 1920 was less than 20 percent.[46] Due to an accompanying rise in agricultural wages, especially those of annual laborers, the direct management of land by landlords using labor services (offered by the servants and other subordinate families) faced serious difficulties. Thus, many landlords sold their lands or began renting them out. On the other hand, many of the former servants and the subordinate families began obtaining an independent position by becoming tenant or tenant-cum-owner cultivators. Because of the rise in land prices, however, it was not easy for them to expand their operations by increasing the amount of land under their ownership. They were therefore enthusiastic about raising the productivity of their small lands by introducing new technology developed in the interwar period.[47] In Saga Prefecture, the new technology introduced by these medium-sized farmers was a system of two crops a year on the basis of mechanical irrigation newly introduced, which has contributed to making Saga the top prefecture in Japan in terms of per-hectare rice output.

This, in essence, is the story of the end of jinushi-tezukuri, and it suggests that the shift from community relations to market relations becomes complete and definite only when the penetration of the exogenous market economy into the agricultural society results in the

46. Toshihiko Isobe, "The Process of Formation of the So-called Saga-Stage," in *Shuyō chitai nōgyō seisan-ryoku keisei-shi* [A history of productivity formation in a major agricultural region], ed. S. Tobata and S. Morinaga, vol. 2 (Tokyo: National Agricultural Research Institute, 1959).
47. Ishikawa and Ohkawa, "Significance of Japan's Experience."

dislocation of the existing practices of land and labor use based on community relations, and the foundation of the existing system of production and management units is thus undermined. It also suggests that simply through the expansion of the market economy without the accompanying development of a productive force expanding employment opportunities, such a rapid shift would not have been possible. (Another finding regarding the productivity increase of the newly emerged, independent cultivators will be taken up later.)

However, what happened in the earlier stage of this shift is also important, mainly from the analytical point of view. In this stage the cultivator families were ambivalent, and the shift in their preferences was only gradual.[48] This can be explained by referring to figure 16.3, which shows the relationship between the aggregate marginal productivity curves (in the market economy context, the aggregate labor demand curves) and the aggregate labor supply curve in the agricultural sector, as was done also in figure 16.2. Curve $m_0$ stands for the marginal productivity curve of labor at the initial stage. When the nonagricultural economy begins to develop and, as a result, employment opportunities for MSL families increase, it is likely that the demand curve of labor in the market economy will shift eastward. However, in a dynamic context, it is not possible for both MSL and non-MSL families to perceive with certainty where a new curve is actually located in each successive stage. Curves $m_1$ and $m_2$ are shown here as examples of numerous possible curves that may appear at any given stage, depending upon the degree of expansion of employment opportunities coming from the nonagricultural economy. Since this degree is unforeseeable, the probabilities of occurrence of these two hypothetical curves are also unknown. The issue of how, in this dynamic context, each individual family determines its institutional preference can be relatively easily described in terms of decision-theory strategy. (This issue is entirely different in nature from the issue of the preferences examined earlier in connection with figure 16.2 in that the labor

48. The relationship between the landlord and one of his tenants in the very early stage of this process is best described, I believe, in a novel called *"Tsuchi"* [Earth] written in 1910 by Takashi Nagatsuka, a well-known naturalist writer in Japan. Here, the alternatives of employment for the tenant were still essentially employment as a pure tenant and employment as tenant-cum-casual laborer, both within the village. Meanwhile, in Rajit Gupta's article "Rural Works Programme: Where It Has Gone Astray" (*Economic and Political Weekly,* May 15, 1971) an interesting case is found in Bihar, India, where the peasants are ambivalent in the face of two alternatives: employment as tenants or laborers of the landlords, and employment as workers outside the village.

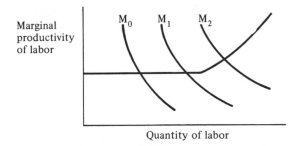

Fig. 16.3: Society's Determination of Employment and Rewards (Wages) in Different Institutions in the Dynamic Context

demand curve under market economy relations can be located with reasonable certainty in the latter issue.) In the earlier stages we are now discussing, the shift of $m_0$ to $m_1$ or $m_2$ would be considered by the families to be not very large. This, together with the generally risk-averting characteristic of MSL families, seems to explain their ambivalence in determining their institutional preferences. Only when the development of the nonagricultural economy becomes significantly rapid, as seen in the case of Japan during and after World War I, does the MSL families' preference for the market principle of employment tend to become a definite trend. For this to be realized, it seems certain that market economy development in the nonagricultural economy must accompany development of its productive force.

### Responses to New Market Opportunities

The second point is related to the question of whether the initial income and wealth differentials among families tend to increase or decrease as a specific part of the impact the above shift to market relations will have upon the class structure of the society.

While the empirical data indicate differing answers to this question, there is a certain tendency in the newly emerged market toward new commercial crops, which gives an especially favorable position to non-MSL families. This arises from the fact that the introduction of these crops in the fields often requires a substantial sum of money, which creates the need for financial scale economies. Thus, in a Mysore village Epstein surveyed, for example, the introduction of a sugarcane crop after the arrival of irrigation water required a considerable amount of working capital for purchasing fertilizer and for investment in processing equipment. Hence, at first only those families that had some ready cash were capable of introducing it. They are today the richest in the village.[49] The case of the introduction of American varieties of tobacco in north China, studied by Chen Han-Seng, presents a similar story. While the market prices of the American varieties were much higher than the native varieties, the costs of production of the American varieties were also much higher than the native varieties, due mainly to the requirement of a larger amount of fertilizer. The American varieties also required investment in drying facilities and their operating costs. These requirements prevented the poorer peasants from easily introducing the American varieties.[50] Similar stories of the different capabilities of responding to new market opportunities among the families of different income and wealth positions are abundant in connection with the recent green revolution.[51] However, there are also quite a few examples in which emergence of a product market benefited the MSL families, although the products here were more often of a labor-intensive nature or of a purely subsistence-crop type.[52]

Similarly, the emergence of a land market is advantageous to those who have money to purchase land, and hence, in principle, to the non-MSL families. There are many examples, however, indicating that the growth of a land market also provides MSL families with opportunities to obtain land and, hence, to acquire an independent position.[53] The emergence of a labor market is in principle advantageous to MSL families. It often happens, however, that when MSL families choose the market economy principle of employment, the landlords retaliate against them by hiring migrant agricultural laborers from outside, thus depriving the resident MSL families of employment opportunities.[54]

These differences in the impact of new market opportunities are explainable also in relation to the conditions of the nonagricultural economy. If the outside market economy development is accompanied

49. Epstein, *Economic Development and Social Change in South India,* pp. 29–30.

50. Chen Han-Seng, *Industrial Capital and Chinese Peasants: A Study of the Livelihood of Chinese Tobacco Cultivators* (Shanghai: Kelly & Walsh, 1939).

51. Ishikawa, *Strategies of Agricultural Development in Asia.*

52. Myint's *Economics of the Developing Countries* provides many such examples. Since, however, they are related to those countries with both surplus land and surplus labor, they are not considered here.

53. Furushima, *Nippon nōgyō-shi,* p. 311; and Andre Beteille, *Caste, Class, and Power: Changing Patterns of Stratification in a Tanjore Village* (Berkeley and Los Angeles: University of California Press; London: Oxford University Press, 1966).

54. Beteille, *Caste, Class, and Power,* p. 130.

by a significant development of the productive force of the nonagricultural economy, the economic position of the MSL families tends to be raised as they participate first in the labor market and then even in the land and product market. The reemergence of the community principle of bringing about scale economies would intensify this tendency.

### Disparity between Market and Productivity Development

My final point deals with the question of whether the disparity between market and productivity development in the nonagricultural sector is likely to result in a similar disparity within the agricultural society. This question is related to an aspect of the relationship between the shift to market relations and the productive force in the agricultural society which is a part of the mechanism at issue.

A few remarks must suffice. First, among the major factors to be studied in connection with this question are: (a) technological progress related to the agricultural inputs and initiated in the nonagricultural sector; (b) that part of the above agricultural inputs which is manufactured in the nonagricultural sector; and (c) agricultural investment induced by (a) and (b). Concerning these factors and their interrelations there are many findings in the existing literature.[55] They suggest a close association between productivity force development inside and outside of the agricultural society. Second, there is the question of who undertakes this induced investment, a question that is closely related to the discussion section before this. It suggests that this undertaking can be made by the former MSL families only when the productive force development in the nonagricultural economy is significant. Third, in the contemporary agricultural society there are still untapped opportunities for increasing the productive force by utilizing traditional but well-articulated technologies such as minor irrigation works and farmyard manures, as I have demonstrated on previous occasions.[56] These opportunities can be tapped once the community principle of bringing about scale economies is implemented. In the present context, where modern inputs are available, these traditional inputs might better

55. Here only two are referred to: Hayami and Ruttan, *Agricultural Development*; and T. W. Schultz, *Transforming Traditional Agriculture* (New Haven: Yale University Press, 1964).

56. See Shigeru Ishikawa, *Economic Development in Asian Perspective* (Tokyo: Kinokuniya Bookstore, 1967); Ishikawa, *Strategies of Agricultural Development in Asia*; and Ishikawa and Ohkawa, "Significance of Japan's Experience."

be used in combination with modern inputs, as was done in Japan after the 1920s. This also suggests that an association between the productivity force development in both sectors would continue to exist.

# Contributors

R. A. Berry, Professor of Economics, University of Toronto.

Robert Evenson, The Agricultural Development Council, University of the Philippines—Los Banos, Los Banos, Laguna.

Walter P. Falcon, Director, Food Research Institute, and Professor of Economics, Stanford University.

John C. H. Fei, Professor of Economics, Yale University, Economic Growth Center.

E. K. Fisk, Professorial Fellow, Department of Economics, The Research School of Pacific Studies, The Australian National University, Canberra.

Yujiro Hayami, Professor, Faculty of Economics, Tokyo Metropolitan University.

Gerald K. Helleiner, Professor of Economics, University of Toronto.

Shigeru Ishikawa, Professor, Institute of Economic Research, Hitotsubashi University, Tokyo.

Z. Kozlowski, Principal Lecturer, Senior Course Tutor, Lanchester Polytechnic, Coventry; Senior Associate Member, St. Antony's College, Oxford University.

Raj Krishna, Senior Economist, World Bank, Washington, D.C. (formerly Professor of Economics, University of Rajasthan, Jaipur, India).

Mahar Mangahas, Associate Professor of Economics, University of the Philippines, Diliman Campus, Quezon City.

James A. Mirrlees, Professor of Economics, Oxford University (Nuffield College).

Hla Myint, Professor of Economics (London School of Economics), University of London.

David M. G. Newbery, Fellow of Churchill College and Lecturer in Faculty of Economics and Politics, University of Cambridge, Cambridge, England.

Gustav Ranis, Professor of Economics, Director, Economic Growth Center, Yale University.

Lloyd G. Reynolds, Professor of Economics, Yale University.

Vernon W. Ruttan, President, Agricultural Development Council, Inc., New York, N.Y.

C. Peter Timmer, Associate Professor of Economics in the Food Research Institute, Stanford University.

Saburo Yamada, Associate Professor, Institute of Oriental Culture, University of Tokyo, and Graduate School of Agricultural Economics, University of Tokyo.

# Index

Absentee ownership: Colombia, 254, 255, 256; 19th-century Europe, 256
African agriculture: traditional issues, 28–31; marginal productivity of labor, 28; rationality, 31; shifting cultivation, 31; smallholders' supply response and crops in various countries, 31–44, 40 (table 2.1); response to innovation, 44–52; extended family system, 46, 47; urban migration, 47; food production seen as paramount, 47
Agrarian community: definition, 457; decision-making power, 458
Agricultural organization, 2–5
Agricultural policy. *See* Policy, agricultural
Agricultural product by major country groups, 414*n*, 416 (table 15.2)
Agricultural sector: as resource reservoir, 14–17; stages of its development, 53–54; Colombia's income distribution compared with other countries, 265, 266 (table 10.5); standard contributions to economic development, 327–54; supplying food and labor, 327–28, 337–44; enlarging domestic market, 327–28, 345, 346; supplying domestic savings, 327, 328, 345, 346; providing foreign exchange, 327, 337–44, 353–54; voluntary vs. compulsory contributions, 328–29, 353; internal role in early stages of development, 329–32, 335, 337; and large densely populated countries, 331, 334; and semi-open economy, 332–37; food self-sufficiency and comparative advantage, 337–54; mutual inconsistency of policies to increase all 4 contributions, 345–54; balanced growth argument, 347–49; savings diversion to agriculture, 350–52; role of foreign loans and investment, 353; role in natural-resource-poor open economies, 356, 360–62; role in closed economy, 356; role in natural-resource-rich open economies, 370; role in economic growth of socialist countries, 440
Agricultural societies, 242
Agriculture: origins and international dispersals, 165–67. *See also* Technological research; Technology transfer
Ahmad, Syed, 175*n*14
Amorphous peasantry, 50
Amortization-receiving landlord, 157
Amortizing peasant, 156
Ardito-Barletta, N., 194
Arromdee, Virach, 382*n*4
Arrow, K. J., 172*n*10
Asian agricultural society: stylized facts, 454–59; measurement of market economy development, 454–55; economic classes and income positions, 455, 459; minimum-subsistence-level families, 456–57; interfamily relations, 457–58, 459, 460; socioeconomic model, 459–60; individual welfare maximization, 460
Ayer, H., 194

Balanced growth, 330, 347–49, 356; in Marxist theory, 416
Baltic republics: collective farm inequalities, 428*n*24
Barber, William J., 74*n*
Bardhan, P. K., 121–27, 132, 135, 139, 158
Bateman, Merrill J., 51*n*84
Berry, R. A., 16, 257*n*, 244*n*19
Bickel, Hans, 382*n*4
Billings, Martin H., 300, 305, 307*n*11
Binswanger, Hans P., 175*n*14
Boserup, Ellen, 7, 8

Bradley, M. B., 446*n*42
Bronstein, M., 429*n*24
Bulgaria: land reform, 420*n;* land not nationalized, 442*n*
Bureaucratic behavior: models of, 181 and *n*25, 183–84
Bush, K., 449*n*47

Canterbery, E. Ray, 382*n*4
Capital deepening, 365, 366, 367
Cash cropping: Africa, 33, 37–41, 44; with supplementary subsistence, 54; in transitional farming, 60; earnings, 453
Cereal grains, 203–09, 204–05 (table 8.4)
Chaudri, D. P., 198
Cheung, Steven N. S., 113, 115, 116, 122, 123, 139
China: balanced growth policy, 21; foodgrain prices, 21; growth of output, 22, 23; rural-urban migration, 22–23; rural full employment, 23; infrastructure activities, 23; compared with Japan, *1880-1905,* 24; land reform, 470*n*28
China, precommunist: share tenancy efficiency, 139; traditional village, 466; equality principle, 467; clan assets, 467; cooperative works, 467; market penetration, 467 and *n;* treaty ports' impact, 468; factor markets, 468; land market, 469; labor exchange practices 469–70; productivity, 470 and *n*28
Cholaj, H., 447*n*43
Clark, M. G., 446*n*42
Class structure, 455; impact of new market opportunities, 493–94
Closed economy, 329, 330; development model of, 17
Closed-family economy, 458
Cocoa, 37, 41, 43
Coffee, 32, 37, 38, 43; Colombia, 254, 255
Collective action, model of, 184 and *n*31
Colombia: characteristics of agriculture, 254–61; output, 254–55; commercial crop sector, 256; land and labor productivity, 256, 280*n,* 282 (table 10.6); heterogeneity and factor proportions, 256, 260, 260 (table 10.3), 282 (table 10.6), 288 (table 10.7); labor/land ratio and sizes of farms, 256, 260, 280*n,* 282 (table 10.6); efficiency of farm size, 257, 257 (table 10.1);

government policies, 258, 259, 265, 288–89; crop percentage grown on small and large farms, 259 (table 10.2); factor market imperfections, 260; credit availability, 260–61, 261 (table 10.4); political power and income distribution, 265, 266 (table 10.5); policy institutions specialized for sizes of farms, 270; foreign exchange market disequilibrium, 290; mechanization policy, 290
Colonial heritage, 357, 359–60, 360*nn*5, 6, 361
Command economy, 459*n*
Commercial family farm, 62–67, 79; Nakajima's model, without labor market, 62–64; with competitive labor market, 64–67
Communist agriculture: growth policy, 412–25; collectivization and collectivist attitude, 415, 419–25; investment in agriculture, 417*n*9; ownership of farm land, 420; land reform, beneficial effects, 420–23, 423*n*; sociological effects, 422–25; containment of capitalist elements, 423–24; supposed inefficiency of small farms, 424, 425; collective agriculture and efficiency problems, 425–36; animal husbandry and private plots, 426–28, 426*nn*17, 18, 427*nn*21, 22; inequalities among collective farms, 428–29, 428*n*24; labor transfer, 430–31, 431*n*-27; state control and planning, 431–34; material incentives for technical crops, 434 and *n*32; procurement, 435; state farms, 436–39; appraisal of policy, 440–45
Communist system of economic growth: theory, 415–19, 424; Marx's law of extended reproduction, 415–17; Stalinist model, 417–19; degradation of agriculture, 417 and *nn*7, 8, 418, 419, 445; ownership in farming, 420, 424; mistrust of peasant, 423–25; priorities, 444–45; efficiency, 445
Community principles of employment, 480–84; decline 490
Community relations: observed forms, 461–75; decline, 474, 490; principal forms, 474–75; economic analysis, 475–88; shift toward market relations, 488–96
Comparative advantage, 330, 333, 335, 337–44

Complementary relations between industry and agriculture, 347–48; and technical linkages, 348

Congo basin, 48

Constant returns to scale, 111, 124

Consumers' surplus, 232, 238

Consumption levels: affecting productivity (productivity hypothesis), 84–106; different levels of, 91–97, 99; and population growth, 106

Contract curve, 365, 366

Contract farming, 109$n$1

Cotton, 36, 39, 41, 43, 45

Cownie, John, 300

Credit facilities, 43, 44, 114, 136; landlord and others for share tenants, 150, 154; landlord for leaseholder, 155

Crop mix, 301, 306–07

Cropping intensity, 301, 306–09

Customary economy, 459$n$

Czechoslovakia: demand for food, 415$n$; land reform, 420$n$; collectivization, 430

Dandekar, V. M., 423$n$

Dean, Edwin, 34

Decision-making power: the collective in agrarian community, 458; independently through the market, 458

Decision-making unit in Africa, 35, 46; role of females, 46; extended family system, 46, 47; in communal tenure system, 46

Development policies to stimulate participation in market economy, 76–78

Diffusion of crop varieties, 165–67; and recent green revolution, 166 (table 7.1), 167; and discovery of America, 167; in 19th century, 167; in Meiji Restoration Japan, 242–43. *See also* Technology transfer

Disguised unemployment, 13, 339, 347, 430; Africa, 28, 29

Double cropping, 10

Dovring, Folke, 7

Dualism, 3, 4, 18, 254$n$, 256$n$7, 273; policy-induced, new dualism, 332–33, 335–36; in closed economy, 356; in open economy, 357

Duff, Bart, 300

East European socialist countries; agricultural output, 412, 413 (table 15.1), 414$n$; shortages, 412; pattern of industrialization, 413–15; income elasticity of demand for food, 414, 444; lag of agriculture, 414, 415; appraisal of general economic growth, 440; appraisal of agricultural growth rate, 440–45, 442 (table 15.5); comparison with USSR and West, 442–43, 443$n$38; maximal growth rate, 443–44; future changes, 445–50; small farm potential, 446–47; Comecon policy for agriculture, 447–48. *See also* Communist agriculture; Communist system

East Germany, collectivization, 430

Economic behavior of farm families: maximizing, "satisficing," optimizing, 5; constraints, 6; response to price and tax changes, 6, 7

Economic intuitions, 264, 265, 269, 291–93

Economies of scale: and community-type activities, 484–85; preference of marginal cultivators, 486; preferences of non-marginal cultivators, 487; resulting choice, 487–88

Education and training, 89, 199–200, 351

Efficiency of production: of fixed-rent and fixed-wage contract, 112; of share tenancy contract, 113, 114, 116

Elasticities: of farm demand for food, 7; of marketings, 7. *See also* Supply response

Employment effects of green revolution, 297–323; direct effects of innovation, 298–307; direct effects of tractorization, 307–09; indirect effects, 310–18; total effects, 318–20

Employment in Asian agricultural communities: community vs. market principle of employment, 480–84; preferences of laborers and landlords, 481–82; resulting choice, 483; conflicts, 482, 483, 484

Enforcement costs, 120, 121, 132; and choice of rental contract, 116–17

Entrepreneurship, 117–20, 137, 359, 360, 361

Epstein, T. Scarlett, 472–73, 493

Equality relationships, 467

Estate economy. *See* Primary product export sector

Ethiopia, 38, 41

Evenson, Robert, 8, 197, 198, 201, 202, 222, 223, 230

Experiment stations, 170, 171, 176;
    Japan, 177; Taiwan, 177; Southeast
    Asia, 179; European privately
    arranged, 238; government initiative,
    Japan, 236–40
Export-led growth, 18–19
Export pessimism, 18, 20, 334, 340,
    341–42
Export substitution, 359, 360, 362,
    372
Extension, 9, 43, 76, 187, 198–200,
    351; value of extension time, 200

Factory economy and wage labor:
    theory, 85–98; profit maximizing
    wage rate under productivity hypoth-
    esis, 87; and unemployment, 88–97;
    constancy of wage rates over time, 88;
    investment in labor quality, 88–89;
    two different consumption levels, 91–
    97; optimum production point, 93–96,
    97–98; government wage subsidies to
    eliminate unemployment, 97–98
FAO *Provisional Indicative World Plan
    for Agricultural Development,* 299–
    300
Farm management studies, Africa, 45
Farm price programs, USA, 186
Farmers' associations, 187
Fei, J. C. H., 12
Felbur, S., 417n8, 430n
Fertilizer: in Nigeria, 48; fertilizer/rice
    price ratio, 177, 178 (table 7.2);
    industry, 348–49
Fixed-rental contracts: utility maximiza-
    tion, 111, 112; and entrepreneurial
    skill, 117–20; and risk aversion, 118;
    and wage employment, 130; model of
    leaseholder, 155–57; with landlord
    financing, 155; income maximization,
    156; compared with share tenant, 156;
    model of leaseholder's landlord, 157;
    income maximization, 157; transaction
    costs, 157n17
Food crop production, 36, 42–43;
    precedence over cash crop, 47
Food supplies: by country groups,
    414n, 416 (table 15.3)
Foreign trade: as incentive for growth,
    334, 335
"Full belly" consumption, 80–83

Geoclimate regions, 202–06
Georgescu-Roegen, Nicolas, 67, 423n
Ghana, 36, 43, 51n84

Gotsch, Carl H., 295
Green revolution, 9, 10, 166 (table 7.1);
    167, 201, 247, 294, 336, 341–42, 348,
    349, 350, 361, 362, 458n, 494;
    capacity transfer stage, 170–71; rice,
    176–80; employment effects, 297–
    323; high-yielding varieties effect,
    302, 303; multiple cropping, 337; and
    international rice prices, 379
Griliches, Zvi, 172, 173, 194, 197

Habakkuk, J. H., 331
Hägerstrand, Torsten, 172n9
Halpern, Joel M., 424n
Hamilton, E. E. Ian, 415n
Havlicek, Jaromir, 415n
Hayami, Y., 9, 197, 198, 223, 390,
    466n18
Heckscher-Ohlin theory of international
    trade, 341
Helleiner, G. K., 59n7
Herer, W., 430n, 434n32, 443n39,
    449n48
Heritability model, 222–23
Hicks, J. R., 175n14, 459n
Hierarchical relationships: Japan, 463,
    465; China, 471, 473
Hill, Polly, 51, 135
Hines, J., 194
Hirschman, Albert, 19, 258n
Hogendorn, Jan S., 38n34
Houck, J., 201
Huffman, W., 200
Hungary: land reform, 420n, 426n19
Hybrid corn: diffusion model, incor-
    porating adaptation, 172, 173; profit-
    ability, 172; and public research
    institutes, 172; and agricultural
    supply firms, 172; sequence of related
    inventions, 194

Imperfect product markets, 134n34
Import substitution, 17, 18; policy
    instruments, 20; squeeze on agricul-
    ture and internal economic effects,
    20–21; in natural-resource-poor open
    economy, 357–61; building of
    domestic market, 357, 360; providing
    foreign exchange, 360; financing
    industrial expansion, 360; government
    policies, 360, 361; prolonged, in
    natural-resource-rich open economy,
    362, 366, 367; backward linkage, 367,
    371, 372
Imports, incentive effect, 336

Income streams per unit of research activity, 202, 208–09; India, 219, 219 (table 8.12)

India: population pressure, 59; and wage rates, 132$n$29; output per acre, 132$n$30; size of holdings and tenancy type, 133–34; research strategy, 179; productivity growth by state, 209–15, 210–12 (table 8.6); factor shares by state, 212 (table 8.7), 214; agricultural research investment, 215–16, 215 (table 8.8), 216 (table 8.9); research publications, 216 (table 8.10); community blocks, 216 (table 8.9), 217; statistical analysis of research and productivity, 217–18, 218 (table 8.12); returns to research investment, 219–20, 219 (table 8.12); extension, 220; transfer of research results between states, 220; size of farm, factor proportions and productivity, 280$n$, 283 (table 10.6); direct employment effect of innovation, Punjab, for wheat, 303–05, 305 (tables 11.2, 11.3); for two-crop mix, 306–07, 307 (table 11.4); of tractorization, two-crop mix, 308–09, 309 (table 11.5); indirect employment effects of agricultural growth, using input-output model, 314–18, 317 (table 11.7); total employment change, 319 (table 11.8); labor-output coefficients computation, 321; marginal propensity to spend, 322–23; technological change and changes in composition of inputs, 323; minimum-subsistence-level families, 458$n;$ income differentials and green revolution, 458$n;$ pre-British village, 471–73, 471$n;$ caste structure, 471; hereditary system of cooperation (*jajimani*), 471, 472; hierarchical relationship, 471, 473; land revenue settlements, 471–72; land reform since independence, 472 and $n$30

Indian Agricultural Research Institute, 216, 220

Indonesia: political economy framework for rice policy, 400–04

Industrial expansion: and employment, unemployment, 347

Infrastructure, 4, 8, 9, 19, 77, 333, 335, 356, 357, 359, 360, 361, and $n$

Input-output model: to measure indirect employment effects, 310–18

Institutional transfer and innovation, 180–89; capacity for technological transfer, 181, 182, 183; institution-building research, 181 and $n$24, 182$n$-26; models of bureaucratic behavior, 181 and $n$25, 183–84; models of collective action, 184 and $n$31; induced institutional change and agricultural productivity, 185–88; role of social sciences, 189

Institutions and organizations: definitions, 180$n$, 182

Intensity of cultivation: enforcement clauses in sharecropping, 113, 115, 116

Interest rate, 143, 148; for share tenants, 151, 152; rate differential for landlord, 153, 154, 157

Interfamily relations, 457–58, 459, 460 and $n$

International agricultural institutes: role in technology transfer, 169, 170–71, 179

International diffusion. *See* Diffusion of crop varieties

International Rice Research Institute, 221

International trade model, 327–54; open economy, 330–33 passim; comparative advantage, 337–44

International trade theory: applicability to LDCs, 18

Investment in agricultural research: output per research dollar, 196 (table 8.2); internal rate of return, 196 (table 8.2); time lag, 197, 219

Investment in agriculture, 16, 351; foreign, 353

Irrigation: effect on employment, 303

Ishikawa, Shigeru, 11, 340, 349

Japan, 89; quantitative aspects of growth, 234–36; industrialization policy, Meiji period, 239; farmers' societies, 242; labor productivity, size of farm and factor proportions, 280$n$, 283 (table 10.6); small farms and taxation, 435–36, 436$n;$ pre-war community relations, 462–66; hierarchical relationship, 463, 465; mutual aid, 463; decline of owner management, 463, 465, 491, 492; landlord-tenant relationships, 464; minor cooperatives, 464 and $n$12, 465 and $n$15, 466; agricultural associa-

Japan (Continued)
  tions and cooperatives, 466; labor
  supply, 492–93
–agricultural research, historical:
  organizational features of government
  initiatives, 236–249; technology
  borrowing phase, 236–37; itinerant
  instructor system, 237, 240–44;
  experiment stations, 237–38, 240, 241,
  243–44; diffusion of farmers' indigenous (*rono*) techniques after land
  reform, 242–43, 245; history of rice
  improvement, 242–43, 245–47;
  research expenditures, 246 (table 9.3);
  crossbreeding projects, 246–47
–agricultural research, modern: organizational features, 225–27; research
  expenditures, 225, 225 (table 9.1),
  227 (table 9.2); extension, 226, 234,
  237; experiment stations, 226–27,
  227 (table 9.2); university research,
  226, 227 (table 9.2)
Jasny, Naum, 427*n*22, 438*n*34
Java, 473 and *n*32
JCRR (Sino-American Joint Commission
  on Rural Reconstruction), 187
Jenicek, Vladimir, 415*n*
Johnson, D. Gale, 113–14, 123, 138
Johnston, Bruce F., 300, 340–41, 345,
  347, 348, 349

Kahan, Arcadius, 413*n*, 434*n*32, 448*n*44,
  449*n*47
Kanel, Don, 294–96
Karcz, J., 426*n*18, 443*n*38, 447*n*44
Kassof, 439*n*, 449*n*47
Kennedy, Charles, 175*n*14
Kenya, 32, 37, 38, 42
Khaldi, N., 200
Khruschev, Nikita, 442
Kilby, P., 348, 349
Kislev, Yoav, 197, 198, 201, 203, 222,
  223
Korea, 356, 361*n*
Koslov, M. 429*n*25
Kravis, Irving, 19
Krishabi system, West Bengal, 136*n*
Kuznets, Simon, 355, 370

Labor: disutility, 11; unlimited supplies
  of, 12, 369 and *n*14; transfer from
  agriculture, 14, 15; surplus, 58, 64,
  355, 357, 361; market imperfections
  and tenancy contracts, 127–32;

  allocation under uncertainty, 128–32,
  136–37; supply function, 368–70,
  477–80, 477*n*, 492–93
–in Africa: seasonal demand, 28, 29;
  marginal productivity, 28, 29;
  backward-sloping supply curve, 30;
  affected by cash economy, 30–31;
  trade-off with other activities, 32, 33,
  44
–input: subsistence economy, 56;
  transitional economy, 68, 71
–productivity: and primitive affluence
  of subsistence farmers, 59; in monetary sector, 60, 63; affected by
  consumption (productivity hypothesis), 84–106; expansion of, 361,
  367, 368; and labor/land ratio, 421,
  428
–supply: complementarity between
  farm and wage labor, 129, 136–37;
  elasticity in share tenancy, 131
Labor/land ratio: share tenancy, 113;
  and productivity, 421, 428
Land availability: Africa, 29, 31; in
  subsistence, 55, 56; population
  pressure, 58, 61; and "ful belly" consumption level, 81–83
Landless peasants, 269
Land ownership distribution, 101
Land Reform, 186, 187–88; and JCRR,
  187; comparison with redistribution
  through tax system, 269*n*19; beneficial
  economic effects, 420–22, 422*n*; in
  East European countries, 420*n*, 423*n*;
  and entrepreneurship, 422–23; other
  sociological effects in socialist countries, 423–25
Land surplus, 11–14; Africa, 29, 31
Latimer, R., 197, 201*n*12
Latin America, 362–71 passim
Leasehold farming. *See* Fixed-rental
  contracts
Leibenstein, Harvey, 456*n*, 478*n*34
Leisure, 121, 142, 151; trade-off with
  productive activity in Africa, 30, 32,
  33, 34, 44
Lewis, W. Arthur, 12, 18, 19, 342–44,
  369, 436*n*
Lipton, Michael, 254*n*2, 264*n*17

Machine tractor stations, 429, 435, 436
Malawi, 34, 39
Malaysia, 83, 362, 473
Management bias, 385

Marginal product of labor: Africa, 28; determining consumption levels, 93–95, 96, 97; in peasant economy with land market, 100–01; under share rental, 113; and size of holding, 120; share tenant's, 151; zero as desired by landlord, 154; leaseholder's, 156; Poland, 430*n*

Marginal product of land, 113, 115

Marginal propensity to spend, 313, 314, 320

Market economy, 454–55, 458, 460; its development changing community relations, 488–96

Marx, Karl, 415–17

McCabe, James, 31*n*12

Mellor, John W., 51, 340–41, 345, 347

Migration, Africa: short-term, 29; rural-urban, 33, 34, 35; connected with cash-crop potentials, 34; and income differentials, 36; and wage rate changes, 39; and extended family system, 47; characteristics of migrants, 51 and *n*82

Minford, A. P. L., 34*n*19

Minimum subsistence level, 456–57, 458*n*

Miracle, Marvin, 48

Monopoly power of landlords, 123, 124–26, 134, 136; Latin America, 134

Montias, J. M., 426*n*20, 432*n*29, 443*n*38

Multiple cropping, 10, 337, 340

Musgrave, P. A., 228

Musialowski, J., 412*n*2

Myint, Hla, 17, 52, 452 and *n*2

Myrdal, Gunnar, 18, 456*n*

Nakajima, Chihiro, 5, 54, 61, 62–67, 68, 77

Natural resources base, 355, 357. *See also* Open economies

Nelson, Richard, 198, 231

Nicholls, W. H., 331, 347, 425*n*15, 426*n*17, 446*n*40

Nigeria, 36, 38, 39, 41, 42, 43, 46, 48, 59*n*7

Non-farm activities, Africa, 29, 30, 48. *See also* Z-goods

Non-indigenous immigrants, 59 and *n*6; and social and political problems, 83

Nove, Alec, 417*n*7, 427*n*21

Olson, Mancur, 184

Open economies: natural-resource-poor, labor abundant (Taiwan), 356–62, 371; import substitution phase, 357–59, 361; export substitution phase, 359, 360, 362; natural-resource-rich, 362–71; 372; prolonged import substitution, 362, 366; "enclave" dynamics, 365–67, 370; terms of trade, 365; enclave-hinterland relations, 368–70; supply curve of labor, 368–70

Open economy and the 4 contributions of agriculture, 17–20, 327–54; export-led growth, 18–20, 21

Opportunity costs of labor, 342, 343

Opportunity wage: for share tenant, 151; for leaseholder, 156

Paarlberg, D., 197, 201*n*12

Pacific islands, 53, 54, 59 and *n*6, 67, 83

Palm oil and kernels, 38, 39, 41

Papadakis, J., 202*n*16, 203, 217

Peasant economy: without factor markets, 98–99; aith land market, 99–101; with labor market, 101–02; with both land and labor markets, 103

Perkins, Dwight, 22

"Permanent" income positions and economic class, 455, 459

Phelps, Edmund, 198

Philippine farmers: "good life" components, 141, 141 (table 6.2); indebtedness, 143 (table 6.3); interest rates, 143; landlord's financing of leaseholder, 155; role expectations, landlords and tenants, 159 (table 6.7)

Philippines: tenure and productivity, 114; land reform, 158; research strategy, 179; as open economy, 362; community relations, 473

Philippine share tenancy: efficiency, 138; decision-making, 140 (table 6.1); *agad* privilege, 143, 148, 153; interest rates, 143, 148; landlord's operating expenses, share in financing, 143, 144 (table 6.4), 148, 149 (table 6.5); rental shares, 144 (table 6.4), 159 (table 6.6); deductible operating expenses, 144 (table 6.4); credit, 150*n*

Plantation farming. *See* Primary product export sector

Poland: livestock production and shortages, 412*n*2; land reform, 420*n*; collectivization abandonment, 429, 430, 447; disguised unemployment,

Poland (Continued)
430 and *n;* production policy failure,
432 and *n*28; planning of agricultural
supply industry, 433–34; state farms,
439*n;* private modern farming, 446*n*41,
447 and *n*43; future of agricultural
structure, 449 and *n*48
Policies, 328, 345, 346, 350; taxation,
7, 17, 72, 78, 330; protection, infant
economy reasoning, 20, 21, 351, 361;
agriculture as infant industry, 350–51.
*See also* Self-sufficiency in food;
Subsidies
Policy, agricultural: and homogeneity
of productive units, 253; and complexities of heterogeneity of productive units, 254, 261–96; goal conflicts,
262–71; political conflicts, 265, 269,
273, 274, 281 and *n*36, 291; income
distribution conflicts, 269; bureaucratic conflicts, 270; non-robustness
of policy, 271–89; frequency distribution of benefits, 271–80; needs of,
pay-offs, costs and pay-off periods for
different subsectors, 273–89; policy
pay-offs, 277, 279; effects of choice
of technique, 278–81, 287–89; effects
of large-farm technology policy, 287–
88; problems of second best and market
imperfections, 289–90; foreign exchange market disequilibrium, 289–90,
290*n*44; errors of economic intuition,
291–93; large-farm and small-farm
policies, 293–96; mutual inconsisten-
cies of policies for open economy,
337–54; policy package in import
substitution, 360, 361; policy stages
from import to export substitution,
371
Population growth, 7–8, 369–70;
Poland, 449 and *n*48
Prebisch, Raul, 18
Preobrazhenskiv, E., 418*n*
Primary-product export sector (nonfood exports), 332–33, 335, 336,
338, 345; Africa, 31, 37, 38; role in
import-substitution phase of natural-
resource-poor open economy, 360–61,
360*nn*5, 6; role in natural-resource-
rich open economy, 370–71
Primitive affluence, 59, 60, 63, 82
Primitive nonmarket organization, 459*n*
Private plots, 424, 426–28, 426*n*19,
427*nn*21, 22

Production functions for agriculture,
4; Africa, 46
Productive force, 457, 459–60, 490,
492, 495
Productivity hypothesis, 84–106;
constancy of wages over time, 88;
training externality, 89

Ranis, G., 12
Rao, C. H. H., 117–20, 133, 134
Rasiński, J., 432*n*28
Rent, average, in share contract, 113
Research. *See* Technological research
Rhodesia, 34, 39, 42, 46, 74*n*
Rice: transfer of high-yielding varieties
from Japan to tropics, 176–80; history
of improvement in Japan, 242–43,
245–47; production, consumption,
yield per hectare, 374, 375 (table
14.1); price ratios to fertilizer, various
Asian countries, 375–77, 376 (table
14.2); international trade flows, 377–
81; concessional sales agreements,
US trade subsidies, 377, 379, 381;
international prices, 379, 381; barter
agreements, 381; international market,
381; licensing, government trade
monopoly, 381–82; cross-section
production function estimation for
9 Asian countries, 382–96, 384 (table
14.3); fertilizer application and rice/
fertilizer price ratio, 383, 386–88;
fertilizer response coefficient, 383–86;
simulation of price ratio impact on
production, 388, 390–93; and of
export surplus, 388, 391 (table 14.4),
392 (table 14.5), 393; potential export
surplus, Burma, Thailand, 393; potential Asian self-sufficiency, 393–95;
resulting shift in trade pattern, 395,
396 (table 14.6)
Rice/fertilizer price ratio, 9, 178, 375–
77, 376 (table 14.2), 383, 386–88,
390–93
Rice policy: political economy framework, 396–400; policy objectives,
397; policy choices, 398; constraints,
398–99; objectives, Asian rice policy,
400, 401 (table 14.7); Indonesia's
framework, 400–04; standard linear
programming model, 405–08
Risk and uncertainty, 6; for African
smallholders, 33, 45; and rental
contracts, 111, 115, 117*n*12, 118,

128–32; in research production function, 231; and minimum subsistence level, 457; and community principle of employment, 481
Risk aversion: and fixed rents, 118; and size of holdings, 118
Romanowski, Jacek, 446*n*41
Rumania: collectivization, 426*n*20, 443*n*38; shortening of crop production cycle, 432*n*29
Ruttan, Vernon W., 9, 114, 134, 197, 198, 201, 223, 393, 466*n*18
Rychlik, T., 438*n*34, 439*n*

Samuelson, Paul A., 175*n*14, 228
Sapre, 308*n*16
Sauer, Carl O., 165
Savings: supplied by agricultural sector growth, 345–52; subsidies for agriculture, 351–52
Savings rates and size of farm, 264*n*17, 289*n*41
Schultz, Theodore W., 5, 20, 203, 224, 230, 231, 347, 428*n*23
Second Enclosure Movement, England, 185–86
Self-sufficiency in food, 330, 333; and comparative advantage, 337–44; as advised by agricultural economists, 337–44, 345; experience of small export economies, 341–44; potential for Southeast Asia, 393–95; Indonesia, 400, 402, 403, 404
Semi-open economy model, 332–37; criticism of its restrictive assumptions, 333, 337; applicability to large, densely populated LDC, 334–35; logical weaknesses, 335–37; policy implications, 337–54
Semi-subsistence. *See* Transitional semi-subsistence farm
Sen, Amartya K., 11, 54, 61, 478*n*34
Sethuraman, S. V., 300
Shadow wage, 13; for rural economy, local employment with family consumption subsidies, 103–05; multiplier effects on family, 105; for urban employment, 105, 106
Share tenancy: theories, 110–27, 138–41, 150–55, 157–61; conventional neoclassical assumptions, 110–11; inefficiency of production, 111–13; landlord's techniques to force intensity of cultivation, 113–16; short-term

lease, 113, 114; contractual labor input, 113, 115; sharing of expenses, 113, 114, 134–36; enforcement costs, 113, 114, 115–116, 121; equilibrium, 121–27; stability of equilibrium, 127; effect of labor market imperfections, 127, 128; elasticity of labor supply, 131; efficiency, 139; bargaining between landlord and share tenant, 139, 157–60; model of share tenant, 150–53, 160–61; income maximization, 151; changes in contractual arrangements, 152; fringe benefits, 153; model of share tenant's landlord, 153–55; income maximization, 153–54; financing role, 154; changes in contractual arrangements, 155; comparison with leaseholder, 156
Shifting cultivation, Africa 31
Sierra Leone, 39
Singh, Arjan, 300, 305, 307*n*11
Sire, Lubo, 417*n*9
Size of farm, 3, 4; and labor intensity, 4; and output, 114, 132 and *nn*30, 31; and entrepreneurial skill, 118; and marginal product of labor, 120; and choice of tenancy contract, 132–34; and productivity, 256, 282 (table 10.6); and policy goal conflicts, 262–71, 293–96; and technological change, 264 and *n*17; and savings rates, 264*n*17, 289*n*41
Skinner, William, 468
Socialist LDCs and agriculture, 21–24; pro-industry bias, 21; China, 21–24. *See also* Communist agriculture; Communist system; East European socialist countries
Social sciences: role in institutional change, 189; public investment in research capacity of, 189, 191
South Africa, 34, 39
Southeast Asian countries, 362
Soviet Union: policy for economic growth, 413*n*; agricultural policy, 417 and *n*, 418; private plot proceeds, 427*nn*21, 22; profitability of state and collective farms, 437 (table 15.4); changes in agricultural policy, 447*n*44; 448*nn*44, 45, 46; grain problem, 448–49, 449*n*47
Specialization, 54, 76–80; and comparative advantage, 330
Spulber, Nicolas, 420*n*

Srinivasan, T. N., 121–27, 132, 135,
    139, 158
"Stagnation" in Latin America, 370
Stalin, Joseph, 417, 418, 436, 442
Staple hypothesis, 18
Strauss, Erich, 448n46
Structural disequilibrium, 476–79
Subsidies: by government for full
    employment, 89, 97–98; by family
    as consumption subsidy for employ-
    ment, 102, 103, 104; as infant industry
    protection, 350, 351, 352
Subsistence economy, 53; supplemen-
    tary cash production, 53, 59–61; Fisk
    model of self-subsistent, non-monetary
    production unit, 54–61; land availabil-
    ity, 55–56; labor input, 56; unused
    labor, 58; primitive affluence and land
    surplus, 58, 59, 60, 63, 82; labor
    productivity, 59 and n7; equilibrium
    between subsistence and cash crop
    production, 61; mistakenly seen as
    obstacle to development, 76, 83.
    *See also* Transitional farm
Sugar cane: diffusion and development,
    169–70; transfer of technology, 201
Supply elasticities of smallholders,
    Africa, 37–41, 40 (table 2.1), 43
Supply response to price changes in
    various African countries, 30–44;
    "normal," 30, 39, 51; and acreage,
    31, 32, 38; and yield, 31, 32, 38;
    models of supply behavior, 36–41;
    measured for cash crops, 37–41,
    40 (table 2.1); for food crops, 36,
    42–43
—to other economic incentives: alter-
    native wage employment, 33, 34, 39,
    41; introduction of quality differen-
    tials, 41; improvements of infrastruc-
    ture, 43–44; socioeconomic factors,
    50, 51

Taiwan: farmers' associations, 186–87;
    land reform, 187; as natural-resource-
    poor open economy, 357–62; initial
    conditions to fuel growth, 357; import
    substitution phase, 357–59; export
    substitution phase, 359, 360, 362;
    wage stability, 359–60; policies in
    import substitution phase, 361
Tanzania, 36, 37, 39, 42, 43, 45
Target income hypothesis, African wage
    labor, 30–31

Technological change, measurement of
    direct employment effects: labor
    coefficient per hectare, 298–309;
    disaggregation of innovation effects,
    298, 300–01; output- and area-
    oriented operations, 301; yield pro-
    jection, 301; irrigation effect, 301;
    crop mix effect, 301, 306–07; model
    for single crop, 302–03; for Punjab
    wheat, 303–05; model for many crops,
    306; for Punjab wheat and rice, 306–
    07; model of tractorization, 307–09
Technological change and agricultural
    growth, measurement of indirect
    employment effects: classification of
    additional demands, 310; model of
    measurement using input-output,
    310–14; income and demand effects,
    312–14; India, 314–18
Technological change and agricultural
    growth, total employment effect:
    model of decomposition of causes,
    318–19; growth of labor force, 320;
    policy implications, 320
Technological change and innovation in
    agriculture, 8–11; African smallholder
    responses, 44–52; and management
    studies, 45–46; and farmer charac-
    teristics, 45, 48–50; characteristics of
    adopters, 45, 48, 50, 51; appropriate
    decision-making unit, 46–48; farm
    level acceptability, 49–50; group
    characteristics, 50; early adopters,
    51; effects, 77, 78; induced innova-
    tion, 175–76; 175n14, 339–41;
    biological-chemical innovation and
    landsaving (Japan), 339, 441; induced
    mechanization (US), 339; induced
    innovation model, 466n18
Technological discovery and diffusion:
    direct commodity studies, 193–95;
    cost-benefit, 193–95; benefit stream,
    193–94; consumer surplus basis, 194;
    hybrid corn study, 194; production
    function studies, 195–98; output per
    research dollar, 196 (table 8.2); rates
    of return, 196 (table 8.2); time lag,
    197, 219; information studies, 198–
    200; transfer studies, 200–03; India,
    209–20
Technological research in agriculture:
    public responsibility, 8, 175, 176, 179,
    187, 229, 232, 248; recommenda-
    tions, 194, 203, 220–21, 223, 248;

rates of return, 196 (table 8.2), 197, 209, 220; obsolescence, 197; research supply prices and income streams, 199 (table 8.3), 202, 208–09; geoclimate regional research contributions, 202, 203–09; intensity and output measured by number of publications, 202, 206, 221; income streams, 202; basic and applied research contribution, 209; India research publications, 216 (table 8.10); demand for, 221, 230, 233, 249; in Japan, 225–27, 236–49; bias, 227; requirements for efficient socially optimal organization, 228–34; its product as public good, 228–29, 233, 238, 248; research production function, 230–31; supply of research workers, 230, 233; linkage with experiment stations, extension, 232, 234, 249; underestimation of returns, 248; interaction with farmers and neighboring disciplines, 249; social returns, 351. *See also* Japan, agricultural research

Technology: choice of, 175 and $n13$

Technology transfer in agriculture, 165–80; phases of, 165–67; material transfer, 167, 168; design (blueprints, prototypes) transfer, 168; capacity (to invent new technology) transfer, 167, 168–69, 176, 180; scientists' migration, 167, 169; role of research, 169; interregional, hybrid corn case, 172–73; international, high yielding rice, 176–80; role of new knowledge in social sciences, 188–91

Tenancy contracts, 109–37; formal and informal, 117, 177$n11$; and entrepreneurial skill, 117–20; effect of labor market imperfections, 127–32, 127$n$; and wage employment, 128–32, 136–37. *See also* Fixed-rental contracts: Share tenancy

Tenure system, 3, 113–37, 138–61

Teriayeva, A., 427$n22$

Thailand, 362, 473

Thirsk, Wayne, 260

Tinbergen, Jan, 396

Tomczak, F., 446$n41$

Tractorization, 303, 307–09

Transaction costs, 157$n17$

Transitional farm with more specialization, 72–83; minimum money income, 72; high effort cost of earning money, 73; wage levels, 73–75; casual labor, 74–75; policy recommendations, 76–78; extension and research, 76; increase of cash crop price, 76–77; taxation, increase of money utility, 78; specialization for market, 79–80; "full belly" consumption, 80; disutility of labor, 81; wage labor commitment, 82–83

Transitional semi-subsistence farm, 53, 61, 67–71; equilibrium of subsistence and case crop production, 61 and $n$, 64, 68; imputation of prices, 67; analysis of non-monetary and monetary parts, 68–71; effect of farm-gate price increase, 77

Uganda, 38, 39, 42

United States: land grant college system, 226; agricultural income distribution, 265, 266 (table 10.5); size of farm, factor proportions, and productivity, 280$n$, 285 (table 10.6)

Urban: migration, Africa, 47; employment and wage policy, 105; unemployment, 347

Utility function of farmer, 141–43

Utility maximization in share tenancy: of tenant, 112, 115; of landlord, 114, 115

Utility of money: transition farming, 72–78

Vavilov, N. I., 165

Vent for surplus, 336, 452, 452$n2$

Wage employment: in tenancy contracts, 128–32, 136–37

Wage labor: of transitional subsistence farming, 60, 73–75; and productivity, 60, 72; high effort cost, 72, 73; supply, Africa, 32, 33, 34, 35, 39; trade-off with other activities, 34–39

Wage rate: gap between casual and average permanent, 132 and $n29$; India, 132$n29$

Wages fund, 361

Warriner, Doreen, 422$n$

Welch, Finis, 198, 200

Welfare maximization: semisubsistence farms, 61, 66, 67, 71; for individual, 460

Welfare optimum: of factory economy, 91–95

West Africa: cocoa production, 16, 37;
    British colonial policy, 333n5
Wharton, Clifton, 33
Wheat, in green revolution, 247; India,
    303–05, 308–09
Windfall profits, 361, 371
Wonnacott, Paul, 478n34

Yield: changes causes by scientific

research, 207, 208, 208 (table 8.5);
    projection, 301
Yugoslavia: demand for food, 415n;
    abandonment of collectivization, 429,
    430, 447


Z-goods, 5, 6, 30, 33, 58

# Economic Growth Center Book Publications

Werner Baer, *Industrialization and Economic Development in Brazil* (1965).

Werner Baer and Isaac Kerstenetzky, eds., *Inflation and Growth in Latin America* (1964).

Bela A. Balassa, *Trade Prospects for Developing Countries* (1964). Out of print.

Thomas B. Birnberg and Stephen A. Resnick, *Colonial Development: An Econometric Study* (1975).

Benjamin I. Cohen, *Multinational Firms and Asian Exports* (1975).

Carlos F. Díaz Alejandro, *Essays on the Economic History of the Argentine Republic* (1970).

Robert Evenson and Yoav Kislev, *Agricultural Research and Productivity* (1975).

John C. H. Fei and Gustav Ranis, *Development of Labor Surplus Economy: Theory and Policy* (1964).

Gerald K. Helleiner, *Peasant Agriculture, Government, and Economic Growth in Nigeria* (1966).

Lawrence R. Klein and Kazushi Ohkawa, eds., *Economic Growth: The Japanese Experience since the Meiji Era* (1968).

A. Lamfalussy, *The United Kingdom and the Six* (1963). Out of print.

Markos J. Mamalakis and Clark W. Reynolds, *Essays on the Chilean Economy* (1965).

Donald C. Mead, *Growth and Structural Change in the Egyptian Economy* (1967).

Richard Moorsteen and Raymond P. Powell, *The Soviet Capital Stock* (1966).

Douglas S. Paauw and John C. H. Fei, *The Transition in Open Dualistic Economies: Theory and Southeast Asian Experience* (1973).

Howard Pack, *Structural Change and Economic Policy in Israel* (1971).

Frederick L. Pryor, *Public Expenditures in Communist and Capitalist Nations* (1968).

Gustav Ranis, ed., *Government and Economic Development* (1971).

Clark W. Reynolds, *The Mexican Economy: Twentieth-Century Structure and Growth* (1970).

Lloyd G. Reynolds, ed., *Agriculture in Development Theory* (1975).

Lloyd G. Reynolds and Peter Gregory, *Wages, Productivity, and Industrialization in Puerto Rico* (1965).

Donald R. Snodgrass, *Ceylon: An Export Economy in Transition* (1966).